Politics and rural society

Politics and rural society

The southern Massif Central
c. 1750–1880

❋❋❋

P. M. JONES

Lecturer in Modern History, University of Birmingham

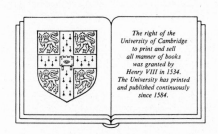

The right of the
University of Cambridge
to print and sell
all manner of books
was granted by
Henry VIII in 1534.
The University has printed
and published continuously
since 1584.

CAMBRIDGE UNIVERSITY PRESS

Cambridge

London   New York   New Rochelle
Melbourne   Sydney

Published by the Press Syndicate of the University of Cambridge
The Pitt Building, Trumpington Street, Cambridge CB2 1RP
32 East 57th Street, New York, NY 10022, USA
10 Stamford Road, Oakleigh, Melbourne 3166, Australia

First published 1985

Printed in Great Britain at the University Press, Cambridge

Library of Congress catalogue card number: 84–21383

British Library cataloguing in publication data
Jones, Peter M.
Politics and rural society: the Southern Massif
Central c. 1750–1880.
1. Peasantry – Massif Central (France) – Political
activity – History – 18th century 2. Peasantry
– Massif Central (France) – Political activity –
History – 19th century 3. Massif Central (France)
– Politics and government
I. Title
306′.2   JN2461
ISBN 0 521 25797 2

For
RICHARD COBB

Contents

Plates

Maps

Figures

Tables

Acknowledgements

Many people helped to bring this work to a successful conclusion and I should not wish their assistance to pass unrecognised. Pride of place must go to the anonymous assessors of several grant-awarding bodies who responded magnificently to repeated claims upon their resources. Without the financial support of the British Academy (Small Grants Research Fund in the Humanities), of the Nuffield Foundation (Social Sciences Small Grants Scheme) and of Birmingham University (Arts Faculty Research Grants Fund and University Field Research and Expeditions Fund), the research for this book could never have been undertaken. That my research proceeded smoothly and with a minimum of time-loss is a tribute to the men and women in charge of the public archives of provincial France. In the Lozère Mademoiselle Hélène Latour and Monsieur Benjamin Bardy acceded unhesitatingly to every importunate request for documents and Monsieur Jean Delmas in the Aveyron, Monsieur Dominique Dupraz in the Ardèche and Monsieur Yves Soulingeas in the Haute-Loire were scarcely less accommodating. The generally welcoming introduction to the more frugal fare of the diocesan record depositories also deserves acknowledgement.

As anyone who has experienced enforced residence in small and seemingly unfriendly towns will testify, the evenings and weekends hang most heavily and I feel a particular debt of gratitude to a number of friends whose hospitality has helped to make the lot of the peripatetic researcher more bearable. The Carrère family did much for my self-confidence (and my French) when I first arrived in Rodez as a postgraduate student in 1971 and the support provided by Bernard and Claude Dausse of Lagarrigue de Druelle goes back to this time as well. At Mende, which might easily pass for the bleakest town in France during the winter months, Madame Vaccero and her husband did much to enliven the dispiriting tedium of the evenings, while Claude and Laurence Petit welcomed me to their flat in Clermont-Ferrand. To the latter couple I owe an unforgettable weekend spent in seasonal pursuit of the amphibious life of the Aubrac plateau.

On the technical side, Sue Offley turned my microscopic handwriting into legible typescript and Béatrice Gilbert and Ceri Crossley of the Birmingham

University French Department tolerated a good deal of questioning on points of French grammar and syntax.

Final thanks must go to my wife, Carolyn, however, for agreeing to an inequitable division of the burdens of child-raising while this book was being researched and written.

University of Birmingham   P. M. JONES
April 1984

Abbreviations

A.D.A.	Archives Départementales de l'Aveyron
A.D.Ard.	Archives Départementales de l'Ardèche
A.D.C.	Archives Départementales du Cantal
A.D.H.-L.	Archives Départementales de la Haute-Loire
A.D.L.	Archives Départementales de la Lozère
A.D.P.-de-D.	Archives Départementales du Puy-de-Dôme
A.E.M.	Archives de l'Evêché de Mende
A.E.R.	Archives de l'Evêché de Rodez
A.N.	Archives Nationales
Ann. E.S.C.	*Annales (Economies, Sociétés, Civilisations)*
Cévennes et Gévaudan	*Cévennes et Gévaudan, 46ᵉ congrès de la Fédération historique de Languedoc méditerranéen, Mende – Florac, 1973*
M.A.T.P.	Archives du Musée des Arts et Traditions Populaires

Introduction

This study of popular politics in a rural context originated in a thesis[1] devoted to the revolutionary Terror in the department of the Aveyron. More precisely, it springs from a sense of dissatisfaction at what can be achieved within the confines of an academic thesis. Exploring the dynamics of grass-roots politics through the medium of the Terror is like watching a roundabout through the wrong end of a telescope. At best the fleeting images offer part-answers to the big 'how' and 'why' questions which the historian is duty-bound to ask. At worst they conceal the complexities of human motivation behind a facade of rhetoric and posturing. One is left wondering who these cardboard revolutionaries strutting in the *comités de surveillance* and the jacobin clubs really were. Whence did they come? And what fate befell them as the receding brilliance of the Republic of the Year Two (1793–4) cast everything into shadow? The Revolution, it is worth recalling, was made by men who had grown to maturity during the *ancien régime* and on them devolved the task of picking up the pieces at the end of the decade. Unavoidably, therefore, revolutionary and post-revolutionary France bore the imprint of the *ancien régime*.

One way or another this insight pervades the present book, for once its subject-matter had been settled the format unfolded naturally. The decision to concentrate upon the evolving political apprehensions of a largely peasant electorate requires little justification. Most readers will be aware that studies of the process of *prise de conscience* in the countryside are few and far between. In contrast to urban social groups, the country dweller plays a strictly walk-on part in most of the standard histories of France in the eighteenth and nineteenth centuries.[2] If the great *jacquerie* which launched the Revolution and the more recently documented provincial insurgency which greeted the news of Louis-Napoléon's *coup* in 1851 are set aside, one might easily conclude that the French peasantry had no history in this period.

---

[1] P. M. Jones, 'The Revolutionary Committees of the Department of the Aveyron, France, 1793–1795', (University of Oxford, D.Phil. thesis, 1977).
[2] An honourable exception is R. Magraw, *France 1815–1914: The Bourgeois Century* (London, 1983).

Social historians have scarcely neglected the study of rural society, but they have chosen instead to split it up into manageable units which is arguably worse. The 'poor', the 'criminal', the 'landed' and the 'landless', the 'mobile' and the 'immobile' attract the attentions of batteries of specialists, while the essential integrity of 'le monde rural' goes by default. Among political historians even this degree of sensitivity is lacking. For them the country dweller remains an enigma: unstudiable because he resists inclusion in any readily identifiable political tradition and hence unstudied.

What is required is a synthesis of the two approaches: a harnessing of the methodology of the social sciences to the preoccupations of the political historian. In retrospect it seems obvious that this was the challenge posed by our earlier study of revolutionary politics in the department of the Aveyron. Little of that thesis has been incorporated in the present work, but the ambition to explain the dynamics of opinion formation in the countryside remains the same. So, too, does the broad territorial context, for subsequent research vindicated our original contention that the department of the Aveyron harboured a rural civilisation of unusual richness and vitality. But this civilisation transcended the borders of the Aveyron to embrace the entire highland plateau of the southern Massif Central. The specific characteristics of village politics on the uplands rising out of the Garonne plain were replicated in the villages overlooking the valley of the Rhône and the Mediterranean littoral. In short, the southern promontories of the Massif Central formed a whole and deserved treatment as such.

The Aveyron became, thus, the pivot for a study which soon encapsulated the departments of the Lozère, the Haute-Loire and the Ardèche too. But it is as well to remember that these administrative categories convey little that is meaningful about the history of the region. They are invoked chiefly as signposts in order to orientate the reader. The best definitions of the scope of this book are geographical and ecological: it concerns the so called 'hautes terres' of the southern Massif Central;[3] that is to say the population living on or above the 500 metre contour. Scant attention is therefore paid to the inhabitants of the lowland periphery of the Ardèche whose historical evolution was quite distinct from that of the mountain peasantry. On the other hand, it is less easy to specify the northerly frontiers of the region for there exists no natural divide separating the southern buttresses of the Massif Central from those of the Monts d'Auvergne. It is to be hoped that the subtle ecological and cultural pressures that helped to differentiate the peasantry of the northern and north-western Massif Central from their near neighbours in the south and south east will emerge in the chapters that follow. Even so, a substantial margin of interpenetration must be allowed for, and we have not hesitated to

---

[3] See A. Fel, *Les Hautes Terres du Massif Central. Tradition paysanne et économie agricole* (Paris, 1962), p. 13.

draw examples from frontier departments when the argument justified so doing.

Nevertheless, in a study which straddles the political watershed of 1789 department labels should be pinned down firmly, for otherwise they will mislead. The Aveyron corresponds to the old province of the Rouergue; the Ardèche to the Vivarais and the Lozère, *grosso modo*, to the Gévaudan which is straightforward enough. Only the Haute-Loire presents a problem. After considerable in-fighting between interested parties, its boundaries were drawn to embrace not only the Velay, but also the Brivadois and a corner of the Gévaudan. The legislators of the Constituent Assembly deemed the diminutive province of the Velay too small to constitute a department in its own right and attached to it a portion of the province of the Auvergne. In so doing, they thrust together two populations who shared little in common beyond physical proximity. The Brivadois was a *pays d'élection* whose administrative centre of gravity lay to the north in the town of Riom, whereas the Velay was a *pays d'état* subject to the political authority of the Estates of Languedoc in Montpellier and the legal jurisdiction of the Parlement of Toulouse. The Gévaudan, likewise, formed part of the highland *arrière pays* of the extensive province of Languedoc while the Rouergue, being a *pays d'élection*, looked westwards to Montauban where the intendant had his seat. That is, until 1779, when Jacques Necker set up the Assemblée Provinciale de la Haute-Guienne which linked the Rouergue and the province of the Quercy (subsequently to become the department of the Lot) in a brief political union. The southern Massif Central, in short, can be described as an administrative no man's land where the three great provinces of the Auvergne, the Languedoc and Guienne converged to form a mountainous cul-de-sac.

The ecclesiastical structures of the *ancien régime* contributed a further layer of administrative incoherence. The diocese of Mende and the Gévaudan dovetailed neatly and so did the diocese of Le Puy and the Velay, more or less. Not so the diocese of Viviers and the Vivarais, however, for this province also embraced a substantial number of parishes belonging to the dioceses of Valence and Vienne. As for the Rouergue, it was divided into two dioceses on the eve of the Revolution. All the parishes to the north of the river Tarn owed allegiance to the bishops of Rodez, while those to the south were subject to the bishops of Vabres. In 1790 this ecclesiastical fabric was hurled into the melting-pot along with so much else and diocesan boundaries were remodelled to coincide with the newly created departments. However, the change proved less than dramatic, for like the provinces, the old dioceses lived on. Rodez regained control of the one hundred and fifty parishes it had lost to Vabres nearly five centuries earlier; the ancient bishopric of Le Puy assumed responsibility for one hundred and thirty-four parishes situated in the Brivadois for the most part; Viviers took over the eighty-nine parishes of the dioceses of Valence and Vienne enclaved in the Vivarais, and the bishopric of Mende emerged from the change of regime pretty much intact. Only one other administrative adjustment deserves mention and that occurred in 1801 when the Concordat reduced the number of *évêchés*. Briefly, the bishoprics of Rodez, Le Puy and Viviers ceased to exist and were merged into the adjacent dioceses of Cahors, St Flour and Mende respectively. But this typically Napoleonic attempt to trim the budget of the restored church soon proved unworkable and the revolutionary format of dioceses contoured around the departments was reinstated in 1823–4.

If the quest for cohesion informs the choice of territorial context for this study, the quest for causality underpins its chronological scope. The narrow time-slice approach is unsuited to the purpose for which this book was written for it fails to capture the secular nature of change within rural society. This is a truism of social history, of course, but one which political historians confronting the evolution of the peasantry have been slow to acknowledge. Examine the dynamics of popular politics through the medium of the Terror and the result is tunnel vision, as we have discovered. Examine the dynamics of popular politics through the medium of a chronological sequence of cathartic events and the structure of political commitment in the countryside begins to emerge. The existence of such a structure – or structures – is probed at several levels, but the demographic cycle provides the basic framework of analysis. After 1750 or thereabouts, the southern Massif Central entered a phase of dynamic population growth which barely faltered before the 1880s. Rural society attained the last apogee in its millennial development. Yet these decades also witnessed the beginnings of the ideological subversion of the rural community by the liberal-democratic state. Naturally, this attrition was not unique to the southern Massif Central; every village in France experienced similar problems of adjustment. But the population of the southern highlands *was* unusual in the degree of resistance it offered to the process of integration. And that resistance flowed, in turn, from the vital stores of energy built up by the rural community in the years of recuperation after 1750.

How the rural community of the southern Massif Central cohered despite a low density human habitat is explored thoroughly in the pages that follow. The issue is important, for it is our contention that individuals acted – and reacted – within a framework of ethnicity and territorialism that effectively segmented the countryside into discrete communities. This is not to re-state the case for 'histoire immobile',[4] nor is it an attempt to chart the evolution of a peasant civilisation in purely anthropological terms. Our intention is rather to examine the interplay of endogenous and exogenous factors which served to crystallise allegiances at the grass roots. The argument outlined, it is true,

---

[4] See E. Le Roy Ladurie, 'L'Histoire immobile', *Ann. E.S.C.*, xxix (1974), 673–92.

lays heavy stress upon the insularity of the rural community, but the temptation to dismiss peasant politics as a contradiction in terms should be resisted. Peasant communities evinced a political character like any other community; what they so often lacked was a definable ideological character. All too frequently, historians have devoted disproportionate energy to labelling the elusive ideological component in peasant behaviour while neglecting the internal architecture of the rural community. This study seeks to redress the balance somewhat. It pays serious attention to so called parish pump conflicts in the belief that they performed a fundamental role in shaping opinion in the countryside.

The vitality of parish pump alignments had a temporal dimension, too, for it seems that the querulousness of the rural community expressed a developing perception of equilibrium and well-being. As the villages repopulated in the decades after 1750, peasant sociability revived and so did the strident tribal loyalties that would bedevil the functioning of representative institutions for a century and more. But community assertiveness reflected more than simply the contours of secular rivalry. It reflected the integrative capacity of rural catholicism. In the southern Massif Central the catholic church exercised a virtual monopoly over all forms of collective expression. Popular culture and the culture of rural catholicism overlapped inextricably. The vigour of the former informed the vigour of the latter and vice versa. Unsurprisingly, since the parish pump issues which established the lines of demarcation between households and between communities often concerned provision for chapels, cemeteries, church schools and the like. In widening the arena of collective expression, the rituals of electoral democracy initially reinforced the purchase of the catholic church upon the rural community. The advent of the ballot-box, that symbol of the new political order, coincided with a fast-flowing tide of popular religiosity in the southern Massif Central and the resultant synthesis found apt expression in the columns of peasant-citizens whom the clergy led to the polls in April 1848. In clericalism, the upland peasantry found a refuge from the encroaching power of the state. A temporary refuge as it turned out, however. With hindsight, it is clear that clericalism performed a dual function. It expressed a rejection of political neologism; a closing of ranks in defence of all that was local and familiar. But it subtly extended the customary range of apprehensions at election times as well. Paradoxically, therefore, enlistment in the cause of religious reaction became the prelude to emancipation, for it sharpened peasant awareness of the national entity and helped to bring to term a certain highly localised conception of politics.

Our study thus ends with rural society on the threshold of a major transformation. By 1886 the demographic cycle which had commenced towards the middle of the eighteenth century was exhausted. A few villages on the most inaccessible plateaux of the Haute-Loire and the Lozère continued to register a net population increase, but haemorrhaging outmigration was already punching great holes in the biological fabric of the region. Having pressed hard against Malthusian restraints for nearly a generation, peasant polyculture won a valuable reprieve. But soon the countryside began to empty and the vitality of an entire agrarian civilisation suffered in consequence. The short-term repercussions of the changing conjuncture should not be overstated, but the trend was unmistakable. By the end of the 1880s, the rural society of the southern Massif Central had passed its apogee. So too in the political domain: railway construction and the siren pressures of national economic integration made the 1880s a make-or-break decade. More potent than either, however, was the furious republican campaign to bring the rural community to heel. Jules Ferry's education laws carried the state's cultural offensive to every peasant's doorstep and rival philosophies were systematically excluded from the class room. The battle for the political loyalties of a rising generation of peasant voters had been won, or so it seemed. The parliamentary come-back of anti-republican forces in the ballot of 1885 produced a rude shock, therefore, and the Opportunists vented their frustrations by releasing a veritable paroxysm of interventionism upon the countryside. In these conditions the outcome could not long remain in doubt. Within a decade the peasantry had learned the lesson of tactical compliance and clericalism ceased to pose a threat to the established political order.

Such, in brief, is the subject-matter of the present book and the reader will find it organised in the following manner. Chapters one, two and three set the scene and treat in turn the regional context, the rural economy and the complex of relationships determining social status in the countryside. Particular emphasis is laid upon settlement patterns, upon the extent of *petite propriété* and upon the structure of the peasant household for these are important building blocks in our argument regarding the process of opinion formation. Chapter four is crucial. It seeks to vindicate the concept of the rural community as a tool for historical analysis and puts forward the idea that a locally rich culture of catholicism provided the principal medium for community expression. Chapter five sets the analysis in the temporal context of the late *ancien régime* and explores the accretions of tradition and prejudice that conditioned the political reflexes of the peasantry after 1789. Atavistic allegiances and bitter memories of seigneurialism and the fiscal aggression of the old monarchy were handed down from one generation to the next irrespective of the surface flux of events which suggests that an enquiry into the new political order ought first to begin with the old. Chapter six provides a corrective to this emphasis on continuity and examines the inception of new political traditions in the countryside under several thematic headings. The invention of electoral democracy is instanced as probably the single greatest achievement of the revolutionary epoch, and the adaptation of its cumbersome mechanisms to a rural environment forms the subject-matter of chapter seven. Not the least institution to be affected by that process of adaptation was the catholic church. The democratic franchise maximised the mobilising potential of rural catholicism and the introduction of universal manhood suffrage in 1848 facilitated the emergence of the church as the first great electoral organisation of the modern age. With an important shift in popular political attitudes impending, chapter eight breaks off from the narrative to take stock of the argument thus far. It proposes a broad classification of the observed sources of political commitment in the countryside and makes use of case studies to suggest ways in which endogenous and exogenous factors interacted. Chapter nine is devoted to the watershed decade of the 1880s in which the stealthy process of political modernisation reached a dramatic and definitive climax. Once the republicans had won control of the parliamentary institutions of the Republic the assault on the bastions of elite power in the countryside became a logical next step. Just how 'modern' was the popular political awareness that emerged from the tussles of the 1880s is discussed in chapter ten. The answer, for what it is worth, is then employed to underpin a number of general observations about the process of peasant politicisation in the course of the nineteenth century.

1

✻✻

The regional context

The roof of France

The plateau of central France culminates in a series of table-lands and escarp-ments which are mostly located along its southern and south-eastern flanks (see maps 1 and 2). Travellers were wont to describe this region as the 'roof of France'. The description is apt for the torrents of the southern massifs drain into the Loire, the Garonne and the Rhône river basins. Hundreds of moun-tain streams splash their way down the steep slopes of the Cévennes. Some of them feed the Allier and Loire rivers which curve northwards for hundreds of kilometres before debouching into the Atlantic; others fuel the Lot and the Tarn to join the Garonne; the remainder combine to form the Hérault, Gard and Ardèche rivers which flow swiftly and unpredictably towards the Mediterranean. Not for nothing were the departments of the southern Massif Central named after their rivers. As physical barriers they were obstacles which could not be ignored. As fissured oases of fertility the role they played was no less crucial. The exception was the department of the Lozère – the veritable roof of France. Named after the highest peak of the southern Cévennes (Mont Lozère, 1699 metres), its highland water-courses discharge their contents in all directions and receive nothing in return. The majority of the communes of the Lozère are situated above the 800 metre contour which makes it the most upland department in France.

Mean altitudes are lower in the Aveyron, the Ardèche and the Haute-Loire, but the broad characteristics of the relief are similar. Five types of terrain can be readily identified. The table-lands known as the Grands Causses (to distinguish them from their lesser neighbours in the Quercy) span the frontier between the Aveyron and the Lozère. These slabs of eroded lime-stone were high, dry and largely uninhabited in the eighteenth century. River valleys provided a more sheltered environment. The rich alluvium of the lower reaches of the Lot and Tarn, and of the Loire around Le Puy, had enabled a prosperous agriculture to develop. More commonly, however, the rivers of the region flowed in steep-sided gorges which made them unsuitable either for settlement or communication. The Jonte and the upper reaches of the Tarn had etched canyons in the limestone that were 500 metres deep in places while the gorges of the Allier made the north-eastern Lozère a virtual cul-de-sac. Volcanic action contributed a third trait to the landscape. The Aubrac, Meygal, Mézenc and Coiron massifs lacked the contoured symmetry of the Puys, but formed well-defined lava fields nevertheless. These volcanic summits (Mont Mézenc culminated at 1751 metres) provided rich grazing for summer flocks. The basalt soils of the lower slopes proved an excellent medium for rye cultivation and were called *planèzes*. In marked contrast were the impoverished crystalline soils which made up the greater part of the terrain of the Massif Central. Granite ramparts such as the Margeride which ran for sixty kilometres between Pinols (Haute-Loire) and Mende (Lozère) were impressive physical barriers, but offered a mediocre context for settlement and agriculture. The schist areas were even less inviting. Unrewarding to work because of high acidity, the land surface was pitted and dissected by

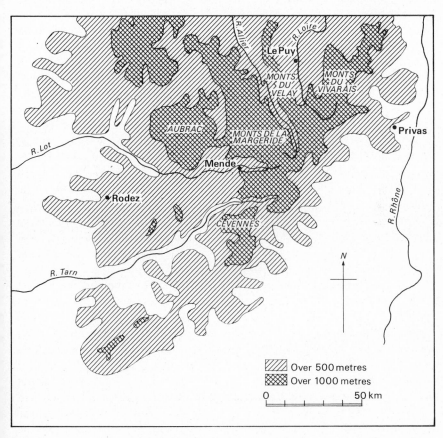

Map 1 The southern Massif Central

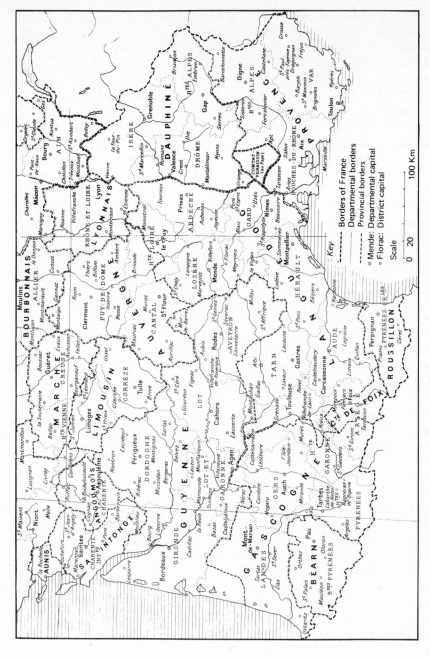

Map 2 The administrative geography of southern France in 1790

erosion. The ségalas and the Cévennes were extreme examples of this type of physical environment. In the ségala of the Rouergue a landscape of exiguous plateaux alternating with damp and diminutive valleys prevailed. The Cévenne escarpments which properly speaking stretched along a north-easterly axis from Le Vigan (Gard) to Privas (Ardèche) possessed a more rugged relief. The plateau element yielded to jagged ribs of decaying and denuded rock (*serres*) which defined steep-sided and elongated valleys. Viewed from surrounding summits the Cévennes gave the appearance of petrified ocean rollers separated by shadowy troughs.

Climatic conditions reflected the intermediate position of the southern Massif Central. It constituted the zone of contact of two quite distinct weather systems whose repercussions extended beyond the physical environment. Along the western and northern flanks of the Massif Central Oceanic influences prevailed unchallenged. The moist Atlantic airstreams encountered the westerly barriers of the Aubrac and the Monts d'Auvergne and shed abundant rainfall upon their summits and nether slopes. These regions were unsuited to intensive arable cultivation and developed a pastoral vocation instead. The carbohydrate needs of the population were met by means of a sophisticated commercial reflex in which fatstock and dairy products were exchanged for grain, wine and other items of daily consumption. Although Oceanic air currents penetrated the southern Massif Central via the Aubrac and the ségala of the Rouergue, they were quickly neutralised by the influence of the Mediterranean. The summits of the Margeride and the plateau of the Velay were conspicuously drier and sunnier. They could be settled and cultivated at altitudes fit only for pasture just a short distance to the west. The rural society which developed in the southern Massif Central was, in part, a response to these conditions.

Terrain, relief and exposure considerably modified this bold pattern. Despite the obstacle posed by the Cévennes, the chalk valley of the Tarn enjoyed a near Mediterranean climate, while damp and cloudy conditions could push far up the valley of the Lot. Even at 1200 metres the causses were torrid during the summer months whereas the adjacent plateau of the Levézou remained temperate. The higher massifs were subject to brusque changes of temperature which in the east posed the principal threat to high altitude farming. From September temperatures plummeted exposing the autumn sowings to frosts until the snows arrived. Most villages in the Margeride and on the Velay plateau had over a hundred days of frost each year. Those situated on the flanks of Mont Mézenc could expect 150 days of frost and Sainte Eulalie,[1] at the head of the Loire, recorded freezing temperatures on 182 days in a year. Frost and snow were virtually unpredictable hazards which might occur at any time. While the wranglings in the Estates-

---

[1] P. Estienne and R. Joly, *Les Régions du Centre* (Paris, 1973), p. 19.

General were moving to a climax in mid-June 1789, snow fell on the plateau of the Palais du Roi and frosts shrivelled crops and the leaves on the trees in the neighbourhood of Mende.[2]

The fundamental climatic distinctions between east and west, the vertiginous changes of elevation and the abrupt juxtaposition of different bedrocks combined to produce a physical environment of spectacular diversity. The southern Massif Central comprised an assortment of natural *pays*, contoured by geography, geology and climate. Improved upon by man, they had fused in places to form ecological zones endowed with specific characteristics. The Aubrac is a case in point. Colonised and cleared by monastic pioneers from the twelfth century onwards, the natural environment was fashioned into pastures of unrivalled quality. The chestnut orchards (*châtaigneraie*) which had burgeoned on the schist slopes of the ségala and the Cévennes by the end of the *ancien régime* were another, if more anarchic, example of this process. A measure of ecological convergence and the inter-dependence of plateau and valley economies helped to mitigate the incoherence of terrain and relief. But in any case the unity of the southern Massif Central as a separate region was scarcely in doubt. Geographically speaking it represented a prolongation of the central plateau and no natural feature divided north from south. Here the frontier was a mental barrier reinforced by history and ancient provincial solidarities. Viewed from the Bas Quercy, the Mediterranean plain and the valley of the Rhône, however, the southern Massif Central was the 'montagne', its inhabitants *gavots* (highlanders) and its hallmark poverty.

Demographic recovery

By the end of Louis XIV's reign the southern Massif Central was underpopulated even in relation to its slender resources. Harvest failure, civil commotions, religious strife, pestilence and the crushing burden of royal taxation (see chapter five) had thinned out the countryside and caused the towns and *bourgs* to contract. Arable and pasture land reverted to heath as entire villages abandoned their taxable possessions and became itinerant. Peasant fertility faltered and the continuity of generations was threatened. The background is important for it helps to explain one of the key features of this society in the nineteenth century – its capacity to absorb sustained growth without significant modification of its economic structures or mental horizons. The pace of recovery varied considerably. In the Vivarais population growth commenced in the 1720s and by mid-century it had gathered sufficient momentum to survive a cycle of poor harvests between 1748 and 1751. The pre-revolutionary decade proved especially propitious and

---

[2] P. J.-B. Delon, *La Révolution en Lozère* (Mende, 1922), p. 49; P. L.-R. Higonnet, *Pont-de-Montvert. Social Structure and Politics in a French Village, 1700–1914* (Cambridge, Mass., 1971), p. 83.

accumulated reserves of vitality with which to withstand the crises of 1788–9 and subsequent years. Thereafter the birth rate fairly rocketed. In 1801 the first prefect of the Ardèche marvelled at the pullulating hordes of children and reported a 'prodigious increase' in population.[3] With the Consulate the department entered a dynamic phase of growth which was reflected in an unbroken curve of demographic advance over the next half century.

Recovery seems to have come later in most other parts, although the evidence is fragmentary which makes generalisation hazardous. Official statistics for the *ancien régime* are incomplete, unstandardised and can be trusted only to provide crude orders of magnitude. The census data of the new regime are scarcely exempt from reproach either. Political and fiscal afterthoughts continued to colour returns well into the nineteenth century.[4] Impressionistically, therefore, the Velay comes closest to the pattern established by the Vivarais. The prosperity of the 1780s was felt here, too, with nearly all parishes recording an increase in population.[5] This growth appears to have been a phenomenon of the second half of the century, but it was well rooted and survived the revolutionary epoch without loss of vitality. The Brivadois, which formed part of the Auvergne until it was amalgamated with the Velay to create the department of the Haute-Loire in 1790, exhibited different characteristics. Recovery was hampered by a heavy burden of seigneurial and fiscal impositions – an enduring feature of the *pays d'élections*. By the Revolution a gentle increase in population had been registered, but the pace was scarcely quickening and the practice of rural migration put even these modest gains at risk.

The itinerant habits of the Auvergnat held little appeal for the inhabitants of the Rouergue in the eighteenth century. But if the Rouergat was sedentary by inclination, it is difficult to make a reliable estimate of numbers at the end of the *ancien régime*.[6] Growth did occur from about mid-century, by which time most of the towns and *bourgs* had made good their losses, but it was uneven. Two prosperous decades were followed by an appalling series of dearths in the 1770s which culminated with the famine of 1777–8. The government made attempts to provision the province, but the demographic repercussions were serious and not fully effaced before the onset of the revolutionary crisis. When royal fiscality and harvest conditions permitted,

[3] Archives Nationales (henceforth A.N.) F[1c] III Ardèche 10, Prefect to Minister of the Interior, Privas, 27 Prairial IX.

[4] On this subject, see M. Leymarie, 'Emigration et structure sociale en Haute-Auvergne à la fin de l'Ancien Régime', *Revue de la Haute-Auvergne* (1956–7), 313–14, who notes sardonically, 'Afin de retarder une augmentation d'impôts, la ville d'Aurillac, par exemple, a éprouvé beaucoup de difficulté pour franchir officiellement le cap des 10,000 et des 20,000 habitants.'

[5] J. Merley, *La Haute-Loire de la fin de l'ancien régime aux débuts de la Troisième République* (2 vols., Le Puy, 1974), i, pp. 44–5.

[6] A. Guéry, 'La Population du Rouergue de la fin du Moyen Age au XVIIIe siècle', *Ann. E.S.C.*, xxviii (1973), 1555–76.

the population of the Rouergue was naturally buoyant. A high birth rate allied to negligible emigration produced dynamic growth in the early decades of the nineteenth century. In the ségala there was a veritable population explosion as the chestnut and the potato held famine at bay and peasant *petite culture* developed unhindered by seigneurialism.

The Lozère was probably the last department to escape the grip of *ancien régime* demography. The elements held the upper hand well into the nineteenth century. In many of the villages of the Upper Gévaudan the population remained stagnant until the Revolution and seventeenth-century levels of fertility were not restored before the 1830s. Arzenc-de-Randon and Chasséradès marked time until the 1780s, at St Sauveur-de-Ginestoux there was little growth before 1795, while at Le Cheylard-l'Evêque the collective memory reckoned that population increase had been a post-revolutionary phenomenon.[7] A census of village common land recorded the existence of sixty households in 1789, but by 1831 this figure had risen to seventy-eight. These were all highland communities situated in the Margeride. Isolated, autarchic and climatically vulnerable, their capacity for self-generated recovery was held in check and throughout the eighteenth century they acted as a brake upon the demographic vitality of the province. In the latter part of the nineteenth century, by contrast, the roles were reversed. As peasant polyculture on the Cévenne valley slopes was pressed to its ecological limits, the plateau came into its own. The population of the Margeride – like that of the ségala region in the Aveyron – continued to increase in response to its own complex dynamics, thereby masking if not staunching the migratory flow towards the Mediterranean plain.

If uninterrupted, or barely interrupted, demographic expansion is a test of the vigour of pre-industrial society, there can be little doubt that the agrarian civilisation of the southern Massif Central crossed an important threshold in the early nineteenth century. A period of sustained growth commenced which can be compared with the cycles cut short by the Black Death in the early fourteenth century and the Wars of Religion in the sixteenth century. This last great epoch was brought to a close by the siren pressures of economic integration. From the 1860s a haemorrhage of definitive migration emptied the Cévennes and the population of the hinterland massifs followed in slow succession. A peasant culture of exceptional richness reached and then passed its zenith. While the most inaccessible villages of the Margeride continued to expand until the First World War, the demographic profile of the region had changed fundamentally (see figure 1). After the staggering losses of that war even these pockets of vitality succumbed.

[7] R.-J. Bernard, 'Démographie et comportements démographiques en Haute-Lozère, XVIIe–XVIIIe–XIXe siècles', *Revue du Gévaudan*, nouv. sér., xxi (1975), 97–100; P. M. Jones, 'Common Rights and Agrarian Individualism in the Southern Massif Central, 1750–1880', in G. Lewis and C. Lucas (eds.), *Beyond the Terror* (Cambridge, 1983), pp. 139–40.

Population statistics provide a foundation for two more observations of particular relevance to this study. The mid-century (1847–51) is commonly taken to mark a crucial watershed in the fortunes of the French countryside. Yet the demographic profile of large parts of the southern Massif Central remained stable or in the ascendant until 1886. Only the Ardèche proved unable to surmount the crisis and the malaise of the Cévennes is recorded in population censuses from 1851 onwards. The contrast with the departments of the western Massif Central (see figure 2) is striking and instructive. In the Corrèze, the Creuse, the Cantal and the uplands of the Lot the potential for steady growth within existing structures had been exhausted by 1848. Malthusian restraints upon peasant *petite culture*, the progress of agricultural specialisation and improved communications undermined the traditional economy. Long-established habits of seasonal and spasmodic migration hardened into definitive migration; village and family solidarities slackened and rural society began to adjust to the pressures of urban markets and urban culture.

The second point to note with regard to the southern Massif Central is that the demographic expansion of the nineteenth century occurred in the countryside. Urbanisation – however measured – was negligible. Towns, or

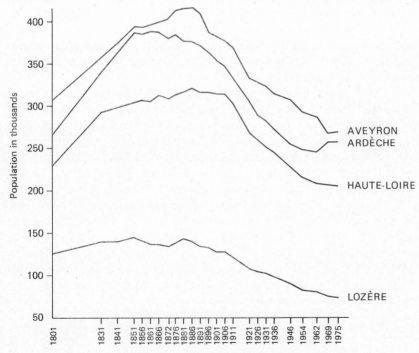

Figure 1 Population change in the southern Massif Central, 1801–1975

Politics and rural society

nucleated settlements of over two thousand inhabitants to adopt the generous administrative definition, were an insignificant feature of the landscape. According to the 1806 census, there were six major centres of population in the Aveyron, in the Ardèche there were five, in the Haute-Loire five, likewise, and in the Lozère three. The ancient cathedral and pilgrim city of Le Puy was by far the largest with just over 12,000 inhabitants. Over the century the rate of growth of the old ecclesiastical and administrative centres was unspectacular: Mende, *chef-lieu* of the Lozère, struggled from about 5,000 to a little over 7,000 inhabitants; Privas, the diminutive capital of the Ardèche, roughly doubled in population to reach 7,000 as did Rodez, capital of the Aveyron, which claimed 14,000 in 1906. Le Puy stagnated until mid-century in stark contrast to its teeming hinterland, but grew swiftly thereafter. The concentration of administrative responsibilities, together with currents of local migration, ensured that the *chefs-lieux de département* continued to expand, but they were too isolated to enjoy sustained commercial prosperity. The great axes of north–south communication by-passed them, and all save for

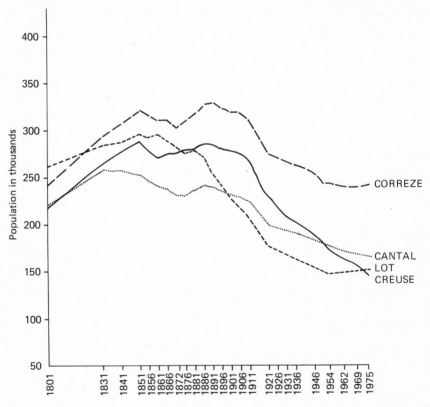

Figure 2 Population change in the western Massif Central, 1801–1975

Privas were situated above the 600 metre contour. The towns which benefited most from the demographic recovery were nearly all located on the margins of the massif. Annonay and Millau were old manufacturing centres with convenient access both to raw materials and to markets: they tripled in size in the course of the century. Aubin and Decazeville were entirely new industrial towns whose development was favoured by easily worked coal and mineral deposits and proximity to a navigable reach of the river Lot.

Sharing characteristics of both town and countryside were the *bourgs*.[8] Situated in the interstices between different climatic and ecological levels, they articulated and lubricated the rural economy. To all intents and purposes, therefore, the *bourg* replaced the town. It mobilised the meagre surpluses of rural production; it supplied aliments and implements beyond the resources of the village and it provided some specialised services. As agriculture recovered from the debilitating crises of the *ancien régime* the *bourgs* recovered, too. Increased productivity, marginal improvements in communications and expanding networks of markets and fairs enhanced their role and swelled their population. The most dynamic were Sauveterre-de-Rouergue and Naucelle, the bulging chestnut 'capitals' of the ségala, and Villefort, the entrepôt of the Cévennes in which the products of the mountain were exchanged for those of the Mediterranean plain. The cattle and textile *bourgs* of the northerly massifs held important fairs, yet lacked a solid agricultural base. In the latter half of the eighteenth century they enjoyed considerable prosperity, but thereafter their fortunes fluctuated. The population of the *bourgs* ringing the pastures of the Aubrac had peaked in most cases by the 1830s.

Beyond the *bourgs* lay the countryside proper and it was here that the balance of the population was located. The mortality of the late seventeenth and early eighteenth centuries removed the better part of a generation from the land and left considerable slack in the rural economy. Over the next one hundred and fifty years this slack was taken up, hesitantly and unevenly it is true, but the overall trend is beyond question. With an unflinching birth rate and declining levels of infant mortality, the villages and hamlets of the southern Massif Central were reinvigorated. By the middle of the nineteenth century the countryside was beginning to bulge at the seams. The labour-intensive agriculture of the Cévennes had reached its natural limits. Sub-

---

8 The *bourg* underlined the shortcomings of the administrative definition of a town. In response to a query by the prefect of the Drôme (21 August 1809), a Napoleonic statistician observed: 'Ce qui distingue les bourgs des simples villages dans le langage ordinaire (car je le répète, il ne saurait être ici d'une distinction légale [*sic*]), il me semble que l'on est convenu de le faire consister en ce que les bourgs ont des marches ou renferment au moins les principaux artisans auxquels les habitants de la campagne ont besoin de recourir. Je sens au surplus que ces lignes de démarcation ne sauroient être bien prononcées et qu'on passe par des nuances presque insensibles des villages aux bourgs' (in R. Le Mée, 'Population agglomérée, population éparse au début du XIXe siècle', *Annales de démographie historique* (1971), 464).

Table I.1 *The rural population (%) of the southern Massif Central*

Department	1806	1831	1856	1861	1872	1881	1891	1901	1911	1921
Ardèche	91.1	90.9	85.2	84.6	85.8	83.9	81.9	81.7	81.8	80.7
Aveyron	89.6	88.5	84.3	81.9	81.4	80.7	82.0	76.4	75.8	75.5
Haute-Loire	87.7	88.3	86.2	86.5	83.0	82.4	81.8	81.1	80.4	80.6
Lozère	92.2	91.2	89.7	88.0	89.4	88.5	88.0	88.5	87.9	87.5
France	81.2	79.5	72.7	71.1	68.9	65.2	62.7	59.1	55.9	53.7

Sources: R. Le Mée, 'Population agglomérée, population éparse', *Annales de démographie historique* (1971), 455–510; *Annuaire statistique de la France: 1881* (Paris, 1881); *Statistique de la France. Résultats du dénombrement de la population en 1856* (Strasbourg, 1859); *Statistique générale de la France. Résultats statistiques du dénombrement de 1891* (Paris, 1894); P. Merlin, *L'Exode rural suivi de deux études sur les migrations par Robert Herin et Robert Nadot* (Paris, 1971), pp. 8–13.

missions to the 'Enquête sur la question du travail agricole et industriel' of 1848 reported that the valley of the Ardèche was terraced 'jusque sur les rochers' at Thueyts.[9] The *conseil-général* of the department of the Aveyron complained that hordes of gleaners pounced upon every ear of corn the harvesters let drop.[10] Nearly everywhere obsessive *défrichement* (land clearing for arable cultivation) caused alarm amongst flockowners and large farmers. When the soil would tolerate no further sub-division, the peasantry became volatile, but with small benefit to the towns of the region. They remained undeveloped and offered strictly limited opportunities for employment. The population surplus drained off towards the cities of the plains of Languedoc and northwards towards Paris and Lyons. In 1893 Cardinal Bourret, bishop of Rodez, remarked wryly that Paris was the largest parish of his diocese.[11]

Habitat

As the preceding paragraphs make clear, the southern Massif Central was a village society. Since society and milieu constantly interacted it is worth looking at the settlement patterns of the region in some detail. The term 'village' provides a suitable starting-point for it is not without ambiguity. In most western peasant societies the modern distinction between village and hamlet

---

[9] V. Chomel, 'Le Département de l'Ardèche à la veille de la Révolution de 1848', *Revue du Vivarais*, lii (1948), 80.

[10] 'C'est au milieu même du gerbier, sous la faucille du moissoneur, que des bandes de femmes, d'enfans, d'hommes quelquefois valides, viennent disputer au propriétaire des épis qu'il est loin d'avoir abandonnés', A.N. F[1c] V Aveyron 4 *Procès-verbal des délibérations du conseil-général*, 31 July 1833.

[11] P. Nauton, *Atlas linguistique et ethnographique du Massif Central* (4 vols., Paris, 1959–63), iv, p. 19.

appears not to have existed.[12] 'Hameau' (hamlet) was a literary expression which hardly ever entered colloquial speech. All settlements lacking the visible substance of the town or, perhaps, the *bourg* were referred to as villages. With extraordinary elasticity the term could even be stretched to embrace the isolated dwelling, but in the Cévennes it was more usual to describe the single farmstead as a *mas*. However useful as tools for habitat analysis, it should be remembered that the distinctions drawn between 'village', 'hamlet' and 'isolated dwelling' are anachronistic and prejudge somewhat the question of peasant sociability (see chapter four). The southern Massif Central was a village society in the cultural rather than the strictly geographical sense.

Where the open fields of northern France ended, the *bocage* country began. In the west the hills of the Perche announced the enclosed landscape of the Armorican massif: in the south the transition was marked by the sad wastes of the Sologne. The Massif Central was not all *bocage*. There were open-field enclaves around Clermont (the *limagnes*) and St Flour (the *planèzes*), but a dissected landscape of woodland, heath, pasture and diminutive arable plots predominated. As the physical environment fragmented, so, too, did the mode of occupation of the soil. The neatly contoured villages of the plains receded to be replaced by settlements of variable size and precarious aspect which appeared to lack either a centre of gravity or a defined agricultural territory (*terroir*). In parts of the Massif Central, habitat dispersion reached record levels. Outsiders concluded that such conditions made social living impossible and historians have often been content to record their observations without further comment. One prefect of the Aveyron likened his department to Siberia, remarking: 'J'ai six cents paroisses qui ne sont composées que d'une foule de hameaux de trois à quatre maisons, ces hameaux sont disseminés ça et là au loin, le chef-lieu de la paroisse ne compte lui-même le plus souvent que cinq à six feux.'[13] This is an accurate description, perhaps, but a false analogy which reveals scant understanding of the mechanisms of peasant sociability in the areas of dispersed habitat.

Systematic analysis of the habitat of the southern Massif Central over time and space is a difficult undertaking. The *ancien régime* generally counted hearths rather than heads and counted them in units which do not reliably equate with the post-1789 commune. Nevertheless, the bold outline of population distribution can be ascertained and sometimes the finer detail as well.

[12] G. Le Bras, *L'Eglise et le village* (Paris, 1976), p. 11 and note 1; P. Bonnaud, ' "La Haie et le hameau": les mots et les choses', *Bulletin de l'Institut de géographie* (Faculté des Lettres, Clermont-Ferrand), xxxviii (1970), 5; R. Cresswell, 'Une Communauté rurale en Irlande', *Travaux et mémoires de l'Institut d'ethnologie* (Université de Paris), lxxiv (1969), 229; C. Pelras, 'Goulien – commune rurale du Cap Sizun (Finistère)', *Bulletin de la société d'anthropologie de Paris*, x (1966), 187.

[13] A.N. F[19] 408 *Cultes*, Prefect to Minister of the Interior, Rodez, 22 September 1808.

Table I.2 *Settlement patterns in the parish of Sénergues*

Settlements	Households per settlement
1	20 (Sénergues)
1	7
1	6
2	5
1	4
9	3
14	2
23	1
Total 52	125

Source: J. Touzery, *Les Bénéfices du diocèse de Rodez* (Rodez, 1906), p. 676.

Data collected in 1771 as part of a massive ecclesiastical enquiry set in train by bishop Champion de Cicé, indicates that the average settlement in the diocese of Rodez contained six households.[14] This is not very helpful since it rounds off the extremes and obliterates the contrasts between ecological zones. Analysis of the same statistics by parishes produces more promising results. In 326 out of 445 parishes over 50 per cent of the population lived outside the *chef-lieu* (the site of the church which was usually the principal settlement), and in 184 parishes the proportion rose to between 83 per cent and 100 per cent.[15] Nonetheless, the spatial distribution of the non-agglomerated population of the parish remains elusive and in order to uncover the balance between village, hamlet and simple farmstead, we have to combine these data with an inspection of the map. The ségala and the Aubrac emerge as the areas of maximum dispersion. As might be expected, the valley villages were well nucleated while those of the causses were thinly distributed but likewise fairly substantial in appearance. The tortuous relief of the ségala seems to have encouraged piecemeal settlement and narrow horizons and loyalties among its scattered population. Hamlets containing two or three households and isolated farms or mills predominated. The parish of Golinhac contained fifty-two 'villages', reported the *curé* in 1771. The biggest of these had approximately one hundred inhabitants, but most consisted of one or two households. In nearby Sénergues a similar level of dispersion obtained. On the eve of the Revolution the parish comprised 1,200 inhabitants grouped as in table I.2.

At first sight the habitat of the Aubrac exhibited identical characteristics.

[14] Guéry, 'La Population du Rouergue', p. 1562.
[15] R. Chartier, M. M. Compère and D. Julia, *L'Education en France du XVIe au XVIIIe siècle* (Paris, 1976), p. 24.

The *curé* of Le Cambon informed the bishop that there were about eighty inhabited places in the parish, 'dont le plus grand nombre n'est composé que d'une ou deux maisons'.[16] However, the Aubrac parishes were of vast proportions. They tended to stretch from the plateau to the valley and integrate several ecological zones in an age old bid for self-sufficiency. The summits were not habitable all the year round and it is likely that many of the highland settlements recorded were summer stations for the herdsmen. What already, strictly speaking, amounted to a pattern of villages and hamlets, became more pronounced to the east and north of the Aubrac massif. Along the declivities of the Margeride in the Upper Gévaudan the hamlets reigned supreme. Too weak to challenge the hegemony of the local village individually, their very numbers conferred on them a certain power to interfere and obstruct. Jealous defenders of their common pastures and collective rights (see chapter three), they were a perpetual irritant to their larger neighbours.

The habitat of the plain of Brioude was marginally more coherent, but not typical of the countryside of the Haute-Loire generally. In this as in other aspects, the synthetic origins of the department are evident. At the close of the Second Empire, the Haute-Loire comprised over 5,000 settlements gathered, rather arbitrarily, into 261 communes. The villages of the Brivadois embraced, on average, fourteen households, while those of the *arrondissements* of Le Puy and Yssingeaux contained thirteen and ten respectively.[17] The *arrondissement* of Yssingeaux roughly corresponded with the Atlantic watershed of the Velay–Vivarais plateau and here extreme dispersion was the rule. The *bourgs* and villages lacked substance and the landscape was dotted with isolated farmsteads. Collectively, if not individually, the non-agglomerated population tended to resist the suzerainty of the *chefs-lieux* and times of political crisis and slackening central control brought these centrifugal tendencies to the fore. The majority of the communes of the plateau were fissured in this way. Some *chefs-lieux* had as many as a hundred tiny satellites in watchful orbit around them. Occasionally the communes were 'hollow', that is to say they lacked a central nucleus altogether, but this was more typical of the Cévennes.

Firmer conclusions can be drawn for the Ardèche where the structure of the countryside has been studied systematically. Working from the 1936 census of population, Bozon[18] discerns four broad types of settlement: a straightforward nucleated habitat of dominant villages situated principally in the valley of the Rhône; a grouped habitat in which the domination of the village was challenged by one or more large hamlets (northern Ardèche); a habitat consisting mainly of hamlets of comparable size and a habitat of almost com-

---

[16] L. Lempereur, *Etat du diocèse de Rodez en 1771* (Rodez, 1906), p. 546.
[17] H. Malègue, *Eléments de statistique générale du département de la Haute-Loire suivis du dictionnaire des lieux habités* (Paris, 1872), p. 85.
[18] P. Bozon, *La Vie rurale en Vivarais: étude géographique* (Valence, 1963), pp. 200–7.

plete dispersion characterised by the isolated dwelling. The Vivarais face of
the Mont Mézenc massif, the plateaux of St Agrève and Vernoux, and the
Cévennes formed the natural habitat of the hamlet and the single farmstead
or *mas*. The phenomenon of the 'hollow' commune or parish occurred
repeatedly, especially in the Lozérian Cévennes, to yield indices of dispersion
approaching 100 per cent (see table I.3). In the canton of St Germain-de-
Calberte isolated dwellings swamped the hamlets entirely. Over 60 per cent
of the settlements forming the communes of St Germain-de-Calberte and
Moissac in 1879 were simple farmsteads.[19] Such figures speak for themselves,
but it is worth remembering that the *maison isolée* of eighteenth and
nineteenth-century census literature is not as helpful as it first appears. The
distinction between mills, châteaux, barns, temporary dwellings and peasant
holdings is not drawn, and, more important for our purposes, the term lends
itself to mistranslation. Strictly speaking, the *maison isolée* was a single
household settlement detached from others. Its inhabitants may also have
been isolated, geographically and psychologically, but this was not a *sine qua
non* of the dispersed habitat. On the volcanic massifs and in the ségala the evidence suggests a rural society bedevilled by a hopeless sense of isolation, yet
the steep walls of the Cévenne valleys could sometimes perform an integrative
role. In linear terms the *mas* were never far apart and often mutually visible.
As the author of a study of one of the Gardon valleys concluded, 'le mas isolé
n'éxiste pas, s'il est isolé sur le terrain, il ne l'est jamais du regard'.[20]

A synoptic view of the rural habitat of the southern Massif Central which
is based on data spanning several generations is necessarily arbitrary. It begs
a number of questions, the most important of which concerns change over
time. How did settlement patterns evolve during a century of dynamic population growth? The time-slice approach suggests that evolution was exceedingly slow. The nineteenth century bequeathed to the twentieth structures
similar to those which it had inherited from the late *ancien régime*. During
periods of demographic growth these structures filled out; during periods of
high mortality they emptied. The broad pattern of settlement, together with
the nuances described above, responded little to cyclical change. This is not
to deny local variations which often struck contemporaries forcibly. In the
areas of most rapid population growth (ségala, the Cévennes) waste land was
brought into cultivation and settlements swarmed up the slopes. The habitat
thickened on the high plateau of the Velay as well. Marginal increases in
productivity and abundant pastures prompted cadets to leave the family
holding and establish precarious households of their own on the edge of the

[19] P. P. Vincens, *Dictionnaire des lieux habités du département de la Lozère* (Mende, 1879), pp.
105–6; Archives Départementales de la Lozère (henceforth A.D.L.) T series [unclassified]
Monographies des instituteurs: St Germain-de-Calberte.
[20] J.-N. Pelen, 'La Vallée Longue en Cévenne. Vie, traditions et proverbes du temps passé' (Université d'Aix, Mémoire de maîtrise, 1972), p. 71.

Table I.3 *Habitat structure in the Lozérian Cévennes c. 1879*

Commune	A	B	C	D	E	F
Barre	3440	31	662	393	269	27.1
Bassurels	4639	24	387	44	343	88.6
Cassagnas	3519	17	645	212	433	67.1
Gabriac	844	22	307	67	240	78.2
Molezon	1476	29	405	33	372	91.9
Pompidou	2280	8	845	287	558	66.0
Ste Croix	1855	21	752	250	502	66.8
St Julien-d'Arpaon	2072	12	559	57	502	89.8
St Andéol-de-Clerguemort	686	30	325	9	316	97.2
St Frézal-de-Ventalon	1689	28	523	0*	523	100.0
St Maurice-de-Ventalon	3851	17	374	50	324	86.6
Vialas	4977	41	2152	528	1624	75.5
Le Collet-de-Dèze	2647	28	1256	400	856	68.1
Moissac	2705	60	660	3	657	99.5
St André-de-Lancize	2285	46	584	39	545	93.3
St Etienne-Vallée-Française	5099	20	1559	302	1257	80.6
St Germain-de-Calberte	3860	125	1516	345	1171	77.2
St Hilaire-de-Lavit	1031	29	367	12	355	96.7
St Julien-des-Points	383	29	175	3	172	98.3
St Martin-de-Boubaux	3140	85	751	21	730	97.2
St Martin-de-Lansuscle	1805	45	548	92	456	83.2
St Michel-de-Dèze	1419	39	609	30	579	95.0
St Privat-de-Vallongue	2387	65	820	32	788	96.1

Key:
A   Area of commune (sq. km.).
B   Number of inhabited settlements.
C   Total population.
D   Population of *chef-lieu.*
E   Population outside *chef-lieu.*
F   Index of dispersion (E/C × 100).
*   no *chef-lieu.*
Source: P. P. Vincens, *Dictionnaire des lieux habités du département de la Lozère* (Mende, 1879).

commons. None of these developments significantly altered existing settlement patterns, though. The steady growth of the first half of the nineteenth century may have enhanced the tendency towards dispersion, but that tendency was already ancient.

Further problems arise in respect of our units of measurement. Communes and parishes varied enormously in size and population and were not generally co-terminous.[21] This limits the comparability of our indices of dispersion. The Cévenne communes were much smaller than those of the causses and

---

[21]   See below, chapter four, pp. 110–11.

Mont Lozère which hemmed them in from the west and the north. The monster communes of the Aubrac were nearly all over 1,500 hectares or fifteen square kilometres (seventy-five square kilometres in the case of St Chély-d'Aubrac), while that of Le Rozier in the valley of the Tarn covered just 192 hectares.[22] Commune and parish can scarcely be considered immutable physical entities either. Each was susceptible to internal pressures which could produce splits and realignments when condoned by the higher authorities. These same authorities were prone to bouts of reorganising zeal, too. In the aftermath of the Concordat, parish boundaries underwent major surgery, but remained fairly stable thereafter. The communes were an altogether more recent creation which required constant adjustment. Sometimes they were contoured around the *ancien régime* fiscal unit – the *communauté d'habitants* – and therefore inherited all the incongruities of that institution. More often they had ecclesiastical or seigneurial antecedents (see chapter four). Whatever their origins, multitudes of tiny, but jealously independent, communes emerged after 1789 only to be extinguished and amalgamated subsequently. Between 1793 and 1945 the number of communes within the territory of the present-day *arrondissement* of Rodez dropped by more than half. François Sainthorent, the first prefect of the Aveyron, was especially ruthless in dismantling the first generation of post-revolutionary communes, but the attrition was uneven and sporadic and many small entities survived. Indeed, Sainthorent's reorganisation of the Aubrac communes proved unworkable and had to be abandoned amid a chorus of complaints in 1837.[23] Each wave of administrative manipulation left its mark on the statistics of the period, however. As a result, the questions we ask of census data which classify population by communes need to be carefully framed. Table I.4 tells us little about settlement patterns, but shows the rough distribution of population in the year in which the commune regained its status as an electoral constituency.

Without some knowledge of habitat, it is difficult to appreciate the realities of politics in the countryside. This applies as much to the logistical aspects of electoral consultation as to the process of decision-making. Equally, it would be difficult to evaluate those theories of rural politicisation which postulate a causal link between habitat and electoral behaviour. What light do settlement patterns shed upon such questions as 'community', 'culture' and 'sociability' which will constitute major themes of this study? Some scholars equate the dispersed habitat with isolation, social deference, vertical solidarities and, consequently, political quietism. Others, in effect, draw the

[22] C. Parain, 'Contribution à une problématique de la communauté villageoise dans le domaine européen', *L'Ethnographie*, lxiv (1970), 42; A.D.L. 2 O 1283 *Administration et comptabilité communales: Le Rozier.*

[23] A. Meynier, 'La Commune rurale française', *Annales de géographie*, liii–lv (1945), 167 and note 3; E. Plagnard, *Prades-d'Aubrac* (Villefranche-de-Rouergue, 1960), pp. 71, 74.

Table I.4 *Distribution of the population of the southern Massif Central by communes (1831)*

Department	Under 500	500–1,000	1,001–1,500	1,501–2,000	2,001–2,500	2,501–3,000	3,001–3,500	3,501–10,000	Total number of communes
Ardèche	73	144	53	28	14	8	2	7	329
Aveyron	13	68	72	45	20	9	6	8	241[a]
Haute-Loire	78	92	44	18	12	8	3	9	264
Lozère	83	62	27	10	4	1	0	2	189

Note:
[a]*Mairies* created on 5 Messidor VIII by prefect Sainthorent from the 579 communes then existing.
Sources: A.N. $F^{1b}I$ 258; F^{1b} Aveyron 3.

opposite conclusion: the regions of scattered settlement were the natural habitat of the small peasant proprietor – a vigorous breed of independent means and radical instincts. The *bourg* poses further problems. In the *bocage* of Upper Brittany[24] they were neither numerous nor influential, apparently, but in Provence they dominated the landscape. Indeed, in the opinion of Maurice Agulhon[25] they played a crucial role in the unfolding political consciousness of the Mediterranean littoral. The southern Massif Central combined the *bourg* with record levels of dispersion. The resulting tension suggests that the *bourg* did not dominate; that it often harboured radical traditions, but was unable to impose them on the surrounding countryside.

Communications

In the course of the 1777–8 dearth in the *généralité* of Montauban,[26] the royal government endeavoured to provision the region from outside. One million *quintaux* (100,000 metric tons) of cereals were purchased. Grain from southern Brittany and Aquitaine was transhipped or embarked in the port of Bordeaux and carried up the Garonne and the Tarn to Montauban and Gaillac. At Gaillac it was unloaded into carts bound for the markets of Villefranche-de-Rouergue and Rodez. Destinations beyond these road ter-

---

[24] T. J. A. Le Goff, *Vannes and its Region: a Study of Town and Country in Eighteenth-Century France* (Oxford, 1981), pp. 205, 239.
[25] M. Agulhon, *La Vie sociale en Provence intérieure au lendemain de la Révolution* (Paris, 1970), pp. 59–61.
[26] H. Guilhamon (ed.), *Journal des voyages en Haute-Guienne de J. F. Henry de Richeprey* (2 vols., Rodez, 1952–67), i, pp. 92–3 and note 1.

mini had to rely upon mule trains to provision their markets. Foodstuffs purchased in Egypt were dispatched by sea to the Languedoc port of Sète from which they could be moved by road as far as Lodève. The limestone ramparts of the Causse du Larzac halted all northbound wheeled traffic and the grain sacks had to be transferred to muleback for the precipitous ascent. On the top of the plateau a good road had existed since the middle of the century and waggons could be employed once more. However, the descent to Millau on the other side of the plateau was if anything more hazardous. Mules alone could carry goods down the steep gradient and at the bottom the river Tarn posed a further obstacle (the bridge at Millau had been swept away in 1758). The expense of this operation was enormous – about 14 million *livres* – although the government recouped most of its outlay by selling the grain at prevailing prices. It has been calculated that the cost of transport from Bordeaux increased retail grain prices in Rodez by 51 per cent on average while transportation from Sète pushed up market prices by some 66 to 80 per cent.[27]

The story of the 1777–8 dearth neatly demonstrates the problem of communications in the southern Massif Central. Disconnected highways, locomotion by mule or bullock team and fallen or infrequent bridges continued to provide the common fare of the traveller for a century after 1750. With the exception of the north-eastern access via the plain of Forez or the valley of the Gier, all other routes into the massif were more arduous than those described above. Entry and exit via the Haute-Auvergne was impractical because the Monts du Cantal were virtually impassable before the Lioran tunnel opened in 1868. Auget de Monthyon,[28] intendant of the Auvergne, remarked in 1770 that haulage between Clermont and Aurillac was more costly than between Clermont and Paris despite the much greater distance involved. The Rhône valley afforded excellent north–south communication, but negligible lateral penetration and the Cévennes were among the last areas to benefit from the transport revolution. Imberdis[29] believes it unlikely that any form of wheeled vehicle reached Clermont or Brioude from either Nîmes or Montpellier before the nineteenth century.

A glance at the map of post roads of France before the Revolution reinforces the point. The southern Massif Central features as a void surrounded by coaching termini (see map 3). The bourgeois of Rodez or Mende who wished to travel to Paris in reasonable comfort had first to make his way on horseback to either Villefranche-de-Rouergue, Aurillac or Le Puy. In 1806 a carriage service linking Rodez to the main road network at St Flour was

[27] R. Sudriès, 'Les Subsistances dans l'Aveyron de 1787 à 1795', *Revue du Rouergue*, iii (1949), 154.

[28] Leymarie, 'Emigration et structure sociale', p. 300.

[29] F. Imberdis, *Le Réseau routier de l'Auvergne au XVIIIe siècle: ses origines et son évolution* (Paris, 1967), p. 263.

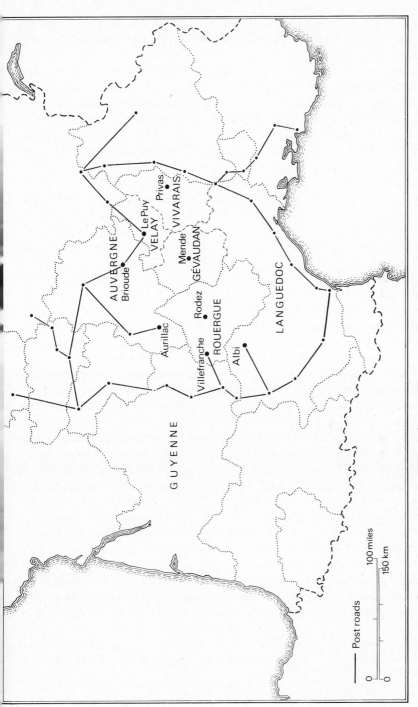

Map 3 Post roads of the southern Massif Central

inaugurated, but it remained irregular until 1845. Weather conditions permitting and barring mishaps, the journey took five days. In 1836 the mail coach broke previous records and covered the distance between Paris and Rodez in two and a half days. But coaches, indeed wheeled passenger vehicles of any description, were an uncommon sight. In 1850 pack mules continued to fill the streets of Privas; the arrival of a mail coach – even the passing of a humble *patache* – attracted throngs of gaping people avid to see the spectacle and receive the news.

Heroic efforts were made to strengthen the road infrastructure of the southern Massif Central in the course of the eighteenth and nineteenth centuries. Despite the neglect of the revolutionary years these efforts produced a fairly steady, cumulative improvement in communications. In 1699 de Boulainvilliers's *Etat de la France*[30] put large areas of the Massif Central out of bounds to wheeled vehicles, while in 1850 Adolphe Blanqui reported that the departments of the Aveyron, Cantal, Haute-Loire, Puy-de-Dôme, Ardèche and Lozère were, 'sans cesse parcouru par des méssageries régulières'.[31] Blanqui's assertions were optimistic in the extreme, but they do reflect the perception among contemporaries that conditions were decisively changing. In the decade of the 1850s the last of the metropolitan prefectures (Mende) was connected to the telegraph line and the railway began to penetrate the region from the West. News could now outpace rumour – at least to the larger centres of population.

Over a broad span of time a picture of relative progress emerges. However, the central question concerns the nature of this evolution. Two points are immediately apparent: the improvement in communications developed from an extremely modest threshold and it was uneven. The task which fell to the intendants and to the provincial estates from about the middle of the seventeenth century was daunting. Instead of making existing roads into better roads, they had to convert mule tracks into carriage ways. Often this was impossible. Pack trains scaled the gradients and kept to the ridges along routes which wheeled vehicles could never follow. As a consequence, entirely new alignments had to be envisaged which entailed enormous expenditure on embankments, cuttings and bridges. New roads linked the towns, but disrupted existing communications and threw ancient patterns of economic, social and spiritual contact into confusion. Arthur Young dimly perceived this when marvelling at the splendid emptiness of *ancien régime* highways. The great road linking Villefranche-de-Rouergue, Rodez and Millau which intendant Lescalopier used forced labour (*corvées*) to build between 1740

---

[30] Cited in G. Boscary, *Evolution agricole et condition des cultivateurs de l'Aveyron pendant le XIXe siècle* (Montpellier, 1909), p. 143.

[31] A.-J. Blanqui, 'Tableau de la situation des classes ouvrières en 1850', *Séances et travaux de l'Académie des sciences morales et politiques*, viii (1850), p. 328.

and 1756, by-passed most of the *bourgs* of the ségala. Through traffic benefited, but local exchange remained hampered by the lack of access roads.

Inherited infrastructure deficiencies meant that the southern Massif Central was not endowed with a basic network of viable, all-weather highways until the second half of the nineteenth century. Indeed, the pioneer period of road-building comfortably overlapped the coming of steam locomotion to the region. As late as 1840 the major lateral road of the Lozère running between Mende and Villefort was not practicable for wheeled vehicles along its entire length. Twenty years later the prefect of this department likened it to 'une île perdue au milieu de la mer et encore, grâce à la vapeur, arriverait-on plus facilement dans une île qu'on arrive à Mende'.[32] Compared with the Rouergue and the Gévaudan, the Velay was well endowed with roads at the end of the *ancien régime*. Le Puy was linked to Lyons via St Etienne and to the valley of the Rhône via Yssingeaux or Le Monastier. Connexions with the Auvergne were tenuous, however. Mules could ply between Le Puy and Brioude in the early eighteenth century, but wheeled vehicles had to make a massive detour via Lyons and Clermont. Road communication with Lower Languedoc was incomplete and with the Gévaudan non-existent. The gorges of the Allier and the Margeride mountains proved formidable barriers which resisted the road engineers and were finally spanned by the railway between 1870 and 1902. In the hinterland of the Ardèche and the Cévennes pockets of mule haulage and sledge transport survived almost to the end of the nineteenth century. The communications revolution came late to these districts, but quickly gathered momentum thereafter. Carts began to appear at Burzet in 1830; by mid-century they had reached St Germain-de-Calberte and in 1875 St Etienne-de-Serres. About thirty of the communes of the Ardèche (9 per cent) remained outside the road network in 1876 and most of these were situated in the Cévennes.[33]

As the modern road infrastructure of the region came into being, the unevenness which had characterised its early development was ironed out. The Revolution probably helped in this respect, for it obliterated the distinction between the *pays d'élections* and the *pays d'états*. Before 1789 the directly administered *élections* of the Rouergue and of the Brivadois were lamentably endowed with roads even by the modest standards of the region. On this evidence the reputation enjoyed by the eighteenth-century intendants as road-builders seems scarcely justified. The adjacent provinces of the Velay, the Vivarais and the Gévaudan were incomparably better served by the Estates of Languedoc. The lassitude of the intendants, the ineffectiveness of the provincial assemblies set up in the *pays d'élections* in the years after 1779 resulted

---

[32] A.N. F¹ᶜ III Lozère 9 Prefect to Minister of the Interior, Mende, 18 June 1864.
[33] G. Bouladou, 'La Vallée du Gardon de St Germain-de-Calberte (Lozère)', *Bulletin de la société languedocienne de géographie* (1946), 43; P. Bozon, *Histoire du peuple vivarois* (Valence, 1966), p. 184.

in bizarre discrepancies in the network. Bits of highway were eventually completed, usually after years of in-fighting over alternative routes, but feeder-roads were ignored and sinuous provincial boundaries played havoc with long-distance communication. The road between Le Puy and Craponne both commenced and terminated in the Velay and the provincial estates had completed the sections under its jurisdiction in 1766. Unfortunately, however, it traversed a wedge of the territory of the Auvergne (*élection* of Brioude) and this portion was still incomplete in 1783. The recalcitrance of the Auvergne was again the cause of an interruption in the important Le Puy–Brioude highway in 1788.[34] Arterial routes through the Rouergue were similarly affected. Communication between Rodez and Toulouse was intercepted on the Rouergue–Albigeois border; between Lyons and Bordeaux on the Rouergue–Gévaudan border and between Paris and Montpellier (highland route) at Marvejols. These were all frontier points between the *pays d'élections* and the *pays d'états*. Jurisdictional squabbles, natural obstacles and the tergiversations of local notables delayed the completion of the axes for decades. In the case of the Paris–Montpellier artery, the descent from the Causse de Sauveterre posed enormous problems and the argument over the alignment lasted for eighty years. Not until 1841 did the Marvejols–Millau section open to traffic.

After the hiatus of the Revolution, the uneven legacy of the *ancien régime* was sorted out in the course of the next half century. Gaps were filled in, gradients were eased and a start was made on local roads. It is doubtful whether these improvements amounted to a revolution in communications, however. Market networks expanded and fairs multiplied, certainly, but if short-range contacts were enhanced, ingress and egress from the Massif remained difficult. As the departmental *conseils-généraux* were wont to lament, the invigorating currents of national 'civilisation' left the region to one side. The building of the railways partially remedied this situation (see table I.5). For the first time the rapid movement of men, goods and ideas became feasible and the consequences were far-reaching. The chronology of railway construction in the region is revealing for it appears to coincide with the apogee of rural society. By 1884 the prefectures of the four departments were all connected to the national railway network and to the capital, although not always directly. In the race for the shortest route between the Mediterranean and Paris, the P.L.M. company had driven a railway up the gorges of the Allier and through the Cévennes to link up Clermont and Alès by 1870. The Midi company capped this in 1888 with a shorter overland route between Béziers and Clermont which included a rail viaduct poised 126 metres above the river Truyère. Although these feats of engineering enabled southern vine-growers to reach northern markets with minimum

---

[34] Merley, *La Haute-Loire*, i, pp. 28–9; M. Chanson, 'L'Assemblée de l'élection de Brioude (1787–1788)', *Revue d'Auvergne* (1888), 388–9.

Table I.5 *The growth in railway communications*

Lines penetrating the southern Massif Central	Date of completion
Arvant (Haute-Loire)–Brioude (Haute-Loire)	1857
Montauban (Tarn-et-Garonne)–St Christophe (Aveyron)	1858
St Christophe (Aveyron)–Rodez (Aveyron)	1860
Livron (Drôme)–Privas (Ardèche)	1862
Firminy (Loire)–Pont-de-Lignon (Haute-Loire)	1863
Pont-de-Lignon (Haute-Loire)–Le Puy (Haute-Loire)	1866
St Rambert-d'Albon (Drôme)–Annonay (Ardèche)	1869
Brioude (Haute-Loire)–Alès (Gard)	1870
Le Puy (Haute-Loire)–St Georges d'Aurac (Haute-Loire)	1874
Millau (Aveyron)–Rodez (Aveyron)	1880
Le Monastier (Lozère)–Mende (Lozère)	1884
Béziers (Hérault)–Neussargues (Cantal)	1888
Mende (Lozère)–La Bastide-St Laurent-les-Bains (Lozère)	1902
Carmaux (Tarn)–Rodez (Aveyron)	1902
Langogne (Lozère)–Le Puy (Haute-Loire)	1912

Sources: R. Caralp-Landon, *Les Chemins de fer dans le Massif Central* (Paris, 1959), table; P. Bozon, *La Vie rurale en Vivarais* (Valence, 1963), p. 276.

delay, they had only a marginal impact upon the archaic economy of the southern Massif Central.

What the region needed were transversal lines which could feed local traffic into the national network. Progress was made in this direction, after 1880, but the secondary lines never proved their economic viability and their coverage remained sketchy. A single-track line pushed eastwards from Rodez to connect with the Béziers–Clermont axis at Sévérac in 1880 and four years later a spur up the valley of the Lot linked Mende to the same axis. An eastward projection of this line to join the Clermont–Alès axis at some convenient point was envisaged in 1881, but not finally achieved until 1902. The Montagne du Goulet seemed insurmountable and so an ambitious attempt was made to cut a passage through it on the model of the Lioran tunnel which had enabled the railway to span the Cantal a decade or so earlier. Revised financial calculations prompted the abandonment of this costly effort after 700 metres of galleries had already been hewn. In 1891 work began on an overland alignment instead which took a single-track line over the exposed plateau of the Palais du Roi to link up with the Clermont–Alès axis at La Bastide. The connexion was made, but it never fulfilled the hopes placed in it. Technical shortcomings ensured that it would never serve as a goods link between Toulouse and Lyons and it also failed to provide the local population with all-weather access to the east and south-east. Constructed at over 1,000 metres, communication was frequently interrupted in the winter and the line has long enjoyed the reputation of being the highest and most snow-swept railway in the country.[35] As for the Ardèche, it was never spanned despite a twentieth-century attempt to link La Levade-d'Ardèche and Le Puy. Privas remained a rail terminus situated at the end of a spur from the Lyons–Avignon line.

The optimism of the Freycinet Plan notwithstanding, large areas of the southern Massif Central remained outside the rail network at the end of the nineteenth century. In such areas the bullock cart survived as the traditional form of locomotion, and the relevant issue continued to be roads, not railways. Much of the northern Ardèche was devoid of rail communications, as were the Cévennes after the failure of plans to build a permanent way linking Le Vigan to Millau and Florac. The largest 'hole' in the network embraced the northern Aveyron and adjacent districts of the Cantal and the Lozère, however. In this vast zone of some fourteen cantons, many of the communes were thirty and forty kilometres from the nearest railway halt. This was a significant drawback in a highland area which was seeking northern outlets for a developing stock-raising and cheese manufacturing economy.

The role of modern communications in the process of historical change should not be overstated, though. Men moved into and out of the Massif despite the obstacles of terrain and habitat and had done so for centuries. The migration of Auvergnats to Paris or Lyons antedated the Grand Central line and the completion of trunk roads, while migration from the Cévennes does not appear to have been hampered by the absence of stations. Conversely, the reluctance of the peasant of the ségala to quit the soil was scarcely diminished by the opening of a rail link between Carmaux and Rodez in 1902. Patterns of migration and social intercourse had deeper roots. Improved overland communications played a more influential role in the economic sphere, although even here they were by no means as consistently corrosive of old insularities and prejudices as is often imagined. The extent to which opportunities were recognised and exploited depended upon cultural as well as ecological factors. The ségala is a classic example of how modern communications could benefit agriculture. Massive rail shipments of lime from Carmaux revitalised the poor schist soils and probably helped to stabilise the rural population as well. A similar benefit might have accrued to the northerly cantons of the Velay plateau which also enjoyed good rail connexions, but here subsistence agriculture was already giving way to commercial stock-raising and the opportunity was ignored. Many contemporary observers assumed that the coming of the railways would free the Massif Central to concentrate on its strengths, basically cattle and timber, and make arable farming redundant. Old habits died hard, however, partly because they were habits and defied economic logic and partly because the provisioning of the region could never be relied upon. There were too many gaps in the

[35] R. Caralp-Landon, *Les Chemins de fer dans le Massif Central. Etude des voies ferrées régionales* (Paris, 1959), pp. 117–36.

network and even in districts which were beginning to feel the pull of remote markets the rural economy was slow to shed its archaic features.

If steam locomotion tended to link rather than integrate the southern Massif Central with the rest of France, there can be little doubt about its impact on popular consciousness. The railway left in its wake a changed sense of time, a sharper perception of the national entity and a disturbed social structure. The new *communes-gares* which it spawned were unlike either the *bourgs* or the villages. They contained a rootless and mobile class of employees and minor officials whose life-style both appalled and attracted the peasantry (see chapter nine). The old elites watched the growth of these railway colonies with misgivings, anxious lest their insubordination should prove contagious. The clergy chronicled the creeping progress of religious indifference while the prefects scrutinised the results of elections for signs of political disaffection.

2

❊❊

The rural economy

The structure of landholding

The modern concept of property developed late in the southern Massif Central. Individual and collective ownership coexisted and interacted. Customary and codified law conflicted and peasant habit respected neither consistently. Much of this confusion was removed by revolutionary and Napoleonic legislation, but the bland slogans of the Declaration of the Rights of Man concerning the 'inviolable' and sacred nature of property should not be taken too literally. Suspiciously feudal forms of tenure survived well into the nineteenth century and the prevalence of common rights in certain regions made freehold ownership something of a myth. The land surface of the southern Massif Central can be grouped under three broad headings: individually owned land; collectively owned land (commons) and land of ill-defined status (usually rocky outcrops, ravines, heath, verges). Two qualifications need to be added: a proportion of individually owned land was held 'indivis', that is to say that it was farmed jointly by members of a household or multi-household group, and some 'waste' land (*landes, terres hermes, terres vaines et vagues*) was in fact abandoned land whose fiscal burden had devolved upon the community of inhabitants (see chapter five, p. 155). The distinctions were never rigid. Land held 'indivis', wastes and fallow were frequently confused with the commons, while the commons were under constant attack from 'owners' arguing that they were the product of a primitive concession. Peasant society was at its most litigious when dealing with matters related to the status of land.

The distinctions drawn above were also subject to dynamic flux. The trend of the period 1750–1880 was firmly in the direction of tillage. In practice this meant a marked increase in the area of land under individual occupation and cultivation at the expense of the commons and wastes. How much land could be drawn from this stock and put under the plough is unclear, however. We have fairly reliable data on common landholdings for the middle of the nineteenth century (see table II.3), but the estimation of waste land is largely inferential. Richeprey[1] noted the existence of extensive heaths in the ségala of the Rouergue before the Revolution and in 1800 Monteil[2] asserted that one-third of the land surface of the Aveyron was waste and non-productive. His estimate excluded fallow land and pasture. It is unlikely that land perpetually barren of crops was any less extensive in the Lozère and on the Velay–Vivarais plateau at this date. The soil of the Brivadois and the Bas Vivarais was probably more effectively colonised. Viewed from the angle of land use, the rural economy contained much slack and it was this slack rather than innovative or intensive agricultural techniques which sustained the population explosion of the early nineteenth century.

Fragmentation was the dominant characteristic of private ownership. Large and compact farms were conspicuous by their rarity. *Petite propriété* had long held sway in the southern Massif Central, but it ramified from about the middle of the eighteenth century as a result of the division of existing holdings and the opening up of new land by squatters (*colons*). The Revolution scarcely modified this secular trend. Monastic estates were swiftly dismembered, but the territorial strength of the nobility and rural bourgeoisie weathered the political storms with remarkable ease. Surveyors and administrators used a variety of square and volume measurements to assess property which have a few advantages, but many shortcomings. They facilitate rough comparisons between localities, but were often inaccurate when applied to slope and terrace agriculture. More seriously, they presuppose criteria of performance and viability which were alien to mountain husbandry. Acreage and affluence did not necessarily coincide, nor were peasant farms compact and balanced as acreage statistics imply. A diminutive hemp field on the banks of the Lot might produce a higher cash-equivalent yield than a hundred-acre holding in the Cévennes. As this example suggests, the key to good husbandry was not acreage but balance between arable and pasture. In an age largely innocent of mineral and artificial fertilisers, the supply of manure was the crucial yardstick of viability. The pioneer agronomist, Amans Rodat,[3] commented wryly in 1839 that he knew of an Aveyronnais farmer whose net yields rose after he had been obliged to sell a portion of his plough-land. In any case peasant society measured property in more concrete terms which conveyed an impression of worth and quality as well as size. Typical of such estimations were phrases like, 'un bien de trois paires de bœufs' (indicative of a substantial peasant proprietor); 'une petite métairie d'une paire de bœufs' (sharecropper) and 'une petite locaterie consistant en une maison et un peu de bien' (day-labourer/plotholder).[4]

---

[1] Guilhamon, *Journal des voyages*, i, pp. 299, 312–14, 324, 327–8; ii, pp. 290, 319, 326, 328.

[2] A.-A. Monteil, *Description du département de l'Aveiron* (2 vols., Paris, *an* X), ii, pp. 46–7.

[3] A. Rodat, *Le Cultivateur aveyronnais: leçons élémentaires d'agriculture pratique et vues sur la science de l'exploitation rurale* (Rodez, 1839), p. 229.

[4] Archives Départementales de l'Aveyron (henceforth A.D.A.) 9L213 *District de Sévérac*, list of suspects, 23 Pluviôse II.

Table II.1 *Crude size of landholdings,*[a] *1882 (hectares)*

Department	0–1	1–5	5–10	10–20	20–30	30–40	40–50
Ardèche	28,000	25,000	12,500	6,500	2,500	1,100	660
Aveyron	38,000	34,500	15,000	7,400	4,000	2,600	1,500
Haute-Loire	22,965	24,372	11,650	7,567	3,075	1,547	684
Lozère	10,763	9,981	6,053	3,502	1,958	1,393	892
France	2,671,667	1,865,878	769,152	431,335	198,041	97,828	56,419

Note:
[a]Land cultivated by a single individual or household whether in the form of a compact farm or scattered parcels.

With all allowances made, it is still not easy to quantify property structures. Variations over space, if not over time, were extreme. Microscopic holdings of under one hectare were perhaps the most clearly defined category. They were common in the hinterland of the towns and *bourgs*, in the river valleys, in the ségala, in parts of the Cévennes and, as the nineteenth century wore on, in the highland parishes of the Aubrac, the Margeride and the Velay. Usually they indicated the presence of either an artisan workforce, lucrative cash crops such as wine, or land clearance on the edge of heaths and commons. The latter phenomenon is clearly evident in the case of the Margeride village of Le Chéylard-l'Evêque.[5] In 1831 all but twelve of seventy-six households held under one hectare and about a third occupied 100 square metres each, effectively the space for a hut and a garden. 'Medium-sized' property, to use contemporary administrative jargon, fluctuated considerably. In the ségala and in the valleys three or four hectares were considered to be respectable, but household sufficiency required at least ten hectares on the highland plateaux and more on the causses. The thresholds of large-scale property likewise shifted through many gradations from perhaps twenty hectares in the ségala and the lowlands of the Ardèche to several hundred hectares on Mont Lozère, the Aubrac and the causses. As the figures reproduced in table II.1 suggest, large landowners were not very numerous but were solidly rooted, especially in the Lozère. The reverse was true of the peasant plotholder whose social significance far outweighed his economic role. A

---

[5] Jones, 'Common Rights and Agrarian Individualism' pp. 139–40.

50–100	100–200	200–300	300–400	400–500	500 and above	Total number of land-holdings	% increase in total number of land-holdings since 1862
590	120	35	10	4	2	77,021	68.85
1,200	700	300	90	12	1	105,303	43.27
451	162	16	13	1	0	72,503	59.87
894	373	179	64	39	12	36,103	71.91
56,866	20,644	5,585	1,653	704	217	6,175,989	91.57

Source: *Statistique agricole de la France (Algérie et colonies) publiée par le Ministre de l'Agriculture. Résultats généraux de l'enquête décennale de 1882* (Nancy, 1887), pp. 282–7.

sampling of property structures in the Lozère during the early nineteenth century indicates that approximately 29 per cent of proprietors possessed little more than 1 per cent of the land.[6]

Possession is a vague term which invites definition. If seigneurial theories of overlordship and the continuing relevance of customary rights are ignored for a moment, a large proportion of the land surface of the southern Massif Central may be described as owner-occupied. Moreover, peasant property increased inexorably during the period in question. However, the convenient categories of freehold, leasehold and sharehold are somewhat blurred by the prevalence of hybrid forms of tenure characteristic of regions of low soil fertility. The *domaine congéable* system of southern Brittany[7] is a case in point and a broadly similar type of lease existed in the southern Massif Central where it went by the name *bail à locaterie perpétuelle* or *bail emphytéotique, dit perpétuel.* Each had the effect of confusing the issue of ownership. The *bail à locaterie perpétuelle* was a lease consented in perpetuity to a tenant and his heirs in return for a small annual rent paid in kind (*rente constituée*). Usually it was conceded by owners who for various reasons were unable to cultivate the land themselves and who were unable to attract tenants on any other terms. In Languedoc, or more exactly in the region subject to the jurisprudence of the Parlement of Toulouse, the legal title to the land remained in the

[6] Y. Maurin, 'La Répartition de la propriété foncière en Lozère au début du XIXe siècle', *Cévennes et Gévaudan, 46e congrès de la Fédération historique de Languedoc méditerranéen,* Mende-Florac, 1973, p. 317.

[7] Le Goff, *Vannes and its Region,* pp. 158–62.

hands of the lessor, but in Provence the *bail à locaterie perpétuelle* did pre-suppose a transfer of property rights. During the Revolution such leases were challenged and tenants were given the opportunity to buy out their *rentes* as though they were feudal dues. The avalanche of petitions addressed to the committees of government from indignant proprietors under threat of expropriation gives some idea of the importance of this form of tenure in the southern provinces of the Massif Central. Wherever the soil was thin and poor and easily exhausted by short-term tenancy, it played a crucial role. Without perpetual leasehold, the Cévennes would revert to sterility, announced one petitioner rather disingenuously. In the ségala the *bail à locaterie perpétuelle* had become widespread during the misery of the last years of Louis XIV's reign. Only on these terms could proprietors find peasant cultivators for their estates. The political tergiversations of the Revolution destroyed the basis for such leases and few were concluded after 1800. Together with sharecropping they declined steadily in the nineteenth century and had become rare even in the Cévennes by the 1880s.[8]

Sharecropping (*métayage*) and renting (*fermage*) offered attractive alternatives to the proprietor. Without actually becoming involved in cultivation, he could choose either to survey or to ignore his tenant. In practice the distinction was not so easily drawn since fixed-term tenants were long required to settle part of their obligations in kind. Sharecropping appealed to the small owner who had perhaps only recently given up farming and who lived nearby. Renting was wasteful but status enhancing and hence appealed to notables and institutional landlords. For obvious reasons these types of tenure were to be found in the areas in which medium and large-scale property predominated, but since they were symptoms of social as well as economic conditions the correlation is not complete. *Métayage* was practised in all the provinces of the southern Massif Central at the end of the *ancien régime* although the trend towards *petite propriété* had already reduced its sway in some districts. Villages composed entirely of sharecroppers existed in the Levézou highlands and much land was farmed on this basis in the Bas Vivarais. Yet, in adjacent districts – the ségala and the Cévennes – owner-exploitation was already well entrenched. The advance of peasant property continued during the post-revolutionary decades and sharecropping bore the brunt. By 1880 *métayage* was virtually extinct in the Aveyron and the Lozère. It survived longer in the Ardèche, but the trend was unmistakable. *Fermage* had never been as extensive and survived rather better. The nationalisation of church lands during the Revolution may have affected tenant farming adversely, but only in so far as those lands were divided up. The major challenge came rather from landlords seeking to bolster the yield of their estates

---

[8] Comte de Tourdonnet, *Situation du métayage en France: rapport sur l'enquête ouverte par la société des agriculteurs de France* (Paris, 1879–80), p. 13.

by hiring direct labour (*maîtres-valets*). Such methods of exploitation were increasingly employed in the Haute-Loire and the Lozère.[9]

The shift away from sharecropping and perpetual leases, the clearing and dividing of land and escalating pressure on the commons were all preliminary symptoms of a rapid expansion of the category of peasant proprietor. At least 50 per cent of the peasantry were owner-exploiters on the eve of the Revolution.[10] By 1882 89 per cent of cultivators could be included in this category.[11] In the ségala and the Cévennes all the land had passed into the hands of the peasantry. Landowning, sharecropping and tenant farming were not mutually exclusive conditions, however (see table II.2); nor did ownership of land presuppose self-sufficiency. The peasant proprietor of official statistics was often the desperately vulnerable proprietor of a potato patch who also rented land and at intervals sold his labour in order to make ends meet. There was nothing coherent about peasant property either. It was nearly always fragmented, often scattered over a wide area and sometimes randomly hacked from heath and highway.

Nearly all property, in fact, exhibited some of these characteristics. Patient accumulation over generations and ecclesiastical donations had resulted in a few well-integrated estates, but even medium-sized holdings tended to include a miscellaneous collection of plots. Jean Velay,[12] a well-to-do rentier of the *bourg* of Florac, acquired by marriage to an heiress in 1663 a substantial patrimony consisting of five compact estates (*domaines*) situated on the causse above Florac; twenty-one assorted patches of land (mostly vines and kitchen gardens); eight other plots (fields and orchards) and seven further oddments of field. By dint of careful management over the next thirty-two years he added a hemp field; another plot of vines; three gardens and twelve more plots of arable. Up to thirty kilometres of mule track separated the outlying parcels and they were cultivated and harvested by direct labour hired as the need arose. The *domaines* were tenanted on renewable leases payable in kind. If the term *domaine* generally indicated a self-sufficient farm, it did not necessarily presuppose a compact holding. The Costy family[13] had occupied the hamlet of Aguès since the thirteenth century and by 1798 their possessions extended to some 117 hectares. Only the cattle pasture and the sapling nursery were adjacent to the farmhouse; the best arable land was near the village of Vimenet two kilometres distant while some of the meadow land

---

[9] *Ibid.*, pp. 297–8. [10] Boscary, *Evolution agricole*, pp. 68–9, 74.
[11] *Statistique agricole de la France (Algérie et colonies) publiée par le Ministre de l'Agriculture. Résultats généraux de l'enquête décennale de 1882* (Nancy, 1882), p. 324.
[12] L. Dupouy, *Les Protestants de Florac de la Révocation de l'Edit de Nantes à l'Edit de Tolérance* (Paris, n.d.), pp. 108–13.
[13] L. Lempereur, 'Une Famille de bourgeoisie rurale en Rouergue: les Costy d'Aguès', *Journal de l'Aveyron*, 20 July 1919 and then weekly until 2 November 1919; P. M. Jones, 'The Rural Bourgeoisie of the Southern Massif Central: a contribution to the study of the social structure of *ancien régime* France', *Social History*, iv (1979), 74–5.

was even further afield. This, then, was the physiognomy of landholding which official statistics derived from fiscal data can scarcely convey. The cultivable land of the southern Massif Central was infinitely divided and would remain so for most of the nineteenth century. In 1866 Durand de Gros, the agronomist and erstwhile utopian socialist, asserted in his evidence to the Agricultural Commission of the Aveyron that, 's'il y a un domaine de quelque étendue, nous le voyons composé de cinquante lambeaux épars, quelquefois dans plusieurs communes'. Choose at random 400 hectares of arable land, he continued,

nous la trouvons en moyenne divisée en 100 lots composés chacun, terme moyen, de huit pièces de diverses natures, bizarrement découpées, séparées par d'assez longues distances, enchevêtrées plus ou moins dans celles des voisins, exerçant ou subissant des servitudes, nécessitant des (*sic*) nombreux chemins et des clôtures coûteuses qui frappent de stérilité une notable partie du sol. Sur chaque lot, nous voyons une famille fournissant moyennement deux travailleurs mâles ou femelles. Chacune d'elles a une paire de bœufs ou une paire de vaches, ou une vache seulement, ou une chèvre. Les gros tenanciers ont en sus 10, 15, 30, 50 brebis. Les forces de ces cent familles s'usent sur ces 400 hectares.[14]

The impact of the Revolution upon the structure of landholding was muted. *Petite propriété*, it is now accepted, antedated 1789 and the tenacious polyculture of the southern Massif Central presupposed the early formation of a class of peasant cultivators. The pressures which shaped and trimmed property structures until the 1880s were mostly evident from about the middle of the eighteenth century. Land hunger, *défrichement*, morcelisation and indebtedness emerged first as agrarian problems of the *ancien régime*. But if the land settlement of the Revolution scarcely benefited the peasantry, either because most land was already in their hands or because they lacked the financial muscle to buy at auction, other revolutionary initiatives certainly reinforced existing trends. The abolition of seigneurial dues and ecclesiastical tithes relieved the soil of a crushing burden of rent and subsequent reforms of the tax system combined to transform the economics of peasant farming in some localities. The beleaguered *pays d'élections* enjoyed the greatest benefits since they were generally subject to oppressive seigneurialism and heavy royal taxation (see chapter five, pp. 160–70). In the Aveyron the demise of harvest dues cut the demands on peasant surplus by about 25 per cent and from the 1820s cadastral adjustments brought further relief.[15] Existing arable surfaces were subdivided, hitherto unviable wastes were reclaimed and land values rose steeply. The enactment of revolutionary and Napoleonic inheritance laws to curtail the *droit d'aînesse* tended in the same direction. Freed from the

---

[14] A.N. ADXIX C43³ *Enquête agricole*, Aveyron, *séance du 27 octobre 1866*.
[15] Archives du Musée des Arts et Traditions Populaires (henceforth M.A.T.P.) *Enquête sur les formes anciennes de l'agriculture*: Aveyron; Boscary, *Evolution agricole*, p. 121.

Table II.2 *Structure of landholding (1862)*

Department	Proprietors (heads of household)			Part-proprietors (heads of household)			Non-proprietors (heads of household)		
	A	B	C	D	E	F	G	H	I
Ardèche	544	23	35,047	6,626	2,352	12,310	4,950	2,084	8,342
Aveyron	492	53	54,274	1,774	1,238	25,687	1,188	731	9,361
Haute-Loire	628	37	41,035	5,695	643	13,154	4,084	211	8,528
Lozère	233	15	14,535	1,662	582	7,808	918	232	4,045
France	47,424	10,215	1,754,934	648,836	203,860	1,134,490	386,533	201,527	869,254

Key:
A Owners employing farm retainers (*maîtres-valets*) to cultivate their property.
B Owners employing farm managers (*régisseurs*) to cultivate their property.
C Owner-exploiters.
D Owner-exploiters farming additional land as tenants.
E Owner-exploiters farming additional land as sharecroppers.
F Owner-exploiters complementing their livelihood with day labour.
G Tenant cultivators.
H Sharecroppers.
I Day-labourers (agricultural proletariat).
Source: *Statistique de la France. Agriculture, résultats généraux de l'enquête décennale de 1862* (Strasbourg, 1868).

constraints of seigneurial *lods et ventes*,[16] and paternal authority as enshrined in Roman Law, property became a commodity and a land market developed. This tendency should not be exaggerated, however. Only in the Auvergne portion of the Haute-Loire did the new inheritance legislation win wide acceptance and,[17] in any case, the soil remained subject to a variety of collective practices which the Revolution challenged but failed to destroy.

Land which was neither privately owned nor waste was common. In the southern Massif Central the commons occupied a pivotal position in the rural economy. They formed an indispensable adjunct to peasant agriculture and hence tended to concentrate and magnify an important category of local rivalries. Such antagonisms were frequently politicised and hence the commons deserve our special attention. All sources agree that collectively owned or collectively exploited property was extensive in the region. Furthermore, it seems to have survived the successive challenges of seigneurial *triages*, revolutionary *partages*, Napoleonic expropriations, nineteenth-century improvement schemes and the time-honoured encroachments of squatters and annexationists to a remarkable degree. While the *landes* of the South West and the commons of Brittany, Burgundy, the Limousin and the High Auvergne declined rapidly in the decades after 1850, those of the southern Massif Central traversed the century very little diminished. In part this was a reflection of the complex status of communal property in a region of dispersed settlement, but principally it underscored the residual stability of agrarian structures. Conditions of access and methods of exploitation evolved in response to demographic pressures, but there was no generalised assault upon the integrity of the public domain.

Mayors and municipal officials tended to view government requests for information on common and waste land with grave suspicion. After all, in 1813–14 the hard-pressed Empire had attempted to strip the communes of their landed assets to the benefit of the Treasury.[18] Land-use statistics should therefore be exploited with care. A reliable census of common landholdings was not compiled until 1863, but it contains a wealth of useful information.[19] As might be expected, the largest concentrations were to be found in the mountain departments of the Alps and the Pyrenees; in the pre-Alps (Jura,

---

[16] Onerous *lods et ventes* could distort the land market. In 1780 Richeprey noted that at St Laurent d'Olt (Rouergue) there had only been one hundred land sales in the previous century. In this seigneurie *lods et ventes* represented 10% *ad valorem* (Guilhamon, *Journal des voyages*, i, p. 73 note 2).

[17] G. Segret, 'La Maison paysanne dans la région de Blesle: étude sur le rôle économique et sociale de l'institution d'héritier du XVIIᵉ siècle à nos jours', *Almanach de Brioude* (1934), 92.

[18] J. Tessier, *La Valeur sociale des biens communaux en France* (Paris, 1906), p. 41; G. Duby and A. Wallon (eds.) *Histoire de la France rurale* (4 vols., Paris, 1975–6), iii, pp. 123–30; A.D.L. *7K4 *Registre de correspondance du préfet*, 25 Prairial X–12 September 1814.

[19] J. de Crisenoy, *Statistique des biens communaux et des sections de communes* (extrait de la *Revue Générale d'Administration*) (Paris, 1887); R. Graffin, *Les Biens communaux en France* (Paris, 1899), tables, reproduces de Crisenoy's statistics, but with numerous errors.

Isère); in the Vosges and in the Massif Central. About 200,000 hectares or 8 per cent of the land surface of the four departments of the Ardèche, Aveyron, Lozère and Haute-Loire was defined as common (see table II.3). This figure takes no account of so-called waste land which we know to have been extensive in the southern Massif Central. Less reliable estimates suggest that in the early nineteenth century waste and common land combined constituted between 30 and 40 per cent of the territory of the Aveyron and over 40 per cent of the Lozère.[20] Generally speaking the most substantial holdings of common land were to be found in the communes situated above the 1000 metre contour, that is to say in the Aubrac, in the Margeride and on the Velay plateau. Some of the villages of the causses, the Cévennes and the Bas Vivarais were also well endowed. By contrast, collectively owned property was meagre in the Brivadois (save for the canton of Pinols) and in the northern Ardèche. The town of Millau possessed over 2,500 hectares of commons on the neighbouring Causse du Larzac, while thinly populated communes such as St Georges-de-Levéjac (Causse de Sauveterre) and St Chély-du-Tarn (Causse Méjean) each enjoyed over 1,500 hectares.[21] Without irrigation the productive potential of the arid expanses of the causses was low, but at higher and wetter altitudes the commons provided rich grazing for transhumant as well as local stock. On the granite and volcanic plateaux intersected by the frontier between the Lozère and the Ardèche there were communes with over 2,000 hectares of collective pasture. Common land was, in fact, the dominant type of property in these districts and in the canton of St Etienne-de-Lugdarès which lay astride the Atlantic and Mediterranean watershed at over 1,000 metres up to 60 per cent of the land surface fell into this category.[22]

To describe the commons as though they were an attribute of the commune is misleading, however. The nineteenth-century commune was an administrative entity grafted on to the countryside. The artificial circumstances of its birth in the regions of dispersed habitat are made painfully evident in the complex juridical status of the commons. In the Massif Central and parts of Brittany and the West, the commons were the patrimony of the villages or of groups of villages. As a late arrival on the scene, the commune inherited from the community of inhabitants (see chapter four) a right to manage the collective property located within its jurisdiction, but the title to such property remained firmly vested in the villages. The new regime merely tidied up this state of affairs and conferred upon the village or hamlet possessing its own commons the status of *section de commune*. The anomaly stemmed from habitat. The extreme levels of settlement fragmentation found

[20] H. Clout (ed.), *Themes in the Historical Geography of France* (London, 1977), pp. 261–70 and figs.

[21] Guilhamon, *Journal des voyages*, i, p. 134 and note; A.-B. Sahut, 'La Propriété sectionale (exemple cévenol)' (Thèse, Institut des Hautes Etudes de Droit Rural et d'Economie Agricole, 1975), p. 140.

[22] Bozon, *La Vie rurale en Vivarais*, pp. 147–53 and fig.

in the *bocages* of the West and the Centre were not characteristic of the country as a whole and 84 per cent of French communes had no dependent sections. In a well-nucleated habitat communal boundaries could be contoured around single settlements whose commons thereby became the property of the commune. The extensive pastures of the Alps and the Pyrenees and the commons of the northern plains were nearly always the patrimony of the commune. In the Hautes-Pyrénées the public domain (woodland as well as pasture) covered 43 per cent of the land surface in 1863 and with a few exceptions it was both owned and managed by the communes. Of 453 communes possessing commons, only 20 had sections with assets of their own. In the Haute-Loire, by contrast, 256 communes out of 260 had dependent sections and the commons were overwhelmingly the property of these villages and hamlets (see table II.4). Just 464 hectares, or 1.3 per cent of the department's stock of common land, were at the disposal of the communes.[23]

It might be argued that the anomalous status of common land in the southern Massif Central made collective ownership something of a fiction. The distribution of common pasture and woodland was haphazardly related to population patterns and access was determined either by residence or by 'immemorial right' customs. Gross disparities both between and within communes existed. Some communes were sub-divided into a dozen or more sections each having its own common land; in others only a handful of sections had significant holdings which they jealously guarded against those less well endowed. Sections varied enormously in size, too. Some were populous and their commons retained the character of collective property, but many were not. Sections consisting of three or four households grouped in a hamlet were not uncommon, indeed there were sections disposing of extensive commons that were occupied by a single *mas*. The section of Chamblard in the commune of La Besseyre-Saint-Mary (Haute-Loire) was one such and the farm of Riffard (eight inhabitants in 1869) in the commune of Connangles (Haute-Loire) was also a section in its own right.[24] In these circumstances the commons became an extension of private property to all intents and purposes, although the proprietor had also to shoulder their entire tax burden.

In theory a section kept the title to its commons even if it ceased to exist as a centre of population. The commune enjoyed the usufruct of that property until such time as the section was re-colonised. In practice, however, a section top-heavy with assets and yet short on *ayant-droits* (beneficiaries) would be picked off by its neighbours. Sectional status was nearly always open to challenge, if only because much of the common land of the southern Massif Central was not only held by the sections, but between the sections. Joint

---

[23] de Crisenoy, *Statistique des biens communaux*.
[24] Tessier, *La Valeur sociale des biens communaux*, p. 306 and note 3.

ownership, originating in many cases from seigneurial concessions to groups of villages, nourished interminable conflicts and the territorial reorganisation of 1789 often added to the friction by allocating villages (baptised sections) to different communes. In some localities the commons were owned and exploited in permutations of daunting complexity. The modern commune of St Privat-d'Allier[25] (Haute-Loire) contains eighteen settlements, but they own common land in twenty-six combinations. The important distinction between ownership which attached to the sections – usually – and management which was a prerogative of the commune did not pass unchallenged, either, even though it was grounded in both pre- and post-revolutionary jurisprudence. When the Estates of the Vivarais mounted an enquiry into the commons in 1767 the communities of inhabitants replied that such possessions were the property of their constituent villages.[26] But the nineteenth-century communes were subject to mounting budgetary pressure as they sought to provide modern amenities for their inhabitants. The temptation to annex the commons and employ the proceeds for the general good was all the greater in that the sections found it difficult to defend their assets effectively. They lacked legal status under the new regime and could not plead in their own right. In 1818 it fell to the sub-prefect of Yssingeaux to warn the municipality of Le Chambon (Haute-Loire) that a proposal to sell off sectional pastures in order to finance the building of a bridge over the river Lignon was illegal unless it could be demonstrated that the bridge would only benefit the inhabitants of that section.[27]

The hybrid status of the commons posed an insuperable obstacle to meaningful collective exploitation in many instances. But even in cases where the common pasture was unequivocally the property of a single hamlet or village, resident householders were not free to profit from it as they saw fit. Access was governed by convention, and over the centuries these conventions had acquired an eminently censitary character. Article eleven of the Custom of the Auvergne stated the position succinctly: only over-wintered stock could be put on the common ('que l'on a hiverné et nourri des foins et pailles provenant des héritages que l'on tient').[28] This custom, known as the *foins et pailles* rule, applied widely across the southern Massif Central and resisted the egalitarian

[25] J.-B. Meyronneinc, 'Des Communautés villageoises aux sections de communes: l'exemple de quelques communes du Devès et de Margeride' (Université de Clermont Ferrand, Institut de Géographie, Mémoire de Maîtrise, 1975); pp. 22–3 and table.

[26] Archives Départementales de l'Ardèche (henceforth A.D.Ard.) C991 Printed circular, 30 January 1767. See, for example, the response of the *communauté* of Dompnac: 'il y a dans notre communauté deux vilages (*sic*) qui possèdent des biens communaux dont chaque vilage a les siens en particulier . . . ces deux vilages ont la plaine (*sic*) propriété de ces biens, elle n'est point commune aux autres vilages de notre communauté ny aux communautés voisines.'

[27] P. M. Jones, 'Parish, Seigneurie and the Community of Inhabitants in Southern Central France during the Eighteenth and Nineteenth Centuries', *Past and Present*, lxxxxi (1981), 86–7.

[28] Parain, 'Contribution à une problématique de la communauté villageoise', p. 53.

Table II.3 *Distribution of common landholdings (1863)*

Department	A	B	C	D	E
Ardèche	552,713	30,994	5.6	14,375	16,619
Aveyron	874,333	54,019	6.2	10,859	43,160
Haute-Loire	496,330	35,018	7.1	464	34,554
Lozère	516,772	78,871	15.2	6,549	72,322

Key:
A   Total area of department in hectares.
B   Total area of commons in hectares.
C   Area of commons as percentage of area of department.
D   Area of commons owned by communes in hectares.
E   Area of commons owned by sections in hectares.
Source: J. de Crisenoy, *Statistique des biens communaux et des sections de communes* (extrait de la *Revue Générale d'Administration*) (Paris, 1887), pp. 22–3.

Table II.4 *Distribution of* Sections de Commune *(1863)*

Department	A	B	C	D	E	F
Ardèche	339	161	47.5	986	28	6.1
Aveyron	283	264	93.3	1,582	30	5.9
Haute-Loire	260	256	98.5	2,881	15	11.2
Lozère	197	171	86.8	1,357	27	7.9

Key:
A   Number of communes.
B   Number of communes with dependant sections.
C   Number of communes with sections as percentage of total number of communes.
D   Total number of sections.
E   Maximum number of sections per commune.
F   Average number of sections per commune possessing sections.
Source: J. de Crisenoy, *Statistique des biens communaux*, pp. 22–3.

reforms of legislators well into the nineteenth century. By gearing access to property holding, it ensured that the biggest proprietors derived the biggest advantage from the commons. If the pastures were exploited directly, village bigwigs had the right to put the most beasts in the common flock; if they were leased to transhumant shepherds (see below, p. 61), village bigwigs obtained the lion's share of the *nuits de fumature* (night soil) and if they were leased for cash, village bigwigs divided up the rental on the basis of tax contributions. The commons, it was argued, were of seigneurial origin and had been ceded to the communities of inhabitants in return for a *censive* assessed on property. Since the large landowners paid most, they enjoyed privileged access to the commons. Where 'immemorial custom' antedated the legislation of the

Revolution, it survived and proprietors exploited their domination of municipal government to extend its sway. Despite instructions to the contrary from the Ministry of the Interior, certain municipalities in the Lozère invoked ancient precedent and continued to apportion the rent yield of their commons on a censitary basis throughout the nineteenth century. In 1902 the municipality of Altier received 617 francs for the lease of a pasture belonging to the section of Chareylasse on Mont Lozère. There were fifteen *ayant-droits* who received between 8 *f. 58 c.* and 128 *f. 70 c.* each. In 1905 the exercise was repeated and the prefect endorsed it, but '*à titre exceptionnel*'.[29]

The *foins et pailles* rule was tempered to allow the landless poor to pasture a minimal number of beasts on the common. Informal cultivation of odd patches was also tolerated – provided the good pasture remained intact. Where the poor were numerous and social deference weak, oligarchic control of the commons was challenged. The common fields and woodland on the outskirts of towns nearly always bore the marks of over-exploitation. But the poor were themselves ambivalent towards the commons. Despite their inferior status as *ayant-droits*, they shared in an ancient conviction that the commons were a heritage which each generation had a sacred duty to preserve and transmit to the next. Invitations to impropriate collective property fell on deaf ears and the political battles of the second half of the nineteenth century were chiefly fought around the questions of access and tillage versus grazing. Even the great revolutionary decree of 10 June 1793 which seemed to fulfil every small peasant's dream left few traces on property structures. The dismemberment of the commons into plots of equal size or value evoked little enthusiasm. Villagers were keenly aware of the disadvantages (loss of pasture, onerous survey fees, the expense of enclosures and access paths etc.) and the advantages (chiefly an increase in arable) were not yet of critical importance. Cereal cultivation at high altitude required large quantities of manure: where was it to come from? Also, the stipulation that division should be 'par tête d'habitant domicilié de tout âge ou sexe'[30] offended the susceptibilities of a society in which the household was the common denominator. This meant that marginals like farm servants, and even children put out to nurse, would be entitled to a share of the commons, objected the primary assembly of the canton of Chaudesaigues (Cantal).[31]

The post-Thermidor petitions of indignant proprietors give the impression that the Revolution had unleashed a spirit of reckless individualism in the countryside. But collective practices and collective exploitation of the commons resisted the facile agrarian egalitarianism preached in Paris. In a few

[29] A.D.L. 2 O 114 *Administration et comptabilité communales*: Altier.
[30] Law of 10 June 1793, section II, article one.
[31] A. Rigaudière, E. Zylberman and R. Mantel, *Etudes d'histoire économique rurale au XVIIIe siècle* (Paris, 1965), p. 52; M. Laurent, 'Le Partage des communaux à Ennezat à l'époque révolutionnaire', *Revue d'Auvergne*, lxxxxii (1978), 193.

localities, and notably on the Causse du Larzac,[32] disputes over methods of exploitation were sufficiently contentious to provoke revolt among the land hungry, but rural *sans-culottes* who had acquired their political education in struggles over the commons were rare. In the southern Massif Central little common land was divided up as a result of the decree of 10 June 1793 and many *partages* seem to have lapsed within a few years. There were numerous procedural grounds on which the divisions could be challenged. At Estables and Fournels in the Lozère, plots were allocated by household rather than by head and the same policy was adopted by the communes of St Alban-d'Ay and Labachère in the Ardèche.[33] The big proprietors and complaisant local authorities exploited these and other shortcomings to question the legality of the operation. Led by two jacobin notables, the poor of Estables fought a long battle to retain their plots and were actually evicted on one occasion before a reprimand from the Ministry of the Interior reached the administration of the department of the Lozère in 1801. The principal deterrent to the division of the commons lay elsewhere, however. Nature intervened on the side of the graziers and within twenty years the tenaciously defended arable plots of the *colons* of Estables had reverted to heath. As the boundary stones were engulfed by heather, collective exploitation resumed. Such was the fate of many attempts to clear the highest, granite slopes of the Lozère. The ecological obstacle proved insurmountable. When a more generalised assault upon the integrity of the commons gathered momentum nearly a century later, the same constraints were soon in evidence. Experts in soil management concluded that the cultivation of commons situated above 1,400 metres was futile; between 1,250 metres and 1,400 metres (the case of Estables) yields were too low and sporadic to return a profit; below 1,250 metres cultivation was usually profitable.[34]

The characteristics of peasant agriculture

Stability was the keynote of agriculture in the southern Massif Central during the period in question. But stability of structure, of orientation, did not preclude flexibility and evolution in the face of demand. If the region experienced no agricultural revolution of classic type before 1880, it nonetheless underwent considerable development. Land clearance, intensified polyculture and the removal of fiscal and seigneurial disincentives effected a quiet revolution in agricultural output. Without any significant structural transformation save for the increased cultivation of the potato, the rural economy kept pace

[32] P. M. Jones, '*La République au village* in the Southern Massif Central, 1789–1799', *The Historical Journal*, xxiii (1980), 796 and notes.
[33] A.N. F³II Lozère 4 Dossier for Estables and Fournels; Meyronneinc, 'Des communautés villageoises aux sections de communes', p. 57; Bozon, *La Vie rurale en Vivarais*, p. 152.
[34] Tessier, *La Valeur sociale des biens communaux*, p. 280.

with a massive growth in population and took major strides towards self-sufficiency. Nor was this achievement bought at the expense of social polarisation. Large landowners retained a rentier mentality and were slow to respond to the commercial opportunities offered by improved communications. For this and other reasons proletarianisation remained limited. With the possible exception of the early decades of the nineteenth century when headlong population increase outstripped the capacity of agriculture to absorb the available labour, wage-earners were being absorbed into, rather than expelled from, the property-owning body politic. As the nineteenth century progressed the signs were mostly in favour of convergence: traditional cottage industries declined, one by one, and the rural economy shifted onto a solidly agricultural footing; *petite propriété* advanced together with owner-occupation of the soil and the peasantry became more homogeneous in social composition and outlook.

The variety and subtlety of peasant polyculture in the *bocage* country is immediately apparent from land registers and plans (*cadastres*) compiled for the purpose of distributing taxation. Jean-François Henry de Richeprey, a surveyor employed by the Provincial Assembly of Haute-Guienne to investigate land use, reported in 1781 that the cultivable surface of the Rouergue and the Quercy could be divided into seven broad categories: gardens, plough-land, meadow land, vineyards, chestnut orchards, woodland and pasture. Under each heading he allowed for degrees or types based on examples collected during his travels in the two provinces. Thus, no fewer than forty-one sub-divisions were required to classify the types of plough-land which he encountered. Richeprey's laborious but rigorous scheme served as the model for the Napoleonic *cadastre* and it illustrates well the contrasting agricultural milieux of the southern Massif Central. Abrupt changes in soil structure, elevation and exposure implied great flexibility of land use which the rural population sought to exploit with the object of attaining self-sufficiency. But the drive for self-sufficiency imposed its own constraints upon land use. Alimentary needs did stubborn battle with ecological laws of diminishing returns as large tracts of unsuitable terrain were ploughed for cereal cultivation. Exhausted by the experience such land lay fallow for decades after two or three harvests, or worse, it fell prey to erosion and was permanently lost as a resource. Although alternative staples had always existed, cereal cultivation for domestic consumption constituted the first priority of peasant agriculture. The best land and, as demographic pressure increased, more marginal land was devoted to the production of bread grains. The only area to have emancipated itself from the burden of producing its own foodstuffs to a significant degree was the Lower Ardèche where the exigencies of the silk-worm industry determined land use and property values.

All the common cereals were grown in the southern Massif Central save, perhaps, for buckwheat which favoured warmer climes. But in the absence of mineral fertilisers all soils would not tolerate all grains. These soil–cereal contrasts were most clearly evident in the Aveyron where the calcareous soils of the causses favoured wheat and the schist soils of the ségala, rye. Indeed, the term 'ségala' derived from the patois noun for rye. A group of ségalis peasants whom Richeprey questioned in 1779 doggedly asserted that when they tried to sow wheat it came up as rye. Be that as it may, the population of the ségala remained shackled to a physically and mentally debilitating diet of coarse rye bread and potatoes until liming became feasible towards the end of the nineteenth century. Pockets of wheat cultivation were also to be found upon the volcanic soils around Brioude and on the marls of the Lower Ardèche, but wheat production was secondary (see table II.5). The staple cereal, the *blé* of peasant parlance, was rye.

Rye tolerated all but the harshest mountain environments and was particularly suited to high altitude volcanic and crystalline soils with an easterly elevation. It required ten or eleven months to reach maturity which made reaping and sowing nearly simultaneous early-autumn activities. But, provided the snows arrived promptly to protect the seedlings from damp and frosts, it withstood the rigours of winter temperatures well. Plentiful rainfall was needed in May and June as the ear filled out and then several months of dry and sunny conditions to bring it to maturity. By intercepting damp, westerly airstreams, the mountains of the Auvergne gave rise to conditions exceptionally favourable to rye cultivation in their lee. Whereas cereal husbandry suffered rapidly diminishing returns over 900 metres or thereabouts on the western flanks of the Massif Central, fields of rye ripened in the *planèze* of St Flour and in the Margeride at 1,200, even 1,300 metres. The impact of this climatic frontier is discernible in agrarian structures, in modes of settlement and ultimately in the divergent development of the two faces of the Massif in the nineteenth century. In the south and south-east, evolution towards a peasant society based on intensive polyculture and owner-occupation was unimpeded. The trend is unmistakable and clearly documented in early nineteenth-century land-use statistics: arable surfaces were more extensive in the high altitude communes of the Margeride than on the lower plateaux of the north and west. In the Cantal, the Corrèze and the Creuse, by contrast, the pastoral vocation of the rural economy was held in check by the necessity of growing cereals for domestic consumption. As modern communications eroded the logic of subsistence farming and brought distant markets within reach, the potential for pastoral specialisation was realised. A restructuring of popular attitudes followed which emphasised further the contrast between east and west.

Rye was not invulnerable to climatic disaster, however, and even in good years yields were pitifully low. The growth in output barely accommodated the needs of a rapidly expanding population and 'subsistence crises' of the

Table II.5 *Rye cultivation as percentage of total area under cereals*

Department	1840	1852	1862	1878	1888	1896	1910	1929
Ardèche	57.4	55.8	49.5	51.6	47.4	46.8	44.4	45.0
Aveyron	37.7	37.7	32.9	25.1	22.2	17.5	16.0	8.3
Haute-Loire	66.8	62.4	59.6	58.3	51.8	46.8	38.7	39.5
Lozère	58.2	55.0	52.0	50.9	53.8	45.4	55.1	54.4
France	17.7	14.3	12.3	12.2	11.0	10.3	8.9	6.5

Sources: Statistique de France. Agriculture (Paris, 1840–1); *Statistique de la France, deuxième série, statistique agricole* (Paris, 1858–60); *Statistique de la France. Agriculture, résultats généraux de l'enquête décennale de 1862* (Strasbourg, 1868); *Annuaire statistique de la France: 1881* (Paris, 1881); *Annuaire statistique de la France: 1896* (Paris, 1898); *Ministère de l'agriculture: statistique agricole annuelle: 1910* (Paris, 1911); *Statistique agricole de la France publiée par le Ministère de l'agriculture. Résultats généraux de l'enquête de 1929* (Paris, 1936).

ancien régime type buffeted the rural economy at intervals throughout the first half of the nineteenth century. A dreadful harvest in 1816 provoked a dearth of European proportions and extremes of misery in the southern Massif Central. Virulent speculation by proprietors anxious to extract the last ounce of profit before the new harvest, exacerbated the situation and the populace threatened to intervene on the market place of Mende in June and July 1817.[35] In the absence of reliable secondary communications, localised dearths would continue to arise until the end of the century, but the last generalised shortage occurred in 1854–5. Market places echoed to the familiar language of price control and at St Chély-d'Apcher (Lozère) the crowd prevented a merchant from moving his grain purchases.[36] Supply mechanisms and production technology lay at the heart of the problem for by the second half of the nineteenth century the region could theoretically meet the carbohydrate requirements of its resident population. The mobilisation of the harvest remained the essential obstacle. Localities producing modest surpluses often found it easier to export their foodstuffs than to provision the denuded markets of their hinterland. As long as rudimentary methods of threshing grain were employed, the climate retained a formidable capacity to obstruct the circulation of foodstuffs, too. In 1710 Louis Jouve,[37] a rural proprietor in the Velay, noted in his journal that the harvest had been good. Rye prices plummeted except for a fortnight after the start when they nearly

[35] A.N. F⁷9675 Prefect Lozère to Minister of the Interior, Mende, 15 July 1817.
[36] A.N. F⁷4067 *Rapports de gendarmerie*, Lozère, 21 November 1855.
[37] Grellet de la Deyte, 'Le Livre de raison de Louis Jouve, sieur de Chadouard, paroisse de Saint Vincent-en-Velay', *Bulletin de la Diana*, xxxv (1957), 85.

tripled. During this period it rained and flailing ceased. Farmers who had completed their threshing hastened to the miller and made a fat profit out of the bread needs of the poor. The example is directly applicable to the period in question. The vagaries of terrain and climate posed obstacles to economic integration which were not swiftly overcome. Even as the threat of famine receded, the problem of artificial, localised shortages endured.

By opening up new land the peasant cultivator could boost his output for a time, but productivity was largely independent of landholding. Grain yields remained low for large and small alike. Elaborating upon an old hypothesis of Henri Sée,[38] Michel Morineau[39] has argued that agriculture displayed few signs of progress before the 1840s. If the science of agronomy advanced in the eighteenth century, cereal productivity emphatically did not. Grain yield ratios exhibited a remarkable stability traceable, in some cases, over centuries. His cartographic representations of rye yields per hectare and rye seed–yield ratios in 1840 show the departments of the southern Massif Central grouped in the lower leagues. The evidence of detailed research bears out these conclusions. Averages are deceptive in a region with manifold qualities of arable; in the Brivadois seed yields oscillated between 2:1 and 6:1 and the best granite soils of the Velay repaid 5 or 6:1. According to a report commissioned by the Committee of Public Safety in 1795, some soils in the Aveyron were capable of returning 7:1. Elsewhere seed yields were lower: about 3:1 in the Lozère and 4.7:1 at best in the Ardèche. No significant changes were registered before 1852.[40]

Substantial improvements in productivity depended upon a reduction of fallow and a shift from biennial to triennial rotation. In an archaic rural economy innocent of fodder crops and super-phosphates, neither was feasible. Arable farming on thin soils demanded huge quantities of animal manure and the fallow was a stratagem for resting the soil and maximising manure production. An hectare under cereals in the Margeride was commonly reckoned to require twenty-five cartloads or about 2.5 metric tons of dung. This was a point which advocates of enlightened farming, and even more sensible observers like Arthur Young, tended to overlook. The fallow was an indispensable adjunct to peasant polyculture, not a monument to

[38] H. Sée, *La Vie économique de la France sous la monarchie censitaire, 1815–1848* (Paris, 1927), pp. 9–47.

[39] M. Morineau, *Les Faux-semblants d'un démarrage économique: agriculture et démographie en France au XVIIIᵉ siècle* (*Cahier des Annales*, 30, Paris, 1971).

[40] Merley, *La Haute-Loire*, i, pp. 113–14; J.-M. Tisseyre and M. Baudot, 'Rapport de Pierre-Joseph Bonnaterre sur l'état du département de l'Aveyron en l'an IV de la République', *Bulletin de la section d'histoire moderne et contemporaine du Comité des travaux historiques et scientifiques*, x (1977), 149; E. Claverie, 'Oppositions et conflits dans une société d'interconnaissance, l'exemple du Haut Gévaudan du XIXᵉ siècle' (Université R. Descartes, Sorbonne, Paris V, Doctorat de IIIᵉ cycle en ethnologie, 1979), p. 12; A. Molinier, 'En Vivarais au XVIIIᵉ siècle: une croissance démographique sans révolution agricole', *Annales du Midi*, lxxxxii (1980), 311.

rural ignorance. In any case biennial crop rotation was by no means the rule. Richeprey divided the arable surface of the Rouergue into four categories: well-fertilised in-field plots which were continuously cropped; land cultivated biennially; land cultivated spasmodically every three or four years; and heath opened up every ten or twelve years. Long fallowing was the norm and only a tiny fraction of the agricultural territory was under crops in any one year. Indeed, the notion of agricultural territory is too formal since it is evocative of the agrarian structures of the northern plains based on fixed *terroirs* and mandatory rotations. As the demographic explosion of the early decades of the nineteenth century intensified land use, a miserable shifting agriculture developed upon the margins of heath and common which eroded further the already blurred distinction between habitually cultivated and habitually non-cultivated land.

Well defined rotation of crops rather than fields was not, in general, a feature of *petite propriété*. A few well sited *domaines* were able to practise triennial rotation – notably those situated on the sotch soils of the causses – and it was on such farms that the first experiments with sainfoin and clover were conducted in the second half of the eighteenth century. The problem of the fallow was tackled in a different way in the ségala. Around the *bourg* of Sauveterre plot farmers kept their heavily fertilized hemp fields in continuous rotation, but still the soil produced only one cereal harvest in three. Fodder crops did not integrate well with an agricultural system biased towards the production of rye. Rye hogged the soil and the margins of high altitude cereal cultivation were too slender to permit any delay during the autumn ploughing and planting season. Even the potato, which the rural population initially regarded as a fodder crop, tended to obstruct the rye cycle. However makeshift in other respects, the peasant smallholding was not flexible enough to tolerate the structural changes which artificial forage cultivation so often required and so-called *prairies artificielles* spread extremely slowly. In the absence of artificial fertilisers, manure remained the key to the fallow. Drove roads were scoured for dung, young children risked life and limb to snatch the precious deposit from beneath cart and carriage, bitter disputes flared over the night folding of summer herds and huge piles of fetid matter obstructed path and alleyway. But the production of manure never reached levels which would permit the wholesale reduction of the fallow. In the Vivarais about 15 per cent of the potential arable surface was under cereals by the end of the *ancien régime*. Calculations suggest that a shift from biennial to triennial rotation would have required between a six and a sevenfold increase in the supply of manure which meant increasing stock by a factor of thirteen.[41] This implied agricultural specialisation which was inimical to the central objective of peasant polyculture. The fallow period survived, therefore. While the

[41] Molinier, 'En Vivarais au XVIIIᵉ siècle', p. 306.

national stock of uncultivated arable land declined swiftly after 1850, the 1882 agricultural survey revealed the survival of a recalcitrant core of heavy fallowing embracing the most mountainous areas of the southern Massif Central. In the Lozère over 30 per cent of the arable land still lay fallow.

When the rye harvest proved deficient, stand-by crops assumed a crucial importance. If the autumn sowings were destroyed by early frosts, oats could be planted in the spring. They had a shorter growing cycle and would tolerate the cool, damp conditions characteristic of the highest plateaux. In some localities a mixture of rye and wheat (*méteil*) was grown, as well. It was difficult to harvest, but helped minimise the losses in years when the climate tended to extremes. The sweet chestnut served as the most important secondary food source, however. It flourished on schist soils of medium altitude and was extensively cultivated in the ségala, the Cévennes and the Vivarais. Orchards occupied the steep slopes which would otherwise have lain waste, but the trees were also planted on plough-land in tandem with rye. In many respects the chestnut deserves to be ranked alongside rye as a food staple. Although of a lower calorific value than cereal, it grew in profusion once the trees reached maturity. The yield of a well established chestnut orchard was much greater than that of an equivalent area planted under rye which had to be rested at intervals. There is evidence that the rural population appreciated this, for in some localities the land surface devoted to chestnuts fluctuated in step with demographic pressures.[42] Certainly the sharp rise in the population of the Vivarais during the second half of the eighteenth century was accompanied by a massive extension of chestnut cultivation. Between 1731 and 1811 the production of chestnuts in the Bas Vivarais virtually doubled.[43] Despite the low esteem in which it was held by a peasantry culturally attached to a cereal diet, the chestnut fully deserved its title of 'arbre à pain' by the nineteenth century. When the failure of the grain harvest coincided with low yields from the chestnut orchards – as happened in 1788–9 – panic spread through the countryside. When the chestnut harvest totally failed in 1816–17, the sub-prefect of Florac[44] reported that 25,000 inhabitants of the Cévennes had lost their means of subsistence for half the year.

The only new crop to find a niche within the cycles of peasant polyculture was the potato. It had been grown in the region on a small scale since the middle of the seventeenth century, but widespread cultivation was chiefly a post-1750 phenomenon. In the Velay and the Haut Vivarais – both areas of precocious demographic growth – the tuber was rapidly added to peasant diet. By 1779 it had become a major food source for the inhabitants of the

[42] J.-R. Pitte, 'Les Origines et l'évolution de la châtaigneraie vivaroise à travers un document cadastral du XVIIIᵉ siècle', *Bulletin de la section de géographie du Comité des travaux historiques et scientifiques*, lxxxii (1975–7), 165–78.

[43] Molinier, 'En Vivarais au XVIIIᵉ siècle', p. 312.

[44] A.D.L. VIM²2 *Rapports du sous-préfet de Florac*, 16 January 1817.

Mézenc plateau. The potato was a near ideal mountain crop. It had a short growth cycle, resisted damp, was immune to storm and hail, combined with oats, if not rye, and gave high yields. But cultural as well as ecological factors delayed its adoption. The Rouergat peasant used the potato to fatten his pig and except in the neighbourhood of Sauveterre, it was not extensively cultivated before the Revolution. Not until the dearth of 1794–5 did the population accept it as a tolerable alternative to cereal consumption.

Nevertheless, the impact of the potato should not be underestimated. At first it served as a carbohydrate supplement and this enabled the traditional agrarian system to provide greater numbers than ever before with the bare minimum for survival. But, by the 1860s, some areas were beginning to export potatoes and the Ardèche as a whole was harvesting 30 per cent more than its actual needs. The subsistence economy and its *sine qua non*, peasant polyculture, was under attack. Yet the structural changes which potato cultivation seemed to herald were slow to materialise. In the Lozère and the Aveyron the potato was domesticated and, if anything, prolonged the equilibrium of peasant farming. Given a more favourable conjuncture the spread of the potato in the mountains and of the chestnut on the lower slopes might have promoted a reorientation of the rural economy. Conditions were not favourable, however. Population pressure remained intense until the 1860s and eroded marginal increases in output; heavy fallowing proved inescapable and pioneer attempts to introduce improved agricultural technology evoked an indifferent response. The horse was rarely employed as a beast of burden and bullock teams provided essential traction throughout the nineteenth century. For this and other reasons, the heavy iron ploughs used in the north were slow to replace the artisanal wooden plough which only scratched the surface. As for the sickle, social and cultural traditions inhibited its replacement with the scythe, while the application of mineral fertilisers to boost yields waited upon modern communications. By the end of the nineteenth century peasant agriculture had reached an important threshold in its millennial cycle. Further development would demand a profound modification of its structures: a twin adjustment to market pressures and a population haemorrhage of monumental proportions. Agricultural commentators described the changes which they perceived variously, but they seemed agreed that the pace of agricultural modernisation quickened markedly in the two decades before the First World War.[45]

Market pressures

Peasant agriculture constituted the backbone of the rural economy, but we should not imagine that it was practised in conditions of complete autarchy.

[45] M.A.T.P. *Enquête sur les formes anciennes de l'agriculture*, Aveyron; Haute-Loire; Lozère.

All peasants had recourse to the market at some point in the year – to buy grain, to purchase or dispose of stock, to hire or sell labour. And where strictly commercial incentives were lacking the state intervened and forced participation. All householders had fiscal obligations, many owed monetary *cens* and *rentes*. Every autumn, when prices were at their lowest, the most vulnerable members of society were driven to part with a proportion of their harvest in order to obtain cash. Self-sufficiency was an ideal which few could realise. Cottage industry tended in the same direction. The rural population derived additional income from activities such as the spinning and weaving of textiles, lacemaking, silk-worm breeding and a host of artisanal crafts, all of which presupposed some degree of economic integration. The problem lies not in recognising the diversity of the peasant economy, but in assessing its implications. Charles Tilly[46] argues that the French countryside was heavily involved in production for regional, national and even international markets by the end of the eighteenth century. This conviction leads him to question interpretations which stress the integrity of the peasantry as a social, economic and cultural group in specific regional contexts. His view that the 'simultaneous' processes of population growth, industrialisation, urbanisation and state consolidation *necessarily* dissolved old solidarities will be discussed in a subsequent chapter,[47] but two other points in his argument invite comment at this juncture.

How market responsive was the countryside in the late eighteenth and nineteenth centuries? With varying degrees of emphasis most regional *thèses* have stressed the tardy development of agricultural capitalism. Production for domestic consumption continued to prevail well into the nineteenth century and market networks remained short-range and geared to the exchange of local produce and the disposal of irregular surpluses. Recent survey histories have consolidated these conclusions.[48] During the July Monarchy market-orientated regions were still exceptions to the rule. Rural France divided into discrete hinterlands which if not entirely self-sufficient were only loosely integrated. Tilly rightly stresses that farming was not the only economic activity practised in the countryside, however. Rural industry was explicitly market orientated and therefore had wider horizons. But this thread in the argument invites criticism, too. Viewed out of context, the processes of rural manufacturing – proto-industrialisation – assume a magnitude and autonomy which they rarely possessed in reality. Cottage industry was an adjunct to agriculture not vice versa. Indeed, in the southern Massif Central,

---

[46] C. Tilly, 'Did the Cake of Custom Break?' in J. M. Merriman (ed.), *Consciousness and Class Experience in Nineteenth-Century Europe* (New York and London, 1979), p. 18.
[47] See below chapter three, pp. 87–95.
[48] T. Kemp, *Economic Forces in French History* (London, 1971), p. 31; R. Price, *An Economic History of Modern France, 1730–1914* (London, 1981), pp. 42–92; H. Clout, *Agriculture in France on the Eve of the Railway Age* (London, 1980), pp. 223–5.

it formed a natural extension of the precarious economy of peasant poly-culture. Cottage production was seasonal, its profits aleatory and insufficient to trigger significant social differentiation in the countryside. The multiple roles of subsistence farmer, village artisan, weaver and day-labourer were linked together in a continuum which exactly reflected the cycle of poly-culture. The silk-worm industry of the Bas Vivarais was the only important exception to this rule. The demand for raw silk in the early nineteenth century was such that land customarily devoted to food production was planted with mulberries instead, but this reorientation was only feasible because sub-sistence farming was already in decline.

The manufacture of textiles, principally woollens and canvas, constituted the most important cottage industry in the southern Massif Central. Worsted yarn and cloth were produced in the villages, finished in centres like Marvejols, La Canourgue, Tournon, Annonay, St Geniez and St Affrique and marketed by merchant-drapers with international contacts. By the end of the *ancien régime* the fabrics of the region were being exported to the Swiss cantons, Genoa, the Levant, the Spanish colonies and Canada (until 1763). In a few localities there were even signs that domestic textile production would shortly dominate the rural economy. Richeprey noted that the clothiers of St Affrique controlled a sizeable workforce of rural spinners who were begin-ning to abandon agriculture in favour of wage labour.[49] But market inte-gration had reached its climax in the 1780s, thereafter the textile industry of the southern Massif Central declined. Large orders for troop uniforms momentarily compensated for the loss of foreign outlets, but by 1815 the trend was unmistakable. Denied access to the rustic markets of the East and the colonies, the poor quality *cadis* of the Aveyron and the Lozère ceased to be the object of international trade. The industry scaled down and relocated to the dismay of the rural population which was accustomed to supplement-ing agricultural activity with dead season spinning or weaving. The contrac-tion coincided with the decades of rapid population growth and the desper-ation it provoked in districts traditionally reliant upon textile out-working is recorded in the columns of the Agricultural Enquiry of 1848.

The cottage textile industry did not collapse, however. The very isolation of the southern Massif Central protected the home market. Domestic con-sumption of rough woollens, linen and canvas remained buoyant and there was a steady ecclesiastical demand for crudely dyed broadcloth until the very end of the nineteenth century. The introduction of mechanised spinning from the 1840s in such centres as Marvejols destroyed the demand for yarn spun by hand in satellite villages, but hand-loom weaving and woolcombing sur-vived until the 1870s, albeit upon a much reduced scale. In the high *bourgs* of the Margeride rural handicrafts were slow to lose their vitality. When the

[49]   Guilhamon, *Journal des voyages*, ii, p. 507.

inhabitants of Auroux deliberated to divide up their common land in 1892, the only objection raised was on behalf of eight or ten weavers who used to spread out their cloth to dry on an adjacent patch of land.[50] It seems, therefore, that the village textile industry of the southern Massif Central retained its archaic characteristics. At the end of the *ancien régime* woollen manufacture, in particular, appeared poised for proto-industrial 'take-off', but the new century brought problems of adjustment and exposed its commercial vulnerability. Far from responding to market changes occurring far from home as Tilly's argument supposes, it retreated into lethargic production for local markets and fairs where quality was unimportant and tastes conservative.

The cultivation of hemp and flax was widespread, particularly on the damper soils of the ségala and the Boutières valleys of the Ardèche. Suitably processed, the plants were woven into coarse fabrics to supply the everyday clothing needs of the rural population. The demand for such fabrics was buoyant and hemp cultivation, particularly, constituted an important extension of the rural economy. Each household endeavoured to grow sufficient to cover its needs and any surplus found a ready local outlet. By contrast the raw silk industry of the Bas Vivarais and the lace and ribbon industries of the Velay were highly commercialised. Manufacture remained dispersed throughout the countryside during the period in question, but urban merchants either supplied or collected the raw materials and exerted considerable control over production. Lace, ribbon and silk production was also vulnerable to fluctuations in demand. The silk and linen lace of the Velay was marketed in Germany, Italy, Spain and England as well as in the rest of France, and the industry expanded fairly steadily until the 1880s, but ribbon-making was more susceptible to changes in fashion. Between 1848 and 1880 it experienced mixed fortunes.[51] The market for raw silk seemed insatiable in the early decades of the nineteenth century and the high prices commanded by cocoons brought real prosperity to the peasantry of the Bas Vivarais and the Cévennes. But in 1850 the silkworm succumbed to a serious infection (*pébrine*). By 1857 the harvest of cocoons had declined by 80 per cent and the dangers inherent in a rural economy geared increasingly to monoculture became painfully evident. Land values crashed and the population migrated in miserable droves towards the plain. After two listless decades the *pébrine* menace was conquered, by Pasteur among others, but the industry never regained its old buoyancy.

The autarchic features of the peasant economy are easily exaggerated and Charles Tilly is rightly critical of modernisation theories which assume, as their point of departure, the existence of a traditional rural society based

---

[50] A.D.L. O 172 *Administration et comptabilité communales*: Auroux.
[51] G. Martin, *Le Tissage du ruban à domicile dans les campagnes du Velay* (Paris and Le Puy, 1913), pp. 30–76; Merley, *La Haute-Loire*, i, pp. 518–19.

solely on land. We should equally be wary of interpretations which assume the immanence of mercantile capitalism, however. Most peasants were affected by market pressures in some way or other, but participation in the market was not the same as producing for the market. And producing for the market did not necessarily entail a greater sensitivity to changes occurring far from the point of manufacture. There were markets and markets and those of the southern Massif Central tended to be short-range. They linked sub-regions and climatic zones and were inadequate for the broader task of national economic integration. Certainly the silk, lace and ribbon industries developed on proto-industrial lines. The lace merchants of Le Puy provided employment for about 50,000 country dwellers in the Velay on the eve of the Revolution and perhaps 130,000 by 1855.[52] At its peak, the production of raw silk probably occupied as many hands. But the organisation of these specialised industries was not typical of rural handicrafts as a whole. In any case, lace-making never acquired the status of an autonomous *métier*, unlike silkworm raising. It provided seasonal employment for a population whose principal activity was agriculture. Unsurprisingly, therefore, the spectrum of occupations in the countryside remained compact. Few fortunes were made out of commerce in the southern Massif Central.

The same might be said of industrial capitalism. Its pull was felt in the lower valley of the Lot around Decazeville, in the Cévennes around La Grand'Combe and Alès and in the hinterland of St Etienne, but concentrated industry scarcely penetrated the region. The obvious exception was the major mining and metallurgical complex which developed at Aubin on the western frontier of the Aveyron during the first half of the nineteenth century. Before the Revolution the mines of Aubin had been exploited in a piecemeal and casual fashion, rather like those of Sainte Florine in the Brivadois and Vialas in the Cévennes. Repeated efforts to regularise coal extraction failed in the face of fierce local resistance, but in 1826 the Compagnie des Houillères et Fonderies de l'Aveyron[53] was founded on the initiative of Duc Elie de Decazes, an early convert to industrial capitalism. The old proprietors were bought out or persuaded to grant concessions and a massive investment in coal-smelting followed. In 1828 the first blast furnace was fired and within four years six more had been added as well as forges and a rolling mill. Efficiency improved with the introduction of the hot-air process and by 1835 the plant was in profit. As the scale of activity increased so did the population and a new commune, appropriately named Decazeville, was formed. By the

[52] Merley, *La Haute-Loire*, i, pp. 123–5; Malègue, *Eléments de statistique générale*, p. 166.
[53] Levêque, 'Histoire des forges de Decazeville', *Bulletin de la Société d'Industrie Minérale*, ix (1916), 5–97, 141–236; G. Daudibertières, 'La Société des Houillères et Fonderies de l'Aveyron et le premier développement industriel de Decazeville', *Mémoires de la société des lettres, sciences et arts de l'Aveyron*, xxviii (1964), 479–95; D. M. Reid, 'Labor Management and the State in an Industrial Town; Decazeville, 1826–1914' (Stanford University, D.Phil. thesis, 1981), pp. 14–19.

middle of the century it counted 7,000 inhabitants. This industrial workforce was slow to shed its peasant mentality, however. The earliest miners were farmers and day-labourers who exploited the coal seams on a seasonal basis. The area lacked technological traditions and the company overseer had to recruit specialist labour from Le Creusot, Fourchambault, the Austrian Tyrol and even Britain in order to line the shafts and construct the furnaces. Factory discipline was gradually imposed, but the industrial workers of the Aubin basin remained a hybrid breed. Often they retained a stake in the land, they continued to attend church in significant numbers and their political behaviour was marked by lingering habits of deference.

The orientation of southern agriculture towards winegrowing which was such a striking feature of the period 1750–1880 had a marginal impact on the Massif Central. Like silk, wine was a cash crop which offered handsome returns in the early nineteenth century provided the natural milieu was favourable and market networks sufficiently developed. In the mountains the conditions were generally hostile to extensive vine cultivation. Monoculture of any description remained inherently risky and commercial viticulture was only practised in the lowlands of the Rouergue and the Vivarais, and in sheltered valleys within reach of urban markets. Nevertheless, *vignerons* constituted an important social group in the cantons of Villefranche-de-Rouergue and Marcillac and the revolution of 1848 revealed them as susceptible to political agitation and collective action as their counterparts in the Midi. The most dramatic extension of viticulture occurred on the lower slopes of the Cévennes, however. By mid-century the greater part of the agricultural territory of the canton of Joyeuse was given over to wine production. Unsurprisingly, therefore, it was on these densely populated slopes that the calamities of the second half of the nineteenth century were most keenly felt. As the *pébrine* laid waste the silk industry, a fungoid blight (oidium) was discovered in vine roots which caused the grapes to rot. It played havoc in the wine-growing districts for about a decade and in 1860 half the harvest of the Ardèche was affected. Barely another decade passed before the vineyards were confronted by a more formidable challenge: the phylloxera insect. Reported first in the Gard, its ravages were soon felt throughout the Cévennes and the Bas Vivarais. In 1882 the crisis finally peaked in the Ardèche with most of the vines either dead or dying. Land values slumped, migration intensified and the shock to the rural economy triggered a reorientation of political attitudes in some communes.

As the physiocrats and their agronomist successors were apt to point out, the natural vocation of the Massif Central lay in animal husbandry. But peasant polyculture required that stock be treated first and foremost as a source of manure for the soil and it was not until modern means of transportation penetrated the region that large-scale dairying and cattle-raising became a feasible option. Even then, the central highlands failed to reap substantial benefits until late in the nineteenth century. In 1867 the agricultural commission of the department of the Lozère complained that the extension of the railway network into adjacent departments had merely exacerbated its economic isolation. Old markets had collapsed and new ones remained beyond the reach of hill farmers denied the advantages of steam locomotion: 'c'est ainsi que l'énorme progression dans la consommation de la viande et des laitages qui s'est produite dans le Midi n'a pas profité au département'.[54] Notwithstanding the obstacles of geography and economic structure, however, some of the potential for stock-raising had been realised during the *ancien régime*. The rich abbatial pastures of the Aubrac and the Mézenc positively invited commercial exploitation and for centuries fatstock had been driven down from the mountains en route for the cities of the littoral. On the drier slopes of the Margeride and Mont Lozère a remarkable synthesis of *petite culture* and commercial sheep-farming had been achieved thanks to the existence of abundant common land. Lowland shepherds took huge flocks up to the pastures each spring and brought them down in the autumn. In return for their herbage, the mountain villages obtained the vital supplies of manure on which high altitude agriculture depended. The summits of the Lozère provided summer grazing for over 300,000 sheep (excluding indigenous flocks) in the middle years of the nineteenth century. Thereafter transhumance slowly declined as the Mediterranean economy shifted towards monoculture.

By the end of the century there were signs that the southern Massif Central was at last realising its potential for animal husbandry. Those areas less reliant on long-distance communications were in the van of change. The growing demand of the Stephanois region for fatstock and dairy products engulfed the north-easterly cantons of the Haute-Loire in a market economy. The insatiable demand of the Roquefort cheese industry for ewe's milk encouraged sheep-rearing on the causses. But progress was uncertain. The railways never quite fulfilled the hopes of those who envisioned the high plateaux as vast reserves of livestock awaiting embarkation for Paris, Lyons and the cities of the Midi. Market forces were filtered, deflected and neutralised by the huge gaps in the network, by problems with gradients which effectively closed a number of lines to heavy freight from the very start. They were filtered, too, by cultural factors, by ancient atavisms. The logic of economic integration was not perceived as clearly by contemporaries as it has been subsequently by historians. While the peasantry of the western highlands of the Massif Central adjusted their cultural horizons in response to outside pressures, those pressures were more uneven to the south east of the Monts d'Auvergne and cultural traditions were tenaciously rooted in the soil of popular catholicism.

[54] A.N. ADXIX C43³ *Enquête agricole* (Paris, 1867), Lozère, p. 65.

Migration

Itinerant labour constituted the most obvious resource of the central high-lands. It circulated freely within the region and was regularly exported to the rest of France and even further afield. In the second half of the nineteenth century the habit of migration in search of seasonal employment was obscured by a trend towards definitive migration, but the traditional forms of labour mobility were never entirely effaced. Two types of seasonal migration can be discerned: short-range movements of harvesters between climatic zones and long-range winter migration towards the lowland plains. The period of *grands travaux* in the countryside offered multiple opportunities for casual work. Haying, harvesting, grape and chestnut picking were activities which called for mutual assistance at village level and, on a larger scale, reciprocal arrangements between villages and localities. Thus the proprietors of the Margeride would await the arrival of teams from the ségala to help bring in their rye harvest. Such was the diversity of altitude and milieu that harvest work was generally available well into September. As time went by the broad pattern of seasonal movements engendered subsidiary patterns of bewildering complexity. The economic logic of rural migration was not lost, but it was deflected by cultural traditions. Landowners in the Levézou uplands adjacent to the ségala were forced to call in harvesters from the Albigeois, while plot farmers in the Margeride preferred to seek work in the *planèze* of St Flour.

Winter migration was characteristic of the highest plateaux of the Auvergne and contiguous districts where the agricultural dead season lasted six months of the year. As soon as the first frosts drove the stock indoors the menfolk made ready to leave. Some headed towards Paris or Lyons, but most took a southerly route, at least until the middle of the nineteenth century. They wintered in the coastal cities of Provence and Languedoc where casual work could usually be had, or else they worked as farm labourers staking the vines and repairing the terraces. The toughest highlanders found employment as sawyers in the forests of the Pyrenees and Catalonia. In April and May the migrants returned home and the agricultural cycle resumed. The hard cash sum or *pécule* which each migrant brought back to his village serves to remind us of the original purpose of the exercise, but winter migration, like harvest migration, rapidly acquired cultural overtones. In some villages virtually all the able-bodied men worked away from home for half the year or so, while the inhabitants of similarly sited villages only a short distance away remained sedentary. Perplexing area differences also seem to bespeak the operation of psychological factors. By the end of the *ancien régime* winter migration was widespread in the Haute-Auvergne and in the *élection* of Brioude and its transformation into a definitive exodus during the early decades of the nineteenth century was not long delayed. In the Gévaudan and the Velay, by contrast, migration during the coldest months of the year was much less prevalent despite comparable milieux. Rural emigration, when it finally affected these provinces, owed little to the habit of seasonal migration. The Auvergnat example had a greater impact upon the neighbouring *pays* of the Rouergue, but the tradition of southerly migration to Languedoc and Aquitaine showed few signs of being replaced by an irrevocable northerly exodus until the last quarter of the nineteenth century. The contingent of Aveyronnais *émigrés* in Paris rapidly overhauled that of the Cantal to stand at about 50,000 on the eve of the First World War, but unlike the Cantaliens, the Aveyronnais mostly arrived after 1875.[55]

Seasonal migration was a rural industry and its roots were probably ancient. Teams of Rouergat *scieurs de long* (log sawyers) had crossed the Pyrenees in search of work since the sixteenth century if not earlier. In the southern Massif Central it performed the same function as the cottage textile industries and served, therefore, to bolster rather than undermine the rural economy. Like spinning, weaving, lace-making and artisanal crafts it enabled peasant households to obtain specie with which to pay taxes and, in good years, to buy land. As important in the highest villages, migration eased the pressure on food stocks during the grimmer months of the year by removing surplus mouths from around the kitchen table. And yet this lucrative, if hazardous, exercise remained compatible with the demands of agriculture in a region in which the seasons telescoped the labour-intensive activities of the farm into five frenetic months between May and September. If we regard seasonal migration as a traditional extension of peasant polyculture akin to rural handicrafts rather than as a symptom of instability and overpopulation, some of the anomalies of its distribution are resolved. It seems likely that the well-attested vigour of domestic industry in the Gévaudan and the Velay rendered long-distance migration unnecessary until the latter part of the nineteenth century. These mountainous outposts of the province of Langudeoc also enjoyed a measure of protection from the fiscal aggression of the *ancien régime* monarchy (see chapter five, pp. 153–60). The Haute-Auvergne, the Brivadois and the Rouergue, on the other hand, enjoyed no such immunity and the monetary demands made upon the peasant household were distinctly greater.

The delicate balance which made seasonal migration an adjunct to agriculture could easily shift, however. Labour mobility brought extraneous influences to bear upon *petite culture* which were potentially destructive of the traditional rural economy. In the western Massif Central where agro-pastoral structures were already under threat at the end of the *ancien régime*, the effect of migration was insidious. The strictly seasonal and limited economic objective of the highland migrations to Languedoc yielded in the face of commercial and speculative migration to Paris which soon shed its seasonal

[55] R. Béteille, *Les Aveyronnais: essai géographique sur l'espace humain* (Poitiers, 1974), pp. 102–13 and figs.

character to become *de facto* emigration. The decay of peasant polyculture and of its traditions was closely linked to the rising curve of definitive migration. As market pressures prompted specialisation and cereal cultivation declined, surplus manpower quit the countryside; as the monetary rewards of urban employment became apparent, cultivation of the land declined further. The cycle of strategic migration to enhance the viability of the peasant smallholding broke down and that impervious domestic culture which accompanied the Auvergnat on his peregrinations no longer filtered his perceptions of the outside world.

The developing rivalry between migration and agriculture in the Auvergne first attracted attention in the second half of the eighteenth century. Influenced by the doctrines of the physiocrats, intendants and sub-delegates deplored the trend and pointed out that it left agriculture short handed. By the mid nineteenth century the attitude of administrators had shifted, however. Migration was now regarded as a source of enrichment provided that the proceeds were injected back into the rural economy. In 1860, the prefect of the Cantal estimated that the income from migration exceeded that derived from stock-raising,[56] although contemporary observers warned that the migrants were no longer in the habit of returning to their department of origin. The cultural habits of generations were slipping, too. The status of the firstborn (*aîné*) declined as offspring came to view the prospect of inheriting the farmstead with apprehension. The cadets could quit the land and use their endowments to set themselves up in business in Paris. A similar trend is evident among the migrant masons of the Creuse. The opportunities for self-advancement inherent in migration and the work habits contracted during long years in the capital, loosened the bonds of the extended family and impaired the efficiency of agriculture.[57] In 1872 the author of a monograph on the commons of the Creuse[58] noted that they generally remained uncultivated except when the collapse of the Paris building trade forced the masons to remain at home.

On the more sheltered southern and south-eastern flanks of the Massif, by contrast, the first waves of emigration were closely geared to the vicissitudes of *petite culture*. A trickle of departures from the congested valleys of the lower Cévennes had developed by 1846 and the calamities of the next two decades turned it into a veritable flood of human misery. The high birth rate of the Velay–Vivarais plateau concealed the progress of emigration in the remainder of the Ardèche and the Haute-Loire until the 1880s, but movement towards the industrial base of St Etienne, towards Lyons and towards the

[56] A. Châtelin, *Les Migrants temporaires en France de 1800 à 1914* (2 vols., Villeneuve-d'Asq, 1976), ii, p. 1034.
[57] A. Corbin, *Archaïsme et modernité en Limousin au XIXᵉ siècle, 1845–1880* (2 vols., Paris, 1975), i, pp. 222–3.
[58] S. Raymon, *Etudes sur les biens communaux du département de la Creuse* (Montluçon, 1872), p. 10.

towns of the lower Rhône valley began in the 1860s. Migration from the Brivadois in the direction of the Limagne and Paris conformed to the Auvergne pattern and was already well established by mid-century. The most northerly cantons of the Aveyron were likewise influenced by their proximity to the Cantal, but there was no large-scale emigration before 1848. The evidence gathered by the Agricultural Enquiry of that year suggests that the villages of the Aubrac continued to practise seasonal migration to Languedoc rather than longer-term migration to Paris. In the rest of the department the population appeared well adjusted to its environment, save for a few localities in which the decline of domestic industry had caused instability. The great exodus was a phenomenon of the final decades of the century. Over-population in relation to resources undoubtedly played a role in triggering the evacuation, especially in the ségala, but the impact of the process of emulation should not be underestimated. The Aveyronnais long hesitated to abandon seasonal migration, but as soon as one village made a success of emigration to the cities others hastened to follow suit. The completion of the railway network greatly facilitated departure and the industrial centres of Decazeville and Carmaux on the fringes of the department offered convenient stopping places on the migration routes to the North and South.

Reduced to an economy of makeshifts for much of the year, the Lozère remained the last great bastion of short-range seasonal migration in the southern Massif Central. As late as 1890 the department was scarcely affected by emigration except in the Cévennes cantons bordering the Ardèche and the Gard. Again the railway provided the opportunity for a decisive shift in popular attitudes. In 1888 the Béziers–Neussargues line opened. For the first time the inhabitants of the causses and the Aubrac were brought within easy reach of the Mediterranean and of Paris. The demographic repercussions in villages bordering the track were immediate (see chapter nine, p. 275). Within a couple of decades periodic migration had become part of the life-style of the mountains. Each autumn young peasants headed for the stations of Aumont and St Chély-d'Apcher to board the express to Paris.

The export of labour, like the export of the products of domestic manufacture, involved rural society in the market, but did it entail other forms of involvement? Michelet[59] was sceptical and remarked that the migrant highlanders of the Auvergne returned home with some money, but few ideas. Yet historians have, on the whole, concluded that migration was an important agent of social and political change. The heterogeneous character of rural population movement invites caution, however. Different environments elicited different responses; different occupations implied different social relationships and migrants from different regions left home with widely differing experiences and expectations. Building workers and water-carriers

[59] Quoted in Châtelin, *Les Migrants temporaires en France*, ii, p. 1029.

plied their trade in the cities, while tinkers toured the villages and lumbermen and sawyers found work in the forests. Some migrants set off singly, others left in teams, families or neighbourhood groups. Many mountain migrants sought the blessing of their parish priests before embarking upon a 'campaign' whereas Martin Nadaud,[60] the apprentice mason of the Creuse, seems scarcely to have set foot in a church beyond his first communion.

The evidence of the southern Massif Central supports Michelet's dictum. Seasonal migration sustained rather than sapped the foundations of the peasant economy, and the southerly destinations which most migrants favoured until the later nineteenth century all fell within the familiar patois-speaking world of greater Languedoc. In any case migration was a group activity which did little violence to mental horizons. The *scieurs de long* of the Rouergue worked in teams drawn from the same family or village. Although they were far from home, they did not integrate with the indigenous population. The Rouergat and Auvergnat lumbermen who worked in Lorraine at the end of the nineteenth century were considered a race apart. Unlike the teams from the Morvan and the Nivernais, they shunned contact and would only come into the *bourgs* and villages on Sundays. Migrant harvest workers possessed a similar *esprit de corps*. They tended to circulate en masse along fixed routes and at fixed times of the year. Impressed by this phenomenon, one of Frédéric Le Play's collaborators observed that:

la population lozérienne n'émigre pas; elle s'épanche périodiquement à jours fixes par familles entières sans distinction de sexe. C'est un flot composé de tous les membres valides de chaque paroisse. On part le dimanche, après la messe, avec la bénédiction du curé, en emportant pour tout bagage un peu de linge, une faucille, un fléau. La journée et au besoin la nuit suffisent pour atteindre les villages où se tiennent des foires spéciales; on se loue par famille entière, en nombre suffisant pour faire un travail donné dans un délai fixe, et chacun se trouve content s'il rapporte 20 à 30 f. au logis.[61]

The reorientation of migration upon a northerly axis upset these habits much less than is commonly assumed. Migrants continued to leave in bands and swiftly formed distinct colonies within the great metropolis. The Aveyronnais, particularly, organised mutual-aid societies known as *amicales* which made a conscious effort to reconstitute the familiar framework of rural life. New arrivals from the Aubrac and the Viadène were welcomed into the bosom of their respective village *amicales* which helped them to find accommodation and employment and tided them over during hard times. By 1914 seventy of these organisations existed in the capital. The Rouergat migrants of the high plateaux took with them to Paris a robust sense of apartness which church leaders were quick to build upon as a prophylactic against the rigours of city life. The regional identity of the Auvergnats was more amorphous,

---

[60] M. Nadaud, *Mémoires de Léonard, ancien garçon maçon* (Paris, 1976), p. 78.
[61] 'Sur les mœurs, l'organisation agricole et le régime d'émigration des montagnes d'Auvergne' in F. Le Play (ed.), *Les Ouvriers des deux mondes*, ii (1858), 354.

however. One of the first waves of nineteenth-century migration, they had also had longer in which to adjust to urban values. Yet if the Cantalian water-carrier[62] whom Le Play's collaborator questioned in 1858 was typical of the Auvergnat migrant in general, the culture of the village remained tenacious. Church attendance gradually succumbed, but political awareness did not grow in proportion. Le Play's *enquêtes* tended to idealise rural virtues and incur suspicion for that reason, but contemporaries whose perspective was somewhat different confirmed his assessment. In 1852 the prefect of the Cantal considered the 40,000 Auvergnat migrants who returned home from the cities each year to be imbued with unspecified 'mauvaises principes', but noted that 'ils s'occupent très peu de politique'.[63]

The cultural armour-plating which enabled the migrants of the southern Massif Central to withstand the pressures of global society was provided by the church. Popular catholicism and popular culture overlapped to a considerable degree (see chapter four) and the clergy fuelled and serviced the cultural traditions of each village and parish. The migrant quit the mountains imbued with an ethic of loyalty to his family, his own small locality and the values represented by the parish priest. These foci of his social existence merged insensibly: household group and village coincided in many instances and the priest was often a kinsman. Years of training since early childhood had inculcated this ethic and the rituals preceding departure – edification in church and secular pageantry in the station-yard – reinforced the message. Refuelling took place when the wanderers returned home: 'les pratiques religieuses, fidèlement suivies pendant l'enfance, sont exigées du jeune homme à chaque retour périodique dans la montagne; il ne vient pas à l'idée de s'y soustraire, car l'exemple est donné par les parents à tous les degrés'.[64] Those whose cultural armour had been pierced were shamefaced; they brought dishonour upon their family and, by extension, upon the clergy.

The evolution of locally-rich religious cultures is only beginning to be investigated and remains *terra incognita*. Even the frontiers are ill-defined. The vigorous popular catholicism of the southern Massif Central extended into the Auvergne to embrace parts of the Cantal, but how far is unclear. The case of Savoy provides an interesting parallel for here, too, we find a pattern of urban migration coexisting with a powerful religious culture. Migrant masons from the high valleys of the Morzine, Samoëns and Thônes worked for part of the year in Geneva, Lausanne and the cities of northern and eastern France. Like their compatriots from the southern dioceses of the Massif

---

[62] 'Porteur d'eau no. 17 de Paris (Seine, France) d'après les renseignements recueillis sur les lieux en avril 1858 par E. Avalle' in F. Le Play (ed.), *Les Ouvriers des deux mondes*, ii (1858), 321–4.

[63] Archives Départementales du Cantal (henceforth A.D.C.) 38M1 Prefect Cantal to Minister of the Interior, Aurillac, 28 June 1852.

[64] 'Sur les mœurs, l'organisation agricole et le régime d'émigration des montagnes d'Auvergne', p. 358.

Central, they set off with the admonitions of their family, neighbours and clerics ringing in their ears. Such conditioning was extremely effective in minimising the threat that migration appeared to pose. More or less consciously, the mountain parishes ensured that their offspring brought in hard cash from their trips to the plains, but precious little else. The pastoral enquiry of 1845 showed the clergy of the high parishes of the diocese of Annecy to be broadly satisfied with the religious zeal of their flock, notwithstanding the practice of migration. The *curé* of Vallorcine complained that Mazzinian doctrines, spreading from the Valais, had been imbibed by a few migrants, but in other parishes attendance at mass during the *retour* and completion of Easter duties was universal.[65]

As seasonal migration hardened into semi-permanent emigration, the habits of detachment, deference and piety waned. On this all sources agree. The first generation migrants had to fend for themselves and those who grew to maturity in the turbulent atmosphere of mid-nineteenth-century Paris sometimes became the carriers of radical opinions. In 1852 the prefect of the Cantal blamed post-*coup* disaffection in the canton of Maurs upon a migrant mason who had returned from the capital after between fifteen and twenty years.[66] The profile of a militant migrant also emerges from the dossier of Jacques-Pierre-Hilaire Barbe who applied for a state pension as a victim of Louis-Napoléon's *coup d'état*. In 1848, after twelve years' residence in the capital, Barbe returned to his home *bourg* of St Félix-de-Sorgues (Aveyron) on family business. An advanced republican and supporter of the National Workshops, he worked tirelessly to make converts: 'les gens du village se rappellent encore les propos absurdes et violents qu'il tenait journellement sur la place publique',[67] wrote the sub-prefect of St Affrique many years later. The passage of time and exposure to political novelty may have eroded the defences of the rustic migrant, but it did not necessarily make the home community more vulnerable. The 'Parisien' who returned having shed his cultural identity often found that he had also shed his power to communicate.

The link between migration, Christianisation, politicisation and, in a broader context, modernisation is by no means straightforward. Even in those regions like the Limousin, the Marche and the Nivernais which are sometimes cited in support of the argument that migration to Paris undermined religious precepts and enhanced political awareness, the evidence is by no means clear cut.[68] The masons of the Creuse rang the changes of modern

---

[65] R. Devos, 'Quelques aspects de la vie religieuse dans le diocèse d'Annecy au milieu du XIXe siècle (d'après une enquête de Mgr. Rendu)', *Cahiers d'histoire*, xi (1966), 68.

[66] A.D.C. 38M1 Prefect Cantal to prefect of police, Aurillac, 19 January 1852.

[67] A.N. F^15 4118 Sub-prefect St Affrique to prefect Aveyron, 2 November 1881.

[68] See Châtelin, *Les Migrants temporaires en France*, ii, pp. 1083–99; A. Corbin, 'Migrations temporaires et société rurale au XIXe siècle: le cas du Limousin', *Revue historique*, ccxxxxvi (1971), 293–334; *Archaïsme et modernité*, i, pp. 196–225, 619–35, 651–2; P. Gratton, *Les Paysans français contre l'agrarisme* (Paris, 1972), pp. 19–20; E. Weber, *Peasants into Frenchmen: The Modernization of Rural France, 1870–1914* (London, 1977), pp. 281–2.

political ideology throughout the nineteenth century, but their propaganda was only one of several forces radicalising opinion in the department. By contrast, the migrant masons of the Haute-Vienne seem to have had a small impact upon the political attitudes of their countrymen. A similar difficulty arises with regard to the migrants of the Nivernais and the Morvan. The lumbermen of Clamecy were instrumental in disseminating socialist doctrines and in 1851 the district exploded in bloody insurrection. But the town was a veritable nest of social conflict and it is not easy to measure the contribution of the *flotteurs de bois*. The adjacent cantons of the Morvan highlands also despatched large contingents of migrants in the direction of Paris. Observers reported a consequent shift in religious and moral habits among the sedentary population, but few signs of political emancipation (see chapter ten, p. 321).

The growth of large-scale urban migration from the middle years of the nineteenth century was accompanied by many of the processes collectively known as modernisation: economic integration, acculturation, secularisation, politicisation. The problem facing the historian is to unravel cause and effect. In a number of instances migration appears to have been a symptom of powerful integrative forces. These forces can be labelled, but their operation, even in concrete historical contexts, is difficult to specify. One theme recurs, however: the role of popular religion in buttressing the particularist values of rural society. Where the threshold of evangelisation was inadequate, or in decline, the peasant lifestyle and its mental armature was potentially vulnerable. Corbin[69] notes the importance of discrepant levels of Christianisation in his study of changing agrarian structures and attitudes in the Limousin. In the rural parishes of the Haute-Vienne religious scepticism was something the migrant took with him to Paris, not something he brought back from his travels. If migrant agnostics became migrant radicals, it is possible that the solutions to the problem of peasant politicisation are to be found in the very nature of a given rural society rather than in the phenomenon of migration. In the southern Massif Central, as in the Alps of Savoy, a rich and impermeable barrier of religious culture filtered the effects of migration throughout the nineteenth century. Long years of residence in the cities of the North doubtless produced Rouergat and Savoyard agnostics, too, but on their return they found a society accustomed to respond to its own peculiar rhythms of change.

[69] Corbin, 'Migrations temporaires et société rurale au XIXe siècle', pp. 325–7; *Archaïsme et modernité*, vol. 1, p. 631.

3

✳✳✳

Social structure and organisation

The enduring stability of the rural economy for much of the nineteenth century helped to perpetuate a social structure characterised by acknowledged hierarchy and consensus. Without doubt the elites wielded considerable economic power over the mass of the population, but there is little evidence to suggest that this power was abused in order to fabricate a spurious conformity. Voluntary social subordination made coercion unnecessary except, perhaps, at election times when the interests of the notables and those of the administration were sometimes opposed.[1] The tenacity of social mores in an age of political upheaval is one of the most striking features of the region. Successive explosions of revolutionary violence restructured the state, but left the fabric of *ancien régime* society intact. The insularity of village life yielded little to outside pressures of whatever provenance; the institutions of village life outlived the *parlements* and the *intendants*, and village hierarchies survived even the most searing attacks of jacobin egalitarianism.

It is now clear that the French Revolution no more destroyed the nobility than it inaugurated peasant property.[2] The seigneurial regime succumbed and labels were changed, but the territorial strength of the old Second Estate kept it alive. Even in the ports and cities, many noble dynasties weathered the storms of the 1790s with remarkable aplomb. And as soon as conditions improved, the work of restoring battered fortunes began. During the Consulate and the Empire large numbers of *émigrés* returned and set about redeeming their estates and asserting their rights as proprietors with the more or less willing connivance of purchasers and tenants. Such activities were also pursued in the southern Massif Central, but on a fairly small scale for little aristocratic property had been confiscated in this region. A few local noble families had made the sad pilgrimage to Paris and the guillotine during the Terror and rather more court nobles with possessions in the South had met the same fate, but the great majority of titled families were *hobereaux*. Unless they drew attention to themselves by participating in royalist insurrections or

---

[1]   See below, chapter seven, pp. 233–8 and chapter nine, pp. 284–95.
[2]   L. Bergeron, *France under Napoleon* (trans. R. R. Palmer, Princeton, 1981), pp. 126–7; G. Chaussinand-Nogaret, *Une Histoire des élites, 1700–1848* (Paris, The Hague, 1975), p. 220.

were denounced to the *comités de surveillance* by their neighbours, they passed the revolutionary decade in grateful obscurity. This reaction was scarcely surprising among a population whose enthusiasm for change cooled rapidly after 1791. The small percentage of noble property which found its way onto the market evoked a hesitant response among potential buyers. In some localities the inhabitants refused to buy, or conspired to buy on behalf of the former owners in the manner of Balzac's Breton hero Michu.[3] In others the coteries of patriots bought as an act of faith, but they rarely enjoyed security of tenure. The *chouannerie* flushed them out of the countryside and many were lucky to escape with their lives. Confidence in the durability of revolutionary institutions had ebbed and the confiscation of noble property disturbed the social order and offended proprieties.

Aristocrats who returned from abroad or who came out of hiding reconstituted their lands, shorn of seigneurial perquisites, without much difficulty. In the Ardèche where about 25 per cent of the nobility had been despoiled, the Vogüé were able to buy back their château at Vogüé and the de Bernis retrieved their possessions at St Marcel-d'Ardèche and St Just. Likewise the de Gaujal who repurchased the château of Tholet (Aveyron). Even where noble estates had been broken up, the new owners were sometimes prepared to hand back their plots in a conscious bid to restore rural equilibrium. In the Aveyron Count Crusy de Marcillac whom Napoléon appointed sub-prefect of Villefranche-de-Rouergue rebuilt his estates in this fashion, and the de Montesquieu endeavoured to do likewise in the Lozère. The mayor of La Malène[4] in the gorges of the Tarn reported that the villagers had defied the *armée révolutionnaire* and hidden Madame de Montesquieu and her three grandsons in a cave during the Terror. In spite of savage reprisals and enormous privations the inhabitants had then clubbed together in order to help the elderly Marquis to buy back his property. Few *émigrés* remained permanently separated from their landed possessions and this fact is reflected in the awards made by the Commission du Milliard des Emigrés at the end of the Restoration. In comparison with the rest of France, the requests for compensation which emanated from the departments of the southern Massif Central (see table III.1) were not very numerous and the sums involved fairly modest.

The lists of major taxpayers compiled by Napoleonic administrators on the morrow of the Revolution confirm the general picture of social stability. Despite the loss of seigneurial dues – by no means a negligible sacrifice in a region in which virtually all wealth was derived from land – the proprietorial strength of the nobility remained significant. At least a third of the thirty 'plus imposés' of the departments of the Aveyron and the Lozère in 1811 were lineage nobles of the *ancien régime*. Nearly as many members of the old nobility figured among the principal taxpayers of the Ardèche and the Haute-

[3] H. de Balzac, *Une Ténébreuse affaire* (Paris, Calmann-Lévy, n.d.).
[4] A.N. F^{1c} III Lozère 8 *Mémoire* of mayor of La Malène to prefect Lozère, 1 July 1814.

Table III.1 *Compensation paid to émigrés (1830)*

Department	Number of decisions of the Commission	Total compensation paid out	Average capital value of each compensation	Number of capital compensations over 225,000f.
Ardèche	52	2,559,121f.	49,213f.	1
Aveyron	129	3,834,024f.	29,271f.	3
Haute-Loire	105	3,073,787f.	29,274f.	1
Lozère	67	1,234,734f.	18,428f.	0
France (av. per department)	243	11,154,672f.	45,904f.	10

Source: Ministère des Finances: *Etats détaillés des liquidations faites par la commission d'indemnité en exécution de la loi du 27 avril 1825 au profit des anciens propriétaires ou ayant-droit des anciens propriétaires de biens-fonds confisqués et aliénés révolutionnairement* (10 vols., Paris, 1826–30).

Loire. The affluence of these aristocratic dynasties was strictly relative. Few were magnates on the scale of their counterparts in the north. In 1813 the prefect of the Lozère scornfully dismissed the local nobility: 'Seules quatre à cinq maisons ont de 25 à 30,000 livres de rentes. Les autres pas plus de 4 à 5,000 ou moins. Il ne faut ici que 150 *f*. d'impôts pour être du 600 plus imposés du département.'[5] But status and wealth imperfectly coincided. The social pre-eminence of the nobility rested upon esteem or public reputation which in turn was largely a matter of ancestry and social proximity. Impoverished *hobereaux* whose material existence scarcely distinguished them from the peasantry clung desperately to the redolent epithets of 'noble homme' or 'messire' and such was the consensus of values in the countryside that the rural population generally accorded them this mark of respect, if not for their own sake then for the sake of their forefathers.

In this sphere the Revolution changed little. The sale of church property rounded off a number of old fortunes, but the stories of rapid social promotion characteristic of periods of civil disorder were mostly without substance. In any case new wealth required several generations of possession before it won acceptance. The nobility continued to provide rural society with its moral leadership, therefore. Indeed, by destroying the judicial and fiscal barriers between noble and non-noble proprietors who nonetheless 'lived nobly', the Revolution probably enhanced the authority of traditional elites in the countryside. By consecrating land, rather than birth, as the condition of access to the political nation, Napoléon tacitly recognised the

[5] Quoted by G. Cholvy, 'Une Chrétienté au XIXᵉ siècle: la Lozère', in *Cévennes et Gévaudan, 46ᵉ congrès*, p. 368 note 19.

converging trends of eighteenth-century society. The ubiquitous lists of principal taxpayers defined the frontiers of an emerging category of rural 'notables'. Essentially the product of a redrawing rather than a reordering of the *ancien régime* social pyramid, the notables swiftly shed their bonapartist loyalties and developed an insular and conservative *esprit de corps* which the regimes of the first half of the nineteenth century were content to endorse. Not until the 1880s did their hegemony falter. The challenge came less from 'nouvelles couches' than from a radical republican regime (see chapter nine) which employed all the means at its disposal to break elite control of the countryside.

The notables

As a generic term for rural elites the plural noun 'notables' has the virtues of convenience and historical accuracy. However, it is not without ambiguity. By consecrating a massive thesis to the theme of the incorporation of the aristocracy and the grand bourgeoisie in the first half of the nineteenth century, A.-J. Tudesq[6] effectively narrowed the concept of the notable. Subsequent studies have rescued the lesser personalities of the countryside from beneath the shadow cast by the magnates, but only to thrust them back into an undifferentiated elite of rural proprietors. The argument has several merits: it redeems the nobility from the myth of their irreversible decline after 1789, and it emphasises the essential continuity between old and new regime social structures. But how undifferentiated was this putative elite in reality? Noble and non-noble proprietors both owned rather than worked the land and tended, therefore, to adopt identical lifestyles; they were no longer distinguishable in the eyes of the law and equality of opportunity among the educated had been decisively vindicated. Yet doubts remain. Did noble and non-noble worthies mix socially and intermarry? Did they exhibit similar political convictions over time and place? Did the ethic of *dérogeance* swiftly decay? In short, did the territorial elites recognise each other as components of a collective leadership at the helm of rural society? The answers to these questions when directed to the social structure of the southern Massif Central are various and inconclusive, and the argument for an undifferentiated elite remains an interesting hypothesis. Perhaps the image of the censitary elector bequeathed by Napoléon is misleading since it implies a unity of outlook and behaviour which never existed outside the electoral college. In any case, we have adopted a more pragmatic definition of the notable as a man of influence and reputation in his locality. Accordingly, the status of rural notable should be extended to the village priest, the legal practitioners and doctors whose professional activities brought them into permanent contact with the inhabi-

[6] A.-J. Tudesq, *Les Grands Notables en France (1840–1849): étude historique d'une psychologie sociale* (2 vols., Paris, 1964).

tants of the countryside, as well as to the ranks of noble and bourgeois land-owners living solely on rent.

The role of the priest as mediator and guardian of the values of the rural community will be discussed in the next chapter. In this context it is sufficient to dwell upon the social background of the secular clergy. Despite some indications to the contrary for the early decades of the eighteenth century, it is likely that the clergy were recruited principally from agricultural families and this tendency was reinforced in the century following. The supposedly peasant origins of old regime *curés* and *vicaires* has been challenged as an historical myth,[7] but there seems little reason to abandon the traditional view as far as the dioceses of the southern Massif Central are concerned. Indeed, matters could scarcely have been otherwise since the dioceses in question were overwhelmingly rural and their clergy indigenous. The church provided an avenue of modest social promotion which appealed directly to the small peasant household of slender means, but numerous offspring. Without doubt the preparation of a son for the priesthood imposed enormous strains upon the family budget, but the rewards were more than commensurate. Ordination eased the problem of inheritance and reflected numberless spiritual blessings upon the entire kinship group, not to mention the high esteem of neighbours. It seems that substantial private and institutional financial aid was forthcoming to assist candidates for the priesthood from these humble milieux. In 1834, Monseigneur de la Brunière informed the Minister of Ecclesiastical Affairs that nearly all the seminarists of the diocese of Mende, belonged to 'des familles pauvres à la vérité, mais très honnêtes, très anciennes dans leur état de petits cultivateurs'.[8] But such recruits needed help, notwithstanding the strict economies practised during their training, and in a subsequent letter he announced that the bursaries to the Grand Séminaire of Mende had each been reduced in value by 50 per cent in order to make them go further.

The notability of the clergy rested on professional rather than social status, therefore. The beneficed cleric was an important figure in the parish. He sat in the village council, dealt with outside authorities, kept vital statistics (until 1792), distributed alms, doubled up as teacher, notary, doctor and scribe, blessed crops and cursed caterpillars. He enjoyed security of tenure until the implications of the Concordat became apparent, and in many parishes could call upon the support of a small army of spiritual outworkers. Wherever the tithe was not impropriated, he was heavily involved in the rural economy and

[7] W. J. Callahan and D. Higgs (eds.), *Church and Society in Catholic Europe of the Eighteenth Century* (Cambridge, 1979), pp. 3, 22; T. Tackett, 'L'Histoire sociale du clergé diocésain dans la France du XVIIIe siècle', *Revue d'histoire moderne et contemporaine*, xxvii (1979), 209; T. Tackett and C. Langlois, 'Ecclesiastical Structures and Clerical Geography on the Eve of the French Revolution', *French Historical Studies*, xi (1980), 368 note 40.

[8] Archives de l'Evêché de Mende (henceforth A.E.M.) Correspondence of Mgr. de la Brunière, 1821–1848, bishop to Minister of Ecclesiastical Affairs, Mende, 10 February 1823.

often practised money-lending as a profitable side-line. Verbal facility with the French language and the capacity to read and write it set him apart from other parishioners and enhanced his intercessory role. But the superficiality of seminary education also exposed his lowly social origins and underlined the ambiguities of a 'notable' status which ultimately rested upon professional vocation rather than inherited loyalties. Dom Bourotte,[9] who despatched questionnaires to the parish clergy whilst working on the *History of Languedoc* in the 1760s, discovered that all the *curés* could write tolerable French, but some respondents in the mountain dioceses spelt phonetically. The familiarity, not to say vulgarity, of a rural clergy largely insulated from Tridentine reforming impulses constantly threatened to undermine its position, too. The peasantry of the southern Massif Central expected its clerics to place themselves at the head of village pageantry, but excessive secular involvement was frowned upon. Deference to the clergy was by no means unconditional, then, although it may have grown in the nineteenth century as some of the traditional areas of conflict lost their potency. The *curé* was honoured and respected as a 'notable' whose claim to moral leadership was without rival, provided that he did not seek to challenge the cultural identity of his parishioners.

The pre-eminence of the nobility, by contrast, was readily acknowledged. Its authority was only seriously questioned on two occasions during the period covered by this study. Between 1789 and 1792 the vicious seigneurialism of the Haute-Guienne, the Haute-Auvergne and the Bas Vivarais which had long since abandoned any pretence of reciprocity brought nemesis upon the nobility. They were not always at fault (see chapter five), but were generally victims. Waves of agrarian violence against châteaux, monastic granaries and *banalités* traversed the region. This brief, and in some ways perplexing, episode readjusted the balance in the countryside. Although the timing and sequence of the disturbances, not to mention the role of shadowy *agents provocateurs*, suggests an ideologically inspired assault upon the aristocracy, the revolts exhibited many characteristics of the peasant *jacqueries* of the seventeenth century. Notable among these was the absence of a *prise de conscience*. Once the irritant of seigneurialism had been removed, the peasantry of the southern Massif Central submitted. When next they took the field, after 1792, it was in defence of a reformed old order. The second opportunity for political emancipation was also a product of circumstance rather than structural change. It arose during the final decades of the nineteenth century as militant republicans struggled to wrest control of the state from the hands of Bonapartists, conservatives and royalists. Democratisation and the systematic manipulation of credits by government eroded the appeal of the notables. Slowly, very slowly in the case of the Lozère, the peasantry recog-

---

[9] A. Molinier, 'Une Enquête politique, économique et sociale en Languedoc au milieu du XVIIIe siècle', *Annales de démographie historique* (1974), 474.

nised the impossibility of continuing to support the old elites in national and local elections. The habits of deference were not destroyed, but henceforth they were tempered by an element of calculation.

The nobility of the southern Massif Central may be characterised as locally numerous, relatively poor, rural and heterogeneous. Heterogeneous because the governments of the *ancien régime* had diluted the noble estate by selling membership on instalments and subsequent regimes had added their own accretions. The Charter granted by the Bourbons in 1814 restored both the *ancien régime* and the Napoleonic nobility as well as providing for new creations. Heterogeneous above all because alongside the lineage nobility, the robe nobility and the barons of the Empire there existed a demi-monde of fake nobles. Until 1789 such families would normally have covered their tracks by purchasing seigneuries and ennobling offices, but in the nineteenth century they were forced to rely on the *particule*. This conglomerate elite was subject to regular osmosis. The *noblesse de race* formed but a tiny fraction of the whole estate and their pecuniary difficulties provided rich pickings for those whose claim to nobility was not yet vindicated. When Jacques Fay, the Marquis de la Tour Maubourg, died in 1713, twelve seigneuries in the Velay were put on the market. Nine of them were purchased by commoners. The long financial decline of the Polignacs presented similar opportunities, as did the bankruptcy of the Marquis de Châteauneuf-Randon during the Revolution.

A strict definition of the nobility based on the names of those who were qualified to attend the electoral assemblies of the Second Estate in the spring of 1789, would confine their numbers to between 200 and 300 families in each of the provinces comprising the southern Massif Central. The status of just over 300 nobles appears to have withstood scrutiny in the Rouergue. These were artificial figures, however, which took little account of social realities as perceived by contemporaries. They ignored a proportion of fief owners and many families whose nobility had never been endorsed, but whose status was tacitly recognised nevertheless. More particularly, they excluded office holders whose *titres d'anoblissement* had not yet matured. This was a grievous omission in the Rouergue where the robe bourgeoisie had invested heavily in offices and the seigneurial regime, and it had a bearing upon political alignments. On the list of thirty-nine individuals of recent bourgeois origins who were refused admission to the noble assemblies we find the names of several future revolutionaries.

A broader definition helps to explain the apparent ubiquity of presumed nobles living in relative poverty and isolation. This stratum of minor nobles is highly evocative of conditions prevailing in the Auvergne and Brittany and a number of writers have commented upon it. The villages of the Haut Vivarais and the Boutières positively teemed with titled families living on diminutive incomes. There were twenty-one noble households at Desaignes by the end of the *ancien régime*, but Desaignes was a *bourg* and the *bourgs* were the natural refuge of impecunious rentiers with frustrated ambitions of an urban lifestyle. Many lived 'près du paysan', both geographically and socially. Twenty-seven nobles lived in the tiny parish of Châteauneuf-de-Vernoux alone at the end of the seventeenth century and the Capitation Enquiry of 1735 revealed that a large number of seigneurs in the Velay lived on their rural estates. The contrast between these *hobereaux* struggling to make ends meet and yet still live decently on a few hundred *livres* and the great feudal dynasties such as the Vogüé or the Levézou de Vezins with upwards of 40,000 *livres* of *rente* could not be more striking. Yet it would be wrong to conclude that the *hobereaux* were without influence. With vast possessions scattered all over the Vivarais, the barons of Vogüé could scarcely fail to exercise considerable power and they remained a force in local and national politics throughout the nineteenth century. The role of the petty nobility was more subtle and ultimately more decisive since their influence was felt in a large number of parishes. It rested less upon a perceived hierarchy of economic power than upon personal relationships regularly serviced in face-to-face communities. Many *hobereaux* were too poor even to put out their land to lease and preserved appearances by farming with the aid of *maîtres-valets*. At this level the status of noble ceased to be a matter of tenure and style of living became intangible and contingent. Like those 'nobles' who presented themselves before the *sénéchaussée* and *bailliage* assemblies of the Second Estate in 1789 dressed in peasant broadcloth and sporting rusty rapiers, the individual could only invoke his lineage and ask for recognition. Such was peasant society's veneration of ancestry that pleas couched in these terms rarely passed unacknowledged.

Alongside the humble scions of ancient aristocratic lineages there existed a category of rustic landowners who sought to emulate the noble lifestyle and win tacit acceptance as members of the Second Estate. Delineated from the peasantry by such pretensions, this 'rural' bourgeoisie constituted a singular feature of the social structure of the southern Massif Central. The term is apposite provided we bear in mind that the French bourgeoisie of the eighteenth and nineteenth centuries evinced a markedly proprietorial character. Possession of landed wealth defined the bourgeoisie almost as much as it defined the nobility, but in the case of the bourgeoisie this essential relationship was masked by migration into the liberal professions. The professions rarely provided an income on a par with land, however; indeed they rarely amounted to a profession in the strict sense of the word. The ubiquitous *avocats*, *notaires*, *officiers de santé* or *médecins* who serviced rural society were first and foremost landed proprietors. Nowhere was this more apparent than in the mountainous provinces of the south where urbanisation and mercantile capitalism were ill-developed and offered scant opportunities for advancement. Possession of the soil or its surplus production were unalterable preconditions of economic independence and social status. The enduring appeal of the rentier lifestyle ought, perhaps, to be regarded as a symptom of modest levels of social stratification as well as isolation. In the southern Massif Central the essential socio-economic divide lay not between the landed and the landless, but between those who owned or controlled sufficient land to be able to withdraw from direct cultivation and those who were forced to seek a living by their own labours. The ambition of every rural household was to acquire enough property to generate the minimal three or four hundred francs which placed the rentier lifestyle within reach. In crossing the threshold of self-sufficiency after generations of patient accumulation, the peasant became a 'propriétaire vivant de ses revenus' and a series of cultural adjustments followed which consecrated his status as a village notable.

The social processes which produced this rural bourgeoisie, like those which thrust its higher echelons into the nobility, were scarcely rapid, but they were continuous until the very end of the nineteenth century when migration interrupted the cycle of renewal. Contemporaries were struck by their numbers and the influence they appeared to exert. A prefect of the Aveyron remarked of his department that it contained few noble families:

mais les campagnes sont habitées par un très grand nombre de familles plébéiennes qui depuis longtemps vivent d'une manière indépendante, possèdent des biens plus ou moins considérables, jouissent d'une considération héréditaire et se sont dans tous les temps rapprochées et presque confondues avec la noblesse par leur manière de vivre et depuis la révolution, par les intérêts qui sont devenus communs.[10]

The comment is revealing and might almost serve as a definition of the rural bourgeoisie for it lays stress upon three of the most important attributes of this social group: residence in the countryside, inherited prestige and an inclination to ape the lifestyle of the nobility.

The social and political significance of the rural bourgeoisie remains ill defined despite recent research on elites. In part this is a by-product of the persistent stereotype which insists that the bourgeoisie were an urban social group essentially engaged in commerce or the liberal professions. Accordingly the rural bourgeoisie are labelled an enriched peasant class of *laboureurs* and *gros fermiers* whose presence in the countryside dissolved old solidarities and fostered polarisation.[11] Such a divergent interpretation serves to remind us of a further obstacle to comparative analysis. The agrarian structures of pre-industrial France exhibited marked contrasts. Social organisation in the *bocage* and the regions of *petite culture* bore only a superficial resemblance to social organisation in the plains where property was concentrated. As efficient farmers producing regular surpluses, as employers of local

[10] A.N. F⁷9635 *Rapport général sur la situation politique de département de l'Aveyron*, 14 March 1823.
[11] See P. Goubert, *L'Ancien régime* (2 vols., Paris, 1969–73), i, p. 225; A. Soboul, *Problèmes paysans de la révolution, 1789–1848* (Paris, 1976), pp. 199–201.

labour, as undisputed masters of their villages the enriched peasantry of the Nord, the Beauvaisis, Burgundy and the East certainly evinced capitalist and bourgeois instincts. The rural bourgeoisie of the southern Massif Central were the product of a more confined environment, however. An environment in which agricultural self-sufficiency was an elusive objective attained by a minority, and in which the opportunities for social differentiation were severely limited. Far from undermining the cohesion of village society, the rentier bourgeoisie provided leadership and professional expertise which would otherwise have had to be drawn from the outside. Like the parish priest, like the *hobereau*, the proprietor 'vivant de ses revenus' provided a landmark and it was around such landmarks that the contours of each rural collectivity were drawn.

It is tempting to argue that the rural bourgeoisie of the southern Massif Central were the product of quite different cultural horizons, too. The mentality which prompted coteries of proprietors to abandon the exploitation of their land and practise a simulacrum of noble living in scruffy manor houses and on diminutive *rentes* was a peculiar feature of meridional society. In Brittany the twin conditions of relative isolation and *petite culture* do not appear to have encouraged the formation of a similar social group. Although the evidence is not conclusive, resident rural landowners who were neither peasant nor noble were not particularly numerous on the eve of the Revolution.[12] Nor had non-noble proprietors penetrated the seigneurial regime to any significant degree. In the South, by contrast, the presence of a rustic bourgeoisie living in symbiosis with the peasantry has been extensively, if not systematically, noted.[13] With nuances, we find them in the Alpine provinces, in Provence, in Languedoc and in Corsica. In this, as in other respects, the example of Savoy offers an interesting parallel for here, too, the countryside supported an elite of proprietors who issued directly from the peasantry. Rent from land formed the bedrock of their economic strength, but as a resident rural elite they also performed a number of collecting functions on behalf of absentee seigneurs and tithe owners. In the 600 rural parishes of Savoy during the reign of Victor Amadeus II (1666–1732) this 'bourgeoisie des champs', as Nicolas terms them,[14] numbered some 1200 families.

The rentier lifestyle which distinguished the bourgeois proprietor from his peasant neighbours implied more than a simple relationship with the soil. The transition from owner-exploiter to modest landlord was rarely accomplished

---

[12] Le Goff, *Vannes and its Region*, pp. 154, 182, 194–5; but see, too, D. M. G. Sutherland, 'The Social Origins of Chouannerie in Upper Brittany' (University of London D.Phil. thesis, 1974), p. 146.

[13] Note the jaundiced remarks of the Marquis de Mirabeau: 'les bourgeois de village et de petite ville, gens qu'on appelle vivant de leur bien, race occupée à médire et à mal faire, et dont je conseillerais de purger la société' (quoted in A. Poitrineau, 'Les Assemblées primaires du bailliage de Salers en 1789', *Revue d'histoire moderne et contemporaine*, xxv (1978), 438).

[14] J. Nicolas, *La Savoie au XVIII* siècle (2 vols., Paris, 1978), i, p. 117.

with speed. *Métayage* offered a convenient resting place on the road to *fermage* and many proprietors preferred to reside on their estates and employ *maîtres-valets* to farm for them. Jean Velay of Florac,[15] on the other hand, lived in the *bourg*, leased his estates on the causse and hired casual labour to work his scattered valley plots. The hereditary tenants of the great ecclesiastical *domaines* of the plateaux pose a further problem. Technically, they were never proprietors and yet they behaved as though they were and therein lies the clue. Bourgeois status, once a certain economic independence had been assured, devolved upon those who satisfied exacting cultural criteria. The subtle semiotics of language, bearing, dress, living conditions, ancestry and education decreed that a wealthy peasant would remain at the pinnacle of one social pyramid, whereas a bourgeois proprietor, however impecunious, held rank in quite another.[16] Recognition could not be wrung from a rural society which was punctilious in matters of status and alert to the fiscal consequences of a casual acceptance of privilege. It matured.

Ancestry alone constituted the distilled social effort of several generations although it could be gilded with the help of a complaisant village priest or notary. The practice of granting courtesy titles was widespread, so widespread in fact that in 1755 the legal fraternity of Largentière publicly declared that:

il est d'usage dans la province du Vivarest (*sic*) de ne point faire précéder de la qualité des nobles les noms de ceux qui n'ont pas véritablement la noblesse, mais de ne donner cette qualité qu'aux nobles et gentils hommes. En quoi la province du Vivarest diffère de la plupart de celles du royaume, où l'on fair précéder du terms de *noble* et honorable homme les noms de toutes personnes, soit nobles soit roturières, qui sont constituées dans quelque dignité.[17]

Nevertheless, village worthies anxious to hasten the pace of social acceptance continued to hoard titles and comb through parish and notarial registers in order to 'rebaptise' their forebears.

The putative bourgeois proprietor encountered rather less difficulty in obtaining the trappings of education; if not for himself, then for his immediate heirs. Before the Revolution the church and the Medical School at Montpellier offered possibilities, especially for younger sons, but legal studies followed by admission to the bar of the *parlement* of Toulouse carried the greatest prestige. Thus Paul Barrot,[18] who devoted a lifetime to exploiting the peasantry of Planchamp in the Cévennes, trained one of his sons as an *avocat* and in so doing unwittingly founded a dynasty of jurists and parliamen-

---

[15] Dupouy, *Les Protestants de Florac*, pp. 108–13.
[16] Jones, 'The Rural Bourgeoisie of the Southern Massif Central', pp. 77–9.
[17] A. Vézian, 'La Qualification de "Noble" en Vivarais', *Revue du Vivarais*, lxxiv (1970), 145.
[18] A.N. BB[18]473 *Justice criminel, Lozère, an VII–an IX*, dossier on J. Bertrand; N. Castan, 'Révoltes populaires en Languedoc au XVIIIe siècle', *Actes du 96e congrès national des sociétés savantes, Toulouse, 1971* (Paris, 1976), ii, pp. 230–3; A. Kuscinski, *Dictionnaire des Conventionnels* (Paris, 1916), p. 35.

tarians. Jean-André was elected to the Convention and his son, Odilon, led the Dynastic Opposition during the July Monarchy. In the 1860s Joseph and Frédéric Barrot (Odilon's nephews) ran consecutively as official candidates in the department of the Lozère. However, in the great majority of cases, the professional qualification of *avocat au parlement* proved to be an adornment, an indication that the holder had imbibed a broader, French-based culture and was suitably equipped to play the role of mediator should the need arise. Few *avocats* actually practised at the bar and even fewer made a living from it.

The most effective short-term remedies for unrequited social ambition were anthropomorphic. During the final decades of the *ancien régime* increasing numbers of *maisons bourgeoises* replete with towers, dovecotes and lordly weather-vanes were constructed. The tendency was especially noticeable in the countryside around the *sénéchaussée* and *bailliage* seats and it continued, scarcely abated, into the nineteenth century. Likewise, bourgeois seigneurs hastened to refurbish the tangible symbols of their social pretensions: *fourches patibulaires* (gibbets) and the lapidary marks of seigneurial jurisdiction. Above all else the rustic bourgeois gentilhomme sought to look the part, however. Dress and toilet were crucial matters for they emitted unmistakable signals to neighbours clad in grubby, homespun smocks and straw-filled clogs. Pierre Costy,[19] *avocat* and the last of a long line of bourgeois proprietors residing in the hamlet of Aguès, died leaving a wardrobe which included green cotton breeches, a black satin jacket, satin waistcoat, cotton stockings and a tricorn hat. Headgear provided a nearly infallible guide to social pretensions and status, so much so that the peasantry referred to the rural bourgeoisie as 'les chapeaux noirs' on occasions.[20] Monteil, the first historian of the Aveyron, remarked that in the valley of the Dourdou bourgeois womenfolk wore a black hat trimmed with a gold ribbon. His aunt refused to doff hers except for a period during the Terror. In the Ardèche the common people wore large, broad-brimmed hats, but those of the nobility and the bourgeoisie were turned up on three sides to form three points or corners. As the tricorn died out in the early decades of the nineteenth century, it was replaced by a no less mistakable ancestor of the stove-pipe hat.

Even more effective in marking out the frontiers of social class was the periwig. The purchase price and cost of upkeep alone placed it beyond the reach of all but a tiny elite, but it represented more than simply an expensive item of clothing. The periwig was a badge of success, an indication that its wearer had arrived and expected to be counted among the ranks of polite society. Hence the pride of François Dubeys of Chambéry in Savoy who noted in his journal the purchase of his first wig for a *louis d'or*, 'laquelle j'ay au

---

[19] Lempereur, 'Une Famille de bourgeoisie rurale', *Journal de L'Aveyron*, 2 November 1919.
[20] A.D.A. 70L *Comité de surveillance*, St Côme, reg. délib., 22 October 1793.

mesme instant porté'.[21] Likewise the case of Jean Gruvel, *procureur*, of Aubais in Languedoc who was so gratified by the admiring compliments that his new wig attracted that he organised a celebration in honour of the event. In the same village, according to its chronicler Pierre Prion, the second consul had initially been content to wear a type of white cap which he took to match the headgear of a *président à mortier* in the *parlement* of Toulouse although he eventually discarded it in favour of a wig. Prion's remarks were tinged with irony, if not scorn, for bourgeois status had eluded him. An impoverished clerk in the seigneurial jurisdiction, he could not afford the robes befitting his rank and was unable, therefore, to take part in village processions.[22] The object of all this cultural manoeuvring was to win respect, and the courtesy title *Sieur* indicated that recognition had been granted and the first stage of social ascension completed. The next stage involved the purchase of an enhancing office. In Rodez at the end of the *ancien régime* only the wives of nobles and *conseillers* in the *présidial* court were permitted the title of *Madame*.

The Revolution frustrated the social promotion of the highest echelons of the robe bourgeoisie. Tantalisingly, ennoblement was pulled from their grasp and they were left to pursue it by stealth throughout the nineteenth century. But the majority of the rural bourgeoisie were unlikely ever to come near this goal. The bonfire of privilege and rank found them busily scaling the lesser economic foot-hills of their ambition. Revolutionary change made a mark here, too, of course. The demise of seigneurial dues and the tithe was a grievous blow to the commoner families which had specialised in providing managerial and collecting services for the nobility and the church. As grain prices escalated from the 1760s, men like Louis Servière, who farmed the rights of the Commanderie of Gap Français in the Gévaudan, made a killing. Yet even at village level the Revolution probably created as many opportunities as it destroyed. Louis Servière's wealth brought his son, Laurent, an education and in 1790 he was elected Justice of the Peace for the canton of Le Pont-de-Montvert. Two years later we find him sitting in the Convention and upon its dissolution he became the Directory's chief executive agent in the Lozère.[23] The administrative and judicial reforms set in train after 1789 launched many a career on a broader stage. Few bourgeois had reason to regret the passing of the parlements, the *présidiaux* and the tax courts of the old regime.

The sale of church property proved a Godsend to the literate, affluent and

---

[21] Nicolas, *La Savoie*, i, p. 344.
[22] E.-G. Léonard, *Mon village sous Louis XV, d'après les mémoires d'un paysan* (Paris, 1941), p. 92.
[23] Higonnet, *Pont-de-Montvert*, pp. 60–4 and *passim*; R. Cuche, 'Le Conventionnel Servière', 29ᵉ *congrès de la Fédération historique du Languedoc méditerranéen et du Roussillon* (Mende, 1955), pp. 111–21; Kuscinski, *Dictionnaire*, p. 563.

ambitious proprietors of the countryside as well. If a few substantial peasants and artisans were able to effect a rapid social transformation by means of speculative purchases, the lion's share was bought by those whose bourgeois status was already assured. The hereditary tenants of the great ecclesiastical institutions were particularly well placed to benefit and wasted no time in removing any lingering doubts about their credentials. The estates of the Domerie of Aubrac mostly fell to rich *fermiers* like Piette Constans of Sagnes and Pierre Baduel of Oustrac. The Baduels originated from St Urcise in the Haute-Auvergne and had leased *montagnes* (pastures) from the Abbey since the 1740s, if not earlier. Combining *fermage* with commercial stock-raising and cheese manufacture, they were the single largest taxpayers in the *bourg* of Laguiole on the eve of the Revolution. Between them these families invested in about half a million *livres*' worth of *biens nationaux* and both figured among the top thirty taxpayers of the department of the Aveyron in 1811. The Baduel dynasty went from strength to strength in the nineteenth century. It forged marriage links with the influential Mayran family of Espalion and rose to a pinnacle of political power and prestige during the Second Empire. In 1878 the sub-prefect of Espalion reported that the *arrondissement* was infeodated to the Bonapartist cause. Casimir Mayran was a senator, Jules Baduel, his son-in-law, was the *conseiller-général* for the canton of St Chély-d'Aubrac and his two brothers, Léon and Henri, were respectively deputy and *conseiller-général* for the canton of Laguiole. The two families had assets worth upwards of six million francs and distributed favours and largesse which the young Republic found difficult to match.[24]

The achievement of the Baduels was untypical of the rural bourgeoisie as a whole, but their unrelenting pursuit of land and the fruits thereof illustrates a form of capital accumulation which the Revolution ultimately fostered rather than inhibited. The egalitarian legislation of the Terror threw those proprietors who had let their possessions on semi-feudal leases into confusion and the hyperinflation of 1795–7 undoubtedly depleted the coteries of small rentiers. But these were momentary panics which were insufficient to destroy the momentum developed during the final decades of the *ancien régime*. Any gaps in the ranks were soon filled from below as the seigneurial and fiscal burden on peasant surplus diminished. The extraordinary continuity of elites across the revolutionary watershed is well attested. A comparison of the tax rolls of the old regime with the lists of censitary electors, mayors and *conseillers-généraux* of the new shows that the *élus* of the 1870s and 1880s were often the direct descendants of the strutting village bigwigs who had

---

[24] A.D.A. C351 Roll of *taille* and *vingtième*, Laguiole, 1786; 8M52 Report of sub-prefect, *arrondissement* Espalion, Espalion, 15 January 1878; P.-A. Verlaguet (ed.), *Vente des biens nationaux du département de l'Aveyron: procès-verbaux d'inventaire et d'adjudication* (3 vols., Millau, 1931–3), i, no. 114; ii, nos. 4289, 4760, 4799, 4965, 4968, 5006, 5059–63, 5065, 5080; G. Maze-Sencier, *M. Casimir Mayran: Souvenirs* (Rodez, n.d. [1892]).

dominated the *communautés d'habitants* a century earlier. The forebears of Urbain Bernié, mayor of St Chély-d'Aubrac in 1876, had been seigneurial notaries and scribes in the *communauté* of Castelnau-de-Mandailles (embracing St Chély) in the decades before the Revolution. At Grèzes the Gaillard clan had long held sway. In 1899 the royalist Dr Gaillard ruled the roost according to the sub-prefect of the *arrondissement* of Marvejols. He had inherited power and prestige from his father, 'Gaillard le riche'[25] who had made a sizeable fortune from money-lending, and his grandfather who was listed among the '600 plus imposés' of the department of the Lozère. Between 1843 and 1933 the Gaillard clan never had fewer than three representatives in the ten member *conseil municipal* of the commune. Dynasties of notaries like the Chaliès of St Léons, the Blanchy of Salles-Curan or the Branche of Paulhaguet crop up with monotonous regularity. Occasionally they clambered out of the rural milieu; more often they vegetated – managing their estates, lending their *rentes* 'à la petite semaine' and dominating local government whatever the regime – seemingly permanent features of the social landscape. Napoleonic land-chopping legislation posed a small obstacle to continuity. Only reproductive failure or generational collapse on the scale of the great exodus of the late nineteenth century proved capable of arresting the cycle. The power of the Gaillard was only eclipsed after 1945, while the Bernié line collapsed without issue during the First World War.

It is true that for much of the period in question the old elites were in some senses imposed upon the countryside. Dynasties of mayors evolved because successive regimes chose to confide power in their hands. Yet nomination did not necessarily imply coercion. In matters of local government, the freedom of action of the central administration was severely limited. Individuals called to the helm of rural society had to carry the confidence of their constituents. Much of the racketeering associated with tax collection before the Revolution stemmed from the failure to combine responsibilities with status. Indubitably, therefore, social recognition preceded administrative recognition, rather than vice versa, and the consent which endorsed notable status came from below. Partly this was based upon forms of obligation (see chapter eight) but the role of economically motivated deference should not be viewed out of context although it can never be fully fathomed either. In a region given increasingly to owner-exploitation, the landlord–tenant relationship was secondary and, in any case, migration gave the tenant the upper hand in some districts from the mid nineteenth century. As long as a proportion of the peasantry faltered on the brink of insolvency economic pressures to conform still applied, but they remained diffuse.

On the other hand, there is much contemporary evidence to suggest that the power of the notables was subscribed. In a picaresque account of a walk-

---

[25] A.D.L. VIM²3 *Arrondissement de Marvejols: situation politique (mai, 1899), notes confidentielles pour M. le Préfet.*

ing tour of the valley of the Ardèche in the 1870s, Albin Mazon[26] and his companion halted for lunch with a peasant family near Vogüé. The only sense that these travellers could collect from their involuntary hosts concerned the names of the local bigwigs: 'Moussu Loouriou [Lauriol]' of St Maurice-d'Ardèche and 'Moussu Tastevi [Tastevin]' of Les Salles. The Tastevin had occupied the *mas* of Les Salles in the commune of Balazuc for centuries. Having prospered in the shadow of the barons of Vogüé, they enjoyed widespread respect and it seemed entirely natural that a scion of the family should become the first mayor of Balazuc in 1790. When he died the assembled inhabitants of St Maurice and Balazuc disputed for the honour of escorting his remains from the estate to the family shrine in the parish church of St Maurice. When his son, also mayor, died these fractious village solemnities were repeated. The role of atavistic loyalties in perpetuating the authority of the notables can scarcely be overstated. The jottings of the *abbé* Cornut on life in Montfauçon – a *bourg* in the Velay – during the 1860s are quite explicit on this point. Under the rubric 'Conditions ou classes', he noted that individuals weighed their social consequence in terms of ancestry, employing the phrase, *bonne souche, vieille souche*. The handful of households thus sanctified by time effectively occupied all local offices, not by virtue of manipulative pressure but because they alone possessed the essential prerequisites: leisure and social esteem. 'Dans ces familles', he continued:

étoient notre seigneur et divers seigneurs de moindre qualité; elles fournissent nos juges, nos consuls, nos maires; elles fournissent encore nos maires, nos adjoints, nos conseillers municipaux. Si les descendants n'ont pas succédé à l'importance de la position sociale des ancêtres, du moins ils ont hérité de la considération et de l'influence que les ancêtres avaient acquises par leurs titres et par leurs places. Il est juste aussi de faire la part des services rendus; le peuple est reconnaissant, et sa gratitude passe de génération en génération, surtout quand elle est personnellement méritée par les dignes enfants de ses anciens maîtres.[27]

By the same token, however, prestige could be clouded by memories of past injustices handed down from one generation to the next. The rapacious seigneurialism of the Brivadois lingered long in popular consciousness, for example. Yet even here defiance and deference were not strict alternatives, but discordant characteristics of a common psyche. In his memoirs the veteran republican, Amédée Saint Ferréol,[28] readily acknowledged the halo of respect which surrounded the bourgeoisie of Brioude until the middle of the nineteenth century.

The pretensions of the rural bourgeoisie and the flexibility of noble status suggest a continuum of social promotion leading inexorably towards an

[26] Francus [A. Mazon], *Voyage . . . le long de la rivière d'Ardèche* (Privas, 1885), pp. 56–9.

[27] Archives Départementales de la Haute-Loire (henceforth A.D. H.-L.) J237/116 *Fonds Convers, Notes Cornut, carnet 35*.

[28] A. Saint Ferréol, *Mes mémoires* (5 vols., 1887–92), i, p. 81.

undifferentiated proprietorial elite. Patently, lifestyle posed no insuperable barrier and in the eyes of many contemporary observers this was the crucial test. At Montfauçon Cornut discerned the existence of two clearly defined classes: 'd'un côté la bourgeoisie ou aristocratie et, de l'autre, le peuple'[29] and the remark of the prefect of the Aveyron[30] that was quoted earlier tended in the same direction. Why, then, is it better to talk of elites in the plural? The clergy scarcely enter the debate and have been included in this analysis as a token reminder of their claim to secular as well as spiritual pre-eminence. They present an interesting example of the professionalisation of status. By the end of the nineteenth century the clergy of the southern Massif Central were closer – socially, culturally and geographically – to their parishioners than they had been for two centuries and more, yet their status had never seemed more assured. Professional vocation provides an unsatisfactory basis upon which to discriminate between the nobility and the bourgeoisie, however. Beyond landowning, most nobles and bourgeois exercised no profession although, among those who did, lineage nobles and *anoblis* were conspicuous in seeking advancement through state service and the career of arms. By contrast, they were much less prominent in commerce and industry. The shadow of *dérogeance* hung heavily in the south and it implies a survival of noble inhibitions which is not evident at first sight. At the lowest levels of petty and pseudo-nobility constant osmosis probably did prevent the erection of significant social barriers, for who was to decree who was or was not noble once the delineating contours of *ancien régime* privilege had been obliterated. Widen the focus to embrace the great aristocratic proprietors and a different picture emerges, however. The de Valady and the de Bonald in the Aveyron, La Rochenégly and de Chambrun in the Lozère, de Bernis and de Vogüé in the Ardèche and the Calemard de Lafayette in the Haute-Loire to mention only the most illustrious houses, constituted an elite which held both the petty nobility and the rural bourgeoisie at arm's length. The distinction is transparent in the ideological arena. The great aristocratic landowners moulded their identity around the Legitimist cause and steadfastly resisted the politics of compromise and fusion until the very end of the nineteenth century. Many *hobereaux* supported the Bourbons with equal enthusiasm (see chapter nine, p. 294). By contrast the rural bourgeoisie lacked a clear political personality. While favouring the censitary system which maximised their influence, they served every regime without compunction. Ever since the Revolution republicanism had recruited its adepts from among the leisured proprietors of the *bourgs* and when the Opportunist vision of a property-owning Republic materialised in the 1880s, the rural bourgeoisie was not slow in pledging its support.

[29] A.D. H.-L. J237/116 *Fonds Convers, Notes Cornut, carnet 25.*
[30] See above p. 78 and note 10.

Towards a definition of the peasantry

In several important respects the preceding analysis has identified the peasantry by default. The peasantry of the southern Massif Central constituted the rural population minus the nobility, bourgeois proprietors and sundry dignitaries. Such an anthropological definition has the virtue of simplicity, but offers little illumination and takes a great deal for granted. It presupposes an extraordinarily compact social spectrum relatively unaffected by the passage of time and isolates the cultural variable at the expense of all others. Many would argue, with Charles Tilly,[31] that labour power furnishes the most appropriate instrument for social dissection since proletarianisation was a key development of the nineteenth century which affected town and country dweller alike. Plainly, it would be absurd to deny that those whom we describe as the peasantry possessed an internal structure based on well-being and prestige, but it would appear equally doctrinaire to reject the suggestion that in a concrete historical context all those who worked for a living in the countryside shared a common mentality. The point at issue is not whether the peasantry of the southern Massif Central were immobile, undifferentiated and egalitarian, but whether the observed levels of mobility, differentiation and inequality were sufficient to provoke diverse forms of cultural behaviour.

Before the Revolution the term *paysan* had a broad colloquial application. In Languedoc, especially, it served as a loose description of all those members of society who were incapable of 'living nobly' and therefore devoid of honour or reputation. Thus, in the eyes of contemporary chroniclers such as Pierre Prion[32] and the *abbé* Favre,[33] the village labourer, artisan, carter or beggar was as much a peasant as the smallholder. After 1789 the pejorative content of the term proved unacceptable, at least officially. Monteil[34] remarked in 1800 that it had become customary to replace *paysan* with *cultivateur* – an altogether more precise expression, but one which still conveyed the flavour of manual toil. Its terminological opposite was *propriétaire* which had gained currency during the late *ancien régime* as a bland synonym for both bourgeois and noble. Since the late nineteenth century the term *cultivateur* has been found wanting and has yielded to the modern euphemism *agriculteur*. How far these semantic changes affected common parlance and reflected shifts in popular attitudes is debatable. The language of oral communication in the countryside was patois (see chapter four) and it is doubtful whether forms with an alien etymology carried much meaning.

---

[31] Tilly, 'Did the Cake of Custom Break?', p. 29.   [32] Léonard, *Mon village sous Louis XV*.
[33] J. B. C. Favre, *Histoire de Jean-l'ont-pris, conte languedocien du XVIIIᵉ siècle* (Paris, 1877).
    Also, E. Le Roy Ladurie, *L'Argent, l'amour et la mort en pays d'oc* (Paris, 1980).
[34] Monteil, *Description du département de l'Aveiron*, i, p. 53.

'Paysan' (*pagès*), by contrast, was a word enshrined in occitanian literature which in turn derived from a rich historical context. Although it has acquired opprobrious adjectival connotations in recent times, its meaning has never entirely shed the ethnographic bias. Even nowadays, the manifestly pejorative epithet 'fils de paysan' implies more than simply a relationship to the soil.

A number of other terms occur in our sources which give clues to the internal hierarchy of the peasantry. Contemporaries referred to *laboureurs, pagès, ménagers, travailleurs de terre, brassiers* and *locataires*, not to mention the phrases employed to differentiate the several categories of vagabond and beggar. While most of these expressions were constant over the time-scale envisaged in this study, there were considerable local and provincial variations. *Laboureur, pagès* and *ménager* were all terms used to identify the most prosperous farmers, those who were adequately endowed with land and the equipment required to cultivate it. *Travailleurs de terre, brassiers* and *locataires* clustered near the opposite end of the social spectrum. They owned insufficient land on which to live; sometimes they owned no land at all. Farm employees (*domestiques, bergers, bouviers* etc.) occupied an adjacent position. The *ménager* appears to have been a regular feature of the country-side in the south-eastern provinces of France, in Provence and Bas-Languedoc especially. The natural habitat of the *laboureur*, by contrast, lay to the south west. In Aquitaine and, more particularly, in the Rouergue the sources give pride of place to the *laboureur* and, less frequently, the *pagès*. The same is true of the Auvergne.

These variations are surely unimportant, however. What counts is the social reality and how we categorise it. *Ménagers* and *laboureurs* were generally long-established and self-sufficient cultivators who had risen over several generations from small beginnings. They possessed sufficient land, stock and draught animals to generate surpluses which guaranteed economic independence and placed them beyond the reach of hunger, even in bad years. As far as the peasant category was concerned their social ascension was complete: they could go no further. Beyond lay the rural bourgeoisie. These 'gros paysans', to use a modern term, are, indeed, sometimes confused with the bourgeoisie. André Armengaud[35] refers to them as 'demi-bourgeois, demi-manants' and notes that in the Tarn and the Tarn-et-Garonne a number even qualified for the vote under the censitary regime. There is little doubt that some rich peasants and millers, particularly, overhauled the most straitened *rentiers*. François Bouissou[36] of Bosc de Quercy who was styled *laboureur* on the tax roll of St Antonin, paid 120 *livres* 6 *sols* 10 *deniers* in *taille* in 1789 – more than many bourgeois proprietors. Furthermore, the prospering peasant almost inevitably became involved in activities beyond the realm of subsist-

[35] A. Armengaud, *Les Populations de l'Est-Aquitain au début de l'époque contemporaine: recherches sur une région moins développée, vers 1845 – vers 1871* (Paris, 1961), p. 84.
[36] A.D.A. C644 *Rôle de taille et de vingtième,* 1789.

ence farming. He expanded the household workforce by recruiting outside labour; he took his surpluses to market or, more likely, lent them to his neighbours in return for services and interest; he cashed in on the seigneurial regime like that archetypal Burgundian *laboureur*, Edmé Rétif, father of Nicolas Rétif de la Bretonne.[37] Such activities were unmistakable signs of imminent social transition and powerful incitements to respect. In the Velay notaries accorded wealthy *ménagers* the title of *maître* and a few were even granted the supreme courtesy of being styled *sieur*. Wealth alone did not provide a means of escape from the peasantry, however. Once again style of life was of critical importance. For all his authority as village patriarch, Edmé Rétif remained a peasant. Aged seventy-three, he died from a fever contracted while scything a water-logged meadow. Before and after the Revolution manual toil was strictly incompatible with bourgeois status.

If the *ménager* or *laboureur* stood at the helm of peasant society, it is much less easy to describe accurately his social and economic inferiors. The convenient classification into 'landed' and 'landless' which some historians and sociologists have sought to generalise is inappropriate. It rests upon the singular example of the social structure of the north-eastern plains which, as virtually any map of peasant property will demonstrate,[38] was untypical of France as a whole. In the *bocages*, in the *pays de petite culture*, landownership was not a variable, but a constant. Apart from the crucial delineation arising out of modes of tenure, the only realistic distinction which can be drawn lies between those who farmed sufficient land for their needs and those who did not. Among those who did not, the proportions in which landholding and wage labour contributed to the household economy varied almost to infinity. Many peasant families survived on the fruits of the soil with occasional recourse to remunerative labour; others combined their labour power with agriculture and systematically and resolutely migrated during the dead season. Neither group enjoyed a healthy margin of economic security and could not, therefore, be ranked with the *laboureurs*. A much larger number, in all probability, relied heavily upon the availability of gainful employment. These were the *travailleurs de terre*, *brassiers* and *locataires*. Yet even the agricultural labourer had a stake in the land, usually a garden or a plot of land on which to grow a little rye or potatoes.

It follows from this that the landless peasant whose survival depended solely upon the market for his labour did not exist in significant numbers in the southern Massif Central. The agrarian structures of the region scarcely permitted the development of a substantial market for anything more than seasonal labour. Large-scale cereal farming was highly localised and shrinking in the course of the nineteenth century if the statistics relating to *fermage*

---

[37] N. Rétif de la Bretonne, *La Vie de mon père* (ed. G. Rougier, Paris, 1970).
[38] For example, H. Le Bras and E. Todd, *L'Invention de la France: atlas anthropologique et politique* (Livre de poche, 1981), p. 345.

can be relied upon. Putative proletarians – younger sons, impoverished artisans, domestics fallen on hard times – either migrated, entered the church, remained within the bosom of the extended family or simply joined the ranks of micro-proprietors. It is important to bear in mind that in many localities the land supply remained elastic well into the second half of the nineteenth century. At the very least, *défrichement* delayed pauperisation. Indeed, the existence of vast tracts of common land in a number of highland communes enabled those who owned no property at all to live rather better than some plotholders in the valleys. These remarks clearly invite a reassessment of the view that discerns in proletarianisation one of the key processes of the nineteenth century. Even generously defined, it is difficult to regard proletarianisation as a massive and accelerating trend in the countryside of the southern Massif Central. In all probability, the proportion of plotholders increased during the immediate post-revolutionary decades when headlong population growth momentarily overtook the rate at which land could be cleared. But this was a passing phase. The precarious *colons* of one generation became the entrenched peasant proprietors of the next. Sober and industrious, they swarmed up the hillsides and on to the plateaux, founding new *mas* and pushing back the frontiers of the heath. By the end of the century the peasantry had triumphantly vindicated its domination of the soil and displayed an impressive degree of homogeneity.

Fiscal and census data leave little room for doubt about the underlying trend towards owner-exploitation, but detailed information on the social and economic realities of daily life for the marginal peasant is sparse. It is an oblique testimony to the threads of continuity that some of the best evidence available derives from the memoirs of those who actually grew up in the countryside during the pre- and post-First World War decades. Maurice Brajon,[39] for instance, was born into a family of day-labourers living in a village near Mende. The fifth child in a straitened household, he was leased as a cowherd at the age of six. Fragmentary documentation does exist for the earlier period, however. In 1844 the Rodez Fourierist, Jules Duval, pioneered an enquiry into agrarian conditions prevailing in the department of the Aveyron. Some of the replies to the questionnaire which he sent out to the parish priests have survived and they tend to confirm the picture of an entirely landowning society. Day-labourers were most numerous in the *bourgs* where work was fairly plentiful. They rented huts in the agglomeration and small plots in the immediate vicinity and were for this reason often referred to as *locataires*. In the villages around St Affrique landless labourers were a rarity, reported the *abbé* Ancessy:

à Calmels, à Viala et à Combez, nous n'avons pas un seul prolétaire; à Saint Yzarn [St

---

[39] M. Brajon and M. Arnaud, *Monsieur Brajon, maître d'école* (Paris, 1977), pp. 17, 64; also, A. Sylvère, *Toinou, le cri d'un enfant auvergnat, pays d'Ambert* (Paris, 1980).

Izaire] on en trouve quelques-uns, à Rebourgues et à Bonnac on en trouve moins; on ne serait peut-être pas éloigné de la vérité en mettant, sur dix familles, une seule de prolétaires, les autres neuf jouissant d'une petite maison, un champ ou jardin.[40]

Micro-property predominated because it was within reach of all but the most feckless, but the plotholder could not grow all the foodstuffs he needed. Many spent half of the active year working for others; at Buzeins on the Causse de Sévérac the *colon* sought employment for 180 days on average and was paid 60 *centimes* per day in winter and 75 *centimes* in summer.[41]

Day-labourers with no stake in the land whatsoever were rather more numerous in the villages of the Velay[42] during the middle years of the nineteenth century, otherwise the plotholder who supplemented his slender agricultural resources with wage labour, cottage industry, gleaning, common grazing and *affouages* represented the norm across the southern Massif Central. The direct testimony gathered by examining magistrates is some-times revealing in this respect. In 1842 a widower burdened with five children from the district of Javols in the Lozère stated: 'je travaille environ la moitié de l'année à la journée et pour le compte des personnes qui veulent bien m'employer, en échange je gagne des pommes de terre et quelques sous; j'ai un revenu de 30 francs par an de mes terres'.[43] If we allow for a degree of variation in the ratio of wage to agricultural labour, his situation was not untypical of a stratum of the peasantry. Sixty years later General Ausset, a *conseiller général* in the department of the Lozère, remarked: 'l'ouvrier purement ouvrier, le prolétaire proprement dit, n'existe pour ainsi dire pas, la presque totalité des travailleurs possèdent un coin de terre qu'ils cultivent avant de louer leurs services à d'autres'.[44]

With reservations, these conclusions might be extended to include the two other categories most vulnerable to proletarianisation: industrial workers and domestic servants. Even at the end of the nineteenth century the indus-trial workforce was small and fragmented. The Aubin–Decazeville mining and metallurgical complex constituted the only sizeable centre of heavy industry in the region and, as we have already noted, its employees were slow to abandon rural habits of mind. On the evidence of the 'Enquête sur les Classes Ouvrières'[45] carried out between 1872 and 1875, the industrial worker and his family remained in regular contact with the soil in all but a few localities. The hands at Jory's spinning mill in Marvejols nearly all owned their houses and adjacent plots of land, and would interrupt industrial work

---

[40] J. Valette, 'Une Enquête sociale dans l'Aveyron en 1848: les habitants de l'Aubrac', *Revue du Rouergue*, xxxiii (1979), 110.

[41] *Ibid.*, p. 117.   [42] Merley, *La Haute-Loire*, i, p. 405 and note 12 *bis*.

[43] Claverie, 'Oppositions et conflits dans une société d'inter-connaissance', p. 26.

[44] C. Causse and A. Tufféry, 'Le Diocèse de Mende au début du XXᵉ siècle' (Université Paul Valery, Montpellier, Mémoire de maîtrise, 1972), p. 28.

[45] See A.N. C3022.

in order to gather the harvest. Many of the miners of Sainte Florine were proprietors, too, and those of Langeac often cultivated plots of land during their spare time. Similar conditions prevailed, naturally, in the semi-concentrated industries such as textile manufacture at St Geniez, gimp threads at Le Puy, silk-ribbon-making at St Didier-de-Séauve and glove-sewing at Millau. In theory, at least, domestic service provided the dis-inherited and unendowed with a chance of accumulating capital and joining the ranks of property-owning society. How realistic a means of social pro-motion this was is difficult to judge, however. Large farms employing retainers on a regular basis were scarcely numerous – except on the causses – and the cash component of farm servants' wages on lesser estates was small. Yet the *abbé* Ancessy considered domestic service to be a reliable, if laborious, method of advancement. Moreover, it coincided nicely with the strategy of late marriage which was widely practised in the southern Massif Central as a primitive technique for limiting births. Lodged, clothed and nourished at the expense of his employer, the farm servant could save virtually the whole of his stipend and,

avec des gages qui paraissent peu de chose la fille arrive à 25 ou 28 ans, le jeune homme à 30 ou 35 ans, ayant l'un et l'autre de quoi s'établir assez advantageusement au point que, pour si peu qu'ils aient 400 ou 500 francs de légitime, ils peuvent former une maison aussi aisée que celle dont nous avons supposé le budget . . .

And the priest added, 'les enfants naturels, qui tournent bien, obtiennent quelquefois ce résultat'.[46]

If most day-labourers were also micro-proprietors, the same is true of the artisans. They existed in large numbers throughout the countryside – a tangible reminder of the insularity of village life. The urban artisan was organised by occupation and status into guilds and fraternities which endowed him with a robust sense of identity. Monteil's[47] description of the sharp contrasts between artisan and winegrower in Villefranche-de-Rouergue on the morrow of the Revolution is eloquent on this point. The noisy coppersmiths wore leather aprons, but their clothes were made of wool rather than rough canvas. They frequented the taverns, enjoyed public spec-tacles and could understand French, although they habitually spoke patois. The *vignerons* were a breed apart, marked physically and emotionally by daily toil up and down the hillsides. Bent by strain and tanned by the sun, they shunned the wine shops and practised the most austere economy in their life-style. Villefranche was a considerable centre of population strategically sited at the intersection of geographical and ecological frontiers. Its craftsmen pro-duced for relatively sophisticated markets and were not representative of arti-sans in general. The typical artisan lived in the *bourg* or village, produced for

---

[46] Valette, 'Une Enquête sociale dans l'Aveyron', pp. 112–13.
[47] Monteil, *Description du département de l'Aveiron*, i, pp. 83–5.

the immediate agricultural hinterland and cultivated a patch of vines or cereals as a secondary occupation. His interests and views converged with those of the small farmer and the two groups frequently intermarried. For most purposes, therefore, the rural artisan may be regarded as forming part of the peasantry.

The middle decades of the nineteenth century saw craft production at its peak. Although there were signs that artisan textile manufacture had entered a crisis, the skills of the mason, blacksmith, wheelwright, barrelmaker, potter, carpenter and clog-maker were in heavy demand. The *bourgs* positively bulged with artisans. About 30 per cent of the households in Chanac and Florac (Lozère) were engaged in handicraft and service activities to some degree and a similar picture emerges from St Sernin-sur-Rance in the Aveyron and Caussade in the adjoining department of the Tarn-et-Garonne. In each case, moreover, the artisan remained in close contact with the soil. At Chanac two-thirds of the plots which dotted the flanks of the causse belonged to the wool carders, weavers, hatmakers, locksmiths and muleteers of the *bourg* and the remainder were exploited by day-labourers. The position of Florac astride the principal artery of the Cévennes made it the centre of gravity of a substantial *arrière pays*. Its handicrafts had steadily prospered since the middle of the eighteenth century and most artisans had come to own their dwellings as well as allotments and patches of vines. For all its urban allures and specialist services Florac retained the appearance of an overgrown agricultural village, however. In 1855 the author of a 'medical topography' noted that the *bourg* contained 362 houses, 185 pigs, almost as many pig-sties and 112 heaps of manure.[48]

From whatever angle we view the social structure of the southern Massif Central the abiding impression is the same: society converged around the possession of the soil. In the period under study the landless rural proletariat was at best a marginal phenomenon of the countryside and in the second half of the nineteenth century it ceased to exist to all intents and purposes. From the 1860s landowners throughout the region deplored the shortage of farm hands. Migration had spoiled the market for wage labour in some districts; in others land clearance had given the *travailleur de terre* access to property. Possession of the soil was a relative matter, of course. A gulf separated the humble *colon* or plotholder from the *ménager* or laboureur. Yet that gulf was bridged by a common relationship to the soil and an archaic mentality which over-rode objective inequalities of condition. As for the artisan, his neighbourhood and emotional ties bound him to the small peasantry. Professionally his outlook was certainly wider, but the small towns and *bourgs* of the mountains rarely provided sufficient stimuli to foster the growth of an independent identity. Outside intervention could always correct these deficiencies

[48] E. Monteils-Pons, *Florac au point de vue de l'hygiène et de la salubrité* (Montpellier, 1855), p. 77.

and precipitate new social alignments, and successive waves of revolutionary apostles sought to do just that. In 1794 the artisans and plotholders of Villecomtal (Aveyron) denounced *paysans* and *bourgeois* in the same breath. But time exposed such attempts at redefinition as essentially artificial. Making the rural artisan or the day-labourer an honorary *sans-culotte* in the style of the Year Two or a *prolétaire* in the style of 1848 did little to alter social realities.

If the abiding reality of rural society was the tendency towards convergence rather than divergence, it is important to conclude with a view of the whole. In the *bourgs* and villages of the southern Massif Central noble and bourgeois as well as peasant cultivator and artisan lived in close mutual proximity. For all the distinctions of rank, for all the parasitical relationships and petty tyrannies that undoubtedly existed, the rural collectivity was more than simply the sum of its parts. The *bourg*, the village, the parish defined the contours of a spiritual community which transcended individual social categories and yet integrated them all. The *hobereau* and the bourgeois proprietor, not to mention the migrant worker and the artisan, had wider horizons to be sure, but outside contacts did not preclude narrow territorial allegiances even among the privileged. In certain circumstances the rural community forgot its internecine squabbles and reacted as of one mind. The challenge of electoral participation was especially liable to evoke this consensual response.

The snapshot glimpses of rural social structure afforded by our sources lend weight to the conclusions outlined above. They bring into focus a world of pullulating villages and *bourgs* in which the privileged and the non-privileged lived cheek by jowl and on terms of rough familiarity which did not, however, preclude a strong attachment to order and hierarchy. Analysis reveals some parallels with the social structure of the Mediterranean littoral which are highly suggestive of a common meridional heritage. The ubiquity of the petty noble, the retired military officer, the bourgeois proprietor is well attested: the *bourg* of Meyrueis (399 households) boasted in its *cahier de doléances* that it was 'très bien habitée puisqu'on y compte dans le moment douze chevaliers de St Louis, nombre d'autres officiers au service de sa majesté, des avocats et une bourgeoisie nombreuse'.[49] The *vœux* of the 'town' of Florac,[50] published in January 1789, were signed by four clerics, eight nobles, ten bourgeois, ten *ménagers*, six *hommes de loi*, one surveyor (*expert*), thirteen merchants, eighteen artisans and four innkeepers. Sixty years later bourgeois households still accounted for some 10 per cent of the

---

[49] C. Lautard, *Convocation de la sénéchaussée de Nîmes aux Etats Généraux de 1789* (Paris, 1923), p. 81.
[50] J. Barbot, 'Au Seuil de la Révolution', *Société des lettres, sciences et arts de la Lozère: Archives Gévaudanaises*, iii (1915–22), 13.

total population. Even a much smaller cévenol community such as Vébron[51] contained eight clerics, two nobles, fifteen bourgeois and seventeen *hommes de loi* on the eve of the Revolution, and when Richeprey visited the crumbling *bourg* of Fons (Quercy) in 1781 he was clearly surprised to discover a dearth of respectable families. 'Pas un particulier que l'on qualifie du titre de Sieur en parlant de luy ou à luy',[52] he noted in his journal. But if the teeming rural bourgeoisie of the highland provinces invites comparison with the village oligarchies of Provence and the plains of Languedoc, it should be remembered that terrain and habitat imposed vigorous restraints which scarcely applied in the Midi. The Mediterranean 'urbanised village' and the structural contrasts it implied had no strict parallel in the mountains. For all their posturing and pretensions, the *bourgs* of the southern Massif Central remained indissolubly a feature of the rural landscape.

The structure of the peasant household

Analysis conceived in terms of social stratification provides at best an opaque image of peasant society. An alternative approach is required if we are to examine our subject in greater detail. Self-evidently the family unit, or rather the household, constituted the elementary cell of rural life, but arguably it played a more active role as well. In the southern Massif Central the household was a complex institution which served as an instrument of subtle social differentiation. It assigned to each individual a fixed status within a kinship group and it furnished the building blocks of an alternative hierarchy within the broader village or parish community. As one writer remarked recently, the patois of Languedoc is unusually rich in words to describe a house. She lists over half a dozen derivations from the root *oustal* which are commonly employed to describe different shapes and sizes of rural dwelling.[53] Such idiomatic precision is highly revealing of popular attitudes for the term *oustal* (also *ostal* and *hostau*) defined more than simply a physical category, a place of residence. It implied an organic entity of family and farmstead and the appurtenances thereof. This is to offer an almost prosaic definition, however. The *oustal* was the mental fulcrum of peasant existence:

'c'est vers lui', wrote Ulysse Rouchon, 'que convergent les pensées de tous ceux qui sont nés sous le même toit; c'est pour lui que l'on travaille et que l'on peine; c'est autour de lui qu'on éprouve les plaisirs du repos; c'est là que se concentrent les affections, les espoirs, les joies et les épreuves, les douleurs et c'est là que se subissent les deuils'.[54]

The household had a metaphysical and timeless dimension, then. It linked the

[51] *Ibid.*   [52] Guilhamon, *Journal des voyages*, ii, p. 108 note 51.
[53] H. Willings, *A Village in the Cévennes* (London, 1979), p. 23.
[54] U. Rouchon, *La Vie paysanne dans la Haute-Loire* (3 vols. in one, Lafitte Reprints, Marseilles, 1977), ii, p. 8.

living with the dead in a permanent communion. Its perpetuation and embellishment transcended the interests of mere individuals and the task of each new generation was to hand on the *oustal*, undivided and undiminished, as a sacred trust to the next.

Family and household were not co-terminous because the household might contain non-kinsmen retainers and, more important, because families were transient. Family patronyms changed, generations came and went, but the name of the *oustal* never changed and ancestors accumulated like so many invisible mentors seated around the hearth. The poverty of patronymics in isolated and endogamous localities[55] and the longevity of the farmstead encouraged a tendency towards substitution. Baptismal names yielded to multifarious sobriquets which made the process of identification and allocation to households much simpler for contemporaries even if it has enormously complicated the task of historians. The substitution of a 'nom de lieu' for a 'nom de famille' was widely practised among those who lived on their lands. Households in jeopardy for want of a male heir were forced to tolerate a break in the strict line of biological succession, but the son-in-law inherited the title as well as the responsibilities of his adoptive *oustal*. Public opinion endorsed the transfer of allegiance by erasing his 'nom de famille' from its memory. This strategy for survival and continuity was not restricted to the southern Massif Central, we find it operating in parts of Brittany[56] and in the Pyrenees,[57] too. Nor was it restricted to peasant households. Bourgeois dynasties which had remained in close contact with the soil evinced a similar preoccupation with the household and its physical location. Jean-Baptiste, the second eldest of Pierre Costy's nine surviving offspring, was known by contemporaries as Laraussie Costy after part of the *domaine*. He signed his name as Laraussie Costy or simply as Laraussie.[58]

The case of the son-in-law who migrates, both physically and emotionally, from one household to another serves to remind us that the extended family constituted the norm in the southern Massif Central throughout the period in question. The influential views of Peter Laslett[59] and others concerning the omnipresence of the nuclear family in Western Europe now stand in need of substantial revision. In France somewhat belated research into the structure

---

[55]   In Lamaison's computerised study of the parish of Ribennes (*circa* 650 inhabitants in 1736), the commonest patronymics were BONNAL (polled 175 times); TICHIT (150); ALLO or D'ALLE (114); DELRANC or RANVIER (113); DUMAS or DELMAS (108) and BOULET (104) (P. Lamaison, 'Parenté, patrimoine et stratégies matrimoniales sur l'ordinateur: une paroisse du Haut Gévaudan du XVIIe au début du XIXe siècle' (Université René Descartes, Sorbonne, Paris V, Doctorat de troisième cycle en ethnologie, 1977), p. 278.

[56]   Pelras, 'Goulien – commune rurale du Cap Sizun', p. 506.

[57]   A. Zink, *Azéreix: la vie d'une communauté rurale à la fin du XVIIIe siècle* (S.E.V.P.E.N., 1969), p. 208.

[58]   Lempereur, 'Une Famille de bourgeoisie rurale', *Journal de l'Aveyron*, 5 October 1919.

[59]   P. Laslett and R. Wall, *Household and Family in Past Time* (Cambridge, 1972).

of domestic groups has undermined the generalisations about the prevalence of nuclear households since the eighteenth century. Once again a rough distinction between North and South seems to be emerging. In the North the conjugal family had long predominated, clearly, but in parts of the Pyrenees and Provence, in Corsica, in the Limousin and in the southern Massif Central the household exhibited varying degrees of complexity throughout its developmental cycle. Moreover, there are signs that in many of these regions the extended family remained the ideal well into the nineteenth century. Indeed, an attempt to map the incidence of complex households in 1975 revealed a lingering core of extended families in the Aveyron and the Lozère.[60]

Information on family structure derives from three sources in the main: the impressionistic observations of contemporaries; microscopic family reconstitution and macroscopic manipulation of census data by computer. All three have a role to play and by matching the literary evidence with quantifiable data we can obtain a reasonable picture of the situation in the southern Massif Central. Computer cartography of the sort alluded to above provides a bold outline. Rather more sophisticated is the attempt by Parish and Schwarz[61] to test the hypotheses of Frédéric Le Play concerning the incidence and distribution of complex households. Using the information contained in the 1856 census and other data, they substantially redeem his reputation as a conscientious empiricist. Although Le Play classified household structures with insufficient rigour his isolation of the stem-family (*famille-souche*) is fully vindicated. The stem-family may be defined as the cohabitation of an elderly couple or ascendant, a married son who has been designated heir, his wife and children, and his unmarried brothers and sisters. As Le Play sought to demonstrate, significant numbers of such households still existed in Brittany, the South West and the Massif Central. Without painstaking local research we can only guess at the nuances in this picture, however. In those regions in which precipuitary systems of inheritance held sway, it is usually possible to calculate the distribution of nuclear and extended families from marriage contracts and wills. Alain Collomp[62] has shown the advantages of this method in a small locality of Haute-Provence. The manifest disadvantage of this economical approach, however, is that it does not offer much penetration. The precise structure of the complex household and the strategies which shaped its development remain mysterious. If these problems are to be resolved there seems little alternative to full-scale family reconstitution and the results of those studies which have been completed to date are

---

[60] Le Bras and Todd, *L'Invention de la France*, pp. 140–1.
[61] W. L. Parish and M. Schwarz, 'Household Complexity in nineteenth-century France', *American Sociological Review*, xxxvii (1972), 154–73.
[62] A. Collomp, 'Famille nucléaire et famille élargie en Haute-Provence au XVIIIᵉ siècle (1703–1734)', *Ann. E.S.C.*, xxvii (1972), 969–75.

Table III.2 *Household structure in southern France, 1644–1861*

Place	Date	Number of households	A	B	C	D	E	D + E
Mostuéjouls[a] (Rouergue)	1690	94	3.2	2.1	51.0	42.6 ⌒		42.6
Laguiole[b] (Rouergue)	1691	214	7.0	3.3	56.1	32.2 ⌒		32.2
Ribennes[c] (Gévaudan)	1736	119	14.3	2.5	38.7	26.9	17.6	44.5
Javols[d] (Lozère)	1836	208	3.4	4.3	67.4	20.3	5.3	25.6
Javols[e] (Lozère)	1861	195	7.7	6.2	69.2	14.9	2.1	17.0
La Courtine[f] (Limousin)	1742–65	?	2.2	1.1	23.1	29.6	43.9	73.5
Tersannes, Nedde, Pageas[g] (Haute-Vienne)	1836	554			52.8	41.6 ⌒		41.6
Corsica[h] (av. of Nebbio, Bastia, Ajaccio)	1769–71	?	2.2	2.9	70.2	6.9	16.5	23.4
Montplaisant[i] (Périgord)	1644	63	11.0	1.6	50.8	15.9	20.6	36.5
St André-les-Alpes[j] (Haute Provence)	1703–34	183			53.0	47.0 ⌒		47.0
Mirabeau[k] (Provence)	1745	120	6.7	0.8	50.8	19.2	22.5	41.7
Bulan[l] (Hautes-Pyrénées)	1793	53	3.7	54.7 ⌒		32	9.4	41.4
Péone[m] (Cté de Nice)	1787	259				41.7 ⌒		41.7
St Martin-de-Vésubie[n] (Cté de Nice)	1718	152	11.2	47.7 ⌒		41.4 ⌒		41.4

Key:
A   Solitaries (as percentage of total number of households)
B   No family links (ditto)
C   Simple family households (ditto)
D   Extended family households (ditto)
E   Multiple family households (ditto)

Notes:
[a] R. Noël, 'L'Etat de la population de Mostuéjouls (Aveyron) en 1690' in *Hommage à Marcel Reinhard: sur la population française au XVIIIe et XIXe siècles* (Paris, 1973), pp. 505–22.
[b] *Ibid.*, 'La Population de la paroisse de Laguiole d'après un recensement de 1691', *Annales de démographie historique* (1967), 197–223.
[c] P. Lamaison, 'Parenté, patrimoine et stratégies matrimoniales', pp. 186–91.
[d] E. Claverie, 'Oppositions et conflits dans une société d'inter-connaissance', pp. 83–91.
[e] *Ibid.*
[f] J.-C. Peyronnet, 'Les Familles de La Courtine en 1759 d'après le manuscrit du curé Michon', *Actes de la rencontre de démographie de 1976 tenue à Clermont-Ferrand* (Clermont-Ferrand, Institut d'études du Massif Central, 1977), 223–49.
[g] *Ibid.*, 'Famille élargie ou famille nucléaire? L'exemple du Limousin au début du XIXe siècle', *Revue d'histoire moderne et contemporaine*, xxii (1975), 568–82.

provided in table III.2. The analytical model is based on that proposed by Laslett.[63]

The shortcomings of such data are transparent. They have a narrow application both over time and place and they tend to 'freeze' family structure at an arbitrary point in the developmental cycle. It has been argued that the restraining effect of eighteenth-century demographic conditions curtailed a natural tendency towards household complexity which time-slice statistics virtually ignore. Low levels of life expectancy among elderly parents and relatives regularly thinned out the *oustal* to leave the young couple and their offspring. Yet a large proportion of the rural population may still have experienced the physical and mental environment of the extended family. On their own, a handful of family reconstitution studies provide a poor foundation for generalisation, but combined with evidence drawn from other sources they do add weight to the argument that the internal architecture of the southern household differed markedly from that of its counterpart in the North. Despite certain discrepancies of computation Peyronnet's analysis of family structure in three parishes in the south-eastern highlands of the Limousin yielded record statistics of household complexity which effectively reverse the conventional picture. And if the affiliations of individuals are tabulated, over 82 per cent of the population (excluding servants) are found to have resided in extended kinship groups. Again, in the case of Ribennes, a remote and mountainous parish of the Gévaudan, Lamaison's impressive computer-based enquiry revealed that under half the households exhibited the classic nuclear profile. By contrast the superiority of the basic family unit is overwhelming in the neighbouring parish of Javols which raises perplexing questions with regard to local cultural variations and trends over time. The evidence of family reconstitution studies in Provence and the South West speaks for itself, but the case of the West is problematic. Le Play maintained, and Parish and Schwarz agreed, that Brittany remained a bastion of the com-

---

Notes to Table III.2 (*cont.*)

[h] J. Dupâquier and L. Jadin, 'Structure of Household and Family in Corsica, 1769–71' in P. Laslett and R. Wall (eds.), *Household and Family in Past Time* (Cambridge, 1972), pp. 290–1.

[i] J. N. Biraben, 'L'Etat des âmes de la paroisse de Montplaisant en 1644', *Annales de démographie historique* (1970), 441–62.

[j] A. Collomp, 'Famille nucléaire et famille élargie en Haute-Provence au XVIIIᵉ siècle (1703–1734)', *Ann. E.S.C.*, xxvii (1972), 969–70.

[k] *Ibid.*, 'Ménage et famille: études comparatives sur la dimension et la structure du groupe domestique', *Ann. E.S.C.*, xxix (1974), 785.

[l] J.-L. Flandrin, *Families in Former Times* (Cambridge, 1979), pp. 73–4 and fig. 7.

[m] Collomp, 'Ménage et famille', p. 785.

[n] *Ibid.*

[63] Laslett and Wall, *Household and Family in Past Time*, p. 31.

plex household in the mid nineteenth century, but Le Goff[64] found few traces of the extended family in the Vannetais at the end of the *ancien régime*. As for the Vendée,[65] a recent study of family structures based on the 1846 census returns for six representative cantons concluded that between a half and two-thirds of the households were nuclear (types A, B and C). The incidence of complex households was greatest in the Vendean *bocage* and coastal villages, but simple family structures constituted 57 per cent of the total even here.

If extended families were numerous in Brittany, they bore little resemblance to those of the South for the provinces of the West were all subject to partible inheritance custom. As far south as Poitou egalitarian prescriptions of varying degrees of severity emasculated the testamentary freedom of the father which was so cherished in the Midi. Under the strict Breton Custom the *oustal* would have lost its *raison d'être* for the impartial endowment of all offspring entailed the fragmentation of the holding. It follows, therefore, that the survival of the *oustal* as both concept and physical reality was bound inextricably to a precipuary system which conferred a large measure of discretion upon the father and demanded self-abasing submission from most other members of the kinship group. In the southern Massif Central, at least, the stem-family and the patriarchal family were one and the same. Testamentary freedom resulting in the endowment of a single heir is often described as an attribute of Roman or Written Law which until 1789 governed the lives of all Frenchmen living south of a zig-zagging line running from the mouth of the Gironde to Geneva. As the map appended to Jean Yver's[66] pioneering study of inheritance law makes plain, this is not strictly true. Pockets of precipuary practice existed in the North, notably in Picardy and Flanders; more important a generous frontier of intermingling practices bisected France from east to west. The Haute-Auvergne and the Brivadois sat astride this frontier, for example. The *bourg* of Blesle acknowledged Roman Law, but its rural hinterland was subject to the Custom of the Auvergne, as was the territory of the adjacent parish of Espalem except for the estates of the Chapter of Brioude which formed an entity under Roman jurisdiction. Less significance attached to these bizarre discrepancies than might appear, however. Law yielded in the face of ecological and cultural imperatives. We have already noted that collective rights continued to flourish in certain districts theoretically subject to Roman Law. Likewise the prescriptions of the Custom in matters of inheritance were regularly contradicted in areas like the Limousin and the Haute-Auvergne which were influenced by the household culture of the South. A study of the registers of three Blesle notaries who

---

[64] Le Goff, *Vannes and its Region*, pp. 213–15.
[65] D. Naud, 'Les Structures familiales en Vendée auXIX[e] siècle', *Société d'émulation de la Vendée* (1977), 50–74.
[66] J. Yver, *Egalité entre héritiers et exclusion des enfants dotés, essai de géographie coutumière* (Paris, 1966).

succeeded one another from 1652 to 1759 leaves no room for doubt on this point. Only twenty eight of some 600 marriage contracts registered between 1652 and 1700 stipulated the division of the inheritance upon the death of the father.[67]

Until the passing of the *ancien régime* the southern Massif Central fell within the orbit of Roman Law and the transmission of property could be arranged in three ways: by immediate and irrevocable donation during the lifetime of the donor; by testament; and by donation to a nominated heir upon his marriage ('institution contractuelle d'héritier'). This latter practice was by far the most common as the example just cited makes plain. Of all the methods employed to ensure the survival of the *oustal* it offered the best guarantees. The marriage of the first son, or the marriage of the son who married first, for Roman Law did not impose primogeniture, was the moment at which the household declared its hand, the moment of truth for cadets, female offspring and elderly parents alike. Once the heir was chosen the hierarchy of the household reassembled around him in anticipation of his assumption of control. Once the heir was chosen every other member of the household was marked in the eyes of village society on a subtle scale of deference and respect. Monteil likened the nominated heirs of the bourgeois families of Rodez to petty kings with the cadets acting as subjects. The status of the firstborn (*aîné*) had acquired almost professional overtones and in conversation on family matters it would be said, 'one is an advocate, one is a doctor and one is the *aîné*'.[68] The researches of Lamaison and Claverie have greatly extended our understanding of these elaborate pecking orders within and between households and they serve to remind us that each rural collectivity possessed an invisible superstructure of biological and emotional obligations as well. The constraints of kinship and household position were tenacious and allowed little freedom of manoeuvre. Each individual's status was figuratively inscribed on his back or, to put it in Claverie's terms, 'chaque individu se déplace avec ce halo autour de lui qu'est l'histoire de son rang, de sa famille, l'histoire des lignées patrimoniales dont il est issu, l'espace et le temps occupés dans le village et sa mémoire par son oustal'.[69]

When the Revolution attempted to extend the rights of the individual into the domain of the family it encountered stiff resistance in many southern departments. On 7 March 1793 the National Convention abolished the 'institution contractuelle' and decreed that all offspring enjoyed equal rights to the estate of their parents. Several months later (law of 17 Nivôse II/6 January 1794) this legislation was made retrospective and in cases where the original donor was still alive or had died since 13 July 1789 the 'institution contractuelle' was revoked. Barely eighteen months elapsed before this

---

[67] Segret, 'La Maison paysanne dans la région de Blesle', p. 60.
[68] Monteil, *Description du département de l'Aveiron*, i, p. 102.
[69] Claverie, 'Oppositions et conflits dans une société d'inter-connaissance', p. 101.

amendment was repealed (law of 19 Fructidor III/5 September 1795) and after further tergiversations during the Directory an attenuated version of the Convention's egalitarian regime was established by the law of 4 Germinal VIII/25 March 1800. This measure introduced the system of the 'disposable portion' which in 1804 was enshrined in the Civil Code. The father retained the right to bestow a quarter of his fortune as he saw fit if he had under four children, a fifth if he had four, a sixth if he had five and so on. The 'institution contractuelle' survived, but the chosen heir might now only receive the 'disposable portion' in addition to his legal entitlement. To guard against fraud article 826 of the Code stipulated that each inheritor could demand a portion of real estate as well as moveable goods.

The inheritance legislation of the Revolution was intended as a bulwark against the political threat of noble primogeniture, but the principal victims were the peasantry. In the southern Massif Central and Provence the Convention's decrees spread pandemonium. The committees of government were inundated with petitions which offer precious direct testimony on the prevalence of the extended family and its inner tensions. The majority expressed shock and horror at the notion of compulsory partible inheritance and issued dire warnings of the social and economic disasters likely to befall the region if testamentary freedom were restricted. A few, what proportion is difficult to gauge, emanated from cadets and they cast a very different light upon the household as an abode of sweetness and light. Joseph Silvestre Blanquet of Marvejols (Lozère) urged the Assembly to extend the blessings of liberty to those whom 'pères et mères immolent sans pitié'. Rigid primogeniture (*sic*), he continued, lay at the heart of many 'haines de famille' and he quoted his own experience as one of the younger of three offspring:

aucun n'a démérité, l'aîné est constitué hériter de la fortune présente et avenir de mes père et mère, à la charge par lui de donner à chacun de ses cadets un neuvième de cette fortune. Pourquoi sept portions seroient-elles dévolus à mon égal en droits? . . . On a voulu me, dit-on, favoriser un mariage avantageux . . . Oh ridicule motif! . . . Et moi, je manque des choses de première nécessité tandis que mon frère est plus que dans l'abondance.[70]

The introduction of the retroactive principle turned dismay and confusion into chaos as disendowed offspring began actions in the courts. A fresh round of petitions flowed from gleeful cadets and desperate inheritors like Jean Veyrat, a *cultivateur* of Villefort in the Cévennes, who had become the heir of his childless brother by 'institution contractuelle':

je scavois combien mon frère étoit fidèle dans ses promesses. Je m'attachai fortement à lui, ses affaires devinrent les miennes. Je cultivai les biens avec force et tous mes travaux prospèrent. Vingt ans se sont passés de la sorte. La mort m'a enlevé mon frère depuis le 14 juillet 1789, et avant la loi trop fameuse de 17 nivôse: l'effet retroactif m'atteignoit. Les héritiers rappellés sont tombés sur moi.[71]

[70] A.N. DIII 138 Petition of J. S. Blanquet, Marvejols, 1 October 1792.
[71] A.N. DIII 139 Petition of J. Veyrat, Villefort, 30 Prairial III.

Veyrat's holding and the benefits of his stewardship over twenty-five years were carved up among the collaterals to leave him and his family without the means of subsistence.

In some districts, around the patriotic *bourg* of Meyrueis notably, the law of 17 Nivôse was respected, but for how long is unclear. Individuals like Veyrat may have retrieved their patrimony after the Year Three. The most widespread reaction, however, was to seek means of circumventing the law and 1793 marked the opening shot in a long century of guerilla warfare between the provisions of the Civil Code and the *oustal* culture of the South. Gross underestimations of the estate, fraudulent divisions and dubious treaties in which the inheritors 'freely' resolved to cede their rights to one of their number were commonly employed until the more obvious loopholes in the legislation were plugged. At Ribennes the common law entitling a creditor to distrain the property of his debtor was turned to good account. In an ingenious deed the father acknowledged an unsettled obligation to the off-spring whom he wished to endow which had the effect of substantially enlarging his inheritance portion. The simplest stratagems proved the most durable, however. Throughout the nineteenth century and into the twentieth, families contrived to sidestep clauses 826 and 832 of the Code and bestow the house and farmland upon a single heir. Such an expedient presupposed a high degree of liquidity, but in the days before the Crédit Agricole the rural money-lender existed for precisely this purpose. Even simpler was the fictitious division in which the patrimony was held 'indivis'.[72]

These subterfuges speak volumes about the survival of the complex house-hold and its peculiar ethos, for their success was conditional upon the con-nivance of the cadets. Despite revolutionary and Napoleonic inheritance legislation, despite the curtailment of testamentary freedom, the brooding presence of the paterfamilias lingered on. By refusing to withdraw their portions, by accepting quite ludicrous valuations, by remaining celibate or by migrating into Holy Orders, less favoured offspring acquiesced in their own disenfranchisement and in so doing paid homage to the values represented by the *oustal*. It would be wrong to draw too rosy a picture, of course. Arrange-ments to hold land 'indivis' often caused trouble among the descendants of the original heirs and cases of forgery and over-boiling tensions between gener-ations make regular reading in the judicial dossiers of the assize courts. But judicial files are exactly the place where we should expect to find such cases; there is plentiful literary evidence that many peasants accepted the logic of the stem-family and the impartible inheritance strategy which buttressed it. And, as far as we can tell, this logic remained compelling until the closing decades of the nineteenth century. The reports submitted to the Agricultural Enquiry of 1867 repeatedly drew attention to the cultural heritage of Roman juris-

[72] See above, chapter two, p. 34.

prudence in the departments of the South. In the Aveyron, we are told, property generally escaped division upon the death of the father 'au moyen d'arrangements de famille, favorisés par les mœurs et les vieilles traditions du droit d'aînesse (*sic*); il arrive assez souvent, par exemple, dans les familles de paysans, que les puînés ne consentent à recevoir leurs droits héréditaires que par dixièmes, ou même par vingtièmes, sans intérêt du capital'.[73] The scanty data on household composition during the latter part of the nineteenth century provides some foundation for this assessment. In 1876 the *bourg* of Sauveterre[74] in the ségala comprised 243 households. Sixty-one of these were dominated by a widower or elderly couple and contained a co-resident child or children with offspring. This was the situation which Edward Barker, the English traveller, found so singular while following in the footsteps of Robert Louis Stevenson across the Velay–Vivarais plateau in the 1880s. Every rural household appeared to contain an old woman, he remarked, upon arriving in the village of Sainte Eulalie (Ardèche) and added trenchantly, 'the parents work incessantly to build up a home, a farm or an inn, or both combined, and when the eldest son or daughter marries they give up that home to the young couple with whom however, they continue to live, always working for their bread but as subordinate figures in the household'.[75]

The custom of the dowry and the 'institution contractuelle' remained widespread in the southern Massif Central until the First World War which serves to remind us of the enduring cohesion of the peasant household. But signs of decline were apparent nearly everywhere by this date. The Agricultural Enquiry of 1867 noted that in the *arrondissement* of Villefranche-de-Rouergue heirs tended to demand division of landed estate as well as movables. Definitive migration had a solvent effect upon household structure, too. Initially it thinned out the collaterals who were often content to depart with a cash endowment in lieu of their legitimate rights, but in areas like the Cantal where the rural exodus became a way of life emigration soon threatened the continuity of generations and thus the very survival of the *oustal*. Near imponderables such as a belated growth of individualism, linked possibly to rapid population increase, also seem to have played a part. The symptoms lay in the manifest tensions between co-resident generations. Elderly parents were less keen than in the past to relinquish control of the household upon the marriage of the designated heir, or so Lamaison[76] has discovered for the period 1670–1790. It is likely that this trend can be extended into the nineteenth century. Some of the anecdotal evidence of family tensions also hints at an important shift in household organisation. When Jean-Antoine Combette, *cultivateur* of Le Buisson (Lozère), fractured his father-in-

[73] A.N. ADXIX C43³ *Enquête agricole*, Aveyron, *rapport de M. Caze*, p. 23.
[74] Béteille, *Les Aveyronnais*, p. 95.
[75] E. Barker, *Through Auvergne on Foot* (London, 1884), p. 125.
[76] Lamaison, 'Parenté, patrimoine et stratégies matrimoniales', pp. 165–6 and fig.

law's skull with a pick after a quarrel over the position of a dung heap, we learn from a statement that Combette and his family lived separately on the ground floor of his father-in-law's house.[77] This may or may not have been significant, after all the passage of a *gendre* from one hearth to another can never have been easy. More revealing is the comment of the mayor of Le Massegros (Lozère) in 1872 during a long-running battle (see chapter nine, p. 279) over the village commons that some cadets, 'quoique vivant dans une même maison, font ménage à part dans des appartements séparés'.[78]

In a pioneering application of the techniques of social anthropology, Claude Karnoouh[79] subjected the electoral behaviour of a small Lorraine village to detailed scrutiny. After much discreet enquiry and observation, he came to the conclusion that the catalysts of allegiance in local elections were kinship and neighbourhood. Village politics were not simply a telescopic reduction of national ideological debate; indeed there was an evident disfunction between state and village polity. The barrier between the two consisted of a vigorous local culture which preserved separatist tendencies in an age of massive centralisation (see chapter ten, p. 309). In essence this is the argument that we have begun to outline for the southern Massif Central. The direct testimony of those who lived in complex households and experienced their suffocating demands is almost entirely beyond our reach,[80] but observation through the prism of documentary evidence provides ample compensation. The incidence of stem- and joint-families among the 900,000 or so inhabitants of the southern Massif Central in 1800 may never be known in mathematical detail. However, it seems reasonable to assert that the extended family group constituted an ideal of rural society at least until the middle of the nineteenth century. This ideal, moreover, proved capable of realisation. For large numbers of bourgeois proprietors, smallholders and artisans it represented the norm.

As both wish and fulfilment the *oustal* added its own intricate relationships to the matrix of obligations and loyalties which formed the mental superstructure of village society. Everything we know about family structures and strategies suggests that the discipline of co-residence nurtured a disciplined response to every challenge confronting the household, whatever the provenance. To a lesser, but still impressive, degree this cohesion extended to non-residential kin. The *oustal* never broke ranks, the kindred (*parenté*) infrequently. In a culture which denied the individuality of the great majority, therefore, we might search in vain for genuine freedom of choice, for expressions of individual opinion. Choice – of an heir or a marriage alliance

[77] A.D.L. 14IIU (361) *Cour d'assises*, Mende, 1864, dossier concerning death of J.-B. Brun.
[78] A.D.L. 2 O 942 Administration et comptabilité communales: Le Massegros, Sarrouy to prefect Lozère, Le Massegros, 7 August 1872.
[79] C. Karnoouh, 'La Démocratie impossible: parenté et politique dans un village lorrain', *Etudes rurales*, lii (1973), 24–56.
[80] But see E. Le Roy Ladurie and D. Vigne, *Inventaire des campagnes* (n.p., 1980), p. 139.

– was the prerogative of a few and there is little reason to suppose that decisions about whom to support in an election were arrived at much differently. The impact of universal manhood suffrage in a given rural society calls for careful assessment, then, for its assumptions were not necessarily those of the peasant electorate. This, at least, was the conclusion drawn by Karnoouh who dubbed village politics an 'unattainable democracy'.

When we explore the conditions attaching to this extraordinary sense of household discipline we are confronted once again with the concept of honour. Despite the isolation of physical milieu, or perhaps because of it, the rural population lived an intensely public existence when the circumstances permitted. Each fair and market day, each trip to the parish church and the tavern on Sundays provided an occasion for ostentatious and truculent display. Pretexts for the assertion of the dignity of one's lineage and the besmirching of rivals were legion and were eagerly sought: 'il a parlé de notre maison avec une sorte de sourire qu'on ne peut pas supporter'[81] is a refrain which occurs constantly in the suits for murder, manslaughter and grievous bodily harm sent before the Assizes of the Lozère in the mid nineteenth century. The sensitivity of the peasants of the high plateaux to remarks uttered in public was notorious. Richeprey drew an unforgettable portrait of the querulous and violent mountaineers of the Aubrac, each armed with a deadly long-bladed penknife. Likewise the highlanders of the Velay were reputed never to leave home, not even to go to mass, without their weapons dangling from leather thongs. The clan, the vendetta and private codes of compensation were regular features of archaic societies which set a high value upon family reputation. As the gendarmerie became better organised in the early decades of the nineteenth century the blood feud lost some of its animus. Yet vengeance killings continued to occur in the taverns of Le Monastier-sur-Gazeille and Les Estables when the cattle fairs of the Mézenc brought the population of a wide area into contact. In 1844 the sub-prefect of Yssingeaux[82] compared the Velay with 'la vieille Ecosse si admirablement décrite par Walter Scott'. It had the same fierce passions, the same antique morality and the same clan chieftains.

[81] E. Claverie, ' "L'Honneur": une société de défis au XIXe siècle', *Ann. E.S.C.*, xxxiv (1979), 753.
[82] A.D. H.-L. 2M²3 *Rapport du sous-préfet d'Yssingeaux*, April 1844.

4

❋❋

An enfolding culture

Until now we have refrained from using the words 'culture' and 'community' as far as possible, on the ground that we should not assume what we are seeking to prove. Yet the concepts which these terms embody underpin much of the argument of this study and require careful explanation. The anthropologist's understanding of 'culture' is at issue here. By 'culture' we have in mind a system of shared values which find expression in what French geographers ever since Vidal de la Blache have called a 'genre de vie' (way of life). Implicitly, therefore, 'culture' is both popular and particularist. The knowledge, customs, attitudes, reactions, manners and apprehensions which the rural population of the southern Massif Central held in common constituted their 'way of life' or 'culture'. A major ambiguity remains, however, for the vigour of inter-village and inter-parish strife suggests that petty 'cultures' survived in the interstices of the broad cultural environment. Accordingly, we shall adopt a two-tier definition which postulates a meridional 'culture' embracing the entire southern Massif Central and specific local 'cultures' differentiated from the common cultural heritage by neighbourhood allegiances.

The definition of 'community' is more troublesome.[1] Some researchers consider the term so value-laden as to positively obstruct proper social analysis. Like the mythical (*sic*) extended family, 'community' is said to be a relic of the simplistic thinking of nineteenth-century writers seeking in history an emotionally satisfying alternative to their own socially mobile age. Phrases like the 'rural community'; 'le monde rural' and 'l'ordre éternel des champs' smack of ethnocentrism which at best misses and at worst conceals the true nature of the historical process in the countryside. Indeed, the most virulent critics of the concept of 'community' hold that it denies the role of individualism, proletarianisation and class conflict altogether. Many rural sociologists would, nevertheless, defend the notion even while jettisoning the term on the grounds of ambiguity. Several alternatives to 'rural community' are currently employed although it may be doubted whether they bring much semantic

[1] See Jones, 'Parish, Seigneurie and the Community of Inhabitants', pp. 74–108.

clarity to the subject. Among the most misleading are simple juxtapositions such as 'village' or 'rural settlement' which convert 'community' into a geographical noun. But expressions like 'local society' or 'rural collectivity' which avoid a physical locus invite criticisms on a different count. They escape the charge of distortion, but only by turning 'community' into an abstraction devoid of reference points. The rejection of the term 'community' on the grounds of ambiguity seems bound to lead to fresh ambiguity, sooner or later, and most historians and anthropologists have ignored the proffered synonyms. For the social and agrarian historian, at least, the word 'community' still describes a reality. But that reality is not self-evident; it needs to be demonstrated. Our conception of the 'rural community' in the southern Massif Central will be explored in the pages that follow. One proposition deserves preliminary statement, however, for it has been foreshadowed in the paragraphs devoted to the impact of migration (chapter two, pp. 62–9), and the question of proletarianisation (chapter three, pp. 87–95). Nowhere in this study is the concept of 'community' employed as the strict opposite of social conflict. Consensual attitudes in some spheres did not preclude conflictual attitudes in others. The peasant psyche – in so far as it is susceptible to identification and analysis – combined reflexes of deference and defiance and we should be wary of assuming that a posture of rebellion necessarily supposed a rejection of the claims of 'community'. By the same token 'culture' is here regarded as a set of values which transcended differences of social condition. These values were cohesive but not exclusive, thus permitting the elites of rural society to officiate in two distinct cultural arenas.

In September 1887 the municipal council of the commune of Le Rozier in the Lozère sought permission to amalgamate with its neighbour, the commune of Peyreleau, across the border in the Aveyron. Le Rozier constituted a tiny physical entity of 192 *hectares*, two settlements and 200 inhabitants separated from Peyreleau by no more than the river Jonte. At a glance the two villages looked indistinguishable and the profile of land holdings indicated a considerable degree of overlap as well. According to the councillors of Le Rozier, 'il a toujours existé et existe fréquents rapports entre ces deux villages de mêmes mœurs, même langage, mêmes coutumes et mêmes intérêts'.[2] Moreover, Peyreleau lacked a burial ground of its own and for the last forty years or so had habitually interred its dead in the cemetery of Le Rozier. The proposal came to nothing, but this is unimportant for it is the process that attracts our attention. We have here, in microcosm, the essential ingredients of community formation. To all appearances the 'snapshot' freezes the process at its climax – the moment of redefinition – when the walls of one human cell are breached and it is subsumed into another.

---

[2] A.D.L. 2 O 1283 *Administration et comptabilité communales*: Le Rozier, deliberation of municipal council of Le Rozier, 18 September 1887.

The example alerts us to the importance of the physical context and many would argue that the sense of community can only develop in conditions of geographical proximity. The community of Le Rozier consisted of a clustered village accommodating eight-tenths of the population, one other settlement and a tiny hinterland bounded by three natural features – the Jonte, the Tarn and the crenellation of the Causse Méjean. An impressive tradition of monographic research has underpinned this interpretation. On the plains of the North, habitat and agrarian structures ensured that the village constituted the rural community to all intents and purposes. The temporal and spiritual authorities merely consecrated this identification by turning the village into a unit of fiscal and parochial administration. Similarly, along the Mediterranean littoral a habitat consisting of substantial *bourgs* and villages provided a generous locus for community. The same is true of the nucleated settlement structures of the Alps and the Pyrenees where the valley context imposed strict limits upon the dimensions of the human group. But what of that broad swathe of western and central France which was thinly inhabited and which lacked a well-ordered landscape? If the rural community is viewed primarily as a by-product of an agglomerated settlement pattern, its existence in these regions must be questioned. This logic has not escaped the attentions of researchers and a number have painted the peasantry of the *bocages* in colours of an anarchic individualism devoid of communitarian scruple. Others have professed to believe in some kind of rural community in the dispersed habitat regions, but have been unable to specify how it functioned. Instructive though it may be as a theoretical exercise, the argument has an air of unreality for evidence of a robust community reflex in the *bocages* is not difficult to find. The mistake occurs at the outset, in an excessively temporal definition of community. The geographical confines of an agglomerated habitat undoubtedly fostered social interaction, but a scattered population devised its own forms of sociability and the rural community, in any case, consisted of more than simply the sum total of possible social relations.

An alternative approach would be to define the rural community as a unit of agricultural production. The relevance of this perspective in the regions of open-field tillage may be taken for granted, but it has superficial attractions for the enclosed landscape of the West and the Centre, too. Peasant polyculture in the *bocages* never developed the social disciplines characteristic of large-scale arable husbandry, but it relied heavily upon collective exploitation of waste and common. Common land, agrarian historians have long asserted, provided a ready basis for the sentiment of community. As we have noted, this is a palpable generalisation. In the southern Massif Central the commons were all too often neither close, compact, nor – in any meaningful sense – collectively owned. Gross inequalities of provision, as between sections, and of access, as between individuals, ensured that common pastures remained a source of perennial conflict rather than consensus. Recently,

Albert Soboul[3] has suggested that the prevalence of mutual aid (*entraide*) helped to define the rural community in regions of scattered settlement. This is a line of enquiry with explanatory potential as the study of Goulien (Finistère) by Charles Pelras[4] has demonstrated, but for the moment it remains largely unexplored.

The impact of institutions with deep historic roots should not be neglected. In many parts of France the seigneurie exerted control over the lives of country dwellers until the very end of the *ancien régime*. And if the apparatus of seigneurialism was dismantled after 1789, its psychological shadow lingered on. The Vicomté of Turenne[5] left a mark on the human landscape which was still perceptible in the twentieth century. However, Turenne was the headquarters of a quite exceptional seigneurie embracing some fifty-seven parishes in the Limousin and thirty-nine in the Quercy. By comparison the seigneurie in the southern Massif Central was in a sorry state (chapter five, pp. 160–70). Defence against the exactions of feudalism provided a powerful incentive to federation, but resistance was not usually organised within the framework of the seigneurie. The sale of fiefs, with or without rights, on the open market had largely destroyed the cohesion of the seigneurie in the second half of the eighteenth century. Only in the Velay had the seigneurial *mandement* retained its antique character and the rural population evinced a strong attachment to some of these archaic jurisdictions. When the Revolution swept to one side the accretions of centuries in order to establish a uniform system of local government based on the commune, the new authorities were bombarded with petitions demanding in some instances the formal recognition of shadowy communities in the process of formation, in others the restoration of ancient entities. Several of these petitions emanated from localities that had constituted *mandements* under the old regime. The prefect of the Haute-Loire admitted that the commune offered little purchase for local loyalties when he remarked before the *conseil-général* in 1854 that 'souvent le véritable élément territorial se trouve dans la section de commune beaucoup plus que dans la commune elle-même'.[6]

The vitality of the Vellavian *mandement* owed something to the fact that it doubled as a unit of civil administration. The boundaries of seigneurial jurisdiction and those of the *communauté d'habitants* coincided. The *communauté d'habitants* was primarily a fiscal unit and in the South where taxation purported to be based on the yield of land, its contours were set out in a register of land holdings known as a *cadastre*. Without any very obvious

---

[3] A. Soboul, 'Problèmes de la communauté rurale en France (XVIIIᵉ–XIXᵉ siècle)' in *Ethnologie et histoire: forces productives et problèmes de transition. Hommage à Charles Parain* (Paris, 1975), pp. 375–6.

[4] Pelras, 'Goulien – commune rurale du Cap Sizun', pp. 520–5.

[5] Y.-M. Bercé, *Histoire des Croquants: étude des soulèvements populaires au XVIIᵉ siècle dans le sud-ouest de la France* (Geneva, 1974), pp. 650–2.

[6] Merley, *La Haute-Loire*, i, p. 419.

reason, historians have deduced from this that the *communauté d'habitants* was, as its title implied, a community and that its boundaries coincided with those of the parish. These generalisations have proved extraordinarily tenacious, despite considerable evidence to the contrary.[7] The case of the southern Massif Central suggests that neither assumption is warranted. Only in the Gévaudan did the *communauté d'habitants* consistently reproduce the physical context of the parish; elsewhere a large measure of institutional incoherence seems to have been the norm. By the end of the *ancien régime* about a third of the *communautés d'habitants* of the Vivarais had a territorial base independent of the parish, while in the Rouergue and the Quercy the boundaries of the two institutions rarely coincided. When in 1780 Richeprey toured the small *pays* of the Carladez situated on the northernmost frontier of the Haute-Guienne, he remarked in his notebook, 'on ne peut assés admirer l'avantage dont jouit cette contrée par la division qu'on a faite anciennement des communautés par paroisse. C'est le premier exemple peut-être dans la province'.[8] Hitherto, his experience had been somewhat different. After questioning the inhabitants of the village of Albaret he recorded, 'Tous les assistants propriétaires dans les diverses communautés désireroient et disent que ce seroit le vœu unanime qu'on les remît en une seule, comme elle ne forme qu'une seule paroisse . . . Nous avons ensuite reconnu qu'il était singulièrement bisarre que les maisons d'un même village appartiennent à cinq à six communautés.'[9]

Unless it can be demonstrated that the parish provided that elusive sense of belonging in the *bocage* the institutional definition of the rural community fails to accommodate all the evidence. Like those definitions that assert the primacy of the nucleated settlement or the unit of agricultural production, it leaves too many loose ends. Many researchers have paused to contemplate the role of the church and organised religious worship in the regions of dispersed habitat,[10] but systematic analysis is rare. In particular, the nature of religious experience among the peasantry and its potential as a factor promoting social integration and cohesion has scarcely been explored. Usually the parish is portrayed, in the words of Pierre de Saint Jacob,[11] as 'the com-

---

[7] On this subject, note the rather contradictory remarks of Le Bras, *L'Eglise et le village*, pp. 89–94.

[8] Guilhamon, *Journal des voyages*, ii, p. 335.   [9] *Ibid.*, i, p. 43 and note 1.

[10] A. Siegfried, *Tableau politique de la France de l'ouest sous la Troisième République* (2nd edn., Paris, 1964), pp. 381–400, 409–41; Le Goff, *Vannes and its Region*, pp. 205, 217–18, 261–4; M. Lagrée, *Mentalités, religion et histoire en Haute-Bretagne au XIXème siècle: le diocèse du Rennes, 1815–1848* (Paris, 1977), pp. 132, 261; Cresswell, 'Une Communauté rurale en Irlande', pp. 98–9, 229; A. D. Rees, *Life in a Welsh Countryside* (Cardiff, 1950), pp. 104–5; P. Burke, *Popular Culture in Early Modern Europe* (London, 1978), p. 109; C. Petitfrère, 'Paysannerie et militantisme politique en Anjou au début de la Révolution (1789–1793)', *Annales de Bretagne et des pays de l'ouest*, lxxxix (1982), 183.

[11] P. de Saint Jacob, *Les Paysans de la Bourgogne du nord au dernier siècle de l'ancien régime* (Dijon, 1960), p. 81.

munity of the faithful' – a classic formulation which implies that the parish was but a dimension of an otherwise ill-defined rural community. Whilst not objecting to this definition, we would allow the parish a greater degree of autonomy. In the shattered physical and human environment of the southern Massif Central, the parish offered a rare framework for collective existence. It defined more than simply a spiritual community, it defined a cultural community. But in order to begin functioning as such, the parish presupposed a degree of convergence in other fields.

Community and kinship

A simple solution to the problem of community in the countryside would be to assert the primacy of the household unit. After all, much of the discussion in the preceding chapter sought to vindicate such a proposition. This is an unhelpful argument, however, for it suggests that the peasant household existed within an emotional void. For all its cohesion the *oustal* was aware of its lineage, of its non-resident kinsmen, of other households and, therefore, of the claims of a larger community. Nevertheless, the argument does alert us to the elasticity of community sentiment: it could coexist on separate and yet complementary planes. To what extent did kinship shape the contours of the rural community and to what extent did these contours reproduce the context of the parish?

The obvious example of kinship performing this role was the association of sharecroppers. These *communautés taisibles* were apparently common in southern France during the fifteenth and sixteenth centuries, but they had mostly disappeared by the end of the *ancien régime*. The co-resident community of the Quittard (four conjugal units plus thirteen servants) at Pinon (Puy-de-Dôme) dissolved in 1818, while that of the Jault (seven conjugal units) at St Benin-des-Bois (Nièvre) began to break up in the 1840s.[12] A few, it seems, survived rather longer in the Montagne Noire.[13] When a *communauté taisible* split up or when a stem-family 'swarmed' the related phenomenon of the heavily endogamous hamlet was born. Although they no longer formed a domestic group, the inhabitants remained linked together by bonds of biological and psychological cousinhood. Such hamlets dominated by a single lineage were numerous in the southern Massif Central. In the parish of Ribennes, for instance, the seven households comprising the hamlet of Laubespin in 1736 shared the same patronymic and a common ancestor, and in the hamlet of Les Pigeyres-Hautes the Pagès family accounted for four out of eight households. As for Les Pigeyres-Basses, it was dominated by a

[12] H. Dussourd, *Au même pot et au même feu ... étude sur les communautés familiales agricoles du centre de la France* (Paris, 1979), pp. 51–9 and *passim*; F. Le Play (ed.), *Les Ouvriers européens* (2nd edn., 6 vols., Tours, 1877–9), v, pp. 188–91; 297–302.
[13] F. Pariset, *Economie rurale, industrie, mœurs et usages de la Montagne Noire (Aude et Tarn)* (Paris, 1882), pp. 164–78.

branch of that most prolific of families, the Tichit. For fine detail of this quality we are indebted to Pierre Lamaison.[14] His spatial reconstruction of genealogical links demonstrates well how kinship networks need to be analysed in the parish setting, for the territory of the parish was indeed the stage on which marriage diplomacy was played out. Some villages were united by long-standing traditions of alliance, others were marked by a resolute tradition of non-alliance and looked instead to the neighbouring *bourg* for marriage partners. When the market for brides dried up or was cornered monopolistically by the larger villages, a proportion of households was forced to rely upon its own genetic resources and practise consanguinous unions. At all costs, 'il faut que la cheminée fume' as the proverb put it.

The marriage market was finite because high levels of territorial endogamy prevailed. The peasant of the southern Massif Central displayed a marked reluctance to have anything more than perfunctory social contact with the outside world. Even migrants tended to draw their spouses from their parishes of origin. Marriage was a rite which engaged the honour of two households and it behove each party to satisfy itself of the reputation of the other. The limits of 'inter-connaissance' varied, but normally they corresponded to the boundaries of the parish or, perhaps, the commune. At Ribennes, Lamaison calculated that 87 per cent of alliances occurred within a radius of fifteen kilometres and 12 per cent of marriage partners lived in the same village. Endogamy of this order remained typical of the region until the middle of the nineteenth century, if not later. A sample analysis of marriage patterns in the canton of Le Bleymard[15] (Lozère) for the decades 1811–20 and 1891–1900 revealed that during the earlier period approximately a third of the alliances involved individuals residing less than a kilometre apart; effectively, therefore, in the same village or hamlet. By 1900 this proportion had declined slightly to 23 per cent. In the southern Cévennes and the lower Ardèche the mid-century economic crisis and rural exodus undermined traditional patterns of endogamy. After a peak in the 1840s decline set in, but it is nonetheless striking that at Burzet[16] (Ardèche) 64 per cent of the marriages concluded between 1863 and 1872 joined parties living within the territory of the commune. The quickening pulse of industrialisation in the St Etienne basin expanded the marriage horizons of the villages of the north-eastern Haute-Loire too. Yet in districts like the ségala where an intensive peasant polyculture overcame the challenge of migration, the rural population remained sedentary and high levels of endogamy have prevailed virtually to

---

14 Lamaison, 'Parenté, patrimoine et stratégies matrimoniales', p. 218.
15 P. J. Perry, 'Mariage et distance dans le canton du Bleymard (Lozère): 1811–1820 et 1891–1900', *Etudes rurales*, lxvii (1977), 69.
16 P. E. Ogden, 'Migration, Marriage and the Collapse of Traditional Peasant Society in France' in P. White and R. Woods (eds.), *The Geographical Impact of Migration* (London, 1980), p. 166 and fig. no. 9.8.

the present. At Najac[17] (Aveyron), according to a case study mounted in the 1960s, about half the marriage partners resided within the parish or within a radius of an hour's walk from the *chef-lieu*.

In conditions such as these marriage between kinsmen was difficult to avoid. But Canon Law forbad union between the descendants of common great-grandparents, that is to say within four degrees or generations. Civil law, enshrined in the Civil Code, was more accommodating and calculated the prohibited degrees slightly differently. In 1917 the catholic church limited the ban to the offspring of common grandparents (the third degree), but during the period under study the marriage of first cousins was reputed consanguinous. What could not be avoided was tolerated, however. Upon application, the church was prepared to grant dispensation for those whose projected alliance fell within the prohibited degrees. Whether the number of requests for dispensations ever accurately reflected the incidence of inter-marriage is unclear. Probably it did not. The parish clergy were generally diligent in hunting out blood relationships and the knowledge that the hier-archy rarely turned down a properly motivated petition for dispensation mili-tated against deliberate concealment, but many parishes were hopelessly inbred and it seems that alliances between cousins were often taken for granted. It should be remembered, too, that the protestants formed the most heavily endogamous section of the population and they escaped the prescrip-tions of Canon Law.

Notwithstanding these qualifications, marriage dispensations on grounds of consanguinity provide excellent material for analysis. The geographical detail and terse arguments which accompanied each individual request cast light upon the physical and cultural dimensions of the rural com-munity, while the quantity and distribution of the dispensations granted per-mit a rough comparative survey of the extent of inbreeding. The concept of the 'isolate' is the most useful tool for this purpose.[18] Defined by its authors as the zone or field of opportunity available to an individual seeking a marriage partner, the isolate has an obvious territorial application. Some of the most exiguous isolates might be expected to occur in islands such as Corsica, or in remote or unfrequented regions such as Brittany, the Massif Central and certain Alpine and Pyrenean valleys. Statistical manipulation of the data relating to consanguinous marriage dispensations confirms this hypothesis. Table IV.1 is based upon a national survey of marriage between kindred and records the number of dispensations granted by departments as a percentage of marriages celebrated in the catholic church during the period 1926–45.

[17] M. Jollivet and H. Mendras (eds.), *Les Collectivités rurales françaises* (2 vols., Paris, 1971–4), i, p. 121.
[18] J. Sutter and L. Tabah, 'Les Notions d'isolat et de population minimum', *Population* (1951), 481–98.

Table IV.1 *Distribution of marriages within the prohibited degrees of kinship, 1926–45*

Department	Consanguinous marriages as % of total catholic marriages
Massif Central	
Ardèche	4.56
Lozère	4.42
Aveyron	4.15
Haute-Loire	4.05
Cantal	3.49
Puy-de-Dôme	3.27
Corrèze	2.56
Creuse	2.15
Haute-Vienne	1.49
Alps	
Savoie (*arrondissement* of St Jean-de-Maurienne)	7.10
Savoie (*arrondissement* of Albertville)	4.46
Hautes-Alpes	3.57
Haute-Savoie	2.33
Basses-Alpes	2.12
West	
Morbihan	4.40
Côtes-du-Nord	3.75
Finistère	3.37
Mayenne	2.90
Loire-Inférieure	2.87
Ille-et-Vilaine (1936–1945)	2.42
Vendée	2.35
Maine-et-Loire	2.32
Pyrenees	
Ariège	2.47
Hautes-Pyrénées	2.17
Basses-Pyrénées	1.95
Corsica	6.85
France (average per department)	1.76

Source: J. Sutter and L. Tabah, 'Fréquence et répartition des mariages consanguins en France', *Population* (1948), 607–30.

Once again the peculiarly introverted character of life in the southern Massif Central is revealed. With the exception of Corsica and the high Maurienne where inbreeding rose with altitude, the region constituted a great bastion of endogamy. All the signs suggest that this was not a new phenomenon. If the crude results presented above are analysed in detail an unmistakable trend away from consanguinous unions emerges: the figure for the Haute-Loire conceals a high of 5.70 per cent for the period 1926–30 and a low of 2.75 per cent for 1941–5. When this decline set in is far from clear since eighteenth and nineteenth-century diocesan records are fragmentary. However, it seems probable, if paradoxical, that marriage among kith and kin was linked to the health of an entire agrarian civilisation. As its self-sufficiency was eroded after 1850 endogamous habits weakened. The long-term trend may be difficult to ascertain, but those bundles of petitions and registers of dispensations that have survived provide a wealth of local information.[19] The regional profile of the isolate is fairly clear: inbreeding followed the contours of the *bocages* and the mountain plateaux. It was endemic in the high Cévennes north of Les Vans, in the Mézenc, along the spine of the Margeride, on the slopes of Mont Lozère, in the Viadène, Aubrac and Levézou highlands of the Aveyron, and in the ségala. By contrast consanguinous unions were less prevalent in the northern, eastern and south-eastern cantons of the Ardèche, in the southern Aveyron and, inferentially, in the Brivadois. In some localities traditions of intermarriage practised over several generations had resulted in monolithic communities of kinsmen. The remote parish of St Etienne-de-Meillas perched on the buttresses of the Levézou above the valley of the Tarn seems to have been totally inbred, while the *curé* of St Etienne-de-Lugdarès in the Tanargue obtained seven marriage dispensations on behalf of his parishioners during the year 1814. A sampling of dispensations accorded by the Evêché of Mende in 1858 and 1886 suggests that comparable levels of consanguinity prevailed in the Margeride parishes of Rieutort-de-Randon, Allenc and Chassérades, and in the parishes of Mas d'Orcières, Cubières and Altier which embraced the denuded northern slopes of Mont Lozère. Habitat rather than crude population size was the principal factor governing the structure of the isolates here, for in these mountain localities the distance between farmsteads and villages was often considerable. The same difficulty arose in the ségala. When the parties to a projected third degree marriage in the parish of Boussac petitioned the ecclesiastical authorities in 1808, they offered the standard excuse: 'la petitesse du lieu de la naissance des exposants; ils sont nés de deux villages dont les habitants sont presque tous parents ou alliés, ou conjoints par affinité spirituelle'.[20] The population of the parish of Boussac totalled some 650 souls grouped in seventeen settlements. The villages in question were situated three or four kilometres apart. The refrain has a familiar ring and it occurs repeatedly in petitions emanating from the depths of the ségala. If the neighbourhood of

[19]   See A.D.A. 3V5; 6V1; 6V3; A.E.M. Marriage dispensations, 1811–1821; M. Riou, 'Ethnologie et histoire au XIXᵉ siècle: les mariages consanguins en Vivarais', *Revue du Vivarais*, lxxxii (1979), 7–14.

[20]   A.D.A. 6V1 *Correspondance et l'Evêché de Rodez.*

the parish constituted the primary locus of intermarriage, it is also possible to detect the existence of kinship networks that united parishes. In the high Aubrac, St Chély and Condom regularly exchanged their sons and daughters and the same was true of the contiguous parishes of Espinas and Verfeil in the Bas Rouergue. Traditions of alliance between parishes presupposed traditions of non-alliance, too. The inhabitants of Rieutord (Ardèche) traditionally looked to Burzet for marriage partners, but during the Revolution they developed the habit of burying their dead in the cemetery of Usclades which was nearer to hand. From the funerary rites for the dead sprang closer ties among the living. These invisible contour lines that linked some localities, but distanced others help to explain much that would otherwise remain impenetrable: the collective violence of the charivari which afflicted some villages like a congenital disease, but not others; the frenetic quality of parish pilgrimages; the tenacity of local enmities and the deceptive randomness of political allegiance.

The logic of inbreeding was not exclusively territorial, however. In addition to the argument based upon geography, the petitioners of Boussac invoked: 'la pauvreté de la fille exposante qui n'a pas une dot suffisante pour trouver à se marier selon sa condition hors de sa parenté'.[21] The relatively advanced age of the bride-to-be was also mentioned. In this case as in nearly every other the application was conceived from the female point of view and it serves to remind us once again that status and family were inescapable denominators. A poor, unendowed spinster of diminishing child-bearing potential was not an attractive match. Her lowly condition and reluctance to migrate compounded the limitations of habitat and drastically curtailed her chances of concluding an alliance outside her kinship group. Canon Law permitting, however, there were circumstances in which the family – in its broadest sense – was more than willing to look after its own. Consanguinous unions, like voluntary celibacy, reduced the financial strain of dowries and simplified inheritance strategies. They also minimised the risk of generational conflict and dissension in the household when a son- or daughter-in-law arrived to take up residence, for the loyalties of kinsfolk were not in doubt. Moreover, blood relationships seem to have excused a measure of promiscuity in the countryside which would not have been tolerated otherwise. The church was sometimes invited to sanction unions that already existed to all intents and purposes.

Clearly the concept of the isolate presupposes more than simply a physical category. Its determinants might equally be occupational or confessional. The protestant isolates of the south are a case in point. Violent persecution in the seventeenth and early eighteenth centuries all but destroyed French Calvinism and the survivors practised systematic in-breeding as a defence

---

[21] *Ibid.*

reflex. Long after official persecution had ceased the psychosis of fear and distrust inhibited relations between the two faiths. Intermarriage was not unknown, but it occurred infrequently. As a consequence, compact, endogamous communities evolved in which genes became isolated. Nearly all the households of a protestant enclave at Orthez (Pyrénées-Atlantiques) were tainted with epilepsy, while at Izeaux in the Isère most of the villagers bore a sixth digit on hand and on foot.[22] Hereditary mutations of this type were undoubtedly the product of inbreeding and as improved communications and migration expanded fields of contact in the nineteenth century they died out. The existence of a large and irreducible sectarian population in the southern Cévennes seems to have preserved the protestant of the southern Massif Central from the genetic repercussions of inbreeding. In the heart of the Cévennes the stray catholic farmsteads were more likely to succumb to this danger. But the protestant outposts strung along the valley of the Tarn and marooned on the plateau of the Velay felt desperately vulnerable. The Calvinist merchants of St Affrique protected their commerce and their faith by the systematic intermarriage of first or second cousins. When the threat of renewed persecution materialised in 1791, they lodged a complaint against the catholic dominated town council. However, the authorities successfully discredited the statements of eleven out of sixteen protestant witnesses on the grounds of inadmissible kinship.[23] At the end of the *ancien régime* the 6,000 protestants of the Velay lived in conditions of near total seclusion. Grouped – loosely – in half a dozen high altitude parishes forming a geographical cul-de-sac between Yssingeaux and the border of the Vivarais, they evinced an extraordinary cohesion. After a passage of arms in the 1750s over the tithe levied by the Chapter of Le Puy, they were left in peace by the authorities. So much so, in fact, that Portalis, the Minister of Public Worship, omitted to include the Calvinists of the Haute-Loire in the post-Concordat reorganisation of French protestantism. The consistory of Le Mazet-St Voy was not established until 1805.[24]

Community and language

Language, like kinship, spoke volumes. The accented, untutored French of François Chabot,[25] the deputy from the Aveyron, at the bar of the Convention vibrantly registered his humble, meridional background. Witness, too, the following remark culled from a statement before the Assizes of the Lozère: ' . . . l'un de ces deux ayant les cheveux d'un rouge ardent et paraissant

---

[22] Cited by Sutter and Tabah, 'Les Notions d'isolat et de population minimum', p. 490.
[23] A.N. F⁷ 3657¹ Aveyron: petition of patriots of St Affrique.
[24] D. Robert, *Les Eglises réformées en France, 1800–1830* (Paris, 1961), p. 157 and notes.
[25] J.M.J.A. de Bonald, *François Chabot, membre de la Convention, 1756–1794* (Paris, 1908), pp. 40–1.

par son langage être du côté de Marvejols'.[26] Voluntarily or involuntarily, the nuances, not to say the choice, of language betrayed status, origins and loyalties. The common linguistic idiom of the southern Massif Central was patois. It survived into the twentieth century as the vernacular tongue. During the period in question no inhabitant of the region was unable to communicate in it save, perhaps, for a few government officials, and for the great majority it was the language of everyday speech. From the start, therefore, the widespread use of an idiom derived from *langue d'oc* marked out the frontiers of a community whose lingua franca was not, in fact, French. In this connexion it is worth reiterating the fundamental contrast between the northern and western Massif Central where the patois of the Auvergne swiftly succumbed to French in the early nineteenth century, and the south and east where the linguistic traditions of the Midi fought a tenacious rearguard action against the imperialism of the national tongue. There was another, more pertinent, way in which the use of patois defined the contours of community, however. As the reported speech of the anonymous redhead indicated, the patois medium contained within it slight but tell-tale variations.

The prevalence of a patois culture before the Revolution has to be inferred. *Ancien régime* officials wasted little time discussing the prejudices of the masses unless they had a bearing upon military preparedness, food supplies or agricultural routines. Public instruction carried a low priority except in those localities where protestantism seemed to pose a threat. Nearly all the surviving documentary evidence for this period is couched in French. Mountain provinces like the Rouergue and the Gévaudan were slow to respond to the edict of Villers-Cotterets (1539) but, by the seventeenth century, the use of *langue d'oc* in official documents had died out. Magistrates interrogated witnesses in patois and notaries employed 'l'idiome du pays' in their dealings with clients, but scarcely a trace of the vernacular entered the record. 1789 marked a watershed, however. The Revolution brought to power the first of many governments obsessed with national unity and seized with the desire to communicate the gospel of liberty. Spurred on by startling evidence of linguistic diversity and the suspicion that 'barbaric tongues' encouraged political dissidence, legislators mounted a series of enquiries into the state of the vernacular.

The *enquête* launched in 1790 by the *abbé* Grégoire[27] was the first systematic attempt to measure the dimensions of patois culture. The forty-nine replies to his questionnaire that have survived provide a valuable retrospect of the situation at the end of the *ancien régime*. As regards the southern

---

[26] Y. Pourcher, 'Criminalité et société: l'exemple de la Lozère au début du XIXème siècle' (Université Paul Valéry, Montpellier III, Mémoire de maîtrise, 1979), p. 92.

[27] A Gazier, *Lettres à Grégoire sur le patois de France, 1790–1794: documents inédits sur la langue, les mœurs et l'état des esprits dans les diverses régions de la France, au début de la Révolution* (Paris, 1880). For Chabot's reply, see pp. 51–79.

Massif Central only François Chabot's response for the department of the Aveyron is extant, unfortunately. However, his remarks are detailed and authoritative; in all probability they applied to much of the region for the National Assembly subsequently decided to arrange for translations of its decrees to be disseminated in these departments, in common with a score of others. Chabot reckoned that the entire population of the Aveyron spoke patois save for a few old soldiers, doctors, lawyers, ecclesiastics, merchants and nobles who ordinarily spoke French. In the district of St Geniez where he lived about 10,000 out of a population of 40,000 could understand some French; about 3,000 were capable of reading it and 2,000 could speak the language. Patois was universal among artisans, whether urban or rural, and there was no town in the department in which the notables were unable to communicate in the vernacular. As for the clergy, they habitually preached and taught the catechism in patois except in the urban parishes of Rodez, Villefranche-de-Rouergue and Millau. This was probably a generalisation for in 1738 the parishioners of Alpuech, in the Aubrac complained that they could not understand their *curé* when he instructed them in French. The comparison with the northern Massif Central is instructive. At Maringues in the Puy-de-Dôme patois was universal, but French was generally understood as well and most peasants could express themselves in it, however maladroitly. Also, preaching in the vernacular had largely died out.

The question of vernacular religious instruction is crucial, not only to the role of the church in the process of community identification, but to the wider issue of peasant politicisation. By continuing to provide edification in the mother tongue the clergy inculcated the belief that the culture of patois and the moral and physical well being of the individual were inter-connected. The French language offered no such guarantees, its reference points were mostly located outside the rural community. If the attitude of the ecclesiastical hierarchy towards patois was not devoid of *arrières pensées*, there were, as we have noted, important practical objections to using the church as a vehicle for linguistic reform. What was the point of using a medium that few could understand? The parish clergy were reluctant to jeopardise the comprehension of spiritual truths in the interests of a national need which they were scarcely better equipped to perceive than their parishioners. Others could pioneer the struggle for linguistic unification if they wished, and with the passing of the Guizot Law in 1833 the rudiments of a state sponsored primary education system slowly took shape. But lay schoolmasters and mistresses brought no magic solution to their task. Learning, if learning there was to be, had first and foremost to be conducted in patois or, perhaps, in a dreadful pidgin ('françois patoisant'). The civil authorities were not unmindful of these difficulties, but could only recommend a policy of attrition mixed with exhortation. In 1835 the prefect of the Aveyron took steps to impose the use of French in village schools, but the excommunication of patois fell on deaf ears.

Three years later an article entitled *Quelques considérations sur le patois* by J.-A. Brouzès[28] of Laguiole revealed the modest progress made since Chabot's survey nearly half a century earlier. 'Les instituteurs devraient, non pas se borner à faire réciter aux enfans une demi-page de grammaire française, mais les obliger rigoureusement à parler toujours français.' In many country schools, 'les enfans parlent toujours patois, même en classe'. As for the parish clergy, they hovered uncertainly between the two languages. Some clerics refused to use French as the medium for instruction ('je pourrais citer un chef-lieu de canton important où le curé a toujours défendu aux enfans des familles pauvres d'apprendre leur catéchisme et leurs prières en français'); others used French missals, but oral communication was conducted in patois ('j'ai vu, en effet, des paroisses où les enfans sont obligés de réciter en patois leur catéchisme qu'ils ont appris en français'). What this exercise demonstrated exactly is open to interpretation.

For all its inadequacies the public instruction provided by the state and increasing numbers of free-lance organisations made a perceptible impact. When a general review of primary education was instituted in 1855, several of the school inspectors of the four departments of the southern Massif Central reported a generation gap between the young who possessed the rudiments of bilingualism and the majority of the population which remained stolidly monolingual. Although superficial, the 'rapports généraux sur la situation de l'enseignement primaire' have the advantage of comprehensiveness. Under the heading 'idiomes et patois locaux' they furnish a useful synopsis of the state of patois across the region. As we conjectured, the vernacular tongue reigned virtually unchallenged in all districts as it had done for centuries. The status of the national language was rising, however, and the numbers of French loan-words entering patois bore witness to this fact. If the rural bourgeoisie of the Cévennes continued to use the popular idiom, the school inspector for the *arrondissement* of Brioude noted that the rural population despised French as 'le partage exclusif des messieurs, comme elles le disent, ou des paysans à prétentions bourgeoises'.[29] As for spiritual instruction, it was still provided in patois in many parishes of the Aveyron and also in the Velay around Le Puy and probably further afield. The school inspector for the *arrondissement* of Espalion echoed the remarks of Brouzès when he observed that the battle for linguistic uniformity had first to be fought in the pulpit and the sacristy: 'si l'instruction religieuse était donnée en français dans toutes les églises le patois serait moins en usage par la raison que les habitants de la campagne tiennent à la langue dans laquelle ils ont appris leur religion'.[30]

---

28 J.-A. Brouzès, 'Quelques considérations sur le patois', *Revue de l'Aveyron et du Lot*, 26 November 1838.

29 A.N. F[17] 9327 *Inspection des écoles primaires*, Haute-Loire, *rapport sur la situation générale de l'instruction primaire dans l'arrondissement de Brioude à la fin de 1855.*

30 A.N. F[17] 9322 *Inspection des écoles primaires*, Aveyron, *rapport général sur la situation de l'enseignement primaire: arrondissement d'Espalion* (1856).

The great enquiry launched by Victor Duruy, the Minister of Education, in 1864 proved the definitive statement on the subject of patois. It gathered evidence suggesting that dialect was the customary spoken language in about a third of the departments of France. The contemporary arithmetic on which this conclusion is based has been published *in extenso* by Eugen Weber.[31] Like all the statistical compilations of the eighteenth and nineteenth centuries these data can be challenged on a number of grounds. It is notable, for instance, that a copyist's error has transposed the findings for the Lozère to imply that the department was entirely French speaking. Nevertheless, when all necessary adjustments and corrections have been made the incidence of patois speaking, measured geographically and demographically, rises rather than declines. As far as the Massif Central is concerned, the results of Duruy's census consolidate the picture outlined. In the west (Creuse, Haute-Vienne, Corrèze) and probably in the Cantal, as well, patois was steadily retreating. In the Puy-de-Dôme the retreat was much slower, while in the south the penetration of French was confined to the two gateways into the mountains: the Limagne of Brioude and the valley of the Rhône. Among the half a million inhabitants of the Aveyron and the Lozère, however, the number of French speakers was statistically negligible. On these remote and economically refractory plateaux, the process of acculturation relied heavily upon the intervention of church and state in the field of educational provision. Hope for change lay with the new generation. But even in this area the Duruy enquiry exposed much unevenness. In 1864 – thirty years after the Guizot Law – 41 per cent of school children (aged between seven and thirteen) in the Haute-Loire were unable either to speak or write in French. In the Lozère this proportion was 26 per cent; in the Aveyron 20 per cent and in the Ardèche 13 per cent.

As all respondents were at pains to point out, French suffered an enormous disadvantage in the competition with patois. It was not a language of verbal communication. Only when more peasants spoke French than did not would the balance tip against the vernacular. This did not happen until the 1880s at the very earliest. A latter-day Restif de la Bretonne eavesdropping on conversations in the streets of Rodez in 1873 would have heard more patois than French. Governments tacitly admitted their powerlessness to force the pace of change by consistently nominating churchmen who could make themselves understood in *langue d'oc* to the bishoprics of the south. Prefects, on the other hand, could rarely speak the local idiom and would certainly refrain from using it in public. The paradox mattered little enough until the struggle for influence between the temporal and the spiritual power was joined in the declining years of Louis-Napoléon's Empire. If patois was not alone in defin-

---

[31] Weber, *Peasants into Frenchmen*, chapter six and appendix. See also M. de Certeau, D. Julia and J. Revel, *Une Politique de la langue: la Révolution française et les patois* (Paris, 1975), pp. 270–2.

ing the limits of peasant awareness by the end of the century, it still commanded an impressive allegiance. In 1901 the newly installed archbishop of Albi, Eudoxe Mignot, whose diocese shared a long frontier with that of the Aveyron mounted an enquiry into the vernacular. According to the clergy patois was still ordinarily spoken in 459 out of 462 parishes.[32] However, French was understood in about two-thirds of the parishes. What an understanding of French actually amounted to is open to discussion, even at this late date. It seems that a decline in the number of patois speakers did not result in a linear gain for the French language or, at least, not immediately. The etiolation of patois thrust a generation of young peasants not into a French dominated polity, but into a twilight world which lacked solid cultural moorings. The consequent danger of emotional and intellectual impoverishment seemed all the more alarming in that it coincided with an assault upon that other sheet anchor of rural habits of mind – the institutional church (see chapter nine). On the eve of the First World War, Paul Roqueplo, a disciple of Le Play and Maurice Barrès, eloquently expressed this concern. In a veritable litany of complaints, he instanced the hostility of the modern schoolmaster towards the vernacular: 'Atteinte aussi la petite patrie dont le patois est le produit et l'expression profonde. Que d'idées, que de choses qui ne peuvent être nommées que par lui et qui, en son absence et en l'absence aussi du français trop mal appris, risquent de demeurer étrangères aux petits paysans diminués dans leur intelligence et leur sensibilité.'[33]

The community of patois speakers contained within it divers lesser communities. The Haute-Loire divided into three distinct but mutually intelligible dialect zones. The *langue d'oc* was spoken throughout the Velay, save in those districts north of Bas-en-Basset where the patois of the Forez prevailed. The idiom of the Brivadois, meanwhile, evoked the ancient link with the Auvergne. In the Ardèche *langue d'oc* prevailed except in the extreme north of the department beyond the river Doux where a Franco-Provençal dialect was current. The *langue d'oc* held sway throughout the Lozère and the Aveyron as well, although Auvergnat or Aquitainian accretions were apparent in some localities. Word stems varied little, but vowel sounds and suffixes tended to be fairly specific. For example, in the Aveyron particular stress was laid upon the *a* vowel in the south and south west; north of the Lot the *e* recurred, while in the centre the patois of the Rouergue, properly speaking, prevailed with its stress upon the *o*. These and other peculiarities of language and pronunciation defined a further series of discrete communities to such an extent that speech revealed as much about an individual's origins as the pattern of his clogs. So striking were these nuances, reported the school

---

[32] J. Faury, *Cléricalisme et anticléricalisme dans le Tarn, 1848–1900* (Toulouse, 1980), pp. 246–8.

[33] P. Roqueplo, *La Dépopulation dans les arrondissements de Mende et de Marvejols (Lozère)* (Rodez, 1914), p. 98.

inspector of the *arrondissement* of Tournon, that 'les habitants d'un village se moquent du language du village voisin'.[34] The patois of Tournon was not that of Le Cheylard, which in turn was not that of Lamastre.

All the signs suggest that language, or more specifically the reactions it evoked, performed a powerful integrative role in the countryside. Each human collectivity made a unique contribution – be it only swear words – to the patois of the region; each human collectivity brought its own mode of speech and pronunciation to bear upon that patois. By exploiting these clues, by mapping the tell-tale shifts in pronunciation, for instance, 'lou pâtres [les bergers]' on the banks of the Loire to 'lou pastres' (in which the *s* is sounded) on the slopes of Mont Mézenc, we may reconstitute the contours of the rural community. The case of the high plateau of the Velay is apposite for the survival of archaic pronunciations and usages in this locality was linked to the survival of an isolated protestant community.[35] The cessation of normal relations with surrounding catholic villages in the latter half of the sixteenth century produced an isolate whose dimensions were as much linguistic as biological. Around 1600 or thereabouts, the patois of the protestant enclave lost contact with the outside world and as the world of patois continued to evolve it was left behind. In all likelihood the same condition developed in remote protestant villages of the southern Cévennes. The spur of religious non-conformity was not a prerequisite, however. Linguistic particularism was endemic and in most cases it appears to have crystallised within the context of the parish. A study of local idiom in the neighbourhood of Saugues[36] (Haute-Loire) illustrates this point well. Sandwiched between the easterly escarpment of the Margeride chain and the gorges of the Allier, the *bourg* of Saugues was, it is true, exceptionally inaccessible. In 1948 the phonetic idiosyncrasies of Saugain patois were found to possess a radius of approximately seven or eight kilometres. Plotted upon a map these linguistic contours follow closely the boundaries of the parish – not the commune. Only the village of Servières and its immediate hinterland remained refractory, but the inhabitants of Servières had a chapel of their own and formed an annex of the main parish.

The extraordinary tenacity of the vernacular in a region such as the southern Massif Central is a subject worthy of study in its own right, but its significance is much reduced if we can accept that the rural population acquired the skills of bilingualism from the middle decades of the nineteenth century. No one acquainted with educational provision at the end of the

[34] A.N. F[17] 9322 *Inspection des écoles primaires*, Ardèche, *arrondissement de Tournon, état de l'instruction primaire*, 3 April 1856.
[35] P. Nauton, 'Le Patois des protestants du Velay' in *Mélanges de linguistique et de littérature romanes offerts à Mario Roques* (4 vols., Baden, 1950–3), iii, pp. 185–93.
[36] P. Nauton, *Le Patois de Saugues (Haute-Loire): aperçu linguistique, terminologie rurale, littérature orale* (Clermont-Ferrand, 1948).

ancien régime or, worse, on the morrow of the Revolution can fail to be impressed by the quantitative effort mounted by church and state in this domain after *circa* 1830. In 1834 the Lozère, for example, possessed just thirty-three state schools and sixty-three private schools. Forty years later and on the eve of Jules Ferry's secularising legislation, the department claimed 852 primary establishments (705 state (60 run by lay orders) and 147 church) for a population of approximately 138,000 inhabitants.[37] But what kind of achievement was this in reality? If it was intended to produce political compliance, then it represented something of a Pyrrhic victory. The Lozère continued to despatch monarchist deputies to Paris twenty years after the proclamation of the Republic. The admirable caution used by historians in constructing evidence has not, in general, been extended to data on literacy. Statistics derived from parish registers and the circumstantial evidence of school building and attendance appear all too frequently in support of simple, linear theories of change in the countryside. The equation of literacy and political radicalism is not challenged as often as it should be; the existence of regional dialects is generally acknowledged, but discounted in favour of the unproven hypothesis of bilingualism, or that which postulates an ill-defined process of ideological osmosis or seepage; the ability to sign is commonly confused with the ability to write. In short, the acquisition of the skills of literacy is telescoped into single, indivisible exercise over which the state exercised preponderant control.

In a recent modernisation study of a village on the edge of the Haute-Loire, James Lehning suggested that the signature may be taken as evidence of 'at least basic instruction in writing'.[38] It is extremely doubtful whether this inference is justified. The departments of the southern Massif Central formed a vast zone of partial literacy in which the cultural anomalies associated with patois speaking and signature writing were compounded for much of the nineteenth century by the custom of teaching reading and writing as entirely separate intellectual activities. The origins of the tradition of signing as a sub-stitute for writing are obscure, unless it be that in an intensely litigious society the art of signing documents was the only writing technique prized by the peasantry. Be that as it may, the untidy pen strokes that passed for signatures on many notarial deeds were scarcely indicative of epistolary talents. In any case, contemporary testimony confirms the suspicion that signing had little to do with literacy. Commenting upon the meagreness of elementary education in the countryside, the first prefect of the Ardèche reported, 'Dans la moitié des communes on trouve à peine quelqu'un qui puisse mettre aveuglement sa

---

[37] G. Géraud, *Notes sur cent ans d'histoire en Lozère (XIXe et XXe siècles)* (Mende, 1969), pp. 19–20; H. Baudrillart, *Les Populations agricoles de la France: 3e série, les populations du Midi* (Paris, 1893), p. 473.

[38] J.R. Lehring, *The Peasants of Marlhes: Economic Development and Family Organization in Nineteenth-Century France* (London, 1980), p. 157.

signature en bas de ce que lui présente un prétendu secrétaire ignorant en vain de ce qu'il croit savoir.'[39] Impatient remarks of this type occur frequently in the administrative correspondence of the first half of the nineteenth century, often accompanied by disparaging observations on the subject of patois. The judicial process brought much interesting information about literacy levels to the surface as well. For instance the interrogation transcript of Antoine Viala of Chastanier (Lozère) in 1843 in which he stated, 'Je ne sais lire n'y écrire, seulement je sais signer pour écrire mon nom.'[40]

It is tempting to dismiss the minimal skill involved in inscribing the letters of one's name as the residual literacy of the common man, but this would be to underestimate a deeply rooted cultural trait. Of the nine principal families (*laboureurs* rather than bourgeois proprietors, it would seem) residing in the causse villages of the commune of Sainte Enimie[41] (Lozère) in 1855, two were unable even to sign; two could fashion the letters of their names with great difficulty and the remainder could only write their names. Anecdotal evidence of this sort scarcely permits generalisation, of course, but the data on literacy contained within the 'Enquête Agricole' of 1848 does help to widen the focus. Unfortunately, the replies elicited were unstandardised and often cryptic. No systematic distinction was drawn between men and women and between generations. More important, the question 'Read and write what?' echoes disconcertingly throughout this otherwise informative compilation. Nevertheless, some of the cantonal commissions were more explicit than others and it seems that in large areas of the Aveyron and the Lozère at least, 'writing' passed as a somewhat exalted description of the ability to sign one's name. Likewise 'reading' was chiefly a liturgical exercise. As the *juge de paix* of the canton of Pont de Salars (Aveyron) put it, 'Peu savent autre chose que lire leur livre de messe et signer.'[42] This was the context in which France embarked upon a second experiment in democracy in 1848 and it puts into perspective the frustrated correspondence of the scores of Parisian militants who hastened to the provinces in order to join in the electoral struggle. Men like Auguste Bibal who reported from the Aubrac that three-quarters of the population could not read his proclamations and had not the slightest notion of the principles of the Republic.[43]

Whilst the state sought to emancipate and convert, the church used its formidable authority in the educational domain to defend and control.The pedagogic approach adopted by each reflected these opposing strategies: the

---

[39] A.N. F^1c III Ardèche 10 Prefect Ardèche to Minister of the Interior, Privas, 27 Prairial IX.
[40] A.D.L. 14IIU (331); *Cour d'assises*, Mende, suit against A. Viala (1843).
[41] A.D.L. 2 O 1420 *Administration et comptabilité communales*: Ste Enimie, *Réponse du Conseil Municipal de Ste Enimie à l'exposé présenté au Conseil-Général de la Lozère* (Nimes, n.d.).
[42] A.N. C947 *Enquête sur la question du travail agricole et industriel (1848)*: Aveyron.
[43] A.N. C938 *Assemblée nationale: enquête sur les événements de mai et juin 1848*: Aveyron, Bibal to *président du comité central de Paris*, Espalion, 12 April 1848.

state taught its pupils to read and write in French; the church was content simply to teach its pupils to read the national language. The dichotomy was pronounced and it added a further layer of half-knowledge to the mongrel literacy of the region. Just how pronounced is revealed in a remarkable survey of the chequered history of literacy edited by François Furet and Jacques Ozouf.[44] They postulate a two-tiered process of acculturation in which the church pioneered the introduction of the French language to the faithful and the state continued and consolidated this effort to ensure that the citizen might also use the national idiom as a tool for communication. Where the institutional presence of the church rivalled that of the state until well into the nineteenth century, the phenomenon of incomplete ('reading only') literacy lingered unseasonably. The available statistical evidence indicates that 'reading only' literacy was a phenomenon of four distinct regions of metropolitan France: the western Pyrenees, the Massif Central, the Alpine departments and a large part of Brittany. In all these regions the catholic church exerted preponderant control over primary education. By all the yardsticks of scholarly achievement, the departments of the southern and south-eastern Massif Central formed a vast and recalcitrant hinterland of semi-literacy among men as well as women. Total illiteracy declined swiftly after about 1830, but it yielded to a largely functional grasp of French based on rote learning rather than comprehension.

The Lozère, the Haute-Loire and the Aveyron headed the list of those departments in which 'reading only' was most prevalent in 1866, followed by the Puy-de-Dôme, the Cantal, the Loire and the Ardèche. In the Haute-Loire 'reading only' literacy had been widespread in all three *arrondissements* until the 1850s when the state began to outflank the church in the field of educational provision. The proportion of men and women who were only able to read plummeted in the Brivadois and around Le Puy, but in the Yssingelais the resourceful *béates* (see chapter nine, p. 281) perpetuated clerical control of primary instruction.[45] The lay teaching orders proved doughty defenders of a particular conception of education in the Aveyron, too. Among the adult male rural population of the *arrondissement* of Rodez in 1866, 31 per cent were totally illiterate, 30 per cent could read but not write and 39 per cent could both read and write. In the *arrondissement* of Millau where the influence of protestantism was still marked, over half the adult males were able to read and write while 15 per cent were only able to read. The proportion of adult females able to read French but not write it was in each case

---

[44] F. Furet and J. Ozouf, *Lire et écrire: l'alphabétisation des français de Calvin à Jules Ferry* (2 vols., Paris, 1977).

[45] V. Parron, *Notice sur l'aptitude militaire en France, suivi d'un essai de statistique générale de la Haute-Loire* (Paris, 1872), pp. 403–4; Malègue, *Eléments de statistique générale*, pp. 246–51; F.-C. Dunglas, *Notice sur les béates de la Haute-Loire, diocèse du Puy* (Paris, 1854).

higher.[46] Once again, a signal contrast between the southern and the western and, to a lesser degree, the northern departments of the Massif Central emerges. In the Creuse, the Corrèze and the Haute-Vienne the retreat of patois and insignificant levels of partial literacy suggest a cultural atmosphere in which the catholic church no longer played a major role. The 'civilisation' of this region proceeded in step with the developing power of the state and the political advantage thereof accrued to the young Republic. The oppressive clericalism of the south posed a much greater obstacle. Whether explicitly or implicitly churchmen used patois to seal off the rural population from outside influences and instruction in French by the *curé* or his auxiliaries was conceived with the same aim in mind. Shorn of the skills of self-expression, reading became a communal and culturally reinforcing experience, especially when nourished upon a diet of devotional literature and almanacs. The historic task of propagating secular education devolved upon the *instituteurs* of the University, the *écoles normales* and sundry other establishments but, with notable exceptions, they failed to live up to the high ideals of republican mythology. Weak in French, profoundly Catholic and practising (even after the Separation), they remained under the thumb of the parish clergy. Many resembled Paulin Chauvet[47] who, in 1878, took up the post of schoolmaster in the tiny commune of St Julien-des-Points (Lozère). The son of a peasant, he had studied with the Frères Ignorantins of Marvejols where he had obtained the *brevet élémentaire*. Under the watchful eye of the *curé*, Chauvet set about imparting his modest skills in reading, writing and arithmetic. Decimals were out of the question for the *frères* preferred to teach the twelve times table which evoked memories of the *ancien régime* rather than the Revolution.

The church as cultural integrator

Sufficient has been said to indicate the claims of the church in the sphere of community formation and it is now necessary to examine this issue in more detail. Throughout the period in question catholicism exhibited a strong penchant for pre-Tridentine forms. Indeed, it is questionable whether a Catholic Reformation, as such, ever affected the upland dioceses of the southern Massif Central. This is not to deny the impact of the Council of Trent, but merely to keep it in perspective. Against the evidence of seminary foundations, missionary activity and pullulating teaching orders, we have to set the stark fact that the nature of popular religious beliefs and the calibre of the secular clergy underwent no fundamental change. Even in 1880 the ideals of the sixteenth- and seventeenth-century reformers – a spiritually aware laity able to distinguish between the sacred and the profane under the guidance

---

[46]   Furet and Ozouf, *Lire et écrire*, pp. 210–12.
[47]   J. Anglade, *La Vie quotidienne dans le Massif Central au XIXe siècle* (Paris, 1971), pp. 213–27.

of a disciplined pastoral body – fell short of realisation. More revealing still is the apparent absence of tension between the laity and a clergy imbued with rigorist principles. When a truly social history of the Gallican church comes to be written this may well turn out to be one of the most pervasive myths of our time. Public and episcopal archives contain an abundant store of documentation on relations between clergy and parishioners and many different images of the parish priest emerge, but that of the village Jansenist interfering with popular culture does not crop up very frequently. Yet, there was a sense in which catholicism experienced a renaissance if not a reformation in this period. Institutionally, rather than doctrinally, the church enhanced its position in the countryside. During the final decades of the *ancien régime* and throughout the century following the church perceptibly gained in authority and prestige. All the ponderable indices from ordination rates to mass attendance percentages seem to agree on this. As for the Revolution, it brought dislocation and chaos for a decade but did little to alter the long-term trend. A full explanation of this process awaits detailed research. However, ruralisation appears to have been an important factor. Increasingly, the church recruited its personnel from agricultural and peasant milieux. The upward permeation of rural values brought rich rewards in terms of social adhesion and submission, but it sapped the independence of the church in matters of dogma and ritual. Rustic recruitment produced a rustic clergy.

The grosser clerical abuses signalled by the Council of Trent had everywhere ceased by the end of the seventeenth century. The Grands Jours of the Auvergne,[48] convened in September 1665, were the last occasion on which priests were indicted for murder and kidnapping. Forswearing, brawling, concubinage and other activities of an eminently unecclesiastical nature were to continue for some years to come, however. Witness, for instance, the following bizarre episode. In 1831 the parish priest of St Sauveur-de-Montagut (Ardèche) supervised a Caesarian operation upon a woman who had died in approximately the fourth month of pregnancy:

à peine avait-elle rendu le dernier soupir que le sieur Pouzet, curé de St Sauveur, ordonna Jean-Jacques Riou du même lieu de lui ouvrir le ventre afin d'en extraire l'enfant qu'elle portait, opération qui fut fait avec un couteau de boucher, en présence du curé, d'Henriette Pouzet sa nièce et de Magdaleine Malheret, femme Valette, mère de la défunte qui lui tenait la bouche entr'ouverte, à l'aide d'une fourchette, pour faciliter un reste de respiration, car on croit généralement que la vie n'était pas entièrement éteinte chez cette malheureuse quand on commença à la dépecer.[49]

The priest defended his conduct arguing that the woman had, in fact, been

[48] A. Lebigre, *Les Grands Jours d'Auvergne: désordres et répression au XVIIe siècle* (Paris, 1976), pp. 122–6.
[49] A.N. F[19] 5767 *Police des cultes*: diocese of Viviers, Mayor St Sauveur-de-Montagut to prefect Ardèche, St Sauveur, 1 April 1831.

dead; that a razor had been used and not a butcher's knife; that he and his niece had not been physically present when the first incision was made and that the foetus had been alive when baptised. The prefect sent the dossier on the affair to Paris and the Ministre des Cultes, or his clerk, appended the following note: 'La bonhomie des aveux et la naïveté du récit font frémir. Quelle barbarie!'[50]

Mercifully such incidents were rare, or at least they were rarely uncovered. But general purpose doctoring long featured in the clergy's repertoire of secular talents, if only because parishioners tended to seek out their priest when they had something physically wrong with them. The example also serves to illustrate the mortal terror which priests in charge of souls could inspire, especially in 'front line' parishes. Two-thirds of the population of St Sauveur-de-Montagut were protestant and the protestant mayor had initially refrained from drawing attention to this deplorable episode for fear of igniting latent animosities. Quaking, superstitious fear formed only one dimension of the relationship between priest and parish, however. Much of the correspondence reaching the bishops and their vicars-general and, after the Concordat, the prefects and ministers of state contained allegations against avaricious, domineering, foul-tongued or lubricious clerics. To all appearances the standards of brutality and rusticity that governed relations among the general population set the tone for the clergy as well. Indeed, when we consider the social composition of the pastoral corps and the intellectual mediocrity of seminary training this could scarcely have been otherwise. Yet the laity retained a dogged conviction, unlinked to Tridentine ideals, that on some occasions, at least, the pastor ought to rise above the depraved behaviour of his flock. Intransigence and 'âpreté de caractère' were commonly voiced criticisms, especially during the Bourbon Restoration which many of the older clerics sought to exploit with almost gloating zeal. One way or another, most were disabused. Laurans,[51] *curé* of St Laurent-les-Bains (Ardèche), for instance, complained to a deputy in the Chambre Introuvable that his parishioners were insufficiently ultra-royalist and suggested that the municipality be replaced. But if the clergy imagined that they could slip back into the multipurpose role they had fulfilled at the end of the *ancien régime*, they were sadly mistaken. First the Revolution and then Napoléon had clarified relations between church and state and the governments of the nineteenth century were anxious to preserve a distinction between matters temporal and matters spiritual. The distinction was somewhat shaky and yielded to political expediency at election times, but it was one which no regime, not even the Restoration, could afford to do without. Thus the prefect of the Lozère invited the higher authorities to concert disciplinary measures

---

[50] *Ibid.*, note pinned to dossier.
[51] A.N. F[19] 5686 *Police des cultes*: diocese of Mende, Laurans to André, St Laurent-les-Bains, 17 November 1815.

against the formidable *desservant* of St Paul-le-Froid who patrolled his parish armed with a cudgel or a shotgun: 'il cherche plustôt à se faire craindre à cause de la force de ses bras qu'à se faire respecter par son exactitude à remplir les devoirs de son ministère'.[52]

Of course, it would be unwise to place too much reliance upon the evidence of petitions and the testy correspondence they produced. Vilification of the parish clergy was a popular leisure activity in the countryside and as the implications of the Concordat sank in, petition-mongering in order to obtain the replacement of an awkward ecclesiastic became more common. Exasperated by the steady stream of complaints, the bishop of Mende remarked in a letter to the Ministre des Cultes that he ignored all such missives as a matter of principle.[53] Nevertheless, the sheer volume of complaint and acrimony cannot be ignored. Priests were routinely accused of inducing the dying into making bequests of various sorts and just as routinely denied the charge. They were routinely accused of uncharitable litigiousness in enforcing their rights and pursuing their debtors; 'Tout le monde sait', reported the *commissaire de police* of Saugues, 'que Monsieur le Curé [of St Christophe d'Allier in the Haute-Loire] fait gérer une boutique de rouennerie au Chambon [Lozère] par une nommée Cécile son ancienne servante; il fournit les fonds et partage les bénéfices.'[54] More seriously, the morality of the parish clergy was repeatedly questioned and the allegations sometimes reached the courts. Schoolroom and catechism class provided both temptation and opportunity, and it is not uncommon to find ecclesiastics cited in the attempted rape and indecent exposure cases coming before the Assises in the middle decades of the nineteenth century. This well attested rusticity is not the whole story, however. For all their shortcomings the clergy of the southern Massif Central presided over a signal re-affirmation of the power of the church in the countryside. With the possible exception of the records of episcopal visitations, no individual source captures the magnitude of this multi-faceted process. The evidence is piecemeal and lacks the poignancy of that which chronicles clerical misdemeanours. Yet even the civil authorities had detected a changed atmosphere by mid-century. In 1858 the prefect of the Haute-Loire reported that rural catholicism was enjoying something of a renaissance.[55] Missions, retreats, pilgrimages, the assiduous propagation of the Cult of the Virgin and the benign political atmosphere during the first decade of the Second Empire filled the churches to overflowing. This incoming tide of religiosity, together with the pride of a clergy at the very height of its power, is reflected in the response of the *curé* of Sainte Croix (Aveyron) to a sugges-

---

[52] *Ibid.*, Prefect Lozère to Minister of the Interior, Mende, 13 January 1819.
[53] *Ibid.*, Bishop Mende to *Ministre des Cultes*, Mende, 24 April 1827.
[54] A.D. H.-L. 7V2 *Commissariat cantonal* of Saugues to prefect Haute-Loire, Saugues, 6 September 1856.
[55] A.D. H.-L. 2M²1 *Rapports des préfets*, 16 March 1858.

tion that he might like to move on after twenty-three years spent in the parish: 'l'année passée, à l'époque du jubilé, je n'ai pas eu *une seule* abstention et cette année-ci, à Pâques, il ne m'a manqué que les jeunes gens et 2 hommes mariés sur une population de 420 adultes. Les premières années, il m'en manquait tous les ans de 25 à 30.'[56]

The growth of a clerical hegemony did not necessarily imply a process of evangelisation, though. Churchmen trumpeted the return of the Voltairian bourgeoisie to the fold and went to extraordinary and illicit lengths to seduce protestant children from the ways of Error, but popular religious beliefs retained all the ambiguities born of too close an association with popular culture. Whilst acknowledging the authority of the church in the countryside, the prefect of the Haute-Loire was careful to point out that it did not rest upon orthodox religious conviction. The ceremonial and placatory aspects of religion were what counted most. Those rituals which demanded physical attendance at church, at a shrine or oratory, at a grave-side evoked a punctilious response from the peasant; most of the spiritual demands of organised religion found him gravely deficient. Attendance at mass, confession and communion, for instance, was never a source of concern for the hierarchy in spite of the obstacles of climate and habitat. The renaissance of the late eighteenth and nineteenth centuries usually consisted of adding a few digits to already impressive totals of *messalisants* and *pascalisants*. This upward curve of religious vitality, as confessional historians are apt to construe it, can only be drawn from the 1820s when measurable indices become plentiful. The trend at the end of the *ancien régime* is known only in broadest outline.[57] One fact is plain, however: the revolutionary climacteric did not fundamentally disturb the church-going habits of the rural population nor, indeed, those of the minute urban population. Dechristianisation in the technical sense ascribed to it by researchers was not a problem in the southern Massif Central. In this respect the clergy taught the laity an unforgettable lesson in the 1820s and 1830s as the handful of village 'Marats' died without the consolation of religion or any prospect of decent burial. In the Aveyron[58] the proportion of adults who completed their Easter duties in the 1870s and 1880s ranged from 94 per cent in the *arrondissement* of St Affrique to 46 per cent in the industrial centre of Aubin–Decazeville. In the Lozère[59] a diocesan

[56] A.N. F^{19} 5853 A. Fraysse to *grand-vicaire*, Ste Croix, 5 July 1880.
[57] Tackett, 'L'Histoire sociale du clergé diocésain dans la France du XVIIIe siècle', p. 205; Tackett and Langlois, 'Ecclesiastical Structures and Clerical Geography on the Eve of the French Revolution', p. 359.
[58] G. Cholvy, 'Le Catholicisme en Rouergue au XIXe et XXe siècles: première approche' in *Etudes sur le Rouergue: actes du 47e congrès d'études de la fédération historique du Languedoc Méditerranéen et du Roussillon, et du 29e congrès d'études de la fédération des sociétés académiques et savantes Languedoc–Pyrénées–Gascogne* (Rodez, 1974), pp. 250–1 and tables.
[59] Causse and Tufféry, 'Le Diocèse de Mende au début du XXe siècle', p. 42 and fig.; A.E.M. *Enquête Boulard.*

survey of 121 catholic parishes in 1909 yielded an average completion rate of 97 per cent. By the time of the Boulard *enquêtes* in the late 1950s the ratio of *pascalisants* in the Aveyron had declined from 81 per cent to 76 per cent, while in the Lozère it had settled at 87 per cent. Ordination rates tell the same story. In 1892 Eugène Melchior de Vogüé[60] commented wryly that a handful of cantons in the high Cévennes produced more sacerdotal vocations than whole dioceses of central France. Nearly all of these recruits to the priesthood found salaried posts in their home or neighbouring dioceses with the result that the church came to control a dense network of agents in the countryside. Not since the sixteenth century had priests been so thick on the ground. In the diocese of Rodez the per capita ratio of parish clergy shifted from 1:363 to 1:300 between 1851 and 1901, notwithstanding the curve of population which continued to rise until 1886.[61]

As far as we can tell popular religion consisted of a rich amalgam of pagan folklore, animist belief and Christian precept. The latter was learnt mechanically and often uncomprehendingly. It had little to do with any formal notion of morality and at heart was based on fear – of the unknown, the uncontrollable. Vague, non-specific, immanent apprehension dogged the footsteps of every peasant and the unanticipated or inexplicable could provoke veritable paroxysms of terror. The Great Fear of 1789 is a case in point, but the eighteenth and nineteenth and early twentieth centuries were littered with instances of mass hysteria and hallucination precipitated by food shortages, ergotism, natural disasters, religious persecution, the closure of temples (in 1685), of churches (in 1791–4; 1905) and incendiarism. In 1848 a respondent of the 'Enquête agricole' made the following entry under the heading of religion and morality:

Dans les campagnes le sentiment de la crainte, c'est-à-dire le jugement de Dieu ou des hommes tient lieu de morale. Chez la femme en général et chez un certain nombre d'hommes une foule d'erreurs, de préjugés et de superstitions viennent les pousser machinalement, tantôt vers le bien, tantôt vers le mal; le sentiment vraiment moral, la satisfaction intérieure, manque, l'intérêt est le mobile le plus puissant dans leurs actions.[62]

The concrete manifestations of popular religiosity shed further light upon the nature of belief. Much as the hierarchy might seek to generalise the Cult of the Virgin, local devotions remained tenacious in the southern Massif Central and the rural population marked time by the calendar of feasts, patron saints' days and pilgrimages. Most saints and shrines had a narrow territory of grace which followed the contours of the parish, but others had a broader catchment area. Between twenty-eight and forty-five parishes par-

[60] Baudrillart, *Les Populations agricoles de la France*, iii, p. 526 note 3.
[61] Jones, 'Parish, Seigneurie and the Community of Inhabitants', p. 97.
[62] A.N. C947 *Enquête sur la question du travail agricole et industriel* (1848): Aveyron, Villefranche-du-Rouergue.

ticipated in the pilgrimage to Our Lady of Ceignac (Rouergue) at the end of the *ancien régime*. Therapeutic shrines also attracted a wide following. Saint Blaise of Aubin was reputed to cure goitre; the spring of Saint Quentin (Haute-Loire) assisted children who were slow in learning to walk, while pilgrims to the hermitage of La Trinité (Haute-Loire) obtained benediction for their lands and stock. According to a mid-nineteenth-century source the officiating priest would bless both man and beast with a *queue de vache* which had been handed down for centuries.[63] The casting out of devils by public exorcism survived into the nineteenth century as an integral feature of popular religious culture, too. Preachers who were specialists in the art attracted large crowds of onlookers from miles around. In capable hands the 'dialogue' of exorcism could be used to drive home any number of lessons ranging from hatred of protestants to hatred of the Civil Constitution of the clergy. Thaumaturgic rituals were equally popular among the laity. To their acute embarrassment bishops on pastoral visits found peasants reaching out to touch their robes and holding up their sick children for blessing as though they were miracle workers. These practices were still widespread in the Lozère in the 1880s.

Recent research suggests that the archaic religious culture of the southern Massif Central was not as anomalous as it might first appear. Rural catholicism in Brittany, in pre-famine Ireland, in Bavaria and along the Atlantic littoral of northern Spain exhibited many of the traits we have discussed here.[64] However, the most original and enduring features of popular religion in this region may prove to have been the tradition of family worship and the related phenomenon of the cult of the dead. Nearly all contemporary observers stressed that the habits of prayer and spiritual rumination began around the hearth. It was here, too, that the *oustal* planted the first notions of its history and genealogy in the minds of each new generation. Little wonder, therefore, if popular religion became heavily impregnated with ancestor worship. The vigour of family worship is well attested. Communal prayer in the evening and catechetical exercises in which the seniors called the questions and the juniors gave the responses were widespread in the mountain parishes of the Lozère. Monseigneur Bourret encountered nearly identical forms of familial piety, or pseudo-piety, during his visits to the parishes of the Aveyron in the 1870s and 1880s. A cultural institution which proved particularly suited to these semi-autonomous expressions of popular religiosity was the *veillée* or gathering of kinsmen or neighbours for sedentary

---

[63] Rouchon, *La Vie paysanne dans la Haute-Loire*, pp. 174–6.

[64] See Pelras, 'Goulien – commune rurale du Cap Sizun', pp. 425–6, 475, 495; Lagrée, *Mentalités, religion et histoire en Haute-Bretagne au XIXème siècle*, pp. 131–2; S. J. Connolly, *Priest and People in Pre-Famine Ireland, 1780–1845* (Dublin, 1982); W. R. Lee, *Population Growth, Economic Development and Social Change in Bavaria, 1750–1850* (New York, 1977), pp. 298–316; W. A. Christian, *Person and God in a Spanish Valley* (New York, 1972).

work, relaxation and edification. The *veillée* was commonplace throughout the southern Massif Central, but in the Velay the efforts of the *béates* had turned it into a brilliantly simple mechanism for the simultaneous transmission of religious truths and the skills of lace-making. The Congrégation des Sœurs de l'Instruction de l'Enfant Jésus,[65] or *béates*, were a teaching order of lay nuns founded at Le Puy in 1688. At first they were regarded rather equivocally by the hierarchy, but by the nineteenth century they had become trusted auxiliaries to the parish clergy rather than rivals in the field of pastoral care. In the 1850s there were approximately 1,400 of these spiritual outworkers, half of whom ministered in the Haute-Loire. Nearly every village in the Velay had its *assemblée* (usually the dwelling of the *béate* constructed at the expense of the local inhabitants) where women and children would congregate to work, gossip and recite under the supervision of the *béate*. George Sand who was well acquainted with the superstitious religiosity of the peasantry of the Velay left an unforgettable, if jaundiced, description of,

des éspèces de communautés de villageoises assises en rond et faisant voltiger leurs bobines en murmurant des litanies ou en chantant des offices en latin, ce qui ne les empêche pas de regarder avidement les passants et d'échanger leurs remarques, tout en répondant *ora pro nobis* à la sœur grise, noire ou bleue qui surveille le travail et la psalmodie.[66]

The cult of the dead and its physical locus, the cemetery, bring us much closer to an understanding of the hybrid role of the church in the countryside. There is overwhelming evidence to indicate that respect for ancestors and the rituals of commemoration and intercession lay at the very heart of popular piety. In areas of creeping religious indifference the rites associated with All Souls' Day were generally the last to succumb and individuals who refused on principle to set foot in a church would nonetheless attend the annual Office for the Dead. In no other sphere, moreover, was the artificiality of the Counter-Reformation more transparent. In matters of death the distinction between the sacred and the profane made very little sense for the rural community perceived itself first and foremost as a community of the living *and* the dead. Pierre Ariès[67] has argued that the cult of the dead and tomb visiting were post-revolutionary developments in the main. Perhaps the model of Romantic piety did have an impact among the educated laity, but it is perversely misleading to suggest that there was no antecedent tradition of commemoration and graveside soliloquy. In the southern Massif Central the reforming efforts of the hierarchy had produced a measure of compliance. Interment within the body of the church had become uncommon by the early nineteenth century and if the burial ground was still, in fact, the churchyard,

---

[65] Dunglas, *Notice sur les béates*.
[66] Quoted in G. Bayssat, *Evolution du monde rural de la Haute-Loire* (Le Puy, n.d. [1955]), p. 177.
[67] P. Ariès, *L'Homme devant la mort* (Paris, 1977), pp. 518–19; 544–9.

most had been equipped with walls and gates. The bishop of Mende found fault with just five cemeteries during a tour of inspection commencing in 1823. But this was mostly cosmetic, albeit expensive cosmetic, which occasioned much grumbling. As the resting place of ancestors, the cemetery remained a place of rendez-vous; a village cross-roads. The graveyard of the parish of Les Albres was crossed by several paths and in 1837 the bishop of Rodez enjoined the parishioners to carry out repairs to the walls ('il leur a fait sentir qu'il ne convenait pas de fouler ainsi aux pieds les cendres de leurs pères').[68] It was not the first time that the matter had been raised and it is doubtful whether the inhabitants could understand the point of the criticism.

This casual familiarity with the dead did not betoken a lack of respect, quite the contrary. In 1883 the *abbé* Pourcher of St Martin-de-Boubaux announced the death of his mother. St Martin-de-Boubaux was an overwhelmingly protestant parish and every morning for twenty years Pourcher had sung high mass to a diminutive catholic congregation consisting of a family of ten plus his mother and niece. Undeterred, he dragged the corpse into the church and propped it up on the front bench so that, as he put it, she should not miss the Office for the Dead. After what must have been an epic journey, he buried his mother alongside her forebears in the cemetery of the parish of Saugues some fifty kilometres to the north. In many ways Pourcher conformed to the caricature of the backwoods *curé*. His religious convictions owed little to Trent and nothing at all to Romantic sensibility. Philippe de Las Cazes,[69] the Sillonist, remembered meeting him as a young man and described him as a pure product of the Middle Ages. Marooned in the midst of the protestant Cévennes, he whiled away the time composing works with titles like *Vie de Sainte Thècle*; *Vie et miracles de Saint Clair*; *Les Heures pieuses des fidèles nobles et villageois*, which he printed in tiny format on a home-made chestnut-wood press.

Putting walls round the cemetery in order to keep out stock and make it 'decent' was one thing, interfering with access was another. Contemporaries were agreed that nothing caused more resentment and indignation than attempts to close, move or in any way alter the spatial organisation of burial grounds. The explosions of wrath that interference of this sort provoked help to illuminate the fundamental structure of the rural community. In both a literal and a figurative sense the cemetery embodied a group of families who frequented the same church or chapel and whose sense of cohesion and identity flowed from that fact. Its physical location, together with that of the church, provided a centre of gravity and the arrangement of graves and plots reproduced the social contours of the human group. Every cemetery betokened a community of the living, therefore, and the destruction or defile-

---

[68] Archives de l'Evêché de Rodez (henceforth A.E.R.) Mgr. Guiraud, *registre des visites pastorales* (1835–1841).
[69] P. de Las Cazes, *Ce n'est rien, rien qu'une vie* (Mende, 1961), pp. 49–54.

ment of a burial ground passed for an act of almost ritualised disfigurement of that community. This was widely understood in the countryside. It was no accident of history that former protestant cemeteries were generally designated for the burial of the unbaptised and suicide cases. The case of St Rémy and Vergezac (Haute-Loire) also serves to illustrate this point. The dispute which divided these villages in the 1820s and 1830s has been discussed elsewhere,[70] but it originated in the decision to transfer the status of *chef-lieu* of both commune and parish from St Rémy to Vergezac. In theory this reorganisation made the church and churchyard of St Rémy redundant and the inhabitants of the new *chef-lieu* wasted no time in dismantling their rivals' church and in closing access to their cemetery. The bishop of St Flour expressed the sense of outrage that resulted from this brutal attempt at community emasculation in a confidential letter to the minister in charge of ecclesiastical affairs:

Ici, Monseigneur, il faut connaître ces montagnards pour concevoir que cette voie de fait est la plus grande insulte que l'on puisse faire à un peuple. Ils tiennent aux cendres de leurs pères, ils tiennent au lieu où ils reposent, ils y vont prier très fréquemment et c'est ce qui est toujours la cause de l'aversion qui règne dans les paroisses qui ont été séparées ou réunies, c'est la perte du cimetière. Ils aiment mieux laisser les cadavres sans sépulture, ils aiment mieux manquer de messes ou aller l'entendre dans une paroisse très eloignée plutôt que de venir au lieu où l'église a été transferée.[71]

Little did it matter what state the cemetery was in (and some were in a quite disgusting state even at the end of the nineteenth century), it remained the dwelling place of ancestral spirits and should remain accessible at all times. Peasants frequented the graves of their forebears in order to intercede for them, to beseech them, to seek advice and to bear witness to the continuity of the *oustal*. The sacred character of the cult of the dead was always in doubt and it caused the church serious misgivings, yet it never withheld its blessing. As with so many facets of popular culture it seemed wiser to temporise or legitimise rather than risk a breach. Accordingly, the feasts of Martinmas and All Souls became hallowed events in the liturgical calendar and they were buttressed by a rich array of special offices, vigils, anniversary masses, lantern processions and bell ringing. The ritual of commemoration preserved the illusion of the eternal peasant household emancipated from the constraints of time and physical space. The *abbé* Sanson[72] noted shortly after the First World War that in some parts of the Cantal families retained the names of deceased kin in the parish necrology for twenty, thirty and even forty years, while in the Cévennes the peasant family actively conspired to minimise the

---

[70] Jones, 'Parish, Seigneurie and the Community of Inhabitants', pp. 103–4.
[71] A.N. F[19] 755[A] Confidential letter of bishop St Flour, St Flour, 21 August 1822.
[72] Abbé Sanson, 'Les Coutumes chrétiennes en Haute-Auvergne', *Revue de la Haute-Auvergne*, xxiv (1922), 375.

dislocation caused by death: 'tant que le père était là, il n'abandonnait pas ses pouvoirs . . . il les conservait même disparu'.[73]

Fear of separation – anomic dread – runs like a thread through the evidence of popular religious convictions that we have at our disposal. The closure or removal of a cemetery imposed a form of spiritual divorce that was profoundly disorientating, but it could also drive a physical wedge between the living and the dead. Each peasant generation expected to mingle its remains with those of preceding generations and the phrase 'mêler leurs cendres à celles de leurs pères' occurs repeatedly in petitions from communities facing cultural extinction. To paraphrase the bishop of St Flour, no more extreme insult could be inflicted upon a population than to deny the bonds of kinship in death as in life. Or, in the graphic language of the inhabitants of the threatened parish of Inos (Lozère): 'Monseigneur [l'évêque] sait le respect et l'attachement des catholiques pour les lieux où reposent les reliques de leurs parents. Il ne voudra pas les forcer dire comme ce sauvage d'amérique, qu'on expulsoit de son territoire, aux ossements de ses pères: levez-vous et quittez votre lieu de repos.'[74] Proposals to disestablish a cemetery on the grounds of hygiene nearly always rubbed on this raw nerve and could produce reactions ranging from resentment and despair to full-scale insurrection. It seems that parishes were prepared to risk any infection short of the plague. When Monseigneur Bourret, bishop of Rodez, arrived in the village of Verrières[75] for a pastoral inspection on the afternoon of 26 May 1876, he was greeted with every sign of filial piety. Not a man to duck issues, Bourret climbed into the pulpit and complimented the inhabitants on having restored the church and churchyard, adding that they need not have bothered to repair the latter since it needed to be replaced. According to the police investigation launched by the public prosecutor of Millau the riot that followed was largely spontaneous. The congregation rushed out of the church, tore down a triumphal arch and a rostrum and built a barricade across the entrance to the cemetery. Pursued by abuse, the bishop retreated to the presbytery which was then assailed with stones. Later that evening he fled across fields to the high road where his carriage was waiting. Humiliated and furious Bourret withdrew the *curé* and placed the church and churchyard of Verrières under an interdict. Warning of the dangers involved in depriving a population of spiritual comforts, the Minister of Justice prevailed upon him to lift it three and a half months later. Few quarrels over cemeteries ended quite so abruptly and violently. At St Urcize (Cantal) the municipality obtained consent for the construction of a new cemetery which was ready for occupation by 1899, where-

---

[73] A near contemporary observation recorded by Pelen, 'La Vallée Longue en Cévenne', p. 81.
[74] A.E.M. Parish dossiers: St Georges-de-Levéjac, *Mémoire pour être présenté à monseigneur l'évêque de Mende relativement au transfert de la paroisse d'Inos au Massegros* (n.d. [1852]).
[75] See A.D.A. 11M7 26 *Troubles de Verrières et St Beauzély, 1876*; A. Maury, 'Le Cardinal Bourret (période 1871–1876)', *Revue du Rouergue*, xxix (1975), 242–7.

upon several inhabitants announced that they wished to exhume the remains of their kith and kin and re-inter them in the new burial ground.

The bishop's interdict forced the villagers of Verrières to seek alternative resting places for their dead, but neighbouring parishes refused to cooperate. The mayor of Vezouillac warned that any attempt to bury alien corpses in his cemetery would provoke '*désordres les plus graves et les plus sérieux*'.[76] Clearly there were limits to the promiscuity of death. The spatial distribution of graves within the cemetery reflected not merely the ties of kinship, but also the fissures and hierarchies within the broader community. Those who had placed themselves beyond the Pale (apostates, for example) and those whose allegiance belonged elsewhere were refused admittance to consecrated ground; those whose claim rested on sufference found their marginality emphasised even in death. The physical remains of the unbaptised and suicide victims had long been relegated to remote corners of the churchyard, but the organic law on cemeteries of 23 Prairial XII (12 June 1804) had unintentionally consolidated these distinctions in the South where protestantism provided a complicating ingredient. In theory Calvinists and Lutherans (and Jews) were entitled to separate cemeteries, but in some parishes these sects numbered few adherents and the municipal authorities were empowered to carry out a division of catholic burial grounds. Unsurprisingly, the church was reluctant to make such concessions and the catholic laity were aghast at the thought that their bones might come into contact with those of 'huguenots'. When a delegation of protestant notables broached this subject with the bishop of Mende in 1823 he retorted by querying whether the followers of Calvin needed to bury their dead communally. This barely concealed enmity encouraged the clergy to worse abuses. In a circular addressd to the bishops and marked 'très confidentielle' the Ministre des Cultes complained that the law was not being upheld, 'Quelquefois, des protestants ont été inhumés dans cette partie du cimetiére qui est affectée à la sépulture des enfants morts sans baptême, des suicidés et même des suppliciés.'[77]

Little changed, it seems. The cemetery continued to serve as a potent instrument of community demarcation throughout the nineteenth century. In 1861 the Calvinist pastor complained that the protestants of St Jean-de-Muzols (Ardèche) were laid to rest alongside suicide victims, alongside, that is to say, those who had forfeited their membership of the indissoluble community of the living and the dead. Anti-clerical legislation in 1881 and 1884 sought to remove the barriers of segregation. Spatial distinctions between catholic and protestant in the cemeteries were abolished, although stillborn children were not admitted to full communion. In the clericalised parishes bordering the Cévennes discrimination against protestants did not cease,

[76] A.D.A. 11M7 26 Minute of prefect Aveyron to Minister of Justice (?), 9 August 1876.
[77] A.E.R. *Administration civile des cultes*, 1830–48: ministerial circular, Paris, 1 September 1846.

however. The death of a protestant at Marvejols in 1887 triggered a bitter politico-religious polemic in the *bourg*. While the *curé* had a grave dug in the annex, the dead woman's offspring had the corpse conveyed by the main entrance into the cemetery.

'Désir fort naturel', reported the sub-prefect, 'si l'on songe au discrédit que le clergé s'est efforcé de jeter sur l'ancien cimetière protestant au moyens d'inqualifiables procédés. Par ordre du clergé en effet, au mépris de la neutralité des cimetières, trois suicidés ont été, *à dessein* depuis la nouvelle loi, inhumés dans l'ancien cimetière protestant, de telle sorte qu'actuellement cette partie du champ de repos commun est désignée par le public et par le clergé sous le nom de "cimetière des suicidés".'[78]

The law prevailed on this occasion, but with the parish priest uttering the word 'desecration' from the pulpit and warning that the cemetery would have to be reconsecrated.

The emotional attachment of a population to its burial grounds serves to underline several important conclusions about the role of the church in the southern Massif Central. In so far as the rural community possessed a territorial context in the eighteenth and nineteenth centuries it was the parish. The *communauté d'habitants* and the seigneurie were brittle by comparison. The parish could reproduce itself like an organic cell; its boundaries were subject to constant piecemeal definition. A broad time focus enables us to chart these shifts and identify the mechanisms of change. Realignment proceeded from two main causes: the desire of the faithful to obtain spiritual and pastoral provision better suited to their needs and the desire of the civil and ecclesiastical powers to achieve a rational and economical distribution of parochial functions. The processes which culminated in the creation of a new parish have been described in detail elsewhere.[79] The decision of a group of families to seek alternative facilities for congregation and worship was often – in a mountainous region – precipitated by topographical or climatic factors, or else by ecological, or demographic dislocation. Restructuring took time since the emergence of a new parish could jeopardise the survival of older entities. The process of community formation and recognition presupposed a concurrent process of decay and dissolution. A century and a half elapsed before the inhabitants of the village of Laviolle and surrounding farmsteads vindicated their claim to independence. Between 1685 when the villagers built a chapel at Laviolle and 1841 when it finally became a parish church, the mother parish of Antraigues (Ardèche) used every conceivable stratagem to halt the secession.

In many instances the bid for ecclesiastical autonomy concealed within it an aspiration to self-government and therein lay the fears of established administrative entities. The victory of Laviolle in 1841 entailed a double

[78] A.D.L. 85 V 1 *Police du culte*: sub-prefect Marvejols to prefect Lozère, Marvejols, 19 March 1887.
[79] Jones, 'Parish, Seigneurie and the Community of Inhabitants', pp. 99–104.

assault upon the integrity of Antraigues for the village emerged as a *chef-lieu de commune* as well as a *chef-lieu de succursale*. Indeed, the creation of a powerful unit of local government after 1789 added a fresh incentive to the well-rehearsed game of community assertion. It also increased the opportunities for friction and misunderstanding between the spiritual and the temporal arm. A tighter parochial network helped the bishops to find livings for their ordinands, but each newly erected parish resulted in a petition for communal status arriving on the prefect's desk. This is only a slight exaggeration. In the parish and commune of St Andéol-de-Fourchades[80] (Ardèche) the village of Le Chambon, which lay at the foot of a steep escarpment, organised a subscription and built a chapel and presbytery of its own. Much to the annoyance of the civil authorities, the bishop was induced to grant Le Chambon the status of parish in 1847. Illusions of administrative independence rapidly burgeoned in this remote river gorge, but the prefect steadfastly refused to split the 1,100 inhabitants of the commune of St Andéol-de-Fourchades into two self-governing entities. Consequently, the tensions found expression in the electoral arena and for the rest of the century the composition of the municipality faithfully recorded the thwarted ambition of the villagers of Le Chambon. In 1854 the municipal councillors were all drawn from the parish of St Andéol-de-Fourchades while the mayor and his *adjoint*, who were appointed by the prefect, were drawn from the parish of Notre-Dame de Chambon. Throughout the Second Empire and the early decades of the Third Republic municipal government remained deadlocked and public works languished. Finally, in 1904, the commune was dismembered.

Officially inspired attempts to alter parish boundaries encountered fierce opposition. When Napoleon, in the aftermath of the Concordat, instructed his prefects and sub-prefects to reorganise the parochial network he provoked an outcry. The measure had been foreshadowed in the Civil Constitution of the Clergy, but even those regions noted for low levels of religious vitality found it objectionable. Describing popular reactions when the idea was first mooted, Gabriel Le Bras remarked wryly: 'L'Eure-et-Loir, par exemple, devint un pays alpestre: des montagnes surgirent dans le Dunois, des torrents dévastèrent la Beauce, la rivière Eure se mit à monter inopinément'.[81] In the departments of the southern Massif Central, the Napoleonic reorganisation elicited reactions akin to panic. Briefly, the entire fabric of community life appeared to be in the melting-pot. Apparently well-established parishes found themselves in competition with shadowy communities in the making which had hitherto achieved no more than *annexe* status. An avalanche of petitions threatened to overwhelm the machinery of local government. The *juge de paix* of the canton of Largentière (Ardèche)

---

[80] A.D. Ard. 9M3 *Circonscriptions territoriales, érections en communes*: St Andéol-de-Fourchades.
[81] Le Bras, *L'Eglise et le village*, p. 119 and note 1.

reported that he had called a meeting of local mayors to discuss the proposal as bidden, but had been left in no doubt as to the strength of feeling on the subject. In the opinion of the mayors the issue was not open to negotiation. Apart from the inhabitants of a few hamlets, everyone wished to maintain the status quo: 'd'après leurs principes religieux, ils regarderoient comme *le plus grand des malheurs* d'être séparés de leur ancienne église, et de n'être pas enterrés *dans le tombeau de leurs pères*'. Various exchanges of villages and of territory might be contemplated, he continued, but the state would gain nothing from this, 'et l'on affligeroit au delà de toute expression des hommes qui ne peuvent pas se faire à l'idée que leurs cendres ne seront pas mêlées à celles de leurs ancêtres. Il faudrait toujours *laisser subsister l'église actuellement existante, je dois répéter.*'[82] Unseemly and even violent scenes occurred as funeral corteges found cemetery gates locked and villagers succumbed to *angst* as their chapels and churches were closed down. And yet, more serious disturbances were avoided, if only because the scope of the reform was soon whittled down. Nomenclature[83] changed and so did many incumbents, but only the tiniest parishes lost their physical identity. In the Ardèche thirty-nine parishes or 12 per cent of the pre-Concordat total were finally sacrificed.[84]

The tardy, but vigorous growth of a parish-dominated religious life in the late eighteenth and nineteenth centuries suggests that Tridentine reforms did not pass entirely unnoticed in the southern Massif Central. The logic of parish discipline as conceived by reformers like St Vincent de Paul should not be taken for granted, however. Regular weekly attendance at mass did not necessarily direct the religious beliefs of the rural masses into orthodox channels and filter out familial and fetishistic accretions. The most intellectually alert among the rural clergy were acutely aware of this dilemma. Their obliquely phrased anxieties add weight to our second conclusion: in the southern Massif Central the catholic church in the person of the parish priest was the custodian, but not the arbiter of popular culture. Attempts to elevate and dogmatise religious experience foundered on the reefs of a fundamental misconception. Though the church might insist upon spiritual values, this was not necessarily the valuation placed upon the institution by a peasant culture lacking alternative means of social integration and self-expression. This conflict of perceptions is brought into sharp focus in G. Bouchard's[85] study of a village in the Sologne and it is likely that it prevailed to a greater or lesser degree throughout the dispersed habitat regions of the Massif Central and the West.

Peasant society was punctilious in its adherence to the formal obligations

[82] A.D. Ard. V26 *Juge de Paix*, Largentière to sub-prefect (n.d. [Messidor an X]).
[83] See Jones, 'Parish, Seigneurie and the Community of Inhabitants', p. 98.
[84] A.D. Ard. V26 *Etat des paroisses supprimées dans le département de l'Ardèche*, Privas, 3 Pluviôse XIII.
[85] G. Bouchard, *Le Village immobile: Sennely-en-Sologne au XVIIIᵉ siècle* (Paris, 1972).

of the faith, but the parish priest was also expected to conform. Within certain limits he was honoured and respected as the symbol of the collectivity, but if he strayed beyond them then he became an outsider. Those who could not accept this self-effacing role were soon disabused. When the *curé* of Balazuc in the Bas Vivarais disbanded the local fraternity of St Antoine on the ground that it had degenerated from its original charitable function, he provoked a minor revolt in the neighbourhood. Gunshots were fired at the presbytery and he was forced to flee. The rattle of shot or stones against the shutters was a traditional means of warning a priest that he had overstepped the mark. Clerical interference in family life was resented, too. A priesthood which even in the nineteenth century had not entirely surmounted the temptations of the flesh and a certain venality was neither qualified nor invited to adopt a rigorous stance on the moral teachings of the gospels.

And yet, if the rural ministry was hedged in by signs warning against trespass, the clergy were clearly expected to intervene in the public activities of life. Paradoxically, but revealingly, the types of parochial leadership prescribed by Trent resulted in friction and conflict more often than not, while the forms of priestly involvement that Trent endeavoured to uproot remained in heavy demand. A third and final conclusion follows naturally from this. In the southern Massif Central catholicism and popular culture overlapped so as to be indistinguishable at certain points. The church exercised a rare monopoly over the opportunities for community self-expression. Every religious celebration was a secular pageant and vice versa: every parish pilgrimage, Patron Saint's day, exorcism and Sunday service exhibited this dual character. It may be surmised that the ecclesiastical hierarchy viewed this state of affairs with serious misgivings, but they clung to it nonetheless. Among a potentially pantheistic population, hybridized Christianity seemed infinitely preferable to paganism. The point merits extension, for the clerical character of village sociability led inevitably to clerical involvement in village politics. As a tradition of electoral consultation developed in the late eighteenth and nineteenth centuries, the church added a further dimension to its secular role. The resemblance between the pageantry of the hustings and the pageantry of the parish pilgrimage was by no means fortuitous.[86]

The clerical component of popular culture enhanced its integrative capacity. Nominal allegiance to catholicism transcended the barriers of social structure, even if it hesitated before the hurdle of territorial particularism. But if the pervasive religious culture of the region fostered a sense of belonging and encouraged conformity of thought and behaviour, we would do well to remember that the rural community remained a fissured whole. A well-delineated hierarchy of honour and prestige presupposed strains and tensions as well as deference, while household and kinship rivalries kept most parishes

---

[86] P. M. Jones, 'An Improbable Democracy: Nineteenth-Century Elections in the Massif Central', *The English Historical Review*, xcvii (1982), 553–4.

in a state of seething discontent. The rural community evinced a Janus-like character. Explored from within it resembled nothing so much as a nest of vipers, but it presented a different face to the outside world. Moreover, it switched from one stance to the other with remarkable facility. As soon as an external threat loomed over the horizon internecine strife ceased and ranks closed. Rival kin groups and rival villagers gaily cudgelled each other on Patron Saints' days ('nous nous sommes battus, pour la bataille'[87] as a defendant before the Assises of the Haute-Loire put it in the mid nineteenth century), but the arrival of the gendarmerie on the scenes gave the signal for a united assault upon the forces of law and order. Migrant harvesters elicited a similar reflex and were annually aggressed out of a mixture of pure relish and atavistic fear. This pathological dislike of strangers extended to all intrusions whether physical or psychological. The point which should be stressed, however, is that they triggered a community response. The complex rituals of democratic politics tended, as we shall see, to evoke an identical reaction.

[87] Merley, *La Haute-Loire*, i, p. 236.

5

‡‡

The burden of the past

Inherited prejudices fused with the enfolding tissue of popular culture to reduce the autonomy of the rural voter even further and candidates for elective office quickly learned how to call forth these stereotyped reactions. During the parliamentary election of 1863 Pierre Calvet-Rogniat,[1] the incumbent deputy for the second electoral constituency of the Aveyron, reminded the electorate of the dangers of voting for his rival, the Legitimist landowner Victor de Bonald,[2] whose family symbolised noble privilege. As polling day drew nearer the clergy worked hard to scotch this 'épouvantail' while countering with the rumour that the government nominee was a protestant. Or, if he were not a protestant, that he was, in the words of the bishop of Rodez, the preferred candidate of the protestants. Seigneurialism, the sectarian confrontation, memories of the fiscal pressures of the *ancien régime* and of its nemesis in the peasant *jacqueries* of 1789–92 cast long shadows over the political landscape of the nineteenth century. Indeed, vestigial traces of powerful forces of historical conditioning can still be detected. Historians of popular religious cultures have noted the enduring impact of ancient diocesan boundaries long after they have been expunged from the official record and Bercé[3] has drawn our attention to the survival of curiously refractory habits of mind in those parishes of the Limousin and the Quercy which once enjoyed substantial fiscal immunities as part of the Vicomté de Turenne.[4] In the southern Cévennes, meanwhile, the ancestral feuding of catholic and protestant still provides a guide to modern electoral alignments.

Atavisms: the confessional divide

French Calvinists were not particularly numerous by the eighteenth and nineteenth centuries. At the time of the Revocation of the Edict of Nantes

---

[1] A. Maury, 'Presbytères et élections en Aveyron au siècle dernier', *Revue du Rouergue*, xxiii (1969), 157–8.

[2] Victor-Marie-Etienne de Bonald was a grandson of the *philosophe* and ultra-royalist Louis-Gabriel-Ambroise de Bonald and nephew of the cardinal Louis-Jacques-Maurice de Bonald.

[3] Bercé, *Histoire des Croquants*, pp. 650–2.   [4] See above, chapter four, p. 110 and note 5.

(1685) they numbered some 4 per cent of the population but, sapped by emigration and repression, they failed to surmount the demographic challenge of the new century. The Act of Toleration (1787) revealed a faith becalmed which claimed the allegiance of no more than 3 per cent of the population and by the 1880s this had dropped to 2 per cent.[5] Yet the regional picture is more telling. Most protestants lived in well-defined nuclei along a broad arc stretching from Poitou in the North to the Dauphiné in the South East. The densest concentrations occurred in the Agenais, the Béarn and in Languedoc. The mountain massifs rising out of the Garonne basin and the Mediterranean plain provided a natural haven for a religious minority which did not enjoy the protection of the law until 1787. Sizeable colonies of protestant merchants and artisans were to be found in most of the *bourgs* dotted along the high valley of the Tarn and its tributaries, while in the Cévennes a protestant peasantry lived in close proximity to its catholic counterpart. Locally the protestants were often in a majority. Throughout the period covered by this study they outnumbered the adherents of the rival confession in the cantons of Barre-des-Cèvennes, St Germain-de-Calberte and Le Pont-de-Montvert in the Lozère; in the canton of Vernoux in the Ardèche and in the communes of Le Chambon sur Lignon and St Voy (renamed Le Mazet–St Voy in 1894) in the Haute-Loire. Indeed, catholic worship lapsed entirely at Le Mazet–St Voy in 1906. Taken together, the Calvinists represented approximately 9 per cent of the total population of the four departments of the southern Massif Central in 1802 compared with 14 per cent in the Drôme (Dauphiné) and 38 per cent in the Gard.

The protestant diaspora exerted an influence out of all proportion to its numbers, however. For better or worse every parish in these departments felt the imprint of the Reform. In part this was merely a tidal legacy of the triumphant protestantism of the sixteenth century which had left an abundant flotsam of crumbling edifices and abandoned cemeteries in the countryside. More important, it was the product of a rich historical tradition of violence and fear which triggered the reflexes of fanaticism among catholics living miles from the nearest protestant stronghold. By the same token Calvinist apprehensions and anxieties transcended the obstacles of geography and terrain. The dramatic events of 1815[6] were to demonstrate once again how local incidents set in a context of national emergency could precipitate a massive sectarian call-to-arms.

The origins of the sectarian confrontation lay in the bitter strife of the sixteenth and early seventeenth centuries. In the south the religionaries as the huguenots were known lost their military and political independence after the siege of St Affrique in 1628 and the sacking of Privas the following year. Their freedom of worship as laid down in the Edict of Nantes survived until 1685.

[5] J. Garrisson-Estèbe, *L'Homme protestant* (Paris, 1980), p. 70.
[6] See below, chapter six, pp. 209–10.

The Revocation marked a watershed in the grim history of relations between catholic and protestant and it set in train the sequence of events that was responsible for the sectarian bitterness of the eighteenth and nineteenth centuries. Once official toleration had been withdrawn Calvinism lost its *raison d'être*. The temples were destroyed, protestants were forcibly admitted to the catholic church and those who could not stomach the prospect fled. New converts who sought to practise their old religion did so under threat of imprisonment and even martyrdom. Nevertheless, many did so – especially after 1715 – and a period of guerilla warfare ensued which continued spasmodically until the Act of Toleration was passed in 1787. The Camisard revolt was undoubtedly the most spectacular episode in this cycle of violence. It flared in the Cévennes between 1702 and 1705 and expressed the desperate resistance of the peasantry in the face of fiscal aggression as well as the anger and despair of embattled huguenots. Unused to the terrain, royal troops made heavy weather of the repression and atrocities were committed by all parties to the conflict. The most savage incident involved the massacre of thirty-nine civilian inhabitants of Fraissinet-de-Fourques (Lozère) by Camisards recruited from the neighbouring villages of Rousses and Vébron. The echoes of this bloody encounter, which also left up to twenty protestant dead, resounded in local and national election results throughout the nineteenth century.

Delirious sectarian fanaticism was not, in fact, the root cause of the enmity between the inhabitants of Fraissinet and those of Rousses and Vébron, which serves to remind us that the confessional divide tended to replicate and consolidate existing neighbourhood alignments. Rousses had long been an outpost of the parish of Fraissinet without even a chapel of its own. Until 1877, moreover, the two villages jointly owned valuable common land whose management, it may safely be presumed, gave rise to frequent disputes. It transpires, too, that Fraissinet and Rousses belonged to different seigneuries. This fact played an important part in the subsequent tragedy for the seigneur of Rousses espoused the Reform and carried his vassals with him while Fraissinet paid homage to Diane de Poitiers-Valentinois, an eminently catholic seigneur. Thus it was that Fraissinet became a redoubt of catholicism surrounded on all sides by Calvinists. And when, after 1685, its militia began to persecute the 'nouveaux convertis', the village seemed to invite an attack. By the end of the Camisard war Fraissinet had lost a fifth of its population.[7]

The tempo of repression tended to fluctuate in accordance with the exigencies of France's foreign policy. Bouts of warfare with the protestant powers of Europe roused fears of subversion from within. On the other hand, ministers were fearful of precipitating another Camisard-style insurrection and used force with care. The movement of troops to the frontiers or the

[7] R. Poujol, *Vébron, histoire d'un village cévenol* (Aix-en-Provence, 1981), pp. 59–61; 155–64; A.D.L. 2 O 661 *Administration et comptabilité communales*: Fraissinet-de-Fourques.

swapping of intendants could also transform the balance of forces at the local level. Thus, when the Vébron[8] military garrison departed in 1742 upon the outbreak of the War of the Austrian Succession, the number of protestants feigning conversion and having recourse to the parish register of births, marriages and deaths tailed off considerably. Generally speaking, however, the most energetic and systematic repression occurred in the first half of the eighteenth century. After the turmoil and multi-faceted unrest of the last years of the reign of Louis XIV, southern protestants found themselves under renewed pressure between 1742 and 1745; between 1751 and 1755 and between 1761 and 1762. Clear signs of a religious revival, evidenced by widespread reports of itinerant pastors and Desert or open-air assemblies stirred the authorities to action. In 1745 the intendant of Montauban ordered punitive measures against the protestants of the Montalbanais and the Bas Rouergue. Prominent members of the Calvinist bourgeoisie in towns like Millau were arrested or suspended from their professions while the tax burden of the entire protestant community was arbitrarily increased. In addition troops were billeted on villagers suspected of having taken part in illicit assemblies. These *dragonnades* proved painful and risked the very outcome that the authorities were anxious to avoid. A clash between a detachment of troops and villagers at Pechboyer[9] near Montauban left four of the latter dead and three injured. Indignant protestant peasants gathered in support of their comrades and provoked in turn a wide-ranging catholic 'fear'. In the crazed imagination of the catholic population a huguenot army 8,500 strong was reported to have cut to pieces four regiments of the line.

It is tempting to argue that collective hallucination leading to violent hysteria was a normal mode of perception among the peasantry of the southern Massif Central. The insecurity of life in an environment in which natural calamity and supernatural intervention were taken for granted made gnawing anxiety an integral component of the peasant psyche. And psychotic fears which mobilised large numbers of men and women occurred too frequently to be dismissed as deviant behaviour. Reports of food shortages, fire-raising, brigandage and ill-specified conspiracies, as during the infamous 'l'onnado de lo poou [Great Fear]' of 1789, could trigger this reflex, not to mention natural catastrophies such as hail, thunderstorms and pestilence. Religious panics were the enduring characteristic of the southern Massif Central, however. A scattered population lived in superstitious dread of separation from its priests and pastors and the confessional confrontation merely accentuated the sense of impending doom. Consternation returned to the Montalbanais in 1761 when the protestant minister, François Rochette,[10] was captured by the

[8] Poujol, *Vébron*, p. 213.
[9] F. Galabert, 'Les Assemblées de protestants dans le Montalbanais en 1744 et 1745', *Bulletin de la Société de l'histoire du protestantisme français*, xlix (1900), 133.
[10] F. Galabert and L. Boscus, *La Ville de Caussade (Tarn-et-Garonne). Ses vicomtes et ses barons* (Montauban, 1908), pp. 227–41.

night watch of Caussade. The news provoked a determined assault upon the town by armed religionaries which in turn precipitated a ripple of fear among the catholic population. Within twenty-four hours Caussade was turned into a fortress as loyalist reinforcements arrived from neighbouring *bourgs*.

Rochette was hanged on the Place du Salin in Toulouse on 19 February 1762. His death coincided with the judicial slaughter of Calas and the imprisonment of the Sirven family of Mazamet and it caused an outcry. After this date the government abandoned repression as a means of achieving religious orthodoxy. But this does not mean that southern protestantism was tolerated from the 1770s as is sometimes suggested. The penal laws were no longer vigorously enforced, yet they remained on the statute book until 1787 and Calvinists were wary of practising their faith openly. Local incidents and frictions constantly reminded them of their equivocal position. When the protestants of St Voy[11] in the Velay combined to resist payment of the tithe – impropriated by the cathedral chapter of Le Puy – they were pursued in the courts and saddled with a huge bill for arrears, damages and expenses. The ideals of the Enlightenment may have suffused the bench of bishops, but the 'front-line' clergy never lost sight of their old quarry. In 1786 the bishop of Rodez[12] reprimanded the *curé* of Millau and the abbess of a local convent for having spirited a young protestant girl away from her parents.

In any case the damage had been done. The memories of the massacre of Fraissinet, of Desert worship, of the *dragonnades* were ineffaceable. A tradition more secular than religious had been established which divided protestant from catholic on every substantial issue. The inception of electoral democracy during the Revolution merely projected this confrontation onto a broader stage. It elaborated a ritual for the settling of old scores which initially paralleled and then replaced the cruder, bloodier strife of the *ancien régime*. The revolutionary climacteric marked out the phases of this transition. Promoted to power by a combination of electoral advantage and superior activism, the protestants found it expedient to use terror against their opponents by 1793. Likewise the catholics when the wheel of fortune spun in their favour after 1794 and again in 1815. At St Affrique[13] the protestant demagogues of the *comité de surveillance* used their powers of arrest to harass those who had ransomed and imprisoned their ancestors, while at Caussade the Terror was also exploited to redress the historic balance. When the news of the decapitation in Paris of sixteen local royalists

[11] L. Mathieu, *La Paroisse de Saint Voy de Bonas* (Le Puy, 1977), pp. 50–2.

[12] J. Bousquet, 'Un Précédent de l'affaire Finaly en Rouergue (1786): Monseigneur Colbert de Castle-Hill, le pensionnat-couvent de l'Arpajonie et les protestants de Millau', *Revue du Rouergue*, vii (1953), 451–73.

[13] P. M. Jones, 'Political Commitment and Rural Society in the Southern Massif Central', *European Studies Review*, x (1980), 346.

including the *curé* reached the *bourg*, protestants congregated in the streets shouting 'Rochette est vengé'.[14]

The apalling butchery of the White Terror in the Gard and neighbouring departments brought to a conclusion the physical confrontation of catholic and protestant. After 1815 the violence was mostly verbal and mostly confined to the electoral arena. Yet the rehabilitation of protestantism as a legally recognised faith had, if anything, increased the opportunities for friction. To the perennial pressure-points of schools, cemeteries and child abductions were added disputes over public religious ceremonies, provisions for the fabric of the two state churches and mixed marriages. In the interests of civil peace a law of 18 Germinal X (8 April 1802) had forbidden religious processions in *bourgs* containing a consistorial church. Notwithstanding this measure protestants had generally been willing to show appropriate respect for the solemnities of the rival religion, however. Yet as catholicism became more militant and royalist in tone that forebearance swiftly evaporated. After the bitter deception of the Hundred Days, few protestants in the Cévennes were prepared to yield on the issue, reported the prefect of the Lozère in 1818.[15] At Florac only three protestants had obeyed local bylaws and draped their houses for the Corpus Christi [Fête-Dieu] procession; at Meyrueis one and at Barre-des-Cévennes two. In addition, all but one of the protestant householders of St Germain-de-Galberte had not even bothered to clean their frontages. Intermittently, the Calvinists refused acknowledgement of the festivals of the catholic church for the rest of the century and the rancorous anti-clericalism of the Combes ministry brought fresh fuel to the conflict. After provocative catholic processions had caused unrest in the *bourg* of Florac throughout 1903, the municipality introduced a bylaw to enforce the provisions of the Napoleonic statute regarding external religious pomp. This ban was still effective in 1931 when the *curé* sought to challenge it in the courts. Despite attempts at conciliation, the affair went to appeal and in 1934 the Conseil d'Etat upheld the municipality's *arrêté*.[16] By this time the issue had lost much of its animus for the clergy no longer insisted upon processing through the protestant quarters of the consistorial *chefs-lieux*, but during the Restoration it had placed protestant notables and office holders in a cruel dilemma. In 1818 Pierre-Bertrand Brun de Villeret, a deputy for the Lozère and a pronounced opponent of the 'ultras', warned that the strong-arm tactics of the sub-prefect of Florac were likely to precipitate the conflagration in the Cévennes that had been so narrowly averted in 1815: 'il s'est conduit pour des affaires de religion à la manière de l'abbé du Chayla'. Honourable servants of the state were being asked to make an intolerable choice. Monsieur Jean Renouard, a Calvinist and a former *commissaire de police*,

[14] *Ibid.*, 346–7.
[15] A.N. BB[18] 984 Prefect Lozère to Minister of the Interior, Mende, 11 June 1818.
[16] A.D.L. 2 O 627 *Administration et comptabilité communales*: Florac, processions.

'me disoit qu'il seroit forcé de rompre pour la vie avec tous ses amis et toute sa famille, si dans une occasion de même nature, il adhéroit encore aux vues de M. le sous-préfet'.[17]

Squabbles over parish allocation and ecclesiastical provision also helped to fan the embers of sectarian tension. The rehabilitation of Calvinism presupposed a massive programme of institutional re-equipment – especially after 1804 when the state shouldered the financial burden of the newly established consistorial churches. Catholics regarded this effort with a jaundiced eye and tended to view money spent on the protestant faith as money lost for their own. The generous ecclesiastical hand-outs of the Restoration redressed the balance somewhat, but the munificence of the July Monarchy seemed to favour the pastorate once more and caused deep suspicion. In the Bas Vivarais – the theatre of the Camps de Jalès[18] of 1790–1 – villagers believed that all the ministers of state were protestants and expected the death of Louis-Philippe to usher in a Regency under the protestant widow of the Duke of Orléans who had died in 1842. The provision of decent places of worship posed the most immediate problem. Most of the temples had been pulled down after the Revocation. That of St Affrique had been rebuilt in 1807 only to be destroyed once more in 1815.[19] Unsurprisingly, catholic taxpayers were reluctant to help restore the edifices of a cult which they did not profess. But the fabric of the catholic church was in need of restoration, too, and Calvinist dominated municipalities were expert in dodging expenditure of this nature. In the Cévennes catholic minorities petitioned endlessly for their clergy to be decently housed. More often than not, the old presbytery had been bought by a protestant during the Revolution. Occasionally the temples had been left intact and reconsecrated for catholic worship which stored up intractable problems for the future. At Vialas (Lozère)[20] local catholics had taken over the well-appointed temple sometime between 1684 and 1686 and it became their parish church. After 1787 the majority community made every effort to retrieve it and during the early years of the Revolution both confessions used the building. The Concordat seemed to settle the matter for the catholic parish of Vialas was disestablished and in 1805 the temple re-emerged in all its old glory. Two years later, however, the government relaxed its budgetary controls and the parish of Vialas was restored. The diminutive congregation of catholics now faced the daunting task of building a new place of worship, a task that was not completed until 1824.

As these examples indicate, protestants and catholics often lived in close

---

[17] A.N. F⁷ 9675 Brun de Villeret to *Monsieur le secrétaire-général* [of the Minister of the Interior?], St Chély-d'Apcher, 26 June 1818.

[18] See below, chapter six, p. 198.

[19] J. Cabantous, *Documents pour servir à l'histoire du protestantisme à Saint Affrique au dix-neuvième siècle* (Montauban, 1896), pp. 11–35.

[20] A.D.L. L189 *Cultes, circonscription des paroisses.*

familiarity despite their manifold differences. Just how close is difficult to gauge. The geography of confessional allegiance tended to be fairly well defined in the *bourgs*, but exhibited no overall pattern in the countryside (see chapter eight, p. 253). At Vernoux,[21] for instance, the catholic population clustered around the church and in the southern quarters of the *bourg*, while the heavily outnumbered protestants were mostly to be found living near the temple and in the quarters of Le Manège and the Place du Cadet. In the rural commune the two faiths intermingled, although the majority of households were Calvinist. Mixed marriages were unusual although, in view of what has been said, it is perhaps surprising that they occurred at all. The bishop of Mende was informed of fifteen such unions when he visited Florac in 1836.[22] Approximately a third of the 2,000 inhabitants of the commune were Calvinists. The centripetal forces which prompted mixed marriages are rarely identified in our sources, but it seems likely that in extreme conditions neighbourhood and kinship pressures cut across confessional rivalries. An incident at Meyrueis[23] in 1808 suggests as much. Baptism of the infant offspring of a mixed marriage was interrupted by an irate father who denied that he had given his consent. The parents were germain cousins and it is probable that the union was a product of household strategy.

What clearly emerges is that Calvinists and catholics were conditioned by distinctive and antagonistic historical traditions and in this sense belonged to separate communities. Nevertheless, the divide was neither constant over time nor unbridgeable and there is evidence to suggest that, in some localities, the peasantry continued to derive nourishment from a cultural tradition which ignored sectarian differences. The notion of a transcendent cultural community embracing catholic and huguenot should not be exaggerated, but the alternative stereotype of 'superstitious' catholicism and bible-thumping Calvinism is repeated too frequently to pass without comment.[24] Common sense, alone, would suggest that where the two confessions lived in close physical contact, inter-penetration occurred routinely. Protestant servants were placed in catholic households and vice versa; protestant and catholic children frequented the same schools and protestant peasants enjoyed the pageantry of catholic festivals much as they would any other kind of spectacle. Of course, they may have hastened to hear the preaching of Jesuit missionaries, or to witness the casting out of devils by priests because their own folklore was deficient. Yet the pastors found plenty of popular culture left to deplore in their sermons. At Vébron in the heart of the Cévennes pastor

---

[21] A. Sabatier, *Religion et politique au XIXe siècle. Le Canton de Vernoux-en-Vivarais* (Vernoux, 1975), pp. 140–3, map and table.
[22] A.E.M. Parish dossiers: Florac.
[23] A.N. F[19] 5686 Consistory of Meyrueis to *Ministre des Cultes*, Meyrueis, 13 December 1808.
[24] E. Le Roy Ladurie, *Les Paysans de Languedoc* (2 vols., Paris, 1966), i, pp. 613–14; Burke, *Popular Culture in Early Modern Europe*, p. 223.

Vincent delivered a long allocution against 'les divins, les conjurateurs, les sorciers et les demi-protestants qui font dire des messes'[25] in 1845. The point which should be stressed, however, is that these convergent tendencies were held in check by bouts of sectarian warfare. When the Jesuit fathers of Florac overplayed their hand and engaged the pastor in a bitter polemic, protestants stopped listening to their sermons and withdrew their children from the school run by the Brothers of the Christian Doctrine. Mixed parishes had to evolve a means of coexistence – however querulous and contingent it may have been. No such compromise was demanded of those areas outside the immediate stress zones. Here the gulf remained unbridged and the clergy wasted no opportunity of building higher the wall of fearful incomprehension. Protestants who strayed into the mountain fortresses of rural catholicism on the eve of the First World War aroused intense curiosity. In the Monts de Lacaune[26] many peasants supposed them to be cyclops while in a village near Mende, Maurice Brajon[27] remembers going to inspect a protestant workman whom the blacksmith had hired. The children of the village expected him to have a black throat.

Atavisms: fiscal aggression

Travellers on the high plateaux of the Massif Central were often mistaken for writ-servers or tax collectors. Occasionally, their requests for shelter and importunate questions provoked an armed insurrection. Be that as it may, we learn from such sources that a century after the Revolution the peasantry continued to refer to state taxes as the *taille*, to their landlords as the *seigneurs*, and to the imposition in support of the church (which was still collected in some localities) as the *dîme*. The continuing use of such archaisms was not peculiar to the southern Massif Central, of course, but the concrete memories which each evoked undoubtedly were. The terms *taille* and *taillaïre* (the tax collector) conjured to the mind images of institutionalised fiscal abuse, of financial racketeering by village potentates and of parties of bailiffs threading their way through the countryside from one farm to the next. Associated with these images we find several of the facets of peasant behaviour already noted: the mixture of explosive defiance and resignation, the ingrained distrust of strangers and the vulnerability to rumour and sudden, unreasoning bouts of fear.

The southern Massif Central fell within the region of the *taille réelle*; that is to say that the principal royal imposition was assessed on land. The extent, status, ownership and yield of the land surfaces in each fiscal unit

---

[25] Poujol, *Vébron*, p. 260. For the full text of this sermon, see P. Joutard, 'Protestantisme populaire et univers magique: le cas cévenol', *Le Monde alpin et rhodanien*, (1977), 166–71.

[26] Faury, *Cléricalisme et anticléricalisme dans le Tarn*, p. 359.

[27] Brajon and Arnaud, *Monsieur Brajon, maître d'école*, p.138.

(*communauté d'habitants*) was enshrined in a register known as a *cadastre* or *compoix*. As part of the Auvergne, the Brivadois, it is true, was subject to the *taille personnelle* or taxation by crude administrative estimation, but from the 1730s elements of the *taille réelle* were introduced here too. In theory this meant that taxes were levied on a scientific basis, but the convenient dichotomy of an arbitrary *taille personnelle* and a judiciously apportioned *taille réelle* so beloved of historians fails to withstand scrutiny. The *cadastres* were not renewed as soil conditions and land exploitation evolved, they were rarely kept up to date and they were compiled in a non-standardised and sometimes highly eccentric fashion. As a result fiscal discrepancies arose between provinces and between households which were out of proportion to the variations in productivity. Such discrepancies were unavoidable in any case for they were inherent to the regime. The monarchy fixed the yield of taxation in advance and employed a quota system to distribute its load. Payment was a matter for collective responsibility, backed by the threat of free billeting and distraint in the event of default. At every level administrative caprice compounded the defects in the *cadastres*.

The Revolution enormously reduced the scale of fiscal maladministration, but the daunting task of cataloguing the land surfaces of France was scarcely begun. This reform awaited the advent of Napóleon and it deserves to be ranked alongside the great achievements of 1789. In the southern Massif Central the compilation of systematic land registers for each commune occupied most of the first half of the nineteenth century. All previous attempts at reform had foundered on the knowledge that the cure would almost certainly be a greater affliction than the disease. Until the fiscal structure of the *ancien régime* was abolished, the abatement of taxation in one locality would probably result in an increased burden elsewhere. The same imperative made tax adjustments as between individuals within the same *communauté d'habitants* infinitely difficult and dangerous. When Colbert[28] ordered an adjustment of the *cadastres* of the *généralité* of Montauban in 1666, the results proved profoundly discouraging. Seventy years later the intendant admitted that this shoddy and ill-advised tinkering had probably made matters worse. In recognition of the fact a fund of 120,000 *l.* was created in 1727 to provide relief to hardpressed communities. It goes without saying that the 'trop allivré' as these sums were called was financed by means of another tax.

When taxpayers could no longer withstand the burden they took to the roads, and during the grim decades marking the end of the reign of Louis XIV they decamped in droves. Entire communities renounced their possessions and lands and joined the miserable stream of humanity heading out of the mountains towards the Languedoc plain. Jean-François Henry de

---

[28] Guilhamon, *Journal des voyages*, i, xxxiv–xxxv.

Richeprey's testimony is invaluable in this respect.[29] Commissioned by the Provincial assembly of Haute-Guienne in October 1780 to begin the groundwork for a new cadastral survey, he tirelessly chronicled the illogicality of fiscal and seigneurial structures which actually undermined wealth production. Much of the waste and heathland covering the plateaux and hillsides of the Rouergue on the eve of the Revolution, had been abandoned earlier in the century. At Boisse[30] the villagers collectively renounced their possessions and handed the keys of their houses to the *receveur* in 1691; at Belmont[31] which enjoyed the reputation of being the most heavily taxed community in the *élection* of Millau, the inhabitants did likewise. Much of the land surface of this community was still waste when Richeprey visited it some decades later. At St Just[32] many households had given up the unequal struggle and migrated across the border into Languedoc; at Najac[33] at least a third of the arable surface had been abandoned. The fiscal malaise left its mark on the *bourgs* as well. At Laguiole[34] the community of inhabitants struggled to pay the *tailles* on crumbling houses long since disowned. The implacability of a government hungry for revenue was not the only canker gnawing at the productive base of the country, of course, and in the Rouergue much land was brought back into cultivation during the second half of the eighteenth century, notwithstanding fiscal and seigneurial disincentives. Nevertheless, intermittent abandonment, distraint, accumulating arrears and ineffective bureaucratic palliatives remained integral features of the *ancien régime* tax system. In the Brivadois and the High Auvergne where cadastration was in its infancy, the anomalies in the distribution of the *taille* were more glaring still. On the eve of the Revolution the Assembly of the *élection* of St Flour reported that in a sample survey of thirty-three parishes, they had discovered eighty-one juridically abandoned landholdings.[35] The northern slopes of the Margeride were littered with deserted settlements whose inhabitants had migrated.

The Gévaudan, the Velay and the Vivarais were *pays d'états* whose fiscal obligations issued from the Estates of Languedoc rather than the intendant. This made little difference in practice since the Estates had long since forfeited financial control to the monarchy. They merely retained the right to distribute the burden of royal impositions as they saw fit. A provincial *compoix* determined the proportions in which taxation was to be allocated between the 'pays' and civil dioceses whereupon diocesan *compoix* laid down the basis of allocation between the communities of inhabitants and so on. Yet, for all the symmetry of this system, it proved inadequate for precisely the same reasons as those already mentioned in connection with the *généralité* of

---

[29] See Guilhamon, *Journal des voyages.*   [30] *Ibid.,* i, p. 182 note 1.   [31] *Ibid.,* i, p. 255.
[32] *Ibid.,* i, p. 300.   [33] *Ibid.,* i, p. 417.   [34] *Ibid.,* i, p. 47.
[35] Archives Départementales du Puy-de-Dôme (henceforth A.D.P.-de-D.) C7373 *Procès-verbal de l'assemblée d'élection de St Flour,* October 1788.

Montauban. The *cadastre* furnished a static image of landholdings and taxable wealth. Without regular and conscientious updating, it quickly became unreliable. The provincial *compoix* of Languedoc was established in 1530 and all attempts to have it modified before 1789 failed. The same may be said of the diocesan *compoix* which were nearly all of sixteenth-century vintage too. At the end of the *ancien régime*, therefore, the *taille* and the *vingtième* were levied in Languedoc according to computations of population density and net income made two centuries earlier. In practice this resulted in a disproportionately heavy burden for the inhabitants of the Toulousain and the Narbonnais whose prosperity had formerly rested on the cultivation of the woad plant. By contrast, the mountain *pays* of the Gévaudan, the Velay, the Vivarais, the dioceses of Nîmes and Alès, and the Albigeois were generally acknowledged to have been under-taxed in relation to the province as a whole.

The burden of taxation punishing agriculture in the *élections* left a deep imprint upon the population. In frontier parishes and those localities subject to onerous seigneurial dues, it distorted the rural economy as well as colouring the popular memory. Travellers crossing into Languedoc from the Brivadois or from the *élection* of Millau were immediately struck by the contrast. The roads were better and not built by conscripted labour; villagers looked more prosperous and less distrustful. At Laguépie[36] – a *bourg* straddling the river border between the Rouergue and Languedoc – the inhabitants informed Richeprey that dwellings in the Rouergue paid fifteen times as much *taille* as those situated in the Albigeois on the opposite bank. Even if this was an exaggeration it is significant to note how keenly the difference was perceived. In any case tell-tale signs of poverty and neglect were everywhere visible. He observed that the portion of the bridge over the Viaur maintained by the Estates was in good repair while the remainder appeared very dilapidated. The implications of this state of affairs for agriculture should not be under-estimated. The inhabitants of Belmont[37] expended most of their energy on the landholdings they had acquired over the border in Languedoc where the *taille* was only a third that levied on their possessions in the Rouergue.

Despite the wealth of anecdotal detail furnished by Richeprey's incomparable survey, or by the enquiry into the *capitation* mounted by the Estates of Languedoc in 1734, the broad contours of royal taxation in the decades before the Revolution are far from clear. The estimates of average per capita direct taxation (*taille, vingtièmes, capitation, accessoires*) made by contemporaries are given in table V.1. These figures beg many questions, but the crude order of magnitude compares favourably with the conclusions drawn from piecemeal evidence. Calculations of this sort shed no light on the relative

[36] Guilhamon, *Journal des voyages*, i, pp. 430–1.   [37] *Ibid.*, i, lxxx; pp. 261–2.

Table V.1 *Average per capita direct taxation*

Region	Date	Estimate
		(taille, vingtièmes, capitation, accessoires)
Brivadois[1] (*élection* of Brioude)	1788	10 *l.* 10 *s.*
Velay[2]	1788	5 *l.* 4 *s.*
Quercy[3]	1790	10 *l.* 0 *s.*
Rouergue[4]	1790	11 *l.* 5 *s.*
Vivarais[5]	1790	4 *l.* 8 *s.*
Gévaudan[6]	1790	7 *l.* 1 *s.*
		(contribution foncière)
Haute-Loire[7]	1791	6 *l.* 3 *s.*
Lot[8]	1791	7 *l.* 9 *s.*
Aveyron[9]	1791	9 *s.* 5 *s.*
Ardèche[10]	1791	4 *l.* 4 *s.*
Lozère[11]	1791	6 *l.* 4 *s.*

Sources: 1 Merley, *La Haute-Loire*, i, p. 89; 2 *Ibid.*; 3 R. Schnerb, *La Péréquation fiscale de l'assemblée constituante, 1790–91* (Clermont-Ferrand, 1936), map 2; 4 to 6 *Ibid.*; 7 to 11 *Ibid.*, map 6.

burden of royal fiscality upon peasant surplus, however. Generalisations on this subject are exceedingly rare although an *expert-féodiste* of Rodez reckoned that state direct taxes deprived the peasant of the Rouergue of about a quarter of his produce at the end of the *ancien régime*. This seems plausible. The Provincial Assembly of Haute-Guienne declared that – ideally – the *taille* should amount to one sixth of net income (income after the tithe and costs of cultivation had been deducted). Richeprey's painstaking enquiries revealed that several notoriously overburdened communities forfeited between 25 and 30 per cent of their net income to pay the *taille* alone, while others paid less than 10 per cent. Within communities the amplitude was often greater. Such was the antiquity of the *cadastres* that individual plots of non-noble land were sometimes assessed at rates *in excess* of their net annual yield while others contributed a mere 1 or 2 per cent. The anomalies of the *taille* were naturally reflected in the *vingtièmes* since these subsidies were also geared to landholding, but the *capitation* presumed to tax all forms of wealth on the basis of cursory inspection. As the protestants[38] of the *élection* of Millau discovered, it proved a tempting target for unscrupulous manipulation. Anachronism and abuse in varying proportions characterised the tax structure of the *pays d'élections* at the end of the *ancien régime*. This much is certain, but further generalisation is hazardous. Computations of the

[38] See above, p. 148.

average tax burden per head of population have an air of unreality for the
intensity of fiscal pressure varied from village to village and even from field
to field. In any case, taxes were paid not by individuals, but by households
and communities. Moreover, they were often paid in conditions and circumstances that greatly aggravated their burden.

The trend of royal taxation was firmly upwards and it affected *pays d'états*
and *pays d'élections* alike. The Breton Estates[39] were able to deflect the
pressure, apparently, but Languedoc bore the full weight of the monarchy's
quest for revenue, perhaps because it enjoyed the dubious blessing of the *taille
réelle*. In this region the opinion was generally held that taxes had doubled in
the two decades prior to the Revolution. The researches of Georges Frêche[40]
lend weight to this conviction. The *taille* rose continuously from 1600 to
1790 with sharp escalations between 1600 and 1626, 1638 and 1661, and
1765 and 1790. In the civil diocese of Lavaur direct royal taxation doubled
between 1751–56 and 1784–90. Inflation and possibly rises in agricultural
productivity must be allowed for, but it is difficult to escape the conclusion
that in certain critical periods – the 1630s and the closing decades of the
ancien régime – the monarchy massively increased its share of peasant
surplus. The trend was no less disquieting across the border in the *élections*
of Haute-Guienne. In June 1643 a Croquant army entered Villefranche-de-
Rouergue[41] voicing the demand that the *taille* be reduced to pre-Richelieu
levels and sporadic anti-fiscal revolts continued to occur in the Quercy until
1707. Between 1723 and 1780 direct taxation per head of population in the
généralité of Montauban (Rouergue and Quercy) tripled on average.[42]

As the monarchy's financial plight deepened, the intendants and agents of
the General Farm increasingly resorted to deceit and coercion and the temper
of the countryside rose accordingly. Attempts by Lescalopier[43] to requisition
labour for road building in the midst of the harvest provoked agrarian disturbances in 1752. The murmurs of discontent assumed a more alarming
character in the late 1770s when the monarch and several other seigneurs
sought to collect a tax known as the *commun de paix*.[44] Imposed in the
twelfth century, this tax supposedly protected the inhabitants of the four
châtellenies of the Rouergue from the attentions of mercenary bands
employed by warring seigneurs. Resistance crystallised first in the ségala and
by 1780 sixty parishes were disaffected in this region alone. The ségala also
bore the brunt of the exactions of the Administration Générale des Domaines

[39] Le Goff, *Vannes and its Region*, p. 128.
[40] G. Frêche, *Toulouse et la région Midi-Pyrénées au siècle des lumières (vers 1670–1789)*
(Mayenne, 1974), p. 503.
[41] E. Le Roy Ladurie, *The Mind and Method of the Historian* (Brighton, 1981), p. 316.
[42] E. Dufour, *Etude sur l'assemblée provinciale de la Haute-Guyenne* (Cahors, 1881), p. 30.
[43] Gaspard César Charles de Lescalopier, intendant of the *généralité* of Montauban from 1740
until 1756, was chiefly remembered for having introduced the *corvée* to the region.
[44] Guilhamon, *Journal des voyages*, i, xlvii; p. 316.

du Roi which Necker had established in 1777. Its local agents were as adept in conjuring up new taxes as were the feudal lawyers in discovering old seigneurial dues. Richeprey reported in 1781 that they had contrived to impose a *droit de lods* in favour of the king without prejudice to the *lods et ventes* due to the immediate seigneur. The duty and arrears of duty over the past twenty-nine years were being claimed from those liable by means of writs, without even offering them the opportunity to make voluntary payment. The peasantry of the ségala resisted sullenly until the events of 1789 unleashed a *jacquerie* on the scale of the Croquant rebellion of the previous century. The rising tension was reflected in the spiralling cost of fiscal repression. In 1779 the intendant admitted that the expense of writs and legal distraint added some 70–80,000 *l.* to the tax liabilities of the *généralité*. A member of the Provincial Assembly of Haute-Guienne proposed the much higher estimate of 150,000 *l.* per annum. The *élection* of Villefranche-de-Rouergue, alone, provided employment for 106 writ-servers instead of the statutory six.[45]

Unscrupulous fiscal policies enforced ruthlessly by unscrupulous officials galvanised the community into a posture of defence. There is, therefore, a sense in which the fiscal aggression of the late *ancien régime* precipitated a *prise de conscience* in the countryside. This is especially noticeable in localities where the fiscal unit – the community of inhabitants – was relatively compact or where it matched the territory of the parish or the seigneurie.[46] No issue was more likely to call forth the reflex of solidarity than that of exemptions – the exemption of land classified as noble – from the *taille*. As the burden of royal taxation escalated, communities contested this kind of privilege with increasing vigour and their desperation focused attention upon the system as a whole. Challenges to the status of land presupposed long and costly litigation and were not embarked upon lightly. Failure in the cumbersome administrative courts of the *ancien régime* could easily mortgage the receipts of a community for a generation. Nevertheless, the intendants and their subordinates noted a wearisome tendency among consuls to launch lawsuits against their seigneurs, especially those of the most recent promotion. The community of Privezac[47] near Rignac was embroiled in a conflict of this type throughout the 1780s and it spilled over into the Revolution. Having purchased the seigneurie and château of Privezac from the Duc de Caylus in 1770, Le Brunet de Paillez, *trésorier de France* and president of the Bureau des Finances of Riom, declared that part of the property was noble and therefore exempt from the *taille*. These pretensions were stoutly resisted and in 1785 a court verdict required Le Brunet de Paillez to pay to the community 5,000 *l.* in arrears of *taille*.

[45] *Ibid.*, i, p. 259 note 1.
[46] As in the Gévaudan and the Velay; see above, chapter four, pp. 110–11.
[47] Guilhamon, *Journal des voyages*, i, p. 389 and note 1.

The embarrassment of the new châtelain of Privezac was unusual and he afterwards claimed that the community had been stirred up by local bourgeois activists. The complaints reaching Richeprey's ears mostly underlined the skill with which large taxpayers contrived to pay little or no tax at all. At Naves[48] the principal inhabitant had acquired an exempting office and thereby side-stepped his share (100 *l.*) of the *capitation* which consequently fell upon the community. At Sainte Croix the bigwigs escaped the *capitation* by strategically withdrawing to Villefranche-de-Rouergue, where assessments were lower, at the start of every winter: 'à leur exemple nombre de nos demy paysans demy bourgeois nous menacaient de donner à ferme leur bien fons (*sic*) et de se retirer à Villefranche où leur taxe ne seroit que 6 *l.* dans le temps qu'ils seroient ici compris dans le rôle pour 60 *l.*'.[49]

The revealing remark of the seigneur of Privezac serves to remind us that the punitive fiscality of the *ancien régime* invigorated the defence mechanisms of the rural community in another way, too. It initiated to positions of leadership a generation of bourgeois proprietors whose new-found prestige and self-confidence received appropriate political recognition in 1789. To be sure, the roles of seigneur, agent of the fisc and village notable were never clear cut. Nor did the counterweight of elite leadership from within the Third Estate come cheap. Many a bourgeois proprietor led his community on a financially ruinous crusade for objects tangential to the general good, and expert advice and helmsmanship was more or less tacitly paid for in the coin of privileged access to the commons and other local amenities. But the *coqs de village* of the revolutionary generation never had the chance to become the petty seigneurs and venal office holders of the next. Brought to maturity by the fiscal and seigneurial struggles of preceding decades and shorn of the ambiguities of *ancien régime* notable status by the Revolution, they glided effortlessly into the positions of power in the countryside.

Atavisms: seigneurialism

Attempts by the monarchy to extend its regalian rights and the issue of fiscal exemptions lead directly to a consideration of seigneurialism. There is no doubting its reality in the southern Massif Central, nor the phenomenon of a seigneurial reaction in the closing decades of the *ancien régime*. Richeprey's splendid domesday survey chronicles the pervasive impact of feudalism on every other page. The ghosts of this servile system were less easily exorcised, however. In 1793 the assembled inhabitants of the canton of Le Cheylard (Ardèche) swore never to suffer 'le retour des privilèges, des dîmes, des rentes,

---

[48]   *Ibid.*, ii, p. 311.
[49]   A.N. DXIV 2 *Comités des Assemblées*, petition of inhabitants of Ste Croix, 29 May 1790.

des lods, des corvées, ni d'aucun autre droit féodal',[50] yet the presentiment that these nightmarish spectres would indeed return lingered on unseasonably. Folk tales of sheaves of corn being carted off to château or monastic granary would continue to excite the apprehension of their grandchildren, even their great-grandchildren. Servile habits of mind lingered on as well. The 'feudalisation' of democratic politics (see chapter nine, pp. 295–304) in which votes were traded for favours – the opening of a new road, perhaps, or the gift of a fine picture to hang above the altar – was partly attributable to the shadow of seigneurialism.

Before the Revolution nearly all land was held by feudal tenure and therefore subject to a variety of seigneurial obligations. In the southern Massif Central these obligations took the form of a harvest tax (*champart*), an annual monetary payment (*censive*), a duty levied on the transmission of property (*lods et ventes*) and other lesser items. Labour service was rare by the eighteenth century, but seigneurs occasionally demanded it. In addition, all landholdings were subject to the ecclesiastical tithe. Seigneurial dues, like the *dîme*, were deducted from gross farm product immediately after the harvest and usually through an intermediary or *fermier des droits féodaux*. The territorial incoherence of the seigneurie in much of the region and the lack of reliable data make precise calculation of the burden on peasant surplus exceedingly difficult. Painstaking research by Leymarie[51] suggests that in the Haute-Auvergne harvest dues deprived the peasant household of at least 10 per cent of the net produce of the land. In the grain-growing *planèze* of St Flour, this rose to over 20 per cent. The fertile plains of Brioude and Issoire were equally if not more heavily burdened. According to one computation,[52] the feudal relationship creamed off 24 per cent of the agricultural product in the Brivadois towards the end of the *ancien régime*. In the Velay, by contrast, it seems that the seigneurial burden was much lighter, 13 per cent. It is questionable whether these figures permit anything more than loose comparison. The results obtained depend upon a number of variables and the method of calculation employed in each case is far from clear. Scientific measurement of the weight of seigneurial dues in the Rouergue has barely commenced. Instead, we have the evidence of informed contemporary opinion. 'Les terres soumises au droit de champart', reported the Provincial Assembly of Haute-Guienne, 'sont condamnées à la stérilité par la nature même de leur institution. Dans la pluspart des terres de cette espèce sur douze gerbes le seigneur

---

[50] C. Riffaterre, 'Les Revendications économiques et sociales des assemblées primaires de juillet 1793', *Commission de recherche et de publication des documents relatifs à la vie économique de la Révolution, Bulletin trimestriel* (1906), 353.

[51] M. Leymarie, 'Les Redevances foncières seigneuriales en Haute-Auvergne', *Annales historiques de la Révolution française*, xl (1968), 327.

[52] *L'Abolition de la féodalité dans le monde occidental* (Colloque du C.N.R.S., Toulouse, 12–16 novembre 1968) (2 vols., Paris, 1971), i, pp. 118–22; ii, pp. 622–3; J.-P. Gutton, *La Sociabilité villageoise dans l'ancienne France* (Paris, 1979), p. 164.

en retire trois, le décimateur une, les impositions en absorbe deux, il faut distraire de celles qui restent deux pour la semence et trois pour les frais de culture.'[53] Richeprey's laborious enquiries lend weight to this generalisation. In many parts of the Quercy and the Rouergue the *champart* alone took between 20 and 25 per cent of gross land incomes.

The southern Massif Central remained a bastion of vigorous seigneur-ialism on a par with Brittany at the end of the *ancien régime*. Of this there can be little doubt. Yet within this region the economic burden of the seigneurial regime varied a good deal. It was intense in the Haute-Auvergne around St Flour, in the Brivadois, in the Bas Vivarais and the Cévennes, and in the ségalas of the Rouergue and the Quercy. Indeed, the peasantry of the *sénéchaussées* of Gourdon, Figeac and Rodez may well have suffered feudal exactions without parallel on the eve of the Revolution. By contrast, it appears to have been much lighter on the high pastoral plateaux of the Aubrac and the Mézenc, throughout the Gévaudan (save for the Cévennes) and in the Haut Vivarais. Ecological differences go some way towards explaining these discrepancies, but the vicissitudes of history seem to have played a more important role. Not surprisingly, the burden was greatest in those localities subject to the *champart* (also called the *quint*) and yet this proportional harvest due was not established in all cereal-growing areas. We encounter it in the Haute-Guienne and the Haute-Auvergne and in the adjacent parishes of the Gévaudan, but it becomes progressively rarer east of these points. The principal seigneurial impositions in the Gévaudan and the Velay were the *censive* – a fixed payment likely to depreciate over time – and the *lods et ventes* which were occasional.

The misfortune of the peasant of the ségala, to cite the most extreme and best documented case, lay in the fact that he paid *all* the major dues and many lesser ones such as the *acaptes* and *arrière acaptes* at maximum rates. Moreover, his temporal and spiritual seigneurs were often one and the same. No question of subscribing a tithe for the upkeep of the parish priest; instead he watched as a sizeable proportion of his harvest was loaded on to the over-seer's wagons each September and carted off to the monastic storehouse from which it would likely be dished out to all and sundry in the form of alms. In localities subject to the institutional lordship of the monastery of Bonnecombe, approximately a quarter of the harvest disappeared in this fashion and there were often *censives* to be paid, too. At Frons,[54] the inhabi-tants avoided cereal cultivation as far as possible and instead planted fruit trees which were exempt from the *champart*. At Jalenques where the

---

[53] A.D.A. C1530 *Procès-verbal des séances de l'Assemblée provinciale de Haute-Guienne*, 13 September 1780, also quoted by J. Bastier, 'Droits féodaux et revenus agricoles en Rouergue à la veille de la Révolution', *Annales du Midi*, lxxxxv (1983), 261–87 whose recently published article is the first systematic attempt to explore the incidence of seigneurial obligations in the Rouergue.
[54] Guilhamon, *Journal des voyages*, ii, p. 300.

seigneurie had been sold in large part to a bourgeois family, Richeprey could find only one comfortably off peasant household. 'Cette communauté est écrasée sous le poids des impositions seigneuriales', he noted, 'tous les grains sont sujets au quint outre la dixme, ce qui revient au quart. Au dessus de ce droit si pernicieux à l'agriculture il sont tenus encore de payer sur ce même fonds où on a levé déjà le quart des grains, une très-forte censive.'[55] *Champart* and *censive* were also collected at Le Bosc, Castelmary, and Lédergues.

Seigneurial obligations, and especially lucrative obligations, were being enforced with greater rigour and efficiency, too. In the South and in the West where the economic dimension of feudalism narrowly outlived the passing of the *ancien régime* seigneurial 'reaction' was endemic. Seigneur and peasant community were locked in subterranean conflict which, if it did not preclude a measure of consensus, presupposed relations of chronic instability as first one party and then the other gained the upper hand. The seigneurial offensive which marked the decades after 1760 was not unique, therefore, but it was specific. In the southern Massif Central a number of converging trends can be identified: the temptation of higher grain prices; the inflationary squeeze affecting the incomes of the petty nobility; the escalating demand for ecclesiastical alms; the preoccupations of rentiers seeking a secure investment; the social ambitions of a flourishing rural bourgeoisie, and by no means least, the emergence to full professional status of a class of entrepreneurs – feudal lawyers and surveyors – who brought a capitalist's zeal to the business of the enforcement and collection of seigneurial dues. As far as the peasantry were concerned the symptoms of these multiple pressures were everywhere similar: a rapid turn-over of seigneurs; a confusing proliferation of petty seigneurs; a growing neglect of non-lucrative seigneurial responsibilities and abusively frequent renewals of the registers of pecuniary obligations (*terriers*). This divorce between rights and responsibilities was, perhaps, the most signal feature of the seigneurial reaction of the late *ancien régime*. Hitherto the skirmishing between lords and their vassals had been conducted within well understood limits and had not called into question the existence of a seigneurial community. In all but a few privileged localities that sense of community had been irretrievably lost by the end of the *ancien régime*. The institutions of seigneurialism were openly and bitterly condemned. The peasantry made over a proportion of their crops to seigneurs whom they never saw and had no compunction about initiating lawsuits in a bid to stem the attrition. Yves and Nicole Castan[56] have drawn our attention

---

[55] *Ibid.*, ii, p. 321.
[56] Y. Castan, 'Attitudes et motivations dans les conflits entre seigneurs et communautés devant le parlement de Toulouse au XVIIIe siècle', *Villes de l'Europe méditerranéenne: de l'Europe occidental du Moyen Age au XIXe siècle* (Actes du Colloque de Nice, 27–28 mars 1969) (Paris, 1969), p. 233 and N. Castan, 'Crime et justice en Languedoc, 1750–1790' (Université de Toulouse-Le Mirail, Thèse de doctorat d'état, 2 vols., 1978), ii, p. 542.

to the growing volume of seigneurial litigation reaching the Parlement of Toulouse in the decades after 1750. In these terms the seigneurial reaction of 1760–89 deserves to be distinguished from those reactions which preceded it. Virulent exploitation of the feudal nexus as a vehicle for surplus extraction had shattered the seigneurial ideal. In 1789 seigneurs all over the southern Massif Central discovered that they could no longer command the loyalty of the peasantry. They had forfeited their claim to the moral leadership of the rural community and were powerless to prevent the abolition of seigneurialism from below.

The worst transgressors were the ecclesiastical foundations. Time and again, Richeprey's peregrinations took him to villages dominated by the monks of Bonnecombe, the chantry priests of Sauveterre, the Commanders of the Order of Malta, the convent of St Sernin-sous-Rodez and the abbey of Belmont, and on nearly every occasion he received chorused complaints about the burden of dues, or the renewal of *terriers*, or the breakdown of policing. At Belmont[57] the villagers were resisting attempts by the monks to extend the *champart* and to subject straw to the tithe, while in the neighbourhood of Lédergues[58] the refurbishing of the *terriers* was in full swing. Bourgeois seigneurs, that is to say wealthy commoners who purchased fiefs principally for the status they conferred, also attracted his attention. Infiltration of the seigneurial regime by members of the Third Estate varied in extent, but it was particularly marked in the Rouergue and in the Cévennes where the territorial cohesion of the seigneurie was already seriously undermined. The declarations of possessions liable to the *vingtième noble* reveal the depth of this penetration: by the end of the *ancien régime* most fief owners in the *élection* of Rodez and the *bailliage* of Millau were bourgeois or *anoblis*.[59] Richeprey denounced their pretensions in thinly veiled terms. After measuring the scale of seigneurial exactions at Najac,[60] he took pains to exclude the 'vrais gentilshommes' from his indictment.

The proliferation of bourgeois seigneurs owed much to the financial embarrassments of court nobles such as the Duc d'Uzès, the Marquis de Châteauneuf-Randon or the Vicomte de Polignac. At intervals throughout the century their creditors forced upon them a liquidation of assets and each sale spawned a new generation of rustic seigneurs who were sometimes little more than enriched peasants. The robe bourgeoisie of the *sénéchaussée* seats and the Parlement belonged to a different category, however. Their investment in the seigneurial regime was more single-minded and often designed to buttress the acquisition of noble status. The intendants were frequently

---

[57] N. Castan, 'Crime et justice en Languedoc', ii, p. 591.
[58] Guilhamon, *Journal des voyages*, i, p. 300; ii, p. 295.
[59] H. Guilhamon, 'Notes sur la noblesse du Rouergue à fin du XVIIIe siècle', *Journal de l'Aveyron*, 15 September 1918.
[60] Guilhamon, *Journal des voyages*, i, p. 424.

importuned to grant redolently feudal titles to distinctly unglamorous collections of seigneuries. In 1759 the intendant of the Auvergne scotched an attempt by Sistrières, *lieutenant général* at the *bailliage* court of Vic-en-Carladès, to have his seigneurial possessions elevated to the status of a *châtellenie*: 'les fiefs et justices dont il demande la réunion sont des objets trop médiocres, trop dispersés et éloignés les uns des autres', he observed. In any case, 'j'ay toujours regardé comme une maxime qu'il falloit être noble ou au moins anobli pour prétendre à de semblables érections'.[61] Etienne-Hippolyte de Julien de Pégayrolles who made an illustrious career in the Parlement of Toulouse clearly had the required status. In the same year he successfully petitioned to have his fiefs in the Levézou erected into a marquisate. But strutting nobles like de Julien were precisely the kind of seigneurs most likely to exploit their possessions to the full. When Richeprey visited St Beauzély, the principal seat of the new marquisate, in 1780, he found the atmosphere heavy with tension. The seigneurial *taille dans les quatre cas* was still in force and the inhabitants had been constrained to repair the château. Moreover, the *cadastre* was not available for inspection and claims were made that the seigneur had tampered with it. He pressed his indelicate enquiries further and noted that the assembled populace seemed on the point of rebellion when 'un des assistants les intimida, les menaca du crédit du seigneur et ceux qui ne se rétractèrent pas, dirent qu'ils ne signeroient pas [the *procès-verbal*] seuls'.[62]

The reaction was not confined to monastic houses, *roturiers* and the *noblesse de robe*, however. It emanated directly from the *hobereaux* nobility whose livelihood was heavily dependent upon the continued payment of seigneurial dues. In the Haute-Auvergne where one out of three nobles contrived to survive on *rentes* amounting to no more than 500 *livres* per annum, the perquisites of the feudal regime were not considered a privilege. Calculations indicate that about a third of their income derived from this source.[63] For the resident seigneur, moreover, dues were an eminently reliable and cost-effective resource. According to a *mémoire* of the municipality of Arpajon (Cantal) there existed no type of income 'plus solide, plus assuré que celui des rentes; il n'est exposé à aucun danger, il ne coûte aucune dépense'.[64] These views were echoed throughout the southern Massif Central and they help to explain the proprietorial indignation which greeted the Assembly's measure of 4 August 1789 and the violence of the peasant riposte. Not all *rentes* were feudal, of course, but nearly all landowners were involved in

[61] A. Poitrineau, 'Aspects de la crise des justices seigneuriales dans l'Auvergne du dix-huitième siècle', *Revue historique de droit français et étranger* (1961), 554.
[62] Guilhamon, *Journal des voyages*, i, pp. 115, 116 and note 2. See also, *abbé* Douais, 'Le Marquis de Pégueirolles, avocat-général, président à mortier au parlement de Toulouse et mainteneur des jeux floraux, 1721–1794', *Mémoires de l'académie des sciences, inscriptions et belles-lettres de Toulouse*, iv (1892), 455–81.
[63] *L'Abolition de la féodalité dans le monde occidental*, ii, pp. 125–6.
[64] *Ibid.*, ii, pp. 122–3.

seigneurialism to some degree. For the *hobereaux* the economic attributes of lordship were crucial and they were not prepared to yield on this issue. The *cahier de doléances* of the nobility of the Haute-Auvergne baldly stated that 'Malgré son amour pour la patrie . . . elle ne peut faire le sacrifice de ses privilèges pécuniaires.'[65] By contrast, the honorific aspects of lordship seemed negotiable. Yet rich and powerful noble dynasties were undermined by the dissolution of the seigneurial regime, too. The Comte d'Antraigues,[66] the future *émigré* leader, enjoyed *rentes* worth 38,000 *livres* per annum in the decade before the Revolution. Three-quarters of this income derived from feudal sources.

In no sphere was the neglect of seigneurial prerogatives more blatant than in that of judicial provision. The desuetude of seigneurial courts stemmed less from a shortage of plaintiffs than a failure of will power on the part of those jointly entrusted with the task of criminal repression. Honorific rights to justice *haute, moyenne et basse* and the tangible symbols thereof were one thing, the expense of police and the pursuit of offenders quite another. With the active encouragement of titular seigneurs, the personnel of these courts conspired to reduce the financial outlay they entailed to an absolute minimum. In practice this led to pluralism, graft, fine-profiteering and studied inactivity in the face of major crime. Paradoxically, the more flagrant the offence the more likely it would pass unpunished. Few seigneuries were equipped with secure prisons and most seigneurs preferred to avoid the expense of arrest and incarceration. *Sieur* Balsa, seigneur of Le Colombiès (Rouergue),[67] stated glumly in his declaration of assets liable to the *vingtième noble* that his judicial prerogatives cost him about 12 *livres* a year, although in 1784 the necessity of having a prisoner escorted to the *sénéchaussée* jail in Villefranche-de-Rouergue had left him 60 *livres* out of pocket.

The decay of seigneurial 'police' exposed the nakedness of an institution more than ever attuned to surplus extraction. It also contributed powerfully to the destabilisation of the countryside on the eve of the Revolution. This is a factor that deserves greater recognition than it has received hitherto. The rising tide of lawlessness, the vagabondage of the late *ancien régime*, was not entirely precipitated by demographic and economic difficulties; it reflected a strategic withdrawal by seigneurs from the business of law enforcement as well as structural weaknesses in the judicial system as a whole. In the southern Massif Central policing was the first casualty of a brisk sellers' market in seigneurial perquisites. As seigneuries were split up, as fiefs without rights of justice or with partial rights changed hands, the moral cohesion of the seigneurial community disintegrated. The inhabitants of quite small localities sometimes complained that they paid dues to a dozen and more seigneurs, but

---

[65] *Ibid.*

[66] C. Jolivet, *La Révolution dans l'Ardèche, 1788–1795* (Largentière, 1930), pp. 17–18.

[67] Jones, 'Parish, Seigneurie and the Community of Inhabitants', 92.

were unsure to whom they should turn in order to obtain judicial redress. In the Cévennes the fragmented habitat had long posed an obstacle to centralised seigneurial control. At the end of the seventeenth century the parish of Frutgères[68] did homage to the barons of Grisac but it had, in addition, eight other seigneurs with high, middle and low justice as well as five 'seigneurs directs' without judicial rights. Each village, each hamlet had a seigneur, in effect, and this seems to have been the case in neighbouring parishes too. Seigneurialism reduced to this scale, it may be assumed, lacked even the most rudimentary apparatus for judicial repression. Yet neglect was not simply a function of size and resources. Some powerful seigneurs in the Velay and the Vivarais were notorious for the nonchalance with which they exercised their powers of police. At the end of the *ancien régime* these provinces were dotted with enclaves in which the royal writ did not run, in which the *maréchaussée* was powerless and the population tyrannised by clan violence and racketeering *hommes de loi*. The lands of the Comte d'Antraigues,[69] for instance, were reputed to shelter robbers and assassins in their dozens.

The tensions subverting the notion of reciprocity which lay at the heart of the seigneurial ideal were even more apparent in the Haute-Auvergne and the Brivadois. Since the Grands Jours of 1665 noble lawlessness had at least been curbed, but it is questionable whether the seigneurs of these highlands had become reliable auxiliaries of the royal judicial and administrative apparatus as one recent author has inferred.[70] Again, chronic jurisdictional confusion and escalating costs tended to result in serious crime going unpunished. Alarmed by the scale of violence in the Auvergne, the government sought to stimulate the zeal of seigneurs and from 1760 the procurators in each assize were required to submit to the sub-delegates regular lists of all offences committed in their localities. With more encouragement from the peasantry, the intendants would probably have encroached further upon the powers of the seigneurs. But the Auvergne was a land impregnated with seigneurialism and the assertive, litigious rural community of the Roman Law provinces had no true counterpart over the border. Nonetheless, the policy of barely disguised coercion adopted by the government after 1760 proved exceedingly irksome to the seigneurs. Each case of cattle rustling, violent assault and murder notified, appeared a monument to their culpability. Compromise seemed inevitable, however. Before 1789 it was quite inconceivable that the Crown should assume the burden of providing justice at the parish level and in an edict of 1771 Terray offered financial inducements to seigneurs who were prepared to investigate serious crimes. The measure may have achieved some

---

[68] A.D.L. G63 *Etat des fiefs situés dans le diocèse de Mende.*
[69] N. Castan, 'Crime et justice en Languedoc', i, p. 234.
[70] I. A. Cameron, *Crime and Repression in the Auvergne and the Guyenne, 1720–1790* (Cambridge, 1981), p. 119.

success in the Auvergne, but in the mountain parishes of Guienne and Languedoc law and order continued to deteriorate.

The seigneurial regime in the southern Massif Central degenerated swiftly in the second half of the eighteenth century. Some large and powerful seigneuries survived and some new holdings were consolidated in defiance of the trend, but they were not exempt from maladministration as we have seen. Degeneration should not be understood as a process resulting in extinction, though. On the contrary, it presupposed a process of adaptation to those roles which seigneurial lordship performed best: surplus extraction and the defining of privilege. This rationalisation singularly clarified perceptions of the institution and prepared the way for the alignments of 1789. On one hand we find the peasantry, that is to say the great bulk of the rural population, and, more ambiguously, the royal intendants; on the other the vested interest of those proprietors who had either been born into the system, or who had bought their way into it, and the considerable authority of the Parlement of Toulouse. As for the peasantry a fundamental shift in attitude had occurred. The validity of seigneurial institutions had rarely been questioned during the violent spasms of the seventeenth century; this was no longer the case after 1730 or thereabouts. The renewal of fiscal pressure coincided with a virulent seigneurial reaction and the once separate issues of the *taille*, the tithe and seigneurial dues merged. Disputes over fiscal exemptions and transparent attempts by the Crown to exploit its regalian rights more rigorously merely confirmed the popular conviction that there was a link between fiscal aggression and seigneurial aggression. And as the climate of fear in the countryside grew more desperate the idea of resistance germinated. Desperation of a different order characterised the monarchy's unscrupulous search for revenue by the 1770s and 1780s. But competition for peasant surplus was not the primary cause of the friction between intendants and seigneurs. This tension lay at the very heart of absolute monarchy – in the restless centralising ambitions of royal officials. The intendants wished to bolster the authority of their subalterns, the syndics, in the villages while the Parlement of Toulouse defended the seigneurs against the creeping administrative encroachment of the state.

Rente formed the very staff of life in a poor and isolated region like the southern Massif Central and rumours that it was to be abolished provoked consternation. The bishop of Mende conspicuously failed to renounce the tithe either on or after 4 August 1789 and the hierarchy received the news that church property had been sacrificed on the altar of national regeneration with extreme ill grace. The anxiety of fief owners on learning the details of the gestures made on their behalf was only surpassed by that of the peasantry when the collectors and tithe proctors turned up in their fields as usual. In the event, proprietorial fears of unilateral expropriation dissipated swiftly, but were soon replaced by fresh forebodings. The attack on feudalism had unleashed an assault upon the *bail à locaterie perpétuelle*[71] and there were doubts as to whether the redemption legislation would take into account the peculiar features of landholding in the mountain provinces of the Centre and the south. It clearly did not, but the peasantry's sense of disillusionment was even greater. In a series of pronouncements between March and July 1790 the Assembly whittled down the concessions of the previous summer: seigneurial *corvées*, *banalités*, *mainmorte*, *triage* and several other rights were abolished without further question, as was the institution of homage and the classification of land as noble or common, but 'useful' rights (to the *cens*, *champart*, *lods et ventes*, etc.) would remain in force until they were bought out. All arrears owing were to be added to the redemption price and peasants who resisted interim payment of redeemable dues were made liable to legal proceedings.

The compensation for monetary dues was calculated by multiplying their annual value by twenty; for harvest dues by multiplying their average annual yield by twenty-five. In the case of casual dues such as *lods et ventes* the redemption arithmetic was more complicated. Taken as a whole the legislation provided for a slow and orderly run-down of seigneurialism, but it pleased no one in the southern Massif Central. Proprietors complained bitterly that the redemption terms left them seriously out of pocket. A revealing collective petition signed by seventeen noble, *anobli* and bourgeois fief owners[72] of the Aveyron explained to the National Assembly that in an impoverished and isolated region with few commercial outlets for capital the value of land and the perquisites thereof had become inflated. Seigneurial dues customarily changed hands at forty times their face value. Moreover, purchasers of fiefs were subject to many expenses such as the cost of renewing *terriers* which could increase the original financial outlay by a sixth. Then there were the inconveniences of re-investing capital which came in by instalments. In short, they urged that the new department authority (which would be dominated by large landowners) be permitted to set the redemption scale it saw fit.

The peasant *jacqueries* of 1789–92 put an end to these pretensions. The freedom to redeem dues, warned the *curé* of Vinezac (Ardèche), 'sera toujours pour le petit peuple une inutile ressource', since the poor were 'jamais en état de compter à la fois une grosse somme d'argent'.[73] Nevertheless, landlords did their best to retrieve something from the wreckage. They profited from

---

[71] See above, chapter two, pp. 37–8.

[72] A. N. DXIV 2 *Comités des Assemblées, représentations adressées à l'assemblée nationale par les possesseurs des anciens fiefs du département de l'aveyron*, 10 May 1790; see also *Très humble et très respectueuse adresse à nos seigneurs de l'assemblée nationale par les habitants de la ville de Sauveterre*, September 1791 and Monteil, *Description du département de l'Aveiron*, ii, pp. 48–9.

[73] P. Sagnac and P. Caron, *Les Comités des droits féodaux et de législation et l'abolition du régime seigneurial, 1789–1793* (Paris, 1907), p. 78.

the abolition of the tithe by raising rents; they profited from the freeing of the grain trade by speculating shamelessly in basic foodstuffs and they employed the compensation paid as a result of the suppression of venal offices to purchase *biens nationaux*. Many hedged their bets in a more cynical fashion and thereby fuelled the pervasive nineteenth-century myth that seigneurialism had only been held at bay, not defeated. Notaries, whose profession had become synonymous with chicanery by the end of the eighteenth century, obligingly drafted contracts which provided for the reactivation of seigneurial dues in the event of a change of regime, or which incorporated their burden as well as that of the *dîme* in leases. On 17 July 1793 the Convention terminated the sorry business of indemnification and liquidated without appeal the remaining seigneurial obligations, but legislation could not remove the psychological shadow of seigneurialism, nor, indeed, the neo-seigneurialism which lived on in a number of localities. Several days after the decree definitively repudiating feudalism the inhabitants of Lédergues (Aveyron)[74] and surrounding villages were convoked in order to express their opinions on the democratic constitution of 1793. Having duly endorsed this ephemeral document, a large number of those present were moved to complain that the former seigneurs continued to collect dues and tithe as leasehold payments.

Atavisms: agrarian uprisings

Collective violence should not be confused with collective protest. Organised tumult, the letting off of firearms and cudgelling were traditional leisure entertainments in the countryside. Charivaris, Saint's Day celebrations, pilgrimages, fairs and the militia ballots could easily degenerate into bloody encounters involving hundreds of participants. Veritable battles were fought between contingents of parishioners on the occasion of the pilgrimage to Notre-Dame-de-Lenne (Rouergue) during the late eighteenth and early nineteenth centuries.[75] This calendared and premeditated popular violence is eloquent testimony to the repressed sociability of a low-density human habitat, but we should be wary of reading too much into it. Inter-parish conflict evinced a timeless character. The tensions of the pre-revolutionary decades may have added poignancy to what one historian has described as a latent 'mentalité d'insurrection',[76] but community bellicosity remained as much a feature of the new regime as of the old.

Collective protest was not endemic. It varied over time and place and presupposed violence to property and persons which was ritualised in form, but

---

[74] Riffaterre, 'Les Revendications économiques et sociales des assemblées primaires', p. 354.
[75] Jones, 'Political Commitment and Rural Society in the Southern Massif Central', pp. 343–4.
[76] H. Hours, 'Emeutes et émotions populaires dans les campagnes du Lyonnais au XVIIIᵉ siècle', *Cahiers d'histoire* (1964), 142.

specific in content and objective. The *jacquerie* provided the time-honoured vehicle for protest in the southern Massif Central and would not be swiftly abandoned. Its sinister unpredictability proved highly effective during the early years of the Revolution. Haemorrhaging agrarian violence had largely ceased by the end of the reign of Louis XIV, it is often suggested, and comparison is made between a rebellious seventeenth century and an apparently quiescent eighteenth century. The contrast relies heavily upon the non-repetition of peasant revolts on the scale of the Croquandages and the Nu-pieds, yet it is only partially valid. Large-scale peasant movements in the Quercy and the Cévennes greeted the inception of the 'siècle des lumières' and from 1787 violent spasms of agrarian unrest regularly punctuated the political life of the nation. Detailed scrutiny of the profile of 'popular emotions' as *ancien régime* administrators were apt to describe disturbances of the peace in the countryside, provides further evidence that the rural history of the eighteenth century was far from quiescent. In the provinces of the southern Massif Central subterranean threads linked the conflagrations associated with the rise of the absolutist state and those which encompassed its demise a century or so later. At intervals they broke the surface and engaged the repressive reflexes of the Royal Council in Versailles and the Parlement in Toulouse, even if they pass unrecognised in the textbook histories of the period. The religious 'fears' and attendant unrest and troop mobilisations of the 1740s, 1750s and early 1760s have already been discussed, but the Masques Armés revolt in the Bas Vivarais provides the most striking example.[77] In the winter of 1783 the small town of Les Vans, more particularly its *hommes de loi*, became the focus of a rebellion which lacked the reputation but none of the intensity of the revolts of the seventeenth century.

In many respects the peasant insurrections of the eighty years between the Camisard Wars and the revolutionary climacteric make for familiar reading. Fiscal pressure, whether actual or imputed, was never far beneath the surface, nor, indeed, was resentment at the licence of billeting sergeants, writ-servers, bailiffs and unscrupulous attorneys. The troubled coexistence of town and country added a further dimension to agrarian conflict. The siege of Caussade by insurgent Calvinists in 1761, or the pillaging of the money-lending lawyers of Les Vans in 1783 were not isolated incidents. Relations between *bourgs* and their satellite villages were rarely harmonious. During the critical winter of 1789–90 the *bourg* of Sauveterre was subjected to repeated assaults by the hard-pressed peasantry of the ségala.[78] The city fathers spent over 4,000 *l.* on bourgeois patrols and repairs to the walls. Dearth, rumoured shortages and

[77] M. Sonenscher, 'Royalists and Patriots: Nîmes and its Hinterland in the late Eighteenth Century' (University of Warwick, D.Phil. thesis, 1977), pp. 374–401; Jolivet, *La Révolution dans l'Ardèche*, p. 22.

[78] A.D.A. L745 Petition of *officiers municipaux* of Sauveterre to administrators of Department of Aveyron, October 1790.

hoarding retained a formidable capacity to mobilise the population, too, as did the perennial confrontations between salt smugglers and officials of the Farm. Attempts by *gabelous* to apprehend a group of smugglers as they passed through Millau in 1773 triggered a massive sympathetic riot.

The disaffection that greeted government interventionism in the field of charitable relief for the poor, the sick and the aged struck a more modern note. In 1752 an *hôpital-général* was established at St Affrique and the parishes of the diocese of Vabres were stripped of their alms in order to endow it. Many communities resisted this typically bureaucratic solution to the problem of mendicity and violence flared repeatedly during the years that followed. The parish of Sainte Eulalie[79] on the Causse du Larzac stood to lose a *rente* of 320 *sétiers* of grain and fought off the agents of the hospital when they came to collect it. The *maréchaussée* received equally short shrift when they tried to execute arrest warrants against the ringleaders. Eventually, in 1773, the mediation of the Commander of the Order of Malta secured the use of the alms for the home community. Not unnaturally, innovations that undermined the precarious economy of the poor were bitterly resented. Monastic houses were no less susceptible to the conventional wisdom of the late *ancien régime* that outdoor relief perpetuated begging and vagrancy, but each attempt to restrict alms hand-outs to the authentically needy triggered an explosion of popular fury. After all, the peasantry regarded ecclesiastical alms in much the same light as the abbeys regarded their feudal dues. The emanations of physiocracy violated customary rights in other areas, too. Surface coal deposits in the district of Aubin[80] had long been exploited by the local inhabitants as an adjunct to subsistence farming, but an *arrêt* of 1744 transferring ownership of the sub-soil to the Crown threatened to terminate this method of extraction. In 1755 a consortium of local proprietors and seigneurs purchased the mining concession and set about enforcing their rights. The peasantry rose in anger and after three major insurrections in the 1760s succeeded in destroying the monopoly.

In one critical respect the *jacqueries* and rebellions that punctuated the closing decades of the *ancien régime* differed from their seventeenth-century forerunners, however. Even before the 'great hope' of 1787–9 kindled ambitions and simplified issues, they had acquired a markedly anti-feudal character. The seigneurial reaction thrust the landlord to the centre of the stage – a position hitherto reserved for the fisc. As the seigneur, as the impropriator of the tithe, as the employer of the despised *homme de loi*, the landlord had become an object of popular resentment. The simmering tensions chronicled by Richeprey, the desperate vigilance of communities subject to the scrutiny of the *commissaires à terrier* and the sporadic acts of

---

[79] Guilhamon, *Journal des voyages*, i, pp. 141 and note 1; 222 and note 1.
[80] *Ibid.*, i, p. 8 note 1.

insurgency against seigneurs who pressed their advantage too far, leave little room for doubt on this point. Yet it is questionable whether the institution of seigneurial stewardship was under general attack before the Revolution. Even in 1789 the great *jacquerie* which was to sweep away the debris of feudalism within four years, retained many archaic characteristics. Not all châteaux were besieged, not all seigneurs were ransomed by their tenants. It seems, rather, that popular furies were unleashed against the excrescences of seigneurial (and fiscal) authority. Once these had been cut away, it is possible that the edifice might have survived in some shape or form had not the logic of revolutionary politics dictated otherwise. For all the intervening trauma, the Revolution failed to breach the traditions of submission and dependence which characterised the rural population of the southern Massif Central. Perhaps the cathartic surgery of 1789–92 removed an irritant in the relationship between lord and peasant and redressed the balance in the countryside. After 1792 the rural community appeared to close ranks around its former seigneurs – little disposed to follow them in risky political adventures, but little disposed to denounce them either.

With the news of events in Paris a dam of resentment broke loose. In late July reverberating currents of fear sowed panic throughout the region. After a moment's breathless expectation huge gatherings of peasants formed and proceeded to move against selected targets. A cycle of agrarian violence began which lasted until the summer of 1792. The principal objects of attack were château archives, granaries and the more offensive trappings of seigneurial privilege, and secondarily the judicial records of the *bailliage* courts and the agents of the fisc. As time went by the assaults became more organised, more sophisticated in motivation and probably less reliant upon the mass support of the peasantry. The main theatres of insurrection were the Cévennes and the Bas Vivarais, and the ségala of the Rouergue – areas which had endured some of the worst excesses of the seigneurial reaction. Reports that châteaux were being pillaged in the Dauphiné crossed the Rhône early in August and precipitated widespread risings along the right bank and further inland. In the Tanargue the violence rapidly acquired the overtones of indiscriminate brigandage, while in the Haut Vivarais the insurgents contented themselves with intimidation and threats of violence. At Bosas,[81] for instance, the seigneur was well liked and the inhabitants left him in peace after destroying his *terriers*. This first spasm of lawlessness came to an abrupt end after a month and before any kind of repression could be organised.

Events followed a rather different pattern in the Rouergue. The denouement of the Great Fear sparked off serious disorders in the Quercy which spilled over into the countryside around Villefranche-de-Rouergue. A notable victim was the seigneur of Privezac whose château was pillaged on

---

[81]   Jolivet, *La Révolution dans l'Ardèche*, p. 139.

30 August. But these spontaneous assaults were isolated and uncoordinated incidents compared with the fermentation that gripped the ségala during the following winter. Once again the contagion travelled down a broad corridor of countryside from the Limousin and the Périgord in the north west to the uplands of the Albigeois in the south where oppressive seigneurialism had long been the norm. The mobilisations corresponded to the *jacquerie* stereotype – sudden concentrations of peasants which rarely remained on a warlike footing for more than a day or two – but they were clearly more than that. Unidentified agitators moving from parish to parish brought a measure of political acumen to the movements. They helped to nurture an awareness among the peasantry that the concessions of 4 August were neither definitive nor irrevocable. The long delay as the Assembly considered how to dismantle the feudal regime pandered to these fears, and the manifest intention of seigneurs and tithe owners to continue to collect their harvest dues in the autumn of 1789 provoked widespread anger. Throughout the ségala rumours circulated to the effect that dues had been abolished purely and simply and that seigneurs were even required to make back-payment. In fact, the decree of 3 May 1790 stated precisely the opposite: arrears due to seigneurs received the full protection of the law. Moreover, time seemed to be running short. According to Louis Louchet, roving agitators were urging a pre-emptive strike: 'il falloit se hâter de se faire soi-même justice; qu'on n'avoir pour cela que trois mois; passé lequel terme il ne seroit plus permis de tirer vengeance des seigneurs'.[82]

The storm broke on 10 December with a series of forays against châteaux in the neighbourhood of Sauveterre. Armed peasants also surrounded the *bourg*. The prompt organisation of patrols by an *ad hoc* committee of well-to-do patriots in Rodez helped to stem the unrest, but the *jacquerie* began again at the end of January. This time the conflagration spread rapidly to embrace the whole of the ségala and several other localities as well. By mid-February the Conseil Permanent of Rodez was receiving reports of outrages by the hour. The inhabitants of Le Claux rose against the *feudiste* commissioned by the seigneur of Firmy to renew his *terriers*, while the population of Firmy itself rebelled against the seigneur's *fermier* who stood accused of employing false weights and measures. In the meantime, the tenants of the Marquis de Valady at Les Vernhettes demanded the reimbursement of the *lods et ventes* they had been required to pay, and the private pews of the Marquis de Buisson were dragged out of the parish church at Bournazel and burnt. When retainers of the marquis tried to remove his archives to a place of safety, the château was surrounded by thousands of armed peasants and they were lucky to escape with their lives. The monks of the abbey of

---

[82] L. Louchet, *Relation des troubles du Rouergue et des moyens employés par la ville de Rodez pour les faire cesser, rédigée d'après les procès-verbaux et les pièces justicatives des faits et de leurs circonstances* (Rodez, 1790), p. 7.

Bonnecombe who enjoyed the reputation of being among the harshest seigneurs in the ségala were repeatedly threatened. On 12 February they were forced to pay to 108 peasants a ransom of 6 *l*. apiece. The monks were rescued by national guardsmen sent out from Rodez, but help was not always so conveniently to hand and many seigneurs fled in terror to the nearest *bourg*. Yet the *bourgs* felt desperately vulnerable, too. Marauding bands encircled Sauveterre again on 14 February.[83]

Within a week the insurrections subsided. A score of châteaux had been threatened or despoiled in the Rouergue and fifteen over the border in the Albigeois. Physical violence against seigneurs was rare; the peasantry were usually content to parley for the restitution of certain payments, the extinction or reduction of others and the removal of the most objectionable features of seigneurial privilege – hunting rights, *banalités* and private pews. Only in aggravated circumstances were châteaux, manors or priories pillaged indiscriminately. In this respect the siren calls of village agitators missed their mark. The rural population seemed more concerned to tilt rather than topple the balance of power in the countryside. Yet the set-piece mobilisations of December 1789 and February 1790 represented only the visible tip of an obscure campaign of petty lawlessness, intimidation and blackmail. These more typical symptoms of crumbling social discipline attracted little publicity and we only learn of them when prudent seigneurs took the trouble to certify their losses before a notary. On 8 December 1789 alleged Antoine Rous, seigneur of Feneyrols, two inhabitants of the village of Arnac induced him to reimburse a fine of 99 *l*. imposed upon them after they had infringed his hunting rights twelve years earlier. A third individual extracted 32 *l*. from him on a similar pretext plus a note cancelling his rent arrears. All three were armed with guns and Rous yielded, so he claimed, under duress ('intimidé de l'hardiesse de laquelle ils appuyent leurs demandes et uniquement pour se soustraire à leurs violences').[84]

The Vivarais remained untouched by the conflagration affecting the south-western flanks of the Massif Central and so, it seems, did the Gévaudan and the Velay. No serious alarms were reported for about eighteen months after February 1790 and it was not until late in 1791 that agrarian unrest began to escalate once more. Reports reached the newly constituted department administration of the Lozère from the Cévennes that roaming bands were forcing proprietors to demolish their towers and turrets, while in the Ardèche assaults upon churches in order to remove the impedimenta of seigneurialism gathered momentum. By the end of the winter the authorities found themselves confronted by a major recrudescence of agrarian conflict. Moreover, the agitation evinced a more organised and politically purposeful character. Two sources of contagion helped to precipitate the call-to-arms. Disturb-

[83] *Ibid.*, p. 12.   [84] R. Granier, *Jadis en Bas-Rouergue* (Montauban, 1947), p. 49 note 17.

ances in the Figeac *arrondissement* of the Lot during February 1792 and in adjacent areas of the Cantal[85] in March and April rekindled anti-seigneurial passions over the border in Aveyron, too. Early in April three châteaux were attacked and their proprietors subjected to a fresh round of spoliation and blackmail. In what had clearly become a ritual of intimidation peasants invaded the fine château of Privezac a second time, even though it no longer belonged to the unfortunate Le Brunet de Paillez whom they had ill treated and robbed two and a half years earlier. They left it a smoke-blackened ruin, which fate was also reserved for the château of Vaureilles a day or so later.[86]

Nearly simultaneous and much more serious insurrections broke out in the lower Ardèche. The renewal of agrarian violence in this bitterly divided corner of the old Bas Vivarais was in part a response to the great *jacquerie* of the South East which Vovelle has brought to light. Between March and September 1792 Provence formed the epicentre of a vast popular revolt that reached as far north as Valence and as far west as the Gard. Agrarian rather than urban unrest was uppermost in the Ardèche and it flared first in those cantons of the lower Cévennes (Jaujac, Thueyts, Montpezat and Antraigues) which had witnessed the worst excesses of August 1789. A score of châteaux and country-houses were invaded and the violence soon spilled out of the mountains and spread southwards to coalesce with the *jacquerie* in the Gard. By May the worst was past and the insurrectionary initiative shifted towards Lower Provence.

The uprisings of 1792 pose many more problems of interpretation than those of 1789–90. Were they solely anti-noble and anti-feudal and therefore the product of continuing efforts to liquidate the heritage of the *ancien régime*, or were they symptoms of new alignments spawned by revolution and only partially subsuming the older categories? It is questionable, too, whether the term *jacquerie* adequately conveys the flavour of the popular mobilisations that affected the region two and three years after the Great Fear. The evidence is ambiguous, which lends weight to our conclusion that the year 1792 marked the joining, or perhaps the overlapping, of old and new traditions of collective protest in the countryside. The anti-seigneurial animus, the *ad hoc* throngs of peasants imbued with a millenarian sense of justice were still features of the risings of 1792. In March four châteaux belonging to the Comte d'Antraigues were sacked in as many days. But the insurgents had other axes to grind as well. Attacks on enclosures mingled with attacks on châteaux; assaults on ecclesiastical foundations spurred on the invasion of forests, and conflicts over church pews became confused with

[85] See J. Dalby, 'The French Revolution in a Rural Environment: the Example of the Department of the Cantal, 1789–1794' (University of Manchester, D.Phil. thesis, 1981), pp. 119–58.

[86] L. Mazars, 'Emeutes et pillages aux châteaux de Pachins, Vaureilles et Privezac', *Les Cahiers rouergats*, iv (1971), 61–3.

conflicts over parish provision and the clerical oath. The whole, meanwhile, was leavened by a recrudescence of confessional rivalries and, as disorder became endemic, a growing taste for brigandage. Protest in the countryside diversified, but it also became institutionalised and organised in fewer hands. Village apparatchiki and rustic cousins of the *sans-culottes* replaced the broad masses of 1789. In the South East pullulating jacobin clubs assumed the task of popular vigilance and national guard detachments channelled the punitive will. As peasant militias set off to pillage the dwellings of 'enemies of the Revolution' rather than those of erstwhile seigneurs on the pretext of searching for firearms, it became clear that the climate had changed. Urban politics, the politics of ideological options, had penetrated the countryside.

6

****

The crystallisation of new traditions

On 12 July 1778 the government established a provincial assembly in the *généralité* of Bourges. This initiative led to similar creations in the Dauphiné, the *généralité* of Montauban and the *généralité* of Moulins over the next two years. The planned assemblies in the Dauphiné and in Moulins proved still-born, but the Assemblée Provinciale du Berry and the Assemblée Provinciale de la Haute-Guienne swiftly took root. They appeared to inaugurate a decade of unprecedented constitutional debate which would, in 1787, result in systematic legislation to extend the scope of such assemblies to every part of France outside the *pays d'états*.[1]

There is no doubt that a new spirit of critical examination was abroad in the years immediately preceding the Revolution, nor that it drew considerable nourishment from the existence in Villefranche-de-Rouergue of an assembly of notables empowered to discuss matters relating to the well-being of the two provinces comprising the *généralité* of Montauban. As prosperity faltered and the burdens on peasant surplus intensified, the *bureau intermédiaire* or permanent bureaucracy of the new body received a steady stream of complaints. By tabling these grievances for general discussion the assembly elevated them onto a higher plane and thereby fostered the atmosphere of reformism. Reformism among the educated was in any case benefiting from a transformation in leisure habits. By the late 1770s even the underdeveloped upland towns of the Massif Central could usually boast a masonic lodge, and in 1779 thirty-five well-to-do inhabitants of St Antonin[2] organised themselves into a 'Société politique et littéraire'. One of their number, the parish priest, was a respondent of the Academy of Arras.[3] Unmistakable signs

---

[1] Studies of the Provincial Assemblies are scarce and of uneven quality. Among the best are Léoncé de Lavergne, *Les Assemblées provinciales sous Louis XVI* (Paris, 1864); G. Boscary, *L'Assemblée provinciale de Haute-Guienne, 1779–1790* (Paris, 1932); P. Renouvin, *Les Assemblées provinciales de 1787, origines, développement, résultats* (Paris, 1921); S. Bétant-Robert, 'L'Assemblée provinciale d'Auvergne à la veille de la Révolution' (Université de Clermont-Ferrand, Mémoire pour Diplôme d'études supérieures d'histoire du droit, 1966).

[2] R. Latouche, *Saint Antonin* (Montauban, 1926), p. 78.

[3] L.-N. Berthe, *Dictionnaire des correspondants de l'académie d'Arras au temps de Robespierre* (Arras, 1969), p. 218.

of an embryonic 'public opinion' began to appear. The Estates of the Vivarais decided to publish the minutes of their deliberations and the members of the Provincial Assembly of Haute-Guienne sought permission to do likewise.

The pioneer provincial assemblies engaged public attention because they appeared to depart from some of the most hallowed principles of *ancien régime* government. Under Necker's unorthodox direction, the administered were invited to participate in the hitherto sacrosanct business of administration. Three important innovations were incorporated into the legislation from the outset: double membership for the Third estate; deliberation in common session and voting by head. The contrast between the resolve of 1778–9 and the shilly-shallying of 1788–9 could hardly be more striking. The body set up in the town and seneschal seat of Villefranche as a compromise between the competing claims of Montauban and Rodez comprised ten ecclesiastics; sixteen nobles; thirteen commoners drawn from the towns and thirteen from the countryside. None of the fifty-two was elected: sixteen were nominated by the monarch and they co-opted the remainder. Moreover, an exacting combination of juridical and fiscal qualifications limited the constituency of eligible persons. For example, nobles were expected to possess four generations of lineage, a fief and property liable to at least 100 *livres* of taxes per annum, while the censitary threshold for a commoner representative of the towns was fixed at 200 *l.* Constituted thus, the assembly met in biennial session under ecclesiastical chairmanship. During the first two years its president was Jérôme-Marie Champion de Cicé, the dynamic bishop of Rodez and confidant of Necker.[4]

The vigour with which the Provincial Assembly of Haute-Guienne interpreted the rather ill-defined responsibilities conferred upon it has already been mentioned. One of its first acts was to commission Richeprey's cadastral survey as part of a wide-ranging enquiry into fiscal anachronisms. Necker's fall from grace in 1781 soon curbed its zeal in this sphere, however. Indeed, his departure placed a question mark over the entire experiment. The assembly survived the crisis, but wisely turned its attention to less contentious subjects such as road-building and agricultural improvements. From beginning to end the intendants were implacable opponents of the provincial assemblies. The mere existence of such bodies in the *pays d'élections* implied a challenge to their authority. In the Haute-Guienne every private and sectional interest that felt vaguely threatened by the apparent determination of the Villefranche assembly to rake over the embers of seigneurial and fiscal privilege invoked the protection of the intendant. Montauban became the headquarters of those who wished to neutralise the work of the *bureau*

---

[4] *Collection des procès-verbaux des séances de l'Assemblée Provinciale de Haute-Guienne tenues à Villefranche, ès années 1779, 1780, 1782, 1784 et 1786 avec la permission du roi* (vol. i, Paris, 1787); J. Egret, *Necker, ministre de Louis XVI, 1776–1790* (Paris, 1975), pp. 137–8.

intermédiaire, sabotage Richeprey's mission and break up the union of the Quercy and the Rouergue which so offended Quercynois. In these alignments and the confrontations they entailed, it is possible to detect a measured politicisation of urban elites. And the integration of the struggle between intendant and assembly into a broader debate helped to shape the contours of educated opinion in 1788–9.

The intendant, Daniel Victor de Trimond, pursued a policy of divide and rule and played on fears that fiscal adjustment would inevitably work to the disadvantage of the Quercy where the average tax threshold was lower. The inhabitants of the Vicomté de Turenne and the grossly under-taxed catholic bourgeoisie of Montauban felt especially vulnerable in this respect. A plan of campaign turning on the venal oligarchies of the towns was concocted and by 1785 the intendant had contrived to fill most of the municipalities of the *généralité* with placemen hostile to the provincial assembly. In 1781 the city fathers of Montauban obligingly sponsored a petition calling for the dissolution of the link between the two provinces. Intendant and sub-delegates guided its passage through the corporations. At Gourdon in the Haut Quercy supporters of the assembly's reforming policies were both numerous and vocal and the Montalbanais proposal was thrown out initially. On the advice of the sub-delegate the dissentient voices were removed from the town council and creatures of the intendancy installed instead. Jean-Baptiste Cavaignac, the source of local resistance and future *conventionnel*, proved to be the principal victim of this administrative purge. In 1787 Gourdon finally adhered to the petition, but Cavaignac rallied the 'principaux habitants et hauts taxés de la ville de Gourdon' and published a counter-resolution.[5] It seems likely that in many localities of the Quercy and the Rouergue the political apprenticeship of the professional and proprietorial bourgeoisie began with the creation of the Provincial Assembly of Haute-Guienne.

Much of the controversy surrounding Necker's assemblies stemmed from the suspicion that they were, in reality, a Trojan horse planted in the midst of the machinery of government. Calonne took the trouble to accompany the unveiling of his assemblies in 1787 with clear signals that they were merely consultative organs subject to the surveillance of the intendants who alone might authorise expenditure. He also softened further the distinctions between the orders and removed the *ex officio* right of the First Estate to the presidency. The most significant feature of the new legislation was its scope, however. Between June and November 1787 regulations were promulgated which established a three-tier hierarchy of assemblies in most *généralités* of the kingdom. Calonne not only endorsed the experiment in provincial assemblies, he provided for *élection* and parish assemblies, too. The reform

---

[5] For this paragraph, see Guilhamon, *Journal des voyages*, i, li–lxiv; ii, p. 276 note 80.

did not apply to the Berry, nor to the Haute-Guienne, and it left the *pays d'états* untouched. Thus, provincial assemblies subsisted in Bourges and Villefranche-de-Rouergue while in neighbouring *généralités* the tri-partite system was introduced.

The reform of 1787 impinged on history so briefly that it has been forgotten and it only affected peripheral areas of the southern Massif Central in any case. Nevertheless, the difficulties which beset the organisation of the subsidiary assemblies prefigured many of the problems encountered by revolutionary administrators after 1789. The *élections* of Brioude, St Flour and Aurillac all formed part of the vast province of the Auvergne and on 8 July an organic law laid down the terms by which the hierarchy of assemblies was to be organised in this region. Clermont-Ferrand became the headquarters of the new provincial assembly and its members convened for the first and, it seems, only occasion in November 1787. Within a year the institution had become an embarrassment: the clamour was all in favour of an Estates-General. Restored to power, Necker informed the intendant of the Auvergne on 15 October 1788 that the king had decided not to summon the provincial assemblies for that year.[6] Nevertheless, the *bureau intermédiaire* continued in obscure existence until September 1790 when it handed over its archives to the officials of the departments fashioned from the old province of the Auvergne. The activities of the *élection* or district assemblies left more substantial traces. At Brioude,[7] for example, the assembly met on 26 October and again the following year. The lower echelons of the new structure survived in the *élections* of St Flour[8] and Aurillac,[9] too. Indeed, the voluminous *procès-verbaux* of the October 1788 sessions (293 pages in the case of St Flour) suggest that the intermediate assemblies had taken vigorous root by the time the revolutionary crisis supervened.

The putative parish assemblies constituted by far the most interesting feature of Calonne's proposals, however. Their proximity to the revolutionary commune which is usually taken to be the source of the municipal liberties of modern France has led to a certain neglect. The legislation of 1787 stipulated that an 'assemblée municipale' be established in every 'communauté' not already in possession of a municipal body. Apart from two *ex officio* members (the seigneur and the parish priest), its composition was elective on the principle of three members for communities of under 100 households, six in the case of communities numbering between 100 and 200 households and nine for those in excess. An executive agent, or syndic, and a scribe were also to be appointed by ballot and the electoral constituency was defined as all those in the 'assemblée de la paroisse' who paid at least 10 *l.* in direct taxes.

---

[6] A.D.P.-de-D. C7356 Necker to Chazérat, Paris 15 October 1788.
[7] A.D.P.-de-D. C7360; C7361.   [8] A.D.P.-de-D. C7371; C7372; C7373.
[9] A.D.P.-de-D. C7358; C7359.

The legislation[10] took no cognisance of the ambiguities inherent in the term 'communauté'. It assumed that parish and *collecte*, as the fiscal community was known in the Auvergne, were one and the same.

Preparations began at once. On 4 August 1787 the intendant published instructions for the formation of the new municipal assemblies and the sub-delegates distributed printed forms (see plate 1) on which to record the results. The elections took place in August and September and by November most of the completed *procès-verbaux* had been returned to the intendant. Predictably, the experience confirmed the inveterate prejudices of the bureaucracy. The sub-delegate of St Flour reported that the reform had missed its mark. Instead, the holding of elections had precipitated 'une terrible combustion dans les parroisses (*sic*) et paroissent nuire à la tranquilité (*sic*) des campagnes et à la société des villes'.[11] On the other hand, the sub-delegate of the *élection* of Aurillac signalled indifference: 'il est certain que les p[aroiss]es ont en g[énér]al beaucoup répugné en ce païs à ce nouveau régime. Les paisans ont craint de n'y rien gagner, de payer d'avantage, d'avoir trop de maîtres, pour me servir de leur expression, ou trop de têtes, de voir une nouvelle division de la taille par un nouveau tarif qu'ils redoutent.'[12] The conduct of elections in the countryside had, indeed, encountered many difficulties, but they were not, in general, a product of peasant incorrigibility. The reform initiative of 1787 brought to light procedural problems which would require several generations of democratic experiment before they could be solved.

Inability to grasp the complex instructions contained within the legislation coupled with poor drafting was responsible for much confusion. Rural electors chose too many or too few candidates; they chose individuals who did not possess the *cens* (fixed at 30 *l.*); they chose individuals linked by close ties of kinship and they found the secret ballot to be quite inoperable. Usually they voted *viva voce*. Critics scoffed and pointed out that independence and maturity could scarcely be expected of an electorate which embraced village artisans, plotholders and day-labourers. In regions of heavy direct taxation such as the Auvergne the 10 *l.* suffrage qualification effectively enfranchised 'le moindre propriétaire'.[13] Remedies were swiftly found for some of these problems. Ministerial circulars ruled on blood affinities in March 1788 and several months later instructed municipal assemblies to keep a book of minutes. The greatest obstacle to a rational system of local government lay in the discrepancy between the basic units of temporal and spiritual jurisdiction,

---

[10] Jourdan, Decrusy and Isambert, *Recueil général des anciennes lois françaises depuis l'an 420 jusqu'à la Révolution* (vol. 28: 1785–1789, Paris, 1927), pp. 374–74.

[11] A.D.P.-de-D. C1803 Sub-delegate *élection* St Flour to intendant (?), St Flour, 31 October 1787.

[12] *Ibid.*, Sub-delegate *élection* Aurillac to intendant, Aurillac, 4 November 1787.

[13] A.D.P.-de-D. 4C11 Observations of the *bureau intermédiaire* of the *élection* of Aurillac on the regulations governing the provincial assemblies (n.d.).

however. This anomaly was never tackled and so survived to bedevil the organisation of the revolutionary commune.

The sub-delegates whose job it was to send out the printed proformas were the first to raise the issue. In the Brivadois the incongruity of parish and *collecte* was not acute, but in the *planèze* and the Carladez highland parishes frequently embraced several fiscal communities. The *élection* of St Flour com-

ELECTION D'AURILLAC.		COMMUNAUTÉ DE		
		NOMBRE DES FEUX EXISTANTS DANS LADITE COMMUNAUTE.		
SEIGNEUR OU SON REPRESENTANT.	NOM.	QUALITÉS.		
C U R É.	NOM.	DÉCIMATEUR.	OU A LA PORTION CONGRUE.	
SYNDIC.	NOM.	Profeffion. Habitation.	Payant en { Taille .. Vingtieme	Sait-il lire? Sait-il écrire? Ou figner feulement?
PREMIER MEMBRE.	NOM.	Qualité. Profeffion. Habitation.	Payant en { Taille. . . Vingtieme	Sait-il lire? Sait-il écrire? Ou figner feulement?
SECOND MEMBRE.	NOM.	Qualité. Profeffion. Habitation.	Payant en { Taille. . . Vingtieme	Sait-il lire? Sait-il écrire? Ou figner feulement?
TROISIEME MEMBRE.	NOM.	Qualité. Profeffion. Habitation.	Payant en { Taille. . . Vingtieme	Sait-il lire? Sait-il écrire? Ou figner feulement?
QUATRIEME MEMBRE.	NOM.	Qualité. Profeffion. Habitation.	Payant en { Taille. . . Vingtieme	Sait-il lire? Sait-il écrire? Ou figner feulement?
CINQUIEME MEMBRE.	NOM.	Qualité. Profeffion. Habitation.	Payant en { Taille. . . Vingtieme	Sait-il lire? Sait-il écrire? Ou figner feulement?
SIXIEME MEMBRE.	NOM.	Qualité. Profeffion. Habitation.	Payant en { Taille. . . Vingtieme	Sait-il lire? Sait-il écrire? Ou figner feulement?
SEPTIEME MEMBRE.	NOM.	Qualité. Profeffion. Habitation.	Payant en { Taille. : . Vingtieme.	Sait-il lire? Sait-il écrire? Ou figner feulement?
HUITIEME MEMBRE.	NOM.	Qualité. Profeffion. Habitation.	Payant en { Taille. . . Vingtieme	Sait-il lire? Sait-il écrire? Ou figner feulement?
NEUVIEME MEMBRE.	NOM.	Qualité. Profeffion. Habitation.	Payant en { Taille. . . Vingtieme	Sait-il lire? Sait-il écrire? Ou figner feulement?
GREFFIER.	NOM.	Qualité. Profeffion. Habitation.		Sait-il écrire? Ou figner feulement?

A AURILLAC, Chez ANTOINE VIALLANES, Imprimeur - Libraire 1787.

1 Proforma used in the municipal elections of August–September 1787

prised 148 *collectes* and 91 parishes. The parish of Neuvéglise,[14] for instance, consisted of 615 taxpayers grouped into five *collectes*. Each *collecte* constituted itself into a municipal assembly. Unintentionally, therefore, the reform had promoted a process of social atomization which would shortly receive added impetus from the centrifugal collapse of 1789. In the case of the tiny village of Buffières (Aveyron)[15] it is possible to explore the stages in this process in some detail. The eighteen taxpayers of Buffières formed a minute fiscal community abutting the highland frontier of the Auvergne with the Rouergue. As such they fell within the ambit of the *élection* of St Flour and were subject to the prescriptions of the edict of June 1787. However, the village lay inside the parish of Lacalm whose territory straddled the border at this point. The *bourg* and parish of Lacalm were indisputably part of the Rouergue and, therefore, beyond the scope of the reform. On 19 August 1787 twelve electors of Buffières chose three of their number to form their municipal assembly and henceforth this microscopic municipality resisted all suggestions that it should either amalgamate with the municipal body (*sic*) of its parish or with that of the nearest parish in the *élection*. The following October the minutes of the *élection* assembly of St Flour noted sourly that Buffières had failed to submit and yet was unable to renew its municipal corps as prescribed by law because all the eligible candidates were already members. Moreover, the municipality included neither the seigneur, nor the *curé*. Before anything could be done the Revolution intervened. On 29 April 1790 the three-member municipal assembly of Buffières (one of whom styled himself 'mayor') successfully petitioned to join the newly constituted commune of Lacalm and, after considerable manoeuvring, the boundary between the Auvergne and the Rouergue was adjusted accordingly. Buffières was not the only small entity to pilot its way through the interstices of late *ancien régime* and revolutionary municipal legislation. The *bureau intermédiaire* tried hard to obtain guidance on the appropriate context for the municipal assembly, but the government was unwilling to adjudicate between the parish and the *collecte*. Ministers were clearly preoccupied with the impending crisis and Necker refused to do more than restate the existing legislation:

Dans ce moment, MM., je verrais beaucoup d'inconvéniens (*sic*) à faire sur cet objet un nouveau réglement général, qui, dans son application, rencontrerait des difficultés comme le précédent. Les vues du conseil sont sans doute qu'il n'y ait qu'une municipalité par paroisse, mais aussi qu'il n'y ait qu'une seule collecte par municipalité, autant que cela sera possible, de sorte que ces trois mots: Paroisse, Municipalité et Collecte deviennent synonimes (*sic*).[16]

---

[14] A.D.P.-de-D. C7372 *Procès-verbal des séances de l'assemblée complète de l'élection de Saint Flour des 22 octobre 1787 et jours suivants.*
[15] *Ibid.*; A.D.P.-de-D. C1805; A.D.A. L702; 2E 105 2.
[16] A.D.P.-de-D. C1818 Necker to *commission intermédiaire* of provincial assembly of the Auvergne (n.d. [October? 1788]).

Circumstances did not favour the provincial assemblies, but the inference that they could have developed into representative bodies is unwarranted. They were established as an expedient by a regime seeking to retain the plenitude of its authority. Members were not elected and their power of decision in matters of substance was negligible. The assemblies were authorised to adjust the burden of taxation between communities and they could make proposals for more fundamental reform, but the edict of June 1787 categorically denied them the right to hinder, delay or in any way alter the demands of the fisc. Pierre Renouvin's[17] judicious rejection of the liberal legend of the provincial assemblies sedulously cultivated by Léoncé de Lavergne[18] has withstood the test of time. As for the intendants, they were not seriously discomfited by the assemblies after 1781 and the intendant of the Auvergne tolerated the amateurish enthusiasms of the provincial and *élection* assemblies in his jurisdiction with reasonably good grace – safe in the knowledge that they were excluded from the decisions determining the yield of taxation. The view advanced recently by R. D. Harris[19] that Necker's pioneer assemblies were modern deliberative bodies retaining little of the traditional estates seems excessive.

The municipal or parish assemblies which flowered briefly in 1787 and 1788 are less easily consigned to an old tradition. Although the reform consolidated the authority of the privileged orders over the rural community, the bulk of the membership of the new bodies was subject to an electoral process which took no account of honorific distinctions. In practice, if not in intention, the suffrage qualifications proved remarkably egalitarian and they were supplemented by regulations of potentially revolutionary import – for example, the stipulation that the municipal assemblies should meet every Sunday even when no business had been tabled for discussion. The issue of fiscal autonomy divides the creations of 1787 from their linear descendants, however. And yet, in a region like the Auvergne where the *taille* remained *personnelle* for the most part, the mere existence of a municipal assembly implied a moral restriction on the discretion of the *consul* or tax collector. Once all these points are weighed the significance of the 1787 reform becomes apparent, but its impact in the countryside remains problematic. On paper, municipal assemblies existed in the Brivadois and the Haute-Auvergne a full two and a half years before the revolutionary communes were organised. According to the *procès-verbaux d'élection* a goodly number of peasants turned out to vote for them and in some localities, according to outside observers, the elections created a ferment. Whether the assemblies continued to meet after the initial summons, and whether they became 'l'école

---

[17] Renouvin, *Les Assemblées provinciales de 1787.*
[18] Léoncé de Lavergne, *Les Assemblées provinciales sous Louis XVI.*
[19] R. D. Harris, *Necker, Reform Statesman of the Ancien Régime* (London, 1979), p. 182.

élémentaire d'une sage administration'[20] as the assembly of the *élection* of Brioude envisaged, seems doubtful, however. Yet the novelty of choosing representatives by ballot should not be underestimated. It offered unsuspected opportunities for the articulation of opinion. An anonymous memorialist painted a dire picture of social subversion. The municipal elections, he claimed, had undermined the reflex of deference:

il est de la connaissance du rédacteur de ce mémoire que dans une certaine paroisse les membres ont été tirés à la courte paille. Que dans une autre plus considérable, où il y a des bourgeois, des avocats, des praticiens on a déposé le sindic qui était de cet ordre, on a nommé à la place un serrurier, les membres ont été élus à l'avenant. Dans une autre la classe des artisans et paysans de campagne étant plus nombreuse et très bruyante, les magistrats et bourgeois se sont retirés, et la composition des membres a été élue en conséquence.[21]

1789: disintegration and reintegration

The collapse of absolute monarchy triggered an explosion of particularism in the countryside. Changes of regime in 1815, 1830 and 1848 produced a similar, if less deafening, detonation. The dammed up rivalries of generations broke loose as villages and parishes jockeyed for position in the new order of things. By 1792 the complex and often chaotic manoeuvring had spawned an administrative and territorial reorganisation which left few visible traces of the institutional infrastructure of the *ancien régime*. While the end-products of this reorganisation are familiar to every student of the French Revolution, the process of redefinition has been little studied. In the southern Massif Central there was nothing pre-ordained about the emergent communes, cantons, districts and departments. They constituted the victors in a neo-Darwinian struggle for survival and recognition which intensified dramatically after 1789. The stampede for the dignity of *chef-lieu* status and the appurtenances thereof produced losers as well as victors and added a fresh layer of petty resentments and thwarted ambitions. Many of the realignments and adjustments fostered during these years of extreme administrative decentralisation have escaped the record, but sufficient evidence remains to suggest a correlation between secular rivalries and postures of hostility or sympathy for the Revolution.

The hiatus of 1789 facilitated several different types of community assertion. Remnants of ecclesiastical, seigneurial and fiscal jurisdictions made determined efforts to secure communal status; diasporas of villages tried to escape the thrall of their *bourgs*; *bourgs* and large or well-sited villages indulged in bitter rivalry to win inclusion in the lists of cantonal seats and towns fought epic battles for administrative and judicial pre-eminence (see

[20] A.D.P.-de-D. C7361 *Procès-verbal de l'assemblée d'élection de Brioude, session du mois d'octobre 1788.*
[21] A.D.P.-de-D. 4C38 *Mémoire sur les municipalités* (n.d.).

chapter eight, pp. 245–6). As the shock-waves of disintegration receded, intimations of administrative grandeur burgeoned in even the most wretched localities and a vast, slow-motion game of musical chairs unfolded as protagonists circled suspiciously around a diminishing supply of *chef-lieu* dignities. Competition was most intense at the level of the commune and it was enhanced by the decision of the legislators to adopt a lowest common denominator solution to the question of municipal liberties under the new regime. During the debates several deputies with experience of the functioning of the provincial assemblies in the Berry and the Haute-Guienne spoke up on behalf of the dispersed habitat regions and Thouret's proposal to agglomerate villages into 'cantonal municipalities' was defeated. On 14 December 1789 the celebrated decree 'pour la constitution des municipalités' swept away the municipal assemblies of 1787 together with the venal corporations and declared that a new municipal body would be formed in each town, *bourg*, parish or community.

The advocates of the lowest common denominator solution were preoccupied with the need to grant a measure of fiscal independence[22] to the countryside and it is doubtful whether they appreciated the administrative and political implications of their victory. The disintegration of authority during these months was beyond the power of any legislator to halt, but it drew further encouragement and a certain justification from the new decree. Furthermore, the Constituent Assembly resolved to tackle the reform of local government from the bottom upwards which meant that for about a year there existed no constituted authority in the departments empowered to curb the pullulating municipalities. By 1790 a stasis had been reached in the Aveyron with a matrix of nine districts, eighty-one cantons and 684 communes officially endorsed. The number of communes roughly matched the number of parishes embraced by the dioceses of Rodez and Vabres, but their origins and boundaries were not usually as straightforward as this. In 1808 the prefect, Sainthorent,[23] claimed that many microscopic communes had been created more or less at whim. The proprietorial bourgeoisie had exploited the chaotic conditions of 1789–90 to elevate the dignity of their manors and *métairies*. Communes comprising a single estate certainly had been established in the district of Rodez and the preliminary survey work for the Napoleonic *cadastre* uncovered all sorts of bizarre anomalies. The territory of the commune of Nauviale was found to contain fifty-two enclaved portions of other communes and several communes in the Levézou mountains were far from compact entities.[24]

[22] Renouvin, *Les Assemblées provinciales de 1787*, pp. 360–9 and notes.
[23] A.N. F^{1b} II Aveyron 3 Prefect to Minister of the Interior, Rodez, 8 July 1808.
[24] A.N. F^2 II Aveyron 1 Extract of register of the prefecture, Aveyron, 25 Ventôse *an* XII; F^2 II Aveyron 3 Report of *directeur des contributions directes* to prefect Aveyron, Rodez, 2 May 1825.

Territorial redefinition was not primarily the work of aspiring bourgeois and seigneurs seeking to convert their fiefs into municipalities, however. It reflected a popular urge, an attempt to actualise a developing perception of community. Usually, therefore, the bid for communal status came as the last act in a long process of emotional secession. The château of La Roque Valzergues (Rouergue) had once been the seat of an important seigneurie embracing about sixty parishes, but by the eighteenth century it subsisted on a much reduced scale and the economic centre of gravity had shifted to Saint Saturnin-de-Lenne, a bustling village situated on the high-road below the old hill-top fort. Officially, La Roque remained the centre of the *mandement*, however. All decisions concerning the seigneurie emanated from La Roque. This situation irked the inhabitants of the more populous settlement who watched emissaries bearing the tax rolls pass through their village on the way to La Roque. They began to intercept the mail addressed to the consuls of the *chef-lieu* and generally to assert their independence. Mounting friction precipitated a trial of strength in the *sénéchaussée* court at Rodez and by the end of the *ancien régime* the two villages were locked in a bitter struggle for preeminence. In 1789 the *conseil politique* of La Roque proceeded to choose its *consuls* for the coming year in the customary fashion, but that autumn the situation was transformed by the publication of the new municipal law. The inhabitants of Saint Saturnin seized the opportunity to assert their separate identity and set up a municipality: 'ils l'ont en effet organisé à leur gré, au mépris des formalités préalables'[25] claimed a petition signed notably by the *curé* of the erstwhile *chef-lieu* parish. La Roque bowed, complainingly, before the force of circumstances and established its own municipality in order to retrieve something from the wreckage. A furious petition reached the Constitution Committee of the National Assembly demanding that Saint Saturnin be called to order, and warning that: 'De cette scission et division des deux parroisses (*sic*) résultent et naîtroient de grands abus. Les habitans de St Saturnin s'érigent en despotes; ils font tout à leur gré, disant qu'ils le veulent ainsi.'[26]

Such confrontations were legion during the winter of 1789–90 as seigneurial, fiscal and ecclesiastical categories succumbed to centrifugal pressures. A spate of petitions and *mémoires* issued from shadowy communities in the making, and from ancient jurisdictions, instancing dark tales of turpitude and deceit. Historians have tended to dismiss the ebb and flow of local animosities as tangential to the process of opinion formation in the countryside and hence unworthy of scientific analysis. Yet so-called 'parish pump' issues constituted the very stuff of politics in a region like the southern Massif Central where territorial particularisms were tenacious. Time and again, these apparently

---

[25] A.N. DIV40 *Comité de constitution*: Albouy, *curé*, and others to *Nosseigneurs*, La Roque, 24 May 1790 [wrongly classified in the file for the Lozère].
[26] *Ibid.*

mundane issues were projected on to the broad canvas of ideological options. A presumption in favour of the Revolution, to put it no more strongly, flourished in villages like Saint Saturnin which had won civil recognition as a result of that event; it flourished, too, in the villages of the Aubin coal basin which had experienced at close quarters the exactions of the old regime, and in the villages of the Causse du Larzac subject to the oppressive lordship of the Order of Malta. Not every social embryo succeeded in its bid for separate existence in 1789–90 and the momentum for redefinition continued only slightly abated during the next few years. But as the process began to overlap the revolutionary climacteric it became as much a symptom as a source of politicisation. In 1791 the villages of Fayet and Mélargues were dismembered from the monster commune of Brusque on the ground that they were imbued with patriotic sentiments while the population of the *bourg* (where an important abbatial foundation had been dissolved) clearly were not. In fact, the commune of Brusque was a transparent descendant of the old community of inhabitants from which the two villages in question had been trying to secede for decades.[27]

The Revolution vested too much power in the commune for proliferation of administratively and politically unreliable municipalities to pass unchecked. Long before the Constitution of the Year Three (1795) initialled a fresh experiment in municipal organisation, *ad hoc* regrouping solutions had been devised by Department and District administrators.[28] The year 1795 and the accession of the Directory witnessed the return to favour of the concept of the cantonal municipality. Commune and municipality ceased to be co-terminous: only towns would be entitled to their own municipality; rural communes (with fewer than 5,000 inhabitants) would be banded together to form collective municipalities. Political control of the new entities was reinforced by the attachment of a non-elected agent of central government (*commissaire du Directoire-Exécutif*) to each 'administration municipale'. In the regions of dispersed habitat and belligerent particularism, this solution posed multiple problems for the rural elector, but was welcomed by administrators. When the Constitution of the Year Eight (1799) undid this reform they abandoned it with marked reluctance. In theory, the law of 28 Pluviôse VIII (17 February 1800) abolished the cantonal municipalities and restored to each rural commune its municipal council, *adjoint* and mayor although these offices ceased to be elective. In practice, the changeover proved less straightforward. Sainthorent,[29] the newly appointed prefect of

---

[27] A.D.A. L701 Constans Labourgade to directory of Department (?) of the Aveyron, St Affrique, 15 March 1791.

[28] The terms Department and District have been capitalised to indicate the administrative body as opposed to the physical context.

[29] A.N. F¹ᵇ II Aveyron 3 Printed *extrait des registres de la préfecture du département de l'Aveiron du 5 messidor an 8 de la République Française*.

the Aveyron, ignored the prescriptions of the law of 28 Pluviôse and agglomerated the municipalities of the 579 surviving communes of the department
into 190 *mairies*. Ministers repeatedly signalled the illegality of Sainthorent's
creations, but administrative inertia and ill will ensured that they survived to
undergo selective and piecemeal reform in the 1830s and 1840s.

When the Minister of the Interior condemned the *mairies* in 1808,
Sainthorent's successor pointed out that a return to the regime prevailing
before the Constitution of the Year Three would entail the reinstatement of
municipalities 'qui ne comptent qu'une population de 25 à 75 âmes parmi
lesqu'elles (*sic*) il ne se trouve que 4 à 12 chefs de famille'.[30] Nevertheless, an
arrêté of 4 October 1808 was promulgated which instructed the municipal
councillors of each *mairie* to meet and discuss how these artificial entities
could be divided up. The result was a rekindling of animosities and a round
of petitioning on a par with 1789–90 as virtually every component commune
demanded its independence. With scarcely concealed impatience the sub-
prefects struggled once more to carve the recalcitrant habitat into viable
administrative units. A draft decree replacing the 190 *mairies* with 346
municipalities was submitted, but the Conseil d'Etat threw it out on the
ground that the proposed communal boundaries failed to coincide with those
of the parishes. The cantonal municipality lived on in disguise, therefore. Yet
even the administrative logic of Sainthorent's reorganisation became questionable as subsequent judicial reforms eroded its foundations. The reshaping
of the jurisdictions of the Justices of the Peace carried out on 7 Fructidor X
(25 August 1802) placed the principal villages of the *mairie* of St Léons in
separate judicial cantons.

As long as the prefects continued to appoint municipal personnel the frictions and tensions engendered by the *mairies* were muffled, but in 1815
Napoleon restored democratic liberties in a desperate bid to catalyse popular
support and galvanise the nation for war. The decree of 30 April 1815
ordered the immediate renewal of the mayors and *adjoints* by election in
accordance with the qualifications laid down in the venerable law of 14
December 1789. Time was short and the studied opportunism of administrators in the department of the Lozère ensured that the decree remained a
dead letter, but in the Aveyron the elections opened a veritable Pandora's Box
of rivalry and recrimination. Electors rebelled against time-serving mayors
appointed by the prefects; they rebelled against the tutelage of the *chefs-lieux
de mairie* and they exploited the novel opportunity for legitimate assembly in
order to settle old scores. In the *mairie* of Laissac the inhabitants of two outlying villages refused to attend the hustings and each chose a municipal body

---

[30] *Ibid.*, Prefect Aveyron to Minister of the Interior, Rodez, 8 July 1808.

of its own instead.[31] At St Léons[32] the venal notary, Joannis, was ousted from the post of mayor, but only to be succeeded by his disreputable father-in-law, the tax-collector Chaliès. At Fayet[33] the electors concluded the business of the day with an attack on those of Brusque and a promise of rendez-vous for the following Sunday. Not since the Directory had the countryside been so disturbed.

The swift defeat of Napoleon ensured that the resurgent pressures of village particularism would be contained. Nevertheless, the electoral ferment of 1815 foreshadowed a resumption of secessionist demands after 1831, for it was in that year that legislators again made municipal office elective.[34] Reform of the *mairies* of the Aveyron could be put off no longer and the work of encadastration offered a judicious means of achieving it. Galvanised by the tabling in the Chamber of Deputies of a Liberal proposal for a municipal franchise in 1829, the prefect pressed ahead with piecemeal reorganisation: 'Je sentais davantage l'urgence de cette mesure depuis la présentation de la loi communale', he reported, adding, 'il est maintenant fort essentiel de terminer ce travail avant l'exécution de la nouvelle loi, car on serait fort embarassé de composer les conseils municipaux'.[35] Progress was made but not quickly enough to avoid the difficulties encountered in 1815. Five years after the re-introduction of municipal elections the prefect admitted that many anomalies still existed: 'Il est vrai, Monsieur le Ministre, que dans l'Aveyron un grand nombre de mairies (ici *mairie* et *commune* ne sont pas deux termes synonimes [*sic*]) sont formées de la réunion de plusieurs communes ayant chacune un rôle particulier.'[36] In fact, by 1836, amalgamations had whittled down the original number of communes from 684 to 480, while Sainthorent's *mairies* had been increased from 190 to 241. The effects of this administrative merry-go-round on ordinary lives can only be guessed at. In all probability it prolonged the conviction that the commune was irrelevant, and perhaps inimical, to the sense of community which resided instead in the parish. When hopes of reform burgeoned briefly in 1808 a petitioner using heroic self-control informed the prefect that the inhabitants of the *succursale* or parish of Rullac had been listed on two separate rolls for tax purposes during the *ancien régime*,

et formait par conséquent deux communautés l'une sous le nom de Rullac et l'autre sous celui de Roufenac, comprenant en tout treize villages; que pendant la révolution les deux rôles furent joints et ne formèrent qu'une seule et même commune sous le nom

[31] In fact the decree only prescribed the renewal of the mayors and *adjoints*, not the *conseil municipal*.

[32] A.D.A. 3M31 *Elections des maires et adjoints des communes, mai–juin 1815*: anonymous letter of complaint to prefect Aveyron, St Léons, 23 May 1815.

[33] *Ibid.*, Mayor of Fayet to sub-prefect *arrondissement* St Affrique, Fayet, 13 July 1815.

[34] See below, chapter seven, p. 218.

[35] A.N. F^2 II Aveyron 1 Prefect to Minister of the Interior, Rodez, 11 March 1829.

[36] *Ibid.*, Prefect to Minister of the Interior, Rodez, 4 April 1836.

de Rullac qui est le chef-lieu de la succursale et le point le plus central de la commune; qu'en l'an 4 leur commune avait un agent municipal à l'administration municipale du ci-devant canton de La Selve; qu'en l'an 8 toutes les communes de ce canton furent réduites en une seule mairie de La Selve, dont les réclamants sont très eloignés, surtout l'ancienne communauté de Roufenac.[37]

And this was only the beginning. By 1982 the commune of Rullac had been amalgamated with that of Saint Cirq, although the parish still survives.

Much of the irritation engendered by the *mairie* solution can be explained in terms of town versus country conflict, for the seats of the *mairies*, like those of their predecessors the *administrations municipales*, were often *bourgs*. In the southern Massif Central relations between the *bourgs* and their village hinterlands were more finely balanced than in the nucleated environment of the Mediterranean plain which the *bourgs* dominated effortlessly. While the peasantry profited from the market facilities provided by the *bourgs*, they also felt exploited by the colonies of 'oisifs' – seigneurs, rentiers and legal officers – which they harboured and subjected them to periodic harassment. The *bourgs*, for their part, were adept practitioners of more subtle forms of aggression. They encroached on their weaker neighbours' commons; they bullied outlying villages into contributing towards the cost of public works of marginal benefit to them and they showed no compunction about invoking rural support in furtherance of their own grandiose ambitions. In 1800 Jean-André Barrot,[38] the deputy for the Lozère, remarked that in his department rural communes would tolerate amalgamation with each other, but would never consent to incorporation with a neighbouring town or *bourg*.

1789 turned out to be a year of unprecedented opportunity for the *bourgs* just as it did for the embryonic communes, but their interests tended to conflict with those of satellite villages. As the scramble for cantonal status began in earnest, the *bourgs* tried to increase their territorial and human substance. Emissaries from the Velay sought to detach the *bourg* of Saugues from the Gévaudan with vague promises of a 'cour de justice'. The ploy worked. Saugues was the seat of an important seigneurie embracing fourteen rural parishes whose inhabitants awoke to discover that they were now a part of the department of the Haute-Loire. The unbridgeable gorges of the Allier dividing the Gévaudan from the Velay had been conjured out of existence. A report which seems to have been drawn up by the Department authorities of the Lozère noted sourly that 'La ville de Saugues était et est encore partagée entre deux partis, le juge et les praticiens sont à la tête de celui qui domine; les cultivateurs sont ceux qui sont opprimés.'[39] The duplicity of the legal

---

[37] *Ibid.*, Inhabitants of *succursale* of Rullac to prefect Aveyron, Rullac, 2 November 1808.
[38] A.N. F² 543 *Délimitation de cantons*: Barrot to Minister of the Interior, 24 Brumaire IX.
[39] A.D.L. L110 *Circonscriptions et dénominations administratives*: unsigned and undated memorandum [1790–1].

bourgeoisie was so transparent that the peasantry made ready to launch an attack on the *bourg*.

Manoeuvres of this type became commonplace as the larger population centres jockeyed for position within and between the new departments. The *bourgs* of Le Malzieu[40] and Serverette (Lozère)[41] sought to impose their administrative hegemony on adjacent communes in a similar autocratic fashion, although with less success. However, the most serious difficulties arose when the rudimentary framework of cantons was put to the test. In the spring of 1790 the active citizens of each commune gathered in cantonal primary assemblies to begin the laborious business of electing the District and Department authorities. These large and unwieldy assemblies seemed purpose-built for the articulation of community grievances. Embittered communes worsted in the struggle for cantonal status refused to attend for fear of setting a precedent; the voters of rival villages refused to enter the same room; dubious communes despatched contingents of voters in the hope of achieving recognition while bona fide communes despatched small armies of voters whose electoral qualifications were dubious to say the least. In the Ardèche the agitation reached fever pitch and violence was only narrowly averted. Several villages in the mountainous hinterland of the canton of Charmes[42] refused to attend the *chef-lieu* on the ground that they would not be safe there. Etienne de Montgolfier, the royal commissioner sent out to supervise the primary assemblies in the Haut Vivarais, reported that the mayor and commander of the National Guard of Charmes had sought his authorisation to disarm the voters as they arrived. In the canton of Vernoux the orderly conduct of the elections was hindered by the civic pride of the 'town' of Chalençon[43] whose electors chose to meet separately, while the inhabitants of Thueyts at the foot of the Tanargue took the unusual step of resisting the cantonal status conferred upon them by the Constituent Assembly. Thueyts had been one of the epicentres of agrarian rebellion eight months earlier and the peasantry feared the dignity of *chef-lieu de canton* for precisely the reason that the bourgeois of Saugues aspired to it: 'ils s'étaient persuadés qu'on voulait leur donner 3 ou 4 juges, beaucoup de procureurs et, comme ils avaient été, disaient-ils, assez vexés par cette engeance, ils n'en voulaient plus',[44] reported the commissioner Duclaux.

It is easy to imagine how such clashes and confrontations, and the aspirations and disappointments they engendered, helped to crystallise loyalties. Yet we should be wary of assuming that territorial allegiances were the only, or even the most important, denominator of political commitment. The

[40] *Ibid., Pétitions en réunion des municipalités et en érection ou division des paroisses* (n.d.).
[41] *Ibid.*
[42] A.N.F.[1c] III Ardèche 10 Montgolfier to Monseigneur [de St Priest], Charmes, 17 April 1790.
[43] *Ibid., Mémoire sur l'assemblée primaire tenue le 24 juin 1791 en la ville de Chalençon.*
[44] A.N. F[1c] III Ardèche 10 Duclaux to Monsieur le Comte [de St Priest], Aubenas, 25 May 1790.

dynamics of mobilisation for or against the Revolution were infinitely complex. In the south-eastern corner of the Rouergue a long history of market rivalry divided the two *bourgs* of St Jean-du-Bruel and Nant.[45] As road communications across the Causse du Larzac improved, the privileged location of St Jean-du-Bruel at the entrance to the Cévennes brought commercial opportunities that were eagerly exploited. Throughout the eighteenth century Nant tried every expedient from force to bribery in a campaign to persuade the *causse* villages to frequent its marketplace, but to no avail. Instead the senior *bourg* had to draw comfort from its acknowledged ecclesiastical and administrative pre-eminence and affected to despise commerce – a convenient posture, for the mercantile families of St Jean-du-Bruel were predominantly Calvinist. Economic and confessional antipathies dovetailed neatly to perpetuate a vigorous tradition of inter-parish warfare. In theory, the irruption of revolutionary politics might have been expected to follow these well-established battle lines, but in fact the alignments were more complicated. Nant, to its relief, obtained the seat of the canton and with its administrative status confirmed became a citadel of patriotism. St Jean-du-Bruel, by contrast, fared badly in the reorganisation of 1789–90 and little better subsequently. Its inhabitants acquired a not entirely deserved reputation for militant royalism. In reality, socio-economic and confessional tensions ensured that neither *bourg* was homogeneously favourable or hostile to the Revolution. Opinion divided and tended to extremes. The Counter-Revolution came early to St Jean-du-Bruel when local royalists sent recruits to the second Camp de Jalès[46] in February 1791. The patriots speedily organised themselves, if only for protection. Likewise at Nant, escalating internal tensions of uncertain origin momentarily clouded older and more straightforward enmities. In any case the dialectic of Revolution in a region characterised more by gladiatorial political combat than mass participation had largely subsumed the older sources of friction by 1792. The rivalry of two mediocre *bourgs* in the Lozère, for instance, became hidden beneath a cloak of revolutionary rhetoric. When, after two years as the seat of a canton, St Sauveur-de-Peyre failed to reward the trust placed in it, the status of *chef-lieu* passed to Le Buisson because its inhabitants were 'républicain'. Yet when these peasants turned 'royaliste' in the Year Three (1794–5), the dignity reverted to St Sauveur-de-Peyre. After the coup of 18 Fructidor V (4 September 1797) republicanism miraculously revived at Le Buisson and the population demanded the elevation of their village once more. Unimpressed and undeceived by this display of opportunism, the Department

---

[45] G. Laurans, *Etude et documents pour l'histoire de Nant* (typescript memoir in A.D.A.). Also A.D.A. L669 *bis*; L706; L713; 67L (2); 8V1.
[46] See below, p. 198.

voted in Brumaire IX (October–November 1800) to amalgamate both localities with the adjacent canton of Aumont.[47]

La République au village

In the controversy over the growth of a national political awareness among the rural population of France the claims of the Revolution of 1789 have been curiously overlooked. To judge from the bold assertions of some contributors to the debate manhood suffrage was invented in March 1848 with the advent of the Second Republic. It may be that the Jacobin experiment in mass political mobilisation deserves, on balance, to be overlooked. But few historians have followed Maurice Agulhon[48] in venturing across the chronological divide in order to put it to the test. Agulhon's sequential histories of Provence contain memorable vignettes of the catalytic process of village politicisation, although he concluded that the legacy of the great Revolution was not of major significance in the development of nineteenth-century republicanism. Whether this judgement is valid for the uplands of the southern Massif Central will be discussed in the remainder of this chapter.

Elections for the new municipal, District and Department bodies; elections for the new Justices of the Peace and the new bishops and *curés* vividly underlined the arrival of a new regime on the scene. Never before had the country dweller been canvassed for so many different purposes and in such a short space of time. The effects of licensing for public discussion topics hitherto inconceivable remain strictly imponderable, but we may assume that electoral consultation triggered a *prise de conscience* of some description. A second, more enduring and more heart-searching growth of awareness issued from the ecclesiastical legislation of the Constituent Assembly. There is abundant evidence to indicate that the dilemma of the clerical oath and the policy it inaugurated powerfully catalysed attitudes in the southern Massif Central. As the time approached when the parish clergy were required to swear allegiance to the constitution early in 1791, public opinion swung sharply. The phases of this transition are beyond the reach of detailed analysis and it is questionable whether the term 'public opinion' has much meaning at this stage. Nevertheless, it seems that in 1791 accumulating prejudices eroded an attitude of benevolent neutrality towards the Revolution. Involuntarily, and not a little paradoxically, the intransigent stance of the catholic church can be counted among the motors of politicisation in this region.

---

[47] A.N. F² 543 *Délimitation de cantons: commissaire du pouvoir exécutif près l'administration municipale du canton du Buisson, ci-devant St Sauveur*, to Minister of the Interior, Coufinhet, 11 Brumaire VI.
[48] Agulhon, *La Vie sociale en Provence intérieure au lendemain de la Révolution*; *La République au village: les populations du Var de la Révolution à la Seconde République* (Paris, 1970). Also chapter ten, p. 314, note 21.

In fact, misgivings in the face of the iconoclasm of the Constituent Assembly were uttered long before the negotiations over the Civil Constitution of the Clergy broke down. The failure of Dom Gerle's motion that catholics alone be entitled to worship publicly provoked consternation in 'front-line' parishes. Toleration of non-conformists was one thing, placing them on an equal footing with the adherents of the majority faith was quite another. For the inhabitants of Murasson,[49] a catholic parish sandwiched between the protestants of the Tarn valley and those of the Castrais, it was clearly too much and on 24 May 1790 they urged the Assembly to declare Roman Catholicism the sole religion of state. A fortnight earlier rekindled sectarian passions had resulted in five deaths at Montauban, while in the department of the Gard the meeting of primary electoral assemblies at Nîmes would shortly give the signal for a savage religious and political confrontation during which between 100 and 300 catholics were massacred. This background of fear and irritation as the monasteries were dissolved and their alms hand-outs ceased, gave an inauspicious start to the Civil Constitution. In the southern Massif Central the parish clergy overwhelmingly rejected the oath, although not without hesitation and heart-searching. Against the condemnations of bitter adversaries of the Revolution such as Monseigneur de Castellane, the bishop of Mende, had to be weighed pecuniary considerations (many *curés* and *vicaires* lived wretchedly on inadequate tithes and *portions congrues*)[50] and an overriding sense of obligation to parishioners. In the Lozère between twenty and thirty clerics swore the oath out of a parochial clergy of 242, but only seventeen of these (7 per cent) adhered unequivocally and unswervingly. In the Ardèche, the Aveyron and the Haute-Loire, by contrast, between 30 and 35 per cent of the clergy swore to uphold the Civil Constitution. However, these figures mask considerable local variations. Almost half (49 per cent) of the clergy of the Brivadois took the oath compared with only 17 per cent in the Velay.[51] This contrast expresses well the manifold discrepancies between the two *pays* which in 1790 had been joined to form the Haute-Loire. The Brivadois was less fervent, more permeable to outside influences and its lower clergy harboured a bitter resentment against the civil and ecclesiastical overlordship of the Chapter of Brioude.

However ideologically motivated may have been the decision over the oath for the clergy, it was not, in general, a matter for debate within the rural community. Parishioners invested much emotional and not a little financial capi-

---

[49] A.N. F^{19} 408 *Cultes*: deliberation of the community of Murasson (Aveyron), 24 May 1790.
[50] In 1790 94 of the 195 parish priests in the diocese of Mende declared incomes not exceeding 500 *l*. (F. Izard, 'Le Clergé paroissial Gévaudanais à la fin du XVIIIe siècle' (Université Paul Valéry, Montpellier III, Mémoire de maîtrise, 1978), p. 69.
[51] For oath-taking statistics, see Izard, 'Le Clergé paroissial', pp. 90–2; Jolivet, *La Révolution dans l'Ardèche*, pp. 253–79; R. P. Mouly, *Concordataires, constitutionnels et 'enfarinés' en Quercy et Rouergue au lendemain de la Révolution* (Rodez, 1945) p. 55; Merley, *La Haute-Loire*, i, p. 276.

tal in their priests and naturally wished to retain them whether they were jurors or non-jurors. Yet the solemn declarations made before the municipalities in the course of 1791 rapidly acquired ideological under-pinnings, for they set in train a series of events which for many priests would end in imprisonment, exile or death. The oath was obligatory for all ecclesiastics carrying out pastoral duties and those who failed to swear it in due form were liable to dismissal and replacement. As this brutal logic was played out country dwellers were drawn into a confrontation with the new regime even as they continued, in many parts of the region, to demolish the foundations of the old. During these critical early years of the Revolution crowd violence exhibited an ambiguous character. It exploded with great paroxysms of rage against the residue of seigneurialism, but it also singled out for attack improving landlords and the newly installed juring clergy who passed for symbols of the new order of things. The hostility which greeted the intruder clerics was born of fears of spiritual separation – the conviction that salvation was linked irretrievably to the ministry of the old incumbent. The inhabitants of the parish of St Jean de Clauselles-les-Bourg urged the administrators of the District of Millau to exempt their priests from the civil oath. They would make any sacrifice rather than be separated from 'la religion de leurs pères, la seule qui puisse les mener au bonheur de la vie futture (*sic*)'.[52] But it soon became more than anomic dread as the peasantry vented its fury, first against the new arrivals and then against the authorities who had allowed the legislation to take effect. Village notables who for social, economic and psychological reasons had failed to adjust to the change of regime began to fish in the troubled waters of the Assembly's religious policies. Aided and abetted by emissaries of the Princes, embryonic counter-revolutionaries sought to catalyse the disaffection into something more sustained, more positive and ideological.

The village of Le Bourg, in fact, had long been a refuge for bandits, who preyed on travellers using the highway across the Causse de Sauveterre; and its seigneur, Antoine Pourquery,[53] turned it into a bastion of militant royalism. By July 1791 disillusionment with the Civil Constitution had reached such a pitch that Pourquery entertained hopes of launching some kind of counter-revolutionary gathering involving a number of parishes at the entrance to the gorges of the Tarn. Viscount Dalbignac's[54] château of Le Triadou became the centre of operations; weapons and powder were

[52] A.D.A. L669 *bis* Petition of inhabitants of Le Bourg to District of Millau, Le Bourg, 29 January? 1791.

[53] M. L. de Santi, 'Notes et documents sur les intrigues royalistes dans le midi de la France de 1792 à 1815', *Mémoires de l'académie des sciences, inscriptions et belles-lettres de Toulouse*, iv (1916), 37–113; D. Higgs, *Ultraroyalism in Toulouse from its Origins to the Revolution of 1830* (Baltimore and London, 1973), p. 40.

[54] A.D.A. 67L (2) *Comité de surveillance* of Rodez, *société populaire* Millau to *société populaire* Rodez, Millau, 16 July 1791.

stockpiled there and its fortifications were improved. These preparations were co-ordinated with more celebrated gatherings in the Bas Vivarais known as the first and second Camps de Jalès.[55] Once again religious fears were paramount. The first gathering took place in August 1790 in the aftermath of the *bagarre de Nîmes*. Between 20,000 and 40,000 catholic peasants drawn from 180 parishes camped in the open countryside around the château of Jalès and threatened to descend on the protestants of the Gard. Although counter-revolutionaries failed to exploit this assembly – probably the largest ever witnessed in the region – its political tone was distinctly ambiguous. By the time the call went out for a fresh demonstration in February 1791 the conflict over the oath had heightened tensions, but the organisers made plain their seditious and insurrectionary intentions and popular support was more measured. It is a signal fact that the success of royalism in the departments of the south hinged on its capacity to play the religious card. Cries of 'Religion in danger!' could mobilise huge armies of peasants at the height of the harvest whereas appeals to the putative monarchical instincts of the country dweller evoked a guarded response. Strictly speaking, popular royalism was probably no more prevalent than popular jacobinism. In the event, Jalès was inundated by patriotic national guardsmen from the Gard and the leaders of the abortive rising were put to flight.

Large-scale mobilisations belied the creeping politicisation that was affecting the region, however. Deprived of their livings, the refractory clergy refused to abandon their parishes and wasted no opportunity to criticise the new regime. More often than not the juring clerics arrived in the villages under armed escort and promptly found themselves engaged in a bitter struggle for the hearts and minds of their parishioners. In many instances these confrontations sowed the seeds of a primitive form of politicisation, for parties tended to coalesce around each priest and before long every issue to affect the community evoked a partisan response. Commissioners sent out by the Department of the Aveyron to investigate a politically motivated murder in the commune of Bozouls[56] reported that the inhabitants were split into two factions. The *curé* and nuns of the local convent led one group while those who objected to clerical control of the commune and who were by definition, therefore, patriots formed another. The local militants of the Year Two (1793–4) naturally emerged from this latter coterie. In his memoirs of the revolutionary years J.-H. de Barrau emphasised the same alignment. The political apprenticeship of the village *sans-culottes* of Carcenac-Salmiech (Aveyron)[57] began with the replacement of the old priest by a juring cleric

[55] Jolivet, *La Révolution dans l'Ardèche*, pp. 209–52; G. Lewis, *The Second Vendée* (Oxford, 1978) pp. 31–7 and *passim*.
[56] A.N. F⁷ 3657¹ *Correspondance et pièces relatives aux troubles et insurrections manifestées dans le département de l'Aveiron, six derniers mois 1791*.
[57] 'Mémoires privés d'un Ruthenois [Justin-Hippolyte de Barrau]', *Journal de l'Aveyron*, 10 March 1900.

named Viguié in 1791. In 1793 Viguié's faction constituted itself into a *comité de surveillance* and took brief control of the commune. The ecclesiastical rupture of 1791 dramatically catalysed opinions in the region, therefore. Even the possessed began to speak the language of politics. The *curé* of Estables (Aveyron)[58] mounted an elaborate charade during which a poor girl imbued with devils denounced the constitutional priest of nearby St Laurent-d'Olt among others. Exorcisms were an integral feature of the religious culture of the region and this one caused a sensation.

The refusal of a majority of the clergy to cooperate with the new regime left parish provision in tatters by the end of 1792. Juring clerics were in desperately short supply and the peasantry of the high plateaux of the Aubrac, the Margeride and the Tanargue found themselves denied spiritual comforts for months on end. Catholicism was reduced to the status of a Desert religion – its plight comparable, momentarily, with that of Calvinism earlier in the century. Superstitious dread gripped the countryside and it leavened the royalist cause. After waiting anxiously, and in vain, for a priest to arrive and say Mass the principal inhabitants of Recoules-d'Aubrac penned the following resolution:

l'heure de la messe étant déjà passée et aucun prêtre ne parroissant (*sic*) pour la dire, alors comme à l'envie se sont fait entendre les soupirs, les gémissemens, les pleurs, les plaintes et les cris. A cette scène qui n'avait rien que d'attendrissant, n'ont pas tardé de succéder des plus violens murmures contre MM. le maire et off[icie]rs municipaux: se (*sic*) sont eux, disent-ils, qui en sont la cause . . . il ne devoient pas publier ce malheureux décret . . . il faut que nous gardions nos prêtres à quel prix que ce soit.[59]

The decree in question was the notorious extradition order of 26 August 1792 against non-jurors. Henceforth priests who refused to accept exile were driven into hiding. As the deliberation quoted above clearly demonstrates, the measure exasperated the peasantry and consolidated the tactical alliance of clericalism and royalism. When Marc-Antoine Charrier of Nasbinals,[60] the parish adjacent to Recoules-d'Aubrac, raised the standard of revolt the following year, the recruits to his Catholic Royal Army were drawn mainly from the communities of the Aubrac plateau. The decree also sent shock waves through the ranks of bourgeois revolutionaries. Sincere, if dilatory, catholics, many administrators had no stomach for the incarceration of priests and with fresh District and Department elections due in November 1792 the manpower reserves of the patriot party dwindled.

As the *menu peuple* of Paris and the great cities awakened to political consciousness, the signs suggested that the arena of debate in the countryside was narrowing. The Revolution (and the Counter-Revolution) had become a

[58] E. Falgairolle, *Les Exorcismes en Lozère en 1792* (Paris, 1894), p. 28.
[59] A.N. F^{19} 444 *Cultes: extrait sur extrait d'une délibération de la commune de Recoules-d'Aubrac*, 30 September 1792.
[60] Delon, *La Révolution en Lozère*, pp. 288–377 and plates.

stage on which minorities engaged in ritualised combat before an audience of sympathetic or indifferent onlookers. In the southern Massif Central, at least, the embryonic politicisation of an immature electorate resulted in a stunted end-product: factionalism. The phenomenon of faction would remain the salient feature of the political landscape of the region for much of the nineteenth century. Indubitably, the logic of revolution favoured this development, for after 1792 the euphoric administrative decentralisation of 1789–90 was rapidly reversed. With internal and external alarms sounding, the Republic found that it could ill afford the freedom of municipalities to protect refractory priests; the freedom of National Guard detachments to manoeuvre like private armies; the freedom of Departments to form coalitions and the freedom of criminal courts to acquit notorious counter-revolutionaries. Officially and unofficially, power devolved upon coteries of militants grouped in the District administrations; in the jacobin clubs and in the police committees (*comités de surveillance*) whose task it was to arrest and detain the heterodox.

These organs, plus the municipalities whose powers remained extensive, became the instruments of factional domination and the embodiment of 'la république au village'. It is worth examining them in some detail for they shed light on the nature of political commitment at the most humble and inarticulate level. Electoral skirmishes and the spilling over of quarrels concerning the clerical oath lay, as we have noted, at the heart of many factional alignments. But the origins of the cliques who monopolised local office during the Year Two were often deeply embedded in the fabric of the *ancien régime*. At St Alban in the Lozère the 'ultra' clique which controlled the *comité de surveillance* consisted of individuals whose sense of cohesion had grown up during anti-seigneurial struggles dating back to 1777. Noé-Jean Atrasic, the seigneur in question, was indicted on numerous counts: 'pour avoir refusé de sortir son banc de l'église et d'abattre ses girouetes (*sic*)'; 'D'avoir menassé (*sic*) un particulier qui plaidoit avec luy pour la restitution des communeaux (*sic*) inféodés', etc.[61] Usually *coqs de village* like Atrasic contrived to move with the times. A local election left uncontested, a seat in the *comité* left unoccupied could make the difference between liberty and proscription. Jean-Victor Chaliès[62] of St Léons weathered changes of regime spanning four decades. He survived a damaging investigation into his activities as notary and self-appointed tax collector, carried out by the *bureau intermédiaire* of the Provincial Assembly of Haute-Guienne in 1781, to emerge, in 1793, as president of the *comité de surveillance*. With the aid of his kinsman, Joannis, he still lorded over the commune in 1815.

In communities which derived a living from the high pastures of the

---

[61] A.D.L. L520 *Comité de surveillance* of St Alban, *reg. dél.*, 20 October 1793; Jones, 'La *République au village* in the Southern Massif Central', pp. 797–8.

[62] See above p. 191. Also Guilhamon, *Journal des voyages*, i, p. 114 note 2.

Aubrac and Mont Lozère, agrarian tensions, either with or without a seigneurial undertow, inevitably bulked large. Led by a local landowner Jean-Pierre Long, the inhabitants of the village of Le Pouget (parish of St Chély-d'Aubrac) served an unwitting apprenticeship to the Revolution when a change of ownership deprived them of pasturing rights on the Montagne de Salacroup in 1777. Long sought to vindicate the community's rights in the courts, but the case was lost and the villagers found themselves saddled with heavy costs. These they were still paying when the Revolution broke out and they drove their stock on to the disputed pasture in defiance. The victory proved short-lived, for the owner, *Veuve* Vivens, obtained a confirmation of the original verdict from the District Tribunal of Espalion and the community was again required to withdraw its beasts. Within a year the creation of the *comités de surveillance* and the first penal measures against 'suspects' transformed the balance of power, however. Girded with the authority of the all-seeing and almighty Republic, Long and his followers proceeded to arrest *Veuve* Vivens and her seven children and to impound the disputed property.[63]

The lineaments of sectarian conflict were never far beneath the surface in the mixed towns and *bourgs* of the Ardèche, the Cévennes and the valley of the Tarn. Adherents to the reformed faith were attracted to the Revolution like moths to light and the jacobin elites which controlled the *comités* and municipalities of towns such as St Affrique, Millau and Florac during the Terror were protestant almost to a man. Factional alignments crystallised around family rivalries, too, even where the spur of religious non-conformity was absent. The appalling bloodshed of the White Terror at Laissac[64] may be traced back to a feud dividing the Pons and Mercier households, their retainers and allies. But the confessional and familial characteristics of village jacobinism have been fully discussed elsewhere.[65] The point which should be emphasised is not that every case of ostensible adhesion to the Revolution (or the Counter-Revolution) can be reduced to considerations of narrow self-interest, but that the political culture of the region was decidedly hybrid. At some point the empirical and the ideological merged, but the stimulus to take sides almost always came from within the rural community.

Authentic examples of disinterested adhesion to the Revolution are not lacking, but they rarely featured the peasantry. Village jacobinism and, we suspect, village royalism were elite phenomena – evidence of ideological seepage into the ranks of the rural bourgeoisie and, possibly, those of artisans dwelling in the *bourgs*. Rural proprietors might bring to the cause a motley collection of villagers, but under conditions of deference and obligation.

---

[63] A.D.A. L682 *bis* Petition of *veuve* Vivens of Salacroup to directory of Department Aveyron, 20 May 1793.
[64] See below, p. 207.
[65] Jones, 'Political Commitment and Rural Society in the Southern Massif Central'; '*La République au village* in the Southern Massif Central'.

Occasionally circumstances arose which catalysed opinion more thoroughly. The vicissitudes of St Geniez-d'Olt, a textile manufacturing centre at the foot of the Aubrac, are a case in point. Yet St Geniez was a *bourg*, even a small town, and we are no longer dealing with the countryside proper. Two facts help to explain the coloration of politics in St Geniez during the Revolution: its vulnerability to attack by royalists encamped in the forests covering the slopes of the Aubrac and its status as the birthplace of François Chabot.[66] Chabot was exceptional among revolutionaries in that he hailed from the people (his father had been employed as a cook by the monks of the Domerie of Aubrac). A talented scholar, he embarked on a career in the church, but made no secret of his unconventional opinions and was reprimanded by the bishop of Rodez in 1788. The Revolution launched him on a fresh career and having assiduously cultivated the patronage of the *abbé* Grégoire,[67] he became, in rapid succession, a *vicaire général* to Grégoire at Bourges, a deputy in the Legislative Assembly and a deputy in the Convention. At Paris the heavily accented interventions of the deputy from the Aveyron became famous – especially his denunciations of the so-called Austrian Committee – and his star continued to rise in the Convention.

A suspicious marriage and involvement in a plot to defraud the East India Company abruptly terminated Chabot's parliamentary career in November 1793, but not until he had consolidated the power of a faction of ultra-revolutionaries in his home town. Repeated royalist alarums in the surrounding mountains had already fixed party lines in St Geniez before Chabot left to seek his fortune in July 1791. Just under two years later he returned to the region as a roving *commissaire* and installed his boyhood cronies in a *comité de surveillance* which was licensed to ransom, arrest and imprison suspects more or less at will. For the next eighteen months this plebeian dictatorship[68] throbbed to the distant heartbeat of the Paris revolution. Of all the *comités* established in the region during the spring and autumn of 1793, that of St Geniez most effectively reproduced the jacobin commitment to fearless political activism. With Chabot and other confidants at the hub of government the faction felt quite invulnerable. Guillaume Serre, the president of the *comité* allegedly informed a woman suspect 'Je puis te tuer sans rien risquer, j'ai carte blanche, les commissaires [i.e. Chabot and his colleague Jean-Baptiste Bo] me l'ont donnée.'[69] When, in the summer of 1793, the girondist authorities of the Department of the Aveyron launched an investigation into the nefarious

---

[66] de Bonald, *François Chabot*, pp. 1–5.   [67] See above, chapter four, p. 119 and note 27.

[68] In the heyday of its authority, the *comité* comprised: 4 weavers, 1 tavern keeper (and part-time weaver); 1 tavern keeper (and part-time wig-maker); 1 saddle-maker; 1 master hatter; 1 wool-comber; 1 cooper; 1 coppersmith; 1 cobbler; 1 dyer; 1 trader; 1 cloth merchant; 1 surgeon; 1 notary and scribe (P. M. Jones, 'The Revolutionary Committees of the Department of the Aveyron, France, 1793–1795', p. 340).

[69] A.D.A. L682 *bis Enquête faite par Delpech sur les exactions de Guillaume Serre, compte-rendu* (n.d. [July 1793]).

activities of the St Geniez jacobins, Chabot procured decrees white-washing his allies and ordering the arrest and transfer to Paris of their calumniators. When the *comité* suggested that the government defray the expenses of working-men who sacrificed their livelihood to become sentinels of the Republic, Chabot's secretary wrote back 'Vous aurés encor (*sic*) vu un décret, rendu sur la motion de notre ami [Chabot], pourque chaque membre reçoive un écu d'indemnité par jour, chaque fois qu'ils se rendront à la séance. Ainsi, voilà votre vœu rempli.'[70] Clearly, Chabot passed for some kind of saviour among his compatriots. Unaware of his impending arrest on 17 November 1793, they wrote, 'Nous t'envoyons une adresse que nous avons cru à propos de faire à la convention; puisque tu es notre Saint, nous t'intercédons pour faire agréer nos vœux; ce sera une grâce de plus pour nous, si tu les fais exaucer.'[71] The language of this petition is redolent of all the cultural and psychological obstacles to political emancipation in a region like the southern Massif Central and it serves as a fitting epitaph to village jacobinism.

Revolution and Counter-Revolution

Impressed by extraordinary continuities of electoral behaviour lasting into the twentieth century, some historians have discerned in the revolutionary experience the emergence of twin dispositions: one hostile and one sympathetic to change. While it would be foolhardy to apply the notion of global political temperaments to the southern Massif Central dogmatically, it is nevertheless true that the Revolution left an important legacy in this region; a legacy, moreover, which frequently betrayed a Manichaean quality. If the Revolution consummated many old traditions, it also launched fresh ones and perpetuated old enmities in a new guise. Jacobins and royalists did not retreat into grateful obscurity once the Revolution moved into calmer waters, they continued to jockey and jostle for position. And when the gladiators of the 1790s went to the grave a fresh generation took up the sword. Opinions may have been easily acquired, but they were not easily shed. Memory – the data-bank of the rural community – saw to that. The founding fathers of the Third Republic in the Ardèche, observed E.-M. de Vogüé, were 'les fils des libéraux protestataires sous l'Empire, les petits-fils des patriotes de la révolution, les arrière-neveux des camisards, et, il faut toujours en revenir là, des combattans huguenots de jadis'.[72] Allegiance was not, apparently, a commodity for electoral transaction. It was too deeply rooted in the soil of clan, religion and locality.

---

[70] J.-L. Rigal, *Comité de surveillance de Saint Geniez-d'Olt. Procès-verbaux et arrêtés* (Rodez, 1942), p. 496 note 1.

[71] A.D.A. 72L(1) *Comité central* of district of St Geniez to Chabot, St Geniez, 24 Brumaire II.

[72] E.-M. de Vogüé, 'Notes sur le Bas Vivarais: II Les Habitans, *Revue des deux mondes*, cxiii (1892), 930.

When the sun set on the mighty Republic of the Year Two, men like Long of St Chély-d'Aubrac or Serre of St Geniez and the cliques of activists they had gathered around them were plunged into a long night of public obloquy. As the self-proclaimed representatives of a government which had exhausted any residual fund of goodwill the peasant may have felt towards the Revolution, they were despised and shunned. No one lifted a finger to help them when their stock were found maimed, their harvests overrun, their ricks set alight or when shots were fired at them through chinks in the shutters. Between 1795 and the *pax Napoleonica* of 1800 hundreds of purchasers of church and *émigré* property, ex-members of the revolutionary committees, patriotic judges and administrators were assassinated, often in circumstances of exemplary barbarity. Thousands had their property laid waste. The killing reached a crescendo in the Ardèche and the Lozère, but petty violence, intimidation and semi-political brigandage were general. The bloodshed of the White Terror was envisaged by its perpetrators as a ritual liquidation of the sins of the Revolution and as a prelude to a co-ordinated royalist rising across the departments of the South. Neither ambition proved justified. The shedding of patriotic and protestant blood in memory of the catholic martyrs of Nîmes merely invigorated and prolonged long-standing rivalries, while the attempts to launch a popular movement in support of the Bourbons foundered amid the caution and distrust of the great mass of the peasantry.

The continuity of factional alignments during the grim post-Thermidor years is truly extraordinary. The Constitution of the Year Three – the founding charter of the Directory regime – retained universal manhood suffrage (subject to exclusions) and opted for a system of annual legislative elections during which local administrative and judicial authorities would also be renewed in part. It nurtured thus an active civic life at the level of the canton and the neo-jacobins soon evolved techniques to manipulate the primary assemblies and retrieve a modicum of power. The tide of reaction flowed too fast and too dangerously for conspicuous supporters of the Revolution to organise a come-back before 1797, but on 18 Fructidor V (4 September 1797) the Directory carried out a *coup* against mounting royalist influence. Election results were overturned by government fiat in about fifty departments, including those of the Aveyron, Lozère, Ardèche and Haute-Loire. Royalist sympathisers – and even moderate republicans – were driven out of office at every level and the penal laws against refractory priests and *émigrés* were reactivated. The stage seemed set for a major neo-jacobin revival and as the militants of the clubs and the *comités* made ready to contest the elections of Germinal VI (March 1798), the factions of the Year Two re-emerged. Analysis of the composition of these factions reveals a continuity of commitment going back to the inception of the Revolution and even earlier. It also reveals a ritual of party politics in a handful of *bourgs* and villages with familiar names on either side of the barricades. Party labels and party epithets conferred an air of ideological grandeur upon the confrontations, but the abiding impression is one of doggedly secular rivalry for local office. In-groups and out-groups fought each other ferociously for control of those elective posts which had a direct and immediate relevance to daily life, such as Justices of the Peace, and each side invoked the rhetoric of national political cal debate in support of its pretensions.

The hustings were seriously disrupted in thirteen out of eighty-one cantons of the Aveyron, in eight out of thirty-six of the Ardèche, six out of thirty-four of the Haute-Loire and in nine out of forty-one of the Lozère. The number and distribution of disputed elections gives a rough idea of the contours of factional conflict. In bitterly divided cantons the electoral assembly split and a proportion of the voters decamped to conduct separate elections elsewhere. The nominees of this schismatic assembly would then compete with those of the mother assembly for the *imprimatur* of the government. The process would often be repeated when the validated electors of the primary assemblies met in common session to choose the deputies to the legislature. Electoral schism was, therefore, the unmistakable sign of violent party conflict. Which faction withdrew and which remained depended on the balance of power at village level, the number of peasants who bothered to trek to the *chef-lieu* in order to vote, and the pressures exerted on the assembled voters during the ballot. Usually, the neo-jacobins were strongest in the *bourgs* and rose early to dominate the proceedings and to deter the denizens of the countryside proper. In the Haute-Loire they discouraged potential moderate voters by insinuating that electoral registration would lead to the imposition of a new military draft and the levying of fresh taxes. But the royalists had become equally adept at managing elections and were better organised at the strategic level. During the long years of reaction they had elaborated an informal organisation known as the Institut Philanthropique which supervised elections in most of the southern departments until the hiatus of Fructidor.

In the event, the revolutionaries were generally outnumbered and outgunned and obliged to fall back on the schism tactic (see table VI.1). Only in the Ardèche where moderates and royalists withdrew in eight cantons did they succeed in forcing their enemies onto the defensive. Yet the deliberations of the primary assemblies were only the first step in this complex ritual. When the departmental electoral assembly met in Privas, royalists staged a fresh schism. While the mother assembly triumphantly elected advanced, and sometimes rather unsavoury, jacobins to the vacant seats in the legislature, administration and judiciary, the royalist leaders reined in their counterrevolutionary zeal and nominated conservative republicans instead. Backed by a good deal of astute lobbying the ploy worked. On 22 Floréal VI (11 May 1798) all the nominations of the pro-jacobin electoral assembly of the Ardèche were revoked in favour of those of the schism assembly. The *coup* of

Table VI.1 *Schism assemblies during the elections of the Year 6 (1798)*

Canton	Neo-jacobin withdrawal	Royalist withdrawal	Other
Ardèche			
Burzet		*	
Jaujac		*	
Lamastre		*	
La Voulte		*	
Le Cheylard		*	
St Fortunat		*	
St Pierreville		*	
Bannes		*	
Aveyron			
Estaing	*		
Gages			*a
La Cavalerie	*		
Le Viala-du-Tarn			*b
Millau (*externe*)	*		
Najac	*		
Rieupeyroux		*	
Rignac		*	
St Geniez	*		
Varen			*c
Villecomtal	*		
Villefranche (section de la Fontaine)	*		
Villefranche (section du Gua)	*		
Cassagnes-Bégonhès			*d
Haute-Loire			
Auzon	*		
Cayres	*		
Fay	*		
Goudet	*		
Le Monastier	*		
St Privat-d'Allier	*		
Lozère			
Allenc	*		
Langogne			*e
La Parade	*		
Le Buisson			*f
Le Malzieu	*		
Mende	*		
St Alban	*		
St Germain-du-Teil	*		
Serverette	*		

Notes:
[a] Gages: conflict of personalities without a clear political coloration.
[b] Le Viala-du-Tarn: conflict of personalities without a clear political coloration.

Floréal set aside the election results in twenty-seven departments and selectively purged the slates of twenty-three others. In the southern Massif Central, it checked the neo-jacobin resurgence. The elections of the Year Seven (1799) evoked a shadowy factional response at best. In the Ardèche the Directorial riposte passed for a second Thermidor. A tidal wave of counterrevolutionary terror engulfed the department and patriots of whatever vintage raced for cover. By the time of Napoléon Bonaparte's *coup d'état* law and order had broken down completely. Government *commissaires* were being killed in sequence; tax receipts were regularly intercepted, and in desperation the Directory resorted to a policy of summary incarceration and execution.

It comes as no surprise, therefore, to find Long orchestrating the proceedings in the primary assembly of the canton of St Chély-d'Aubrac;[73] Chabot's former secretary and six erstwhile members of the *comité de surveillance* leading a neo-jacobin schism at St Geniez[74] and Atrasic and his son-in-law combatting neo-jacobin electoral manoeuvres at St Alban.[75] Death alone blurred party alignments – spectacularly so in some instances. The hustings at Laissac[76] were subdued to say the least after a *chouan* band led by Mercier and the Bastide brothers raided the *bourg* one summer's night in 1795. They left the entire 'ultra' faction either dead or injured. As those who had made a name for themselves during the Year Two departed, village jacobinism lost much of its *raison d'être* and the politicised feuding of the 1790s abated. The restoration of firm central control under the Consulate removed the conditions of personal and material insecurity which had helped to promote factionalism in the first place, but the success of Napoléon's policy of internal pacification is chiefly attributable to a combination of constitutional reform and *realpolitik*. After 1802 there was very little opportunity for the kind of electoral rivalry which the Constitution of the Year Three had institutional-

Notes to Table VI.1 (*cont.*)
[c] Varen: conflict of personalities without a clear political coloration.
[d] Cassagnes-Bégonhès: schism occasioned by territorial particularism.
[e] Langogne: election disputed by rival clienteles of 'patriots'.
[f] Le Buisson: schism occasioned by territorial particularism.
Sources: A.N. F[1c]III Ardèche 2; C532; A.D.A. L612*bis*; L612*ter*; L613; C. Jolivet, *L'Agitation contre-révolutionnaire dans l'Ardèche sous le Directoire* (Lyons, 1930), p. 66; E. Delcambre, *La Période du Directoire dans la Haute-Loire. Les Commissariats de Montfleury et de Portal (messidor an IV – floréal an VI)* (fascicle 2, Rodez, 1941), pp. 274–7.

[73] A.D.A. L610 *Elections, an* VI.
[74] A.D.A. L613 *Elections, an* VI. Also, Jones, '*La République au village* in the Southern Massif Central', p. 809.
[75] Delon, *La Révolution en Lozère*, pp. 689–90.
[76] A.D.A. 90L Criminal Tribunal of the Aveyron (Nivôse–Ventôse *an* VII), *procès-verbal* of the municipality of Laissac, 19 Messidor III.

ised. Nearly all local offices were filled by appointment and a complex system of minutely supervised, infrequent and indirect elections replaced the hustings of the revolutionary period. In these conditions village factionalism simply ran out of steam.

Factional alignments and shadowy party loyalties survived better in the larger *bourgs* and towns where a resident professional bourgeoisie clung tenaciously to postures adopted during the Revolution and actively proselytised among craftsmen and small landowners. The continuity is especially noticeable in centres of mixed population, for the religious imperative helped to maintain party cohesion and encouraged a process of laying-on of hands between generations. In Millau[77] the judicial reform of 8 Pluviôse IX (28 January 1801) which reduced the numbers of Justices of the Peace provoked a fresh outbreak of factional strife. As soon as the shape of the new constituencies became known party chiefs began to prepare their candidates and work on the passions of the voters in readiness for the contest. The *juge de paix* elections of the Year Ten proved, in fact, to be the last direct and democratic electoral consultation for thirteen years. Not until the municipal renewal of the Hundred Days would ordinary citizens again be called to the polls to choose their representatives. Conducted within unfamiliar constituencies and over several days, the hustings for the new judges and their deputies caused havoc in many localities and the First Consul promptly introduced fresh legislation to dilute their democratic character.

After the recrudescence of party conflict over the post of *juge de paix* and a bitter neo-jacobin inspired campaign of vilification against the sub-prefect, Jean-Pierre Randon,[78] Millau returned to a state of uneasy calm during the Empire. The prefect of the Aveyron was undeceived, however, and reported in 1808 that sectarian political combat had been suspended pending fresh opportunities, not abandoned. Opportunity beckoned once more when Napoléon landed *en route* from Elba in March 1815. His epic march on Paris and subsequent defeat at Waterloo in June lasted just long enough for the protestant revolutionaries of the South to compromise themselves. At Millau the old faction sprang into action like a well-oiled machine. Unlike village jacobinism which royalist attrition and the passing of time had virtually effaced by this date, it possessed extraordinary regenerative capacity. At the helm stood six ex-members of the *comité de surveillance* of the Year Two and a couple of dozen militants of roughly the same generation whose political indentures had been sealed during the strife surrounding the Monarchist Club of Millau in 1791, or during the neo-jacobin resurgence of the Year Six. Beneath them lay a younger generation for whom the battles of the Revol-

[77] A.N. F¹ᵇ II Aveyron 10 Sub-prefect *arrondissement* Millau to Minister of the Interior, Millau, 12 Germinal X.
[78] A.N. F¹ᵇ II Aveyron 10 Sub-prefect *arrondissement* Millau to prefect Aveyron, Millau, 29 Germinal X.

ution were, at best, blurred childhood memories, but whose allegiances were scarcely in doubt. The mutually reinforcing disciplines of religion and household left little room for manoeuvre. Restoration prefects clearly perceived this and wrote off the Calvinists *en masse* as beyond political redemption. Invited to identify the most notorious opponents of the government in Millau, the sub-prefect listed about thirty individuals and labelled the rest by households: the Montets, the Loirettes, the Caldesaigues, the Cabantous, the Carrières (save for Jean Carrière *père* et *fils*), the Buscarlets, the Relluchs and the Nazons.[79]

Three dramatic changes of regime between April 1814 and July 1815 not only rekindled factional in-fighting in pursuit of local office, they sent spasms of fear through the mixed population of the southern Massif Central. During these tense months the slightest incident precipitated a sectarian call-to-arms, but violence was held in check until the fate of the resurrected Empire became clear. The denouement of Waterloo triggered the largest popular mobilisations the region had witnessed since the days of the Camps de Jalès. As General Gilly, the Bonapartist commander, retreated from Nîmes the White Terror broke out in his wake. Protestants fled in fear from the Gard and many followed Gilly into the Cévennes where they spread the alarm among the indigenous population. In consequence, the protestant cantons of the Lozère rose and gathered their forces at Florac in readiness for combat. This caused the population of the adjacent catholic cantons of Sainte Enimie and St Georges-de-Levéjac to take fright and their mobilisation alarmed in turn the Calvinists of the Tarn valley. To the north, meanwhile, René de Bernis, the special envoy of the Duc d'Angoulême, had organised a shadow cabinet of local magnates noted for their devotion to the Bourbon cause who took over the reins of power from the Napoleonic prefect of the Lozère. With more enthusiasm than political acumen, these scions of ancient noble houses gathered together a motley collection of forces and threatened the protestants from the rear. Detachments moved on Rodez to await reinforcements before engaging the Calvinists of Millau. In the event, the rising in the Cévennes hung fire. With the discreet backing of the Duc de Bernis, Lozéran de Fressac – the interim prefect of the Lozère – managed to restrain the more ardent royalists and avoid a confrontation. As a result the conflagration in the Gard never spread to the Lozère or the Aveyron, although it spilled over into the Ardèche.

If the numerical strength of Calvinism in the Cévennes held the catholic royalist murder gangs at bay during the summer of 1815, the isolated and exposed protestant communities of the southern Aveyron had every reason to be grateful that the ramparts of the Cévennes lay between them and the *miquelets* of the Gard. At St Affrique the municipal elections licensed by the

---

[79] A.N. F⁷ 9635 Sub-prefect *arrondissement* Millau to prefect Aveyron, Millau, 23 May 1816.

Emperor's decree of 30 April 1815 finally took place several days after the battle of Waterloo, but before its significance could be fully digested. The broad franchise favoured the poorer and more numerous community and a catholic, Jean-Baptiste Roques, defeated the out-going protestant mayor. However, popular rejoicing at this signal victory was abruptly cut short when a royal decree dated 7 July annulled all the elections held during the Hundred Days and imposed the *status quo ante*. This had the paradoxical effect of restoring to office the same protestant appointee since his mayoral functions antedated Napoléon's return. As indignation mounted the prefect tried to retrieve the situation by suspending the effect of the decree and restoring Roques, together with two catholic *adjoints*. Nevertheless, on 19 August a catholic crowd battered down the portals of the protestant temple, pillaged and burned it amid reminders of the desecration of catholic churches in 1793–4. Then they proceeded to ransack the house of a former member of the local *comité de surveillance*.[80]

The violent clashes which took place in St Affrique, Millau and Florac in 1815 and 1816 had as their back-drop the White Terror. They were not solely the product of recrudescent party conflict. Yet the bloody legacy of the White Terror brought into sharper focus allegiances which might otherwise have become blurred over time. Bonapartist nostalgia mingled with an older tradition of republicanism to consolidate the politicisation of the protestant artisans of the *bourgs*. In the aftermath of sinister riots in Millau the judicial authorities attached much significance to a conversation between the wives of four leather-dressers, one of whom reportedly announced: 'La Montagne va percer; Bonaparte reviendra bientôt, laissez les chanter, bientôt elles ne chanteront ni ne riront pas tant.'[81] Lyrical invocations of this type kept the agents of the government on constant alert throughout 1816. Indeed, tension reached breaking point once more when the news of the dissolution of the Chambre Introuvable penetrated the Cévennes just as the total failure of the chestnut harvest was becoming apparent. Hope against hope of a political settlement more favourable to Calvinism became confused with the first intimations of economic catastrophe and found expression in a fresh outbreak of prophetism.

The White Terror, the judicial repression of the loi Decazes and the political offensive mounted by the Ultra-Royalists finally cemented the alliance of small-town bourgeois, merchants and artisans that would constitute the backbone of republicanism for the rest of the century. In July 1822 the prefect of the Aveyron informed the Minister of Police that a secret society of 'misérables ouvriers' had been discovered in Millau. Its affiliates met in a

---

[80] L. Raylet, 'Les Evénements de 1815 à Saint Affrique', *Journal de l'Aveyron*, 9, 16 October 1932.
[81] A.N. F⁷ 9635 *Procureur du Roi au criminel près la cour d'assises et prévotale et le tribunal civil de Rodez* to prefect Aveyron, Rodez, 18 June 1816.

room crudely painted to resemble a masonic lodge. Suppression and prosecutions followed in due course, but several months later the prefect felt it necessary to modify his earlier description. Not all the members had turned out to be poor workmen:

> on n'y voit point à la vérité figurer les hommes les plus influents et les plus considérables du parti libéral; mais tous ces sociétaires sont bien connus par des opinions très hostiles contre le Gouvernement, tous sont au-dessus de la dernière classe et plusieurs sont des fabricants assés aisés. On voit parmi eux quelques petits propriétaires, un avoué et un huissier.[82]

The *avoué* in question was a former notary named Joseph-François Lagarde[83] who had migrated to Paris as a youth and succeeded in establishing a substantial practice. An ageing, ailing and prosperous rentier, Lagarde returned to Millau in the early years of the Restoration and for reasons which the prefect could not fathom his reappearance in the town seemed to galvanize local revolutionaries. Lagarde passed for a folk hero among the initiated. A vintage jacobin, he had consistently exhibited republican convictions since the earliest days of the Revolution. On the night of 9 Thermidor he had spoken out in support of Robespierre in the Paris Jacobin Club and had earned a spell in prison in consequence; through the long years of the Directory he had clung to his faith and, while opposing the return of the Bourbons in 1814, he had rejoiced in Napoléon's downfall. In Millau, meanwhile, Lagarde *père* served a more modest apprenticeship to the Republic and became a member of the local *comité de surveillance*. Less fortunate than his eldest son, he was assassinated by a *chouan* gang in Prairial IV (May–June 1796).

Men like Lagarde with personal memories of the gladiators of the Revolution were rare. But Lagarde's remarkable career perfectly exemplifies the process of laying-on of hands which nourished and perpetuated the revolutionary tradition in the nineteenth century. In the southern Massif Central the Revolution and, indeed, the Counter-Revolution were experienced through a prism of tenacious familial and sectarian loyalties. The nuances of ideology mattered little for the act of adhesion did not usually imply a political choice in the modern sense; that is to say, a choice between alternative philosophies. If the imperatives of commitment were ultimately biological rather than ideological, however, it is nonetheless true that faith could burgeon *a posteriori*. With the passing of generations and the flux of regimes opinion was apt to shift its moorings. The Opportunists' spectacular siege of the countryside in the 1880s[84] encouraged several impeccably royalist dynasties to change their colours as the interventionist power of government threatened to undermine their status as notables. There were few travellers in

[82] A.N. F⁷ 6694 Prefect Aveyron to Minister of Police, Rodez, 14 July 1822.
[83] *Ibid.*, Prefect Aveyron to Minister of Police, Rodez, 1 November 1822; *Préfect de Police de Paris* to Minister of the Interior, Paris, 18 December 1822; F⁷ 4758 Dossier on J.-F. Lagarde.
[84] See below, chapter nine, pp. 284–304.

the opposite direction, however, and as E.-M. de Vogüé has testified the dominant impression is one of continuity rather than discontinuity between generations. No single source illustrates this fact more strikingly than the personal files of the victims of Louis-Napoléon's *coup d'état* in December 1851. The lists of those implicated in the insurrections at St Affrique and Millau read like a roll-call of the families who had dominated these communes during the revolutionary Terror.[85]

Our discussion of the birth pangs of a tradition of village and *bourg* radicalism has inevitably shifted the focus from the great mass of the rural population, and yet the peasant vote preoccupied revolutionaries and counter-revolutionaries alike. Some historians have discerned a kernel of autonomous and self-sustaining peasant revolution imprisoned within the lineaments of 'bourgeois' revolution, but the peasantry tended to react to revolution rather than act in it. Indeed, they ceased even to react after 1792. What, then, did two and a half decades of insistent and intermittently tumultuous change signify in the countryside? A chance to settle scores with the local seigneur? A windfall opportunity to press the claims of the rural community over common, fallow and forest? A breath of fresh air which momentarily stirred the suffocating atmosphere of social deference? All these things, perhaps, but we would do well to avoid exaggerating the impact that the Revolution had – indeed, could have had – on a peasantry possessing vital reserves of economic and cultural stability. The peasantry of the Aveyron epitomised that stability, but the phenomenon of a deeply rooted peasant *petite culture* operating well within the thresholds of economic viability was general throughout the region, at least until the 1850s. Equilibrium and a perception of well-being made for political quiescence. A Restoration prefect of the Aveyron commented tellingly that, 'Les mots de droit, de liberté, d'égalité, avec lesquels on a soulevé ou agité d'autres provinces, seraient à peine entendus ici; et c'est une chose singulièrement remarquable que la subordination volontaire dans laquelle le paysan Aveyronnais est resté envers ceux qui le dominaient autre fois.'[86]

It is tempting, therefore, to regard both the Revolution and the Counter-Revolution as spectator sports since neither engaged the majority of the inhabitants of the southern Massif Central. The Revolution drew its activists from the ranks of the rural bourgeoisie (many of whom passed for petty seigneurs); from among the artisans and small traders of the *bourgs* and villages and from among a section of the very poor, but so, one suspects, did the Counter-Revolution. The absence of mass support for the royalist cause is one of the most striking features of the Counter-Revolution in the southern Massif Central. In the Vendée about two-thirds of the insurgents were drawn from the peasantry. The circumspection of country dwellers evidently con-

---

[85] Jones, 'Political Commitment and Rural Society in the Southern Massif Central', pp. 348–9.
[86] A.N. F[7] 9635 Prefect to Minister of the Interior, Rodez, 15 February 1825.

fused the counter-revolutionary leaders in charge of operations in the South and it helps to explain their failure to foment a sustained revolt even in the exceptionally favourable conditions of the Year Seven (1799). Yet the peasantry were clearly prepared to risk life and limb in defence of religion – be it Calvinism or their own peculiar brand of catholicism. And from 1791 the name of religion was invoked repeatedly in order to enlist them into a political cause. In the long run, therefore, the church may have done more to promote political awareness than the state.

Yet it would be foolish to imply an ignorance of the altering structures of the state, but for the efforts of priests and pastors. Even spectators participate in the sense that they show an awareness of what is taking place. The Revolution involved the country dweller whether he liked it or not; his freedom lay rather in how little or how much he chose to participate. Ignorance and indifference should not be confused. If the peasantry of the southern Massif Central evinced an indifference towards the Revolution, it was studied, and studied indifference is surely a political response. The country dweller, remarked another Restoration prefect, 's'attache, si l'on peut même employer ce terme, au gouvernement qui le gêne le moins'.[87] If the French Revolution taught the peasant anything, it taught him the lesson of regimism, a lesson which the nineteenth century could only reinforce.

[87]   A.N. F⁷ 8998 Prefect Aveyron to Minister of Police, Rodez, 26 May 1816.

7

❋❋

The democratic challenge

The pioneer experiments in electoral democracy conducted by successive revolutionary legislatures threatened to transform power relationships at village level. Between 1789 and 1815 distant affairs of state became matters for public consultation and deliberation while governments attached ideological reference points to the most trivial parish-pump issues. The magical rituals of the hustings, of 'universal suffrage' (a neologism imported from England) suggested the dawn of a new age in which every institution would be subjected to popular sanction. The following extract, culled from a civic catechism published for the guidance of rural voters, is typical of this first flush of enthusiasm for electoral democracy: 'Demande: Qu'est-ce qu'une élection? Réponse: C'est le plus bel attribut d'un homme libre, que de choisir ceux qui doivent lui donner les lois.'[1]

That the revolutionary Declaration of the Rights of Man did not immediately create a free nation may be taken for granted. Yet it is a persistent theme in liberal historiography that, sooner or later, the electoral process did facilitate a *prise de conscience* among both town and country dwellers. In reviewing nearly a century of faltering experience of electoral politics, this chapter raises certain objections to the usual interpretation of linear democratic integration. The southern Massif Central provided a poor proving ground for ballot-box politics. Habitat posed formidable problems of electoral organisation; the cultural vitality of the rural community rebuffed external ideological stimuli; familial and confessional ties reduced the autonomy of the individual voter and the lingering strength of deference cut across alternative political postures. But if the great lurches towards democracy which occurred in the 1790s, in 1848 and in the 1880s failed to evoke a commensurate response from the peasant, the challenge of the franchise triggered other developments which left durable marks on rural habits of mind. The electoral process furnished an alternative arena for gladiatorial combat between clienteles, kin-networks and territorial groups. By the end of the nineteenth century inter-community strife had lost much of its ritualistic savagery and

---

[1] Archives Communales de St Flour K⁵13 *Petit catéchisme des droits et devoirs d'élection pour l'an V* (Ventôse, Aurillac).

the pacification owed a good deal to the growth of electoral politics. As Francis Pomponi[2] has remarked of Corsica – a society similar in many ways to that of the southern Massif Central – the ballot box overhauled firepower as a method of settling local power struggles. More important, the inception of electoral democracy foreshadowed a massive escalation of interventionism in the countryside. The interventionist role of the state was visibly expanding during the final decades of the *ancien régime*, but in the century that followed the power of the administration became all pervading. Elections were too important to be left to people and the management of democracy, even the sanitised democracy of the censitary regimes, preoccupied the prefects and their subordinates. Few nineteenth-century governments professed a belief in the virtues of electoral neutrality and none, it seems, withdrew from the electoral arena altogether. This is scarcely surprising for the distinction between opposition and sedition which lies at the heart of parliamentary politics developed slowly and painfully. The general election of April 1848 which occasioned the extraordinary sight of something over eight million Frenchmen trudging to the polls also marked the entry of the catholic church into politics. And the mobilisation of peasant voters as catholics rather than as citizens was surely the most striking development of the period.

The inception of electoral democracy

The habits of democracy were alien to the popular culture of the southern Massif Central. The point deserves stressing for a number of authors[3] have explained the vigorous, if volatile, political commitment of the Mediterranean departments in terms of antecedent folklore and rooted traditions of municipal autonomy. The ramparts of the causses and the Cévennes certainly overlooked the Midi, but the peasantry of these high plateaux held little in common with the population of the littoral. Only in the southernmost cantons of the Ardèche and in the *bourgs* of the Tarn valley was the ostentatious, outdoor *sociabilité* familiar to students of the Var or the Pyrénées-Orientales much in evidence. In the mountains the sense of community rested less on communal traditions than on a transcendent psychology of belonging expressed through the intensely hierarchic rituals of the catholic church (see chapter four). The assumption that municipal freedoms tended necessarily

---

[2] F. Pomponi, 'Pouvoir et abus de pouvoir des maires corses au XIXᵉ siècle', *Etudes rurales*, lxiii–lxiv (1976), 155.

[3] See, for example, Agulhon, *The Republic in the Village*; R. Bezucha, 'Mask of Revolution: A Study of Popular Culture during the Second French Republic' in R. Price (ed.), *Revolution and Reaction. 1848 and the Second French Republic* (London, 1975), pp. 236–53; P. McPhee, 'Popular Culture, Symbolism and Rural Radicalism in Nineteenth-Century France', *The Journal of Peasant Studies*, v (1978), 238–53; 'On Rural Politics in Nineteenth-Century France: The Example of Rodès, 1789–1851', *Comparative Studies in Society and History*, xxiii (1981), 248–77.

towards a democratisation of village life is, in any case, open to question. In lower Languedoc[4] weaker royal and seigneurial controls over the rural community do not appear to have encouraged internal power sharing, nor did the existence of consular institutions provide a democratic safeguard. Whether in the plains, or in the mountains, the rural community was usually an oligarchy. Its 'independence' was defended by a small group of bourgeois and *laboureurs* gathered together in a 'conseil politique'. In this respect the local government changes introduced by the Revolution and the immediate post-revolutionary regimes were less dramatic than is generally assumed. *Ancien régime* village life already evinced a markedly censitary character.

The 1787 municipal reform placed that censitary principle on a firm legislative basis and in the process initiated a section of the population of the southern Massif Central to the experience of elections. What proportion of the peasantry of the Brivadois and the Haute-Auvergne attended the hustings in the summer of 1787 is unclear. In the absence of census data, we can do little more than speculate. Nevertheless, contemporaries complained that the censitary threshold[5] was too low and insufficiently discriminatory which argues for a fairly democratic franchise, and the surviving *procès-verbaux* show that the electoral assemblies rarely numbered fewer than twenty voters. In the larger population centres the hustings commonly attracted in excess of 100 participants. The problems which this first practical experiment in representative local government encountered are more fully documented and it is worth enumerating them for they bedevilled the functioning of electoral democracy in this region throughout the nineteenth century.

As has already been suggested, the most intractable problem arising from the 1787 edict related to the constituency of the new municipal or parish assemblies. The dispersed habitat of the southern Massif Central defied neat administrative compartmentalisation and the muddled boundaries of *communauté d'habitants* and parish discussed in preceding chapters became the source of untold difficulties. The stipulation that the nomination of the new municipalities be conducted by *scrutin* – that is to say by secret ballot – caused dismay and confusion, too. The concept of balloting lay outside the experience of the peasantry and in the villages many elections were carried out *viva voce*. It may be argued that voting by public acclamation conveyed the full flavour of classical democracy, but in the context of the southern Massif Central it gave full rein to all the mechanisms of social deference. The electoral principle also projected household and kinship rivalries on to a fresh plane. Naturally enough, the peasantry envisaged the municipalities in severely domestic terms and more often than not they became instruments of

---

[4]   G. Fournier, 'Des Conseils politiques aux conseils municipaux dans les diocèses civils de Carcassonne, Narbonne, et Béziers (1750–1791)' (Université de Toulouse-Le Mirail, Thèse de troisième cycle, 2 vols., 1974), i, p. 218 and *passim*.
[5]   See above, chapter six, p. 182.

factional domination. In 1788 the government issued the first in a litany of warnings that the 'conseil municipal' should not resemble a 'conseil de famille' ('les deux frères, le père et le fils, le beaupère et le gendre, ne peuvent être à la fois membres de l'assemblée municipale de leur communauté').[6] For its part, the *élection* assembly of Brioude[7] became the first representative body to point out that the problem of *parenté* was inseparable from that of habitat.

At least the 1787 edict did not insist upon the conduct of elections on the basis of absolute majorities, for this was the major stumbling-block of the revolutionaries' attempts to construct a democratic franchise. For the men of 1789 anything less than *pluralité absolue* seemed an intolerable affront to liberty and equality. Instead they condemned the rural voter to hours and even days of fruitless balloting, and in the process did incalculable damage to the prestige of France's burgeoning representative institutions. The municipal law of 14 December 1789[8] introduced to the whole of the southern Massif Central a complicated set of electoral regulations – so complicated, in fact, that the Constitution Committee found itself obliged to issue several important 'Explications' in the months that followed. Mayors and *procureurs* were to be chosen by absolute majority even if this necessitated three ballots; the permanent municipal officers were likewise to be elected by absolute majority with the proviso that a relative majority would suffice if a third round of voting became necessary. Only the *notables* could expect to be chosen by simple majority in one round. The franchise was restricted, of course, but it is unlikely that the censitary threshold excluded many peasant farmers in the southern Massif Central. Accordingly, the hustings tended to be time wasting and tumultuous. In the villages the three distinct electoral operations required to complete the *corps municipal* might take several days, while in the *bourgs* and towns the added complication of electoral constituencies ('sections électorales') further prolonged the process. The hustings for the new District and Department bodies presented similar problems, but on a grander scale for they were held in the *chefs-lieux de canton*.[9] Moreover, all these institutions of local government were subject to annual or biennial renewal and for a decade after 1789 the rural voter was expected to be in semi-permanent electoral trajectory. When we consider that the rustic mayors of the patois-speaking South were notoriously ignorant of their civic responsibilities, it is remarkable that the decentralised administrative structures set in place by the Revolution survived as long as they did. Yet we should be wary of the siren simplicity of the bundles of *procès-verbaux d'élection* preserved in the public

6 A.D.P.-de-D. C7356 M. de Lambert to *commission intermédiaire* of provincial assembly of the Auvergne (6 March 1788).
7 A.D.P.-de-D. C7361 *Procès-verbal de l'assemblée d'élection de Brioude, session du mois d'octobre 1788.*
8 *Archives parlementaires de 1787 à 1860 (première série, 1787–99)*, x, 564–71.
9 See above, chapter six, p. 193.

archives. From the earliest years of the Revolution, from 1787, indeed, there existed a gulf between the theory and the practice of elections in the country-side. After 1795 that gulf became a chasm as the Republic lost control of large areas of the Ardèche and the Lozère to the *chouannerie*. Local officials sub-mitted *procès-verbaux* when pressured to do so, but much of the machinery of electoral democracy had ceased to function.

Napoléon's judgement that people were tired of elections was probably correct except in so far as he applied it to the *justices de paix*. After 1800 the democratic experiments of the revolutionary epoch were fudged in favour of a system based on nomination and co-option. Henceforth, mayors, *adjoints* and municipal councillors were all chosen by the government and imposed on the countryside with mandates of between five and twenty years. Resig-nations apart, the rotation of officials virtually halted. The first renewal of municipal councillors did not occur until 1812. Democratic controls over the judiciary fared slightly better. Between 1800 and 1814 the periodic replace-ment of the *juge de paix* provided the only opportunity for popular elections in the countryside. Initially the *juge de paix* was directly elected for a three year term by all citizens without distinction. The hustings might last a total of eight days and the successful candidate was expected to obtain an absolute majority of the votes cast. After 1802, however, the Consul-for-Life intro-duced an element of discretionary power in this sphere, too. The assembled citizenry retained the right to vote, but were required to sanction two candi-dates leaving the final choice to the government. And in order that such elec-tions did not occur too frequently the mandate of the *juge de paix* was extended to ten years.

Only the desperate circumstances of the Hundred Days prompted Napoléon to reconsider these arrangements. In a decree of 30 April 1815 following swiftly upon the Acte Additionnel the Emperor restored some of the municipal freedoms of the revolutionary era. Communes were invited to submit their nominee mayors and *adjoints* (but not the municipal councillors) to the test of the hustings and the 25-year-old law of 14 December 1789 was resurrected for the purpose. In case no one could remember how elections had been conducted under this venerable statute, the relevant articles were printed as an addendum to the text of the decree. The significance of this momentary resuscitation of municipal liberties – such as it was – has already been discussed.[10] In chronological terms its impact was slight for the restored Bourbons evinced little enthusiasm for local elections and prefectoral nominees swiftly resumed the leadership of village life. Not until 1831, in fact, did the liberal and decentralising tradition of the early years of the Revolution take root once more. In that year Louis-Philippe gave his blessing to the first sustained experiment in local democracy in over three decades.

[10]   See above, chapter six, pp. 190–1.

The revised Charter announced a series of measures intended to widen the base of the political nation. The best known and least significant of these reforms marginally increased the numbers entitled to participate in parliamentary elections. With the *cens* pegged at 200 *f.* instead of 300 *f.* and a prescribed minimum of 150 voters in each constituency, the electorate increased from 100,000 to 170,000 in a nation comprising between seven and eight million adult males. More important were the law of 21 March 1831 which established elective municipal councils and the law of 22 June 1833 which opened the administrative councils (*conseils-généraux*) of the departments and of the *arrondissements* to elections conducted on a cantonal basis. The former enfranchised one in four adult males; the latter perhaps one in forty. To be sure, this fell a long way short of universal manhood suffrage, but the law of 21 March 1831, in particular, marked an important milestone on the road towards democratic local government. Henceforth the members of the *conseil municipal* held their places at the behest of a mixed electorate of village tax payers and notables enfranchised by virtue of their professional status. If not exactly popular, this electorate was nonetheless fairly broad for the franchise tended to favour rural communes. In the departments of the southern Massif Central the average *cens* appears to have worked out at between 13 *f.* 05 *c.* and 19 *f.* 98*c.*[11] The procedures adopted for the conduct of the hustings suggest a degree of progress when compared with the provisions in force during the Revolution. Polling took place in the *chef-lieu de commune*, but with the qualification that the prefect might authorise the subdivision of the communal constituency should the need arise. This concession was of supreme importance to the dispersed population of the southern Massif Central. The hustings for the selection of municipal councillors (*notables* had been abolished in 1795) presupposed two rounds of voting instead of three, and small communes with under 500 inhabitants were exempted from the customary prohibitions on kinship. Each of these modifications of past practice took sensible account of the obstacles to participatory democracy in the countryside. If the institutions of representative government were to evoke a positive response from the peasantry they had to be contoured around the salient features of the rural community.

The July Monarchy hesitated to throw open the posts of mayor and *adjoint* to popular sanction. They continued to be appointed as in the past, though with the important proviso that they be drawn from the ranks of the municipal councillors. Complete democratisation of local government waited upon the revolution of 1848 and was accomplished by a law of 3 July 1848.[12] In fact, this measure bore an interim character. It reproduced the statutes of

---

[11] A.N. F^{1b} I 257 *Tableaux contenant des renseignements statistiques sur les élections municipales de 1834.*

[12] *Bulletin des lois de la République Française* (Xième série, tome deuxième, nos. 48–111) (Paris, 1849), pp. 2–5.

21 March 1831 and 22 June 1833 with two modifications: universal manhood suffrage and the election of mayors and *adjoints*. After fresh elections had renewed the *conseils municipaux*, the councillors would themselves choose the individuals to fill these posts from among their own number. Although the executive arm continued to nominate to these posts in large communes and towns and although the prefects retained the power to suspend democratically elected mayors, the new law dramatically curtailed the interventionist power of government in the countryside. The troubled history of the Second Republic soon revealed this experiment in unlimited grassroots democracy to be a colossal hostage to political fortunes. Unfriendly municipalities possessed formidable powers of obstruction. More worrying, given the atmosphere of incipient politicisation, municipalities were responsible for compiling the electoral register and therefore well placed to undermine the calculations of central government. In the aftermath of the law of 31 May 1850 which was designed to disenfranchise the most radical section of the adult male population, the sub-prefect of Largentière reported: 'Si le maire est bon tout marche à moitié bien, il affiche l'avertissement, porte sur la liste les électeurs sujets à déclaration qu'il sait dévoués à l'ordre et raie faute de déclarations tous les rouges qui devraient faire cette déclaration en temps opportun. Mais l'inverse a bien souvent lieu car nous ne choisissons pas les maires.'[13]

Long before the extinction of parliamentary democracy by Louis-Napoléon's *coup d'état*, the Republic was seeking support for a more restrictive municipal charter. Canvassed by the Minister of the Interior[14] in the late summer of 1849, the *conseils-généraux* of the Aveyron and the Ardèche opined in favour of a return to the Orleanist system of nomination of mayors and *adjoints* from within the municipal council. But in the wake of the uprisings of December 1851 even this solution seemed to offer insufficient guarantees of executive freedom. The constitution of the emergent Second Empire insisted that the appointment of mayors was a prerogative of central government which admitted of no qualification. They would be drawn either from within the municipal council or from outside it as policy dictated. At least the councillors remained subject to democratic sanction (decree of 7 July 1852), although this decision aroused misgivings among some supporters of the regime. In 1854 the Interior Ministry again sponsored an internal debate on the wisdom of applying the electoral principle to local government. The prefect of the Aveyron willingly conceded that a system of blanket nomination would be the neatest administrative solution, but warned that it would also be politically inept. If parliamentary elections left peasant voters unmoved, municipal elections stirred all the passions:

[13]	A.D.Ard. 2M341 Sub-prefect Largentière to prefect Ardèche, Largentière, 6 February 1851.
[14]	A.N. F[1c] V Aveyron 4 *Procès-verbaux des séances du conseil-général*, 1849; F[1c] V Ardèche 4 *Extrait du registre des délibérations du conseil-général*, 27 August–8 September 1849.

Il est impossible, en effet, de se dissimuler que si les électeurs ruraux sont d'une complète indifférence lorsqu'il s'agit de nommer un député et des membres du conseil-général [of the Department] ou d'arrond[issemen]t, fonctions dont l'importance échappe presque généralement à leur intelligence, cette indifférence disparaît lorsqu'ils ont à élire les conseillers municipaux, c'est à dire ceux auxquels est confiée la mission de décider les questions qui s'agittent (*sic*) chaque jour sous leurs yeux.[15]

The balance between nomination and representation was a fine one, and rather artificial at that. While ministers and their subordinates claimed that the power to appoint mayors from outside the *conseil municipal* enabled them to forestall or neutralise factional rivalries, the electoral apathy which gripped the countryside for a decade after 1852 was only partly induced by legislative adjustments. Indeed, such conflicts as continued to arise were often directly attributable to the hybrid nature of the Napoleonic municipal regime. Democratically elected village worthies disliked having nominee mayors foisted upon them and they devised novel methods of expressing their displeasure. The *conseil municipal* of La Cavalerie[16] used the tactic of resigning *en bloc* in a bid to browbeat the prefect into dismissing their mayor. In any case, the justification for mayoral nomination really lay elsewhere. The system of managed elections perfected by the Second Empire presupposed that the mayor was an agent of government rather than the defender of municipal liberties. His primary task was to galvanise the peasantry into a massive and 'spontaneous' endorsement of the official candidate at election times.

A sense of tradition as well as repugnance at the cynical manipulation of the democratic franchise by Napoléon III ensured that the Third Republic would revert to the precedents of 1789–92 and 1848. Such was the revulsion, indeed, that a ministerial circular[17] warned the prefects not to interfere in the parliamentary by-election campaign of June–July 1871. This was, perhaps, the only occasion in the nineteenth century when a government positively ordered its employees to vacate the electoral arena. Yet the advent of a durable village democracy was slow to materialise for the character of the regime itself hung in the balance until the end of the decade. Between 1871 and 1884 the battle for the control of the countryside was fought more tenaciously than at any time since the Revolution. The Opportunist and Radical politicians espoused the cause of municipal autonomy, while conservatives invoked the policies and even the methods of Bonapartism in an effort to prolong the authority of the traditional elites at village level. Each new law – and there were five major measures dealing with the municipalities during these years – marked a twist in the parliamentary struggle.

With the promise that a definitive municipal statute would follow in due course, the National Assembly dismissed all the mayors and *adjoints* who had

---

[15] A.D.A. 8M¹ 33 Note of prefect Aveyron.
[16] A.D.A. 8M¹ 35 Sub-prefect Millau to prefect Aveyron, Millau, 30 September 1864.
[17] A.D.A. 3M422. Ministerial circular, Versailles, 24 June 1871.

not been selected from the ranks of municipal councillors on 14 April 1871. Henceforth, these posts would be tied firmly to the *conseil municipal* and in the interim provision was made for the existing councillors to fill the vacancies. This decision would, in time, have restored the experiment in democratic accountability launched by the Second Republic, but the fall of Thiers momentarily arrested the process. The election of Marshal MacMahon to the presidency foreshadowed a resumption of governmental interventionism in all its forms. As of 20 January 1874 all mayors and *adjoints* became liable to nomination: by the President in the case of towns and administrative centres and by the local prefect in the case of rural communes. Moreover, the government of 'Moral Order' as the Marshal's intended seven year term of office became known, claimed the right to draw the mayors and *adjoints* from outside the municipal council as had the Second Empire. The law of 20 January 1874 cashiering civic dignitaries by ministerial fiat and substituting placemen brought to term a certain conception of local government. It did not linger long on the statute book for, by degrees, the republicans were winning control of the Republic. After the decisive elections for a new Chamber of Deputies in 1876, rural communes retrieved the right to choose their own mayors and *adjoints* (interim law of 12 August 1876); and after the Senate elections and the resignation of MacMahon early in 1879 the republicans found the way clear for a thorough-going democratisation of the institutions of local government.

The long-promised and long-awaited charter of municipal liberties was promulgated on 5 April 1884.[18] It comprised 168 articles covering nearly every aspect of public administration from common land to cemeteries. More particularly, it represented a summation and distillation of nearly a century of intermittent electoral practice in the countryside. The enduring achievement of the measure was to settle the issue of authority at village level: henceforth authority flowed from below. The artificial distinction between appointed municipal officials and elected municipal councillors was abandoned and the institutions of local government were harmonised. Since 1884 no regime, save that presided over by Marshal Pétain between 1940 and 1944, has challenged this principle. Yet the organising mechanisms of electoral democracy had undergone a number of modifications over the decades. During the early years of the Revolution the mayors (and the *procureurs*) had been directly elected by the constituency of active citizens which was admirably democratic, but exceedingly time-consuming. The July Monarchy introduced the practice of selecting the mayor and *adjoint* from the *conseil municipal* and it was this system – suitably amended – that eventually prevailed. The character of the hustings had changed sensibly over the century, too. In 1787 the majority of peasant electors voted *viva voce* and if many

---

[18] *Bulletin des lois de la République Française* (XIIième série, premier semestre de 1884, tome 28, nos. 825–54) (Paris, 1884) pp. 369–408.

peasants continued, in the nineteenth century, to verbally communicate their preferences to a literate third party, there was, at least, a general appreciation that voting was performed with ballot slips and in conditions of utmost formality. In recognition of this fact the municipal statute of 1884 attached stringent conditions to the act of voting: ballot slips were to consist of unmarked white paper and were to be completed outside the polling station. They should be folded or sealed before being handed to the presiding officer. The statute also reiterated the injunction against kinsmen enshrined in the law of 21 March 1831. Thus, in a commune numbering fewer than 500 inhabitants, nothing prevented the electoral muscle of a 'famille nombreuse' such as the Gaillard[19] of Grèzes from packing the municipal council with fathers, sons, brothers and in-laws.

Techniques of influence: uses and abuses of the democratic franchise

Local government elections nurtured elementary forms of political life at parish and village level. Parliamentary or legislative elections and plebiscites contrived to focus the burgeoning civic awareness of a predominantly rural electorate on more distant objectives. The prefects perceived the distinction in terms of ideology: local elections were about parish-pump affairs and relatively unimportant; national elections were about matters of state and therefore of great moment. Neither assumption was strictly warranted, of course, but that is not our present concern. What is significant is that the prefects and subaltern officials devoted a considerable amount of time and talent to electoral prognostication. And prognostication was but one step removed from intervention. Yet electoral management demanded skills of increasing sophistication as the nineteenth century proceeded. Techniques devised to secure the election of 'ministerial' candidates by narrow colleges of censitary electors were not adequate to the task of returning docile deputies under conditions of universal manhood suffrage. After a moment's hesitation during which the catholic church and even the *démocrates-socialistes* of 1849–51 outpaced government as an electoral organisation, the prefects took up the challenge. The orchestrated democracy of the Second Empire was the obvious outcome, but in the southern Massif Central the climax of interventionism coincided with the advent of the Opportunist Republic. In the 1880s the prefects of these highly clericalised departments developed techniques for controlling the expression of opinion which were reminiscent of the Revolutionary Terror.

Preoccupation with the parliamentary franchise only became acute in 1848 when all adult males became eligible to vote. At the last general election of the July Monarchy in August 1846 the electoral *cens* conferred voting

---

[19] See above, chapter three, p. 84.

rights on about 2.8 per cent of the adult male population.[20] Before 1848, therefore, the number of peasant proprietors qualified to attend the electoral colleges was infinitesimal. Yet the great leap forward accomplished by the Second Republic rested on precedents set over half a century earlier which should not be ignored.

It would be tedious and probably unenlightening to examine the legislation governing the conduct of parliamentary elections before 1848 in the same detail as we have used for local elections. For all the achievements of the Revolution, it can be argued that the acquisition of authentic democratic institutions waited upon the founding of the Second Republic. Between 1789 and 1831 nearly all parliamentary elections were indirect: that is to say that the voters chose electors who in turn chose the deputies. Often, of course, they were inhibited by a franchise qualification as well. Until the July Monarchy pioneered direct elections, the only legislation to countenance the abandonment of two-tier voting was the celebrated Constitution of the Year Two (1793) which was never put into operation and the law of 5 February 1817[21] establishing a single electoral assembly in each department which was swiftly repealed. Yet certain features of the regulations in force during these decades are worth mentioning for the light they shed on the functioning of primary electoral assemblies. One such was the dogged insistence on absolute majorities. Until 1848, complicated and time-consuming multiple balloting was virtually unavoidable since the statutes prescribed *pluralité absolue* for the first ballot. Parliamentary elections, like local elections, could last days and often degenerated into factional struggles. Moreover, the secret ballot had yet to prove its *bona fides* with the result that the organisation of the hustings had few precedents to draw upon. In 1793 Danton argued that voting by ballot slip was potentially counter-revolutionary ('Je demande que le riche puisse écrire, et que le pauvre puisse parler')[22] – a view that was loudly endorsed by the militants of the Paris Sections.

Ballot slips would, in fact, provide a fertile medium for misunderstanding and manipulation. The laws in vigour from the time of the Revolution until the end of the nineteenth century tended to assume that prospective voters would either write out their own slips or make use of ready-printed slips distributed by candidates. Illiterate 'active' citizens wishing to participate in the elections to the Legislative Assembly of 1791 were instructed to enlist the help of the three oldest voters or the three officiating scrutineers. And all slips had to be completed on a narrow table within view of the presiding officials. Evenly cut white paper was sometimes provided, sometimes not; there were no envelopes and a variety of receptacles were employed as ballot boxes. Such

---

[20] S. Kent, *Electoral Procedure under Louis Philippe* (New Haven, 1937), p. 25.
[21] G. D. Weill, *Les Elections législatives depuis 1789. Histoire de la législation et des mœurs* (Paris, 1895), p. 83.
[22] *Ibid.*, p. 24.

makeshift arrangements contrasted strongly with the detailed provisions governing the choice of the presiding officers, the electoral contest between the candidates and the drawing-up of the *procès-verbal*. Little by little the scope for intimidation was reduced, but it was a slow and piecemeal process. Not until 1861 did the government despatch legally certified ballot-boxes to communes that had failed to procure suitable (i.e. lockable) containers of their own and squabbles over illegible slips and coloured or otherwise marked slips occurred routinely. At Firmy[23] in the heart of the Aubin–Decazeville industrial basin, the factory overseers interfered in the polling as a matter of course. During the general election of 1881 they organised an unofficial electoral 'bureau' of trusty employees who shadowed the activities of the official 'bureau' led by the mayor. As each workman approached the ballot-box he was left in little doubt as to where his loyalties ought to lie. As long as voters were enjoined, or at least encouraged, to declare their preferences more or less openly, these rather crude techniques of influence would continue to pay dividends. Not until 1913, in fact, were the first really effective steps taken to enforce the secret ballot. A law of that year introduced the voting booth to protect the privacy of the voter as he filled in his slip and the envelope in which to enclose it.

That the infancy of the secret ballot lasted until the eve of the First World War owed as much to political calculation as to inexperience. By tradition and by necessity, the mayors and Justices of the Peace presided over the hustings in the countryside and for most of the nineteenth century such officials were liegemen. Their dominating presence only inches away from the ballot-box afforded governments a window on the electoral process. The opportunities for abuse with a nudge and a wink from the prefects were legion. Country mayors could make adjustments to the electoral register; they could omit certain hamlets and farmsteads from the electoral summons, or fail to apprise intending voters of the location of the hustings. In remote and upland parishes grapevine communication could not be relied upon – the more so if the mayors gave insufficient warning of forthcoming elections as sometimes happened. Usually, of course, balloting took place on Sundays in the parochial *chef-lieu*, for the peasantry were exceedingly reluctant to make unnecessary journeys. Yet even the hour at which the hustings commenced could influence the results of an election. Notwithstanding the temptations of the wine shop, most country dwellers would not long delay their departure for home once Mass had been celebrated. In October 1877 dozens of rural mayors petitioned the prefect of the Aveyron with the request that balloting in the forthcoming parliamentary election be synchronised with the ending of Mass. 'Si le scrutin ne s'ouvrait qu'à huit heures', wrote the mayor of the village of St Saturnin where First Mass was over by 7 a.m., 'il est certain que

---

[23] A.D.A. 3M440 Petition of the secretary and *assesseurs* of the *bureau de vote* of Firmy, 23 September 1881.

bon nombre d'électeurs et des meilleurs ne pourraient attendre l'heure d'ouverture.'[24] The prefect – a MacMahon nominee seeking a massive mobilisation of the conservative electorate in the aftermath of the Seize Mai crisis – graciously acceded to these 'spontaneous' requests.

Nevertheless, the freedom of manoeuvre which governments willingly accorded to village magistrates when it suited them could also backfire humiliatingly. We have already noted what a hostage to political fortune was the decision of the Second Republic to release the mayors from executive controls.[25] Moreover, village notables evinced a tiresome habit of practising highly personal forms of electoral manipulation which imperfectly coincided with those desired by central government. After the parliamentary by-elections of March 1850 the sub-prefect of Tournon (Ardèche) reported that:

Le maire de Silhac qui est protestant, n'a ouvert le scrutin que le dimanche à midi, de sorte que les catholiques qui forment les deux tiers [*sic*, they formed one third] de la population de cette commune et qui voulaient voter à la sortie de la messe qui se dit de huit à neuf heures du matin, obligés de rester sur la place publique ou à la porte de la Mairie, se sont lassés d'attendre et se sont retirés, la plupart sans voter.[26]

But all this was small beer – likely only to affect the results of individual polling stations and on an *ad hoc* basis. Two other variables which may be summarised as the 'debate on electoral constituencies' and the 'politics of *sectionnement*' powerfully conditioned electoral participation in the countryside. The debate on the appropriate constituency framework for France's burgeoning democracy did not become acute until 1848. The tradition of voting within multi-member constituencies based on the departments (*scrutin de liste*) went back to the Revolution, but the July Monarchy, in particular, favoured the single-member constituency (*scrutin d'arrondissement*) based usually upon the administrative sub-division of the department known as the *arrondissement*. The latter arrangement narrowed the horizons of the voter and minimised the risk of social insubordination that elections entailed. Accordingly, the embattled Second Republic opted for the broader constituency to ensure that republican votes were deployed to best effect. When the peasantry went to the polls in April 1848 they were invited to cast as many votes as there were parliamentary seats allocated to each department. In practice this resulted in a list system of voting as interested parties distributed ready-made lists of candidates. Yet these printed lists had no legal existence and the count was carried out by individual named rather than by list. It is questionable whether rural voters fully appreciated these subtleties, however. Daniel Stern claimed that peasants were taken aback by the pre-fabricated slips: 'Mais le gouvernement a déjà choisi, disaient-ils, pourquoi nous fait-on voter?'[27]

[24] A.D.A. 3M439 Mayor St Saturnin to prefect Aveyron, St Saturnin, 3 October 1877.
[25] See above, p. 220.   [26] Sabatier, *Religion et politique*, p. 241.
[27] D. Stern, *Histoire de la Révolution de 1848* (2 vols., Paris, 1862), i, p. 199 note 1.

Be that as it may, the debate on electoral constituencies had become ideologically laden. Between 1848 and 1889 the law on this subject changed no fewer than five times: the Second Empire reinstated the single-member constituency in 1852; the Third Republic abolished it once more in 1871; in 1875 a law re-established the single-member constituency in time for the elections of 1876, but it was abolished again in 1885. Four years later fears of a Boulangist steam-roller prompted a return to single-member districts and there the matter rested – ever controversial – until after the First World War. Until the 1880s the republicans remained persuaded that the best hopes of neutralising the authority of village notables and of completing the political education of the peasantry lay with the list system and the broad constituency. But as the republic took root and established an elite of its own in the countryside, the tactical situation altered and the Opportunists discovered unsuspected merits in the *scrutin d'arrondissement* which enabled them to bottle up their political enemies. In the general election of 1881 moderate and radical republican candidates captured six out of seven seats in the Aveyron even though they only gained 43 per cent of votes cast.[28]

Important though these logistical calculations were, the debate on constituency organisation impinged on the peasant electorate in a more concrete fashion, however. The single-member constituency assumed that the ballot would be conducted in the *chef-lieu de commune*, for the act of voting under the watchful eye of local priest and local landowner maximised the bonds of community. The multi-member department constituency, on the other hand, was associated with balloting in the *chef-lieu de canton* and had been ever since the Revolution. Democrats argued that voting in the village in conditions of universal male suffrage was potentially counter-revolutionary, while voting in the *bourg* put physical and psychological distance between the peasant and his overlords. It also offered the considerable advantage of exposing rustic voters to the propaganda of the coteries of bourgeois republicans who made up a section of the rentier class in nearly every *bourg*. The debate on electoral constituencies engendered, therefore, a further debate on the location of the 'bureaux de vote' and further opportunities for manipulation. Between 1848 and 1889 there was something like a score of national electoral consultations of one shape or form in the departments of the southern Massif Central and voting oscillated between commune and canton. Indeed, the situation was still more confusing for, as we shall see, the creation of *sections électorales* added another layer of complexity.

Calculations that cantonal hustings would encourage detached and dispassionate voting fell short of the mark in the southern Massif Central. Far from neutralising or transcending local particularisms, cantonal voting

---

[28] A.D.A. 3M444 *Tableaux* of election results compiled in response to the circular of the prefect Aveyron, Rodez, 13 September 1888. See also table IX.2.

simply enlarged the arena for conflict. The vicinity of the polling station became a battle-ground – literally so on occasions – as rival columns of communal voters besported themselves in a ritual affirmation of their collective identity. After initial excitement and exuberance – the ballots of April and December 1848 were the first time most Frenchmen had participated in a national election – enthusiasm for the long march to the *chef-lieu de canton* cooled, however. In 1870 most communes deplored the new Republic's determination to restore cantonal voting. The solicitous, if manipulative, electoral arrangements of the Second Empire had won many friends among the peasantry. In the ségala around the *bourg* of Sauveterre, territorial particularism was positively ferocious and several mayors warned the prefect that the peasantry would boycott the hustings if they were held in the *chef-lieu*. 'En 1848', reported the mayor of Colombiès:

des faits regretables (*sic*) ont eu lieu à Sauveterre, à l'époque où le vote de tout le canton avait lieu au chef-lieu, entre les habitants de Sauveterre d'un côté et les électeurs des communes qui forment la zone de la montagne de l'autre, des coups de feu ont été essuyés pour ces derniers. Ces souvenirs sont encore présents à l'esprit de nos populations; les haines et les rancunes de part et d'autre sont loin d'être éteints, vouloir réunir aujourd'hui ces populations au chef-lieu du canton, ce serait à mon avis, plus qu'imprudent.[29]

Similar tales reached the ears of the prefects from all over the region: the commune of Le Viala-du-Tarn (Aveyron)[30] blithely ignored all instructions to the contrary and constituted itself into an illegal 'bureau de vote'. As a result the turn-out in March 1871 was low, although the inclement season and the sudden scheduling of the ballot for a Wednesday were contributory factors. In the department of the Aveyron 45 per cent of registered voters abstained and in individual cantons this proportion reached 70 per cent. By contrast, no more than 25 per cent of the electorate abstained in the general election of 1876 and in the heavily *dirigiste* election of 1877 which saw the reappearance of official candidatures the abstention rate dropped to about 21 per cent.[31] In 1876 and 1877 voting had taken place within the commune.

Abstentionism could, of course, denote incomparably greater awareness of political issues than rote participation in elections and evidence exists to underline the fact. In some localities protestants expressed their opposition to Louis-Napoléon's *coup d'état* by conspicuous abstention in the plebiscite of December 1851 and in the 1880s Legitimists frequently withdrew their supporters from the electoral arena when monarchist candidatures failed to materialise. Yet the principal obstacles to electoral participation were climate, terrain and, above all, habitat. As historians of the Burgundian and the

---

[29] A.D.A. 3M422 Mayor Colombiès to prefect Aveyron, Colombiès, 18 September 1870.
[30] *Ibid.*, Note attached to *procès-verbaux d'élection*, 11 February 1871.
[31] Figures derived from A.N. C3448 and A.D.A. 3M422; 3M425; 3M439. See also table IX.3.

Alpine departments have noted,[32] there is usually a positive correlation between abstentionism and the dispersed habitat. On the whole, the scattered population of the high plateaux of the southern Massif Central attended the hustings less assiduously than did the well-nucleated population of the valleys.

Habitat, indeed, provides us with the key to much of the contentiousness surrounding the issue of canton versus commune voting. The peasantry agreed to participate in the electoral process on condition that they were permitted to do so as communities. Voting in a remote and unfamiliar *chef-lieu de canton* offered small consolation, for the canton was at best a shadowy entity. But voting in the *chef-lieu de commune* was scarcely ideal either. We have already remarked on how insubstantial was the commune as a forum of collective life in large areas of the region. The common-sense solution was to acknowledge the strength of territorialism and to allow voting to take place within a village or parish context, yet the conversion of each village and parish into a *section électorale* posed formidable logistical problems and raised important questions of principle. This, in turn, gave rise to what we have called 'the politics of *sectionnement*'. The creation of sub-communal constituencies in order to accommodate local pride and sectional interests was first laid out in detail in the municipal law of 21 March 1831 and in 1848 the accumulated experience of running municipal elections was brought to bear upon the parliamentary franchise. Before 1876 republican governments were reluctant to countenance the establishment of multiple electoral sections or 'bureaux de vote', however. To have done so would have been to undermine the stated purpose of the *scrutin de liste*. Yet a refusal to allow sub-constituencies was manifestly unjust in mountain regions where the cantons covered a vast area and there was also the risk of mass abstention from the polls. On the other hand, a low turn-out might favour the republicans who were acutely conscious of their minority status in the countryside.

In fact, the provisional executive which assumed power upon the abdication of Louis-Philippe was the only government to adhere rigorously to the principle of polling in the cantons. As far as we can tell, the vast majority of Frenchmen either voted in the towns and *bourgs* or they did not vote at all in April 1848. That they were prepared to do so on such a massive scale (abstentions averaged 16 per cent) suggested that the electoral arrangements had won popular approval, but contemporaries hesitated to draw this conclusion. There was a feeling that the feat could not be achieved twice and that truly representative democracy demanded communal voting. These misgivings came to the fore during the debates on the constitution when an amendment

---

[32] P. Lévêque, 'La Bourgogne de la Monarchie de Juillet au Second Empire' (Université de Paris IV, Thèse de doctorat d'état, 6 vols., 1977), iii, p. 1252; P. Rambaud and M. Vincienne, *Les Transformations d'une société rurale: la Maurienne, 1562–1962* (Paris, 1964), pp. 197–8. Also chapter eight, pp. 228–9.

to shift the hustings to the commune was tabled. It was defeated, but the Assembly agreed that in future ballots principle should be tempered with policy. The elections for the presidency of the Republic soon put this decision to the test and exposed the dangers of *ad hoc* provisions. In the southern Massif Central, a prefectoral dispensation in favour of one outlying village swiftly brought an avalanche of similar requests for a separate 'bureau de vote'. Local administrators discovered that they could do no right; indeed, their intervention threatened to accentuate the tribal characteristics of the hustings as rival villages and parishes squared up to one another. The decision to locate a subsidiary polling station in the commune of Cros de Géorand at the northern extremity of the elongated canton of Montpezat (Ardèche) placated some villages and enraged others. On being informed that his constituents would be required to vote at Cros de Géorand rather than at Montpezat, the mayor of Usclades warned that the two villages were at daggers drawn. At the hustings held the previous April, two individuals from Cros de Géorand had murdered a voter from Usclades.[33]

Accordingly, for the legislative elections of May 1849 strict cantonal voting was relaxed. In the department of the Aveyron every canton was divided into four electoral sections (one of which was the *chef-lieu*). Thus, in the canton of Sauveterre where columns of voters arriving from the countryside had been ambushed the year before, 'bureaux de vote' were established in the villages of Gramond, Castanet and Colombiès.[34] But the hesitant palliatives of the Republic paled before the achievements of the Second Empire. Bonapartism aimed to bring democracy to the doorstep. With the ideological objection to communal voting removed, the prefects made no bones about their willingness to take the polls to the voter rather than vice versa and readily acceded to requests for *sections électorales*. On the eve of the plebiscite of November 1852 the sub-prefect of St Affrique reported: 'J'ai multiplié autant que possible et que le temps me l'a permis les sections électorales dans les communes.'[35] The only threat to the regime appeared to be electoral inertia and during these decades the peasantry were permitted to cast their ballots in unities of as little as sixty voters. yet the logistical strains which Caesarian democracy imposed on the countryside of the southern Massif Central came close to defeating the object of the exercise. Who would police the ubiquitous 'bureaux de vote'? Where else could they convene but in the official residences of the parish clergy? This possibility seemed much less congenial after the Emperor's Italian policy strained relations with the catholic church. The mayor of St Basile (Ardèche) grumbled that the establishment of three polling stations in his commune (for the legislative elections of 1863) 'nécessite la présence de 18 personnes pendant 2 jours et la

[33] A.D. Ard. 2M519 Mayor Usclades to sub-prefect Largentière, Usclades, 4 December 1848.
[34] A.D.A. 3M61 Printed 'Avis aux électeurs'.
[35] A.D.A. 3M76 Sub-prefect St Affrique to prefect Aveyron, St Affrique, 19 November 1852.

disposition de 3 locaux. Or, les conseillers municipaux en exercise sont au nombre de 11, tous sachant signer, mais dont 3 ne savent ni lire ni écrire'.[36]

As we have seen, the proclamation of the Republic in September 1870 rekindled the issue of electoral constituencies. But the Government of National Defence took note of the practical difficulties inherent in holding elections in the *chefs-lieux de canton*. While a decree of 30 September asserted the general principle of cantonal voting, a ministerial circular issued several days later informed the prefects that they might divide cantons into two or three electoral sections and even more in exceptional circumstances. A further telegraphic message interpreted this to mean '3 circonscriptions au plus par canton'.[37] In fact, the general election of February 1871 which had originally been scheduled to take place the preceding October proved to be the last occasion on which any serious attempt was made to restrict voting to the cantons. The young Republic learned more from the Empire than it cared to admit and in 1876 and 1885, in particular, the prefects granted requests for *sections électorales* with cynical abandon. The commune of Nant[38] on the Causse du Larzac was divided into as many as five *sections* in time for the elections of 1876. Manipulation of this sort reached its zenith during the period of Moral Order, however. In the Aveyron the 14,548 potential voters comprising the electorate of the Rodez I constituency were divided into fifty-nine *sections électorales* for the purposes of the 1877 contest.[39] Wherever possible the prefect based these sub-constituencies upon the parishes. Thus, the commune of La Bastide-L'Evêque was carved up into its four constituent parishes of La Bastide, Cabanès, Cadour and Teulières. Electoral logic put asunder what administrative logic had put together.

These strictures prompt a final comment on the nature of voting. In the countryside and perhaps in the towns, too (after all, in 1848 Parisian workers were urged by their representatives in the Luxembourg Commission to march to the polls in craft groups),[40] electoral participation was generally a symptom of collective consciousness. The same point could, with reservations, be made of non-participation. Indeed, it is difficult to see how voting could have taken any other form for the 'technology' of late eighteenth- and nineteenth-century elections positively enforced regimentation. The modern stereotype of voters frequenting the polling station at their own convenience is entirely misplaced. During the period covered by this study electoral legislation required voters to attend the polls *en masse*. They therefore tended to

[36] A.D. Ard. 2M346 Mayor St Basile to sub-prefect Tournon, St Basile, 23 April 1869. In 1857 8.3% of the electoral constituencies of the Ardèche contained fewer than 100 registered voters (2M344).

[37] A.D.A. 3M422 Telegraphic communication from the Minister of the Interior.

[38] A.D.A. 3M425 Dossier headed *sections de vote*.

[39] A.D.A. 3M439 *Bureaux de vote: 1ère circonscription de Rodez*.

[40] W. H. Sewell, Jr, *Work and Revolution in France: the Language of Labour from the Old Regime to 1848* (Cambridge, 1980), p. 262.

arrive *en masse* and to go home *en masse*. For example, the Convention decreed on 25 Fructidor III (11 September 1795) that voters would be called upon to cast their slips by name and in turn. In turn meant by order of inscription on the electoral register and – if necessary – by order of commune with the most distant communes voting first. A ministerial instruction circulated prior to the abortive elections of 16 October 1870 reiterated that voters were to be admitted to the polls in set order: 'si une commune ne se trouvait pas à son rang au moment où ses électeurs seront appelés à entrer dans la salle, on passerait à la commune suivante et l'autre reprendrait ensuite son rang'.[41]

Communal voting in formations which maximised social discipline militated against an individualistic perception of the issues raised by the electoral process. In the southern Massif Central, indeed, those issues were often lost sight of altogether. But this does not mean that peasant political behaviour was in some sense non-rational. Merely that groups of rural voters bound by ancient allegiances possessed an apprehension of rationality which the theories of political scientists seem unable to comprehend. William Brustein, for instance, has chided the pioneers of French regional history and geography for 'overemphasising the role of nonrational (*sic*) factors such as party loyalty, past relative deprivation, tradition, and ethnic solidarity' and holds that 'voters are strategic actors who vote for those candidates or programs that will provide them with the greatest benefits'.[42] This latter contention is not without merit for there is evidence that the priorities of the rural electorate were changing by the 1880s, but it rests on premises which are dubious in the extreme. Whether in the 1880s or in earlier decades, popular electoral participation in the departments of the southern Massif Central expressed first and foremost a sense of collective awareness. We have already noted how the familial and cultural traditions of an unusually homogeneous peasant society inhibited the autonomy of the individual; and the ostentatious, belligerent and above all public character of the hustings (which Brustein appears to doubt) reduced that freedom still further. The collective response did not, of itself, preclude an acceptance of political neologism, however. After Louis-Napoléon's *coup d'état*, the sub-prefect of Brioude reported that Jean-Pierre Joseph Martin of Berbezit 'est venu voter en 1848 portant le drapeau en tête de sa commune, toute dévouée au parti socialiste'.[43] Yet radicalisation of opinion achieved by this means tended to be hybrid, volatile and, after 1851, a victim of the economic and political conjuncture. As the final section of this chapter will illustrate, the communitarian response could usually be relied on to produce a vote in support of the traditional status quo.

[41] A.D.A. 3M422 Ministerial circular, Tours, 6 october 1870.
[42] W. Brustein, 'A Regional Mode-of-Production Analysis of Political Behaviour: the Cases of Western and Mediterranean France', *Politics and Society*, x (1981), 356; 367.
[43] A.D. H.-L. 7V2 Sub-prefect Brioude to prefect Haute-Loire, Brioude, 29 December 1851.

The emergence of the catholic church as an electoral organisation

For most Frenchmen the advent of direct democracy in 1848 represented a staggering leap in the dark. In Paris the Academy of Sciences[44] wondered whether the exercise was arithmetically feasible, while a parliamentary candidate in the Lozère concluded – after a particularly tumultuous electoral meeting at Marvejols – that 'le hazard fera l'élection; les électeurs ignorants, et il y en a beaucoup, jetteront dans l'urne le bulletin qui se présentera le premier au bout des doigts'.[45] In the event neither the arithmetic, nor the logistics of cantonal voting posed insuperable obstacles, but the very scale of democratic politics placed a premium on organisation and the institution which responded to this challenge most incisively and effectively was the catholic church. To be sure, the clergy had long been involved in politics. During the Revolution clerical Jeremiahs had done much to undermine confidence in representative government and Carlist clerics had used the same ploy – with less success – after 1830. In parishes scattered all over the southern Massif Central strong-minded ecclesiastics conspicuously absented themselves from requiem masses in honour of the 'Trois Glorieuses', or refrained from uttering the words 'Ludovicum Philippum' in public prayers. None of this chiselling opposition enjoyed the publicly declared support of the hierarchy, however. Monseigneur de la Brunière, bishop of Mende, warned his clergy to keep their own counsel at election times and Monseigneur Giraud, bishop of Rodez, did likewise.[46]

All this changed in 1848. The collapse of the despised July Monarchy and the opening of the electoral arena to all comers galvanised opinion of every conceivable hue. For the first time the church entered the lists armed with offensive rather than purely defensive and obstructionist political weaponry; for the first time since the Civil Constitution the clergy preached politics from the pulpit with the blessing of the bishops; for the first time the clerical effort was orchestrated in support of lists of 'bon parti' candidates endorsed by the *évêchés*. In the departments of the southern Massif Central, in short, the dawn of direct democracy was accompanied by the emergence of the catholic church as a tremendously powerful and technically sophisticated electoral organisation. An obvious comparison can be made with the incursion of the Irish clergy into the electoral arena which helped to secure a victory for Daniel O'Connell in the Clare by-election of 1828.[47]

That the clergy were able to induce the peasantry to trek to the *chef-lieu* in April 1848 and vote for clerical candidates says much for the authority of the

[44] Weill, *Les Elections législatives depuis 1789*, p. 168.
[45] A.D.L. F2818 Belviala to Vicomte Charles de la Rochenégly, Marvejols, 5 April 1848.
[46] A.E.M. Bishop to Prefect, Mende, 12 June 1834; A.N. F[19] 2570 Copy of letter of prefect Aveyron, Rodez, 12 March 1832.
[47] J. H. Whyte, 'The Influence of the Catholic Clergy on Elections in Nineteenth-Century Ireland', *The English Historical Review*, cccxciv (1960), 240–1.

catholic church as an institution. That they were able to repeat the demonstration – albeit less successfully – in May 1849 when the *démocrates-socialistes* were primed to contest the election is even more remarkable. The nature of clerical control and its limitations has already been explored (see chapter four), but it is worth noting that the inception of mass democracy in the middle of the nineteenth century coincided with an in-coming tide of popular religiosity and a re-affirmation of parish discipline. Important elements in this process were the improving ratios of parish clergy per head of population and the diminishing social distance – which had never been great – between cleric and countryman.[48] We know, too, that cantonal voting presupposed a somewhat military style of electoral mobilisation and that many contingents of voters were led to the polls either by their parish priest, their mayor, their local landowner or by all three. Plentiful evidence exists to underpin this latter point, of which Alexis de Tocqueville's description of voting in the department of the Manche is the most eloquent.[49] We also know that polling for the Constituent Assembly commenced on 23 April and resumed the following day in populous cantons. This was a particularly unfortunate choice of date as far as the protagonists of the young Republic were concerned, for the 23rd was Easter Sunday and the peasantry reached the hustings in a state of spiritual exaltation. All over the region the 'grand' messe' was brought forward to the crack of dawn and, after suitable edification, the voters assembled outside the church porch and with banners unfurled made ready for the march to the *chef-lieu*.

The impetuous agents of the Paris Club des Clubs who had been despatched to the provinces to proselytise for the Republic could only chronicle the impending disaster. Full of foreboding, Marie and Peillon reported from the Haute-Loire that 'les habitants des campagnes du Puy marchent pour ainsi dire tous d'accord avec leurs curés et feront ce que ces derniers conseilleront', and as polling began, 'ce que nous voyons tous les jours nous ferait presque désirer que les habitants de la campagne de la Haute-Loire fussent désherités d'un droit qu'ils ne comprennent pas et dont nous craignons qu'ils en fassent mauvais usage, fanatisés qu'ils sont par les prêtres'.[50] From the Ardèche Barruel announced: 'Hier les élections ont commencé, à 7 heures du matin les communes arrivaient, on a commencé par Privas; sur les 8 heures j'ai vu arriver avec peine des communes avec le curé en tête, avec des bulletins cachetés. Ils avaient la consigne de ne les laisser voir par personne.'[51] Delegates in the Lozère and the Aveyron recounted a similar story. While deploring the damage which the forty-five *centimes* tax was

[48] See above, chapter four, pp. 128–44.
[49] Quoted in Jones, 'An Improbable Democracy', pp. 530–1.
[50] A.N. C939 L. Marie and Peillon to *président du comité central de Paris* (Club of Clubs), Le Puy, 16 and 24 April 1848.
[51] A.N. C938 Barruel to *président du comité central de Paris* (Club of Clubs), Privas, 24 April 1848.

doing to republican candidates, Garnier warned that the clergy was 'tout puissant [underlined]'[52] in the Lozère and campaigning on a common platform with the Legitimists. Meanwhile from Espalion at the foot of the Aubrac, Bibal reported:

L'on a voté toute la journée. L'ensemble des électeurs est admirable au premier à bord, toutes les communes arrivent drapeau en tête et chantant la Marseillaise, mais là finit cette union. Les gredins de prêtres nous volent impunément. Je deviens fou de rage; ils ont tous d'un commun accord imposé des listes à leurs paroissiens, au confessionnal, à l'église et chez eux.[53]

The results bore out these gloomy prognostications. Between them the clergy and the aristocracy celebrated a resounding victory. In the Haute-Loire seven out of eight seats fell to conservative candidates; in the Ardèche only one place out of nine went to a republican; in the Aveyron one in ten and in the Lozère where the protestant vote promoted Edouard Commandré, a long-standing republican, to the delegation, one in four. In Rodez the republicans vented their anger by organising a charivari which penetrated the courtyard of the episcopal palace and which the journal of Monseigneur Croizier described rather melodramatically as the 'sac de l'évêché'.[54] In the Lozère the notoriety of clerical intervention in the elections reached the ears of the deputies in Paris and the Assembly voted to suspend two of the successful candidates – the *abbé* Fayet, bishop of Orleans (born in Mende of peasant stock), and the Legitimist Desmolles – pending an enquiry. The documents gathered together for this electoral enquiry shed precious light on the abiding strength of ancient prejudices in the countryside. The *curé* of Badaroux, for instance, allegedly warned his flock in a pulpit allocution that 'les protestants au nombre de quatre ou cinq mille marchaient comme un seul homme et ne manqueraient pas de réussir d'envoyer à l'assemblée quatre candidats de leur choix si les catholiques ne s'entendaient pas mieux.'[55] The *curé* of St Etienne-de-Valdonnez likewise stood accused of advising his parishioners on how to vote: 'leur fesant (*sic*) observer que les mal-intentionnés fesait (*sic*) courir le bruit que le clergé voulait les dîmes et les censives; mais que cela n'était pas vrai'.[56]

Notwithstanding a damning catalogue of abuse, Fayet and Desmolles retained their seats and again demonstrated the formidable capacity of a clerical *mot d'ordre* to command votes during the presidential elections of

---

[52] A.N. C939 F. Garnier to *président du comité central de Paris* (Club of Clubs), Mende, 20 April 1848.

[53] A.N. C938 Bibal to *président du comité central de Paris* (Club of Clubs), Espalion, 23 April 1848, 8 p.m.

[54] A.E.R. *Journal et visites pastorales, 1842–1855, Mgr. Croizier*, 29 April 1848.

[55] A.D.L. IVM⁴ 1–9 Extract from the minutes of the *juge de paix* of the canton of Mende, 23 April 1848, 4 p.m.

[56] *Ibid.*, Statement recorded before M. A. Trincald, *premier suppléant du tribunal de paix du canton de Mende*, 26 April 1848, 4 p.m.

December 1848. Fayet despatched an open letter to all bishops urging the choice of Cavaignac on the ground that he offered the best guarantees for religion and in the Lozère the General took nearly 33 per cent of the votes cast, in the Ardèche 27 per cent and in the Haute-Loire 20 per cent compared with only 11 per cent in the Aveyron and a national average of 19.5 per cent.[57] In fact, a convincing interpretation of what happened during the presidential ballot is as remote for the departments of the southern Massif Central as it is for the rest of France. The presence of two candidates of the 'party of order' confused alignments and created some odd bed-fellows. Two facts are plain, however: even in the Lozère Louis-Napoléon Bonaparte collected two out of every three votes cast and the candidature of Ledru-Rollin failed to register significantly except in a few cantons of the Haute-Loire and the Ardèche. While the clergy of the Lozère and the Ardèche worked dutifully for the victory of General Cavaignac, it seems likely that the Legitimists threw their weight behind Louis-Napoléon and in this they were supported by the bishop of Rodez, the spiritual leader of the Aveyronnais clergy. Yet many protestants also voted for Cavaignac in the belief that the catholics would rally masssively to the cause of Louis-Napoléon and the freedom of education. In the Lozère[58] the General took 47 per cent of the popular vote in the *arrondissement* of Florac where Calvinists constituted a slight majority of the population compared with 24 per cent and 31 per cent respectively in the homogeneously catholic *arrondissements* of Marvejols and Mende. Similarly, in the Ardèche[59] the predominantly protestant canton of Vernoux voted massively for Cavaignac, but so did ardently catholic communes like Sainte Eulalie in the Monts du Vivarais, while Lalouvesc – the pilgrim centre and a veritable citadel of Roman Catholicism – voted unanimously for Louis-Napoléon. Clearly there existed a certain tension, or rather a failure of communication, within the ranks of the notables which divided loyalties and fragmented the vote. In spite of appearances, the southern Massif Central was a bastion of clericalism rather than of Legitimism, although the political import of this nuance was not fully plumbed until the 1880s. We would be unwise to press ingenious global explanations in the absence of conclusive evidence, however. As this study has repeatedly emphasised, the rationality of popular electoral behaviour often lay at a deeper level. Is it pure coincidence that Sainte Eulalie chose Cavaignac while Burzet, the *chef-lieu de canton*, chose Louis-Napoléon, or Ruoms chose Louis-Napoléon while the protestants of the *chef-lieu*, Vallon, opted for Cavaignac?[60]

The testing time for the church as an electoral force was only beginning,

[57] A.N. BII 963; 968; 999; 1006. Also M. Agulhon, *The Republican Experiment, 1848–1852* (Cambridge, 1983), pp. 71–3 and figs.
[58] A.D.L. IVM^2 1–7 Elections, results by cantons.
[59] Sabatier, *Religion et politique*, p. 194; M. Riou, 'L'Election présidentielle de décembre 1848 en Ardèche', *Revue du Vivarais*, lxxviii (1974), 89–93.
[60] Riou, 'L'Election présidentielle de décembre 1848 en Ardèche, 89–93.

however. The parliamentary election for the renewal of the Assembly in May 1849 took place in a countryside weighed down by debt (especially in the ségala), alienated by the forty-five *centimes* levy and infiltrated by *démocrate-socialiste* propaganda. In the Aveyron a composite list of clericals and conservatives dominated the polls without difficulty. Perhaps two out of the eight representatives sent to Paris could be considered staunch republicans. Likewise in the Lozère where the future social reformer and senator Théophile Roussel,[61] ousted Commandré after a portion of the protestant vote shifted its moorings. The republican bridgehead was held, but not extended. Further east, however, the election revealed the 'party of order' to be in considerable disarray. The Ardèche and the Haute-Loire numbered among the sixteen departments which cast a majority of votes in support of *démocrate-socialiste* candidates. In the Ardèche they captured six out of eight seats, while in the Haute-Loire they swept the board completely. With hindsight it is clear that the republican victory in this latter department was foreshadowed in the elections of the preceding year, for the cantons of the *arrondissement* of Brioude had voted massively for the most radical list, and by May 1849 only eight of the twenty-eight cantons comprising the Haute-Loire were still resisting the *démocrates-socialistes*. Such was the proselytising zeal of the Brioude clubists, indeed, that by May 1850 there were signs that the democratic contagion had infected adjacent communes in the Lozère.

What was happening? Had the general election of 1849 revealed that a fundamental restructuring of popular attitudes was in progress in the southern Massif Central, or had it prefigured a vigorous but shortlived crisis of political authority in the countryside such as the region experienced between 1789 and 1794? Detailed discussion of these interesting hypotheses must await our final chapter, but it is worth remarking that a broad chronological perspective tends to minimise the *démocrate-socialiste* break-through, such as it was, of 1849–50. The tide of socialist democracy rose and it fell leaving few traces. Repression after Louis-Napoléon's *coup d'état* and a pervasive defeatism had something to do with it, of course, yet socialist democracy never acquired the status of a mass political movement in the southern Massif Central. Moreover, what energy it still possessed after the *coup* was largely sublimated into the concept of Caesarean democracy.

Arguably, therefore, the notables resumed a position of social and political pre-eminence in rural society which had never been seriously challenged. After the debacle following upon its neutralist stance in the contest of 1849, government rediscovered the merits of electoral management while the church temporarily forgot its equivocations of December 1848 and rallied to

---

[61] A.D.L. IVM⁴ 10–12 *Elections, Assemblée Législative, 1849*. During a long parliamentary career spanning five decades, Jean-Baptiste Victor Théophile Roussel (1816–1903) earned a reputation as a campaigner for child welfare legislation. The law of 23 December 1874 protecting new-born children bears his name.

the cause of Napoléon – the guardian of the social order. Bishop Croizier[62] was returning from a tour of inspection when the first reports of disturbances in Rodez following the *coup* reached his ears and he prudently turned off the highway and billeted himself on the *curé* of Flavin. Not until calm had been restored did he complete his journey on 5 December 1851. The experience had a chastening effect and the clergy's support for the new status quo was scarcely in doubt when the referendum on the *coup* took place a fortnight later. Yet Legitimist prelates like Croizier regarded Louis-Napoléon as a necessary evil and drew small comfort from the proclamation of the Second Empire a year later. The bishop had committed all the resources of the church to the defence of the social order, wrote the prefect of the Aveyron,[63] but had conspicuously failed to endorse the establishment of an hereditary Empire. Nevertheless, the Aveyronnais peasantry cast as many 'Yes' ballots in November 1852 as they had done the previous December.

The ecclesiastical hierarchy considered it inadvisable to seek independent political representation when the elections to the new legislative body took place in February–March 1852. Those clerics and Legitimists who stood, did so as official candidates. Yet even during the early years of the Second Empire when the Bonapartist synthesis seemed to be working and the storm clouds of Italian nationalism remained safely beneath the horizon, relations between church and state exhibited a certain fragility. In Rodez, Legitimists sowed discord between the prefecture and the *évêché* until Croizier died in 1855 and the government replaced him with a more amenable cleric. In the Ardèche, meanwhile, the sectarian feud complicated the tasks of imperial administrators just as it had those of their predecessors. With a by-election pending for 1854 in the electoral *arrondissement* of Privas, the government chose a protestant to be the official candidate and instructed the prefect to recommend him to the predominantly catholic electorate. This spectacular act of insensitivity prompted an independent landowner to enter the lists in order to provide catholics with an alternative choice.[64]

Above all else, it was the Italian war which restored to the clergy an autonomous political role. As the social and political repercussions of that bloody Easter campaign of 1859 reverberated, the public utterances of the parish clergy struck an unaccustomed note of vehemence. The *curé* of Beauzac (Haute-Loire)[65] alleged that the Emperor had started hostilities in order to further the aims of the 'reds', while the *curé* of Versols (Aveyron)[66]

---

[62] A.E.R. *Journal et visites pastorales, 1842–1855, Mgr. Croizier*, 2 December 1851.
[63] A.N. F^{19} 2570 Prefect Aveyron to *Ministre de l'Instruction Publique et des Cultes*, Rodez, 16 July 1853.
[64] A.N. F^{1c} III Ardèche 5 Dossier on by-election of 30 April–1 May 1854.
[65] A. Rivet, *La Vie politique dans le département de la Haute-Loire de 1815 à 1974* (Le Puy, 1979), p. 291.
[66] A.E.R. *Liasse (1848–1870), divers*: Copy of letter of sub-prefect St Affrique to prefect Aveyron (n.d. [1860]).

repeatedly sermonised his parishioners on the plight of the Holy See. The bishops, meanwhile, expressed their disquiet in a series of pastoral letters which were read out in every parish. As the government strove vainly to win concessions from Pius IX, Monseigneur Delalle[67] of Rodez issued a 'mandement' for Easter 1860 which enjoined the Pope to stand firm. Monseigneur de Morlhon[68] of Le Puy was more circumspect and took care to lay the major responsibility for the train of events at the door of the Italian government, but Foulquier,[69] the bishop of Mende, backed up his public pronouncements with a letter to the Emperor giving full expression to his misgivings.

The timely approach of legislative elections ensured that the so-called Roman Question would be discussed at greater length and in greater depth than any other issue to confront the Second Empire until that time. Indeed, it is scarcely an exaggeration to suggest that the spectres conjured forth by Garibaldi's designs on the Papal States aroused opinion in the region from the torpid state into which it had fallen during the previous decade. The reanimation of local political life provoked by the re-entry of the clergy into the electoral arena was especially fervent in the Lozère where the cause of catholicism and liberal monarchism found a talented defender in the person of Aldebert-Dominique-Joseph de Chambrun.[70] The public career of the Comte de Chambrun began under the star of Louis-Napoléon Bonaparte. After a brief spell in the prefectoral corps during the testing months of 1850–1, he married advantageously, resigned his post and took up foreign travel. On returning to the Lozère, he was invited to contest the elections of 1857 as an official candidate in place of the ex-constituent, Desmolles, whose inactivity as a deputy had caused general dissatisfaction. He stood accused of failing to look after the interests of the department – the most damning indictment that could be levelled against a political representative in the nineteenth century.

The prestige of the de Chambrun name had a most pleasing effect on the voters and the government congratulated itself on its choice. But then the violence perpetrated against the Holy See intervened to embitter relations between church and state. In 1863 de Chambrun stood as an independent and hostile candidate with the support of the *évêché*. The administration gave its patronage to Joseph Barrot, grandson of the *conventionnel* Jean-Antoine

---

[67] *Ibid.*, Prefect to bishop of Rodez, Rodez, 14 February 1860.

[68] Rivet, *La Vie politique dans le département de la Haute-Loire*, p. 291.

[69] A.E.M. *Correspondance des évêques*: Minute of letter of Foulquier to Emperor, Mende, 9 October 1861.

[70] For the details of de Chambrun's political career given below, see L. Costecalde, *Biographie du Comte Aldebert de Chambrun (1821–1898)* (Mende, 1934) and M. Masseguin, 'Les Parlementaires royalistes lozériens de 1815 à 1893' (Université de Montpellier, Diplôme d'études supérieures, 1958), pp. 73–84.

Barrot,[71] which did nothing to enhance his *éclat* in the eyes of the voters. Scenting disaster as pulpit politicians turned the election into a matter of conscience, the prefect used every conceivable stratagem to hinder de Chambrun's progress. When he fell sick at Villefort gendarmes were posted outside his bedroom door in a bid, presumably, to deter callers, and the electioneering of Madame de Chambrun was also conducted in the intimidating presence of the gendarmerie. Notwithstanding these unmistakable marks of official displeasure, the peasantry rallied massively to the 'bon parti'. The government's nominee was defeated humiliatingly by 17,871 votes to 9,405. Moreover, the lesson was repeated in 1869. Having inflicted a crushing defeat on Joseph Barrot, the clergy meted out similar treatment to his younger brother, Frédéric, six years later (de Chambrun: 17,897 votes; Frédéric Barrot: 14,379 votes). Buoyed up by two remarkable victories achieved in the face of blatant administrative pressure, the clergy of the Lozère had acquired a taste for politics by the end of the Second Empire. More to the point, their combativeness in support of the Comte de Chambrun had laid the foundations of a formidable electoral machine which would come into its own in the 1870s and 1880s.

In the Aveyron, and also in the Haute-Loire, catholic opposition to the Empire tended to be more closely identified with the ideology of Legitimism. This must be accounted as one reason why the regime proved better able to defend its position in these departments than in the Lozère. De Chambrun's antecedents were suitably royalist, of course, but his monarchism was tempered by pragmatism. His family belonged to the *rallié* rather than the *émigré* wing of the local nobility. The Calemard de Lafayette of the Haute-Loire and the de Bonald of the Aveyron were steeped in the traditions of the *ancien régime*, by contrast, and peasant support for them was coloured by recollections of seigneurialism. In 1863 Charles Calemard de Lafayette[72] decided against standing in the Le Puy–Yssingeaux constituency after taking soundings with the *curés*, while in the Aveyron clerico-Legitimist candidates had to be content with local successes. Despite a campaign of exceptional virulence in the Millau–St Affrique constituency, Victor de Bonald,[73]the grandson of the *philosophe*, failed to unseat the incumbent official candidate, Pierre Calvet-Rogniat, either in 1863 or 1869.

Yet neither the church nor the Legitimist aristocracy could afford to push their opposition to extremes however much they might have disliked the Second Empire. Behind Bonapartism lay republicanism – albeit a long way behind in the southern Massif Central. Memories of the confusion of 1849–

---

71 See above, chapter three, pp. 80–1.
72 Rivet, *La Vie politique*, p. 291. Charles Calemard was the son of pierre Calemard who had represented the Haute-Loire as a Legitimist deputy during the July Monarchy and the nephew of François Calemard who had represented the department during the Restoration.
73 A.D.A. 5M10; 5M10 *bis*; 5M11. Also above, chapter five, p. 145 and note 2.

51 when the authority of the notables had faltered remained fresh and served as a constant reminder of the dangers of headlong descent into party politics. Moreover, the regime had a knack of presenting its opponents with unpalatable alternatives and of forcing them back into line. It is in this light that we should interpret the plebiscite of May 1870. Few catholics or Legitimists were prepared to align themselves with the Calvinists and the republicans and vote against the liberal reforms. With the exception of a handful of irreconcilable clerics, the church rallied to the defence of the social order as it had done in 1851. If sizeable minorities of 'No' ballots were cast in the Brivadois, the lower Ardèche (the old Bas Vivarais) and the Cévennes, elsewhere the peasantry voted *en masse* for the status quo. In the Aveyron 4 per cent of voters and barely 2 per cent in the Lozère (excluding the mixed *arrondissement* of Florac) rejected the Empire. In each case there had been a record turnout of, respectively, 83 per cent and 85 per cent.[74] The debt which the regime owed to the church was patent and the prefect of the Aveyron was gracious enough to acknowledge it. As polling drew to a close, he penned the following letter to Bishop Delalle of Rodez:

Aujourd'hui la parole est au scrutin, et à l'heure même où je n'ai plus qu'à attendre la décision du peuple, j'ai à cœur de vous dire que vous l'avez éclairée par votre haute adhésion au plébiscite et que bien des votes acquis à la cause de l'ordre et de l'Empire sont votre œuvre. Merci mille fois d'avoir fait appel au patriotisme des populations qui vous suivent d'autant plus volontiers dans vos avis qu'elles vous connaissent depuis bien des années.[75]

[74] A.D. Ard. 2M276 Results by departments in *Moniteur des Communes*, 13 May 1870.
[75] A.E.R. *Liasse (1848–1870), divers*: Prefect Aveyron to bishop of Rodez, Rodez, 8 May 1870.

8

✲✲✲

The sources of political allegiance

The cumbersome mechanisms of electoral democracy conditioned political behaviour in the countryside to a degree unrecognised. Historians have been slow to acknowledge that the questions of 'when', 'where' and 'how' to vote often coloured the issue of 'for whom' to vote. But with the peasant elector making his way to the hustings in a cohort of neighbours and kinsmen, it becomes possible to take stock of our argument and to set out what it implies more explicitly.

The process of *prise de conscience politique* among country dwellers in the late eighteenth and nineteenth centuries was extraordinarily complex and calls for multi-disciplinary analysis. Empirical studies of peasant politicisation are rare and it would be unwise to assume that the case of the southern Massif Central is in any sense typical. Nevertheless, our enquiry into the sources of political allegiance in the four departments of the Ardèche, the Aveyron, the Haute-Loire and the Lozère has focused upon several of the factors which André Siegfried delineated in his pioneer study of electoral dualism in the West of France. Published over seventy years ago, the *Tableau politique de la France de l'Ouest* (Paris, 1913) remains an impressive and fertile analysis of grass-roots political behaviour. While Siegfried's diagnosis of the role performed by property structures was overly schematic and he took insufficient account of the contingent, cultural and psychological facets of rural electoral mobilisation, his thesis contained one idea of particular merit: it placed community before polity. The formative influences upon political opinion should be sought, first and foremost, within the *milieu* from which the voter was drawn. That this insight has informed our approach to the subject of peasant politicisation in the southern Massif Central needs no emphasising. In fact, Siegfried was well aware of the parallels between the two regions for, towards the end of his life, he applied his theories to the department of the Ardèche.[1]

If voting in the countryside was primarily an experience conditioned by group reflexes, it follows that the history of the peasantry in an age of

---

[1] A. Siegfried, *Géographie électorale de l'Ardèche sous la IIIᵉ République* (Paris, 1949).

participatory democracy is perforce regional, or even local, history. A methodology based on microscopic analysis is unavoidable if we are to detect the rhythms of opinion formation at parish and sub-parish level. In this chapter an attempt is made to classify the observed sources of rural political commitment under a number of thematic headings: habitat; territorialism; household structure; confessional rivalries and social structure. This typology owes much to Siegfried, but does not provide a sufficient explanation of peasant politicisation in itself. We should be wary of portraying the peasant inhabitant of the Massif Central as merely the passive recipient of multifarious conditioning forces. The peasantry possessed a voice of its own and a cultural medium through which to articulate its beliefs and opinions. In reality, the chemistry of political allegiance was a compound of internal and external factors – the product of an interaction of historical and environmental criteria with external ideological stimuli.

The human habitat described in chapter one rarely exercised a determining influence on political options, but it left a shadowy imprint on election returns nonetheless. High levels of abstentionism in parliamentary elections marked out the entire Massif Central, but the lofty mountain spines of the Margeride and the Monts du Vivarais, and the tortured relief of the Cévennes posed particular obstacles to the habits of ballot-box democracy. In these areas even attendance at local elections was likely to be patchy. In 1848 the first democratic municipal election in over fifty years mobilised just 140 voters (36.2 per cent) in the commune of Araules (Haute-Loire).[2] Those present at the hustings complained that news of the impending election had reached them by public rumour. By the time the preliminaries had been completed it was dusk – candles illuminated the 'bureau' – and numbers had dwindled to fifty. The 392 registered electors of the commune of Araules resided in a scatter of thirty-nine settlements and isolated farms dotted along the flanks of Mont Meygal. By contrast, abstentionism, whether in local or national elections, was less marked in the *limagne* of Brioude and in the upper valley of the Loire and it is tempting to invoke a variant of Siegfried's 'law of altitudes' as an explanation. Yet Siegfried's contention that in the department of the Ardèche altitude played the decisive role in shaping political attitudes ('au-dessus de 800 et surtout de 1000 mètres, on vote à Droite, tandis qu'au-dessous de 300 mètres on vote à Gauche')[3] smacks of geographical and ecological determinism and fails to accommodate all the facts. High altitudes and refractory habitat structures rarely inhibited the electoral mobilisation of Calvinists. Moreover, they voted for the perceived Left whether they happened to live above the 1000 metre contour as in the Monts du Vivarais or below the 500 metre contour as in the Bas Vivarais. In any case we should be

---

[2] A.D. H.-L. 4M27 Protest of 'un grand nombre d'électeurs' to sub-prefect Yssingeaux, Araules, 2 August 1848.
[3] Siegfried, *Géographie électorale de l'Ardèche*, p. 113.

wary of harnessing too closely participation in the routines of global society and ecological factors. Peasants suffered their physical environment and were marked by it, but they could also defy it. For the population of the ségala, or the Cévennes, or the snow-swept plateaux, Sunday attendance at church was just such an act of ritual defiance. Isolation, in short, could trigger compensatory reflexes of sociability and it is likely that in some parishes elections came to play an integrative role in the course of the nineteenth century. While noting a positive correlation between abstentionism, altitude and habitat dispersion, a study of the Alpine valley of the Arc also found evidence of the reverse process in two remote cantons, 'comme si l'isolement cherchait à se compenser par un essai d'adhésion à la société'.[4]

The physical environment contoured political expression in a general fashion at best, therefore. But the imperatives of climate and topography did not act in a vacuum. They combined with multiple human factors and therein lies the relevance of habitat to the question of opinion formation. We have already described how the pattern of settlement could enormously complicate the logistical aspects of electoral consultation. And settlement dispersion, in particular, had an important bearing upon the matrix of social relationships and rivalries in the countryside. Perhaps the most striking feature of this human landscape was the dichotomy between *bourg* and village. *Bourgs* were numerous in the southern Massif Central for they suffered little competition from towns, but their bustling self-importance is deceptive. The literate professional classes and rentiers of these overgrown villages never succeeded in imposing their cultural and political stereotypes on the surrounding countryside. To be sure, the *bourgs* housed a rustic bourgeoisie which did more than any other social group in the nineteenth century to keep the flame of jacobinism burning brightly. But that flame cast a small shadow which rarely extended beyond the circles of clients and kinsmen. The model of politicisation which Maurice Agulhon[5] has elaborated for the inland districts of Provence scarcely applies to the thinly populated escarpments of the southern Massif Central, therefore. Some form of cultural osmosis may be taken for granted, but the political consciousness of the *gavot* (highlander) – such as it was by the 1880s – sprang from other sources.

The economic implications of a fissured countryside need to be approached with similar caution. While the *bourgs* were usually entrepôts and nearly always centres of usury it would be wrong to assume, therefore, that the *bourgs* in some sense controlled the rural population. During the time span of this study the battle honours in 'town versus country' disputes were fairly evenly distributed. Village diasporas lived in fear of *bourg* imperialism and were adept at combining to meet the threat, while the more highly

[4] Rambaud and Vincienne, *Les Transformations d'une société rurale*, p. 198.
[5] Agulhon, *The Republic in the Village* (Cambridge, 1982).

specialised population of the *bourgs* were vulnerable to starvation tactics and armed assaults. And yet a number of accounts of politicisation have emphasised the integrative role performed by market networks geared, in the first instance, to the *bourgs*. Ted Margadant,[6] in particular, has pioneered this line of enquiry and concluded that the profile of popular insurgency in 1851 owed much to 'proto-urbanisation' or the quickening pace of exchange between cities, towns, *bourgs* and villages. Reduced to its essentials, this argument resembles an economic variant of Agulhon's thesis and it is equally inapplicable to the southern Massif Central. Sustained population growth in the early decades of the nineteenth century tended to enhance the rural characteristics of these departments rather than their urban characteristics, and with the notable exception of the silk-worm industry in the lower Ardèche, there is little reason to suppose that the peasant economy was becoming more market orientated and monetarised. Some *bourgs* did exert a measure of control over a hinterland of agricultural labour, especially during the dead season. The textile *bourgs* of the Tarn and Lot valleys are a case in point, but they were mostly in the doldrums by the early nineteenth century. On the other hand, the great majority of peasant households practised traditional polyculture and could afford to regard the market-place with a certain detachment. As for the mobilisations of 1851, it is difficult to explain the geography of militancy by reference to any clear pattern of economic relationships, whether in the southern Massif Central or in the country at large.

Contemplation of the troubled co-existence of *bourg* and village from a territorial point of view is rather more revealing. Territorialism constituted the very stuff of politics in the southern Massif Central and it seems that territorial particularism increased in keeping with the general sense of well-being during the first half of the nineteenth century. Demographic pressure had a solvent effect upon old solidarities and new communities emerged to challenge the hegemony of long-established entities. Several decades of administrative efforts to carve up the dispersed habitat into orderly units simply helped to speed up this process of territorial redefinition. Each commune and parish created after 1789 added further strands to complex webs of local animosities and allegiances. As we have seen, the towns and the *bourgs* occupied the intersecting points in this filigree mesh of petty rivalries: during the early years of the Revolution epic battles were fought between Rodez and Villefranche-de-Rouergue for dominance in the new department of the Aveyron; between Aurillac and St Flour for *chef-lieu* status in the new department of the Cantal and between the towns of the Haut and the Bas Vivarais for pre-eminence in the Ardèche. Traces of these rancorous disputes

---

[6] T. W. Margadant, *French Peasants in Revolt* (Princeton, 1979); 'Proto-Urban Development and Political Mobilisation during the Second Republic' in J. M. Merriman (ed.), *French Cities in the Nineteenth Century* (London, 1982), pp. 92–116.

survived into the nineteenth century, but they represented little more than the tip of the iceberg as far as the politics of territorial particularism were concerned. The issue of whether the Criminal Assizes and the administrative headquarters of the department of the Aveyron should be located in Villefranche or Rodez – both of which had been seats of *présidial* courts – was of supreme importance to the robe bourgeoisie, but it left the rural population largely unmoved. By contrast, the vexatious issue of the cantonal *chefs-lieux* and the Justices of the Peace, of communal and sub-communal boundaries transformed every peasant into a political animal.

The forms of territorial rivalry which aroused most passion can be grouped as follows:

> the confrontation of *bourgs* for cantonal status
> the confrontation of villages for communal status
> the confrontation of villages for parochial status

To which may be added internal conflict between:

> cantonal seats and village diasporas
> communal seats and outlying *sections*
> parochial seats and outlying *annexes*

These categories should not be interpreted rigidly, however. By its very nature the process of territorial redefinition presupposed a repercussive effect and internecine squabbles between rival villages could easily escalate to the point where they threatened to plunge into the melting-pot the community fabric of an entire locality. Feuding which traversed cantonal frontiers could be relied upon to produce this result and was especially feared by the authorities. Nor, indeed, should the concept of territorial particularism be considered in isolation, for territorial conflict between belligerent communities was often contoured around socio-economic polarities, household rivalries and confessional differences. This latter point applies particularly to the southern Cévennes, for even a cursory inspection of election results reveals the link between political temperament and religious topography in this area. The bitterly contested parliamentary election of 1885 in the department of the Lozère witnessed a massive protestant mobilisation in support of Léon Boyer, the republican candidate. The communes of the canton of Barre were solid for Boyer and so were those of the canton of St Germain-de-Calberte, all, that is, save for the catholic enclave of St Julien-des-Points.[7]

At least the catholic community of St Julien-des-Points enjoyed the measure of local autonomy inherent in communal status. The most intractable territorial feuding generally occurred within communes; that is to say between *bourg* or village *chefs-lieux* and disaffected *sections*. In many such instances it is more appropriate to talk in terms of ecological rivalries, for the dissected relief of the southern Massif Central dissected communes and

---

[7] A.N. C4524 *Elections législatives*, 1885: Lozère.

parishes, too. As human needs and purposes altered centrifugal pressures developed which threatened to explode these precarious entities. Ecological strains constituted a regular ingredient of inter-village strife in the region of the Grands Causses of the Aveyron and the Lozère where vertiginous shifts in altitude created difficulties for communities which straddled both plain and valley. The communes of St Rome-de-Tarn, La Malène and Sainte Enimie in the valley of the Tarn all had outlying settlements situated on the plateau. More important, the common pastures belonging to each community tended to be located on the plateau, while the plotholders who relied most heavily upon these assets resided in the *bourg* at river level. A sense of physical isolation emphasised, perhaps, by disagreements over the management of common land combined, therefore, to sustain a perception of separateness. All that was required to precipitate the birth of a new social embryo was the intervention of a professional midwife and the turbulent village bourgeoisie of the southern Massif Central were particularly skilled in operations of this sort.

In 1840 Jean-Pierre-Baptiste Barrandon,[8] a rentier with substantial possessions in the causse hamlets above Sainte Enimie, launched a petition demanding that these outlying dependencies of the commune of Sainte Enimie be permitted to form a new commune centred on the village of Champerboux. The proposal caused general dismay in the *bourg* for most of the community's stock of common land lay on the causse and within the perimeter of the projected commune. Such was the consternation, indeed, that Barrandon abandoned the idea and publicly retracted his petition in order to quell the discontent. But this was only the beginning. Fourteen years later a group of causse proprietors which included Barrandon, but which was led by the magistrate Monestier of Banassac, resurrected the proposal. During the ensuing conflict the poorer inhabitants of Sainte Enimie threatened to invade and divide up the causse pastures, while Monestier's personal ambitions were exposed in a polemical brochure published under the auspices of the municipal council of Sainte Enimie. Monestier, it was revealed, owned estates both at Banassac in the canton of La Canourgue and in the village of Roussac which lay within the disputed territory of the commune of Sainte Enimie: 'Si je pouvais enlever Roussac à Ste Enimie, et l'englober dans le canton de La Canourgue, se dit M. Monestier, comme il me serait commode d'appeler devant le juge de paix de ma ville d'affection mes petits débiteurs de Roussac et de réprimer devant ce magistrat, les contraventions que divers pourraient se permettre sur mes propriétés.'[9] Our source of information is scarcely impartial, but the accusation rings true for an affair

[8] A.D.L. 2 O 1420 *Administration et comptabilité communales*: Sainte Enimie, Deltour, *maire*, to sub-prefect Florac, Sainte Enimie, 21 July 1855.
[9] *Ibid., Réponse du Conseil Municipal de Sainte Enimie à l'exposé présenté au Conseil Général de la Lozère, par MM. de Lhermet et Monestier* (Nîmes, n.d.).

of this kind was typical of the way in which village bigwigs used and were used by the rural community. Cutting the umbilical was not easy, however, and the projected commune of Champerboux never saw the light of day. Instead, a deepening sense of umbrage poisoned relations between causse and valley folk for the remainder of the century. Only at election times did Champerboux enjoy a fleeting independence as a *section électorale* and its disenchantment took the form of a persistent tendency to contradict the political preferences of the *chef-lieu*.

Such antagonisms were legion. If the balance of temporal motivations varied from locality to locality, the broad contours of inter-community strife altered very little. And these stress zones and fault lines naturally helped to pattern the political relief of the region. When, in 1792, the villagers of Livinhac-le-Haut (Aveyron) charged that the inhabitants of Flagnac on the opposite shore of the river Lot were lacking in revolutionary zeal, the District administration of Aubin merely noted that, 'Depuis longtemps les habitants de Livinhac-le-Supérieur (*sic*) nourissent une vraie antipathie pour ceux de Flagnac. Il y a environ huit ans qu'ils s'étaient déclaré une espèce de guerre civile. Le sang coula alors. Le cy-devant évêque de Rodez trouva le moyen de réprimer les excès mais il n'étouffa pas le germe de discussion.'[10] In the same matter of fact way the sub-prefect of St Affrique reported similar difficulties in the ominously named commune of St Jean-et-St Paul nearly three-quarters of a century later. The two villages from which the commune had been constructed were separated by six kilometres of footpaths and since each entity possessed a parish church the social and cultural life of the commune remained neatly compartmentalised. Except, that is, at election times; in 1865 the sub-prefect pressed the case for dismemberment as the politically expedient solution. Up to 300 votes were at stake for, 'il est de notoriété publique que quand St Jean vote blanc, St Paul vote noir'.[11]

It may be, of course, that the tenacity of local particularism in the southern Massif Central was merely the visible dimension of an obscure process of bargaining between the centre and the periphery. We have already noted how the growth of electoral democracy in the course of the nineteenth century gave a voice to even the tiniest social embryo. It massively reinforced that dependence on central power which was the hallmark of politics in all the poor and mountainous regions of France. But, by the same token, participatory democracy exposed the weaknesses of an administrative system which was unused to coping with registered dissent, with voters who failed to participate or who expressed the 'wrong' preferences. Small entities with unrequited ambitions for territorial or administrative recognition quickly learned how to exploit the susceptibilities of prefects and subaltern officials. Thus, when the first *section électorale* of the commune of Clairvaux

[10] Jones, 'Political Commitment and Rural Society in the Southern Massif Central', p. 343.
[11] A.D.A 11M725 Sub-prefect St Affrique to prefect Aveyron, St Affrique, 27 April 1865.

(Aveyron) gave a massive majority to the republican list in the parliamentary election of 1885 and the second *section* (Bruéjouls) voted overwhelmingly for the conservative candidates, we might reasonably deduce a state of inter-village rivalry.[12] Indeed, the village of Bruéjouls was the seat of an ancient parish and had been complaining about the imperialism of its larger neighbour for some time. Yet we should admit, too, the possibility that the electoral contest enabled the dissatisfied inhabitants of Bruéjouls to articulate their grievances in a more positive fashion; to signal to the higher authorities the political wisdom of allowing them to form a commune of their own.

This signalling system is more explicit in the case of the commune of Martiel which, like the majority of the communes of the Aveyron, was an artificial entity created by subsuming parishes. In May 1870 the communal voters gave their verdict on Napoléon III's liberal reforms within two electoral constituencies which had effectively been contoured around the parishes of Martiel and Elbès. On the day after the ballot, the local schoolmaster transmitted the results to the prefect. The *chef-lieu* voted overwhelmingly 'Yes' (308 to 8 with one blank or spoilt paper) whereas Elbès voted 'No' (58 to 42 with 29 blank or spoilt papers). 'J'ai compris', he commented, 'qu'on désire vivement que le résultat afférent à la section de Martiel fut remarqué par l'administration.'[13] The Second Empire was especially vulnerable to this kind of bargaining, for the regime sought to bring its peculiar brand of managed democracy to every peasant's doorstep and officials of government were expected to do their utmost to ensure political conformism. Woe betide the deputy who omitted to keep the interests of his constituents in the forefront of his mind. During the parliamentary elections of 1869 the inhabitants of St Ilpize[14] reproached Barthélemy de Romeuf, the incumbent member in the Le Puy–Brioude *arrondissement*, for having failed to secure a government subsidy for a bridge over the river Allier. In May 1870 they expressed their disillusionment more forcibly and voted 'No' in the plebiscite by a majority of over six to one.

The ubiquity of neighbourhood enmities and of calculations of local interest invites us to consider the role of kinship as a catalyst of opinion in the countryside. Kinship and territorialism were mutually reinforcing concepts among the peasantry of the southern Massif Central: with quite exceptional measures of endogamy obtaining until the very end of the nineteenth century, loyalty to village or to parish merged insensibly with loyalty to kindred. The structure of the peasant household as described in chapter four, the persistence of the marriage contract, of the dowry, of impartible inheritance

[12] A.N. C4466 *Elections législatives*, 1885: Aveyron.
[13] Jones, 'An Improbable Democracy', p. 547; A.N. BII 1235 *Votes populaires, plébiscite de 1870*, Aveyron.
[14] A. Rivet, 'LesDébuts de la IIIᵉ République en Haute-Loire: les élections de Guyot-Montpeyroux (1868–1876)', *Mélanges en l'honneur de Etienne Fournial* (St Etienne, 1978), p. 306; A.N. BII 1266 *Votes populaires, plébiscite de 1870*, Haute-Loire.

strategies and of high levels of consanguinity all suggest that the perception of 'famille' provided the sheet anchor of popular consciousness. It may be inferred, therefore, that household and kin-group had an important bearing on political behaviour. Just what bearing, exactly, is more difficult to specify, but two approaches to the problem offer the best results. We may explore the political allegiances of a given family or kin-group over time, that is to say over several generations. Alternatively, we can try to elucidate the opinions of individual members of a residential or kin-group. The latter task is infinitely more difficult than the former. Voting was a private act and we lack an analytical tool comparable with the poll-books available to British social historians. For participants, of course, the ballot held few secrets, but for historians the evidence on individual motivation is fragmentary, circumstantial and indirect. On the other hand, the data relating to kin-groups and lineages is highly selective and spot-lights the political behaviour of bourgeois rather than peasant households.

Of course, we might retreat from the empirical objective altogether and seek refuge in generalities and mechanistic models of how kinship affected political options. The recent work of Emmanuel Todd (and his collaborator Hervé Le Bras)[15] has underlined the potential and also the shortcomings of the theoretical approach. Boldly asserting the failure of both liberal and Marxist sociology to explain perceived differences in political attitudes, Todd brings the techniques of social anthropology to bear upon the puzzle of electoral behaviour. His hypothesis that 'la sensibilité politique dépend en effet étroitement du mode dominant d'affectivité familiale'[16] enlivens the debate, but does little to advance the argument. The identification of right-wing voting habits with simple or nuclear family structure and left-wing postures with a hybrid type of complex or extended family structure in many ways reverses the accepted correlation. In Brittany, in the Basque country, in the southern Massif Central – all regions in which the patriarchal extended family continued to flourish in the nineteenth century – the peasantry voted by tradition for the Right. This Todd notes and accommodates by introducing a questionable distinction between authoritarian and non-authoritarian (or 'communitarian') family structures. The latter provided the emotional environment most conducive to democratic ideas and were to be found in the North, the Midi and the South West apparently, but he implies that the patriarchal or authoritarian household would also have oriented its members towards an acceptance of left-wing politics had it not been for the countervailing pressure of the catholic church. This is surely the point to grasp. Schematic analysis of kinship systems tells us little about the process of opinion formation on its own. However, the study of household structure in

15 H. Le Bras and E. Todd, *L'Invention de la France*; also E. Todd, *La Troisième planète: structures familiales et systèmes idéologiques* (Paris, 1983).
16 Le Bras and Todd, *L'Invention de la France*, p. 9.

conjunction with other variables can be more rewarding, and the relationship between kinship, family structure and clericalism deserves particular attention.

In the absence of poll-books, we might resort to the *listes d'émargement*. Unfortunately, these manuscript 'listes d'appel et d'inscription des votants' as they were officially termed were usually lost or destroyed soon after an election and only a few copies have survived. As documents designed to guard against electoral fraud they were subjected to considerable abuse. Nonetheless, where they have survived, it becomes possible to trace the contours of rural political commitment in more detail. Voting, it must be emphasised, was an elaborate public ritual in which only the last act was accomplished by individuals in conditions of ostensible secrecy. Peasant electors presented themselves before the 'bureau' in communal or village formations, this we know. But the *listes d'émargement* suggest that peasants cast their votes in coherent and disciplined family groups, and this we could only surmise hitherto. Did bloc voting in family units result in similar political options? The circumstantial evidence points strongly in this direction. The *listes* shed useful light on age and household structure as well. An undated 'liste d'appel et d'inscription des votants' for the commune of Araules[17] in the eastern highlands of the old Velay affords us a glimpse of numerous multi-generational households attending the hustings during the Second Empire. While most families counted no more than one, two or three adult males, the village of Recharingues contained stem-families disposing of considerable electoral muscle. In 1863 (?) the Besson household boasted six eligible males whose ages ranged from twenty-six to seventy-eight. Five of them turned out to vote. The Faure counted seven adult males aged between twenty-six and sixty-five, of whom five voted; the Perbet eight adult males aged between twenty-eight and sixty-eight, all of whom voted, and so on.

The testimony of contemporaries well placed to pass judgement upon the process of politicisation in the countryside provides additional support for the hypothesis that considerations of kin and household strategy played a primary role in determining electoral choice. After the combative legislative election of 1889 when the clergy renewed their challenge to the institutions of the Republic throughout the southern Massif Central (see chapter nine), the schoolmaster of a small village in the Lozère wrote: 'Monsieur le Préfet ne sera pas étonné de cela quand je lui dirai que sur les 63 électeurs de la commune, 50 au moins sont parents entre eux, et la plupart appartiennent aux familles Moulin, Robert et Brunel. Ces familles sont toutes acharnées contre le gouvernement.'[18] Whether in the aftermath of national or of local elections, comments of this type reached the prefects with tedious frequency. Yet we should resist the temptation to belittle their significance. Allegations

---

[17] A.D. H.-L. 4M27 *Liste d'appel et d'inscription des votants, Araules, 1ère section*.
[18] A.D.L. IVM⁴ 25 Robert, *instituteur*, to prefect Lozère, Sainte Eulalie, 30 October 1889.

of ethnicity, like allegations of parochialism, clothed defeat in a convenient rhetoric, but they also struck at the heart of politics in the countryside. Forced on to the defensive by the growth of secular ideology in the second half of the nineteenth century, the catholic church quickly discovered how to exploit the potential of kin and household solidarities, but jacobins and republicans had long exploited the same mechanisms. Another item in the prefectoral dossier on the 1889 elections in the Lozère consisted of a list of individuals, grouped by communes, 'qui n'ont pas été hostiles'. Alongside the tally of the fourteen republicans of the village of Malbouzon we find the following observations: 'maire; père du maire; frère du maire; frère du maire; cousin du maire; cousin du maire; beaupère du maire; oncle du maire'.[19] Apart from two rural proprietors and a tenant farmer (of whom?), the remainder were state employees and necessarily, therefore, republicans.

It follows from this example that kinship also performed a vertical integrative function. The perception of generic belonging exercised a potent influence upon the political options of each succeeding generation. An act of self-conscious adhesion to a set of values might be re-enacted as a family tradition in which the original ideological reference-point lost all but symbolic meaning. As the news of the capture of Napoléon III and the fall of the Second Empire filtered into the countryside, one Boutin of St Georges-d'Aurac prefaced an offer of assistance to the new republican prefect of the Haute-Loire with the remark: 'je suis fils d'une des victimes de décembre [1851] et le petit-fils d'un membre du District du Puy'.[20] Continuities of political commitment stretching back to the Revolution were not uncommon in the southern Massif Central and the protestant merchant dynasties of St Affrique and Millau may be cited as extreme examples of this principle.[21] But the phenomenon poses several problems of interpretation. Most of the documented cases of visceral jacobinism, or republicanism, or Legitimism cast light upon the behaviour of village elites and it remains an open question whether peasant and artisan households nourished political allegiances in quite the same fashion. Boutin was a public notary and rural mayor who must, therefore, have been exceedingly discreet about his affiliations and sympathies prior to September 1870. A more fundamental difficulty has already been mentioned and it stems from our use of terms. In what sense is a third generation commitment to the Republic still 'political'? Does it remain an ideal, or has it become an atavism, a purely cultural tradition?

As Todd and others have observed, the link between kin and household structures and opinion formation seems palpable. And yet the subject defies really satisfactory analysis. In part, the difficulty is one of sources, but even if we were able to penetrate the secrecy of the ballot it is unlikely that the result-

[19] *Ibid.*
[20] A.D. H.-L. 6M140 Boutin to prefect Haute-Loire, St Georges-d'Aurac, 17 September 1870.
[21] See above, chapter six, pp. 208–12.

ing evidence would permit us to establish neat correlations. The outstanding problem, therefore, remains the peasant psyche. We need to penetrate the imagination of the rural voter, to discover how he ordered a set of complex variables and how those variables were catalysed by external stimuli. Viewed from one angle popular political reflexes appear to be conditioned by the physical environment; from another by ethnic factors; from a third by confessional differences. While it is often convenient to group these variables together, it should be remembered that they were not necessarily complementary. Loyalty to household and kindred must have cut across loyalty to the larger community on occasions. As for the process by which such conflicts were resolved, it can only be guessed at.

By contrast, confessional alignments generally followed the fissures of kinship. Catholic and protestant exchanged offspring in marriage on rare occasions, but religion tended to demarcate rather than to divide households. As the minority affiliation, Calvinism evinced the most striking familial characteristics. The narrow horizons of daily intercourse and several generations of spasmodic persecution conspired to turn village protestantism into a dense network of kindred. Clan organisation seemed ideally suited to the defensive posture which huguenots had been forced to adopt for much of the eighteenth century, but it mortgaged the future. Imprisoned within a framework of consistories by Napoléon, Calvinism vegetated. In 1847 pastor Bourbon of Gatuzières (Lozère) put his finger on the problem in a condemnation of the consistory of Meyrueis. 'Ce consistoire', he wrote to the Ministre de Justice et des Cultes, 'a seize membres, quatre pasteurs et douze anciens. Sur ces seize membres, sept sont proches parents, M. le Président a pour collègue un fils, et parmi les anciens un beaufrère, un neveu et trois cousins germains, un huitième est cousin du neuveu du président; il y a entre ces huit membres d'autres alliances, trois d'entre'eux, par exemple, sont beaufrères.'[22]

The confessional divide was also reflected in the topography of the region – albeit in a crude and distorted fashion. By the time of the Edict of Toleration (1787) protestantism was restricted to six main areas: the *bourgs* of the upper Tarn valley and its tributaries; the Cévennes; the districts of Vallon and Vals in the Bas Vivarais; the Eyrieux region to the north of Privas and the vicinity of Le Mazet–St Voy on the Velay–Vivarais border. The population of the *bourgs* in these localities was often mixed, but in the villages and hamlets it seems to have been unusual for protestant and catholic families to occupy adjacent farmsteads. A reconstruction of the religious topography of the three rural communes of Les Vastres, Fay and Le Mazet (subsequently Le Mazet–St Voy) in 1851 established that roughly 84 per cent of the 109 villages and hamlets then existing adhered monolithically to one sect and in

---

[22]   A.N. F[19] 10471 *Mémoire* of pastor Bourbon, Meyrueis, 9 October 1847.

12 per cent one sect predominated, while catholic and protestant households were evenly matched in only a handful of hamlets (4 per cent) mostly situated in the commune of Les Vastres.[23] Alain Sabatier's[24] scrutiny of the sectarian geography of four communes in the canton of Vernoux (Ardèche) confirms this picture, although it should be noted that in the latter region, particularly, extreme habitat dispersion prevailed and many families lived on isolated farmsteads.

Questions of physical proximity between catholic and protestant made little difference in practice, however, for practically the whole of the southern Massif Central was susceptible to a sectarian call-to-arms. As the official persecution of Calvinists subsided, the tensions and fears which had nourished two centuries of intermittent warfare subsided also. The atrocities of 1815 in the department of the Gard were an anachronistic by-product of exceptional circumstances, for the legal guarantees and constitutional experiments of the revolutionary epoch had introduced alternative means of resolving inter-community friction. In the nineteenth century the rhetoric of struggle replaced atavistic violence, the hustings the old battle-grounds. Confrontation and mutual suspicion continued to underpin relations between protestant and catholic, but it only surfaced at election times and in manageable proportions. Nevertheless, the rivalry between the two confessions remained intense and it tended to override all other considerations in the electoral arena.

Conflict between obligations to kin and obligations to sect was rare, as we have suggested. On the contrary, the tenacious household loyalties of the southern Massif Central massively reinforced the mobilising potential of Calvinism. As for the petty territorial hostilities which formed the stuff of electoral politics in a department like the Aveyron, the sectarian rallying-cry transcended them. Protestant villages were probably no less belligerent than their catholic counterparts, but decades of officially inspired intolerance had taught them perspicacity and they grasped the issues more readily at election times. Among Calvinists the perceived interests of their faith likewise transcended social class. Despite some evidence that protestant merchant clothiers baulked at the revolutionary Terror in towns like St Affrique and Millau, protestants of all social conditions, whether urban or rural, tended to identify with the Left. In the Year Two (1793–4) they were disproportionately represented in the *comités de surveillance* and in 1849–51 they were disproportionately numerous in the montagnard secret societies. André Siegfried's oft quoted dictum that 'un patron protestant est protestant avant d'être patron'[25] holds good. Moreover, southern Calvinism obeyed the

[23]   J.-C. Gouly, 'Protestants et catholiques en Haute-Loire au milieu du XIXe siècle', *Cahiers de la Haute-Loire* (1970), 91.
[24]   Sabatier, *Religion et politique*, pp. 140–1 and map 4.
[25]   Siegfried, *Géographie électorale de l'Ardèche*, p. 70.

'toujours à gauche' principle after 1789 and consistently adopted extreme positions in the political spectrum, be they jacobin, Bonapartist or *démocrate-socialiste*. With the intrusion of Radicalism and socialism in the final decade of the nineteenth century, and the *ralliement*[26] (which eased the sectarian confrontation), allegiances became more fluid and it is likely that protestantism lost some of its political homogeneity. Yet the identification of protestantism with left-wing electoral preferences has survived into the twentieth century substantially unaltered. After the presidential elections of December 1965, *Le Monde*,[27] the authoritative Paris daily, published a feature drawing attention to striking continuities of political allegiance in the departments of the Centre and the South. The protestant villages of the southern Cévennes voted solidly for Mitterand, the candidate of the Left, while adjacent catholics, with few exceptions, voted to renew the mandate of General de Gaulle.

The political homogeneity of Calvinism is not difficult to demonstrate; nor is the reflex it could trigger within the catholic community. From the time of the Revolution onwards the confrontation can be read in election returns, especially in the returns of local elections, for the embattled protestant generation of the late *ancien régime* sought first and foremost to secure its physical well-being by winning control of the municipalities, Districts and Departments.[28] With the inception of universal and direct democracy in 1848, however, the stakes were dramatically raised and the perception of confessional rivalry magnified. Positions hardened and conflict escalated – was escalated notably by a catholic clergy which had never lost sight of its old quarry and which was determined to mobilise the electoral strength of the majority faith to maximum effect. As government agents whose responsibilities included the management of elections, the prefects and their subalterns faced the task of coping with this seismic rift and for half a century after 1848 calculations regarding the activism and probable voting intentions of the protestant electorate were never far from their minds. The unnerving success of the *démocrates-socialistes* in the Ardèche during the election of May 1849 owed much to the example of disciplined voting provided by the protestants. With a by-election impending, the sub-prefect of the Largentière asked rhetorically: 'les protestants du département qui, par horreur des blancs ont voté pour les rouges, persisteront-ils dans cette voie? Je le crains.'[29]

---

26 See below, chapter ten, p. 305.
27 *Le Monde*, 4 January 1966, 'De la Montagne à M. Mitterand' and 'L'Election dans les Cévennes'. For similar remarks applicable to the legislative elections of March 1973, see Pelen, 'La Vallée Longue en Cévenne', p. 16.
28 See the lament of the catholic minority of St Christol (Ardèche) who complained that the electoral principle had placed the municipality and the National Guard in the hands of the protestants (A.N. DIV 17 A *Nosseigneurs, nos libérateurs composant l'assemblée nationale*, 15 March 1790).
29 A.D. Ard. 2M339 Sub-prefect Largentière to prefect Ardèche, Largentière, 2 July 1849.

The die was cast. When the department of the Ardèche went to the polls again in March 1850 few illusions remained on the subject of the protestant vote. Marie Félix Imbault de Latourette, the candidate of the moderates and a veiled Legitimist, beat the *démocrate-socialiste* contender Lazare Hippolyte Carnot, but thanks only to the catholic peasantry of the highlands and the extreme north of the department. The government could draw little comfort from the result for as the sub-prefect of Tournon pointed out, 'la proportion entre le nombre des électeurs inscrits et celui des votants est en raison inverse de la loyauté du vote. Dans mon arrondissement la proportion moyenne est 63 votants sur 100 électeurs; dans 6 bons cantons de 60 sur 100, dans les cantons douteux de 66 sur 100, dans trois cantons mauvais de 72 sur 100.'[30] Unsurprisingly, the predominantly protestant communes of the Eyrieux featured prominently in the sub-prefect's list of dubious and disloyal localities. As the example of the canton of Vernoux demonstrates, the Calvinists were ardent and active supporters of the Left (see table VIII.1).

While ingrained suspicion continued to bedevil the functioning of local government, sectarian rivalries eased in the sphere of parliamentary elections during the Second Empire. Only when the government misjudged the atmosphere of calm as in the case of Dautheville's[31] candidature in the Ardèche in 1854 were passions rekindled on a significant scale. In general the Calvinists were divided in their responses to the Bonapartist phenomenon. Many supported the official candidates – the more so when those candidates were protestants (as was often the case in the Ardèche), or when they were confronted by Legitimist opponents. Republican challengers naturally attracted their allegiance, but when the regime turned voting into an issue of confidence, as in the plebiscite of May 1870, protestants hesitated to condemn it. In the Calvinist fortress communes of Le Chambon sur Lignon and St Voy (Haute-Loire) most voters chose to dodge the issue; 75 per cent of those attending the polls declared themselves in favour of the liberal reforms and 25 per cent against, but an unprecedented 57 per cent of the electorate failed to turn up to the polls.[32]

The resurrection of the Republic restored to Calvinism its unity and sense of political purpose, however. Protestant notables and peasants alike, rallied to the new regime swiftly and, it would appear, unhesitatingly. And as militant, ultramontane catholicism harnessed the catholic peasantry to the cause of Legitimism, that identification with the birth struggle of the young Republic became almost visceral. When MacMahon threw down a challenge to the republican majority which had dominated the Chamber since the renewal of 1876, a bitterly divisive election campaign ensued. It established the battle lines of sectarian and party conflict for the next decade and a half. The protestants of Le Chambon sur Lignon and St Voy voted for the republican

---

[30] A.D. Ard. 2M340 Sub-prefect Tournon to prefect Ardèche, Tournon, 20 March 1850.
[31] See above, chapter seven, p. 238.   [32] *La Haute-Loire*, 10 May 1870.

Table VIII.1 *Canton of Vernoux (Ardèche): voting correlated to religious affiliation. By-election of March 1850*

A	B	C	D	E	F	G	H	I	
Boffres	396	353	89.1	49	13.9	304	86.1	74.7	(in 1861)
Chalençon	342	255	74.6	155	60.8	100	39.2	37.4	(in 1861)
St Apollinaire-de-Rias	170	115	67.6	9	7.8	106	92.2	87.1	(in 1851)
St Félix-de-Châteauneuf[a]	135	123	91.1	32	26.0	91	74.0	70.6	(in 1856)
St Jean-Chambre	320	168	52.5	39	23.2	129	76.8	62.5	(in 1851)
St Maurice-en-Chalençon	162	139	85.8	1	0.7	138	99.3	91.1	(in 1872)
Silhac	409	284	69.4	76	26.8	208	73.2	67.1	(in 1851)
St Julien-le-Roux }[b] Vernoux	903	631	69.9	299	47.4	332	52.6	61.0	(c. 1851–61)
Canton	2837	2068	72.9	660	31.9	1408	68.0	64.0	(in 1850)

Notes:
[a] Subsequently renamed Châteauneuf-de-Vernoux.
[b] Votes cast in a single electoral constituency.

Key:
A   Commune.
B   Registered voters.
C   Votes cast.
D   Percentage turn-out.
E   Votes for Latourette.
F   Percentage of votes cast for Latourette.
G   Votes for Carnot.
H   Percentage of votes cast for Carnot.
I   Protestants as percentage of total population.

Sources: A. Sabatier, *Religion et politique au XIXe siècle: le canton de Vernoux-en-Vivarais* (Vernoux, 1975), p. 135; A.D. Ard, 2M340 *Élections législatives*, March 1850.

257

Alexandre de Lagrevol almost to a man, while the mixed population of the adjacent communes of Araules and St Jeures split on sectarian lines.[33] These alignments reproduced and underscored territorial and topographical polarities of the type already discussed. Araules I (the electoral section of the catholic *bourg*) opted overwhelmingly for the outgoing conservative deputy, but Araules II (principally the protestant village of Montbuzat) voted decisively for Lagrevol. The legislative election of October 1877 and the subsequent invalidations[34] which brought to a term the crisis of Seize Mai evoked a commensurate response in the department of the Lozère. Amid a record turn-out of 81.9 per cent, the catholic communes forming the western sector of the *arrondissement* of Florac declared in favour of the official candidate, Eugène de Joly, while the predominantly protestant villages of the Lozérian Cévennes mobilised in defence of the outgoing republican deputy, Théophile Roussel. Thus, at Fraissinet-de-Fourques – scene of the massacre of 1703 – 87.8 per cent of the votes cast were for Joly compared with only 32.7 per cent in the neighbouring and rival village of Rousses.[35]

Statistical correlations and percentages demonstrate the link between religious affiliation and electoral preference in global terms, but scarcely penetrate to the heart of the issue with which this chapter is concerned: the process of politicisation as it affected individuals within individual communities. The statistical approach rests upon certain untested assumptions and leaves a number of questions unanswered. Did cross-voting occur? Did protestantism everywhere evince comparable levels of discipline and activism? Such detailed evidence as we possess would suggest that discipline rather than activism constituted the most reliable feature of protestantism as a political phenomenon. For all the mingling of cultures and day-to-day activities in 'front-line' parishes, cross-voting in elections was unusual. Normally discipline and activism went hand in hand, but as the spiritual unity of Desert or pre-revolutionary Calvinism crumbled small groups seceded from the consistories to found free churches based on an ethic of renunciation which extended to the political structures of the state. Dissident protestant sects, known variously as 'Darbystes' or 'Plymouthistes' or 'Mômiers' had become quite widespread by the 1870s and although they never succeeded in challenging the hegemony of the established consistorial churches, they constituted an additional complicating feature of village life in places like St Voy (Haute-Loire) and St Agrève (Ardèche). Invited to comment on the failure of many able-bodied men to fulfil their responsibilities as citizens in the legislative elections of 1876, the mayor of St Agrève recorded forty abstentions

---

[33]   A.N. C3873 *Elections législatives*, 1877: Haute-Loire.
[34]   See below, chapter nine, p. 300.
[35]   A.N. C3487 *Elections législatives*, 1877: Lozère. Also chapter five, p. 147.

under the heading: 'Hommes qui professent la religion dissidente (appelés mômiers) et qui prennent rarement part au vote.'[36]

Large questions remain, however. Does the observed statistical correlation between sectarian allegiance and political bias have any substance at the level of daily human perceptions? More important, we are bound to ask what force the term 'political' conveys in this context. The first point poses few serious difficulties. Sufficient testimony survives to indicate that electors were mutually recognisable – on grounds of religion as well as on grounds of kinship and territorial allegiance. The signal of recognition might often be in code ('vous avez la bouche bien noire, vous avez l'air d'un huguenot',[37] interjected the *curé* of Chirols (Ardèche) as a voter whom he suspected of republican sympathies approached the urn), but there was no mistaking it. The perplexing issue of whether the manifest orientation of southern protestantism can be described as a properly ideological adherence to left-wing political options calls for lengthier consideration, however. Siegfried argued that the organic qualities of the protestant faith – its quasi-democratic organisation and emphasis upon individual responsibility – made for an intrinsic left-wing bias. Others have explained the political culture of southern protestantism primarily in terms of historical conditioning; in terms, that is, of a persecuted minority's reflex of resistance to central authority. Familial, communal and territorial traditions preserved and perpetuated a set of archaic stereotypes which allowed scant latitude for the questioning and redefining of relationships. For all its vaunted freedom of conscience, southern protestantism was a mental prison whose peasant inmates were scarcely more capable of construing the meaning of contemporary ideological debate than their catholic counterparts.

This was the view favoured by the prefects, at least until the 1870s. The political incorrigibility of the Calvinist minority amounted to 'rage de parti' and that was all. Even when data painstakingly collated by subaltern officials indicated that protestant peasants were uncommonly literate and zealous in performing their duties as citizens (payment of taxes, military service, voting, etc.), the prefects rarely offered a more complex analysis of the protestant phenomenon. Nevertheless, their diagnosis was surely correct in many respects. It must be emphasised that in the southern Massif Central Calvinism evinced a markedly rural character and adherents reacted as peasants even before they reacted as Calvinists. As for the vulnerable, excitable and clannish protestant coteries of the *bourgs*, they were certainly more susceptible to external ideological stimuli. Yet they lived in nightmare fear of persecution, too, and archaic postures constantly intruded upon their political consciousness. The concatenation of a predominantly rural Calvinism and advanced democratic and even socialist ideology poses, thus, a delicate problem of

---

[36] A.D. Ard. 2M349 Mayor St Agrève to prefect Ardèche, St Agrève, 14 March 1876.
[37] A.D. Ard. 5M41 Certified statement of Félix Picaud, Chirols, 25 October 1885.

interpretation. Was the ideological orientation of peasant Calvinism a function of protestant theology or was it, rather, the by-product of powerful forces of social conditioning? The latter seems more likely in the context of the southern Massif Central and it is worth noting that André Encrevé[38] – the historian who has done most to illuminate this aspect of electoral behaviour – concludes that the participation of the Calvinist peasantry of the south in the insurrections that greeted Louis-Napoléon's *coup d'état* in December 1851 reveals more about their fear of catholicism than their commitment to socialist ideas.

And yet the argument for continuity should not be pushed too far. The fact remains that between the late eighteenth century and the late nineteenth century a substantial tradition of electoral democracy evolved in France which coloured the outlook of protestants and catholics alike. New and in some ways more familiar political habits displaced the old sources of commitment. Under the exceptional integrative pressures of the Third Republic, Calvinism ceased to resemble a *mentalité* masquerading as an ideology and acquired autonomous political reference points. In a sense the priorities which had informed the electoral mobilisation of protestants hitherto were reversed. Sectarian prejudice became a function of irreconcilable ideological differences rather than vice versa. To all appearances this transition took place in the 1870s and 1880s and it gave the age-old distinction between catholic and protestant a new lease of life.

An extraordinary sense of cohesion or social discipline underpinned popular electoral behaviour. Protestants, especially, evinced a a powerful *esprit de corps*, but the point holds for catholic voters, too, and it is worth pondering how these communal mobilisations were achieved. Many would argue that conformism was an unnatural state achieved by coercion or, at the very least, by economically enforced deference. After all, the peasantry attended the hustings in well-drilled squadrons often accompanied by a General Staff of village notables. Clearly the parish clergy, local châtelains, village schoolmasters and the like played a conspicuous role in mobilising and aligning the electorate, but we should be wary of assuming that the peasantry were thereby deprived of any vestige of electoral autonomy. In December 1848 the rural population of the southern Massif Central departments vindicated its independence by voting for Louis-Napoléon Bonaparte to assume the presidency of the Republic despite the advice of village pundits, and the phenomenon of reappraisal of old allegiances was repeated the following year. These were isolated moments in a long century of political quiescence, of course, but they suggest that the authority of the notables was not so much imposed as subscribed.

---

[38] A. Encrevé, 'Protestantisme et politique: les protestants du Midi en décembre 1851' in *Droite et Gauche en Languedoc-Roussillon: Actes du colloque de Montpellier, 9–10 juin 1973* (Montpellier, 1975), pp. 161–95.

Perhaps the channels of bribery and corruption were discreet, but it is a singular fact that allegations of mercenary pressure on electors were rare and virtually unknown before the embittered ballot of October 1877 which brought the Seize Mai emergency to an end. Most candidates found it unnecessary to resort to such tactics. A few mundane cases of heavy-handed electioneering by local proprietors have been documented, but they tend rather to exemplify the complexity of the phenomenon of deference. An almost caricatural instance of attempted 'social control' can be found in the private correspondence of Vicomte Charles de La Rochenégly of Booz (Lozère) with Eugène Paradan, a local bourgeois proprietor, on the subject of the parliamentary elections of 1837 – or so it would seem. Both men were heavily committed to the candidature of Emile-Auguste Chazot and in colourful and ironical prose Paradan commented upon their quest for votes:

. . . et ce calin de Vieillevigne? Il vous disait hier qu'il n'avait pas pris d'engagements; il vous proposait d'être Le *Pastre*! Acceptez et parquez cette brebis docile dans les gras pacages de Chardonnet.[39] Ah! ce serait délicieux. Obtenez un pareil résultat et vous serez un vrai magicien. Du reste vous rendez d'assez nombreuses services à vos administrés; vous vous occupez de leurs intérêts de toute nature avec un tel zèle et un tel dévouement qu'il est impossible qu'ils ne se rendent pas à un désir de votre part exprimé avec clarté et insistance.[40]

Paradan's role as political adviser to the local aristocracy developed further in the years that followed. Apprising the viscount that Louis-Napoléon's *coup d'état* had unleashed disturbances in nearby Rodez, he warned against precipitate measures of defence: 'Tenons nos populations au courant de tout ce qui se passe, mêlons-nous avec elles et pénétrons-les bien de l'idée que nous avons tous les mêmes intérêts.'[41]

Electoral compliance could be contrived, then, but as even Paradan acknowledged it turned on the lubricating oils of reciprocity. The mechanics of this process are illustrated well in a second batch of letters addressed by the deputy Jean-Pierre André to his confidant Auguste Vachin. André hailed from a respected proprietorial family of Sainte Enimie, the catholic *bourg* at the head of the gorges of the Tarn. An ardent royalist, his parliamentary career began in 1795 when the electors of the Lozère sent him to sit in the Council of Five Hundred, only to be curtailed two years later by the anti-royalist purge of 18 Fructidor V (4 September 1797). In 1815 Louis XVIII ennobled him and endorsed, thus, he resumed his career as a deputy until the July Revolution intervened. Solicited by various parties, André entered the electoral lists once more in 1834 when he ran as a Legitimist challenger in the *arrondissement* of Florac and it is this episode which is related in his corre-

---

[39] A hamlet five kilometres from the château of Booz.
[40] A.D.L. F2809 Paradan to 'Monsieur et cher voisin [La Rochenégly]', La Canourgue, n.d.
[41] *Ibid.*, Paradan to 'Monsieur et cher voisin [La Rochenégly]', La Canourgue, 7 December 1851.

spondence with Vachin. Like that of any rural notable, André's power-base consisted of a matrix of ancestoral allegiances, petty services dutifully performed and territorial loyalties embracing the canton of Sainte Enimie. Imagine his dismay, therefore, when several electors unilaterally altered the rules of the game and he lost the election by two votes. Anticipating defeat (college elections were lengthy affairs), he remarked to Vachin,

Ce que vous me dites du canton de Ste Enimie comble la mesure de la plus noire ingratitude. Les nombreux électeurs avoint (*sic*) constamment voté pour moy comme un seul homme; je les ai obligés [i.e. done them favours] presque tous; il en est deux surtout, Paradan et Olivier, qui ont reçu des témoignages de mon affection; je ne puis ni deviner ni comprendre les motifs de leur défection. Je n'aurai garde de leur adresser aucun reproche, ils seraient trop confus et humiliés![42]

The patronage exercised by titled aristocrats such as La Rochenégly or by scions of the rural bourgeoisie such as André is not to be reduced to a set of economic variables. Landlords relied upon the votes of tenants and a clientele of artisans and agricultural labourers, but the relationship was informed by a spirit of mutual benefit which rendered coercion otiose. In any case, the structure of landholding in the region refracted economically enforced deference. The trend lay firmly in the direction of *petite propriété* and owner-exploitation, as suggested in chapter two. By the end of our period, sharecropping – the source of much landlord abuse in central and southwestern France – had dwindled to the point of insignificance. Tenant farming, too, was in sharp decline save, perhaps, on the high plateaux of the Lozère and the Haute-Loire. In 1877 a wealthy proprietor of Landos in the mountains of the Devès could still write in the following terms to Henri Vinay, the Moral Order candidate in the *arrondissement* of Le Puy II: 'je serai demain, jour de marché, à Pradelles où je patronnerai votre candidature. Je vous garantis au mois 30 votes . . . parmi mes parents, mes fermiers, mes amis.'[43] But electioneering which lined up tenants and farm servants like feudal levies was neither necessary, nor particularly profitable in an age in which votes were counted in their thousands.

In short, it would seem that the myriad peasant proprietors who determined the issue of every parliamentary election after that of August 1846 conceived of politics as first and foremost an extension of their cultural being. The perception of belonging to a cultural community or, more accurately, a series of discrete cultural communities embedded in a framework of broader consensual values is an idea which has been discussed at length in chapter four. Its relevance to the subject of opinion formation in the electoral arena is transparent. In the countryside of the southern Massif Central the usefulness of academic distinctions between elite and popular culture is questionable. There existed, rather, a 'peasant' culture in which every member of the

[42] A.D.L. F427 André to Vachin, Orthez, 14 June 1834.
[43] Rivet, *La Vie politique*, p. 412.

two days later they excited little more than curiosity. Several individuals profited from their overnight stop in the tavern to engage them in conversation on their beliefs, reported the sub-prefect, while 'au dehors la curiosité avait réuni quelques personnes qui attendaient le moment où ils sortiraient du café pour voir leur costume'.[48] In short, the local population seemed neither for nor against this novel intrusion of contemporary ideological debate.

As far as we can tell the Saint Simonian gospel made few converts among the citizenry of Brioude, but the impartial hearing which they gave it accurately reflected the receptive and mobile state of public opinion. In 1834 a young republican of ennobled bourgeois stock, Amédée de Saint Ferréol, established a branch of the Société des Droits de l'Homme in the town and with the help of Jules Maigne, son of a local wax merchant, began to build up a republican nucleus in Brioude and its village hinterland.[49] Saint Ferréol and Maigne had acquired their political education at source: during law studies in Paris they had established contact with Barbès, Blanqui, Buchez, Raspail and other members of the radical avant-garde. The crystallisation of opinion in the district owed everything to this singular ideological admixture. In April 1848 the democratic list led by Saint Ferréol and Maigne polled heavily in the cantons of the Brivadois, albeit fruitlessly since the embryonic *démocrate-socialiste* bridgehead was swamped by the support for clerical or Legitimist candidates elsewhere in the department. But the following year proved more auspicious; socialist democracy expanded its slender toehold in the west to embrace the north and parts of the centre of the department. In consequence, Saint Ferréol, Maigne and several other democrats were despatched to Paris after the legislative elections of May 1849. Several turbulent years followed which served only to strengthen republican sentiment in the Brivadois. Maigne bore the deputy's sash for less than a month before falling victim to the repression following the abortive Montagnard insurrection of 13 June. He was excluded and imprisoned, but the voters retorted by electing his brother, Françisque, in his place.[50] Saint Ferréol narrowly avoided proscription until December 1851 when he fled abroad having played a prominent role in organising resistance to the *coup d'état*. Neither was permanently removed from the political scene, however. In June 1853 the sub-prefect of Brioude reported that Saint Ferréol had returned from his enforced exile and seemed little chastened by the experience. 'Les cultivateurs se sont préoccupés d'une manière plus spéciale que les ouvriers de la présence de cet ancien chef,'[51] he noted ominously. Jules Maigne, meanwhile, refused any compromise with the Second Empire and left France for Switzerland after his

[48]   *Ibid.*, Sub-prefect Brioude to prefect Haute-Loire, Brioude, 15 June 1833.
[49]   Rivet, *La Vie politique*, pp. 506–9, 572–5.
[50]   A.D. H.-L. 3M³11 *Elections législatives*, March 1850.
[51]   A.D. H.-L. 2M²2 Sub-prefect Brioude to prefect Haute-Loire, Brioude, 18 June 1853.

release from prison in 1859. His brother, Françisque, returned to Blesle – a *bourg* situated some twenty-five kilometres from Brioude – where he discreetly combined the roles of country doctor and political evangelist. In common with so many veteran 'quarante huitards', Saint Ferréol and Jules Maigne resumed their careers as public representatives in the 1870s and 1880s.

For all their public notoriety, Saint Ferréol and the Maigne brothers epitomised the phenomenon of small-town radicalism – the linear descendant of small-town jacobinism. Exalted briefly by the revolution of 1848 and the opportunities it brought in its wake, the threshold of their ambition remained modest as did the radius of their influence. Outside the Brivadois their appeal was limited; in Le Puy and, *a fortiori*, Yssingeaux their names were scarcely known. Yet the combination of a fertile medium, a restless and underoccupied local bourgeoisie and a catalysing event such as 1848 'produced' an enduring and ideologically sensitive commitment to left-wing politics among the mass of the population. The role of the medium should be emphasised for, while village and small-town jacobins and radicals were a familiar species, the formalisation of opinion in the Brivadois was untypical of the region as a whole. Republicanism clearly made emotional and intellectual sense to the peasant communities of the plain of Brioude, but it did so as part and parcel of a general flux in social and cultural relationships. The vigorous injection of ideology provided by Saint Ferréol and his comrades probably did no more than hasten the process. We know, for example, that linguistic usage had ceased to mask the socio-economic disparities within the community and tended rather to accentuate them,[52] and there exists tell-tale evidence of a decline in the traditional forms of social deference. Two days before the contested legislative election of May–June 1863 the sub-prefect of Brioude chided the official candidate, Barthélemy de Romeuf, for imagining that the prestige of the family name rendered electioneering unnecessary: 'M. de Romeuf se prétend satisfait des visites qu'il a rendues. Mais le danger n'est pas là. C'est le vigneron, c'est l'ouvrier et le paysan, dont il ne se préoccupe pas, qui paraissent vouloir sortir de leur inanition et pas en sa faveur.'[53] By the 1870s and 1880s the authority of notables who had hesitated to switch to the winning side was ebbing fast. One such revealed to the sub-prefect of Brioude at the height of the Seize Mai crisis that he no longer understood the mentality of the electorate in his locality:

la confiance est complètement déplacée. Il y a quelques années nos populations venaient d'elles-mêmes et spontanément se renseigner, à certains moments, auprès des personnes pouvant les bien conseiller; il n'en est plus de même maintenant. Elles vont puiser leur inspiration auprès de cette masse nouvelle (*sic*) des chemins de fer, dont

---

[52]   See above, chapter four, p. 121.
[53]   A.D. H.-L. 3M^{2}12 Sub-prefect Brioude to prefect Haute-Loire, Brioude, 29 May 1863.

l'esprit est des plus mauvais et qui flattent leurs mauvaises passions par le mensonge, les corrompent et les éloignent des personnes qui pourraient les diriger mieux.[54]

Small-town radicalism was an enduring characteristic of the political culture of the region. Notwithstanding the instances mentioned, it posed less of a threat to established attitudes and relationships than might appear to have been the case, however. Such was the level of distrust between town and country that *bourg* militancy often provoked a resistance to political novelty among the peasantry. This reflex is particularly noticeable in localities riven by confessional differences. Less enduring, but more perplexing to the authorities was the phenomenon of the village propagandist. The heyday of the isolated village propagandist fell roughly between 1789 and the 1880s for he flourished in the interstices of an unevenly acculturated society. The bringer of good news, the narrator of bad news, he appeared in multiple guises as the local proprietor, the neighbourhood land surveyor, the tavern-keeper, the schoolmaster and even as the parish priest or the pastor. These village bread-oven orators whose education distinguished them from the common herd, but whose vocation or personal predilections placed them in daily contact with the peasantry, were viewed with deep suspicion by the prefects and their subordinates. They rarely accomplished a durable politicisation of the rural masses, if only because they acted upon the peasantry in a void, but their intervention could be highly embarrassing. Moreover, like sectarian alignments and territorial rivalries, the activism of village propagandists helps to explain the convoluted results that elections could throw up.

The legacy of neo-jacobinism in the countryside which has been described in chapter six derived largely from this source. The proselytizing zeal of individual rural proprietors rather than the existence of an antecedent fertile class of village artisans or poor peasants may be considered the principal factor in the strange outbreak of *babeuvisme* at Rieupeyroux[55] deep in the Aveyronnais ségala and of agrarian socialism at Estables (Lozère)[56] on the high slopes of the Margeride. The point may be extended to the nineteenth century, too: at Campagnac (Aveyron)[57] 104 voters (out of 314) chose François-Vincent Raspail for the presidency of the Second Republic in December 1848. Raspail collected only three other scattered votes in the entire department. The motivations which determined this impressive endorsement of the 'communist' candidate are difficult to fathom, but the interventionism of a radically-minded bourgeois proprietor offers the most likely explanation. The *bourg* of Campagnac had boasted a militant coterie

---

54 A.N. C3485 *Elections législatives*, 1877: Haute-Loire, Charles to sub-prefect Brioude, Langeac, 9 July 1877.
55 Jones, '*La République au village* in the Southern Massif Central', pp. 809–10.
56 Jones, 'Common Rights and Agrarian Individualism', pp. 133–5.
57 A.D.A. 4M114 *Election du président de la République, relevé par canton des suffrages obtenus par les divers candidats*; 1M112a Prefect Aveyron to *général de division* Gouvion, Rodez, 22 messidor IX.

once before, in the Year Two (1793–4), which serves to remind us that the factors contributing to the growth of political awareness among the peasantry can never be isolated with total clarity, but neither Campagnac, Estables, nor Rieupeyroux showed any other inclination for left-wing politics in the course of the nineteenth century. Ideological contamination via democratic patronage was not – on its own – sufficient to effect a *prise de conscience*.

We are left, therefore, with a complex model of peasant politicisation based on the interaction of endogenous and exogenous factors. Territorial imperatives; household structure and strategies; confessional rivalries and social hierarchy all moulded the attitudes of country dwellers in varying degrees, while secular ideology provided categories for debate. The community learned to express its loyalties in the language of the polity. But in so doing symbols acquired substance: abstract reference points actually replaced the archaic allegiances which they had once typified. In this fashion the experience of electoral democracy slowly integrated the recalcitrant rural population of the southern Massif Central. It is arguable whether this process represented a significant extension of the horizons of the ordinary peasant voter, however. He may have approached the electoral urn in a state of religious intoxication, or girded with village pride, or fired by a vision of 'la Belle [the social and democratic Republic]', but in each case his reflexes as an individual were conditioned by adherence to a primary group.

The crisp differences of opinion between catholic and protestant in the zones in which they came into close contact illustrate well this curious dialectic of internal and external factors. The sectarian divide was, as we have suggested, an incontrovertible fact of life for many peasants in the southern Massif Central. So much so, indeed, that it became a kind of ideological bench-mark. Calvinism presupposed left-wing political options, *ergo* left-wing political options presupposed adherence to Calvinism. Several staunchly catholic communities in the throes of political radicalisation appear to have accepted the logic of this statement in the course of the nineteenth century and it seems that this process of cross-referencing was far from uncommon. Both Vigier[58] and Agulhon[59] have uncovered cases of a broadly similar identification in the departments of the South East. In the highlands where the role of creeping religious indifference can be discounted, the collective repudiation of the catholic church was not undertaken lightly. Usually it occurred in an atmosphere of intense popular irritation following attempts by the ecclesiastical hierarchy to switch parish priests, or in consequence of a refusal by the hierarchy to meet demands for an adjustment to the existing parish network. Nonetheless, it is worth noting that these pseudo-

[58] P. Vigier, *La Seconde République dans la région alpine: étude politique et sociale* (2 vols., Paris, 1963), i, pp. 149–53, ii, 112–15.
[59] Agulhon, *The Republic in the Village*, pp. 105–11.

conversions often coincided with the period 1849–51, that is to say with the *démocrate–socialiste* onslaught on the countryside.

Two examples drawn from the Brivadois illustrate well how the weapon of defiant protestantism could be used to delineate political attitudes. The village of Paulhac[60] on the outskirts of Brioude was better placed than most to respond to the heartbeat of national ideological debate. In the aftermath of the 1830 revolution two factions emerged which may be loosely described as the Carlist party and the liberal party since they identified themselves with these standpoints in all but name. Carlist sentiment derived principally from the matrix of loyalties that the local magnate – the Marquis de Miramon – and the parish priest were able to exploit, while liberal-republicanism was nourished on the root-stock of the resident bourgeoisie, as in Brioude. The municipal law of 21 March 1831 provided the first opportunity for a trial of strength and four hotly contested elections had to be held before the new council could be sworn in. The parties were finely balanced and remained so through several generations of protagonists over the next fifty years.

It is likely that the blatant and partisan electioneering of *curé* Cros left bitter memories which temporarily receded upon the arrival of a new priest, the *abbé* Martin, who succeeded in winning the affection of most of the population. Certainly, once the revolution of 1848 had rekindled local political rivalries, we find Martin a popular figure in the expanding ranks of the *démocrate–socialiste* Left. Disconcerted by the advent of universal manhood suffrage and deprived of clerical support, the château party lost control of the municipality and sought outside aid to redress the balance in their favour. Early in 1851 a prefectoral *arrêté* suspended the popular, and radical, mayor and *adjoint* from office, while an episcopal instruction replaced the *abbé* Martin with a more compliant *desservant*. At this point the commune rebelled. The new spiritual incumbent arrived to the accompaniment of a menacing *charivari* and murmurs of 'Nous ne voulons plus de prêtre, puisqu'on a retiré le nôtre; nous ne voulons plus aller à l'Eglise, il pourra dire sa Messe seul. Nous voulons un ministre protestant et nous l'aurons bientôt.'[61] In fact the spiritual migration of the parish had already been taken in hand by those who were chiefly responsible for its political migration: the republican bourgeoisie of the neighbourhood. On 4 August 1851 a pastor named Collins and supposedly supplied by the consistory of St Voy took up residence in Paulhac. To the evident dismay of the authorities he seems to have performed all the duties associated with the role of priest. The local population, meanwhile, showed every sign of satisfaction at having embraced a faith which harmonised with their political convictions. When a leading

[60] For Paulhac, see A.D. H.-L. 4M167; 2M²2; 2M²1; 3M³12; 6M93; *La Haute-Loire*, 10 May 1870 and J. Villain, *La France moderne (Haute-Loire)* (St Etienne, 1906), entry for Miramon.
[61] A.D. H.-L. 4M167 Gendarmerie report to prefect Haute-Loire, Le Puy, 15 July 1851.

Brivadois radical died leaving instructions that his coffin should not on any account be taken into a church, a substantial contingent of Paulhac villagers accompanied the funeral cortège on the way to the cemetery. The Napoleonic *coup d'état* brought an end to this curious experiment in political and religious cross-referencing.

At Paulhac the decision to defect was a calculated and provocative gamble following upon two decades of intermittent party feuding. At Torsiac,[62] by contrast, the tensions which finally precipitated a similar course of action remained ideologically unfocused except for a brief period between 1848 and 1851. The source of dispute in this riverain commune near the border between the Haute-Loire and the Puy-de-Dôme might be described as a variation upon the theme of territorial conflict. The commune comprised two ancient parishes, each of which possessed a church and a presbytery of sorts although the seat of the seigneurial *mandement* and the château were situated in the village of Torsiac. In this respect the situation of Torsiac and its subordinate parish of Brugeilles was comparable with that of La Roque Valzergues and St Saturnin-de-Lenne discussed earlier.[63] If we allow for the chronological discrepancy, both Brugeilles and St Saturnin-de-Lenne may be described as dynamic villages experiencing slow but remorseless demographic expansion whose inhabitants increasingly clamoured for seigneurial and civil status.

In the early decades of the nineteenth century all the omens seemed favourable to Brugeilles. Finding the manse uninhabitable, the priest appointed to the parish of Torsiac after the Concordat chose instead to reside in Brugeilles, and in 1825 the dilapidated and insalubrious *chef-lieu* church was effectively closed down by an episcopal interdict. The crumbling building was emptied of its furniture and ornaments and public worship was concentrated instead at Brugeilles. As seat of a parish and of a commune, Torsiac seemed destined for extinction and doubtless would have been disestablished in due course had it not been for the local squire, Adrien de Torsiac, who decided to make the château of Torsiac the permanent residence of his family. Anxious to restore the dignity of his erstwhile seigneurial seat, de Torsiac took an active part in the rebuilding of the church and presbytery and the work was completed shortly before the revolution of 1848. The villagers of Brugeilles viewed this unexpected turn of events with dismay fearing that it not only dispelled any hope of communal status, but also presaged the demise of their own parish. Dismay turned to anger and outright rebellion as the inhabitants of Torsiac repossessed their church furniture and ornaments backed by an impressive force of gendarmes.

---

[62] For Torsiac, see A. Lavialle, 'Monographie paroissiale de Torsiac, canton de Blesle', *Bulletin de la société d'agriculture*, iii–iv (1903), 49–60; A.D. H.-L. 4M268; 6M93; J.-C. Gouly, 'Protestants et catholiques en Haute-Loire au milieu du XIXe siècle', 102–3 and Villain, *La France moderne (Haute-Loire)*, entry for Torsiac.

[63] See above, chapter six, p. 188.

This rape (for that was how it was seen) of Brugeilles's church occurred in 1849. Already the villagers had given expression to their sense of outrage by calling in a protestant pastor. But why Brugeilles should react in this fashion whereas the inhabitants of Saint Rémy[64] whose church suffered a similar fate did not, remains an open question. At Brugeilles the decision to secede from the catholic church seems to have antedated the revolution of 1848 by several weeks. Nevertheless, the identification of defiant protestantism with political radicalism developed swiftly in the months that followed. The cell of *démocrates–socialistes* grouped around Françisque Maigne in the adjacent *bourg* of Blesle played the crucial role in this process. Indeed, the expedient of seeking a Calvinist preacher may have been suggested by Maigne in the first place. Be that as it may, the village of Brugeilles became an outpost of Brivadois socialist democracy in contrast to the *chef-lieu* which owed everything to the de Torsiac family. When the news of Jules Maigne's arrest after the shambolic insurrection of 13 June 1849 reached local ears, millenarian excitement took hold of the population of Brugeilles. François Lapirot, described by the sub-prefect as a peasant cultivator, roamed the commune urging a preemptive strike against the 'blancs', singing snatches from the Marseillaise and shouting 'A bas la calotte, à bas les jesuites, à bas les usuriers.'[65] Local issues and the imbibed rhetoric of national ideological debate merged to precipitate an embryonic political consciousness. The subsequent judicial indictment against one Jouve, an elected officer of the commune and a more circumspect radical, neatly summarised the levels of this consciousness: 'Le S[ieu]r Jouve, adjoint de la commune de Torsiac, était présent à cette scène et non seulement il ne chercha point à arrêter Lapirot, mais celuici lui ayant dit qu'il fallait aller *chez le curé*, Jouve lui répondit qu'il fallait aller à Blesle s'informer si l'ordre de tuer les blancs était arrivé.'[66]

[64] See above, chapter four, p. 137.
[65] A.D. H.-L. 6M93 Interrogation of Françoise Pascal of Brugeilles.
[66] *Ibid.*, *Procureur de la République près le tribunal civil de Brioude* to prefect Haute-Loire, Brioude, 14 August 1849.

9

✳✳

Admission to the polity

From the 1880s the scattered population of the southern Massif Central began to live *à l'heure de Paris*. Most strikingly in 1884 when Mende – the last prefecture in France to acquire a railway station – was connected to the national network. Henceforth railway time would bring increasing precision and formality to the rituals of electoral democracy. As the physical horizon receded the mental horizon of village life widened perceptibly. The inhabitants of the Lozère, commented an inspector of schools in 1880, 'disent volontiers qu'ils sont *en* Lozère, tandis qu'au delà des monts, ils vont *en* France'.[1] His remark was nicely timed for the sense of cultural apartness which distinguished the history of all four departments of the southern Massif Central was about to be subjected to some rude shocks. With the benefit of hindsight it is apparent that rural society had reached a plateau by the final quarter of the nineteenth century – a plateau of economic well-being, social cohesion and cultural vitality. But this climax was scarcely substantial or prolonged. It amounted to little more than the hiatus between consecutive agrarian cycles of expansion and contraction. Continued growth on the pattern of previous decades required a continuance of physical isolation and the continuing appeal of values which discerned in peasant farming a way of life as well as a system of land management. To be sure, the population of these uplands had rarely, if ever, lived a totally separate existence. The scale and continuity of seasonal migration from the southern Massif Central serves to remind us that isolation is a loaded term. Yet the very continuity of that quest for seasonal employment provides the essential clue. Until the later nineteenth century the recourse of the Aveyronnais or Lozérian peasant to the resources of global society was largely contingent and expedient, that is to say it was designed to sustain his existing way of life. By the 1880s – earlier in the Brivadois and the southern Ardèche – this reasoning had ceased to apply, however. Traditional short-term migration had all but ceased in the face of a massive, definitive exodus from the soil. The implications of this transition were far-reaching.

---

[1] A.N. F^{17} 9267 *Inspection générale de 1880: rapport d'ensemble sur le département de la Lozère.*

Although socially minded catholic writers sounded the alarm in the decade before the First World War, the partial erosion of the economic foundations of rural society proceeded slowly and elicited little comment from among the actors. Contemporaries noticed the change in retrospect and were more inclined to point to the trauma of 1914–18 as marking the ultimate and insurmountable crisis of the *ancien régime*. In what sense, therefore, can we bring this study to term with the founding of the Third Republic? The vindication of the 1880s as a turning-point falls squarely within the domain of political history. In the 1880s the psychological and cultural separatism of the peasantry of the southern Massif Central was broken, not by new roads and railways, not by the siren pressures of the market-place, nor even by the repercussive effects of rural depopulation although all these factors played a part, but by government interventionism. After the abortive experiments of 1793–4 and 1848–51 the aptly dubbed Opportunist politicians of the 1880s finally devised a method of grafting republican democracy upon catholic and conservative root stock. In the 1880s 'la république au village' became a reality, but this synthesis owed everything to opportunism and little or nothing to ideology.

Apogee of a rural society

The census of 1881 revealed that for the first time the proportion of the French working population engaged in agriculture had dropped below half. In the four departments of the southern Massif Central, by contrast, roughly three-quarters of the labour force remained tied to the land and that figure would not swiftly diminish. Indeed, the agricultural character of the region intensified in the second and third quarters of the nineteenth century as rural handicrafts declined and waste or common land was cleared for arable cultivation. The census also revealed that the social pyramid had become more compact, principally owing to the departure of the lowliest echelon of day-labourers and plot-farmers. An undifferentiated proprietorial elite continued to occupy the apex of village society and showed few, if any, signs of wishing to abandon the countryside, but the mendicant armies which had invested isolated farmsteads and intimidated reapers in the fields in the late eighteenth and early nineteenth centuries were now a thing of the past. With the easing of demographic pressure two of the most enduring hallmarks of *ancien régime* peasant society – vagabondage and indebtedness – ceased to be subjects for routine correspondence between officials.

Initially, therefore, the rural exodus performed the same function as seasonal migration. It relieved the overloading strain of a century of uninhibited population expansion and left the traditional structures of peasant society better able to cope. However, the purgative migration of agricultural labourers, impoverished artisans and younger sons set in train a haemorrhage of life blood which eventually punctured the reproductive buoyancy of an entire agrarian civilisation. The opening up of the region by spectacular feats of civil engineering set in motion a similar process, for the improvements to the road network tended to favour the old market economy based on the *bourg*. By 1850 the great inter-departmental axes had been completed although the Lozère, as always, remained poorly served. In the second half of the century the substantial subsidies offered by government were usually earmarked for the construction and repair of secondary roads which benefited local entrepôts. The rash of fairs founded during these decades underlines the way in which the building of access roads served initially to perpetuate one of the more archaic features of the rural economy.

The researches of Jean Merley[2] on the Haute-Loire enable us to capture this process in some detail. Beginning in the 1840s the state started to finance road building on an ambitious scale and it encouraged local authorities to do likewise. Central government provided 44,916 *f.* for the purpose of cutting new roads in the department of the Haute-Loire in 1841, but five years later this allocation had risen to 673,127 *f.* During the Second Republic funding tailed off temporarily, but with the establishment of the Second Empire infrastructure became a priority item on the agenda of government. Between 1851 and 1880 ministers pledged approximately 250,000 *f.* each year to the task of road building. To these sums should be added the department's own resources. In 1851 the *conseil-général* raised 522,052 *f.* for the purposes of road repair and construction and by 1880 this activity accounted for a little over half the department's budgeted expenditure (compared with 7 per cent allocated to primary education). For three decades, in short, it seems that expenditure on road building and maintenance never dropped below three-quarters of a million *francs* per annum. The participation of village worthies in this tremendous effort was all the more enthusiastic in that most of the money was applied to the improvement and extension of by-roads (*chemins vicinaux*) which directly and immediately benefited the rural population (see table IX.1). This willingness to face up to the task of integrating a dispersed habitat, but relative indifference to the problems posed by long-distance communication, has a venerable history in the southern Massif Central. In 1834 the newly constituted *conseil-général* of the Haute-Loire was rebuked by the prefect for its reluctance to vote funds for anything other than *chemins vicinaux*.

Railway construction was destined to have a much greater impact. While the building of country roads in the second half of the nineteenth century helped to promote a sense of rural cohesion, steam locomotion proved disruptive in almost every conceivable sense. Moreover, the age of the train came

---

[2] J. Merley, *L'Industrie en Haute-Loire de la fin de la Monarchie de Juillet aux débuts de la Troisième République* (Centre d'histoire économique et sociale de la région lyonnaise, Université de Lyon II, 1972), pp. 139–41.

Table IX.1 *Road communications in the department of the Haute-Loire (in kilometres)*

Type of road	Length in 1851	Length in 1880	Percentage increase
Routes nationales	325	358	10.15
Routes départementales	457	468	2.4
Chemins de grande communication[a]	414	432	4.34
Chemins d'intérêt commun[b]	296	530	79.05
Chemins vicinaux ordinaires[c]	2352	3807	61.86

Notes:
[a] Village roads maintained by the communes with financial assistance from the Department authorities.
[b] Village roads whose maintenance was shared by several communes.
[c] Village roads maintained from the communal budget with occasional financial assistance from the Department authorities.
Source: J. Merley, *L'Industrie en Haute-Loire de la fin de la Monarchie de Juillet aux débuts de la Troisième République* (Centre d'histoire économique et sociale de la région lyonnaise, Université de Lyon II, 1972), p. 140.

late to the southern Massif Central and it intruded upon a society already showing symptoms of a generalised loss of demographic and cultural equilibrium. The economic repercussions of railway penetration are, perhaps, the most difficult to specify. The challenge of construction in difficult terrain provided unskilled work for thousands of under-employed villagers whose agricultural holdings were highly marginal. And when the numberless cuttings and embankments and tunnels had been completed, the new stations seemed to beckon the way to an easier and more fulfilling life on the plains. The steady northward push of the Béziers–Neussargues line (opened along its entire length in 1888) brought to a definitive climax the population of many communes situated on the confines of the Aveyron and the Lozère. Within five years of the arrival of the Chemin de Fer du Midi in 1882 the population of the commune of Auxillac (Lozère) had plummeted by twelve per cent.[3]

The effects of steam locomotion upon the agricultural and industrial structures of the region can best be described as patchy. Late nineteenth-century prefects envisioned the Massif Central as a vast natural park producing livestock, dairy products, timber and even hydro-electric power for the consumer cities of the lowlands. Once, that is, modern communications had freed the indigenous population from the tiresome necessity of growing its own food. Some modern historians have extolled the potent combination of communications and markets in analogous terms. The reality proved much less dramatic, for the railways that eventually spanned the region were built in

[3] Roqueplo, *La Dépopulation*, p. 40.

answer to perceived national needs, whether economic or political. Local lines serving local interests were certainly projected, but few were built. Occasionally, the chosen route accommodated both national and local needs: thus the line between Le Puy and Saint Etienne (via Pont-de-Lignon) did much to invigorate and commercialise the cereal and animal husbandry of the north-eastern Haute-Loire and the belated construction of a line between Rodez and Albi (via Carmaux) performed the same service for the Aveyronnais ségala.[4] Generally speaking, however, the impact of steam locomotion upon the rural economy proved unspectacular. Notwithstanding vastly improved communications, market pressures hesitated in the face of an array of social, cultural and geographical obstacles. In the last analysis the station-yard where migrants assembled each autumn posed a greater challenge to peasant polyculture than the stock-yard.

The impact of railway construction on local trade and industry tended to be both specific and localised. As the rail-head advanced it created a corridor of economic renewal which sucked in artisanal and industrial enterprise, but left peripheral centres all but denuded of non-agricultural activities. The building of the Brioude–Alès section of the Clermont-Ferrand–Nîmes axis illustrates this point well for it made the fortunes of such *bourgs* as Langeac (Haute-Loire) and Langogne (Lozère) which happened to be situated on the route adopted by the engineers. The establishment of railway workshops and the construction of a spur to the mines of Marsanges turned Langeac into a miniature industrial town, while Langogne became an embarkation point for cattle and timber. By contrast, the rival *bourg* of Pradelles (Haute-Loire) ten kilometres to the north east of Langogne saw its prosperity abruptly curtailed after 1873. The important *bourg* of Le Monastier-sur-Gazeille (Haute-Loire) suffered a similar fate upon the opening of the transversal line between Le Puy and St Georges-d'Aurac the following year. For centuries the merchants of Le Monastier had provisioned the Vellavian capital with the products of the Midi, but high-speed rail communications re-routed this trade to the west. Road haulage over the Monts du Vivarais was, therefore, one of the earliest casualties of the transport revolution. River navigation on the Allier below Brioude suffered more grievously still. The rail-head offered a cheaper and more efficient method of despatching the coals of the Brassac basin than river barges and as steam locomotives pushed their way upstream the boat-building industries on the banks of the Allier folded. Their collapse triggered in turn a crisis in the forest economy of the adjacent plateau of La Chaise-Dieu.

Those influences which may be described as cultural are less easily measured. Yet we would do well not to underestimate their potency for the railway decades of the 1870s and 1880s were also decades in which the war

---

[4] See above, chapter one, p. 32.

against local particularisms was waged on many fronts. The burgeoning awareness of the discipline of time – time as measured by the station clock and the whistle of the Paris mail train rather than by the church belfry – has already been mentioned. But *all* the cultural and political connotations of steam locomotion proved corrosive of the attitudes which had hitherto structured the rural community. Small wonder that the founding fathers of republicanism lyricised the building of railways and the building of schools in the same breath. Each in its separate way pressed forward the central task of the 1880s: integration.

Intimations of a durable shift in the values and outlook of the peasant masses can be discerned as early as the 1830s and 1840s in localities such as the Brivadois and the turbulent villages of the lower Ardèche, but by the 1880s these tell-tale signs had become more abundant and widespread. The penultimate decade of the nineteenth century witnessed the culmination of three generations of population growth in most villages of the southern and south-eastern Massif Central and demography remains the best indicator of the well-being of an agrarian civilisation limited by Malthusian restraints for much of the period covered by this study. The birth rate held firm for a further two decades, but outmigration ensured that population densities stood still or declined. The downward drift of agricultural prices cannot be totally ignored, either, for commercial wheat-growing had established a bridgehead in parts of the Aveyron and the north-eastern Haute-Loire during the second half of the century. Just as high cereal and fatstock prices had soothed acceptance of the Republic in the early 1870s, the economic malaise of the early 1880s helped to boost support for anti-republican candidates in the elections of 1885. Migration, massive and rather desperate migration, remains the salient feature of these years, however. Peasants of both sexes voted with their feet, and while many quit the countryside with every intention of returning in due course, it is difficult to escape the conclusion that the exodus expressed a partial rejection of the values which had hitherto informed peasant society.

Dissatisfaction – or just plain doubt about the future – was already evident in a number of spheres. While noting, in 1866, the abiding strength of paternal authority over offspring, the minutes of the Agricultural Enquiry for the Aveyron nonetheless recorded that peasant households contained fewer children than formerly.[5] By the 1880s the co-habitation of generations was no longer an inflexible rule. Siblings who had earlier been tacitly excluded from household inheritance arrangements began to demand their legal rights. Disinherited cadets (or *aînés*) stepped forward to record before the notary their dissent from the practice of generations, while land held 'indivis' occasioned friction and discontent between heirs.[6] There is some evidence, too, which

[5] A.N. ADXIX C43³ *Enquête agricole: Aveyron*.
[6] E. Claverie, 'L' "Ousta" et le notaire: le système de dévolution des biens en Margeride lozérienne au XIXe siècle', *Ethnologie française*, xi (1981), 336.

suggests that popular culture was losing its animus. The *charivari* and the *fête patronale* no longer excited ferocious passions by the turn of the century and the gendarmerie could afford to spend less time policing such assemblies. Even the legendary 'esprit processif' of the highland peasantry eased somewhat. Between 1829 and 1869 the number of suits brought before the civil courts of the Haute-Loire declined by about a half, while in the Aveyron and the Lozère litigation pending before the Justices of the Peace likewise declined in the course of the century.[7] The precise significance of these trends is difficult to specify. Was rural society becoming more law abiding? Minor assault and defamation constituted the staple fare of first instance courts both before and after the Revolution and a drop in the bulk of litigation (despite rising population) may have reflected a relaxation of the code of honour which regulated the social space between individuals and kinship groups. Forest, fishing and hunting offences remained endemic, but the rural community persistently refused to acknowledge that these were also infractions of the law.

Railway construction merely added to this climate of uncertainty and incipient renewal. It brought considerable, if temporary, material disturbance; unprecedented opportunities for social and geographical mobility and, in the conditions of the 1870s and 1880s, political contagion. As the Chemin de Fer du Midi skirted round the causses and scaled the Aubrac, the non-native population of the Lozère approximately doubled to reach 6.4 per cent in 1882.[8] Clerics and conservative village notables triumphantly identified the railway gangs as rootless aliens, but the navvies and assorted specialists soon moved on – too soon for the comfort of local republicans. The danger to the fabric of rural society lay rather in what the railway pioneers left behind them. Railway *bourgs* or *communes-gares* mushroomed along the flanks of the permanent way and relayed urban culture and urban styles of living to the innermost recesses of the countryside. The peasantry resisted, but in a half-hearted and equivocal fashion. The balance of political power within the rural community oscillated sharply during the final decades of the nineteenth century. Democratisation of the municipalities and bitter struggles over the management of common land emphasised social and economic disparities as never before.[9] The coming of the railway and its human impedimenta complicated these alignments in bizarre and unforeseeable ways.

Disposing of vast holdings of common pasture, the causse communities

---

[7] Malègue, *Eléments de statistique générale*, p. 285; B. Schnapper, 'Pour une géographie des mentalités judiciaires: la litigiosité en France au XIXᵉ siècle', *Ann. E.S.C.*, xxxiv (1979), 410; *Atlas de la France rurale* (Cahiers de la Fondation nationale des sciences politiques, Paris, 1968), maps 62, 63.

[8] Roqueplo, *La Dépopulation*, pp. 36–7.

[9] Jones, 'Common Rights and Agrarian Individualism', pp. 144–9.

bordering the Chemin de Fer du Midi were among the first to register the presence of increasing numbers of railway employees and other *fonction-naires* in their midst. At Le Massegros (Lozère) which developed from nothing into an important administrative centre during the period covered by this study, flock-owners successfully fought off attempts to divide up and cultivate the commons until the 1870s and 1880s. Their efforts ultimately failed, but the evolving social structure of the *bourg* ensured that the issues were by no means clear cut. In 1888 several inhabitants wrote to the prefect in order to disassociate themselves from a petition calling for the partition of a common known as La Devèse which they had earlier signed. 'Si j'ai signé la petition', wrote Casimir Fages, 'c'est qu'on m'avait dit que les employés du gouvernement et les étrangers qui étaient venus habiter Le Massegros n'auraient pas droit au partage. D'après ce qu'on dit ils y ont droit comme les autres et cela ne me paraît pas juste.'[10]

Willy-nilly, the traditional agrarian community comprising notables, artisans and an assortment of peasants was being redefined. State employees ought not to be admitted to the *partage* 'au détriment des vrais enfants du village',[11] declared another repentant petitioner. They were birds of passage with no stake in the community. But depopulation and widening horizons rendered the notion of 'enfant du village' much more equivocal than it had been a generation earlier. The toiling peasant distrusted the local official with a foot in each camp, yet cherished a secret ambition to join him on the pay-roll of state. For a century and more the catholic church had satisfied this desire for modest social elevation, until the 1880s, that is, when the Republic undermined the power of the church as a social institution.[12] Henceforth ambitious peasant households looked to the state, but the state exacted a high political price in return for the coveted status of *salarié*. Employees, their kith and kin – in short anyone beholden to bountiful Marianne – had little choice but to adopt, or affect, an attitude of obsequious republicanism. It comes as no surprise, therefore, to discover that the map of radical opinion during the formative years of the Third Republic corresponds in no small measure to the map of railway communications. After 1877 every *commune-gare* could be described as a republican bridgehead. A questionnaire completed by the clergy of the diocese of Mende revealed that in 1902 'good' journals (such as *La Croix de la Lozère* or *La Croix de Paris*) were distributed in virtually all catholic parishes, while subscribers to 'bad' newspapers (principally *La Dépêche de Toulouse*; *Le Petit Journal* and *Le Moniteur de la Lozère*) tended to reside either in parishes touched by the railway, or in the northerly parishes of the Aubrac and the Margeride whose sons and daughters had migrated to

---

[10] A.D.L. 2 O 942 *Administration et comptabilité communales*: Le Massegros, Fages to prefect Lozère, (n.d.).
[11] *Ibid.*, Galière to prefect Lozère (n.d.).   [12] See below, p. 303.

Paris. 'Sur la ligne, toutes sortes de journaux',[13] reported the incumbent of Arcomie, while his counterpart in the parish of Montjézieu noted: '*La Dépêche* pour l'institutrice qu'elle lit en présence de ses élèves et communique à 4 ou 5 personnes.'[14]

A village schoolmistress would scarcely have dared to subscribe to *La Dépêche de Toulouse* twenty years earlier. Nor would it have profited her to lecture her pupils, for the church maintained a careful scrutiny of teaching personnel and French was not the language of everyday oral communication. Education, in the sense of formal schooling, played no small part in that complex process of integration which contrived the eclipse of rural society. But if the mere existence of rail and carriage-ways promoted cultural intercourse, it is less certain that schools and scholarly instruction were predestined to perform a similar role. After generally low thresholds of institutional provision in the late eighteenth and early nineteenth centuries, the southern Massif Central departments embarked upon an ambitious and sustained programme of school building in the second half of the nineteenth century. By 1881–2 the Lozère headed the national league-table with a primary school for every 175 inhabitants. The department of the Aveyron occupied eleventh place, while the Ardèche and the Haute-Loire held the thirtieth and forty-seventh position respectively.[15] Infrastructure was one thing, however, pupil attendance rates and pedagogy were another. 'Comment se fait-il', exclaimed Henri Malègue, the author of a statistical treatise on the Haute-Loire in 1872, 'que nous ayons tant d'écoles, tant d'élèves et si peu d'instruction?'[16]

The explanation of the paradox, as perceived by republicans imbued with positivist ideas, lay in the fact that education was a sphere in which the spiritual and the temporal arm disputed for jurisdiction. Consciously or not, the state had perpetuated clerical hegemony over education by its unwillingness or inability to exercise responsibility in this domain. Such informality mattered little so long as church and state pursued agreed objectives, but in the later 1870s the expectations of each party to the agreement diverged irrevocably and confrontation took the place of compromise. What the church called elementary instruction, the state refused to dignify by any such name and instead it set about training a corps of lay primary-school teachers, fashioning a non-denominational syllabus and building more schools. To ensure that future generations, at least, understood the duties of citizenship, basic schooling was made compulsory and free. The enacting of this legislation, known collectively as the Ferry education laws, occupied much of the 1880s and nowhere did it provoke more popular resistance than in the southern Massif Central.

The ramifications of clerical influence in the field of primary education

---

[13] C. Causse and A. Tufféry, 'Le Diocèse de Mende au début du XXᵉ siècle', p. 119.
[14] *Ibid.*, p. 117.   [15] A.D. H.-L. T56 *Statistique de l'enseignement primaire* (Paris, 1884).
[16] Cited in Merley, *L'Industrie en Haute-Loire*, p. 246.

have already been discussed in chapter four under the heading 'Community and Language'. Nevertheless, it is worth drawing out the implications of a system of schooling which sought to neutralise untoward elements of secular ideology. As constituted prior to 1880, the catholic monopoly of basic instruction effectively reinforced and prolonged the cultural impermeability of rural society. Conversely, the arrival of Ferry's teacher-missionaries in the countryside and the retreat of the lay orders from the educational sphere exposed the flanks of peasant particularism at a crucial moment when attacks were under way from other quarters. Admittedly, the clergy had not been totally unresponsive to change. Diligent efforts were made to teach in French, if only for liturgical reasons, although progress on this front remained painfully slow. Two English visitors to the mines of Decazeville left an illuminating account of a dinner-party held in their honour by a rich peasant proprietor of the environs. Two of the guests (the mayors of St Martin-de-Bouillac and Cuzac) proved incapable of uttering a word of French, while the host explained that he translated in his mind from patois as he spoke. This improbable encounter took place in 1887.[17] Weakness in the national idiom; excessive reliance on rote learning; neglect of handwriting and appalling ignorance of general culture mitigated only by grotesquely partisan history textbooks: these were the stock complaints of schools' inspectors in the 1870s and early 1880s. One such denounced the lay sister in charge of the communal school of Le Cayrol (Aveyron). Apparently she used as a primer the '*Histoire de France* de l'abbé Courval où l'on qualifiait de brigands à la figure hideuse, les républicains de l'assemblée constituante.'[18]

Anxious always to clothe their assault upon the edifice of church education in arguments of pedagogic principle the republican politicians of the 1880s reserved the *béates* of the Haute-Loire for special attention. The Demoiselles de l'Instruction, or *béates*, were probably the oldest, most numerous and – in the formal sense – least qualified female teaching order. On the eve of their dissolution, government officials calculated that some 16,800 children frequented 882 *béate* schools (known as *assemblées*) in the department. These figures are taken from a report submitted to the Minister of Education in 1880.[19] By the time the order was finally banned from teaching six years later, their numbers had begun to decline. On the other hand, F.-C. Dunglas,[20] the Rector of the Academy of the Haute-Loire, who published a vindication of the *béates* in 1854 reckoned that the congregation counted approximately 1,400 lay sisters, of whom 756 were fixed in the Haute-Loire and the remainder in adjacent departments. The guiding objective of the

---

[17] G. C. Davies and Mrs Broughall, *Our Home in Aveyron with Studies of Peasant Life and Customs in Aveyron and the Lot* (Edinburgh and London, 1891), p. 138.
[18] A.N. F^{17} 9255 *Inspection générale de 1881*: Aveyron.
[19] A.N. F^{17} 9265 *Rapport d'ensemble sur la Haute-Loire* (1880).
[20] Dunglas, *Notice sur les béates*.

Demoiselles was to edify and instruct poor peasant girls who might otherwise escape the attentions of the church, although it is worth noting that in 1880 27 per cent of those reputed to attend the *assemblées* were boys. Nevertheless, the first public criticisms of the *béates* drew attention to their virtual monopoly over female educational provision. In 1878 the Minister of Education reminded the prefect of the Haute-Loire that, despite the law of 10 April 1867, many communes in his department had made no attempt to equip themselves with a state primary school for girls. Three years later a ministerial circular from Jules Ferry reiterated the point. Although twenty-seven new primary schools for girls opened during the first seven months of 1882, there still remained eighty-four communes with over 500 inhabitants which had failed to comply. By 1892 this figure had dropped to twenty-seven.[21]

With state education fast becoming a science, indeed, a science of state, the *béates* were soon condemned on other counts, too. If the *béates* succeeded in teaching the principles of lace-making, they succeeded in little else, announced the government report of 1880 sententiously: 'Quant à la lecture, on peut hardiment affirmer que la plupart des béates ne le savent pas, du moins comme on l'entend aujourd'hui dans nos écoles . . . elles se bornent à faire assembler des lettres et réunir des sons, mais les enfants qui sortent de leurs écoles ne peuvent lire bien couramment que dans le catéchisme qu'ils savent par cœur.' As for writing, 'il y a peu de béates qui se hasardent jusqu'à enseigner l'écriture et l'orthographe'.[22] Dogmatic and derisive though these judgements may appear, they can be corroborated from other sources. Literary sources confirm the survival of an archaic 'reading only' culture in the highlands of the Haute-Loire as in much of the southern Massif Central,[23] while the custom of 'manuscrire' scarcely enhanced intellectual development. The teaching of reading via close textual scrutiny of old documents or manuscripts such as notarial deeds, wills, contracts of marriage and the like was widely practised by the *béates*. It compensated for a chronic shortage of printed material – even devotional works were in scant supply at village level – and it was highly functional. The peasantry acquired some notions of how to construe the deeds that would be most relevant to them in their daily lives. In short, then, the bishops of Le Puy controlled an army of spiritual outworkers whose pedagogic methods did nothing to undermine and everything to sustain the cultural status quo.

The signal achievement of the *béates* lay in the fact that they brought basic

---

[21] A.N. F[17] 9265 *Ministre d'instruction publique* to prefect Haute-Loire, Paris, 29 August 1878; A. Rivet, 'L'Application des lois Jules Ferry en Haute-Loire (1880–1892)', *Actes du 92ème congrès national des sociétés savantes, Strasbourg et Colmar 1967: section d'histoire moderne et contemporaine* (3 vols., Paris, 1970), iii, p. 66.
[22] A.N. F[17] 9265 *Rapport d'ensemble sur la Haute-Loire* (1880).
[23] See above, chapter four, p. 127 and notes 44 and 45.

instruction to every peasant's door-step at very little cost. If the Republic wished to compete in this field it could scarcely do less and the 1880s ushered in a massive and state-subsidised programme of school building. The commissioning of hamlet schools accounted for most of the expenditure and there were several reasons for this. By 1880 all the *chefs-lieux* possessed a state primary school, while the coverage of subsidiary villages was patchy. Historic factors played a part. In the Aveyron, for instance, the artificiality of the communes bedevilled the process of equipping outlying parishes with schools, just as it bedevilled every other process that depended on co-operation among municipal councillors. Moreover, many *chefs-lieux* establishments had fallen under the control of the teaching orders and could not immediately be laicised, while the countryside proper offered greater scope for the republican propaganda effort. It should be remembered, too, that the protestant community actively solicited the establishment of hamlet schools as part of its strategy for survival. In 1880 the Calvinist *bourg* of Le Pont-de-Montvert[24] obtained a grant of 35,000 *f.* towards the cost of building new schools in the villages of Grizac (120 inhabitants); Finiels (66); Prat Soubeyran (20) and Villeneuve (46).

In fact the Lozère had taken great strides towards the completion of an auxiliary infrastructure of hamlet schools even before Ferry's celebrated law of 20 March 1883 enjoining communes to make provision for 'hameaux distants les uns des autres de 3 km et réunissant au moins vingt enfants d'âge scolaire' was enacted. With some exaggeration the annual report of the schools inspector for 1880 announced that 'tous les hameaux de quelque importance et distants de 1 à 2 kilometres d'une école publique possèdent une école régulièrement créée'.[25] Nevertheless, 235 schemes for school building or repair reached the Minister from the Lozère between June 1878 and May 1880. In the Ardèche, the Aveyron and the Haute-Loire the drive to establish hamlet schools came slightly later, that is to say after the 1883 legislation. Schools alone could not compensate for the manifold weaknesses of the Republic in this region, however, for the problem lay at one remove, in what was taught and by whom. After chronicling an unrivalled record of building, the schools inspector of the Lozère admitted the sober reality: 670 state schools were attended by 18,170 pupils while 72 church schools opened their doors to 6294 pupils.[26] The orders ran the biggest and most efficient establishments in the comfortable knowledge that the parish clergy would supervise the lay *instituteurs* in the villages. Ineluctably, therefore, the renewed struggle for 'la république au village' resulted in a crusade against clericalism.

[24] Higonnet, *Pont de Montvert*, p. 111.
[25] A.N. F[17] 9267 *Inspection générale de 1880*: Lozère.   [26] *Ibid.*

Resistance: clericalism versus republicanism

The resignation of President MacMahon and the republican victory in the Senate elections of 1879 brought to an end a decade of political turbulence during which first royalism and then Moral Order conservatism had threatened to overturn the regime. Unassailable from either the Right or the Left, the Opportunists embarked upon a programme of reforms to liberalise the statutes governing the press, rights of association, trade unions, local government, divorce and access to elementary education. The myth of the Revolution was sedulously rehabilitated, too: parliament returned to Paris, the Marseillaise became the national anthem, and the anniversary of the fall of the Bastille a public holiday. In the words of Gambetta, the Republic had entered upon its 'organic and creative period'. This at least was the view from Paris. In much of rural France the consolidation of the regime was greeted with pragmatic indifference, while parts of the West and the South West offered considerable resistance to the republican idea. In the southern Massif Central resistance was orchestrated by the church on behalf of the peasantry and it attracted the repressive rather than the creative energies of government. By 1893 the republican bridgehead had been secured in this region, too, but at the expense of another decade of sterile political conflict.

Bridgehead is an apt description, for the politicians of the 1880s entertained few illusions about the convictions of the peasantry of these uplands. The object was to 'capture' them for the Republic; conversion would hopefully occur at some later stage. Yet even capturing them proved a formidable task and demanded unremitting and unscrupulous administrative pressure. The profile of parliamentary election results provided in table IX.2 records all the twists and turns in this protracted struggle. The struggle was not between the Republic and the peasantry, however, at least not directly. Most country dwellers practised regimism and for most, regimism supposed a posture of obedience to various emanations of conservative rule. What caused confusion once the certainties of Moral Order had dissolved was the sharp dichotomy of political ethos which developed between central and local government. Republicans dominated the Republic, but the church and conservative-minded village notables still operated the levers of local power and patronage. Momentarily, the instinct towards regimism missed its target; the peasantry committed its destiny to a clerico-Legitimist order which then proceeded to crumble under the weight of the republican assault.

The parish clergy of the southern Massif Central already possessed considerable expertise in the matter of elections.[27] That knowledge had been acquired pragmatically and not without misgivings, however. In the 1870s and 1880s the clergy entered the electoral arena in an altogether different

---

[27] See above, chapter seven, pp. 233–41.

Table IX.2 *Political stance of successful candidates in parliamentary general elections, 1871–1893*

	1871	1876	1877	1881	1885	1886[d]	1889	1893
Ardèche								
Republicans[a]	0	5	4	6	0	6	2	4
Anti-republicans[b]	8	1	2	0	6	0	3	0
Ralliés[c]	0	0	0	0	0	0	0	1
Aveyron								
Republicans	0	2	2	6	0		0	6
Anti-republicans	8	5	5	1	6		6	1
Ralliés	0	0	0	0	0		0	0
Haute-Loire								
Republicans	0	2	2	2	4		2	4
Anti-republicans	6	2	2	2	1		2	0
Ralliés	0	0	0	0	0		0	0
Lozère								
Republicans	1	2	1	3	0	3	1	3
Anti-republicans	2	1	2	0	3	0	2	0
Ralliés	0	0	0	0	0	0	0	0

Notes:
[a] All nuances from moderate republican (Centre Left) to Radical.
[b] Monarchists, Bonapartists.
[c] *Droite constitutionnelle.*
[d] Outcome of rescheduled elections in the Ardèche and the Lozère following the annulment of the 1885 ballot.
Sources: A.N. C3448; C3452; C3466; C3485–7; C4466; C4524; C3734; C3739 and A. Daniel, *L'Année politique*, Paris, 1876–93.

mood. Ultramontane ideas had blurred the distinction between matters spiritual and matters temporal, and republican incursions into the field of educational provision provided added justification for a posture of combat. From this historic conjuncture was born the policy of clericalism which the Robert dictionary succinctly defines as the 'opinion de ceux qui sont partisans d'une immixtion du clergé dans la politique'[28] and Gambetta identified as the principal threat to the infant Republic. The threat appeared all the more redoubtable in that the bishops of this Bretagne du Midi[29] were also ultramontane in outlook and little disposed to rein in the zeal of their clergy. Ernest Bourret, bishop of Rodez from 1871 until 1896, was the most power-

[28] P. Robert, *Dictionnaire alphabétique et analogique de la langue française* (7 vols., Paris, 1953–72), i, p. 797.
[29] An expression ascribed to Pope Pius IX, see J. Gadille, *La Pensée et l'action politiques des évêques français au début de la IIIème République, 1870–1883* (2 vols., Paris, 1967), i, p. 175 and note 2.

ful. He staunchly defended the Legitimist cause in the Aveyron throughout the 1870s, but became persuaded of the need for a *rapprochement* with the Republic in the 1880s. His change of heart evoked little enthusiasm among the clergy, but it won him a cardinal's hat in 1893. Having served as one of Bourret's *vicaires-généraux*, Julien Costes, bishop of Mende (1876–88), was no stranger to electoral management and clerical journalism, either. As for the youthful Joseph Bonnet, bishop of Viviers between 1876 and 1923, he remained an implacable opponent of the Republic until the day of his death. A spell as curate in the divided bourg of Meyrueis (Lozère) had turned him into a rabid anti-protestant and several years spent in the entourage of Monseigneur Dabert of Périgueux completed his ultramontane education. An anonymous official in the prefecture of the Ardèche portrayed him as 'ardent, vif mais rétréci par le fanatisme, autoritaire, étroit et entêté; paysan fanatique de la montagne qui n'a jamais connu que le monde clérical'.[30] Only the bishops of Le Puy seemed ready to cooperate with the civil power from the outset. Auguste Lebreton (1863–87) made no secret of his ultramontane convictions, but urged his clergy to refrain from explicit involvement in elections, while Fulbert Petit (1887–94) was almost unique on the bench of bishops in coming from republican stock. Like his mentor, Monseigneur Ardin of La Rochelle, he preached submission to the civil power.

Neither Lebreton, nor Petit were locals, however, and they experienced difficulty in controlling their clergy. The rest were drawn from the introspective world of the central plateau. Bourret hailed from St Etienne-de-Lugdarès (Ardèche), Bonnet from Langogne (Lozère) several miles to the north and Costes from a parish near Villefranche-de-Rouergue (Aveyron). All were of humble parentage, all spoke patois and all three toured their dioceses incessantly. The devotion which they inspired among the laity was legendary. After a visit to the episcopal city of Rodez in 1873, the bishop of Châlons wrote Bourret a congratulatory letter which concluded, 'Vous êtes seigneur du Moyen Age.'[31] Bourret was indeed formidable. As the spiritual leader of a numerous and youthful clergy, he exercised considerable powers of patronage and tirelessly solicited the promotion of his most able protégés and lieutenants. Thus, by 1880, he had managed to fill the dioceses of Mende, Viviers and St Flour with tough-minded and intransigent prelates. This policy mortgaged the future, however, as Bourret was shortly to recognise. It minimised the prospects of a reconciliation between church and state in the later 1880s and early 1890s. As table IX.2 indicates, the politics of *ralliement* attracted little support in the region.

Conservatives and clerics entered the parliamentary election campaign of 1881 in a dispirited mood. The repudiation of Moral Order by the electorate in 1877 had left them without policies, while the exclusion[32] of seventy-seven

---

[30]   A.D. Ard. V155 *Renseignements sur M[onsei]g[neu]r Bonnet, évêque de Viviers* (n.d.).
[31]   Gadille, *La Pensée et l'action politiques*, i, p. 174 and note 2.   [32]   See below, p. 300.

right-wing deputies from the Chamber and the purging of the *mairies* and sundry other branches of the administration had left them without influence. In the event many voters used the freedom from administrative pressure to stay at home and the Right proved the losers. Just under a hundred conservative deputies (divisible equally into monarchists and Bonapartists) finally took their seats compared with 457 republicans. In the four departments of the southern Massif Central, too, 1881 marked a low point in the fortunes of all who opposed the Republic. The invalidation of those conservative candidates who had succeeded in gaining election in October 1877 (Vinay in Le Puy-Sud; Malartre in Yssingeaux and Lauriol in Largentière II) taught the peasantry a sharp political lesson. Without a rallying cry, without a riveting issue the conservatives seemed incapable of halting the slide towards a *de facto* acceptance of the Republic. In the Ardèche, the Haute-Loire and the Lozère (but not in the Aveyron) electoral participation dropped substantially when compared with 1877.[33] Republican candidates swept the board taking seventeen out of twenty constituencies.

The rallying cry that conservative elites so badly needed if they were to halt the erosion of their power base was provided by the Republic: 'l'école sans Dieu'. The issues were, in chronological order, the expulsion decrees against the congregations and the laicising legislation applied to schools and teaching personnel. The congregations or orders were integral to the religious culture of the region. They embodied many of the traditions of *ancien régime* piety and their resurgence in the nineteenth century seemed to underline the superficial character of the revolutionary watershed. They also underpinned a hierarchic social system which subordinated the will of the individual to that of the group. Many a peasant household's strategy for survival was based on the assumption that surplus offspring would take Holy Orders. The attack on the congregations seemed calculated to repeat the cardinal mistakes of the 1790s, therefore. It offended religious sensibilities, it subverted social relationships and it anticipated the systematic attempt to secularise primary education initiated by Jules Ferry in 1882.

Details of the numbers of orders affected by the legislation of March 1880 in the Ardèche and the Lozère are scanty. The Jesuit fathers in charge of the shrine of Lalouvesc (Ardèche) were forcibly expelled and in the Lozère the Jesuits relinquished control of the Grand Seminary of Mende, otherwise the two departments emerged unscathed, it seems. In the Haute-Loire and the Aveyron, by contrast, lay orders of dubious status abounded. Often they were female and committed to teaching or the care of the sick. In addition to 882 *béates*, the department of the Haute-Loire[34] contained a further 1,200 'religieuses institutrices' belonging to twenty-seven orders and grouped in

[33] M.-T. and A. Lancelot, *Atlas des circonscriptions électorales en France depuis 1875* (Cahiers de la Fondation nationale des sciences politiques, Paris, 1970), p. 86.
[34] A.N. F^{17} 9265 *Rapport d'ensemble sur la Haute-Loire* (1880).

253 establishments. The Aveyron[35] boasted ten male orders and twenty-five female orders operating in 460 localities – an average of one and a half communities per commune. The female component of this task force topped a thousand. Virtually all these lay sisters were natives of the department and firmly embedded in its social fabric. In the words of the prefect, 'on est obligé de reconnaître qu'elles tiennent une grande place dans la vie sociale du pays: en effet il est peu de familles dont un des membres ne se voue à la vie religieuse'.[36] As regular customers for rough-quality serge the orders played an important role in the economic life of the region, too. The merchant clothiers of Marvejols (Lozère) were adversely affected by the closure of male religious houses and they urged the government to reconsider 'l'application des décrets aux congregations de femmes'.[37]

The most serious and intended consequence of the measures against the orders was to rid primary education of clerical influence, however. The prefect of the Aveyron went on to point out that the so-called unauthorised orders supplied the teaching personnel for more than 150 state primary schools. And yet no one except for a few administrators appointed since 1877 seemed particularly irked by this state of affairs: 'l'état de l'opinion est tel que, dans les cités les plus républicaines aucune assemblée municipale n'a pris l'initiative de demander la substitution de l'enseignement laïque à l'enseignement congréganiste'.[38] His comment prefigures the magnitude of the changes that were to take place within the next few years. The progressive exclusion of the local *sœurs* or *béates* from village schools caused considerable emotional and social upset, but the government's determination to banish the crucifix from the schoolroom and the catechism from the syllabus (hence the slogan 'école sans Dieu') caused positive anguish. The discovery that protestants were disproportionately represented among the students being prepared in the new *écoles normales* to take on the role of the teaching orders merely accentuated the spiritual anxieties of the catholic peasantry.

The political reaction marked by five years of anti-clerical legislation was manifested at the polls in 1885. To the astonishment of republican politicians the right-wing parties staged an electoral comeback. In the first round of balloting conservative candidates were returned in droves and while the republicans retrieved the situation in the second round, they lost control of thirteen departments. The Ardèche, the Aveyron and the Lozère were among this number for in the southern Massif Central republican sentiment tended to be localised and numerically weak and the reversion to a list system of voting within departmental constituencies (as in 1848 and 1871) produced

[35] A.N. F[17] 9255 *Inspection générale de 1880*: Aveyron.
[36] A.N. F[7] 12313 Prefect Aveyron to Minister of the Interior, Rodez, 3 September 1880.
[37] A.N. F[19] 12317 J.-B. Monteils, deputy for Lozère, to Minister of the Interior, Paris, 15 November 1880.
[38] A.N. F[7] 12313 Prefect Aveyron to Minister of the Interior, Rodez, 3 September 1880.

the worst possible results for the regime. In the Ardèche, list voting released the conservative majorities of the mountains and the north of the department to crush the radicalism of the *arrondissement* of Privas. In the Aveyron, the electoral muscle of the Aubrac and the ségala overwhelmed the republican citadels of Decazeville, Villefranche-de-Rouergue and Millau, while in the Lozère the catholic peasantry of the Margeride out-voted the protestant peasantry of the Cévennes. Only the broad-based support for the Republic in the Brivadois and the neighbourhood of Le Puy preserved the Haute-Loire from a conservative landslide, but narrowly, for the Right took 49.5 per cent of the popular vote.[39]

The electoral debacle of 1885 marked an important political watershed in the region. It ensured that the founding struggle for the Republic (as opposed to Gambetta's 'organic and creative period') would endure a further eight years. In the context of this study the sociological implications of the 1885 ballot should not be overlooked either. It marked the culminating point of a cycle within the broader process of integration which had commenced with the laicisation campaign. In most of the region the contest precipitated an electoral mobilisation on the scale of 1877 (see table IX.3). To be sure, the initiation was to electoral politics and not to the republic, but once the peasantry grasped the point of democratic politics there was no knowing where it might be led. The major responsibility for this signal development must be ascribed to the hierarchy of the catholic church. Since 1848 virtually all governments of whatever political hue had considered it their duty to offer guidance to voters at election times, but the church had hesitated – even in 1877 – to exert to the full its authority in this domain. By 1885 the ultra-montane bishops of the southern Massif Central considered that the fate of the catholic faith itself was at stake and felt justified in commenting on the approaching elections in the most uncompromising and unmistakable tone. Thus church and state conspired jointly to nationalise politics by lecturing the peasant elector on his rights and duties. On the eve of the first ballot *La Semaine Religieuse du Diocèse du Puy-en-Velay* which was edited by a team of ecclesiastical journalists and distributed in every parish urged: 'Votez donc sans abstention. S'absentir, dit M[onsei]g[neu]r Lavigerie [archbishop of Algiers], ce serait trahir sa foi, ou, pour employer une expression plus française encore, ce serait déserter devant l'ennemi.'[40] And as hopes rose in anticipation of the second ballot: 'Electeurs catholiques, vous voterez donc, vous voterez tous, vous voterez en catholiques, sous l'œil de Dieu qui vous voit, au nom de l'Eglise, qui vous le commande, et pour la France qui l'attend.'[41] The point could easily be extended for the electoral contest was

[39] Rivet, *La Vie politique*, pp. 78–9.
[40] *La Semaine Religieuse du Diocèse du Puy-en-Velay*, 2 October 1885.
[41] *Ibid.*, 16 October 1885.

Table IX.3 *Electoral mobilisation (Legislative elections, 1871–93)*

Department	1871			1876			1877		
	A	B	C	A	B	C	A	B	C
Ardèche	115,623	73,015	63.16	109,052	80,117*	73.45	110,360	91,686	83.08
Aveyron	118,742	65,678	55.31	112,325	85,457*	76.08	115,012	90,123	78.36
Haute-Loire	—	—	—	78,902	62,084*	78.68	82,781	65,357	78.95
Lozère	—	25,502	—	37,507	27,809*	74.14	37,906	31,061	81.94
France	—	—	—	9,696,461	7,367,275*	75.97	9,948,070	8,012,714	80.55

Key:
A   Registered voters.
B   Votes cast *minus* blank and spoilt ballot papers (*suffrages exprimés*).
C   Percentage turn-out.
*   Votes cast *including* blank and spoilt ballot papers (*votants*).

fought out within multi-member constituencies which, republicans had long insisted, focused attention on issues rather than personalities. Unfortunately the conservative candidates had the pick of the slogans and if rural voters trudged to the polls with thoughts of 'l'école sans Dieu' or the 'massacre of Tonkin' in their minds, it was because the church had planted them there.

Officials on the spot cannot have been too surprised by the verdict of the polls. The debate over the Ferry laws had echoed disconcertingly in the elections for the *conseils-généraux* held in August 1883 and more particularly in the municipal elections of May 1884 which were destined to influence the composition of the Senate. Increasingly, broader issues were blurring the old particularisms. The seepage of ideology or the fusing of local preoccupations and nation-wide categories of debate is exemplified in the tensions which divided the commune of Borée (Ardèche)[42] between 1881 and 1884. The village of Borée was situated a little above the 1,100 metres contour on the southern flank of Mont Mézenc, that is to say on the Velay–Vivarais plateau which officials of the prefecture generally regarded as beyond political redemption. Nevertheless, under the leadership of an energetic mayor a new municipality was installed in 1881 which the sub-prefect of Tournon subsequently labelled as 'republican'. Just how republican the new administration was at this juncture remains unclear, but it was soon judged by its actions, for Pouzet, the mayor, became involved in a dispute with the curate over the boundaries of his garden which resulted in the latter's redeployment. This minor, but ominous, skirmish prepared the ground for a full-scale confrontation between the civil and the spiritual power when Charreyre, the parish priest, launched a stinging pulpit attack on parents who sent their offspring to the lay primary school in the village. During the reprisals that followed the Borée affair became an important issue of principle. The government cast the villagers in the role of stout-hearted defenders of republican

[42]   For a file on the Borée affair, see A.D. Ard. 2M698 also V141.

	1881			1885			1889			1893	
A	B	C	A	B	C	A	B	C	A	B	C
112,815	76,930	68.19	111,845	87,930	78.62	113,792	93,445	82.12	112,074	82,695	76.38
117,815	92,375	78.41	118,271	94,030	79.50	118,667	96,463	81.29	116,374	90,017	77.35
86,256	61,057	70.79	86,968	70,326	80.86	89,600	64,038	71.47	89,945	65,618	72.95
40,497	25,710	63.49	38,719	31,318	80.88	38,753	30,487	78.67	37,976	29,316	77.20
10,124,830	6,944,531	68.59	10,181,095	7,896,062	77.56	10,689,592	7,977,447	74.63	10,446,178	7,427,354	71.10

Sources: M.-T. and A. Lancelot, *Atlas des circonscriptions électorales en France depuis 1875* (Paris, 1970); H. Avenel, *Comment vote la France. Dix-huit ans de suffrage universel, 1876–93* (Paris, 1894); E. Duguet, *Les Députés et les cahiers électoraux de 1889* (Paris, n.d.); P. Goumain-Cornille and R. Martin, *Les Cahiers électoraux de 1881* (Paris, 1882); *Annuaire Statistique de la France: 1881* (Paris, 1881); A.N. C3448; C3452; C3466.

democracy marooned in a wilderness of clerico-royalism, while bishop Bonnet made unscrupulous use of his spiritual authority in order to force the villagers into a posture of submission.

In March 1883 the Minister of the Interior withheld Charreyre's ecclesiastical stipend and the bishop riposted by withdrawing the priest altogether. For the next fifteen months the celebration of Mass ceased at Borée and in May 1884 the provision of the sacraments for the dying also terminated. With a fresh municipal election called for the month of May, Bonnet clearly hoped that Pouzet and his team would be turned out. In the event a riot disrupted polling. The electoral urn was smashed and the electoral list torn to pieces. The duel between the authorities and the spiritual privations of the local population continued throughout the summer, therefore, until September when the hustings were reconvened. Each side girded itself for the contest and all attention was fixed on Borée. The Republic issued warnings and made promises; the bishop dangled the prospect of a replacement for Charreyre enticingly, and the squabble over the curate's garden was patched up. In a long letter to the prefect from which the bulk of our knowledge of the affair is derived, the sub-prefect of Tournon summarised the position: 'Si, par suite de l'absence d'un desservant, M. Pouzet n'était pas réélu, son échec semblerait démontrer, dans cette partie de l'arrondissement, qu'un maire, alors même qu'il est soutenu par ses chefs administratifs, ne peut pas lutter contre un curé appuyé par l'Evêque.'[43] On the eve of polling a squadron of gendarmes took up positions in the village, while the sub-prefect discreetly stationed himself in the nearby *bourg* of St Martin-de-Valamas in case of need. Amid tense and disciplined balloting the clerical list carried the day and Pouzet was thrown out.

Incidents such as the Borée affair, coupled with the dramatic reversal of political fortunes worked by the general election of October 1885, exasper-

[43] A.D. Ard. 2M698 Sub-prefect Tournon to prefect Ardèche, Tournon, 16 July 1884.

ated the republicans and produced demands for more aggressive government interventionism. All over the southern Massif Central subaltern officials set to work collating and documenting instances of clerical meddling. Allegations of more or less explicit electioneering by members of the clergy poured into the prefectures. One hundred and seven instances were cited in the department of the Aveyron alone.[44] Allegations of government complicity in the massacre of '24,000 chrétiens au Tonkin' had done serious harm to the Republic in the Ardèche, while in the mixed *bourg* of Vals (Ardèche)[45] a handbill urging catholic republican voters to expunge from their ballot slips the names of three protestant candidates was brought to light. In Rodez and Viviers retreats had been organised prior to the elections which large numbers of parish clergy attended. Moreover, bishop Bourret prescribed special prayers for the Feast of the Rosary throughout the month of October in a 'mandement' which was read out in every parish church on the morning of the first ballot. How much weight we should attach to such facts is questionable, however, for the civil authorities were falling victim to their own propaganda. Sane assessment of the extent of clerical intervention yielded before a paranoid desire to explain every single vote cast for conservative candidates in terms of 'ingérence cléricale'. Debating whether the *curé* of Colombiès should be disciplined, the prefect of the Aveyron remarked in a letter to the minister that,

les renseignements que j'avais recueillis jusqu'ici sur le compte de cet ecclésiastique ne lui étaient pas défavorables, mais en présence des résultats de la com[mu]ne de Colombiès, où les candidats réactionnaires ont obtenu 431 voix contre 57 données aux candidats républicains, écart qui ne peut être attribué qu'à l'influence du clergé, je fais prendre un supplément d'informations sur l'attitude de M. Maurel au cours de la période électorale.[46]

Civic denunciation on the model, if not the scale, of the Year Two (1793–4), came back into fashion in the late autumn of 1885 and it is likely that many of the scores of priests deprived of their stipends by way of punishment were guilty of quite trivial offences which would not have attracted comment in quieter times.

By far the sanest assessment of the debacle issued from the anonymous pen of a correspondent of the Paris daily *Le Temps*.[47] Writing from Rodez a matter of days after the second ballot, he drew attention to the fact that the 1885 election had given expression to a massive realignment of conservative opinion in the department of the Aveyron. After discussion with interested parties he offered two interrelated explanations of the result: revulsion against the 'lois Ferry' and a crisis of confidence in the durability of the

---

[44] A.N. F[19] 5930 Prefect Aveyron to *Ministre des Cultes*, Rodez, 12 November 1885.
[45] A.D. Ard. 2M351 *Aux électeurs républicains* (n.d.).
[46] A.N. F[19] 3017 Prefect Aveyron to *Ministre des Cultes*, Rodez, 24 October 1885.
[47] A.N. F[19] 5930 *Enquête électorale: département de l'Aveyron*, Rodez, 30 October 1885.

regime. The impact of the laicisation measures can be taken for granted, but the malaise which eroded support for the Republic went deeper and calls for further discussion. The crisis, it seems, was one of authority: 'le paysan aveyronnais est essentiellement administratif. Il a toujours voté dans le sens gouvernemental, avec une régularité et une constance remarquables.' Why had this instinctive regimism faltered in 1885? Because the regime had failed to exert itself with sufficient vigour, even aggression, during the electoral campaign. Supposing that the conservative parties no longer possessed the capacity to endanger the Republic, ministers had encouraged their subordinates to drop their militant guard. Local officials and public functionaries made a show of impartiality. Meanwhile, new laws on the press and public meetings in 1881 and the Municipal Charter of 1884 marked a considerable retreat by the state from the role of electoral *dirigisme*. The peasant voter waited in vain for a *mot d'ordre* from the prefect and in its absence fell victim to the sedulously propagated illusion that the 'bon parti' would shortly be taking over the reins of government. A vote for the Right became a vote for conscience *and* for jobs.

The parents who besieged the *instituteurs* and *institutrices* on the morrow of the elections in the expectation that the catechism would be restored to the school curriculum succeeded only in demonstrating the extreme political naivety of the peasant electorate.[48] 1885 was a local, not a national, victory and even that proved shortlived. The republican majority in the Chamber voted to annul the results in the Ardèche, the Lozère and three other departments which had returned conservative slates on the pretext of 'inadmissable' clerical intervention and corruption. Fresh elections were called for February 1886 and this time the Republic made no mistake: the voters of the Ardèche and the Lozère were induced to repudiate the deputies whom they had elected only four months earlier. A full description of the 'admissible' forms of government intervention and corruption which produced this *volte-face* must await our final section. In truth, both the republicans and their opponents used tactics of the most unprincipled opportunism in order to sway the electorate. The prefects manipulated employees of state with all the cynicism of their Moral Order and Bonapartist forebears, while the *évêché* of Mende circulated a notorious *Catéchisme de l'électeur* which provided unambiguous answers to such questions as 'Y a-t-il obligation de bien voter?'; 'Serait ce donc une faute grave que de voter mal?' and 'Un électeur est-il donc obligé de se confesser d'avoir mal voté?'[49]

If the shock of 1885 and the hollow victories of 1886 did little to settle the ultimate political complexion of the region, they did at least clear away a number of misconceptions which had hitherto clouded the republican electoral effort. Since the peasantry of these uplands would not come naturally to

[48] A.D.L. IVM⁴24 Minute of prefectoral report, Mende, 14 February 1886.
[49] *Ibid.*, *Catéchisme de l'électeur: de l'obligation de bien voter* (n.d.).

that nebulous entity which called itself the Republic, a tangible and militant Republic must come to them. 'Quand donc le gouvernement républicain aura-t-il la force de se faire respecter de ses adversaires, non pas qu'on veuille les terroriser, mais au moins faudrait-il leur faire comprendre que la maison n'est plus à eux'[50] enquired a village radical of the Ardèche in 1880. His question passed largely unanswered until the later 1880s when a determined attempt was made to establish a permanent republican presence in the countryside by means of *comités* and *cercles*. But the *réseau* of these latter-day jacobin clubs was desperately thin and it could scarcely compete with the organisational scope of the catholic church. In 1889 the clergy again mounted an electoral campaign which vindicated conservative strength in the Aveyron and wiped out many of the republican gains of 1885–6 in the Ardèche, Haute-Loire and the Lozère. The prefects seemed agreed that clerical meddling had increased since 1885 with younger priests aged under forty chiefly to blame. In the Aveyron bishop Bourret earned oblique praise for his refusal to exploit Boulangism, but Bonnet in the Ardèche had allowed his clergy to give the General discreet support ('non sans doute par sympathie pour lui, mais pour faire échec à la candidature républicaine')[51] during a by-election held in July 1888, and the following year a Boulangist candidate was elected with clerical support in the *arrondissement* of Largentière.

The Lozère remained the great redoubt of clerico-Legitimist politics, however. Bishop Costes retired in 1888 and was replaced by François Baptifolier who hesitated to allow his clergy to openly attack the Republic from the pulpit. But in this ancient fief of the count-bishops of Mende the confessional was a more effective weapon than the pulpit and the clergy made voting a 'cas de conscience'. And lest any elector mistook his duty, the *Catéchisme de l'électeur* reappeared and was printed in local clerical press organs. By the end of the century piety alone could not win elections, however. The survival of royalist electoral hopes relied heavily upon the willingness of a class of *hobereaux* and wealthier landowners to use their resources in a cause which most observers considered lost since the death of the Comte de Chambord. In 1889 the successful conservative candidates in the *arrondissements* of Mende and Marvejols had each lubricated the wheels of piety and deference to the tune of approximately 25,000 f. according to a prefectoral estimate. Such sums reflected the escalating costs of elections in the 1880s as the Republic perfected its strategy of patronage. Bernard Anatole de Colombet[52] was typical of this class of backwoods royalists. A country gentleman with a bent for agricultural experimentation, he was elected to the National Assembly in 1871 as a member for the Lozère. In a body of incorrigibly conservative parliamentarians he nonetheless stood out as an uncompromising royalist and

---

[50] A.D. Ard. 5M41 E. Julliers to prefect Ardèche, St André-de-Cruzières, 10 May 1880.
[51] A.N. F[19] 2596 Extract from a report by *procureur général* of Nîmes, 27 July 1888.
[52] Masseguin, 'Les Parlementaires royalistes lozériens de 1815 à 1893', pp. 85–9.

was compared with the Comte René de Bernis – the illustrious Ultra-Royalist who had represented the Lozère during the Restoration. Colombet retreated to the Senate between 1876 and 1879, but stood again for the Chamber in 1885 only to be disqualified along with the other successful candidates and beaten in the re-scheduled elections of 1886. Three years later he both won and held the seat for the *arrondissement* of Mende taking nearly 60 per cent of the vote despite a strong republican challenger, but this proved the last occasion on which an undisguised Legitimist sat in the Chamber as a member for the Lozère. In 1893 the peasantry backed his republican opponent, Maurice Bourrillon, who was a commoner, a doctor and very much a symbol of the new political order.[53]

Acquiescence: the 'milch cow' state

In 1906 the *comité d'action républicaine* of Sainte Colombe-de-Peyre (Lozère) criticised their mayor for privately referring to the Republic as 'une bonne vache à lait dont il faut tirer tout ce qu'on peut, quitte à lui donner ensuite le coup de pied à la première occasion'.[54] The mayor of another village in the Lozère expressed the same sentiment more politely: 'la commune de St Léger-de-Peyre ne peut être que démocratique et républicaine d'abord parce qu'elle est très pauvre et ensuite parce qu'elle a sans cesse recours aux libéralités de l'Etat pour les inondations qui ont lieu sur son territoire accidenté'.[55] By implication, then, the population of the southern Massif Central were won for the Republic by a process of attrition which progressively detached them from their old cultural moorings and incorporated them within a broader polity. The principal casualty in this process was the church – the institutional church – not the faith, for the peasantry adjusted its electoral stance while maintaining the highest standards of public piety. The battles of the 1880s fuelled demands for the abrogation of the Concordat which followed within two decades. The catholic church had effectively curtailed the first experiment in republican democracy in the 1790s. It had striven successfully to seal off large areas of the southern Massif Central from renewed contamination upon the proclamation of the Second Republic in 1848. In the 1880s it met its match: an avowedly liberal regime which was prepared to use the coercive power at its disposal unblushingly. Above all, a regime able to wield the carrot as well as the stick. What distinguished the founding fathers of the Third Republic from their illustrious forebears who

---

[53] G. Géraud, *Notes sur cent ans d'histoire en Lozère (XIXe et XXe siècles)*, p. 11; A. Runel, 'Opinion, mentalités, idéologie: le traditionalisme en Lozère (1930–45) d'après les almanachs locaux' (Université de Paris I, Mémoire de Maîtrise, 1973–4), p. 13.

[54] A.D.L. VIM10 10 *Comité d'action républicaine* of Sainte Colombe-de-Peyre to sub-prefect Marvejols, Sainte Colombe-de-Peyre, 16 June 1906.

[55] A.D.L. IVM⁴25 Mayor (?) St Léger-de-Peyre to prefect Lozère, St Léger-de-Peyre, 4 November 1889.

had launched the First Republic was not the use of terror tactics to secure political compliance for this was a matter of degree, but the ample pecuniary resources of state. In building roads and railways, in purging patois and the catechism from the schoolroom, in resisting the theocratic tendencies of an unbridled clergy, the republicans shattered the cultural universe of the peasantry beyond repair. But at the same time they wooed the peasant elector with flattering attention, with a thousand trifling subsidies and with the enticing prospect of signing on to the pay-roll of state.

The bureaucratisation of village life proceeded apace in the final decades of the nineteenth century. Reliable statistics are scarce, but France enjoyed the reputation of being the most bureaucratic state in Europe in 1848 with the Ministry of the Interior alone employing 203,000 individuals.[56] The big-spending departments of state – Public Works, Finances, Cultes and Education – were chiefly responsible for the growing army of salaried officials. Between 1869 and 1887 the budget of the Ministry of Education rose from 38 million francs to 170 million francs.[57] Plentiful anecdotal evidence exists to suggest that impoverished mountain villages regarded the pullulating ranks of officialdom as a considerable economic blessing. Among the fifteen-hundred-odd inhabitants of the *bourg* of Le Pont-de-Montvert (Lozère)[58] in the 1890s we find one protestant pastor, one priest, four male teachers, two female teachers, three road menders, two tax collectors, one forest guard, three policemen and two postmen. All were state employees and their collective spending power generously compensated for the decline in local craft industry. Indeed, by the 1880s, announcements of newly created posts in the Civil Service featured regularly in the public prints and it is permitted to ask whether bureaucratisation had become an instrument of policy. Senators, deputies and prefects certainly relied on the governments of the day to maintain a steady flow of spoils and favours. On reading reports of new openings in the state agency for children in care ('de nouveaux emplois d'inspecteurs et sous-inspecteurs des enfants assistés'),[59] the prefect of the Ardèche wasted no time in submitting his recommendations.

The enviable security of a toe-hold in the bureaucracy had been regarded as the fitting reward for unstinting political loyalty ever since the time of the Parisian *sans-culottes*, but never before had a regime sought to purchase support in such a blatant fashion. Never before in this region had a republican regime successfully challenged the power of the notables. Hitherto the authority of the notables had derived from two sources: the delegated authority of government and the subscribed authority of the peasantry. With the system

[56] Kent, *Electoral Procedure under Louis Philippe*, p. 125.
[57] G. d'Avenel, 'L'Extension du fonctionnarisme depuis 1870', *Revue des deux mondes* (1 March 1888), 102.
[58] Higonnet, *Pont-de-Montvert*, p. 105.
[59] A.D. Ard. 5M40 Cabinet of prefect Ardèche to *Monsieur le Sous-Directeur* (?), Privas, 14 August 1879.

of political clientage pioneered by the Opportunists threatening to outbid them in the electoral arena, the notables found themselves confronted with a stark choice. They could continue to resist and risk political and social extinction or they could come to terms with the regime and regroup on the right of the republican spectrum, alongside the Opportunists whose ardour for reform would shortly cool. Most chose the latter course and the death of Chambord in 1883, followed by the first timid steps towards the creation of a catholic centre party, made the compromise easier than it might have been. Thus, while de Colombet's royalist convictions were widely respected, his political stance and public utterances were already an anachronism by 1893. For the old dynasties the future lay in frank acceptance of the Republic as the regime desired by the vast majority of Frenchmen. Even as de Colombet was defeated, a *rallié* nobleman and bearer of an illustrious name, Eugène Melchior de Vogüé, was elected in the Ardèche.[60]

Like the peasantry, the notables also responded to the imperatives of regimism in the final analysis. But this development could scarcely have been predicted and the Republic took steps to cultivate a political elite of its own. Gambetta's 'new social strata' figured prominently in this republican vanguard and yet the phrase is apt to mislead for there was nothing fundamentally new about the doctors, veterinary surgeons, pharmacists, notaries, functionaries and businessmen who aligned themselves with the regime at an early date. All were drawn from the ample ranks of the proprietorial bourgeoisie which had emerged from the shadow of the nobility in the eighteenth century and acquired a vocation for state service in 1789. While striking examples of imperturbable republicanism handed on from father to son have been recorded,[61] among Calvinists especially, most members of the proprietorial bourgeoisie were political chameleons. The republican zealots of the 1870s and 1880s tended to come from old rather than new families and to have Bonapartist fathers and Orleanist grandfathers. What is noticeable, however, is the retreat of rentiers, and more especially of noble rentiers, from positions of local influence. This development is often associated with the definitive democratisation of municipal government between 1882 and 1884 – the so-called 'revolution of the *mairies*' – but it did not wait upon the event. In the Haute-Loire,[62] which was the first of the southern Massif Central departments to rally to the Republic, the conservative parties lost control of the municipalities in the early 1870s: a fact underlined by their failure to ensure the election of a single conservative senator either in 1876 or 1879. In the Lozère, by contrast, analysis of the composition of the *conseil-général*

---

[60] A. Coront-Ducluzeau, 'Une Election mémorable: le vicomte E.-M. de Vogüé, député de l'Ardèche (1893–1898)', *Revue du Vivarais*, lxxiii (1969), 177–89.

[61] See above, chapter six, pp. 211–12. Also Jones, 'Political Commitment and Rural Society in the Southern Massif Central', pp. 348–50.

[62] A. Rivet, 'L'Image de la Droite (1871–1881)', *Cahiers de la Haute-Loire*, (1979), 187.

Table IX.4 *Social composition of the* conseil-général *of the Lozère at the end of the nineteenth century*

	1875	1881	1890	1900
Doctors, lawyers and barristers	8	9	9	10
Rentiers (noble and non-noble)	12	13	7	8
Magistrates, judges	4	1	1	3
Merchants, industrialists	0	1	1	0
Public functionaries, civil engineers	0	0	3	3
'Noms à particules (titled individuals)'	9	7	4	3

Source: G. Géraud, *Notes sur cent ans d'histoire en Lozère (XIXe et XXe siècles)* (Mende, 1969), p. 14.

suggests that the retreat of the titled and the rise of the professions was barely perceptible before the 1880s (see table IX.4).

Doctors, particularly, had a reputation for radicalism stretching back to the Revolution and it comes as no surprise to find them disproportionately represented in the republican movement. Who better to organise a system of political patronage than a professional group whose *métier* presupposed an extensive and submissive clientele. Reporting the lone republican success of the philanthropic physician, Théophile Roussel, in the elections of 1871, the prefect of the Lozère recalled: 'J'avais dit l'autre jour au ministre que tout ce qu'on pouvait espérer dans la Lozère c'était la nomination de M[onsieu]r Roussel, non parce que mais quoique républicain.'[63] Engineers constituted a more recent professional category, however. Their status rose in step with expenditure on road and rail communications in the second half of the nineteenth century and they came to be looked upon as a new breed of inter-cessors with privileged access to government. In some respects they were reminiscent of the politically committed 'experts' of the 1790s who parcelled the *biens nationaux* for auction and assisted the peasantry to divide up the commons. Conscious of their electoral appeal, local republican caucuses fre-quently selected engineers to run against conservative candidates. The manifesto of the Ministry of Public Works engineer, Léon Boyer, whom the Comité Républicain de Marvejols (Lozère) put up to contest the elections of 1885 dwelt long on the blessings which Boyer had already bestowed on the *arrondissement* and might yet bestow. What better choice for deputy than an

enfant du pays, que vous connaissez tous, qui a déjà rendu de grands services dans la Lozère en faisant construire toutes les lignes de chemin de fer de notre arrondissement. Il peut en rendre de plus grands encore si, aux influences qu'il s'est déjà acquises par son mérite incontestable et les fonctions qu'il a remplies auprès du Ministère etc. etc.[64]

[63] A.N. C3452 *Elections législatives*, 1871 Telegraphic message of prefect Lozère to Minister of the Interior, Mende, 9 February 1871.
[64] A.N. C4524 *Eléctions législatives*, 1885 *Le comité républicain de Marvejols aux électeurs de la Lozère.*

Creeping bureaucratisation and the emergence of a pioneer corps of republican notables enjoying the confidence of government were necessary preliminary steps towards the creation of a 'milch cow' state. After the political tergiversations of the 1870s and the unanticipated reverse of 1885, the Opportunists resolved upon a policy of firm measures to destroy the influence of their right-wing opponents. This policy consisted of a mixture of threats and bribery: adversaries were intimidated and the hesitant, the uncommitted and the apathetic were wooed simultaneously. The coercive features of the republican onslaught can be summarised in one word: *fiches*. In the 1880s the apparatus of 'la féodalité radicale' more commonly associated with the period of the Combes Ministry (1902–5) was introduced to the departments of the southern Massif Central. Republican *comités*, village schoolmasters and other trustees compiled detailed statements of the political proclivities of their neighbours in reply to prefectoral enquiries couched in the following terms: 'Privas, le [blank] 188 [blank]; Monsieur [blank], J'ai l'honneur de vous prier de bien vouloir me faire parvenir, le plustôt possible, des renseignements sur la conduite privée, la situation de fortune et de famille, les antécédents, l'attitude et l'opinion politiques de M. [blank].'[65] Delegates were posted to keep an eye on 'reactionary' mayors; secret agents reported on the hustings; political files were opened on every state employee. These techniques of surveillance had all been used during the revolutionary Terror. Indeed, there is a striking resemblance between the *tableaux* of suspects compiled by the *comités de surveillance* in 1794 and the *fiches* compiled by the republican *comités* in the 1880s. None of these underhand manoeuvres was unique to the Left, however. During the period of Moral Order the Right used nearly identical tactics in order to intimidate the opposition. What marked out the Opportunist onslaught was the scale of the inquisition and the self-righteousness with which it was conducted.

The Lozère and the Ardèche bore the brunt of government interventionism, for once the results of the 1885 elections in these departments had been set aside the prefects moved heaven and earth to ensure a republican victory. As far as we can tell memoranda and notes giving details of the balance of the parties were submitted for virtually every commune in the Lozère. By 1889 these notes had become institutionalised and were drafted on proforma sheets headed 'Liste des personnes notoirement républicaines'. In the protestant Cévennes where the Republic enjoyed mass support these 'listes' could be lengthy and complex documents. Thus we find the vital details of over a hundred republicans recorded at Meyrueis[66] which tend, incidentally, to confirm the impression that politics, like religion, was a family tradition within the Calvinist community. Informants in some other protestant communes chose the easier task of listing opponents of the regime under a revised

[65] A.D. Ard. 5M43.
[66] A.D.L. IVM⁴25 *Elections législatives*, 1889 *Listes des personnes notoirement républicaines*.

rubric in which the word 'républicaines' was crossed out and replaced with 'réactionnaires'. Few such *fiches* have survived in the Ardèche, for in this department the repression seems to have been concerted in Paris with republican deputies and senators playing the leading role. Powerful 'barons' such as François-Antoine Boissy d'Anglas and Camille Vielfaure kept the prefecture busy with a constant stream of letters written on Chamber of Deputies or Senate notepaper urging the dismissal, transfer or promotion of this or that schoolmaster, postman, road mender and so on.[67]

When local repression missed its mark the argument shifted to Paris in any case. The Chamber of Deputies, in common with earlier legislative bodies, reserved to itself the right to examine the credentials of its members and in the 1870s and 1880s this power was abused to annul the elections of members whose political affiliations were unacceptable to the majority. In 1876 a republican house challenged about forty elections and rid itself of ten monarchist or Bonapartist opponents in this fashion; after the bitter confrontation of October 1877 over 130 elections were challenged and 77 conservative *élus* required to seek a fresh mandate; in 1881 fifteen elections failed to pass muster and eight were eventually cancelled; in 1885 the election results of five departments were set aside in their entirety; in 1889 fifty results were challenged and fourteen Boulangist candidates numbered among those weeded out.[68] The breaking of elections on the ground that government interventionism had failed while opposition interventionism had succeeded only too well, had, in short, become a weapon of policy. A weapon, moreover, whose effects were profoundly demoralising, for the republicans concentrated their fire on the recalcitrant departments of the southern Massif Central and the Breton peninsula where the clergy continued to incite the peasantry to a posture of resistance. What was the point of following the *curé* to the polls if the resultant victory of the conservative candidate was likely to be set aside on the flimsiest of pretexts? What, indeed, was the point of pursuing a feud which placed the voter, his household, his kinsmen and perhaps the entire village beyond the pale of government patronage.

Government patronage was, of course, the pendant to the policy of coercion. The strategy was summarised by the *secrétaire de mairie* of a small commune in the Lozère who announced that he conducted the affairs of the locality on the principle of 'La justice à tout le monde, les faveurs aux amis de la République'.[69] What this suspect dichotomy amounted to in practice was electoral corruption. Whether the concept of corruption means much in this context is debatable, however. The Republic simply paid out small sums to its supporters while denying political enemies access to the cornucopia of funds

[67] See A.D. Ard. 5M41.
[68] J.-P. Charnay, *Les Scrutins politiques en France de 1815 à 1962: contestations et invalidations* (Cahiers de la Fondation nationale des sciences politiques, Paris, 1964), pp. 80–94.
[69] A.D.L. IIIM^{5}5 Delon, *instituteur*, to prefect Lozère, Montredon, 29 October 1893.

and favours. It made no bones about the fact and the precedents were by no means one-sided. Subsidies were generally disbursed by the prefects on the recommendation of subaltern officials and in the form of compensation for cattle loss, storm-damage and other accidents to which peasant farming was prone. However, not all victims of cattle disease, lightning, hail and flood succeeded in attracting the attention of government. Nor, it seems, were all those receiving relief bona fide applicants. Performance in the polling station determined the fate of the great majority of claims. Thus Bonnet, *adjoint* of the commune of Ribennes (Lozère), wrote to the prefect two days after the re-scheduled legislative election of 1886 with the news that the republican candidates had emerged with a narrow lead. 'Mes administrés', he added, 'ont fait un grand nombre de demandes de secours pour pertes de bestiaux. Je me propose de vous signaler ceux qui méritent les faveurs du Gouvernement.'[70] Nearly identical letters arrived on the prefect's desk from other communes of the *arrondissement* of Mende.

Institutionalised venality underpinned the republican electoral effort in 1889, too. The mayor of Salelles (Lozère) terminated his list of 'notorious republicans' with the observation: 'Je compte que cette liste servira dans la distribution de secours aux inondés, en accordant une large part à ceux des réclamants qui y figurent; ce sera là le meilleur moyen que je connaisse pour faire ouvrir les yeux aux autres, d'autant plus qu'avant les élections, je leur disais assez qu'ils n'auraient aucun secours si la commune ne fournissait pas une majorité républicaine'.[71] How much money was expended in this fashion is difficult to judge, but an undated scrap of paper emanating from the prefecture of the Lozère makes for interesting reading. On one side it is inscribed: 'Pour M. Valentin, huissier, avec prière de communiquer à Monsieur Pelisse [republican deputy in the *arrondissement* of Marvejols between 1881–5 and 1886–9] et aux autres personnes intéressées [signed].' On the other: 'Sommes accordées ou sur le point d'être allouées, pour pertes de bestiaux dans la C[ommu]ne de St Amans.' There follows a list of eighty names (three subsequently crossed out) with varying sums recorded against each and totalling 430 *f*. And in conclusion the remark: 'Ces sommes ne seront mandatées qu'après les élections.'[72] The document bears the stamp of Maître Hermantier, *avocat* of Mende.

Most of the evidence detailing the extent of venality in the 1880s comes from the Lozère, but this seems to reflect the uneven quality of our source material rather than eccentric policies pursued by the prefecture at Mende. Officials in all four departments faced similar problems and they tended to cope with them in similar ways. In any case, the distribution of pecuniary incentives under the guise of compensation was only one of a number of

---

[70] A.D.L. IVM⁴24 Bonnet, *adjoint*, to prefect Lozère, Ribennes, 16 February 1886.
[71] A.D.L. IVM⁴25 Mayor Salelles to prefect Lozère, Salelles, 11 December 1889.
[72] A.D.L. IVM⁴25.

inducements available to 'le parti du manche (the party in power)'. Much of the daily postbag of senators, deputies, prefects, *conseillers-généraux* and other potential patrons consisted of petitions requesting jobs, transfers, promotions, pensions and a thousand and one different exemptions involving the bending of the rules by someone in authority. This vast reservoir of administrative discretion was tapped by the Opportunists in a determined effort to drive home the political lesson that the old notables in alliance with the church could no longer compete with the state in the exercise of patronage. For example, the burden of compulsory military service was almost universally resented in the southern Massif Central and the republicans skilfully exploited the scope of the law to ensure that sons with household responsibilities escaped conscription. Charles Seignobos, the long-serving republican deputy for the Ardèche who narrowly defeated a monarchist opponent in a by-election in April 1890 wrote enthusiastically to the prefect: 'Je prends la liberté de venir vous recommander quelques demandes de soutiens de famille très-intéressantes . . . il y en a deux *d'absolument indispensables* . . . 3 de *nécessaires* . . . une de très *utile*.'[73] Boissy d'Anglas entertained the long-suffering prefect of the Ardèche to a long correspondence on this subject, too. The object of his solicitations was the son of a veteran republican, 'un des rares de la commune de Saint André-des-Effrangeas'. Gounon *père*, the militant in question, could play a crucial role in the forthcoming elections reasoned Boissy: 'je n'ai jamais eu dans cette commune que 3 ou 4 voix contre 250. Si je pouvais obtenir le retour de son fils [from the army] cette faveur le stimulerait et produirait bon effet sur ces paysans en leur prouvant qu'ils ont intérêt à se mettre du côté de la République.'[74] In this matter the perspicacious deputy met his match, however, for the colonel-in-charge politely resisted the suggestion that he should release Gounon *fils*. The politicisation of the Army waited upon the arrival of the Radicals in power.

But few areas of national life escaped the attention of the Opportunists. Even the tax authorities bowed to political pressure. A few days before the legislative elections of 1889 Albert Fabre, a licensee of Lablachère (Ardèche), informed his deputy that he had been fined a large sum for alleged irregularities concerning the sale of liquor. The wheels were set in motion and within a fortnight a generous compromise had been reached. Fabre's fine was reduced from 585 *f.* 55 *c.* to 40 *f.* plus costs, 'en raison de l'intervention de l'honorable Vielfaure'.[75] The church and the great Legitimist proprietors could not compete in this league, or at least, not for long. Their republican adversaries wasted no opportunity of reminding the electorate that a vote for the Right was a wasted vote in so far as roads, railways and jobs were con-

[73] A.D. Ard. 5M41 Seignobos to prefect Ardèche, Paris, 29 June 1891.
[74] *Ibid.*, Boissy d'Anglas to prefect Ardèche, Paris, 2 April 1889.
[75] *Ibid.*, *Premier commis* at *Direction des contributions indirectes* to prefect Ardèche, Privas, 25 September 1889.

cerned. There were signs, moreover, that the conservative camp realised as much. In a revealing pastoral letter[76] destined to be read out in all the parishes of the Ardèche in December 1885, bishop Bonnet chided the faithful for their lack of confidence in the future role of the church in a secular society. Families were hesitating before sending their children to be taught by the Frères and the Sœurs. Worse, families were using the Grand Seminary as an inexpensive secondary school for their sons only to divert them into lucrative civilian careers at the end of their training. For significant numbers of peasants in the poor villages of the uplands, 'getting on in life' had ceased to be synonymous with entering the church. This was why the issue of church schools bulked so large. The republicans condemned them on political grounds, but the bishops viewed them as nurseries of spiritual vocations, as barometers of the health of the church at large.

The apocalyptic urgency which men like Bonnet injected into the defence of the teaching orders proved misplaced for rural catholicism turned out to be far stronger than its institutional under-pinnings. Even so, the retreat – if not the defeat – of clericalism did not mark an unequivocal advance for the Republic. The peasantry slipped into a twilight world which lacked clear cultural and political landmarks. After a period of studied *attentisme* 'la république au village' triumphed, but the commitment to the politics of the national entity, like all forms of regimism, remained shallow, circumstantial and mercenary. In this region village republicanism never acquired the ideological buoyancy and autonomy of which steadfast political opinion is made. Nor, on the other hand, did it ever relinquish the primary link with personality, kinship and sect. Indeed, the word 'triumph' implies a transfer of allegiances altogether too grandiose and definitive. It would be more accurate to describe the Republic as having been launched in the 1880s. Sea trials were only just beginning and fresh clerical squalls were looming on the horizon. If the vessel survived at all, it did so because constant efforts were made to keep it afloat. Left to its own devices and deprived of outside stimulus, village republicanism quickly foundered.

This was the disheartening experience of the republicans of St Colombe-de-Peyre (Lozère) who conjured up two turbulent decades of village politics in a long and revealing epistle addressed to the sub-prefect of Marvejols. Their testimony has already received a passing mention at the beginning of this section. It is worth returning to for no other account captures more vividly the vicissitudes and ambiguities of republicanism at the grass roots. In St Colombe-de-Peyre a new age dawned in 1884 when two self-styled republicans won admission to the municipal council. At that time alignments simply reflected diverse attitudes towards the building of a communal school. Only Monsieur Fleisch, the *instituteur*, could be considered a convinced (that

---

[76] *Ibid.*, Pastoral letter of bishop of Viviers, 20 December 1885.

is, ideological) republican. Nonetheless, the elected mayor, Boissonade, pressed forward the building of the school and his political education likewise appeared to advance under the supervision of the schoolmaster. In 1887 the progressive minority in the council was unable to prevent the nomination of two conservative senatorial delegates, but with the renewal of 1888 three more republicans entered the council. Soon only one conservative municipal officer remained and the commune turned in solid majorities for the republican candidates in the parliamentary elections of 1889, 1893 and 1898. Republicans were despatched as delegates to the Senate elections, too. However, the steady political integration of the commune abruptly ceased in 1899 when a new *instituteur* took over the role of *secrétaire de mairie*. Mayor Boissonade began dining at the presbytery and in the legislative election of 1902 the clerical candidate took most of the votes. Then, in 1904, with the renewal of the municipality pending, Boissonade entered the lists at the head of a slate of 'reactionaries' which included 'tous les conseillers de fabrique qui furent autrefois ses mortels ennemis'. He could scarcely fail to win for all the conservatives gave him their support and also, 'bon nombre de républicains pour lesquels il incarnait l'idée républicaine et qui ne s'expliquèrent pas au premier abord ce brusque revirement. Seuls les plus clairvoyants evitèrent le piège.' Profiting from the immaturity of the electorate and the misplaced confidence of the prefecture, Boissonade succeeded in reconciling the irreconcilable. In 1906 he again mobilised support for the clerical candidate in the general election while plausibly insisting: 'c'est nous les amis du gouvernement, c'est nous qui avons le pouvoir, c'est nous qui sommes les dispensateurs de toutes les faveurs'.[77]

[77] A.D.L. VIM10 10 *Comité d'action républicaine* of Sainte Colombe-de-Peyre to sub-prefect Marvejols, Sainte Colombe-de-Peyre, 16 June 1906.

10

****

Politicisation in traditional societies

A decade of guerilla warfare between church and state forced upon the peasantry of the southern Massif Central a *prise de conscience* unlike anything it had experienced since 1789. The unbridled interventionism of the 1880s resulted in a precarious political synthesis combining the demands of the polity with the salient features of local culture. In 1893 a general election occasioned the extraordinary spectacle of thousands of catholic peasants trudging to the polls in order to vote for more-or-less anti-clerical republican candidates. What had happened? The Republic had scarcely changed its stripes, nor had catholicism lost its purchase on the rural population. In this region all the indices record an affirmation of formal and informal piety during the course of the nineteenth century. The *ralliement* preached discreetly by Leo XIII since 1889 must be accounted a partial explanation, if only because it undermined the clerico-Legitimist alliance, but the imperatives of the *ralliement* seem rather to have coincided with a more fundamental shift in electoral behaviour. The Constitutional Right (*ralliés*) ventured few candidates in the southern Massif Central and would-be conservative voters tended to express their submission to papal dictates by abstaining. The majority of the electorate were busy cementing political compromise of a different type. If republican rhetoric had failed to lift the consciousness of the peasant voter, the blandishments of government had instructed him in the wisdom of tactical compliance. The rural elector learned to serve both God and mammon as incarnated in the 'milch-cow' state. Voting in parliamentary elections for the apostles of anti-clericalism under the very noses of a domineering parish clergy required courage and determination and therein lies the magnitude of the *prise de conscience* accomplished in the final decades of the century. Yet the evolution of a dualist political mentality was less remarkable than it may appear, for the peasantry of these highlands had long maintained a functional attitude towards the church. The task of the priest was to serve and reflect the interests of the rural community: such was the tradition of Gallicanism as understood at the grass roots. But ultramontane catholicism reversed this order of priorities and prompted the belated discovery that the rural community was a civil as well as a spiritual entity.

The growth of electoral pragmatism at the expense of the rampant clericalism which had characterised the 1880s was not unique to the southern Massif Central. The phenomenon has been noted in several penurious departments of the South. After two decades of unflinching support for conservative candidates, the catholic peasantry of the Lot[1] abandoned the 'bon parti' in 1889 and elected a slate of republicans. The peasantry of the eastern highlands of the Cantal[2] trod a similar path as did that of the Puy-de-Dôme.[3] Writing of the diocese of St Flour in 1905, the *abbé* Rouchy observed that the electorate tended to choose candidates hostile to the church – not from motives of anti-clericalism, 'leur plus puissant mobile est, en définitive, l'espoir de s'attirer les faveurs gouvernementales'.[4] As for the diocese of Clermont, Abel Poitrineau has remarked on the facility with which 'la majorité de la population votait radical, mais respectait les traditions religieuses'.[5] This symbiosis could also be found in the plains where the peasantry of the Tarn[6] switched allegiances at roughly the same moment as their neighbours in the Aveyron. Again, the conversion to republican institutions seems to have been largely circumstantial and lacking in ideological repercussions. For many, perhaps a majority, of country dwellers voting had become a cynical offertory to the regime in power which did not entail 'une révolution en profondeur des attitudes mentales et des comportements sociaux'.[7]

The *ralliement* of the peasantry should, therefore, be construed principally as a rallying to a source of power rather than to an ideology. The exponents of *ralliement* proper urged acceptance of the Republic on more intellectual grounds, but their efforts resulted in a qualified failure both locally and nationally. Whether this crabbed acceptance of 'la république au village' as we have charted it can be dignified as a process of politicisation seems a matter of interpretation. A political conversion which failed to unleash 'une révolution en profondeur des attitudes mentales et des comportements sociaux' sounds most unpromising. Yet it should be remembered that in the conditions of the southern Massif Central the decision to ignore a clerical *mot d'ordre* at election times was in itself an act of emancipation of prime importance. Furthermore, as Eugen Weber has most recently pointed out, the condition of politicisation has less to do with support for one ideology or another than an awareness of the existence of political choice. On this count, too, we must allow that the rural population evinced a grasp of one of the central

[1] J. Calvet, 'Monographie religieuse d'un diocèse français, Cahors', *Revue catholique des églises*, (1905), 77–9.
[2] C. Rouchy, 'Monographie religieuse d'un diocèse français: le diocèse de Saint Flour en 1905', *Revue catholique des églises*, (1905), 550–1.
[3] A. Poitrineau (ed.), *Le Diocèse de Clermont* (Paris, 1979), p. 245.
[4] Rouchy, 'Monographie religieuse', p. 551.
[5] Poitrineau (ed.), *Le Diocèse de Clermont*, p. 245.
[6] Faury, *Cléricalisme et anticléricalisme dans le Tarn*, p. 231. [7] *Ibid.*, p. 492.

attributes of politicisation. It opted for the Republic in defiance of the church and over the heads of the notables.

However, an interpretation of popular politicisation which relegates the element of ideology – regarded by many historians as the stuff of politics – necessarily poses problems. Possible solutions to these problems have been offered in the preceding chapters and they can be summarised by reference to a number of inter-locking concepts which underpin this study. The notion that the 'peasantry' constituted an identifiable whole is a recurrent theme of our analysis. This ethnocentric approach can be criticised on the ground that it glosses important socio-economic cleavages in the countryside; that, in short, it inhibits perception of the village as the forum of class conflict. Yet eminent historians of rural France writing before and since the incorporation of social science methodology have continued to employ the concept of the peasantry as an analytical tool. Used skilfully it need not imply that social stratification was non-existent, that tensions were solely biological in origin, that village life was fundamentally harmonious; whereas the alternative postulate appears so firmly wedded to the principle of conflict that it makes scant allowance for consensual modes of behaviour. In the southern Massif Central socio-economic contrasts were muted by extreme sub-division of arable surfaces; by *petite culture* which yielded small and irregular surpluses; by the frailty of the cash nexus and by a low threshold of proletarianisation. During the period envisaged by our study the economic structures of the region consolidated around the self-sufficient proprietor and his household labour force. Tillage of waste and common land increased, landless agricultural labourers and farm servants acceded to property and *fermage* of all types sharply declined. Nonetheless, the palpable socio-economic disparities between *laboureurs* and *colons* led to violent conflict on occasions, notably regarding access to the commons, but such conflict was episodic rather than endemic. It jeopardised consensual attitudes in the political domain twice: in 1793–4 when revolutionary legislation momentarily extended the enticing prospect of an egalitarian division of common land and in the 1870s and 1880s when *allotissement* of the commons reappeared on the agenda of village political life and worked a similar *prise de conscience* among the poor. In conclusion, therefore, we would support the judgement of Paul Bois whose analysis of the dynamics of politicisation in the department of the Sarthe provides a model for studies of this sort: 'la société paysanne constitue un tout dont la complexité ne détruit pas l'homogénéité morale'.[8]

Taken on its own, Bois' proposition scarcely presses the argument very far, however. How did the collective personality – the 'moral homogeneity' – of the peasantry bear upon its political attitudes? Our answer has been to advance the concept of 'community'. The idea of community follows

---

[8] P. Bois, *Paysans de l'ouest; des structures économiques et sociales aux options politiques depuis l'époque révolutionnaire dans le Sarthe* (Le Mans, 1960), p. 447.

naturally from that of a single, identifiable peasantry and yet it arouses even greater misgivings among those engaged upon historical research. Geographers may invoke the confines of physical space while anthropologists chart the frontiers of ethnicity, but social historians remain ill at ease with the concept – fearful lest an admission of its validity undermine such operative tools of the trade as class conflict and social mobility. It is true that the concept of community poses particular problems of interpretation in the southern Massif Central. While habitat and collective agricultural practices contoured the rural community unmistakably on the openfield plains of the North and North East, neither habitat nor the constraints of crop rotation help us to identify the rural community of the *bocage* country and the highland plateaux. Moreover, the migratory instincts of a rural population subject to chronic under-employment during the winter months appear to militate against the development of a pronounced sense of belonging.

In order to meet these strictures we have abandoned the traditional outlines and introduced instead the notion of the 'cultural' community. Culture in this sense is defined as the matrix of custom, costume, signs, manners and language which enabled individuals to identify with one another. The cultural community transcended the limitations of physical space and tolerated considerable social and geographical mobility. Alan Macfarlane's influential debunking of the pre-modern English rural community is worth mentioning in this respect for it rests upon the assumption that isolation is a physical condition geared solely to the level of mobility prevailing at any one time. Since short-range geographical mobility had been the norm in England since the fifteenth century, if not earlier: 'Any particular community in England in the past was probably no more isolated than a Chicago suburb or twentieth-century Banbury.'[9] In the southern Massif Central it would be more appropriate to suggest that the rural community originated in the efforts of generations to compensate for low levels of sociability. Its locus was the parish church whose Sunday offices provided the only regular medium for extra-familial social interaction; its confines usually those of the parish. This, together with the logistical presence of the catholic church throughout the region, helps to explain the quasi-religious content of popular culture. The link with the church may also be held to account for the dynamic character of the rural community, for it was the parish priest who defined and inculcated its values, who galvanised migrants to resist the temptations of global society during their peregrinations.

The mutually reinforcing synthesis of seasonal migration and community values must be emphasised for the community postulate is too frequently portrayed in static and other-worldly terms. If the peasantry formed a whole society, they also formed a part society, but it does not follow from

[9] A. Macfarlane, *Reconstructing Historical Communities* (Cambridge, 1977), p. 9.

Redfield's[10] insight that widening geographical horizons and encroaching market pressures necessarily broadened the mind. Loyalties were not swiftly transferred from one entity to another, especially when migrants continued to practise their faith and to practise endogamy. Until the final decades of the nineteenth century when all the resources of the state were marshalled against the remaining pockets of cultural separatism, the peasantry of the southern Massif Central could afford to adopt a functional attitude towards the emanations of global society. Even after this date it is unlikely that the pressures of the cash nexus and acquisitive individualism disrupted social relationships in the countryside to the extent that is commonly assumed. The rural community evinced a capacity for survival in the interstices of an industrial economy which points up the contrasts between French and British economic development over the past century. Etienne Juillard[11] has noted how the heyday of the rural community coincided with the first phase of industrialisation in lower Alsace (Bas-Rhin). Good rail communications and low levels of industrial concentration enabled a sedentary rural population to divide its labour between the land and the factory. Two distinct life styles grew up, in consequence, which often involved one and the same individual. The mentality of these peasant proletarians has been explored by the ethnographer, Claude Karnoouh, on the basis of field research carried out in an unexceptional village of the Meurthe-et-Moselle during the 1960s and it holds some surprises for the unwary. Divided roughly equally into peasant cultivators and factory workers, the village nevertheless retained its 'cohérence culturelle traditionnelle'.[12] On returning to the village each evening, the wage earners shed the solidarities of the workplace and re-engaged their reflexes as peasants.

These examples suggest that the cultural superstructures of rural society were only loosely related to prevailing socio-economic infrastructures and the proposition is an axiom of our study. Bois,[13] too, concluded that commonly held traditions could override economic and social realities (*sic*) in specific historical contexts, if only for a time. Of course, the unevenness of wealth and social condition in the southern Massif Central was slight compared with the gross inequalities of the northern plains, yet the point is worth making for the rural community is sometimes portrayed as the spurious construct of a resident bourgeoisie. Such evidence as we have found to suggest that a dominant landlord class manufactured cultural homogeneity and thereby contrived political acquiescence has been discussed in detail. Even

---

[10] R. Redfield, *The Little Community: Viewpoints for the Study of a Human Whole* (Stockholm, Chicago, 1955); *Peasant Society and Culture: an Anthropological Approach to Civilization* (Chicago, 1956).

[11] E. Juillard, *La Vie rurale dans la plaine de Basse-Alsace: essai de géographie sociale* (Paris, 1953), pp. 398–9.

[12] Karnoouh, 'La Démocratie impossible', p. 35.   [13] Bois, *Paysans de l'ouest*, xi.

allowing for forms of persuasion which have left few traces, it is difficult to make out a case for the view that postures of conformism reproduced over several generations were artificially induced, however. Communities derived their identities from bodies of lore which every resident member, whether high-born or low-born, imbibed to some degree.

Individuals differentiated themselves within communities, but in ways which did not call into question the whole. It would be quite wrong to suppose that subscription to a common set of values removed all sources of conflict. In the *oustal*-based society of the southern Massif Central, conflict was usually articulated and resolved in the following fashion: kindred *a* competes with kindred *b* for influence, but both *a* and *b* admit the pre-eminent authority of collectivity *c*. In this light we have described the rural community as Janus-faced: the united and impregnable aspect it presented to the outside world belied an internal architecture of seething malice and envy. As an emanation of global society electoral politics tended to evoke the inscrutable face, but in moments of tension and turmoil politicisation penetrated deeper and flowed down the fault-lines which marked off households, clienteles and neighbourhood groups.

The fault-lines which differentiated entire communities are less easily specified, however, for here it must be acknowledged that our hypothesis of the culturally determined community can lead to ambiguity. The *oustal* culture of the southern Massif Central was just that – the culture of a region. When we apply it to discrete communities the proposition loses much of its explanatory value. Allowance must, therefore, be made for the territorial context of the rural community which was provided by the parish. But parish boundaries were not immutable and it would be more exact to think in terms of the catchment area of a chapel and its burial ground, which may also have constituted the parish church. The camaraderie of death in a communal burial ground which had admitted generation upon generation of mutually familiar and mutually intelligible human beings tempered the dominant culture of the region with infinite local variations which articulated community consciousness. Around the cult of the dead, there developed a festive culture for the living based on pilgrimages, processions and Saint's Day celebrations which naturally differed from community to community or, to follow contemporary usage, from bell tower to bell tower. And around this vibrant communion of the living with the dead there clustered, in turn, numberless secular signs of mutual recognition and demarcation: nuances of dress, of speech and of manner. If the pattern of a man's clogs offered substantial clues as to his background, the pattern of his clogs *and* the lilt of his patois would generally betray his provenance with pin-point accuracy. Sustained and perpetuated by intensive endogamy, it was these inflections in the dominant culture which gave the rural community its specificity.

Welded together in discrete biologically and culturally determined communities, the peasantry possessed a *mentalité*, or perhaps we should say *mentalités*. This neologism derives from the *Annales* school of historiography and although the term has been used sparingly throughout our study, the notion is integral to it and invoked frequently in the form of references to 'temperament'; to 'popular attitudes' and to 'collective personality'. Lacking firm contours, the study of *mentalité* risks becoming a branch of metaphysics in the hands of some of its practitioners. Yet this need not result: Michel Vovelle has shown us how to look for structure and shape in a difficult realm of enquiry and has vindicated the study of *mentalité* as 'la fine pointe de l'histoire sociale'.[14] In a somewhat empirical vein we have followed his example. Our attempt to identify and account for the motor elements of popular attitudes rests upon the twin assumptions that *mentalité* has a causality, but that it is also capable of outliving its concrete *raison d'être* (the image of the peasants of Mont Lozère who continued to grow cereals at inhospitable altitudes when ready-baked bread could be obtained from the *boulangerie* springs to mind). The quest for causality explains the chronological scope of this book for attitudes, unlike opinions perhaps, were tempered by memory over a broad time scale. Arguably, our study should have traced the development of an unusually potent rural catholicism to its pre-Tridentine origins, but this proved impracticable. Instead, we have retreated no further than the late *ancien régime*, for the final decades of the eighteenth century provide a sufficient glimpse of the traditions, both old and new, that were to structure popular attitudes for the next hundred years or so. In a region in which both Revolution and Counter-Revolution left the bulk of the rural population unmoved, the traditions of the *ancien régime* continued to exert a preponderant influence. These we have described as atavisms and their legacy hung over the peasantry like a pall, inhibiting and suffocating independent intellectual development. The perenniality of sectarian prejudice can be taken for granted, but the uneven burdens of royal fiscality and seigneurialism left an undoubted, if less measurable, impression on popular consciousness, too. In 1880 the prefect of the Aveyron reported that the expulsion of the Trappists of Bonnecombe[15] in accordance with the legislation against unauthorised orders was unlikely to excite opposition among the local population. It would seem that the pre-revolutionary notoriety of the abbey as a seigneurial exploiter (see chapter five, p. 162) had not evaporated even a century later.

Mentalité should not be confused with *idéologie*, however. The aversion of the peasantry of the ségala for the abbey of Bonnecombe was a collective attitude of mind deriving from folk memories of exploitation and the *jacquerie* of 1789–90. It never hardened into a coherent opinion measurable

[14] M. Vovelle, *Idéologies et mentalités* (Paris, 1982), p. 17.
[15] A.N. F⁷ 12313 Prefect Aveyron to *Ministre de l'intérieur et des cultes*, Rodez, 15 June 1880.

in electoral terms, at least not during the period spanned by our study. Traditions were not bound to work in unison to accelerate popular consciousness, nor, indeed, were they bound to exert a braking influence. The scattered villages of the Aveyronnais ségala were subject to conflicting traditions in the nineteenth century: victims of *ancien régime* fiscality and seigneurialism they counted among the most conspicuous beneficiaries of the revolutionary settlement, yet the region was also noted as a bastion of supine catholicism and endemic illiteracy. The consequence: a politically quiescent rural population interspersed with pockets of *bourg* radicalism. In the Brivadois, by contrast, the legacy of tradition possessed a more homogeneous character for here the liquidation of an oppressive *ancien régime* was not filtered through the medium of an omniscient clergy and it set in motion a process of emancipation which eventually transformed a vaguely reformist *mentalité* into a coherent left-wing ideology.

But the Brivadois was not typical. Throughout most of the southern Massif Central and for most of the period in question politics were a function of *mentalité*. By this we mean that political commitment was fashioned from the raw materials of *mentalité* and not from the store of abstractions which made up what were, generally speaking, nation-wide ideologies. The sources of political commitment have been discussed at length in chapter eight and it is noteworthy that the catalysts of allegiance tended to lie inside, rather than outside, the rural community. Family structures, household rivalries, sectarian antipathies, social hierarchies and territorialism, to recall only the most obvious categories, conspired to mould attitudes, and therefore political attitudes, in the countryside. The content of political allegiance – thus fashioned – was inherently unstable and susceptible to colonisation by exogenous factors when pressed beyond the range of normal parochial apprehensions, but the secular residuum, what is sometimes rather casually labelled 'la politique du clocher', was never entirely absent.

Recourse to that interesting phrase begs questions about our concept of politics, however. In essence, the preceding chapters offer an extended answer to a single question: in what ways and under what pressure did the rural population come to terms with the precocious growth of the liberal state in France? By implication, therefore, the prolonged and painful birth of electoral politics between 1787 and the 1880s provides the subject-matter of our study. It may be objected that such a focus refines the meaning of politics to an unacceptable degree. Some have argued that there existed an antecedent tradition of democratic freedom and self-government within the French countryside which the inception of electoral politics subsumed and concealed from view. Collective decision-making was certainly not the invention of the liberal state, but it is exceedingly difficult to synthesise disparate and discontinuous references to forms of village democracy into an alternative political tradition. Maurice Agulhon[16] and others who have examined the robust sense of municipal autonomy which distinguished village life in Provence and the Bas-Languedoc may fairly claim to have identified an alternative political tradition of some substance, yet it seems only to have flourished in the society of the Mediterranean littoral. Even so, the link between municipal autonomy and properly democratic decision-making is by no means self evident. In the southern Massif Central the mass of the rural population served no discernible apprenticeship to the concept of political freedom prior to 1787. Save perhaps for the Bas Vivarais, the habits of democracy were alien to the popular culture of the region.

While Claude Mesliand[17] has argued, on the basis of research into rural Provence concerning the early decades of the Third Republic, that no essential distinction need be made between village politics and the politics of the national entity, most scholars have found it necessary to adopt a two-tier concept of politics. Agulhon[18] distinguished between local and national politics as did most of the contributors to a recent colloquium entitled 'Les Paysans et la Politique (1750–1850)',[19] although the Tillys[20] have employed the dichotomy more subtly and have described the eighteenth and nineteenth centuries as the period during which 'the locus of relevant politics shifted'. The distinction clearly has operative value, if only because contemporaries used it unhesitatingly. Successive generations of apostles despatched into the countryside to preach the republican gospel invoked the difficulties they had faced in seeking to substitute the disinterested politics of ideas for 'la politique du clocher'. But therein lies the difficulty, for the dichotomy categorises the content of political commitment much too neatly. We would not wish to argue that the ideological reference points of national politics automatically suffused the deliberations of the *conseils municipaux*, but it is worth considering the alternative hypothesis. When referring to 'local elections' and 'national elections' we have endeavoured to refrain from drawing the net too tightly, for the implication that the peasant voter adjusted his behaviour according to whether he was electing a councillor or a member of the legislature should be resisted. The omnipresence of *mentalité* makes generic distinctions of this type highly problematic.

For this reason the polarities of 'archaicism' and 'modernity' no longer

[16] Agulhon, *The Republic in the Village*; L. A. Loubère, *Radicalism in Mediterranean France: its Rise and Decline, 1848–1914* (Albany, 1974); T. Judt, *Socialism in Provence, 1871–1914: a Study in the Origins of the Modern French Left* (Cambridge, 1979).
[17] C. Mesliand, 'Gauche et Droite dans les campagnes provençales sous la IIIième République', *Etudes rurales*, lxiii–lxiv (1976), 207–8.
[18] Agulhon, *The Republic in the Village*, xiv–xv.
[19] 'Les Paysans et la politique (1750–1850)', *Annales de Bretagne et des pays de l'ouest*, lxxxix (1982).
[20] L. A. Tilly and C. Tilly (eds.), *Class Conflict and Collective Action* (Beverly Hills, London, 1981), p. 17.

provide an adequate theoretical framework for the debate about politicisation in the French countryside. Launched by Agulhon[21] with his ground-breaking enquiry into the expanding consciousness of the population of the Var, the model received swift endorsement in Alain Corbin's[22] pioneer study of three departments of the western Massif Central captioned *Archaïsme et modernité en Limousin au XIXᵉ siècle*. It might be thought that Corbin's material was much less amenable to this kind of interpretation, but nevertheless the model has become something of an orthodoxy – helped by the fact that few historians have taken up the challenge to explore other regions of rural France over a similar time-scale. Yet, both Agulhon's and Corbin's approach to the problem of politicisation is weakened by an inadequate appreciation of the potentialities of ethnographic data. Inevitably so, since ethnography and social anthropology are recent additions to the analytical tool-bag of the European historian. The immediate consequences of bringing the new methodology to bear upon a key issue in political and social history is a shift of focus. Distinctions such as 'archaicism' and 'modernity' are blurred and the traditional order of priorities according to which change occupies the foreground and continuity the background is effectively reversed. Pressed to extremes, the approach can result in virtually a new genre of rural social history. Eugen Weber has provided us with an outstanding example.[23]

We would not wish to reject the tension inherent in the 'archaicism–modernity' dichotomy altogether, rather to reformulate it. The cautious confrontation between the peasantry of the southern Massif Central and the integrative pressures of democracy provides an object lesson in the coexistence of 'archaicism *within* modernity'. Embedded in the encroaching structures of the liberal state, the peasantry exploited the electoral arena to pursue a range of secular interests which made eminent sense at the level of small, endogamous communities. In so doing, it made a nonsense of the central concept of participatory democracy as applied to traditional societies which supposed the release of the individual from the constraints of primary allegiances. Man is born to ethnicity, comments A. H. Somjee[24] in his study of the democratic process in India, and the dictum sheds light upon the electoral behaviour of peasant society in nineteenth-century France, as well.

---

[21] Expounded in a doctoral thesis (M. Agulhon, 'Un Mouvement populaire au temps de 1848: histoire des populations du Var dans la première moitié du 19ᶦᵉᵐᵉ siècle' (Université de Paris, Thèse de doctorat d'état, 12 vols., 1969)) and published in four distinct works entitled: *Pénitents et Francs-Maçons de l'ancienne Provence* (Paris, 1968); *La Vie sociale en Provence intérieure au lendemain de la Révolution* (Paris, 1970); *Une Ville ouvrière au temps du socialisme utopique: Toulon de 1815 à 1851* (Paris, The Hague, 1970); *La République au village (les populations du Var de la Révolution à la Seconde République)* (Paris, 1970), translated as *The Republic in the village: the people of the Var from the French Revolution to the Second Republic* (Cambridge, Paris, 1982).

[22] A. Corbin, *Archaïsme et modernité*.   [23] Weber, *Peasants into Frenchmen*.

[24] A.H. Somjee, *The Democratic Process in a Developing Society* (London, 1979), p. 7.

Whether literally or figuratively, the rustic voter approached the hustings in a cohort of family and kinsmen, in a cohort of neighbours, in a cohort of co-religionaries, or in some other primary reference group. Yet it would be a mistake to deduce that resistance to the precepts of electoral democracy was somehow wilful or contrived, on the analogy of present-day electorates which sometimes choose to ignore the wider ideological ramifications of decision-taking. Such evidence as we have uncovered indicates that the concession of the franchise, in 1787, in 1789 and in 1848, left the peasantry frankly bemused. They interpreted the institution of manhood suffrage as best they could, that is to say within the limits of their physical and cultural horizons. They sought advice from the traditional mentors of the rural community and they gave voice to a variety of local grievances and ambitions. In 1789 this process of consultation resulted in the *cahiers de doléances* – documents which captured the essence of peasant political apprehensions on the eve of the Age of Liberty. Never again would the people petition their governors in such a fashion and the *cahiers* appeared to mark the end of a long chapter of French history. But did they in reality? Attitudes changed more slowly than institutions and in regions like the southern Massif Central the conception of relevant politics embodied in the *cahiers* lingered on unseasonably.

How long before 'the locus of relevant politics shifted' and, in the event, how far this transition proceeded are matters discussed in the latter part of our study. The 1880s seem to mark an important stage in the evolving symbiosis of archaicism and modernity. By the end of that decade, it is likely that conflict between church and state had inculcated a heightened awareness of the gravity of electoral participation. This is not to argue that endogenous factors ceased to provide the rationale for political commitment, but to suggest that a process of cross-fertilisation took place in which, for instance, a proposal to construct a village school, or to convert a stretch of common into allotments, became laden with ideological significance. Obviously, the dating of such a process is approximate: the 1880s saw the Opportunists force the southern Massif Central departments into a posture of political compliance, but the concomitant cultural changes worked by the communications revolution and by Ferry's education laws took longer to achieve. The process is still continuing as a detailed scrutiny of behaviour during recent elections would doubtless show. The inter-penetration of endogenous and exogenous factors gradually destroys the specificity of each, however, and the distinction between archaic and modern political perceptions no longer provides a helpful framework for analysis.

One reason why the distinction ceases to have much operative value is that widening cultural horizons and the growth of elementary education made possible the development of relationships of complicity between the central power and the rural electorate. Instead of voting in mechanical obedience to the multiple pressures of ethnicity, the peasantry learned how to use the ballot box as a bargaining device. Votes were cast bearing the appropriate party label and in return governments tacitly agreed to accept the evidence of political conversion at face value and to enquire no further. Tactical voting on a scale sufficient to attract the attentions of government presupposed a capacity to synthesise material and abstract considerations into a coherent political philosophy. The first indications that the rural electorate had acquired such a capacity can be traced back to the final years of the Second Empire,[25] but this kind of compromise was principally the achievement of the 1880s. In the hands of the Opportunists and then those of the Radicals, the policy of 'votes for favours' consummated a hybrid politicisation of the rural electorate. And this hybrid politicisation has since become the hallmark of the region. Traditional allegiances subsist, especially among protestants, but the ideological content of politics is no longer widely ignored as an alien, and therefore irrelevant, intrusion. Instead, ideology has become a commodity to be auctioned to the highest bidder. With the crucial legislative elections of March 1978 in the offing, *Le Monde* published region-by-region surveys of voters' intentions. Its correspondent in the Lozère reported that the controversial hydro-electric project requiring the evacuation of the village of Naussac now seemed unlikely to damage the electoral chances of the government candidate: 'C'est l'hiver et, dit-on, les premières indemnités offertes aux propriétaires expropriés ont été assez substantielles pour calmer les esprits.'[26]

Reconsideration of the 'archaicism–modernity' model necessarily invites a reconsideration of periodisation. Agulhon's influential arguments suggest that the crystallisation of democratic opinion was somehow preordained once the Second Republic had been proclaimed, and to the sceptical eye it seems that his reasoning has been expanded to embrace every department which recorded a healthy vote for the *démocrates-socialistes* – the jacobin socialist party – in the elections of May 1849. On these insubstantial foundations rests the current conviction that the period 1848–51 witnessed the moment of 'breakthrough' when the political consciousness of the rural masses shifted onto a higher, more ideologically aware, plane.[27] There are several objections to this interpretation of the process of peasant politicisation. Notwithstanding the contribution of Corbin, it now seems less likely than it did a decade ago that the experience of the Var can shed much light upon the evolution of opinion in the hinterland of France. Secondly, the scale of the *dém-soc* 'breakthrough' should be kept in perspective; the legislative election of 1849 marked a signal victory for the party of order even though

---

[25] See above, chapter eight, p. 249.
[26] *Le Monde*, 12 January 1978, 'La préparation des élections législatives: IV Languedoc-Roussillon'.
[27] For a clear statement of this point of view, see McPhee, 'Popular Culture, Symbolism and Rural Radicalism in Nineteenth-Century France', pp. 238–9 and *passim*.

sixteen out of eighty five departments gave a majority of votes cast to the *dém-soc* lists. Thirdly, it is far from certain that the mobilisation of support behind the slogans of socialist democracy between 1849 and 1851 can be taken to indicate that a significant section of the rural electorate had shifted their political moorings in a definitive and irrevocable fashion.

The first criticism scarcely requires restating except, perhaps, to add that – in retrospect – it seems slightly odd that the Var should ever have prompted a search for analogies in the first place. Not least because Agulhon has relatively little to say about the dynamics of specifically peasant politicisation, and what he does say supports the thesis that the participation of the peasantry in the *montagnard* political movement and the subsequent insurrection should be measured chiefly in archaic terms. This is a point of fundamental disagreement between Agulhon and Margadant[28] who also defends the significance of the Second Republic as a moment of political transition, but from a rather different angle. Our second criticism bears upon questions of scope and balance which are intrinsic to the historian's craft. Apprehension of significance – of those factors and forces which are consequential and those which are not – is never an easy matter in the realm of social history, and rural social history poses the problem in its most acute form. We may widen the focus of enquiry in the interests of breadth of coverage and risk the blurring of the significant into the insignificant, or we may narrow the focus and concentrate on conflict, perhaps, at the expense of consensus. The current preoccupation with the electoral appeal of socialist democracy and the proliferation of *montagnard* secret societies presents this difficulty. Clearly, the efforts of democrats to stem the tide of reaction after 1848 constitute more than an historical footnote and scholars like Vigier[29] and Agulhon deserve our thanks for rescuing the provincial risings of 1851 from historiographical neglect. But how much significance we attach to the *dém-soc* epic of 1849–51 depends again on focus: whether we can discern an antecedent tradition of democratic radicalism and whether the *dém-soc* initiative issued in at least a partial transformation of relationships in the countryside. On both counts the *longue durée* approach tends to minimise the importance of the mid-century crisis of political authority. It is a frequently overlooked fact that the first apprenticeship to manhood suffrage and the institutions of republican democracy was served between 1792 and 1799. Jacobinism and neo-jacobinism need to be weighed in the balance before we can pronounce upon the novelty of socialist democracy. The so-called *montagnard* secret societies, surely, betray a link with the past. On the other hand, the phenomenon of socialist democracy should also be weighed in terms of its promise for the future.

[28] T. W. Margadant, 'Peasant Protest in the Second Republic', *The Journal of Interdisciplinary History*, v (1974–75), 130.
[29] Vigier, *La Seconde République dans la région alpine*.

This point provides the substance for our third criticism of the thesis which traces to the Second Republic the inception of peasant political consciousness. Against the evidence of a structural, and hence durable, transformation of attitudes must be set the evidence that the conversion of large numbers of peasant voters to the programme of socialist democracy in the elections of 1849 and 1850 was purely conjunctural, that is to say, the product of a crisis of political leadership combined with a crisis in the rural economy. The example of the southern Massif Central lends support to the latter hypothesis, for none of the profiles we have drawn was fundamentally disturbed by the advent of a lingering economic recession in 1846, or by the advent of the Republic in 1848. The cycle of demographic growth resumed; low levels of market penetration insulated peasant polyculture from the price slump, although craft activity in some of the *bourgs* weathered the malaise less effectively, and social solidarities reformed around the traditional elites. The *dém-soc* enthusiasms of the Brivadois and the lower Ardèche drew considerable inspiration from the crisis of artisan production which hit the *bourgs*, but more, perhaps, from the antecedent traditions of political radicalism which had marked out the Auvergne portion of the Haute-Loire and the old Bas Vivarais ever since the great Revolution.

The case for a mid-century structural transformation of popular politics can be made most effectively by concentrating on the departments of the Mediterranean littoral and the sub-Alpine departments of the South East. These regions of precocious and well-rooted *dém-soc* activity seem to have shared a vocation for left-wing political options, for in the 1880s they emerged as the principal bastions of Radicalism and Radical-Socialism (Bouches-du-Rhône, Vaucluse, Var, Basses-Alpes, Drôme, Hérault, Pyénées-Orientales). The 'fit' was not perfect: in the Hérault[30] the *dém-socs* took only 30 per cent of the popular vote in 1849 compared with a national average of 34.8 per cent and yet the department proved an early and easy convert to Radicalism. Nevertheless, the element of continuity is impressive and well documented. In the Var[31] the repression following the insurrections of 1851 drove opposition underground for a time, but it also ensured that the embryonic democratic movement avoided entanglement in the Bonapartist snare. With the switch to 'liberal' Empire the militant traditions of the region quickly became visible once more and by 1870 the 'Var rouge' had become a byword. In 1876 the department despatched two Radicals and two moderate republicans to Paris; in 1881 the Radicals swept the board, taking all four constituencies. Unmistakable continuities of political allegiance distinguished the department of the Pyrénées-Orientales situated at the opposite extremity of the coastal plain, too. A skilfully contrived list of *dém-socs*

---

[30] Loubère, *Radicalism in Mediterranean France*, pp. 40, 118–19, 126–7.
[31] Agulhon, *The Republic in the Village*, xvi; Judt, *Socialism in Provence*, p. 55.

leavened with several less doctrinaire republican personalities enabled the Left to take almost 67 per cent of votes cast in 1849 and to establish the mould for subsequent political alignments. As Loubère[32] has pointed out, the cantons which still resisted the Radicals in the 1880s tended to be those which had also offered resistance to *montagnard* penetration in 1848–9.

The sixteen departments which appeared to pledge their support for the idea of 'la république démocratique et sociale' did not all fall within the ambit of the peculiar culture of the South, however. A compact group of departments occupying the western approaches to the Massif Central (Creuse, Corrèze, Dordogne, Haute-Vienne) also sent entire slates of *dém-soc* candidates to sit in the Assembly, as did a second group of departments flanking the central highlands to the north (Allier, Cher, Nièvre, Saône-et-Loire). Nevertheless, the character of peasant politicisation in these zones was much less consistent and it is questionable whether the electoral contest of 1849 can be said to have laid the foundations for a durable alteration of popular attitudes. The radicalism of the western buttresses of the Massif Central defies analysis in the terms applied to the departments of the South and Agulhon[33] has even referred to the results of the 1849 ballot in the Limousin as a 'surprise vote'. The human habitat of the Limousin and adjacent districts was quite different from that of Provence; literacy levels were much lower; cultural diffusion less pronounced and the relay class of village worthies less numerous and less active in the cause of democracy. Indeed, the exiguous role of the notable provides the most striking contrast between the social structure of the western plateaux of the Massif Central and that of the plateaux of the south and south east. The low threshold of cultural diffusion may surprise since the economy of the Creuse department, especially, relied upon the periodic displacement of large numbers of building workers to Paris and Lyons, but Corbin[34] makes it clear that migrants were no more committed to the *dém-socs* than any other section of the rural population.

In short, the rural population of the western Massif Central took a rather different route to radicalism in 1849 from that taken by the inhabitants of the bustling villages of the Mediterranean plain. Circumstance and ingrained prejudices against proprietary wealth and the clergy combined to determine allegiances. The support for the *dém-socs* crystallised from several identifiable sources: the nullity of the conservative electoral campaign compared with the vigour of the *montagnard* propaganda effort; the persistence of malaise in the countryside, especially in the non-migrant districts which bore the brunt of the economic crisis, and the influence of the radical city of Limoges. Recent research on the organisational underpinnings of socialist

[32] Loubère, *Radicalism in Mediterranean France*, pp. 119–21 and maps 4, 5.
[33] Agulhon, *The Republic in the Village*, xvi.
[34] Corbin, *Archaïsme et modernité*, ii, pp. 735–7, 753–4, 830–1.

democracy has done much to clarify our understanding of the phenomenon[35] and it seems likely that the very activism of its cadres in the Limousin provided the peasantry with the leadership which the notables seemed incapable of assuming. Activism allied to programmatic flexibility, that is, for *dém-soc* ideology was nothing if not eclectic. There was nothing specifically socialist about it and a great deal that harked back to Robespierre and the jacobinism of 1793. If the *dém-socs* succeeded in rallying the voters of the Limousin by reworking the anti-fiscal and anti-sumptuary themes of the Revolution, they failed to establish their credentials as political messiahs bearing news of an authentically new political vision.

Their failure to establish a niche in the political consciousness of the rural electorate is recorded in the history of the region between 1848 and 1851. Corbin acknowledges as much, although he remains attached to the concept of structural change and reluctant to define the significance of the 1849 ballot in purely conjunctural terms. Nevertheless, it is clear from his analysis that the Second Republic did not break the mould of politics. Atavistic allegiances and a certain cultural immobilism prevented the Limousin peasantry from fully comprehending the crucial distinction between Bonapartism and socialist democracy. Martin Nadaud[36] himself describes how, as a child, he was raised on *Bulletins de la Grande Armée* collected by his father and how, as a migrant mason working in the capital, his political education advanced through Bonapartism to republicanism and utopian socialism. Nadaud was a trail blazer, however. Only six months before the *dém-soc* landslide of 1849, the electorate of the Creuse and the Haute-Vienne voted Louis-Napoléon Bonaparte into power as president of the Republic by a margin unequalled anywhere in France. Cavaignac and Ledru-Rollin did correspondingly badly, save in the Corrèze where Ledru-Rollin pushed Cavaignac into third place and bettered his performance in the country at large. It seems that the peasantry voted for the nephew of the Emperor or they did not vote at all, and the migrant peasantry voted for Louis-Napoléon in greater numbers than did the sedentary peasantry. These electoral gyrations raise important questions about the character of political attitudes in the region. Are we simply dealing with an immature electorate? Are we striving to interpret non-ideological alignments in gratuitously ideological terms? Corbin[37] notes, for instance, that town versus country polarities provide a more satisfactory explanation of the results in some districts – a hypothesis that we have found useful in the southern Massif Central.

Subsequent behaviour provides a more compelling answer, however, for

---

[35] T. W. Margadant, 'Modernisation and Insurgency in December 1851: a Case Study of the Drôme' in R. Price (ed.), *Revolution and Reaction: 1848 and the Second French Republic* (London, 1975), pp. 254–79; *French Peasants in Revolt*.

[36] Nadaud, *Mémoires de Léonard*, pp. 69, 77, 141, 227 and *passim*.

[37] Corbin, *Archaïsme et modernité*, ii, p. 735.

the *dém-soc* enthusiasms of the spring of 1849 ebbed almost as quickly as they had flowed. With the return of prosperity the masons found work and returned to their primitive Bonapartist allegiance, while the uncertain rise of fatstock prices nudged the bulk of the peasantry in a similar direction. Between the summer of 1850 and the autumn of 1851 the Left's bridgehead in the Limousin 'broke up', in the words of Corbin.[38] The quiescence of the countryside on receipt of the news of Louis-Napoléon's *coup d'état* was less a symptom of heavy-handed repression than of conversion to Bonapartism. In the final analysis, Bonapartism, sedulously buttressed with an array of social and democratic myths, proved more appealing than socialist democracy. Not until the elections of 1869 did republicanism succeed in nibbling at peasant support for the Empire in the Limousin, and the shift in allegiances was restricted to certain cantons of the north-eastern Haute-Vienne and the north-western Creuse. The republican reconquest did not begin in earnest until the 1870s.

Hence Agulhon's description of the 1849 ballot in the Limousin region as a 'surprise vote' and it might be argued that the *dém-soc* 'breakthrough' in the departments bordering the northern ramparts of the Massif Central poses a similar problem of interpretation. In the Nièvre, for instance, which figures on Margadant's[39] Richter Scale of conflict as the centre of a 'major armed mobilization' in December 1851, radicalism tended to fluctuate in keeping with the vicissitudes of a rural economy oriented towards the export of timber. As the conjuncture improved the democratic energies of forest workers and lumberjacks were sublimated into a durable Bonapartist affiliation. That Bonapartism (and also Boulangism) competed for votes in the same marketplace as socialist democracy is also apparent from a weighty study of the Burgundian departments of the Côte-d'Or and the Saône-et-Loire undertaken by Pierre Lévêque.[40] By the yardstick of the 1849 ballot the Saône-et-Loire emerged as perhaps the most vehemently left-wing department in France, yet the *dém-socs* proved congenitally incapable of establishing their identity in the eyes of the electorate – the more so when confronted by a Bonapartist propaganda machine playing on the theme of popular anti-fiscalism as in the Limousin. After making a promising start in the Constituent Assembly elections of April 1848, perhaps three-quarters of the Left's electorate defected from Ledru-Rollin to Louis-Napoléon in the contest for the presidency, estimates Lévêque.[41] The collapse of democratic hopes was general, but especially pronounced in the Saône-et-Loire. Six months later these voters shuttled back across the political spectrum, although we would do well not to exaggerate the distance involved. A slate of twelve *dém-soc*

---

[38] *Ibid.*, pp. 743, 830.
[39] Margadant, *French Peasants in Revolt*, p. 11.
[40] P. Lévêque, 'La Bourgogne de la Monarchie de Juillet au Second Empire'.
[41] *Ibid.*, iii, p. 1271.

candidates headed nominally by Ledru-Rollin set off for Paris endorsed by 66 per cent of the electorate of the Saône-et-Loire.

But again the Mountain seemed unable to capitalise on its success and establish a durable political partnership with the peasantry. The sophisticated network of semi-clandestine organisations which in the South sustained popular support for the programme of the Left between 1849 and 1851 was conspicuous by its absence in the Burgundian departments. Pierre Joigneaux, the influential *montagnard* deputy for the Côte-d'Or and editor of *La Feuille du Village*, considered the recourse to conspiracy unnecessary. In any case the *dém-soc* triumph of 1849 defies analysis conceived in conventional structural terms. Lévêque[42] notes that the conservative list performed best in open-field areas where small and medium-sized farms predominated, where literacy was above average and religious devotion below average. By contrast, the *dém-socs* reigned supreme in the south-western sector of the province: a region of *bocage*, large estates, generalised illiteracy and entrenched catholicism. An 'archaic' route to political consciousness comparable to that taken by the peasantry of the Limousin and certain cantons of the Aveyronnais ségala? Perhaps, but it was a politicisation that lacked stamina as well as ideological consistency. Although Margadant[43] classifies the Saône-et-Loire as a theatre of a major armed mobilisation in December 1851, the reality was much less glorious. For all its 'red' connotations, the department never became a focus for resistance on the scale of the Var, the Basses-Alpes, or even the Nièvre. As for the peasantry, they generally avoided involvement in the resistance to the *coup*.

It is tempting to conclude with Corbin[44] that Bonapartism may well have provided the peasantry with their first initiation to politics. Perhaps the extraordinary presidential ballot of December 1848 can tell us more about the evolving apprehensions of millions of provincial Frenchmen in the second half of the nineteenth century than the parliamentary election of May 1849. In which case it is time for historians to expend as much effort exploring the Napleonic 'interregnum' of 1848–70 as they have hitherto expended on decoding the *dém-soc* enigma of 1849–51. Karl Marx long ago pointed the way when he described the hustings of 10 December 1848 as 'the day of the *peasant insurrection*'.[45] The attention recently paid to the provincial insurgency of December 1851 with its supposed focus of moral outrage at the unconstitutional actions of the Prince-President seems to have arbitrarily separated the tangled threads of democratic republicanism and Bonapartism. The conundrum of Bonapartism, after all, lay in its capacity to synthesise authoritarianism and populism and this was precisely the conundrum which

---

[42] *Ibid.*, iv, p. 1358.   [43] Margadant, *French Peasants in Revolt*, p. 11.
[44] Corbin, *Archaïsme et modernité*, p. 843.
[45] K. Marx, *The Class Struggles in France, 1848 to 1850* in Karl Marx and Frederick Engels, *Collected Works* (38 vols., London, 1975–82), x, p. 80.

Marat and Robespierre bequeathed to the Left in the nineteenth century. Even in districts where the repression of the Commissions Mixtes provided a stark reminder of the gulf between the theory and the practice of Caesarian democracy, Bonapartism showed itself able to win support among adherents to socialist democracy. The radical tradition of the *arrondissement* of St Affrique (Aveyron)[46] was neutralised in this fashion during the Second Empire. Bonapartism sapped the foundations of political dissent, while migration and a faltering birth-rate depleted the Calvinist community and softened the contours of sectarian rivalry.

But could Bonapartism attract support from the Left without sacrificing the confidence of the Right? Several historians have suggested that the massive endorsement of Louis-Napoléon in December 1848 expressed a popular determination to outflank the traditional mediator class in the countryside who had urged the choice of Cavaignac for the presidency in many districts. The corollary would seem to be that the imperial regime retained peasant support by distancing itself from the Right and by pioneering forms of doorstep democracy. Corbin finds much to commend this approach in his study of the Limousin. The regime put down roots by cultivating the neo-jacobin prejudices of the rural voters: it appeared democratic, socially reforming, anti-noble and anti-church. In short, it could be taken, or mistaken, for being hostile towards the notables and anxious to project a direct link between the Emperor and the people. Some support for this interesting thesis can be elicited from the regional histories of Philippe Vigier[47] and André Armengaud.[48] In the sub-Alpine departments of the Basses-Alpes, the Drôme and the Isère, and also in the Pyrenean departments of the Ariège and in the Haute-Garonne, the new regime worked hard to detach the rural population from their mentors. But at this level the regime amounted to little more than the prefect and his corps of administrators. The bias towards or against the notables tended to derive from internal factors such as the propaganda line pursued by individual prefects, the relative strength of established elites and the role of the local catholic clergy. Circumstances could combine to catalyse Bonapartism into a force for social and political emancipation, then, but we should be wary of assuming that the Napoleonic model of plebiscitary democracy automatically released the peasantry from the bonds of deference.

In the southern Massif Central the Second Empire enlisted the notables and in return the notables supplied the regime with its official candidates, prefects and subordinate officials. While individual prefects occasionally over-

---

[46] A.D.A. 8M¹ 41 Sub-prefect St Affrique to prefect Aveyron, St Affrique, 5 July 1865.
[47] Vigier, *La Seconde République dans la région alpine*, i, pp. 312–26.
[48] Armengaud, *Les Populations de l'Est-Aquitain au début de l'époque contemporaine*, pp. 384–5, 397–400.

stepped the mark, as in the case of Dautheville's candidature in the Ardèche,[49] they generally acknowledged the force of particularism in the electoral life of the region and accepted that will-power alone would not overcome it. Peasants would be led to the hustings by their village bigwigs or they would not be led at all, therefore it was politic to work in partnership with local elites. And such, as far as we can tell, had always been the intention of the regime. If the Second Republic pioneered the *scrutin de liste* linked to cantonal polling in order to raise the consciousness of the rural elector, the Second Empire restored the single-member constituency and sub-divided communes into microscopic electoral units for precisely the opposite reason. Of course, the partnership did not preclude a measure of carefully calculated opposition on the part of the clergy and the great Legitimist families, but this opposition was carefully calculated specifically in order that it should not jeopardise the regime. In any case, the domestic repercussions of the Emperor's Italian venture were far from wholly damaging. The threat to the papacy roused clerical ire, but the encouragement given to Italian nationalism was applauded by liberals and democrats.

Corbin's timely reminder that Bonapartism could promote mass political awareness awaits further research, but there appears to be no reason for supposing that it performed this role in the southern Massif Central. We are left, therefore, with a chronology of politicisation which makes few concessions to the concept of progressive structural renewal. Neither the Second Republic, nor the Second Empire can be regarded as major stepping stones on the road to peasant emancipation. The radicalism of 1848–51 showed signs of wilting even before the Napoleonic regime curtailed democratic freedoms, and to all intents and purposes the republican conquest of the countryside in the 1870s and 1880s was launched from scratch. Thus, Agulhon's evocation of politicisation as 'a series of surreptitious injections of ideas that acted as catalysts and set off sudden general mutations'[50] seems inappropriate. Politicisation by stealth was not a measurable phenomenon in the southern Massif Central and we would favour, instead, a more brutal metaphor. The region experienced the pressures of political integration as a process of irruption. At intervals the issues and postures that constituted the politics of global society penetrated the rural community, catalysed internal tensions and alignments and momentarily endowed them with ideological reference points. But the process was cyclical rather than linear, for it failed to trigger general mutations. Unable to extract substantial nourishment from within the community and reliant always on outside reinforcement, the catalytic reaction lapsed and internal tensions and alignments reverted to their natural state. We should, therefore, envisage the politicisation of the peasantry of the southern Massif Central as a dialectical process of imprinting and efface-

[49] See above, chapter seven, p. 238.   [50] Agulhon, *The Republic in the Village*, p. 112.

ment; shallow ideological imprinting, that is, and rapid effacement in the absence of further stimulus. In the final analysis, the failure of politicisation to advance by any measurable criteria can only be explained in terms of the impermeability of the rural community. When structural changes brought the cultural autonomy of the upland peasantry to term in the 1870s and 1880s political integration entered its definitive stage. Yet the colonisation of the rural community by the nation-state remained a decidedly hybrid affair in which local particularisms and radical ideology interacted. It is for this reason that we have rejected the stereotyped polarities of 'archaicism' and 'modernity' as a model for analysis. If the political history of the southern Massif Central departments can be said to demonstrate anything at all, it is the extraordinary capacity of supposedly archaic modes of behaviour to adapt to the conditions of modern electoral democracy.

In this respect the obvious comparison lies with the West: another region in which peasant political apprehensions retained an irreducible component of traditionalism. Structural similarities of habitat and landholding provide a point of departure for analysis, but it is questionable whether the subtleties of political outlook can be measured in purely Siegfriedian terms. Rigorous comparison between the southern Massif Central and the dozen or so departments forming western France will only be possible when more monographs of the stature and scope of Paul Bois's[51] study of the Sarthe have been completed. Nonetheless, it is worth noting the parallels and contrasts as they appear to date. In addition to broadly comparable patterns of habitat dispersion and land tenure, the West retained a community-based social structure curiously similar to that obtaining in the southern Massif Central. As in the South, the rural community expressed the sociable instincts of a scattered *bocage* population whose convocation by the priest for Sunday Mass provided the principal occasion for intercourse. Its locus was, therefore, the parish and its sense of identity owed much to the culture of catholicism. Modest levels of market penetration and social stratification helped to buttress that sense of identity, while linguistic insularity posed a further barrier to the permeation of urban, francophone values.

On the other hand, certain elements in the equation we have elaborated for the southern Massif Central appear to be missing. *Bourgs* and the rentier class of rural bourgeois whose struttings did much to crystallise opinion in the southern Massif Central were inconspicuous features of the Breton landscape.[52] And, in the absence of the honour-laden distinctions which distanced bourgeois from peasant in southern villages, it seems unlikely that the western peasant household possessed the cohesion and internal discipline of the

---

[51] Bois, *Paysans de l'ouest*.
[52] See Le Goff, *Vannes and its Region*, pp. 182, 194–5, 239; D. Sutherland, *The Chouans: the Social Origins of Popular Counter-Revolution in Upper Brittany, 1770–1796* (Oxford, 1982), pp. 23–4, 126.

oustal. Both the Breton and the Norman Customs curtailed paternal testamentary freedom and treated heirs in the direct line of succession as equals. More important than these pathological distinctions, perhaps, was the impact of history. The West generally escaped the savage crisis of the late *ancien régime*: seigneurial obligations and the tithe seem to have creamed off a much lower percentage of peasant surplus than tended to be the case in the southern Massif Central. The Estates of Brittany deflected fiscal pressure and sent the monarchy in search of easier prey elsewhere, and a gentler profile of demographic growth spared the region from the extremes of land abandonment, mendicity and vagabondage which burdened peasant polyculture in the South on the eve of the Revolution. In contrast, the installation of the new regime between 1789 and 1792 provoked deeper resentment. New and more onerous taxes, tergiversations over the status of quasi-feudal forms of leasehold tenure and irritation at the swelling ranks of busybodying officialdom, prompted a comparison between the old and the new regimes which was entirely unfavourable to the latter. Unlike the peasantry of the southern Massif Central, the peasantry of the western *bocages* concluded that they had gained nothing from the Revolution and sacrificed a good deal. Their desperate disillusionment found expression in the Counter-Revolution: the Vendée rebellion and the Breton *chouannerie* were above all peasant-based resistance movements. In the southern Massif Central the royalist call to arms evoked a guarded response from the rural community, however. Peasant dislike of conscription, requisitions and the religious policies pursued by the new regime was tempered by memories of rampant seigneurialism and the fiscal aggression of the old monarchy. In short, it seems that the traditionalism of the West sprang primarily from the experience of the Revolution, whereas the social and political conservatism of the southern Massif Central was more thoroughly anchored to attitudes inherited from the *ancien régime*.

Nevertheless, the all-pervading presence of Roman Catholicism provides a thread which finally unites the two regions, for both the West and the southern Massif Central were lands of priests. They shared a common religious culture and a common propensity to mobilise in response to a clerical *mot d'ordre*. In the latter part of the nineteenth century the clergy of the Breton dioceses, in particular, exploited this facility to devastating effect. Priests shepherded columns of peasant-citizens to the hustings in the Léon (Finistère) and in the Norman *bocage* (Manche, Calvados, Orne) in much the same fashion as did their contemporaries in the Ardèche or the Lozère. Clericalism proved a great initiator to democratic politics and the opportunities for mass control intrinsic to democratic politics made the fortune of clericalism. Yet it is somewhat casuistical to invoke clericalism as the ultimate determinant of political behaviour. Bois[53] invites us to consider clericalism either as a facet of

[53] Bois, *Paysans de l'ouest*, pp. 25–7.

peasant political behaviour or as an explanation of that behaviour, pointing out that it cannot logically have been both. Our answer to this objection is unequivocal: the peasantry of the southern Massif Central paid ostentatious lip-service to the external obligations of the catholic faith, but never conceded to the clergy a right of oversight in matters temporal as well as spiritual. Indeed, many rural incumbents were saddened to discover how little freedom of action they enjoyed in view of the elasticity of the temporal sphere. Thus, if the rural population responded to a clerical *mot d'ordre* at election times they did so largely as a matter of choice. Clericalism, even at the height of the struggle over the Ferry Laws in the 1880s, could never have passed muster as an opinion in its own right. It was an agent of opinion: resistible and increasingly resisted as first the Opportunists and then the Radicals prompted the peasantry to weigh the implications of voting for clerical or royalist candidates. Hence the paradox with which we commenced this survey of popular political attitudes in an age which witnessed the invention of ballot-box democracy. The highland peasant breathed social and political conservatism through every fibre of his being and yet, by the late nineteenth century, he had learned to use his vote as a tactical weapon in order to salvage at least a portion of the familiar status quo. If recognition of the necessity for compromise between competing loyalties and allegiances constitutes the hallmark of democratic politics, there can be no doubt that he had come of age as a citizen.

Bibliography

MANUSCRIPT SOURCES

Archives Nationales, Paris

Section Ancienne: Ancien Régime

Série H (Administration locales et comptabilités diverses)
$H^1$1600 *Correspondance et mémoires sur les assemblées provinciales, particulière-ment en Haute-Guienne et Berry, 1779–88*
$H^1$1601 *Ibid*
$H^1$1602 *Ibid*
$H^1$1603 *Ibid*

Série TT (Affaires et biens des protestants)
TT253 *Religionnaires fugitifs, Meyrueis; Millau*
TT268 *Protestantisme à St Affrique, 1568–1734*

Section Moderne: après 1789

Série AD (Imprimés)
ADXIX^{x}2 *Statistique de la France*
ADXIX^{x}3 *Ibid*
ADXIX^{x}6 *Résultats statistiques du recensement général de la population, 1901*
ADXIX C43^3 *Enquête agricole, 1867: Aveyron; Haute-Loire; Lozère; Ardèche*

Série B (Elections et votes)
BII 17 *Constitution de 1793*
BII 963 *Election du président de la République, 1848: Ardèche*
BII 968 *Election du président de la République, 1848: Aveyron*
BII 999 *Election du président de la République, 1848: Haute-Loire*
BII 1230^{AB} *Votes populaires, plébiscite de 1870: Ardèche*
BII 1235 *Votes populaires, plébiscite de 1870: Aveyron*
BII 1266 *Votes populaires, plébiscite de 1870: Haute-Loire*
BII 1271 *Votes populaires, plébiscite de 1870: Lozère*

Série BB (Ministère de la Justice)
BB^{3}61 *Affaires criminelles, 1789–1834*
BB^{3}77 *Ibid*
BB^{3}105 *Ibid*
BB^{3}106 *Ibid*
BB^{3}127 *Ibid*
BB^{3}131 *Ibid*
BB^{3}149 *Ibid*
BB^{3}151 *Ibid*
BB^{3}166 *Ibid*
BB^{3}175 *Ibid*
BB^{16}75 *Correspondance générale de la division civile: Aveyron*
BB^{16}76 *Ibid*
BB^{16}77 *Ibid*
BB^{16}79 *Ibid*
BB^{16}419 *Correspondance générale de la division civile: Lozère*
BB^{16}420 *Ibid*
BB^{16}421 *Ibid*
BB^{16}422 *Ibid*
BB^{16}423 *Ibid*
BB^{18}163 *Correspondance générale de la division criminelle: Aveyron*
BB^{18}164 *Ibid*
BB^{18}165 *Ibid*
BB^{18}166 *Ibid*
BB^{18}167 *Ibid*
BB^{18}471 *Correspondance générale de la division criminelle: Lozère*
BB^{18}472 *Ibid*
BB^{18}473 *Ibid*
BB^{18}474 *Ibid*
BB^{18}475 *Ibid*
BB^{18}984 *Resistance of protestants to Fête-Dieu, Florac, C. 1818*
BB^{18}1187 *Situation de la ville de Villefranche, août 1830*
BB^{18}1462 *Quarante-cinq centimes, 1848*
BB^{30}380 *Rapports politiques des procureurs généraux: cour de Montpellier*
BB^{30}382 *Rapports politiques des procureurs généraux: cour de Nîmes*
BB^{30}392^A *Affaires politiques de 1850 à 1860*
BB^{30}393 *Ibid*
BB^{30}441 *Cabinet du M. Justice: cour de Montpellier*

Série C (Assemblées Nationales)
C431 *Assemblées du Directoire*
C485 *Ibid*
C511 *Ibid*
C532 *Ibid*
C551 *Ibid*
C938 *Assemblée constituante: enquête sur les événements de 1848*
C939 *Ibid*
C945 *Assemblée constituante: enquête sur le travail agricole et industriel, 1848–9: Ardèche*
C947 *Assemblée constituante: enquête sur le travail agricole et industriel, 1848–9: Aveyron*

C957 *Assemblée constituante: enquête sur le travail agricole et industriel, 1848–9: Lozère*
C1178 *Elections, 1815–30: Aveyron*
C1246 *Elections, 1815–47: Lozère*
C1327 *Elections générales, avril 1848: Haute-Loire; Lozère*
C3022 *Chambre des députés: enquête sur les classes ouvrières, 1872–5: Lozère; Haute-Loire; Aveyron; Ardèche*
C3448 *Assemblée nationale, 1871–6, élections: Ardèche; Aveyron*
C3452 *Assemblée nationale, 1871–6, élections: Haute-Loire; Lozère*
C3466 *Chambre des députés, 1876–7, élections: Haute-Loire; Lozère*
C3485 *Chambre des députés, 1877–81, élections: Haute-Loire*
C3486 *Ibid*
C3487 *Chambre des députés, 1877–81, élections: Lozère*
C3503 *Chambre des députés, 1881–5, élections: Aveyron*
C3528 *Assemblée nationale, 1871–6, élections: Aveyron*
C3564 *Assemblée nationale, 1871–6, élections: Lozère*
C3734 *Chambre des députés, 1876–7, élections: Ardèche*
C3739 *Chambre des députés, 1876–7, élections: Aveyron*
C3770 *Chambre des députés, 1876–7, élections: Haute-Loire*
C3822[A] *Chambre des députés, 1876–7, élections partielles: Haute-Loire*
C3873 *Chambre des députés, 1877–81, élections: Haute-Loire*
C4466 *Chambre des députés, 1885–9, élections: Aveyron*
C4524 *Chambre des députés, 1885–9, élections: Lozère*
C5301 *Chambre des députés, 1885–9, élections: Ardèche; Aveyron*

Série D (Missions des représentants du peuple et comités des Assemblées)
DIII 138 *Comité de Législation: Lozère*
DIII 139 *Ibid*
DIV 17 *Comité de Législation: Ardèche*
DIV 40 *Comité de Législation: Lozère*
DXIV 2 *Comité des Droits Féodaux: Aveyron*
DXIV 5 *Comité des Droits Féodaux: Lozère*

Série F (Versements des Ministères et des Administrations qui en dépendent)
$F^{1b}I$ 257 *Renouvellement des conseils municipaux, 1834–71*
$F^{1b}I$ 258 *Ibid*
$F^{1b}II$ Ardèche 1 *Personnel administratif, 1789–1884*
$F^{1b}II$ Ardèche 2 *Ibid*
$F^{1b}II$ Ardèche 3 *Ibid*
$F^{1b}II$ Ardèche 5 *Ibid*
$F^{1b}II$ Ardèche 6 *Ibid*
$F^{1b}II$ Ardèche 7 *Ibid*
$F^{1b}II$ Ardèche 8 *Ibid*
$F^{1b}II$ Aveyron 1 *Personnel administratif, 1789–1884*
$F^{1b}II$ Aveyron 2 *Ibid*
$F^{1b}II$ Aveyron 3 *Ibid*
$F^{1b}II$ Aveyron 4 *Ibid*
$F^{1b}II$ Aveyron 7 *Ibid*
$F^{1b}II$ Aveyron 8 *Ibid*
$F^{1b}II$ Aveyron 9 *Ibid*
$F^{1b}II$ Aveyron 10 *Ibid*

F^{1b}II Aveyron 11 *Ibid*
F^{1b}II Aveyron 12 *Ibid*
F^{1b}II Aveyron 13 *Ibid*
F^{1b}II Aveyron 14 *Ibid*
F^{1b}II Aveyron 15 *Ibid*
F^{1b}II Aveyron 16 *Ibid*
F^{1b}II Aveyron 17 *Ibid*
F^{1b}II Lozère 1 *Personnel administratif, 1789–1884*
F^{1b}II Lozère 2 *Ibid*
F^{1b}II Lozère 3 *Ibid*
F^{1b}II Lozère 4 *Ibid*
F^{1c}II 54 *Esprit public, élections: objets généraux, 1832–42*
F^{1c}III Ardèche 1 *Esprit public, élections, 1789–1870*
F^{1c}III Ardèche 2 *Ibid*
F^{1c}III Ardèche 4 *Ibid*
F^{1c}III Ardèche 5 *Ibid*
F^{1c}III Ardèche 10 *Ibid*
F^{1c}III Ardèche 11 *Ibid*
F^{1c}III Haute-Loire 1 *Esprit public, élections, 1789–1877*
F^{1c}III Haute-Loire 2 *Ibid*
F^{1c}III Haute-Loire 3 *Ibid*
F^{1c}III Lozère 1 *Esprit public, élections, 1789–1870*
F^{1c}III Lozère 2 *Ibid*
F^{1c}III Lozère 3 *Ibid*
F^{1c}III Lozère 4 *Ibid*
F^{1c}III Lozère 8 *Ibid*
F^{1c}III Lozère 9 *Ibid*
F^{1c}V Ardèche 3 *Conseils-généraux, 1825–33*
F^{1c}V Ardèche 4 *Conseils-généraux, 1834–58*
F^{1c}V Aveyron 4 *Conseils-généraux, 1833–52*
F^{1c}V Haute-Loire 2 *Conseils-généraux, 1817–33*
F^{1c}V Haute-Loire 3 *Conseils-généraux, 1834–52*
F^{1c}V Lozère 3 *Conseils-généraux, 1828–51*
F^{2}543 *Administration départementale: délimitation de cantons, Lot-Lozère, 1792–1840*
F^{2}II Aveyron 1 *Administration départementale: délimitation de communes*
F^{2}II Aveyron 2 *Ibid*
F^{2}II Aveyron 3 *Ibid*
F^{2}II Haute-Loire 1 *Administration départementale: délimitation de communes*
F^{3}II Lozère 1 *Administration communale: Lozère, 1790–1848*
F^{3}II Lozère 2 *Ibid*
F^{3}II Lozère 3 *Ibid*
F^{3}II Lozère 4 *Ibid*
F^{3}II Lozère 5 *Ibid*
F^{3}II Lozère 6 *Ibid*
F^{3}II Lozère 7 *Ibid*
F^{7}3657^I *Police générale: classement départemental, 1790–1830*
F^{7}3936 *Police générale: gendarmerie, Aveyron*
F^{7}3937 *Ibid*
F^{7}3938 *Ibid*
F^{7}4065 *Police générale: gendarmerie, Lozère*

$F^7$4067 *Ibid*

$F^7$4758 *Comité de sûreté générale: dossiers individuels*

$F^7$6694 *Affaires politiques: associations, loges maçonniques*

$F^7$6770 *Situation politique des départements: Lozère, 1815–30*

$F^7$6779 *Situation politique des départements: gendarmerie, Aveyron*

$F^7$6781 *Situation politique des départements: gendarmerie, Lozère*

$F^7$7407 *Police générale: affaires diverses*

$F^7$8990 *Police générale: affaires administratives, 1814–19*

$F^7$8998 *Ibid*

$F^7$9635 *Ibid*

$F^7$9675 *Ibid*

$F^7$9842 *Police générale: commissaires de police, an XIII–1847*

$F^7$9876 *Police générale: individus surveillés, loi du 29 octobre 1815*

$F^7$12313 *Police générale: congrégations non autorisées, 1880–1901*

F^{10}2315 *Agriculture: mise en valeur des communaux, 1860–1900*

F^{15}3967 *Hospices et secours: victimes du 2 décembre 1851*

F^{15}3973 *Ibid*

F^{15}4118 *Ibid*

F^{15}4133 *Ibid*

F^{15}4154 *Ibid*

F^{15}4165 *Ibid*

F^{15}4218 *Ibid*

F^{17*}88 *Enseignement primaire: enquête de 1833, Aveyron*

F^{17*}122 *Enseignement primaire: enquête de 1833, Lozère*

F^{17}9253 *Inspection de l'enseignement primaire: Ardèche, 1847–93*

F^{17}9255 *Inspection de l'enseignement primaire: Aveyron, 1847–93*

F^{17}9265 *Inspection de l'enseignement primaire: Haute-Loire, 1847–93*

F^{17}9267 *Inspection de l'enseignement primaire: Lozère, 1847–93*

F^{17}9322 *Inspection de l'enseignement primaire: Aveyron; Ardèche, 1855–6*

F^{17}9327 *Inspection de l'enseignement primaire: Haute-Loire, 1817–90*

F^{17}9328 *Inspection de l'enseignement primaire: Lozère, 1817–90*

F^{17}10294 *Enseignement primaire: personnel et affaires diverses, Ardèche; Aveyron*

F^{17}10311 *Enseignement primaire: personnel et affaires diverses, Aveyron*

F^{17}10550 *Enseignement primaire: états de situation des écoles primaires, 1880–1, Ardèche; Aveyron*

F^{17}10556 *Enseignement primaire: états de situation des écoles primaires, 1880–1, Lozère*

F^{19*}1 *Cultes: paroisses du département de l'Aveyron*

F^{19}403 *Cultes: affaires des cultes, Ardèche, 1790–1822*

F^{19}408 *Cultes: affaires des cultes, Aveyron, 1790–1821*

F^{19}444 *Cultes: affaires des cultes, Lozère, 1791–1822*

F^{19}755^A *Cultes: réunions et disjonctions de succursales, diocèse du Puy, an XII–1843*

F^{19}756^A *Cultes: réunions et disjonctions de succursales, diocèse de Rodez, an XII–1820*

F^{19}2124 *Cultes: succursales érigées, 1847, Rodez à Soissons*

F^{19}2127 *Cultes: succursales érigées, 1848, Orléans à Viviers*

F^{19}2129 *Cultes: succursales érigées, 1849, Le Mans à Viviers*

F^{19}2537 *Cultes: diocèse de Mende, évêques, dossiers personnels*

F^{19}2563 *Cultes: diocèse du Puy, évêques, dossiers personnels*

F^{19}2570 *Cultes: diocèse de Rodez, évêques, dossiers personnels*

F^{19}2571 *Ibid*

F^{19}2596 *Cultes: diocèse de Viviers, évêques, dossiers personnels*
F^{19}3016 *Cultes: diocèse de Rodez, curés, dossiers personnels*
F^{19}3017 *Ibid*
F^{19}3063 *Cultes: diocèse de Viviers, curés, dossiers personnels*
F^{19}3064 *Ibid*
F^{19}5686 *Cultes: police des cultes, diocèse de Mende, an XI–1827*
F^{19}5708 *Cultes: police des cultes, diocèse de Viviers, an XI–1829*
F^{19}5767 *Cultes: police des cultes, diocèse de Viviers, 1830–50*
F^{19}5824 *Cultes: police des cultes, diocèse de Mende, 1850–89*
F^{19}5848 *Cultes: police des cultes, diocèse du Puy, 1862–86*
F^{19}5853 *Cultes: police des cultes, diocèse de Rodez, 1850–80*
F^{19}5877 *Cultes: police des cultes, diocèse de Viviers, 1850–89*
F^{19}5927 *Cultes: police des cultes, diocèse du Puy, 1880–1905*
F^{19}5930 *Cultes: police des cultes, diocèse de Rodez, 1880–1905*
F^{19}5946 *Cultes: police des cultes, diocèse de Viviers, 1880–1905*
F^{19}6071 *Cultes: décrets de 1880, Ardèche, Aveyron*
F^{19}6073 *Cultes: décrets de 1880, Haute-Loire*
F^{19}10467 *Cultes: administration des cultes non catholiques*
F^{19}10471 *Ibid*
F^{19}12317 *Cultes: congrégations, Jura–Lozère, 1880–1901*

Archives Départementales de l'Ardèche, Privas

Série A (Actes du pouvoir souverain et Domaine public)
A5 *Pièces imprimées, 1762–85*

Série C (Administrations provinciales)
C991 *Enquiry into the commons, 1767*
C1083 *Mémoires sur les justices seigneuriales* [Dom Vaissette's Enquiry]
C1084 *Ibid*
C1085 *Ibid*

Série L (Révolution)
L267 *Assemblées électorales: délibérations et correspondance, 1790–an VII*
L269 *Procès-verbaux des assemblées primaires, an VI*
L344 *Circonscriptions territoriales, 1790–1*
L345 *Divisions de districts en cantons, 1790–an VII*
L356 *Correspondance sur des affaires communales, 1790*
L798 *Circonscriptions territoriales, 1791–2*

Série M (Administration générale [post-1800])
2M273 *Elections: élection du président de la République, 1848*
2M274 *Elections: plébiscite des 20 et 21 décembre 1851*
2M275 *Elections: plébiscite des 21–22 novembre 1852*
2M276 *Elections: plébiscite du 8 mai 1870*
2M337 *Elections législatives: Assemblée Constituante, 1848*
2M338 *Elections législatives: Assemblée Législative, 1849*
2M339 *Elections législatives: élection partielle du 8 juillet 1849*
2M340 *Elections législatives: élection partielle du 10 mars 1850*
2M341 *Elections législatives: electoral law of 31 May 1850*

2M344 *Elections législatives: 21–22 juin 1857*
2M345 *Elections législatives: élection partielle des 24–25 juillet 1864*
2M346 *Elections législatives: 23–24 mai 1869*
2M347 *Elections législatives: 8 février 1871*
2M348 *Ibid*
2M349 *Elections législatives: 20 février 1876*
2M350 *Elections législatives: procès-verbaux de recensement des votes, 1877–1914*
2M351 *Elections législatives: 1881–5; 1886*
2M352 *Elections législatives: 1889–96*
2M391 *Elections cantonales: conseil-général et conseils d'arrondissement, 1848–50*
2M474 *Conseils municipaux: sections électorales, 1831–51*
2M498 *Conseils municipaux: protestations, 1840*
2M512 *Conseils municipaux: procès-verbaux d'élection, arrondissement de Largentière, 1846*
2M518 *Conseils municipaux: 1848*
2M519 *Conseils municipaux: protestations, 1848*
2M524 *Conseils municipaux: 1852–5*
2M653 *Conseils municipaux: 1815–18*
2M657 *Maires et adjoints: 1819–20*
2M664 *Maires et adjoints: plaintes, 1829*
2M682 *Conseils municipaux: plaintes, 1850–65*
2M690 *Maires et adjoints: plaintes, 1864–5*
2M698 *Conseils municipaux: plaintes, 1871–92*
2M699 *Conseils municipaux: révocations, suspensions, 1872–80*
2M700 *Conseils municipaux: nominations, 1874–5*
2M708 *Conseils municipaux: révocations, 1881–93*
5M7 *Police politique: 1814–18*
5M9 *Police politique: 1841–51*
5M10 *Police politique: 1848–52*
5M11 *Police politique: 1849–51*
5M13 *Police politique: 1850–2*
5M14 *Police politique: coup d'état du 2 décembre 1851*
5M15 *Police politique: mouvements insurrectionnels, 4–6 décembre 1851*
5M31 *Police politique: 1858–60*
5M38 *Police politique: 1869–76*
5M40 *Police politique: 1871–9*
5M41 *Police politique: 1880–5*
5M42 *Police politique: 1880–9*
5M43 *Police politique: 1885–98*
5M44 *Police politique: 1889–1901*
6M44 *Sûreté générale: rapports de police, 1833–5*
6M58 *Sûreté générale: rapports de police, 1861–2*
6M59 *Sûreté générale: rapports de police, 1863–6*
9M3 *Circonscriptions territoriales: érections en communes*
9M5 *Ibid*
9M6 *Ibid*
9M8 *Circonscriptions territoriales: réunions de communes*
9M10 *Circonscriptions territoriales: réunions de sections en communes*
9M11 *Ibid*
9M18 *Circonscriptions territoriales: projets d'érections en communes non réalisés*
10M58 *Population: recensement par familles, arrondissement de Privas, 1820*

12M182 *Agriculture: statistiques agricoles, 1853–6*
12M188 *Agriculture: statistiques agricoles, 1877–8*
15M1 *Travail: enquête sur le travail, 1848–1938*

Série O (Administration et comptabilité communales [unclassified])
O no. 60 *Loubaresse à Lyas, 1828–1939*
O no. 108 *Borée, 1836–1932*
O no. 109 *Ibid*
O no. 110 *Ibid*
O no. 130 *Usclades à Uzer, 1811–1939*

Série T (Enseignement)
T71 *Instruction primaire: correspondance, 1882–7*
T363 *Instruction primaire: laïcisation, 1879–84*

Série V (Cultes)
V8 *Pièces relatives à la circonscription des paroisses et succursales, an X*
V26 *Pièces relatives à la circonscription des paroisses et succursales, 1807*
V27 *Tableau des succursales, 1807*
V53 *Demandes pour l'érection d'églises en succursales, 1819–29*
V141 *Pèlerinages, processions, agitation cléricale, 1872–86*
V155 *Affaires diverses, 1879–93*

Archives Départementales de l'Aveyron, Rodez

Série C (Administrations provinciales)
C351 *Rôle de taille et vingtième, Laguiole, 1786*
C644 *Rôle de taille et vingtième, St Antonin, 1789*
C1530 *Assemblée provinciale de Haute-Guienne: procès-verbaux des séances, 1779–*
     86
C1598 *Déclarations des biens, revenus et rentes nobles, 1781–6*
C1599 *Ibid*
C1600 *Ibid*
C1601 *Ibid*
C1604 *Ibid*
C1605 *Ibid*
C1606 *Ibid*
C1607 *Ibid*
C1610 *Ibid*
C1611 *Ibid*
C1612 *Ibid*
C1613 *Ibid*
C1675 *Administration provinciale de Haute-Guienne*

Série 2E (Communes)
2E 1052 *Délibérations municipales de Lacalm, 1790–an III*
2E 1053 *Délibérations municipales de Lacalm, an VII–1831*
2E 216 17 *Etat-civil de l'église réformée de St Affrique, 1756–90*
2E 221 2 *St Beauzély: registres paroissiaux, 1735–92*
2E 222 14 *St Chély-d'Aubrac: rôle des défricheurs de Bonnefont, 1792–3*
2E 275 24 *Sévérac: partage des biens communaux, 1793*

Série G (Clergé séculier)
G113 *Visites pastorales de Mgr. de Saléon, évêque de Rodez, circa 1738*

Série J (Dons et acquisitions)
J134 *Lettres de Vernhet de Laumière, 1848–9*
48J34 *Famille Rouvelet: correspondance, 1830–44*
48J35 *Famille Rouvelet: correspondance, 1830–35*
48J36 *Famille Rouvelet: correspondance, 1849–55*

Série L (Révolution [interim classification])
For the definitive inventory of this series, see J.-M. Tisseyre, *Répertoire numérique de la série L. Tome 1: administrations du département, des districts, des municipalités de cantons. Comités de surveillance à comités révolutionnaires (1790–an VII)* (Rodez, Archives départementales, 1977).
L610 *Elections, an VI, assemblées primaires*
L611 *Ibid*
L612 *Ibid*
L612 *bis Ibid*
L612 *ter Ibid*
L613 *Ibid*
L614 *Elections, an VI, liste des électeurs*
L615 *Elections, an VI, registres de la remise des procès-verbaux des assemblées primaires*
L669 *bis Administration du département: troubles, 1790–2*
L682 *bis Administration du département; enquête Delpech, 1793*
L697 *Délimitation et constitution du département, 1790–1819*
L701 *Modifications de circonscriptions territoriales: municipalités, 1790–1*
L702 *Désunions et réunions des municipalités, cantons et districts*
L706 *Administration du département: troubles et brigandages, an IV*
L745 *Troubles à Sauveterre, 1790*
9L213 *District de Sévérac: tableaux des détenus, an II*
67L(2) *Comité de surveillance de Rodez: correspondance reçue, 1790–3*
70L *Comité de surveillance de St Côme: registre de délibérations, 1793–an II*
72L(1) *Comité de surveillance de St Geniez: correspondance reçue, an II*
90L *Tribunal Criminel de l'Aveyron, an VII*

Série M (Administration générale [post-1800])
This series awaits classification and all class-marks are provisional.
M *Registre des arrêtés de M. le préfet, an VIII–an X*
M *Elections législatives: 1871*
M *Elections législatives: 1876*
1M28 *Correspondance préfectorale: enregistrement des lettres ministérielles, 1813–15*
1M37 *Correspondance intérieure et ministérielle, 1815–16*
1M112a *Correspondance secrète, an VIII–an X*
1M142 *Correspondance avec M. d'état chargé de la police, an XIII–1808*
1M314 *Registre de correspondance, minutes, 1813–15*
1M319 *Loi du 27 avril 1825: indémnité aux émigrés, registre de correspondance, 1828–32*
1M320 *Loi du 27 avril 1825: indémnité aux émigrés, registre de correspondance, 1825–8*

1M350 *Correspondance ministérielle, 1828–31*
3M29 *Sénatus-consulte du 20 mai 1815 sur l'Acte additionnel*
3M31 *Cent Jours: élections des maires et adjoints, mai–juin 1815*
3M47 *Monarchie de Juillet: élections aux conseils municipaux*
3M52 *Monarchie de Juillet: élections municipales, 1840–6*
3M60 *Seconde République: élections législatives, avril 1848*
3M61 *Seconde République: élections législatives, mai 1849*
3M68 *Seconde République: élections aux fonctions de maire et d'adjoint, 1848–51*
3M69 *Seconde République: élections aux conseils municipaux*
3M70 *Ibid*
3M71 *Ibid*
3M72 *Ibid*
3M75 *Renseignements sur la composition des conseils municipaux, 1852*
3M76 *Second Empire: plébiscite des 21–22 novembre 1852*
3M79 *Second Empire: élections au corps législatif, septembre 1853*
3M80 *Second Empire: élections au corps législatif, juin 1857*
3M422 *Elections à l'Assemblée Nationale, vote du 8 février 1871*
3M425 *Elections législatives, janvier 1876*
3M439 *Elections législatives, octobre 1877*
3M440 *Elections législatives, août 1881*
3M441 *Election complémentaire, arrondissement d'Espalion, 18 mai–1 juin 1884*
3M442 *Elections législatives, octobre 1885*
3M443 *Election complémentaire, 27 février 1887*
3M444 *Elections législatives, septembre–octobre 1889*
3M445 *Elections législatives, août–septembre 1893*
4M114 *Election du président de la République, décembre 1848*
4M115 *Plébiscite pour Louis-Napoléon Bonaparte, décembre 1851*
4M115 *bis Référendum–plébiscite sur le rétablissement de la dignité impériale, novembre 1852*
4M116 *Evénements de décembre 1851: inculpés politiques*
4M116 *bis Ibid*
4M117 *Evénements de décembre 1851: travaux de la commission mixte départementale*
4M118 *Evénements de décembre 1851: inculpés politiques*
4M121 *Coup d'état de 1851: pensions accordées aux victimes, 1881–1915*
4M122 *Plébiscite du 8 mai 1870*
4M^{1}136 *Electeurs communaux de l'arrondissement de Millau, 1840*
4M^{1}138 *Electeurs communaux des arrondissements de Rodez et de Villefranche, 1843*
5M10 *Elections législatives, 1863*
5M10 *bis Polémique entre Mgr. Delalle et Calvet-Rogniat, député*
5M11 *Elections législatives, 1869*
8M52 *Maires et adjoints, 1876–8*
8M54 *Elections municipales, 1878*
8M^{1}15 *Maires et adjoints, 1815–59*
8M^{1}30 *Maires et adjoints, 1843–60*
8M^{1}33 *Réorganisation municipale, 1852–4*
8M^{1}35 *Elections municipales, 1855–69*
8M^{1}41 *Maires et adjoints, 1865–7*
8M^{1}56 *Renseignements sur les municipalités, 1881*
8M^{1}58 *Maires et adjoints, 1881–1913*

8M¹58 *bis Ibid*
11M¹62 *Rapports politiques adressés au M. de l'Intérieur, 1860–4*
11M¹63 *Rapports politiques adressés au M. de l'Intérieur, 1868–72*
11M7 24 *Police générale, 1852–62*
11M7 25 *Sûreté générale, 1851–95*
11M7 26 *Troubles de Verrières et de St Beauzély, 1876*

Série O (Administration et comptabilité communales)
22 O 197 *Prades-d'Aubrac*
22 O 222 *St Chély-d'Aubrac*

Série V (Cultes)
3V5 *Correspondance du clergé avec l'évêché, 1823–6*
3V9 *Clergé: affaires ecclésiastiques diverses, 1876–1905*
6V1 *Correspondance de l'évêché de Rodez, 1787–1810*
6V3 *Correspondance de l'évêché de Rodez, 1825–41*
8V1 *Réclamations relatives au choix des curés et succursales, an VII–an XII*
8V8 *Affaires ecclésiastiques, 1857–87*
9V2 *Objets de police relatifs aux plaintes, an IV–1809*
9V3 *Plaintes, 1849–96*
15V1 *Circonscriptions des paroisses et des succursales, 1792–1808*
15V5 *Circonscriptions paroissiales, an X–1809*
15V7 *Etats des succursales proposées, 1807–8*
34V7 *Culte protestant, 1857–1901*

Fonds (recent deposits)
Fonds Alengrin
Fonds Bouzat

Archives Départementales du Cantal, Aurillac

Série M (Administration générale [post-1800])
2M2 *Plébiscite du 8 mai 1870*
36M1 *Monarchie de Juillet: police politique*
38M1 *Coup d'état du 2 décembre 1851*

Série O (Administration et comptabilité communales)
0216 *St Urcize*
0241 *La Trinitat*

Série V (Cultes)
1V18 *Chapelles et annexes*
1V76 *Curés, desservants, vicaires, aumôniers*
1V126 *Etablissements publics et édifices*

Archives Départementales de la Haute-Loire, Le Puy

Série C (Administrations provinciales)
C7343 [501C] *Reçus de mandes, concordances des mandements et les paroisses vellaves, 1790*

Série J (Dons et acquisitions)
J237/116 *Fonds Convers: notes de l'abbé Cornut*

Série M (Administration générale [post-1800])
2M^{2}1 *Rapports des préfets, an VIII–an XIV; 1813–73*
2M^{2}2 *Rapports des sous-préfets de Brioude, an VIII–an IX; 1816–19*
2M^{2}3 *Rapports des sous-préfets d'Yssingeaux, an VII–an IX; 1817–*
2M^{3}3 *Circonscriptions administratives: cantons, an IX; 1816–1909*
3M^{1}9 *Elections: président de la République, 1848*
3M^{1}10 *Elections à l'Assemblée constituante, 1848*
3M^{1}11 *Rétablissement de l'Empire: 1851–2, plébiscite*
3M^{1}12 *Plébiscite de 1870: procès-verbaux d'élection*
3M^{1}14 *Vote sur le plébiscite, 1870*
3M^{1}15 *Elections législatives: février 1871*
3M^{3}10 *Elections législatives: 1839–48*
3M^{3}11 *Elections des représentants du peuple à l'Assemblée nationale législative, 1849–50*
3M^{3}12 *Elections législatives: 1850–9*
3M^{3}13 *Elections législatives: 1876–9*
3M^{3}14 *Elections législatives: 1885*
4M4 *Administration municipale: décrets, circulaires, 1815–18*
4M6 *Maires et adjoints, 1809–80*
4M27 *Araules: maires, adjoints, élections, 1817–1938*
4M101 *Croisances: maires, adjoints, élections, 1815–1938*
4M124 *Goudet: maires, adjoints, élections, 1815–1938*
4M132 *Langeac: maires, adjoints, élections, an VIII–1938*
4M167 *Paulhac: maires, adjoints, élections, 1816–1938*
4M268 *Torsiac: maires, adjoints, élections, 1830–1938*
4M278 *Vergezac: maires, adjoints, élections, 1830–1938*
5M45 *Restauration: rixes et agressions, 1816–24*
5M72 *Police générale: correspondance et affaires diverses, 1848–51*
5M73 *Seconde République: crimes et délits, 1848–51*
6M83 *Saint Simoniens, 1833*
6M93 *Seconde République: politique générale, 1848–51*
6M99 *Seconde République: troubles, complots, émeutes, 1848–51*
6M100 *Seconde République: cris et écrits séditieux, 1848–51*
6M104 *Seconde République: affaire Cussinel frères, 1850–1*
6M105 *Seconde République: victimes du coup d'état, décembre 1851*
6M106 *Seconde République: événements politiques du 2 décembre 1851*
6M106 *bis Ibid*
6M140 *Affaires politiques diverses, 1870–1940*
6M142 *Manifestation de St Victor de Malescours, 1880*
17M5 *Tableau statistique comparatif du département, 1844; 1862*
17M^{1}12 *Statistiques agricoles quinquennales, par cantons, 1852*
18M41 *Enquête sur le métayage, 1936*
18M42 *Agriculture: modes de location et d'exploitation, 1855–*

Série O (Administration et comptabilité communales)
51 O III *Le Chambon sur Lignon: biens communaux, 1818–1954*
147 O III *Paulhac: biens communaux, 1845–1951*
147 O IV *Paulhac: bâtiments et mobilier*

154 O III *Pradelles: biens communaux, 1806–1945*
154 O IV *Pradelles: bâtiments et mobilier*
234 O III *Saugues: biens communaux, 1792–*
257 O I *Vergezac: circonscriptions territoriales, 1806–73*
257 O III *Vergezac: biens communaux, 1833–1954*
257 O IV *Vergezac: bâtiments et mobilier*
257 O VIII *Vergezac: cimetière et concessions*

Série S (Travaux publics et transports)
S463 *Statistique: chemins de fer, 1875–6*
S464 *Statistique: chemins de fer, 1887–8*
S465 *Ibid*

Série T (Enseignement)
T55 *Statistique de l'enseignement primaire, 1892–7*
T56 *Statistique de l'enseignement primaire, 1881–2*
T61 *Conseil départemental de l'instruction publique de la Haute-Loire, 1859–80*

Série V (Cultes)
4V1 *Circonscriptions paroissiales*
6V1 *Police du culte*
7V2 *Personnel*
11V3 *Culte protestant: personnel, 1804–93*

Archives Départementales de la Lozère, Mende

Série B (Cours et juridictions)
161B$^{1-3}$ *Juridictions secondaires: Estables, 1749–90*
226B *Pièces concernant David et Pierre Causse de Gatuzières*
279B$^{14-21}$ *Juridictions secondaires: Le Malzieu, 1765–77*
302B *Juridictions secondaires: La Méjanelle, 1777–90*
343B^{15} *Juridictions secondaires: Meyrueis, 1787–9*
411B^{1} *Juridictions secondaires: Peyre, 1770–*
475B^{1} *Juridictions secondaires: St Alban, 1754–80*
475B^{2} *Juridictions secondaires: St Alban, 1781–91*
483B$^{1-2}$ *Juridictions secondaires: Ste Croix-Vallée-Française, 1688–1791*

Série C (Administrations provinciales)
C20 *Registre des déclarations de biens nobles pour le vingtième noble, 1757–9*
C30 *Etat des communautés du diocèse en ce qui concerne les impositions, 1680–1753*
C34 *Procès-verbaux de vérification de la capitation, 1734*
C466 *Etat contenant les noms des communautés du diocèse de Mende, 1736*
C943 *Déclarations des droits et biens nobles, 1750–80*

Série E (Communes)
E03 *Allenc*
E08 *Arzenc-de-Randon*
E69 *Fraissinet-de-Fourques*
E90 *Le Malzieu ville*
E155 *Communautés d'habitants: St Germain-de-Calberte*

E194 *Communautés d'habitants: Vialas*
E865 *Communautés d'habitants: Florac, 1769–90*
E874 *Communautés d'habitants: Le Malzieu, 1639–1793*
E945 *Communautés d'habitants: St Julien-d'Arpaon, 1527–1789*
2E 874 *Titres de communautés d'habitants: La Malzieu*

Série F (Fonds divers)
F427 *Fonds Vachin*
F1177 *Registre des délibérations des chefs et principaux royalistes du département de la Lozère, 1815* [copy]
F1274 *Lettres adressées au Comte de Chambrun, 1815*
F2808 *Lettres d'Honoré Charrier*
F2809 *Fonds Larochenégly*
F2810 *Ibid*
F2815 *Ibid*
F2818 *Ibid*

Série G (Clergé séculier)
G63 *Etat des fiefs situés dans le diocèse de Mende*
G773 *Edit du Roi portant règlement sur l'administration de la justice dans le Vivarais et le Gévaudan, 1767*
G1871 *Livre-journal du Prieur-curé d'Estables, 1716–29*

Série J (Dons et acquisitions)
1J87 *Correspondance de Mgr. de la Brunière, évêque de Mende, 1825*
7J16 *Fonds St Amand*
7J56 *Ibid*
8J56 *Fonds Boyer, Florac, an IV–1848*
8J148 *Journal de Madamoiselle des Molinets, 1871–6*
13J15 *Fonds Valgalier*
17J46 *Documents concernant Charrier de Chirac*

Série K (Lois, ordonnances, arrêtés depuis 1800)
7K2 *Registres de correspondance du préfet, 1806–7*
*7K4 *Registre de correspondance du préfet, an X–1814*

Série L (Révolution)
L*1 *Collection des lois*
L110 *Circonscriptions et dénominations administratives, 1789–an IV*
L112 *Administration du département*
L127 *Lettres saisies, 1792*
L189 *Circonscription des paroisses, 1790–an VIII*
L190 *Etat des revenus du clergé, 1790*
L191 *Traitement des ecclésiastiques*
L206 *District de Florac: correspondance, an II*
L387 *District de Villefort: cultes, 1790*
L499 *Comité de surveillance d'Albaret-le-Comtal*
L500 *Comité de surveillance d'Allenc*
L501 *Comité de surveillance d'Aumont*
L502 *Comité de surveillance d'Auroux*
L503 *Comité de surveillance de Bagnols-les-Bains*

L504 *Comité de surveillance de La Canourgue*
L506 *Ibid*
L507 *Comité de surveillance de Chanac*
L508 *Comité de surveillance de Châteauneuf-de-Randon*
L509 *Comité de surveillance de Chaudeyrac*
L510 *Comité de surveillance de Chirac*
L511 *Comité de surveillance de Grandrieu*
L512 *Comité de surveillance de Lachamp*
L513 *Comité de surveillance de Langogne*
L514 *Ibid*
L515 *Comité de surveillance du Malzieu*
L516 *Ibid*
L517 *Ibid*
L518 *Comité de surveillance de Mende*
L519 *Ibid*
L520 *Comité de surveillance de St Alban*
L521 *Ibid*
L522 *Comité de surveillance de St Chély-d'Apcher*
L523 *Ibid*
L524 *Ibid*
L525 *Ibid*
L526 *Ibid*
L527 *Ibid*
L528 *Ibid*
L529 *Comité de surveillance de Sainte Enimie*
L530 *Comité de surveillance de Serverette*
L531 *Comité de surveillance de Villefort*
IIL3 *District de Florac: élections, juge de paix*
IIL87[1-13] *Tribunaux de district: Meyrueis*
IIL273 *Jugements arbitraux, actes des tribunaux de famille*

Série M (Administration générale [post-1800])
Seriously depleted by a fire in 1887, this series awaits classification. All class-marks are provisional.

IIM[5]3 *Préfets: dossiers individuels*
IIM[7]3 *Sous-préfets de Florac: dossiers individuels*
IIM[7]4 *Sous-préfets de Marvejols: dossiers individuels*
IIIM[5]2 *Maires, adjoints, conseillers municipaux, 1892–1953*
IIIM[5]3 *Plaintes et poursuites contre les maires, adjoints, 1806–1939*
IIIM[5]5 *Maires, adjoints, conseillers municipaux, 1888–*
IVM[1]5 *Elections: liste définitive des six cents contribuables les plus imposés du département de la Lozère, 1811*
IVM[2]1–7 *Plébiscites, référendums, élections des Présidents de la République*
IVM[4]1–9 *Elections législatives: 1816–48*
IVM[4]10–12 *Elections législatives: 1849–52*
IVM[4]13–19 *Elections législatives: 1851–77*
IVM[4]20–23 *Elections législatives: 1879–85*
IVM[4]24–25 *Elections législatives: 1886–89*
IVM[4]26–29 *Elections législatives: 1893–1905*
IVM[5]1 *Elections cantonales, 1833*
IVM[7]1–17 *Elections municipales, 1848–88*

IVM^{8}48 *Elections municipales: Chirac*
IVM^{8}57 *Elections municipales: La Fage-Montivernoux*
IVM^{8}60 *Elections municipales: Florac*
IVM^{8}61 *Elections municipales: Fontanes*
IVM^{8}62 *Elections municipales: Fontans*
IVM^{8}64 *Elections municipales: Fraissinet-de-Fourques*
IVM^{8}71 *Elections municipales: Grèzes*
IVM^{8}93 *Elections municipales: Le Massegros*
IVM^{8}98 *Elections municipales: Le Monestier*
IVM^{8}104 *Elections municipales: Naussac*
IVM^{8}125 *Elections municipales: Le Recoux*
IVM^{8}130 *Elections municipales: Les Rousses*
IVM^{8}146 *Elections municipales: Sainte Enimie*
IVM^{8}198 *Elections municipales: Villefort*
VIM^{2}2 *Rapports du sous-préfecture de Florac, an X–1881*
VIM^{2}3 *Rapports du sous-préfecture de Marvejols, an X–1923*
VIM^{2}4 *Comptes-rendus: chefs-lieux de canton*
VIM^{2}6 *Rapports du commissaire de police, canton de Langogne, 1880–1*
VIM^{2}11 *Rapports du commissaire de police, canton de Meyrueis, 1881–*
VIM^{8}7 *Banquets politiques, 1851*
VIM^{9}2 *Evénements à caractère politique*
VIM^{9}3 *Actes de nature à troubler l'ordre public, 1816–1900*
VIM10 2 *Boulangisme*
VIM10 3 *Royalisme*
VIM10 10 *Activités des partis: comités d'action républicaine, 1885–1936*

Série O (Administration et comptabilité communales)
2 O 114 *Altier*
2 O 172 *Auroux*
2 O 438 *Chasséradès, biens*
2 O 484 *Chaudeyrac, biens*
2 O 487 *Chaudeyrac, contentieux*
2 O 493 *Chaulhac*
2 O 510 *Le Cheylard-L'Evêque, biens*
2 O 517 *Chirac, église*
2 O 535 *Collet-de-Dèze, temple, église*
2 O 585 *Estables*
2 O 594 *La Fage-Montivernoux*
2 O 627 *Florac, contentieux*
2 O 661 *Fraissinet-de-Fourques*
2 O 817 *Lanuéjols, biens*
2 O 821 *Lanuéjols, contentieux*
2 O 864 *Luc, biens*
2 O 876 *Malbouzon, contentieux*
2 O 940 *Le Massegros*
2 O 942 *Ibid*
2 O 945 *Ibid*
2 O 1014 *Montbrun, contentieux*
2 O 1104 *Pelouse*
2 O 1223 *Le Recoux*
2 O 1225 *Ibid*

2 O 1283 *Le Rozier*
2 O 1292 *St Alban, biens*
2 O 1293 *Ibid*
2 O 1406 *St Denis-en-Margeride, biens*
2 O 1420 *Sainte Enimie, contentieux*
2 O 1493 *St Georges-de-Levéjac*
2 O 1688 *St Pierre-le-Vieux*
2 O 1758 *Les Salces*
2 O 1804 *Termes, biens*

Série T (Enseignement [unclassified])
T *Monographies des instituteurs, circa 1862: St Germain-de-Calberte*
T *Monographies des instituteurs, circa 1862: Albaret-le-Comtal*
T *Monographies des instituteurs, circa 1862: Auxillac*
T *Monographies des instituteurs, circa 1862: Rousses*
T *Monographies des instituteurs, circa 1862: Le Rozier*
T *Monographies des instituteurs, circa 1862: La Tieule*
T891 *Langogne: collège du Sacré-Cœur*

Série U (Justice [unclassified])
14IIU (331) *Cour d'assizes, Mende*
14IIU (338) *Ibid*
14IIU (344) *Ibid*
14IIU (345) *Ibid*
14IIU (346) *Ibid*
14IIU (347) *Ibid*
14IIU (348) *Ibid*
14IIU (359) *Ibid*
14IIU (360) *Ibid*
14IIU (361) *Ibid*
14 *ter* IIU 1 *Cour prévotale, 1816–32*
15IIU 3 *Tribunal correctionnel de Florac, 1811–25*
27IIU 21 *Tribunal de première instance de Florac, an VIII–1816*
27IIU 25 *Ibid*
27IIU 27 *Ibid*
27IIU 38 *Ibid*
31 *bis* IIU *Dossier relatif aux études et notaires: Tichit, notaire à La Fage-Montivernoux*
43IIU 52 *Tribunal de première instance de Marvejols, an XIII–1837*
43IIU 54 *Ibid*
43IIU 55 *Ibid*
43IIU 57 *Ibid*
43IIU 77 *Ibid*
43IIU 89 *Ibid*
43IIU 94 *Ibid*
43IIU 100 *Ibid*
43IIU 115 *Ibid*
43IIU 137 *Ibid*
43IIU 154 *Ibid*

Série V (Cultes)
11 V 1 *Renseignements sur l'esprit politique du clergé, 1830–1905*
59 V 1 *Circonscriptions paroissiales, an X–1887*
62 V 1 *Chapelles non autorisées*
85 V 1 *Police du culte, an XIII–1905*

Archives Départementales du Puy-de-Dôme, Clermont-Ferrand

Série C (Administration générale [post-1800])
C1803 *Intendance: affaires communales, 1787*
C1804 *Intendance: procès-verbaux d'Assemblées paroissiales, 1787*
C1805 *Ibid*
C1806 *Ibid*
C1815 *Ibid*
C1818 *Intendance*
C7354 *Intendance*
C7356 *Intendance*
C7358 *Intendance: procès-verbal de l'Assemblée d'élection d'Aurillac, 1787*
C7359 *Intendance: procès-verbal de l'Assemblée d'élection d'Aurillac, 1788*
C7360 *Intendance: procès-verbal de l'Assemblée d'élection de Brioude, 1787*
C7361 *Intendance: procès-verbal de l'Assemblée d'élection de Brioude, 1788*
C7371 *Intendance: procès -verbal des séances de l'Assemblée préliminaire d'élection de St Flour, 1787*
C7372 *Intendance: procès-verbal de l'Assemblée complète de l'élection de St Flour, 1787*
C7373 *Intendance: procès-verbal de l'Assemblée d'élection de St Flour, 1788*
4C4 *Liste des municipalités, arrondissement de Brioude*
4C11 *Observations du bureau intermédiaire de l'Assemblée d'élection d'Aurillac*
4C36 *Intendance*
4C38 *Intendance*

Archives Communales de Millau (Aveyron)

GG14 *Etat-civil de l'église réformée de Millau, 1737–84*
GG15 *Etat-civil de l'église réformée de Millau, 1760–76*
GG16 *Etat-civil de l'église réformée de Millau, 1776–92*
GG17 *Etat-civil de l'église réformée de Millau, 1781–92*

Archives Communales de Rodez (Aveyron)

BB21 *Procès-verbaux des délibérations du conseil politique établi à Rodez dans l'assemblée générale du 9 août 1789 au 22 février 1790*

Archives Communales de St Flour (Cantal)

D^{3}21 *Pétition et délibération du canton de St Hippolyte (Aveyron)*
K^{5}13 *Petite catéchisme des droits et devoirs d'élection pour l'an V, Aurillac, Ventôse*
P^{1}44 *Pièces relatives à l'épiscopat de Mgr. de Belmont, 1er évêque concordataire de St Flour*

P^{1}52 *bis Registre des lettres adressées à l'évêque de St Flour par le Ministre des cultes, 1802–6*

P^{1}52 *ter Cahier d'enregistrement des lettres écrites par Mgr. de Belmont, évêque de St Flour, 1802–3*

S18 *bis Minutes de rapports présentés au préfet en l'an VIII par le conseil d'arrondissement de St Flour*

Archives de l'Evêché du Puy (Haute-Loire)

Journal de Louis Gaspard Broussard, curé
Correspondance des évêques: paroisse de Lavoûte-Chilhac

Archives de l'Evêché de Mende (Lozère)

Visites pastorales de Mgr. Brulley de la Brunière, 1823–36; 1837–41
Correspondance des évêques: Mgr. Brulley de la Brunière, 1821–48
Correspondance des évêques: Mgr. Foulquier, 1849–78
Correspondance des évêques: Mgr. Costes, 1876–89
Correspondance des évêques: Mgr. Baptifolier, 1887–1900
Dossiers des paroisses: St Martin-de-Boubaux
Dossiers des paroisses: Meyrueis
Dossiers des paroisses: Les Salces
Dossiers des paroisses: Servières
Dossiers des paroisses: St Georges-de-Levéjac
Dossiers des paroisses: Florac
Dispenses de mariage, 1811–21
Dispenses de mariage, 1858–87
Enquête Boulard: diocèse de Mende

Archives de l'Evêché de Rodez (Aveyron)

Mgr. Bourret: politique aveyronnaise, élections, 1876–83
Mgr. Bourret: sonnerie des cloches, 1885
Mgr. Bourret: suspensions de traitement, 1884–93
Mgr. Bourret: procès-verbaux de la visite diocésaine, 1879
Mgr. Guiraud: registre des visites pastorales, 1835–41
Mgr. Croizier: journal et visites pastorales, 1842–55
Administration civile des cultes: 1830–48
Administration civile des cultes: liasse, 1848–70, divers
Dossiers des paroisses: Castanet
Documents sur Sylvestre Agussol, curé, 1784–1813

Archives du Musée des Arts et Traditions Populaires, Paris

Enquête sur les formes anciennes de l'agriculture: Aveyron; Haute-Loire; Lozère

PRINTED SOURCES AND OFFICIAL PUBLICATIONS

Album graphique de la statistique générale de la France. Paris, 1907
Annuaire du département de la Haute-Loire. Le Puy, 1835

Annuaire du département de la Lozère: l'année 1850. Mende, 1850
Annuaire ecclésiastique: diocèse de Mende. Mende, 1980
Annuaire ecclésiastique: diocèse de Rodez et de Vabres. Rodez, 1981
Annuaire statistique de la France: 1881. Paris, 1881
Annuaire statistique de la France: 1896. Paris, 1898
Annuaire statistique du département de l'Aveyron. Rodez, 1834
Archives parlementaires de 1787 à 1860. Recueil complet des débats législatifs et politiques des chambres françaises (première série, 1787–99), 92 vols., Paris, 1862–1980
Bulletin des lois de la République Française (Xième série, tome 2, nos. 48–111). Paris, 1849
Bulletin des lois de la République Française (XIIième série, premier semestre de 1884, tome 28, nos. 825–54). Paris, 1884
Collection des procès-verbaux des séances de l'Assemblée Provinciale de Haute-Guienne tenues à Villefranche, ès années 1779, 1780, 1782, 1784 et 1786 avec la permission du roi, vol. 1, Paris, 1787
Délibérations de l'Administration départementale de la Lozère et de son Directoire de 1790 à 1800 (Documents relatifs à l'histoire du Gévaudan, publiés par la Société d'agriculture, industrie, sciences et arts de la Lozère), tome 4, Mende, 1884
Département de la Lozère: Procès-verbal du Conseil Général, session de 1844
La France ecclésiastique: almanach-annuaire du clergé pour l'an de grâce 1892. Paris, 1892
La France ecclésiastique: almanach-annuaire du clergé pour l'année 1851. Paris, 1851
Lozère: atlas agricole (d'après le recensement général de l'agriculture, 1970–1). Mende, 1974
Ministère de l'Agriculture: statistique agricole annuelle: 1910. Paris, 1911
Ministère des Finances: bulletin de statistique et de législation comparée, xvi (1884)
Ministère des Finances: Etats détaillés des liquidations faites par la commission d'indemnité en exécution de la loi du 27 avril 1825 au profit des anciens propriétaires ou ayant-droit des anciens propriétaires de biens-fonds confisqués et aliénés révolutionnairement, 10 vols., Paris, 1826–30
Ordo à l'usage du diocèse de Saint Flour pour l'année 1966. St Flour, 1966
Statistique de France. Agriculture. Paris, 1840–1
Statistique de la France, deuxième série, statistique agricole. Paris, 1858–60
Statistique de la France. Agriculture, résultats généraux de l'enquête décennale de 1862. Strasbourg, 1868
Statistique agricole de la France (Algérie et colonies) publiée par le Ministre de l'Agriculture. Résultats généraux de l'enquête décennale de 1882. Nancy, 1882
Statistique agricole de la France publiée par le Ministère de l'Agriculture. Résultats généraux de l'enquête de 1929. Paris, 1936
Statistique de la France. Résultats du dénombrement de la population en 1856. Strasbourg, 1859
Statistique générale de la France. Résultats statistiques du dénombrement de 1891. Paris, 1894.
Recueil des usages locaux approuvés par la commission centrale départementale [*Aveyron*]. Rodez, 1906
Usages locaux des six cantons de l'arrondissement de Mauriac [*Cantal*]. Aurillac, 1878
Usages locaux du département de la Haute-Loire. Le Puy, 1865

PRESS

Feuille villageoise de l'Aveyron, 1806–7
Gazette du Rouergue, 1832–5
Journal de l'Aveyron, 1796–1944
Journal officiel de la République, 11 juin 1878
La Haute-Loire, 1870–1
La Semaine religieuse du Diocèse de Viviers, 1882–3
La Semaine religieuse du Diocèse du Puy-en-Velay, 1881–9
L'Echo des Montagnes, 7 mai 1848
Le Monde, 4 janvier 1966
Le Monde, 12 janvier 1978
Le Républicain de l'Aveyron, 1870–1
Le Temps, 30 octobre 1885

SECONDARY SOURCES

Agulhon, M. *Pénitents et Francs-Maçons de l'ancienne Provence*. Paris, 1968
  'Un Mouvement populaire au temps de 1848: histoire des populations du Var dans la première moitié du 19ième siècle' (Université de Paris, Thèse de doctorat d'état, 12 vols., 1969)
  La Vie sociale en Provence intérieure au lendemain de la Révolution. Paris, 1970
  Une Ville ouvrière au temps du socialisme utopique: Toulon de 1815 à 1851. Paris, The Hague, 1970
  La République au village (les populations du Var de la Révolution à la Seconde République). Paris, 1970. Translated as *The Republic in the village: the people of the Var from the French Revolution to the Second Republic*. Cambridge, 1982
  The Republican Experiment, 1848–1852. Cambridge, 1983
Albaric, P.-M. 'Aspects de la vie religieuse à Millau, 1870–1890' (Université Paul Valéry, Montpellier III, Mémoire de maîtrise, 1972)
Allignol, C. and A. *De l'Etat actuel du clergé en France et en particulier des curés ruraux appelés desservants*. Paris, 1839
Angeville, A. *Essai sur la statistique de la population française*. Reprint, Paris, The Hague, 1969
Anglade, J. *La Vie quotidienne dans le Massif Central au XIXe siècle*. Paris, 1971
Ariès, P. *L'Homme devant la mort*. Paris, 1977
Armengaud, A. *Les Populations de l'Est-Aquitain audébut de l'époque contemporaine: recherches sur une région moins développée, vers 1845–vers 1871*. Paris, 1961
Atlas administratif de l'Empire Français. Geneva, 1973
Atlas de la France rurale (Cahiers de la Fondation nationale des sciences politiques, Paris, 1968)
Aucoc, L. *Des sections de communes et des biens communaux qui leur appartiennent*. Paris, 1864
Avenel, G. d' 'L'Extension du fonctionnarisme depuis 1870', *Revue des deux mondes*, 1 March 1888
Avenel, H. *Comment vote la France. Dix-huit ans de suffrage universel, 1876–93*. Paris, 1894
Balzac, H. de *Une Ténébreuse Affaire*. Calmann-Lévy, Paris, n.d.
Barbot, J. 'Au Seuil de la Révolution', *Société des lettres, sciences et arts de la Lozère: Archives Gévaudanaises*, iii (1915–22), 1–20

Barker, E. *Through Auvergne on Foot*. London, 1884

Barral, P. *Le Département de l'Isère sous la Troisième République, 1870–1940*. Paris, 1962

    Les Agrariens français de Méline à Pisani. Paris, 1968

Barrau, H. de *Documens historiques et généalogiques sur les familles et les hommes remarquables de Rouergue dans les temps anciens et modernes*. 4 vols., Rodez, 1853–60

Bastid, P. *Doctrines et institutions politiques de la Seconde République*, 2 vols., Paris, 1945

Bastier, J. 'Droits féodaux et revenus agricoles en Rouergue à la veille de la Révolution', *Annales du Midi*, lxxxxv (1983), 261–87

Baudrillart, H. *Les Populations agricoles de la France: 3e série, les populations du Midi*. Paris, 1893

Bayssat, G. *Evolution du monde rural de la Haute-Loire*. Le Puy, n.d. [1955]

Bercé, Y.-M. *Histoire des Croquants: étude des soulèvements populaires au XVIIe siècle dans le sud-ouest de la France*. Geneva, 1974

Bergeron, L. *France under Napoleon*. Translated by R. R. Palmer, Princeton, 1981

Bernard, R.-J. 'Démographie et comportements démographiques en Haute-Lozère, XVIIe – XVIIIe – XIXe siècles', *Revue du Gévaudan*, nouv. sér., xxi (1975), 97–107

Bernis, R. de *Précis de ce qui s'est passé en 1815 dans les départements du Gard et de la Lozère et réfutation de plusieurs des pamphlets qui ont défiguré ces événements*. Paris, 1818

Berthe, L.-N. *Dictionnaire des correspondants de l'académie d'Arras au temps de Robespierre*. Arras, 1969

Best, C. *Dissertation sur les biens communaux de la Haute-Loire*. Le Puy, 1860

Bétant-Robert, S. 'L'Assemblée provinciale d'Auvergne à la veille de la Révolution' (Université de Clermont-Ferrand, Mémoire pour Diplôme d'études supérieures d'histoire du droit, 1966)

Béteille, R. *Les Aveyronnais: essai géographique sur l'espace humain*. Poitiers, 1974

Bezucha, R. 'Mask of Revolution: A Study of Popular Culture during the Second French Republic' in R. Price (ed.), *Revolution and Reaction. 1848 and the Second French Republic*. London, 1975, pp. 236–53

Bidault, E. *Code électoral*, 7th edn, Paris, 1876

    Electeurs et éligibles. Paris, 1877.

Biraben, J. N. 'L'Etat des âmes de la paroisse de Montplaisant en 1644', *Annales de démographie historique* (1970), 441–62

Blanqui, A.-J. 'Tableau de la situation des classes ouvrières en 1850', *Séances et travaux de l'Académie des sciences morales et politiques*, viii (1850), 313–34

Bloch, M. *French Rural History: an Essay on its Basic Characteristics*. Oxford, 1966

Bois, P. *Paysans de l'ouest: des structures économiques et sociales aux options politiques depuis l'époque révolutionnaire dans le Sarthe*. Le Mans, 1960

Bonald, J. M. J. A. de *François Chabot, membre de la Convention, 1756–1794*. Paris, 1908

Bonnaud, P. ' "La Haie et le hameau": les mots et les choses', *Bulletin de l'Institut de géographie* (Faculté des Lettres, Clermont-Ferrand), xxxviii (1970), 1–27

Bornes, M. 'Les Saints Guérisseurs en Bas Rouergue' (Université de Montpellier, Thèse de troisième cycle, 1969)

Boscary, G. *Evolution agricole et condition des cultivateurs de l'Aveyron pendant le XIXe siècle*. Montpellier, 1909

    L'Assemblée provinciale de Haute-Guienne, 1779–1790. Paris, 1932

Bouchard, G. *Le Village immobile: Senneley-en-Sologne au XVIIIe siècle.* Paris, 1972
Bouladou, G. 'La Vallée du Gardon de St Germain-de-Calberte (Lozère)', *Bulletin de la société languedocienne de géographie* (1946), 38–59
Boulard, F. *Essor ou déclin du clergé français?* Paris, 1950
Bousquet, J. 'Un Précédent de l'affaire Finaly en Rouergue (1786): Monseigneur Colbert de Castle-Hill, le pensionnat-couvent de l'Arpajonie et les protestants de Millau', *Revue du Rouergue*, vii (1954), 451–73
    Enquêtes folkloriques en Rouergue, 1900–1954. Paris, 1958
Bozon, P. *La Vie rurale en Vivarais: étude géographique.* Valence, 1963
    Histoire du peuple vivarois. Valence, 1966
Brajon, M. and Arnaud, M. *Monsieur Brajon, maître d'école.* Paris, 1977
Brouzès, J.-A. 'Quelques considérations sur le patois', *Revue de l'Aveyron et du Lot*, 26 November 1838
Brustein, W. 'A Regional Mode-of-Production Analysis of Political Behaviour: the Cases of Western and Mediterranean France', *Politics and Society*, x (1981), 355–98
Buisson, F. E. *Dictionnaire de pédagogie et d'instruction primaire*, 4 vols., Paris, 1878–87
Burke, P. *Popular Culture in Early Modern Europe.* London, 1978
Cabantous, J. *Documents pour servir à l'histoire du protestantisme à Saint Affrique au dix-neuvième siècle.* Montauban, 1896
Callahan, W. J. and Higgs, D. (eds.), *Church and Society in Catholic Europe of the Eighteenth Century.* Cambridge, 1979
Calvet, J. 'Monographie religieuse d'un diocèse français, Cahors', *Revue catholique des églises* (1905), 65–87
Cameron, I. A. *Crime and Repression in the Auvergne and the Guyenne, 1720–1790.* Cambridge, 1981
Caralp-Landon, R. *Les Chemins de fer dans le Massif Central. Etude des voies ferrées régionales.* Paris, 1959
Castan, N. 'Révoltes populaires en Languedoc au XVIIIe siècle', *Actes du 96e congrès national des sociétés savantes, Toulouse, 1971* (Paris, 1976), ii, 223–34
    'Crime et justice en Languedoc, 1750–1790' (Université de Toulouse-Le Mirail, Thèse de doctorat d'état, 2 vols., 1978)
Castan, Y. 'Attitudes et motivations dans les conflits entre seigneurs et communautés devant le parlement de Toulouse au XVIIIe siècle', *Villes de l'Europe méditerranéenne: de l'Europe occidental du Moyen Age au XIXe siècle (Actes du Colloque de Nice, 27–28 mars 1969)* (Paris, 1969), 233–9
Catéchisme du diocèse de Mende. Dijon, 1835
Causse, G. and Tufféry, A. 'Le Diocèse de Mende au début du XXe siècle' (Université Paul Valéry, Montpellier, Mémoire de maîtrise, 1972)
Certeau, M. de and Julia, D. and Revel, J. *Une Politique de la langue: la Révolution française et les patois.* Paris, 1975
Chanson, M. 'L'Assemblée de l'élection de Brioude (1787–1788)', *Revue d'Auvergne* (1888), 285–303; 379–98
Charnay, J.-P. *Les Scrutins politiques en France de 1815 à 1962: contestations et invalidations* (Cahiers de la Fondation nationale des sciences politiques, Paris, 1964)
Charra, W. 'Notes sur l'évolution des Causses de Quercy au cours du XIXe siècle', *Revue géographique des Pyrénées et du Sud-Ouest*, xx (1949), 175–221
Chartier, R. and Compère, M. M. and Julia, D. *L'Education en France du XVIe au XVIIIe siècle.* Paris, 1976

Châtelin, A. *Les Migrants temporaires en France de 1800 à 1914*, 2 vols., Villeneuve-d'Asq, 1976

Chaussinand-Nogaret, G. *Une Histoire des élites, 1700–1848*. Paris, The Hague, 1975

Chiva, I. *Rural Communities: Problems, Methods and Types of Research* (Reports and Papers in the Social Sciences, no. 10, Unesco, 1958)

Cholvy, G. 'Le Catholicisme en Rouergue au XIXe et XXe siècles: première approche' in *Etudes sur le Rouergue: actes du 47e congrès d'études de la fédération historique du Languedoc Méditerranéen et du Roussillon, et du 29e congrès d'études de la fédération des sociétés académiques et savantes Languedoc–Pyrénées-Gascogne* (Rodez, 1974), 249–67

   'Une Chrétienté au XIXe siècle: La Lozère', *Cévennes et Gévaudan 46e congrès de la Fédération historique de Languedoc méditerranéen, Mende-Florac, 1973*, 365–82

Chomel, V. 'Le Département de l'Ardèche à la veille de la Révolution de 1848', *Revue du Vivarais*, lii (1948), 31–52, 69–97; liii (1949), 32–51

Christian, W. A. *Person and God in a Spanish Valley*. New York, 1972

Clark, C. and Haswell, M. R. *The Economics of Subsistence Agriculture*, 4th edn, London, 1970

Claverie, E. 'Oppositions et conflits dans une société d'inter-connaissance, l'exemple du Haut Gévaudan di XIXe siècle' (Université R. Descartes, Sorbonne, Paris V, Doctorat de troisième cycle en ethnologie, 1979)

   ' "L'Honneur": une société de défis au XIXe siècle', *Ann. E.S.C.*, xxxiv (1979), 744–59

   'L' "Ousta" et le notaire: le système de dévolution des biens en Margeride lozérienne au XIXe siècle', *Ethnologie française*, xi (1981), 329–38

Clout, H. (ed.) *Themes in the Historical Geography of France*. London, 1977

   Agriculture in France on the Eve of the Railway Age. London, 1980

Collomp, A. 'Famille nucléaire et famille élargie en Haute-Provence au XVIIIe siècle (1703–1734)', *Ann. E.S.C.*, xxvii (1972), 969–75

   'Ménage et famille: études comparatives sur la dimension et la structure du groupe domestique', *Ann. E.S.C.*, xxix (1974), 777–86

Connolly, S. J. *Priest and People in Pre-Famine Ireland, 1780–1845*. Dublin, 1982

Corbin, A. 'Migrations temporaires et société rurale au XIXe siècle: le cas du Limousin', *Revue historique*, ccxxxxvi (1971), 293–334

   Archaïsme et modernité en Limousin au XIXe siècle, 1845–1880, 2 vols., Paris, 1975

Cornut, *abbé* 'Croyances populaires à Monfauçon et Dunières au siècle dernier', *Cahiers de la Haute-Loire* (1968), 91–9

Coront-Ducluzeau, A. 'Une Election mémorable: le vicomte E.-M. de Vogüé, député de l'Ardèche (1893–1898)', *Revue du Vivarais*, lxxiii (1969), 177–89

Costecalde, L. *Biographie du Comte Aldebert de Chambrun (1821–1898)*. Mende, 1934

Cresswell, R. 'Une Communauté rurale en Irlande', *Travaux et mémoires de l'Institut d'ethnologie* (Université de Paris), lxxiv (1969)

Crisenoy, J. de *Statistique des biens communaux et des sections de communes* (extrait de la *Revue Générale d'Administration*). Paris, 1887

Cuche, R. 'Le Conventionnel Servière', *29e congrès de la Fédération historique du Languedoc méditerranéen et du Roussillon* (Mende, 1955), 111–21

Dalby, J. 'The French Revolution in a Rural Environment: the Example of the Department of the Cantal, 1789–1794' (University of Manchester, D.Phil. thesis,

1981)

Daniel, A. *L'Année politique*. Paris, 1876–93

Darcissac, E. 'Une Enfance en pays protestant à la fin du XIXe siècle', *Cahiers de la Haute-Loire*, (1972), 187–220

Daudibertières, G. 'La Société des Houillères et Fonderies de l'Aveyron et le premier développement industriel de Decazeville', *Mémoires de la société des lettres, sciences et arts de l'Aveyron*, xxviii (1964), 479–95

Davies, G. C. and Broughall, Mrs *Our Home in Aveyron with Studies of Peasant Life and Customs in Aveyron and the Lot*, Edinburgh and London, 1891

Delcambre, E. *La Période du Directoire dans la Haute-Loire. Les Commissariats de Montfleury et de Portal (messidor an IV–floréal an VI)*, fascicle 2, Rodez, 1941
Le Coup d'état jacobin du 18 fructidor an V et ses répercussions dans la Haute-Loire. Rodez, 1942

Delon, P. J.-B. *La Révolution en Lozère*. Mende, 1922

Deribier de Cheissac, *Description statistique du département de la Haute-Loire*. Paris, Le Puy, 1824

Deribier du Châtelet, *Dictionnaire statistique du département du Cantal*, 6 vols., Aurillac, 1852–7

Deslandres, M. *Histoire constitutionnelle de la France*, 3 vols., Paris, 1933–7

Devos, R. 'Quelques aspects de la vie religieuse dans le diocèse d'Annecy au milieu du XIXe siècle (d'après une enquête de Mgr. Rendu)', *Cahiers d'histoire*, xi (1966), 49–83

Donat, J. *Une Communauté rurale à la fin de l'ancien régime*. Montauban, 1926

Douais, *abbé* 'Le Marquis de Pégueirolles, avocat-général, président à mortier au parlement de Toulouse et mainteneur des jeux floraux, 1721–1794', *Mémoires de l'académie des sciences, inscriptions et belles-lettres de Toulouse*, iv (1892), 455–81

Duby, G. and Wallon, A. (eds.) *Histoire de la France rurale*, 4 vols., Paris, 1975–6

Dufour, E. *Etude sur l'assemblée provinciale de la Haute-Guyenne*. Cahors, 1881

Duguet, E. *Les Députés et les cahiers électoraux de 1889*. Paris, n.d.

Dunglas, F.-C. *Notice sur les béates de la Haute-Loire, diocèse du Puy*. Paris, 1854

Dupâquier, J. and Jadin, L. 'Structure of Household and Family in Corsica, 1769–71', in P. Laslett and R. Wall (eds.), *Household and Family in Past Time*. Cambridge, 1972, pp. 283–97.

Dupouy, L. *Les Protestants de Florac de la Révocation de l'Edit de Nantes à l'Edit de Tolérance*. Paris, n.d.

Dussourd, H. *Au même pot et au même feu . . . étude sur les communautés familiales agricoles du centre de la France*. Paris, 1979

Egret, J. *Necker, ministre de Louis XVI, 1776–1790*. Paris, 1975

Encrevé, A. 'Protestantisme et politique: les protestants du Midi en décembre 1851', in *Droite et Gauche en Languedoc-Roussillon: Actes du colloque de Montpellier, 9–10 juin 1973* (Montpellier, 1975), pp. 161–95

Estienne, P. and Joly, R. *Les Régions du Centre*. Paris, 1973

Fabre, D. and Lacroix, J. *La Vie quotidienne des paysans du Languedoc au XIXe siècle*. Paris, 1973

Falgairolle, E. *Les Exorcismes en Lozère en 1792*. Paris, 1894

Faury, J. *Cléricalisme et anticléricalisme dans le Tarn, 1848–1900*. Toulouse, 1980

Favre, J. B. C. *Histoire de Jean-l'ont-pris, conte languedocien du XVIIIe siècle*. Paris, 1877

Fel, A. 'Notes de géographie humaine sur la montagne de Margeride', *Bulletin de l'Institut de géographie* (Faculté des Lettres, Clermont-Ferrand), iii (1953), 71–82

Les Hautes Terres du Massif Central. Tradition paysanne et économie agricole. Paris, 1962

Fine-Souriac, A. 'A propos de la famille-souche pyrénéenne au XIXe siècle: quelques réflexions de méthode', *Revue d'histoire moderne et contemporaine*, xxv (1978), 99–110

Flandrin, J.-L. *Families in Former Times.* Cambridge, 1979

Fournier, G. 'Des Conseils politiques aux conseils municipaux dans les diocèses civils de Carcassonne, Narbonne, et Béziers (1750–1791)' (Université de Toulouse-Le Mirail, Thèse de troisième cycle, 2 vols., 1974)

Francus [A. Mazon] *Voyage . . . le long de la rivière d'Ardèche.* Privas, 1885

Frêche, G. *Toulouse et la région Midi-Pyrénées au siècle des lumières (vers 1670–1789).* Mayenne, 1974

Furet, F. and Ozouf, J. *Lire et écrier: l'alphabétisation des Français de Calvin à Jules Ferry*, 2 vols., Paris, 1977

Gadille, J. *La Pensée et l'action politiques des évêques français au début de la IIIième République, 1870–1883*, 2 vols., Paris, 1967
Guide des archives diocésaines françaises. Lyons, 1971

Galabert, F. 'Les Assemblées de protestants dans le Montalbanais en 1744 et 1745', *Bulletin de la Société de l'histoire du protestantisme français*, xlix (1900), 132–51

Galabert, F. and Boscus, L. *La Ville de Caussade (Tarn-et-Garonne). Ses vicomtes et ses barons.* Montauban, 1908

Garaud, M. *La Révolution et la propriété foncière.* Paris, 1958

Garrisson-Estèbe, J. *L'Homme protestant.* Paris, 1980

Gaussin, P.-R. 'La Ville du Puy et ses pèlerinages', *Revue de géographie de Lyon*, xxvi (1951), 243–71

Gazier, A. *Lettres à Grégoire sur le patois de France, 1790–1794: documents inédits sur la langue, les mœurs et l'état des esprits dans les diverses régions de la France, au début de la Révolution.* Paris, 1880

Géraud, G. *Notes sur cents ans d'histoire en Lozère (XIXe et XXe siècles).* Mende, 1969

Girard, L. and Prost, A. and Gossez, R. *Les Conseillers généraux en 1870.* Paris, 1967

Godechot, J. *Les Institutions de la France sous la Révolution et l'Empire.* Paris, 1968

Goubert, P. 'En Rouergue: structures agraires et cadastres au XVIIIe siècle', *Ann. E.S.C.*, ix (1954), 382–6
L'Ancien régime, 2 vols., Paris, 1969–73

Gouly, J.-C. 'Protestants et catholiques en Haute-Loire au milieu du XIXe siècle', *Cahiers de la Haute-Loire*, (1970), 85–110

Goumain-Cornille, P. and Martin, R. *Les Cahiers électoraux de 1881.* Paris, 1882

Graffin, R. *Les Biens communaux en France.* Paris, 1899

Granier, R. *Jadis en Bas-Rouergue.* Montauban, 1947

Gratton, P. *Les Paysans français contre l'agrarisme.* Paris, 1972

Grellet de la Deyte, 'Le Livre de raison de Louis Jouve, sieur de Chadouard, paroisse de Saint Vincent-en-Velay', *Bulletin de la Diana*, xxxv (1957), 77–88

Guéry, A. 'La Population du Rouergue de la fin du Moyen Age au XVIIIe siècle', *Ann. E.S.C.*, xxviii (1973), 1555–76

Guilhamon, H. 'Notes sur la noblesse du Rouergue à la fin du XVIIIe siècle', *Journal de l'Aveyron*, 15 September 1918

Guilhamon, H. (ed.) *Journal des voyages en Haute-Guienne de J. F. Henry de Richeprey*, 2 vols., Rodez, 1952–67

Gutton, J.-P. *La Sociabilité villageoise dans l'ancienne France*. Paris, 1979

Harris, R. D. *Necker, Reform Statesman of the Ancien Régime*. London, 1979

Higgs, D. 'Politics and Landownership among the French Nobility after the Revolution', *European Studies Review*, i (1971), 105–21
   Ultraroyalism in Toulouse from its origins to the Revolution of 1830. Baltimore and London, 1973

Higonnet, P. L.-R. *Pont-de-Montvert. Social structure and Politics in a French Village, 1700–1914*. Cambridge, Mass., 1971

Hood, J. N. 'Patterns of Popular Protest in the French Revolution: The Conceptual Contribution of the Gard', *Journal of Modern History*, xxxxviii (1976), 259–93

Hours, H. 'Emeutes et émotions populaires dans les campagnes du Lyonnais au XVIIIᵉ siècle', *Cahiers d'histoire*, (1964), 137–53

Houssel, J.-P. (ed.) *Histoire des paysans français du XVIIIᵉ siècle à nos jours*. Roanne, 1976

Huard, R. 'La Préhistoire des partis: le parti républicain dans le Gard de 1848 à 1881' (Université de Paris IV, Thèse de doctorat d'état, 5 vols., 1977)

Hunt, L. 'The Political Geography of Revolutionary France', *The Journal of Interdisciplinary History*, xiv (1984), 535–59

Imberdis, F. *Le Réseau routier de l'Auvergne au XVIIIᵉ siècle: ses origines et son évolution*. Paris, 1967

Isambert, F. and Terrenoire, J.-P. *Atlas de la pratique religieuse des catholiques en France, d'après les enquêtes diocésaines et urbaines du chanoine F. Boulard (1898–1977)*. Paris, 1980

Izard, F. 'Le Clergé paroissial Gévaudanais à la fin du XVIIIᵉ siècle' (Université Paul Valéry, Montpellier III, Mémoire de maîtrise, 1978)

Jarriot, J. 'Pour une histoire de la communauté villageoise en Rouergue à la fin de l'ancien régime', *Revue du Rouergue*, xxvii (1973), 19–26

Jerphanion, G. T. *Statistique du département de la Lozère*. Paris, *an* X

Jolivet, C. *La Révolution dans l'Ardèche, 1788–1795*. Largentière, 1930
   L'Agitation contre-révolutionnaire dans l'Ardèche sous le Directoire. Lyons, 1930

Jollivet, M. and Mendras, H. (eds.) *Les Collectivités rurales françaises*, 2 vols., Paris, 1971–4

Jolly, J. (ed.) *Dictionnaire des parlementaires français: notices biographiques sur les ministres, députés et sénateurs français de 1889 à 1940*, 8 vols., Paris, 1960–77

Jones, P. M. 'The Revolutionary Committees of the Department of the Aveyron, France, 1793–1795' (University of Oxford, D.Phil. thesis, 1977)
   'The Rural Bourgeoisie of the Southern Massif Central: a contribution to the study of the social structure of *ancien régime* France', *Social History*, iv (1979), 65–83
   'Political Commitment and Rural Society in the Southern Massif Central', *European Studies Review*, x (1980), 337–56
   '*La République au village* in the Southern Massif Central, 1789–1799', *The Historical Journal*, xxiii (1980), 793–812
   'Parish, Seigneurie and the Community of Inhabitants in Southern Central France during the Eighteenth and Nineteenth Centuries', *Past and Present*, lxxxxi (1981), 74–108
   'An Improbable Democracy: Nineteenth-Century Elections in the Massif Central', *The English Historical Review*, xcvii (1982), 530–57
   'Common Rights and Agrarian Individualism in the Southern Massif Central,

1750–1880', in G. Lewis and C. Lucas (eds.), *Beyond the Terror*, Cambridge, 1983, pp. 121–51

Jourda de Vaux, G. de *Le Nobiliaire du Velay et de l'ancien diocèse du Puy*, 7 vols., Lyon, 1924–33

Jourdan, Decrusy and Isambert *Recueil général des anciennes lois françaises depuis l'an 420 jusqu'à la Révolution*, vol. 28: *1785–1789*. Paris, 1927

Joutard, P. 'Protestantisme populaire et univers magique: le cas cévenol', *Le Monde alpin et rhodanien* (1977), 145–71

Judt, T. *Socialism in Provence, 1871–1914: a Study in the Origins of the Modern French Left*. Cambridge, 1979

Juillard, E. *La Vie rurale dans la plaine de Basse-Alsace: essai de géographie sociale*. Paris, 1953

Karnoouh, G. 'La Démocratie impossible: parenté et politique dans un village lorrain', *Etudes rurales*, lii (1973), 24–56

Kemp, T. *Economic Forces in French History*. London, 1971

Kent, S. *Electoral Procedure under Louis Philippe*. New Haven, 1937

Kuscinski, A. *Dictionnaire des Conventionnels*. Paris, 1916

L'Abolition de la féodalité dans le monde occidental (Colloque du C.N.R.S., Toulouse, 12–16 novembre 1968), 2 vols., Paris, 1971

Lagrée, M. *Mentalités, religion et histoire en Haute-Bretagne au XIXème siècle: le diocèse de Rennes, 1815–1848*. Paris, 1977

Lamaison, P. 'Parenté, patrimoine et stratégies matrimoniales sur l'ordinateur: une paroisse du Haut Gévaudan du XVIIe au début du XIXe siècle' (Université René Descartes, Sorbonne, Paris V, Doctorat de troisième cycle en ethnologie, 1977)
  'Des foires et des marchés en Haute-Lozère', *Etudes rurales*, lxxviii–lxxxx (1980), 199–230

Lancelot, M.-T. and A. *Atlas des circonscriptions électorales en France depuis 1875* (Cahiers de la Fondation nationale des sciences politiques, Paris, 1970)

Landsberger, H. A. (ed.) *Rural Protest: Peasant Movements and Social Change*. London, 1974

Las Cazes, P. de *Ce n'est rien, rien qu'une vie*. Mende, 1961

Laslett, P. and Wall, R. *Household and Family in Past Time*. Cambridge, 1972

Latouche, R. *Saint Antonin*. Montauban, 1926

L'Aubrac: étude ethnologique, linguistique, agronomique et économique d'un établissement humain, 4 vols., Paris, 1970–3

Laurans, G. *Etude et documents pour l'histoire de Nant* [typescript memoir in A.D.A.]

Laurent, M. 'Le Partage des communaux à Ennezat à l'époque révolutionnaire', *Revue d'Auvergne*, lxxxxii (1978), 167–95

Lautard, C. *Convocation de la sénéchaussée de Nîmes aux Etats Généraux de 1789*. Paris, 1923

Lavergne, Léoncé de *Les Assemblées provinciales sous Louis XVI*. Paris, 1864

Lavialle, A. 'Monographie paroissiale de Torsiac, canton de Blesle', *Bulletin de la société d'agriculture*, iii–iv (1903), 49–60

Lebigre, A. *Les Grands Jours d'Auvergne: désordres et répression au XVIIe siècle*. Paris, 1976

Le Bras, G. *L'Eglise et le village*. Paris, 1976

Le Bras, H. and Todd, E. *L'Invention de la France: atlas anthropologique et politique*. Livre de poche, 1981

Lebrun, F. *Les Hommes et la mort en Anjou aux 17e et 18e siècles*. Paris, 1971

Le Clère, B. and Wright, V. *Les Préfets du Second Empire* (Cahiers de la Fondation nationale des sciences politiques, Paris, 1973)

Lee, W. R. *Population Growth, Economic Development and Social Change in Bavaria, 1750–1850.* New York, 1977

Le Goff, T. J. A. 'A Social and Economic Study of the Town of Vannes and its Region during the Eighteenth Century' (London University, D.Phil. thesis, 1977) *Vannes and its Region: a Study of Town and Country in Eighteenth-Century France.* Oxford, 1981

Lehring, J. R. *The Peasants of Marlhes: Economic Development and Family Organization in Nineteenth-Century France.* London, 1980

Le Mée, R. 'Population agglomérée, population éparse au début du XIXe siècle', *Annales de démographie historique* (1971), 455–510

Lempereur, L. *Etat du diocèse de Rodez en 1771.* Rodez, 1906 'Une Famille de bourgeoisie rurale en Rouergue: les Costy d'Aguès', *Journal de l'Aveyron*, 20 July 1919, weekly until 2 November 1919

Léonard, E.-G. *Mon village sous Louis XV, d'après les mémoires d'un paysan.* Paris, 1941

Le Play, F. (ed.) *Les Ouvriers européens*, 2nd edn, 6 vols., Tours, 1877–9

Lequin, Y. *Les Ouvriers de la région lyonnaise.* Lyons, 1979

Le Roy Ladurie, E. *Les Paysans de Languedoc*, 2 vols., Paris, 1966 'L'Histoire immobile', *Ann. E.S.C.*, xxix (1974), 673–92 *L'Argent, l'amour et la mort en pays d'oc.* Paris, 1980 *The Mind and Method of the Historian.* Brighton, 1981

Le Roy Ladurie, E. and Vigne, D. *Inventaire des campagnes.* n.p., 1980

Lescure, Vicomte de *Armorial du Gévaudan.* Lyons, 1929

Les Etats provinciaux comparés avec les administrations provinciales suivis des principes relatifs aux Etats Généraux à l'usage de ceux qui se destinent à concourir à l'intérêt public. Paris, 1789

'Les Paysans et la politique (1750–1850)', *Annales de Bretagne et des pays de l'ouest*, lxxxix (1982)

Levêque, 'Histoire des forges de Decazeville', *Bulletin de la Société d'Industrie Minérale*, ix (1916), 5–97, 141–236

Lévêque, P. 'La Bourgogne de la Monarchie de Juillet au Second Empire' (Université de Paris IV, Thèse de doctorat d'état, 6 vols., 1977)

Lévi-Strauss, L. and Mendras, H. 'Survey of Peasant Studies: Rural Studies in France', *Journal of Peasant Studies*, i (1974), 363–78

Lewis, G. *The Second Vendée: The Continuity of Counter-revolution in the Department of the Gard, 1789–1815.* Oxford, 1978

Lexpert, A. *L'Organisation judiciaire de l'ancien pays de Vivarais.* Aubenas, 1921

Leymarie, M. 'Emigration et structure sociale en Haute-Auvergne à la fin de l'Ancien Régime', *Revue de la Haute-Auvergne* (1956–7), 296–323 'Les Redevances foncières seigneuriales en Haute-Auvergne', *Annales historiques de la Révolution française*, xl (1968), 299–380

Loubère, L. A. *Radicalism in Mediterranean France: its Rise and Decline, 1848–1914.* Albany, 1974.

Louchet, L. *Relation des troubles du Rouergue et des moyens employés par la ville de Rodez pour les faire cesser, rédigée d'après les procès-verbaux et les pièces justificatives des faits et de leurs circonstances.* Rodez, 1790

Lucas, C. 'The Problem of the Midi in the French Revolution', *Transactions of the Royal Historical Society*, xxviii (1978), 1–26

Macfarlane, A. *Reconstructing Historical Communities.* Cambridge, 1977

McPhee, P. 'Popular Culture, Symbolism and Rural Radicalism in Nineteenth-Century France', *The Journal of Peasant Studies*, v (1978), 238–53

'A Reconsideration of the "Peasantry" of Nineteenth-Century France', *Peasant Studies*, ix (1981), 5–25

'On Rural Politics in Nineteenth-Century France: The Example of Rodès, 1789–1851', *Comparative Studies in Society and History*, xxiii (1981), 248–77

Magraw, R. 'Pierre Joigneaux and Socialist Propaganda in the French Countryside, 1849–1851', *French Historical Studies*, x (1978), 599–640

France 1815–1914: The Bourgeois Century. London, 1983

Malègue, H. *Eléments de statistique générale du département de la Haute-Loire suivis du dictionnaire des lieux habités*. Paris, 1872

Margadant, T. W. 'Peasant Protest in the Second Republic', *The Journal of Interdisciplinary History*, v (1974–5), 119–30

'Modernisation and Insurgency in December 1851: a Case Study of the Drôme' in R. Price (ed.), *Revolution and Reaction: 1848 and the Second French Republic*, London, 1975, pp. 254–79

French Peasants in Revolt: the Insurrection of 1851. Princeton, 1979

'Proto-Urban Development and Political Mobilisation during the Second Republic' in J. M. Merriman (ed.), *French Cities in the Nineteenth Century*, London, 1982, pp. 92–116

Marres, P. *Les Grands Causses: étude de géographie humaine*. Tours, 1935

Martin, G. *Le Tissage du ruban à domicile dans les campagnes du Velay*. Paris and Le Puy, 1913

Marx, K. *The Class Struggles in France, 1848 to 1850* in Karl Marx and Frederick Engels, *Collected Works*, 38 vols., vol. 10, London, 1975–82

Masseguin, M. 'Les Parlementaires royalistes lozériens de 1815 à 1893' (Université de Montpellier, Diplôme d'études supérieures, 1958)

Mathieu, L. *La Paroisse de Saint Voy de Bonas*. Le Puy, 1977

Maurain, J. *La Politique ecclésiastique du Second Empire de 1851 à 1869*. Paris, 1940

Maurin, Y. 'La Répartition de la propriété foncière en Lozère au début du XIXe siècle', *Cévennes et Gévaudan, 46e congrès de la Fédération historique de Languedoc méditerranéen, Mende-Florac, 1973*, 309–35

Maury, A. 'Presbytères et élections en Aveyron au siècle dernier', *Revue du Rouergue*, xxiii (1969), 157–64

'Le Cardinal Bourret (période 1871–1876)', *Revue du Rouergue*, xxix (1975), 5–30, 241–55

Mazars, L. 'Emeutes et pillages aux châteaux de Pachins, Vaureilles et Privezac', *Les Cahiers rouergats*, iv (1971), 55–63

Maze-Sencier, G. *M. Casimir Mayran: Souvenirs*. Rodez, n.d. [1892]

'Mémoires privés d'un Ruthenois [Justin-Hippolyte de Barrau]', *Journal de l'Aveyron*, 10 March 1900

Merley, J. 'Le Velay dans la première partie du XVIIIe siècle: les mandements vellaves et l'enquête de 1734 sur le capitation', *Cahiers de la Haute-Loire*, (1965), 69–155

L'Industrie en Haute-Loire de la fin de la Monarchie de Juillet aux débuts de la Troisième République (Centre d'histoire économique et sociale de la région lyonnaise, Université de Lyon II, 1972)

La Haute-Loire de la fin de l'ancien régime aux débuts de la Troisième République, 2 vols., Le Puy, 1974

Merlin, P. *L'Exode rural suivi de deux études sur les migrations par Robert Herin et Robert Nadot*. Paris, 1971

Merriman, J. M. *Agony of the Republic: Repression of the Left in Revolutionary France, 1848–51*. London, 1978

Mesliand, C. 'Gauche et Droite dans les campagnes provençales sous la IIIième République', *Etudes rurales*, lxiii–lxiv, (1976), 207–34

Meynier, A. *Ségalas, Levézou, Châtaigneraie: étude géographique*. Aurillac, 1931

'La Commune rurale française', *Annales de géographie*, liii–lv (1945), 161–79

Meynier, A. *Les Coups d'état du Directoire*, 3 vols., Paris, 1927

Meyronneinc, J.-B. 'Des Communautés villageoises aux sections de communes: l'exemple de quelques communes du Devès et de Margeride' (Université de Clermont-Ferrand, Institut de Géographie, mémoire de maîtrise, 1975)

Molinier, A. 'Une Enquête politique, économique et sociale en Languedoc au milieu du XVIIIe siècle', *Annales de démographie historique*, (1974), 451–78

'En Vivarais au XVIIIe siècle: une croissance démographique sans révolution agricole', *Annales du Midi*, lxxxxii (1980), 301–16

Paroisses et communes de France: Ardèche. Paris, 1976

Monteil, A.-A. *Description du département de l'Aveiron*, 2 vols., Paris, *an* X

Monteils-Pons, E. *Florac au point de vue de l'hygiène et de la salubrité*. Montpellier, 1855

Morineau, M. *Les Faux-semblants d'un démarrage économique: agriculture et démographie en France au XVIIIe siècle* (*Cahier des Annales*, 30, Paris, 1971)

Mouly, R. P. *Concordataires, constitutionnels et 'enfarinés' en Quercy et Rouergue au lendemain de la Révolution*. Rodez, 1945

Mours, S. *Le Protestantisme en Vivarais et en Velay des origines à nos jours*. Valence, 1949

Nadaud, M. *Mémoires de Léonard, ancien garçon maçon*. Paris, 1976

Naud, D. 'Les Structures familiales en Vendée au XIXe siècle', *Société d'émulation de la Vendée* (1977), 50–74

Nauton, P. *Le Patois de Saugues (Haute-Loire): aperçu linguistique, terminologie rurale, littérature orale*. Clermont-Ferrand, 1948

'Le Patois des protestants du Velay' in *Mélanges de linguistique et de littérature romanes offerts à Mario Roques*, 4 vols., Baden, 1950–3, iii, 185–93

Atlas linguistique et ethnographique du Massif Central, 4 vols., Paris, 1959–63

Nicolas, J. *La Savoie au XVIIIe siècle*, 2 vols., Paris, 1978

Noël, R. 'La Population de la paroisse de Laguiole d'après un recensement de 1691', *Annales de démographie historique* (1967), 197–223

'L'Etat de la population de Mostuéjouls (Aveyron) en 1690' in *Hommage à Marcel Reinhard: sur la population française au XVIIIe et XIXe siècles*, Paris, 1973, pp. 505–22

Ogden, P. 'Expression spatiale des contacts humains et changements de la société: l'exemple de l'Ardèche, 1860–1970', *Revue de géographie de Lyon*, xxxxix (1974), 191–209

'Migration, marriage and the collapse of traditional peasant society in France' in P. White and R. Woods (eds.), *The Geographical Impact of Migration*, London, 1980, pp. 153–79

Parain, C. 'Contribution à une problématique de la communauté villageoise dans le domaine européen', *L'Ethnographie*, lxiv (1970), 34–60

Parieu, F. de *Essai sur la statistique agricole du département du Cantal*. Paris, 1864

Pariset, F. *Economie rurale, industrie, mœurs et usages de la Montagne Noire (Aude et Tarn)*. Paris, 1882

Parish, W. L. and Schwarz, M. 'Household Complexity in nineteenth-century France', *American Sociological Review*, xxxvii (1972), 154–73

Parron, V. *Notice sur l'aptitude militaire en France, suivi d'un essai de statistique générale de la Haute-Loire*. Paris, 1872

Pataut, J. *Sociologie électorale de la Nièvre*. Paris, 1953
Pelen, J.-N. 'La Vallée Longue en Cévenne. Vie, traditions et proverbes du temps passé' (Université d'Aix, Mémoire de maîtrise, 1972)
Pelras, C. 'Goulien – commune rurale du Cap Sizun (Finistère)', *Bulletin de la société d'anthropologie de Paris*, x (1966), 147–587
Perié, J.-M. 'Le Clergé aveyronnais sous la IIIe République' in *Etudes sur le Rouergue*. Rodez, 1974, pp. 269–81
Perry, P.-J. 'Mariage et distance dans le canton du Bleymard (Lozère): 1811–1820 et 1891–1900', *Etudes rurales*, lxvii (1977), 61–70
Petitfrère, C. 'Blanc et bleus d'Anjou, 1789–1793' (Université de Toulouse II, Thèse [de doctorat], 2 vols., 1977)
'Paysannerie et militantisme politique en Anjou au début de la Révolution (1789–1793)', *Annales de Bretagne et des pays de l'ouest*, lxxxix (1982), 173–85
Peyrolles, J. *La Révolution de 1848 au Puy et en Haute-Loire*. Le Puy, 1944
Peyronnet, J.-C. 'Famille élargie ou famille nucléaire? L'exemple du Limousin au début du XIXe siècle', *Revue d'histoire moderne et contemporaine*, xxii (1975), 568–82
'Les Familles de La Courtine en 1759 d'après le manuscrit du curé Michon', *Actes de la rencontre de démographie de 1976 tenue à Clermont-Ferrand* (Clermont-Ferrand, Institut d'études du Massif Central, 1977), 223–49
Pilenco, A. *Les Mœurs électorales en France, régime censitaire*. Paris, 1928
Pitte, J.-R. 'Les Origines et l'évolution de la châtaigneraie vivaroise à travers un document cadastral du XVIIIe siècle', *Bulletin de la section de géographie du Comité des travaux historiques et scientifiques*, lxxxii (1975–77), 165–78
Pitt-Rivers, J. 'Social class in a French village', *Anthropological Quarterly*, xxxiii (1960), 1–13
Plagnard, E. *Prades-d'Aubrac*. Villefranche-de-Rouergue, 1960
Poitrineau, A. 'Aspects de la crise des justices seigneuriales dans l'Auvergne du dix-huitième siècle', *Revue historique de droit français et étranger* (1961), 552–70
La Vie rurale en Basse Auvergne au XVIIIe siècle. Paris, 1965
'Les Assemblées primaires du bailliage de Salers en 1789', *Revue d'histoire moderne et contemporaine*, xxv (1978), 419–42
(ed.) *Le Diocèse de Clermont*. Paris, 1979
Pomponi, F. 'Pouvoir et abus de pouvour des maires corses au XIXe siècle', *Etudes rurales*, lxiii–lxiv (1976), 153–69
Ponteil, F. *Les Institutions de la France de 1814 à 1870*. Paris, 1966
'Porteur d'eau n. 17 de Paris (Seine, France) d'après les renseignements recueillis sur les lieux en avril 1858 par E. Avalle' in F. Le Play (ed.), *Les Ouvriers des deux mondes*, ii (1858), 321–51
Poujol, R. *Vébron, histoire d'un village cévenol*. Aix-en-Provence, 1981
Poulat, E. *Les 'Semaines Religieuses': approche socio-historique et bibliographique des bulletins diocésains français*. Lyons, 1972
Pourcher, Y. 'Criminalité et société: l'exemple de la Lozère au début du XIXième siècle' (Université Paul Valéry, Montpellier III, Mémoire de maîtrise, 1979)
Pouthas, C.-H. *La Population française pendant la première moitié du XIXe siècle*. Paris, 1956
Price, R. *An Economic History of Modern France, 1730–1914*. London, 1981
Quéniart, J. *Les Hommes, l'église et Dieu dans la France du XVIIIe siècle*. Paris, 1978
Rambaud, P. and Vincienne, M. *Les Transformations d'une société rurale: la Maurienne, 1562–1962*. Paris, 1964

Raylet, L. 'Les Evénements de 1815 à Saint Affrique', *Journal de l'Aveyron*, 9, 16 October 1932

Raymon, S. *Etude sur les biens communaux du département de la Creuse.* Montluçon, 1872

Redfield, R. *The Little Community: Viewpoints for the Study of a Human Whole.* Stockholm, Chicago, 1955
Peasant Society and Culture: an Anthropological Approach to Civilization. Chicago, 1956

Rees, A. D. *Life in a Welsh Countryside.* Cardiff, 1950

Regné, J. *Etat comparatif des paroissiaux catholiques et protestants du département et des communes de l'Ardèche.* Annonay, 1927

Reid, D. M. 'Labor management and the state in an industrial town: Decazeville, 1826–1914' (Stanford University, Ph.D. thesis, 1981)

Renouvin, P. *Les Assemblées provinciales de 1787, origines, développement, résultats.* Paris, 1921

Rétif de la Bretonne, N. *La Vie de mon père.* (ed. G. Rougier), Paris, 1970

Reynier, E. *La Seconde République dans l'Ardèche (1848–52).* Privas, 1948

Riffaterre, C. 'Les Revendications économiques et sociales des assemblées primaires de juillet 1793', *Commission de recherche et de publication des documents relatifs à la vie économique de la Révolution, Bulletin trimestriel* (1906), 321–80

Rigal, J.-L. *Comité de surveillance de Saint Geniez-d'Olt. Procès-verbaux et arrêtés.* Rodez, 1942

Rigaudière, A. and Zylberman, E. and Mantel, R. *Etudes d'histoire économique rurale au XVIIIᵉ siècle.* Paris, 1965

Riou, M. 'L'Election présidentielle de décembre 1848 en Ardèche', *Revue du Vivarais*, lxxviii (1974), 82–96
'Ethnologie et histoire au XIXᵉ siècle: les mariages consanguins en Vivarais', *Revue du Vivarais*, lxxxii (1979), 7–14

Rivet, A. 'L'Application des lois Jules Ferry en Haute-Loire (1880–1892)', *Actes du 92ᵉᵐᵉ congrès national des sociétés savantes, Strasbourg et Colmar 1967: section d'histoire moderne et contemporaine* (3 vols., Paris, 1970), iii, 65–91
'Les Débuts de la IIIᵉ République en Haute-Loire: les élections de Guyot-Montpeyroux (1868–1876)', *Mélanges en l'honneur de Etienne Fournial.* St Etienne, 1978, 306–15
'Des "ministres" laïques au XIXᵉ siècle? Les béates de la Haute-Loire', *Revue de l'histoire de l'église en France*, lxiv (1978), 27–38
'L'Image de la Droite (1871–1881)', *Cahiers de la Haute-Loire*, (1979), 169–90
La Vie politique dans le département de la Haute-Loire de 1815 à 1974. Le Puy, 1979

Robert, D. *Les Eglises réformées en France, 1800–1830.* Paris, 1961

Robert, P. *Dictionnaire alphabétique et analogique de la langue française*, 7 vols., Paris, 1953–72

Robert, A. and Cougny, G. *Dictionnaire des parlementaires français, comprenant tous les membres des Assemblées françaises et tous les ministres français depuis . . . 1789 jusqu'au 1ᵉʳ mai 1889*, 5 vols., Paris, 1889–91

Rodat, A. *Le Cultivateur aveyronnais: leçons élémentaires d'agriculture pratique et vues sur la science de l'exploitation rurale.* Rodez, 1839

Root, H.-L. 'En Bourgogne: l'état et la communauté rurale, 1661–1789', *Ann. E.S.C.*, xxxvii (1982), 288–302

Roqueplo, P. *La Dépopulation dans les arrondissements de Mende et de Marvejols (Lozère)*. Rodez, 1914

Rouchon, U. *La Vie paysanne dans la Haute-Loire*, 3 vols. in one, Lafitte Reprints, Marseilles, 1977

Rouchy, C. 'Monographie religieuse d'un diocèse français: le diocèse de Saint Flour en 1905', *Revue catholique des églises*, (1905), 533–53

Royer, C. 'Les Buronniers de l'Aubrac' (Université de Paris, Institut d'ethnologie, Thèse de doctorat de troisième cycle, 2 vols., 1966)

Runel, A. 'Opinion, mentalités, idéologie: le traditionalisme en Lozère (1930–1945) d'après les almanachs locaux' (Université de Paris I, Mémoire de maîtrise, 1973–4)

Sabatier, A. *Religion et politique au XIXe siècle. Le canton de Vernoux-en-Vivarais*. Vernoux, 1975

Saby, M. *Allègre et sa région au fil des siècles*. Le Puy, 1976

Sagnac, P. and Caron, P. *Les Comités des droits féodaux et de législation et l'abolition du régime seigneurial, 1789–1793*. Paris, 1907

Sahut, A.-B. 'La Propriété sectionale (exemple cévenol)' (Thèse, Institut des Hautes Etudes de Droit Rural et d'Economie Agricole, 1975)

Saint Ferréol, A. *Mes Mémoires*, 5 vols., 1887–92

Saint Jacob, P. de *Les Paysans de la Bourgogne du nord au dernier siècle de l'ancien régime*. Dijon, 1960

Sanson, *abbé* 'Les Coutumes chrétiennes en Haute-Auvergne', *Revue de la Haute-Auvergne*, xxiv (1922), 357–77

Santi, M. L. de 'Notes et documents sur les intrigues royalistes dans le midi de la France de 1792 à 1815', *Mémoires de l'académie des sciences, inscriptions et belles-lettres de Toulouse*, iv (1916), 37–113

Schnapper, B. 'Pour une géographie des mentalités judiciaires: la litigiosité en France au XIXe siècle', *Ann. E.S.C.*, xxxiv (1979), 399–419

Schnerb, R. *La Péréquation fiscale de l'assemblée constituante, 1790–91*. Clermont-Ferrand, 1936

Schram, S. R. *Protestantism and Politics in France*. Alençon, 1954

Sée, H. *La Vie économique de la France sous la monarchie censitaire, 1815–1848*. Paris, 1927

Segondy, L. 'L'Enseignement secondaire libre et les petits séminaires dans l'académie de Montpellier (1854–1924)' (Université de Montpellier, Thèse de troisième cycle, 1974)

Segret, G. 'La Maison paysanne dans la région de Blesle: étude sur le rôle économique et sociale de l'institution d'hériter du XVIIe siècle à nos jours', *Almanach de Brioude*, (1934), 59–101

Seignebos, C. *L'Evolution de la 3e République*. Paris, 1912

Seignolle, C. *Le Folklore du Languedoc. Gard – Hérault – Lozère*. Paris, 1977

Sewell Jr, W. H. *Work and Revolution in France: the Language of Labour from the Old Regime to 1848*. Cambridge, 1980

Siegfried, A. *Tableau politique de la France de l'ouest sous la Troisième République*. Paris, 1913 (2nd edn 1964)

Géographie électorale de l'Ardèche sous la IIIe République. Paris, 1949

Soboul, A. 'Problèmes de la communauté rurale en France (XVIIIe–XIXe siècle)' in *Ethnologie et histoire: forces productives et problèmes de transition. Hommage à Charles Parain*. Paris, 1975, pp. 369–95

Problèmes paysans de la révolution, 1789–1848. Paris, 1976

Somjee, A. H. *The Democratic Process in a Developing Society.* London, 1979
Sonenscher, M. 'Royalists and Patriots: Nîmes and its Hinterland in the late Eighteenth Century' (University of Warwick, D.Phil. thesis, 1977)
Stern, D. *Histoire de la Révolution de 1848,* 2 vols., Paris, 1862
Sudriès, R. 'Les Subsistances dans l'Aveyron de 1787 à 1795', *Revue de Rouergue,* iii (1949), 147–71
'Sur les mœurs, l'organisation agricole et le régime d'émigration des montagnes d'Auvergne' in F. Le Play (ed.), *Les Ouvriers des deux mondes,* ii (1858), 351–62
Sutherland, D. M. G. 'The Social Origins of Chouannerie in Upper Brittany' (University of London, D.Phil. thesis, 1974)
    The Chouans: the Social Origins of Popular Counter-Revolution in Upper Brittany, 1770–1796. Oxford, 1982
Sutter, J. and Tabah, L. 'Fréquence et répartition des mariages consanguins en France', *Population,* (1948), 607–30
    'Les Notions d'isolat et de population minimum', *Population* (1951), 481–98
Sylvère, A. *Toinou, le cri d'un enfant auvergnat, pays d'Ambert.* Paris, 1980
Tackett, T. 'L'Histoire sociale du clergé diocésain dans la France du XVIIIe siècle', *Revue d'histoire moderne et contemporaine,* xxvii (1979), 198–234
Tackett, T. and Langlois, C. 'Ecclesiastical Structures and Clerical Geography on the Eve of the French Revolution', *French Historical Studies,* xi (1980), 352–70
Tessier, J. *La Valeur sociale des biens communaux en France.* Paris, 1906
Thomson, J. K. J. *Clermont-de-Lodève 1633–1789: Fluctuations in the prosperity of a Languedocian cloth-making town.* Cambridge, 1982
Tilly, C. 'Did the Cake of Custom Break?' in J. M. Merriman (ed.), *Consciousness and Class Experience in Nineteenth-Century Europe,* New York and London, 1979, pp. 17–44
Tilly, L. A. and Tilly, C. (eds.), *Class Conflict and Collective Action.* Beverly Hills, London, 1981
Tisseyre, J.-M. and Baudot, M. 'Rapport de Pierre-Joseph Bonnaterre sur l'état du département de l'Aveyron en l'an IV de la République', *Bulletin de la section d'histoire moderne et contemporaine du Comité des travaux historiques et scientifiques,* x (1977), 135–201
Todd, E. *La Troisième planète: structures familiales et systèmes idéologiques.* Paris, 1983
Tourdonnet, Comte de *Situation du métayage en France: rapport sur l'enquête ouverte par la société des agriculteurs de France.* Paris, 1879–80
Touzery, J. *Les Bénéfices du diocèse de Rodez.* Rodez, 1906
Tudesq, A.-J. *Les Grands Notables en France (1840–1849): étude historique d'une psychologie sociale,* 2 vols., Paris, 1964
Valette, J. 'Une Enquête sociale dans l'Aveyron en 1848: les habitants de l'Aubrac', *Revue du Rouergue,* xxxiii (1979), 107–23
Vaylet, J. *L'Abbé Bessou.* Rodez, 1919
Vayssier, A. *Dictionnaire patois-français du département de l'Aveyron.* Rodez, 1879
Verlaguet, P.-A. (ed.), *Vente des biens nationaux du département de l'Aveyron: procès-verbaux d'inventaire et d'adjudication,* 3 vols., Millau, 1931–3
Vézian, A. 'La Qualification de "Noble" en Vivarais', *Revue du Vivarais,* lxxiv (1970), 145–9
Vigier, P. *La Seconde République dans la région alpine: étude politique et sociale,* 2 vols., Paris, 1963
    'Elections municipales et prises de conscience politique sous la Monarchie de

juillet', in *La France au XIXe siècle. Mélanges Charles-Hippolyte Pouthas.* Paris, 1973, pp. 276–86

Vila, S. 'Les Milieux populaires et la République dans l'Hérault de 1815 à 1852. Mutations dans les comportements politiques' (Université de Paris I, Thèse de troisième cycle, 2 vols., 1976)

Villain, J. *La France moderne (Haute-Loire).* St Etienne, 1906

Vincens, P. P. *Dictionnaire des lieux habités du département de la Lozère.* Mende, 1879

Vogüé, E.-M. 'Notes sur le Bas Vivarais: I Le Pays', *Revue des deux mondes,* cxiii (1892), 448–65

'Notes sur le Bas Vivarais: II Les Habitans', *Revue des deux mondes,* cxiii (1892), 921–36

Vovelle, M. 'Les Troubles sociaux en Provence, 1750–1792', *Actes du 93e congrès des sociétés savantes: section d'histoire moderne et contemporaine, Tours,* ii (1968), 325–72

Idéologies et mentalités. Paris, 1982

'Peut-on parler de "mentalités paysannes" à l'époque napoléonienne?', *Le Monde alpin et rhodanien* (1982), 193–209

Weber, E. *Peasants into Frenchmen: the modernization of rural France, 1870–1914.* London, 1977

'The Second French Republic, Politics and the Peasant', *French Historical Studies,* xi (1980), 521–50

'Comment la Politique Vint aux Paysans: A Second Look at Peasant Politicization', *The American Historical Review,* lxxxvii (1982), 357–89

Weill, G. D. *Les Elections législatives depuis 1789. Histoire de la législation et des mœurs.* Paris, 1895

Weyd, P.-M. *Les Forêts de la Lozère.* Paris, Lille, 1911

Whyte, J. H. 'The Influence of the Catholic Clergy on Elections in Nineteenth-Century Ireland', *The English Historical Review,* cccxciv (1960), 239–59

Willings, H. *A Village in the Cévennes.* London, 1979

Yver, J. *Egalité entre héritiers et exclusion des enfants dotés, essai de géographie coutumière.* Paris, 1966

Zink, A. *Azéreix: la vie d'une communauté rurale à la fin du XVIIIe siècle.* S.E.V.P.E.N., 1969

Index